SILAS T
SAMUEL

THE

H I S T O R Y

AND

A N T I Q U I T I E S

OF

HARWICH AND *DOVERCOURT*

IN THE COUNTY OF ESSEX

TO WHICH IS ADDED A LARGE

A P P E N D I X

C O N T A I N I N G

THE NATURAL HISTORY OF THE SEA-COAST AND COUNTRY ABOUT HARWICH, PARTICULARLY THE CLIFF, THE FOSSILS, PLANTS, TREES BIRDS AND FISHES, &c.

Elibron Classics
www.elibron.com

THE

HISTORY

AND

ANTIQUITIES

OF

HARWICH and *DOVERCOURT,*

In the County of *Essex,*

By SILAS TAYLOR, Gent.

To which is added a large

APPENDIX

CONTAINING

The Natural Hiftory of the Sea-Coast and Country about *Harwich,* particularly the Cliff, the Fossils, Plants, Trees, Birds and Fishes, &c.

Illuftrated with Variety of COPPER PLATES.

By *SAMUEL DALE,*

Author of the Pharmacologia.

The Second Edition.

LONDON:

Printed for C. Davis in *Pater-nofter Row,* T. Osborn in *Gray's-Inn,* and H. Lintot at the *Crofs Keys* againft St. *Dunftan's* Church in *Fleet-ftreet.* MDCCXXXII.

TO

Sir *HANS SLOANE*, Bart.

PRESIDENT

OF THE

COLLEGE of PHYSICIANS,

AND OF THE

ROYAL SOCIETY of *London*;

AND

Firſt Phyſician to His MAJESTY:

THESE

NOTES and OBSERVATIONS

ON THE

HISTORY *and* ANTIQUITIES

OF

Harwich and *Dovercourt*,

ARE,

In grateful Acknowledgment of his many Favours, humbly dedicated by

His obliged and obedient Servant,

Samuel Dale.

TO THE

R E A D E R.

THE Foundation of the following *History* was a MS. of Collections made about the Year 1676. by one Mr. *Silas Domville* alias *Taylor*, Keeper of the King's-Stores at *Harwich*, not long before his Death; this his Curiosity might prompt him to, he living at the Place, and being a Lover of *Antiquities*, a Person of Leisure, and a Member of the *Corporation*, whereby he had access to the Books and Records both of the Church and Borough. Whether he designed ever to publish these his Collections, or only writ them for the Satisfaction of himself and Friends is to me unknown: But whatever were his Intentions, they were prevented by the Thread of his Life being not long after cut off; and dying in Debt, all his MSS. and Papers were, together with his Goods, seized on by his Creditors, and so disperfed.

This MS coming into my Hands some Years after, thro' the Favour of a Friend, the Curiosity of it made

me

me defirous of copying it, not only as it related to a Place in the County in which I was an Inhabitant, but alfo becaufe I had before been divers times at the Place, to obferve the natural Curiofities thereof; but efpecially the *Cliff*, whofe various imbedded *Foffils* I had there difcovered; the firft Invention of which the late Dr. *Woodward* in publick Company attributed to me. Afterwards, whatever I found in my Reading relating unto *Harwich*, I tranfcribed into the Left-hand Page of my Copy, (the *Original* being only written on the Right) and thus I continued to do for divers Years without any View or Defign of publifhing them myfelf, not being without Hopes, that they might be of fome ufe to a better Hand, who might undertake the Publication either of a *General Hiftory* of *England*, or particular one of this *County*; for which Caufe I never declined lending them to any of my Acquaintance, whofe Curiofity might lead them to defire a Perufal : But after a long Waiting without Effect, befides, Years encreafing upon me, and being loth that they fhould be altogether buried in Oblivion, by their being after my Deceafe torn to pieces as wafte Papers, or deftroyed by *Mice* and *Vermin*; I refolved to fend them abroad myfelf, in the Drefs they now appear.

Our

Our Author Mr. *Taylor* divided his Collections into five Heads. The firſt of which was the *Topography* of the Place, where in the Chapel or Church he gives an Account of Alterations therein made by the ſeveral Changes of Religion, in the Reigns of King *Edward* VI. Queen *Mary* I. and her Siſter Queen *Elizabeth*; but what the Mutations were in thoſe times at the Mother Church of *Dovercourt*, he is altogether ſilent: He hath likewiſe inſerted an Account of ſome Monuments then exiſting in the *Chapel* of *Harwich* with their *Epitaphs*, but not of all that were then in being; and he likewiſe mentions other Stones there, but ſtript of their Braſſes, which was a Fault not only of later times, but began ſoon after, if not with the *Reformation*, as doth appear by the Proclamations publiſhed to reſtrain ſuch Enormities, and the ſtrict Prohibition of it by Queen *Elizabeth*. At *Dovercourt* he barely mentions a *Gild of St. George:* This I was in great hopes to have got ſome Light into, its Foundation, *&c.* through the Peruſal of ſome old Writings, which the Reverend Vicar of the Pariſh told me were kept in the Cheſt of that Church, which I had his Leave to look into; but though I made two Journeys on purpoſe, yet could I at neither of them find the Church-wardens both together at Liberty to afford me that Satisfaction. Nor was it with leſs Difficulty that

a Suca Succeffion of the Lords of the Manor are continued unto the prefent time. Nor am I alone herein, it being the Complaint of divers *Antiquarians*, that when they have waited on certain Gentlemen to enquire fome things relating to their Anceftors, Predeceffors, or other things about their Eftates, they have been looked upon as Perfons that had fome ill Defign upon them.

The next Head which Mr. *Taylor* treats of, is that of the *Natural Accidents* and *Productions*; but altho' he hath here a large Field for *Natural Hiftory*, yet he is fo very fhort, that in many Parts thereof there is little more than the Names of the things.

His third Head is of the *Defpotical* or *Dynaftical* Concerns of the Town. Befides *Uluvin* no other Lord thereof is mentioned before the Conqueft. At the *general Survey* it was in the Hands of the *Veres* Earls of *Guifnes* and from them it defcended to divers Lords until the Reign of Queen *Elizabeth*, when, on the Attainder of *Thomas* Duke of *Norfolk*, it came into the Crown, where it remained until King *James* I. fold it to *George Whitmore*, Efq; whofe Son *William* was poffeffed of it, when Mr. *Taylor* finifhed his Account. Our Author hath added hiftorical Matters to every one of the faid Lords, chiefly extracted from *Dugdale's Baronage*.

The

The fourth Head is of the *Municipal, Political* or *Civil* Conftitution of the Place, in drawing up which he (being one of the capital Burgeffes) had free Accefs to the publick *Charters,* &c. of the Corporation, to extract whatever he judged proper for his Defign.

The fifth and laft Head contains the *Hiftorical* Part, in which he confeffeth himfelf much to feek, having but little to fay of it.

Thus I have given a fhort Abftract of our Author's Performance, in the Publication of which I have all along kept the *Original Text* intire, printing it on the upper Part of the feveral Pages, and in a larger Character than the Additions or Notes, which are moftly printed in two Columns with a fmaller Letter, and referred by diftinct Letters to the feveral Places they belong to; fo that at firft Sight it may be feen which was *Original,* and which *Addition.*

Perhaps fome may object againft this Publication as needlefs, having been before done by others, as by the R. R. Editor of *Cambden's Britannia,* in the Additions to *Effex.* Then by *Newcourt* in his *Repertorium*; and laftly, by the *Compilers* of *Magna Britannia nova* in the Article of *Effex.* To this it may be anfwered, that what

what was publifhed by all thefe were but *Fragments* of Mr. *Taylor's* MS. and none of them coming any thing near the whole of it.

What is further to be added, is an Account of the Additions to this Work; and as they are numerous and very large, the fhorter Account of them may fuffice, that fo the Work itfelf may not be here anticipated; but as fome may be expected, a few things fhall be here taken Notice of. *Camulodunum* tho' a Station mentioned by *Antoninus*, yet where it ftood hath been the Controverfy among the *Literati*, of which a large Abftract is inferted in the *Appendix*. It was firft taken from the *Britons* by *Claudius* Anno D. xliv. who placed a Garrifon of *Veterans* therein; who behaving them-felves infolently towards the neighbouring *Britons*, provoked *Boadicia* Widow of *Prafutagus* King of the *Iceni* to raife an Army, and being affifted by the *Tri-nobants* retook it, put the Garrifon to the Sword, and burnt the Place. *Tacitus* makes it an unfortified Place of little Strength, and therefore there is fome Impro-bability that *Colchefter* fhould be it. Befides by the Nearnefs of *Caftle - Camps* to the *Iceni*, the *Roman* Garrifon might be troublefome to that Kingdom, which might occafion *Boadicia* their Queen to de-ftroy it.

The

The large Number of natural Productions hath given room to infert a *Synopfis* of the *Plants*, and divers *Farrago's* of *Animals.* Thefe indeed might all have been made much larger, had the Publifher there refided, but he dwelling more than thirty Miles from the Place, and being continually employed in his Profeffion, could not afford more time than perhaps one Day or two in a Year, and that in the Summer Months; when other Seafons might have afforded him the Sight of many more Species of *Animals*, efpecially *Birds*.

The whole of the *Dynaftical* Part is augmnted by inlarging the Hiftories, and correcting fome Miftaks about the feveral Lords of the Soil; to which is added a Continuation down to the prefent Poffeffor.　In the *Political* Part are added a Lift of the *Mayors*, *Recorders* and *Parliament Men*, none of which were done by Mr. *Taylor*.　And in the laft Part there is an Addition of hiftorical Matters to the prefent time.　To all which are added Fourteen large and curious Cuts, four of which are of the *Foffils* found in the *Cliff.*

In compiling the whole, many Authors have been confulted, of which a Catalogue is here added, containing their Names, the Title of the Book, the Place where printed, and time of Edition.

Who

Who this Mr. *Taylor* was the Reader may be desirous to know, but the time since he died being about fifty two Years, there can be but few Persons now living that personally knew him; and old Age must have so far obliterated their Memories, that they can give but a very slender Account of him: I shall therefore for the Information of my Readers give the following Account, which I have transcribed from *Wood's Athenæ Oxonienses*, Ed. 1692. Part II. p. 464. N. 414.

Silas Domville *or* D'omvill *alias* Taylor, *Son of* Silvanus Taylor *a Committee Man for* Herefordshire *in the time of the Rebellion,* &c. *was born at* Harley *near* Much Wenlock *in* Shropshire *on the* 16. *of* July 1624. *bred in the Free-Schools at* Westminster *and* Shrewsbury, *became a* Commoner *of* New-Inn *in the Beginning of the Year* 1641. *but being soon after called thence, without the taking of a Degree, upon the Eruption of the* Civil Wars, *he took part with the Rebels upon his Father's Instance, and at length became a* Captain *under* Colonel, *afterwards* Major General Edward Massey; *and when the Wars ceased he was made by his Father's Endeavours a Sequestrator of the Royalists in* Hereford-shire, *and had in those times great Power there; which he used so civilly and obligingly, that he was beloved by*

2   *all*

all the King's Party. His Father settled upon him a good Estate in Church-Lands *which he had bought, and had the Moiety of the* Bishop *of* Hereford's *Palace in* Hereford *settled on him, on which he laid out much Money in building and altering. Upon the rising of Sir* George Booth *in* Cheshire, *in the Beginning of* August 1659. *he received a Commission to be a Captain of a Troop of Horse for the* Militia *of the* City *of* Westminster, *and shewed himself very active in that Employment; but at the* King's Return *he lost all, and was in a Manner ruined. Soon after by the Favour of certain Persons whom he had before obliged, he became* Commissary *of the Ammunition and warlike Provision at* Dunkirk, *and five Years after (about* 1665.) *he was by the Endeavours of Sir* Paul Neile *and others made Keeper of the* King's Store-Houses *for Shipping, and other marine Matters at* Harwich, *a Sea-port Town in* Essex ; *where he continued to the time of his Death. This Person being a great Lover of* Antiquities, *did in the times of Usurpation ransack the* Library *belonging to the Church of* Hereford, *of most, or at least the best* MSS. *therein, and also Garble the* MSS. *in the Library of the Church of* Worcester, *and the Evidences pertaining thereunto; among which, as I have heard, he got the Original Grant of King* Edgar : *Whence the Kings of* England *derive their Right to the Sovereignty of the Seas, which is printed in Mr.* Selden's *Book call'd* Mare

b   Clausum,

Claufum, Lib. II. *He had got alfo into his Hands a Quarto* MS. *of great* Antiquity, *which treated of the* Philofopher's Stone *in* Hieroglyphicks, *with fome few* Latin *Verfes underneath: And being limned with very great Curiofity, it was prefented to the View of his Majefty King* Charles II. *who offered one hundred Pounds for it; but was refufed by the Owner.*

This Perfon, commonly call'd Captain Taylor, *hath written,* The Hiftory of Gavel-Kind, *with the* Etymology *thereof; containing alfo an Affertion that our* Englifh *Laws are for the moft Part, thofe that were ufed by the ancient* Britons, *notwithftanding the feveral Conquefts of the* Romans, Saxons, Danes *and* Normans; *with fome Obfervations and Remarks upon many efpecial Occurrences of* Britifh *and* Englifh *Hiftory. To which is added, a fhort Hiftory of* William *the* Conqueror, *written in* Latin *by an anonymous Author, in the time of* Henry I. London 1663. *Quarto. The Original of which laft Piece is in the* Archives *of* Bodly's Library, *communicated to him by Dr.* Thomas Barlow *the Head Keeper of that* Library.

He had alfo written and publifhed feveral Pamphlets before the Reftoration of King Charles II. *but his Name being not put to them, he would never after own them.*

He

*He alfo laboured four Years or more in collecting va-
rious* Antiquities, *as* Arms, Monumental Infcriptions,
&c. in many Places of Herefordfhire, *during his Employment there under the two* Protectors: *which being
now, or at leaft lately in the Hands of Sir* Edward
Harley *of* Brompton Brian, *may ferve as an* Apparatus
for him, who fhall hereafter write the Antiquities *of
that* County.

He wrote alfo The Defcription of *Harwich,* with
all its Appurtenances and Antiquities.

*He had great Skill not only in the practical, but theo-
retical Part of* Mufick; *did compofe feveral* Leffons,
fome of which were tried, and played in the publick
School *of that Faculty in this Univerfity, while Dr.*
Wilfon *held the Chair, before his Majefty's Reftoration;
and after that time, being well acquainted with that
moft admired* Organift *to the* Queen, *call'd* Matthew
Lock, *he compofed feveral* Anthems; *two or more of
which were fung in his* Majefty's Chapel; *which being
well performed, his Majefty was pleafed to tell the Author that he liked them.*

He had alfo good Skill in the Mathematicks,. *and the*
Tongues, *and might have proved excellent in them,*
b 2   *had*

had his Continuance in the Univerſity *been longer, or had he not ſpent moſt of his time in military Matters.*

He died on the fourth day of November **1678**. *and was buried in the Chancel of the Church of* Harwich.

There are ſome further Accounts of this Mr. Taylor, *which he gives of himſelf in the following* Hiſtory, *p.* **238**. *And likewiſe in his Title Page to his* Hiſtory of Gavel-Kind; *he ſtiles himſelf* Silas Taylor, *Gent.*

A CATA-

A

C A T A L O G U E

O F

A U T H O R S

Made ufe of in the compiling this Work, with the Place and Time of the Publication of each.

A.

A *Ldrovandus Ulyſſes* De Piſcibus.   *Bononiæ* 1638
            De Anguibus,   *Ib.*   1642
            Ornithologia I.   *Ib.*   16
                   II.   16
                  III.   1637
            De Infeƈtis, *Ib.*   1658

Allen Benjamin. The Natural Hiſtory of the Chalibeat, and purging Waters of *England.*   *London* 1699

Aſhmole Elias. The Hiſtory of the Order of the Garter.   *London* 1715

Aubrey John. The Natural Hiſtory and Antiquities of the County of *Surrey,* V. Vol.   *London* 1723

Baker

B.

Baker Richard.   A Chronicle of the Kings of *England.*
                                                London 1643

Barrelierus Jacobus.   Plantæ per Galliam, Hispaniam &
                   Italiam, observatæ, Iconibus Æneis
                   exhibitæ.   *Parisiis* 1714

Bartholinus Thomas.   Acta Medica & Philosophica Hafni-
                   ensia, Vol. I.   *Hafniæ* 1673
                        Vol. II.   1675
                        Vol. III.   1677

Bauhinus Casparus.   Phytopinax seu Enumeratio Plantarum.
                                          Basileæ 1596
                   Prodromus Theatri Botanici.   *Ib.* 1671
                   Pinax Theatri Botanici.   *Ib.* 1671
                   Theatri Botanici five Historiæ
                   Botanicæ Liber Primus.   *Ib.* 1658

Bauhinus Johannes.   Historia Plantarum.   *Ebroduni* 1650, 1651

Baxter William.   Glossarium Antiquitatum Britannicarum.
                                          London 1719

Behrens H.   The Natural History of *Hartz-Forest.*   *London* 1730

Bellonius Petrus.   De Aquatilibus, Lib. II.   *Paris* 1553
                 L'Histoire de la Nature des Oyseaux. *Paris* 1555

Boccone Paulus modo *Sylvius.*   Icones & Descriptiones Ra-
                   riorum Plantarum.   *Oxford* 1674
                   Museo di Fisica.   *Venetia* 1697
                   Museo de Piante rare.   *Ib.* 1697

Boerhaave Hermannus.   Index alter Plantarum.   *Lugduni*
                                   Batavorum 1720

Bonannus Philippus.   Recreatio Mentis & Oculi.   *Romæ* 1684

Bradley Richard.   A Course of Lectures upon the Materia
                   Medica.   *London* 1730

z

                                     A Bre-

A Breviary of *Suffolk*, MS. penes *Edward*
          Earl of *Oxford* and *Mortimer*.

Brome James.   An Hiſtorical Account of three Years
          Travels over *England*, &c.   *London* 1700
Brooke Ralph.   A Catalogue, &c. of the Kings, Princes,
          Dukes, &c. of *England*.   *London* 1619
          A Diſcovery of certain Errors.   *London* 1723
          A ſecond Diſcovery of Errors.   *London* 1723
Burton William. A Commentary on Antoninus.   *London* 1658

C.

Cambden William.   Britannia.   *London* 1695
Camerarius Joachimus.   De Plantis Epitome. *Francofurt ad*
                                Mænum 1586
Carlton George, Biſhop of *Chicheſter.*   A thankful Remem-
          brance of God's Mercy.   *London* 1625
Chabræus Dominicus.   Stirpium Icones & Sciagraphia.
                                Geneva 1677
Childrey Joſhua.   Britannia Baconica, or the Natural Ra-
          rities of *England*, &c.   *London* 1661
Churchill Winſton.   Divi Britannici.   *London* 1675
Cluſius Carolus.   Rariorum Plantarum Hiſtoria.   *Antwerp* 1601
          Exoticorum Libri Decem.   *Ib.* 1605
Collins Arthur.   The Peerage of *England*.   *London* 1710
Collins John.   Salt and Fiſhery.   *London* 1682
Columna Fabius.   Minus cognitarum Plantarum Ecphraſis.
                                Roma 1616
Commelinus Johannes.   Catalogus Plantarum Indigenarum
                Hollandiæ.   *Amſtelodami* 1683

Dale

D.

Dale Robert.   Catalogue of the Nobility of *England.*
                                                    London 1697
Dale Samuel.   Pharmacologia feu Manuduétio ad Materiam
                 Medicam.   *London* 1710
Daniel Samuel.   A Colleétion of the Hiftory of *England.*
                                                    London
Derham William.   Philofophical Experiments and Obferva-
                    tions.   *London* 1726
                    Phyfico-Theology, or a Demonftration
                    of the Being and Attributes of God.
                                                    London 1713
Dodonæus Rembertus.   Stirpium Hiftoriæ Pemptades fex five
                        Libri xxx.   *Antverpiæ* 1616
Donatus Anton.   Trattato de Simplici.   *Venet.* 1631
Dugdale William.   Monafticon Anglicanum.   *London* 1655

E.

Evelyn John.   Silva, or a Difcourfe of Foreft Trees.
                                                    London 1679

F.

Fox John.   Book of Martyrs.

Gale

G.

Gale Thomas. Antonini Iter Britanniarum. London 1709
Gerard John. The Herbal or General History of Plants.
London 1597
Gesnerus Conradus. Historiæ Animalium Lib. III. sc. de
Avium Natura. Francofurt. 1617
Historiæ Animalium Lib. IV. sc. de
Piscium & Aquatilium Animantium
Natura. Francofurt. 1620
Godwin Morgan. Annals of England. London 1630
Gottsched Johannes. Flora Prussica, &c. Regiomont. 1703
Gouldman Francis. Dictionary. Cambridge 1678
Grew Nehemiah. Musæum Regalis Societatis. London 1681
Guillim John. A Display of Heraldry. London 1638

H.

Hartmannus Philippus Jacobus. Succincta Succini Prussici
Historia & Demonstratio. Philos. Transf. N. 248.
Heers Henricus ab. Observationes in Fontano Spadanacreno
Lugd. Bat. 1685
Heide Antonius de Anatome Mytuli. Amstelodam. 1684
Helmont J. B. Van. Opera. Elziver 1652
Helwing M. Georg. And. Lithographiæ Angiburgicæ Pars I.
Regiomont. 1717
Pars II. Lipsiæ 1720
Hermannus Paulus. Horti Academici Lugduno-Batavi Ca-
talogus. Lugd. Bat. 1687

Historia

Hiftoria Generalis Plantarum.   *Lugduni* 1587

Hofmannus Cafparus.   De   Medicamentis   Officinalibus.
                                          Paris. 1647

Hollinfhed.

Holloway Benjamin.   Introduction to Woodward's Natural
           Hiftory of the Earth, &c.   *London* 1726

Hook Robert.   Micrographia.   *London* 1665

How Guilielmus.   Stirpium Illuftrationes Lobelii.   *London* 1655

I.

Imperatus Ferr.   Hiftoria Naturale.   *Venetia* 1672

Johnfonus Thomas.   Iter Cantianum I.   1629

                  II.   1632

                  Mercurius Botanicus I.   *London* 1634

                  On Gerard's Herbal.   *London* 1636

                  Mercurius Botanicus II.   *London* 1641

Jonftonus Joannes.   De Avibus.   *Amftelodam.* 1657

                  De Pifcibus.   *Ib.*

                  De Infectis.   *Ib.*

                  De exanguibus aquaticis.   *Ib.*

K.

Kennet White.   Parochial Antiquities.   *Oxford* 1695

L.

Lachmund Fredericus. Orictographia Hildeſhemenſis. *Hil-*
deſheim 1669
Laet Joannes de. De Gemmis & Lapidibus. *Lugd. Bat.* 1647
Lambard William. The Perambulation of *Kent. London* 1657
Langius Car. Nich. Hiſtoria lapidum figuratorum Helvetiæ.
Venetiis 1708
Methodus Nova Teſtacea Marina.
Lucernæ 1722
Lawrence Thomas. Mercurius Centralis, or a Diſcourſe of
ſubterranean Cockle, &c. *London* 1664
Leland John. Itinerary of *England.* *Oxon* 1710
Le Neve John. Monumenta Anglicana in 4. Vol. *London* 1717
Lewis John. Hiſtory and Antiquities of the Iſle of *Thanet*
in *Kent.* *London* 1723
Hiſtory and Antiquities of *Feverſham.* *London* 1727
Luidius Edwardus. Lithophylacii Britannici Ichnographia.
London 1699
Liſter Martin. Hiſtoria Animalium Angliæ. *London* 1678
Hiſtoria ſeu Methodus Conchyliorum.
London 1685
Exercitatio Anatomica altera. *London* 1695
Exercitatio Anatomica tertia. *London* 1696
Lobelius Matthias. Stirpium Adverſaria. *London* 1605
Plantarum ſeu Stirpium Hiſtoria. *Lon-*
don 1576
Plantarum ſeu Stirpium Icones. *Ant-*
verpiæ 1581
Lydiat Thomas de Origine Fontium. *London* 1605

M.

Madox. Firma Burgi. *London*

Magnol Petrus. Botanicum Monfpelienfe. *Monfpelii* 1686

    Hortus Regius Monfpelienfis *Ib.* 1697

Martyn William. The Hiftory and Lives of the Kings of
     England. *London* 1628

Matthiolus Petrus Andreas. Commentarii in fex Libros Diof-
      coridis. *Venetiis* 1565

     Compendium de Plantis. *Ib.* 1571

Merret Chriftophorus. Pinax rerum naturalium Britannica-
     rum. *London* 1667

Mills Thomas. The Catalogue of Honour. *London* 1610

Monti Jofephus. Catalogi Stirpium Agri Bononienfis Pro-
     dromus. *Bononiæ* 1719

Morrifon Robert. Plantarum Hiftoria univerfalis Oxonienfis.
        Oxon 1680

Morton John. The Natural Hiftory of *Northamptonfhire.*
        London 1712

Moufetus Thomas. Infectorum Theatrum. *London* 1634

N.

Newcourt Richard. Repertorium Ecclefiafticum. *London* 1708

O.

An Account of the Origin of Foffil-Shells. *London* 1705
        Parkinfon

P.

Parkinson John. Theatrum Botanicum. *London* 1640

Petiver James. Mufei centuria I. II. &c. concordia Graminum.

Philofophical Tranfactions of the Royal Society. *London*

Phytologia Britannica. *London* 1650

Plot Robert. The Natural Hiftory of *Oxfordfhire.* *Oxon* 1677

The Natural Hiftory of *Staffordfhire.* *Oxford* 1686

Plukenet Leonardus. Almageftum Botanicum. *London* 1696

Almagefti Botanici Mantiffa. *London* 1700

Phytographiæ Pars I. II. &c. *Ib.* 1691

Pontedera Julius. Compendium **Tabularum** Botanicarum

Patavii 1718

Poynter John. Britannia Romana. *Oxford* 1724

Q.

Quincy John. Lexicon Phyfico-Medicum. *London* 1719

A Complete *Englifh* Difpenfatory. *Ib.* 1718

R.

Ray John. Hiftoria Plantarum *Tom.* I. II. III. *London* 1686

Ornithology *Ib.* 1678

Synopfis methodica Stirpium Britannicarum III.

London 1724

Fafciculus Stirpium Britannicarum. *London* 1688

Ray

Ray John. Three Phyfico-Theological Difcourfes. *London* 1713
Synopfis Methodica Avium & Pifcium. *London* 1713
Rondeletius Gulielmus De Pifcibus marinis. *Lugduni* 1554
Univerfæ aquatilium Hiftoriæ Pars al-
tera. *Ib.* 1555

S.

Salmon Nathaniel. New Survey of *England*, Part I. &c.
London 1728
Salvianus Hippolitus. Hiftoria Aquatilium. *Romæ* 1557
Sammes Aylett. The Antiquities of ancient *Britain. London* 1676
Sandford Francis. A Genealogical Hiftory of the Kings of
England. London 1677
Scheuchzer Johannes. Operis Agroftographici Idea. *Tiguri* 1719
Agroftographia five Graminum &c.
Hiftoria. Ib. 1715
Scheuchzer Johannes Jacobus. Specimen Lithographiæ Hel-
veticæ curiofæ. *Tiguri* 1702
Schonevelde Stephanus. Icthyologia. *Hamburgi* 1624
Schwenckfeld Gafparus. Theriotrophium *Lignicii* 1603
Scilla Agoftino. Lettere i Corpi marini che petrificati.
Naples 1670
Skinner Stephanus. Etymologicon Linguæ Anglicanæ. *Lon-
don* 1671
Sloane Sir Hans. Voyage to the Iflands, &c. of *Jamaica.*
Vol. II. *London* 1725
Sprat Thomas. The Hiftory of the Royal Society. *London* 1702
Steno Nicholaus. The Prodromus to a Differtation concern-
ing Solids, &c. *London* 1671
Canis Carchariæ diffectum caput. *Am-
ftelodami* 1669

Stillingfleet

Stillingfleet Edward.   Origines Britannicæ.   *London* 1685
Stukeley William.   Itinerarium curiosum.   *London* 1724

T.

Taylor Silas.   The Hiſtory of Gavel-kind.   *London* 1663
Tyrrell James.   The general Hiſtory of *England.*   *London* 1696
Threlkeld Caleb.   Synopſis Stirpium Hibernicarum.   *Dublin* 1727
Tour through Great Britain, *&c.*   *London*
Tournefort Joſephus Pitton.   Inſtitutiones Rei Herbariæ.
Paris 1700
Truſſel John.   Continuation, *&c.* of the Hiſtory of *England.*
London 1641

V.

Vaillant Sebaſtien.   Botanicon Pariſienſe.   *à Leide* 1727
Vincent Auguſtine.   A Diſcovery of Errors, *&c.*   *London* 1622

W.

Warburton John.   New and correct Map of *Middleſex, Eſſex*
and *Hartfordſhire.*
Weaver John.   Ancient funeral Monuments.   *London* 1631
Willughbeius Franciſcus.   Ornithologia.   *London* 1676
Hiſtoria Piſcium.   *Oxon* 1686
Wittie Robert.   Scarbrough-Spaw.   *York* 1668
Wood.   Athenæ Oxonienſes, Vol. II.   *Oxon* 1692

Woodward

Woodward John. An Effay towards the Natural Hiftory of
the Earth. *London* 1695
An Attempt towards a Natural Hiftory of
Foffils. *London* 1729
Wormius Olaus. Mufeum. *Lugduni Bat.* 1655

Y.

York James. A brief Catalogue of the Reigns, &c. of the
Kings of *England.*

THE

Tab. 1. Page 1.

A.The Gate with the greater Light Houſe. over it B. The Town-Hall. C. The Chapple. of S.
Nicholas. D. Store-Houſe s to the Rope Walk. E. Shotley in Suffolk. F. the Road to London. G.
Part of the Marſh. H. the Rope-Walke. and may to the Cliff

R. Sheppard Sculp.

THE

H I S T O R Y

A N D

A N T I Q U I T I E S

O F

HARWICH and *DOVERCOURT.*

THE Town or Borough of *Harwich* fometimes
written *Villa*, but now commonly *Burgus*, and
Lordſhip and Pariſh of *Dovercourt*, judged to
be in 5 2 Degrees of North Latitude and (as ſome more
curious have obſerv'd) 12 Minutes, are ſituate in the
Eaſtern Part of this County ⁱ

ⁱ *Eſſex*, lying in the Hundreds
of *Tendering*, and bearing *North-
Eaſt* from *London*, from which
it is diſtant by Computation ſixty
two Miles, but by Admeaſure-
ment according to the *new Map*
ſeventy two Miles five Furlongs; and according to *Ogilby's
Roads* ſeventy Miles ſix Furlongs.

B While

While the *Britains* maintained their Dominion and Right in this Ifle, the *Ifthmus* (whereon are fituated thefe two Towns) was in the Territory of the *Trinobants*, [b] from whofe Government the *Romans* forced it [c].   But

[b] Of which Kingdom *Cunobeline*, *Kynobelin*, or *Kymbelain* was King, in the eighteenth Year of whofe Reign, but as fome think the twenty third, our Saviour *Jefus Chrift* was born: This King civiliz'd the *Britains*, which it is thought he was mov'd to by an Emulation of the *Roman Majefty*, whereof he had been an Eye-witnefs, when his Father *Tenantius*, under pretence of fending him to congratulate *Auguftus* upon his Succefs againft *Mark Anthony*, left him as an Hoftage at *Rome:* He did endeavour by his own Example to bring his Countrymen into the *Roman* Fafhion of living; imitating them in the Manner of their Houfes, eating, drinking, and Clothes: Coining Money in Gold and Silver inftead of their rufty Iron and Copper Rings, valued by weight; making their Money in *Medals* or *Plates*, on the one Side whereof was fome Device quaint enough for the In-

2

vention of thofe times; on the other the Face of the King; fome of which have been preferv'd unto this Day, *Churchill*'s *Divi Brit.* p. 62. There are divers of thefe Coins in *Cambden* and *Speed*, which may be feen in *Camb. Brit. ed.* 1695. among the *Nummi Britannici*, Tab. I. one of which I have in my Poffeffion, having a Head and CAMV. on the one Side, as in Nº. 21, perhaps of the God *Camulus*, under which Name *Mars* is by *Cambden* faid to be worfhip'd by the *Britains*, *Brit.* p. 348. and on the reverfe *Victory* fitting in a Chair with the right Hand extended, and underneath CVNO.

[c] Soon after the Death of *Cunobeline* (whofe Reign according to *Jeoffrey* of *Monmouth* was about fixty Years) *Claudius* the Emperor fent *Plautius* the *Prætor* of *Gaul* to invade *Britain*, who having flain *Togodumnus*, and routed *Caratacus* Sons to *Cunobeline*, of which

which he fent word to the Emperor, who embarking at *Geſſoriacum*, landed in *Britain* and joining his Forces, which waited for him near the *Thames*, he paſs'd that River, fought with the *Britains*, overcame them, taking *Camulodunum* the chief City of *Cunobeline*, and return'd to *Rome*; leaving the Government to *Plautius*, with Orders to fubdue thofe that remain'd unconquer'd. So under the *Romans* the aforefaid Kingdom became part of the Province of *Flavia Cæſarienſis*, over which *Agricola* was Governor under the Emperor *Domitian*.

From the Beginning of this King's Reign *(Belinarvirag)* we date the Dominion of the *Romans* in this Iſle; *Julius Cæſar* had the Honour of being the firſt Aggreſſor: *Claudius* laid the Superſtructure upon his Foundation; *Domitian* had the good Fortune to perfect the Work, *Churchill's Div. Brit. p.* 64. Our laſt quoted Author names twelve of the *Roman* Emperors that were perfonally in *Britain*, viz. *Julius Cæſar, Claudius, Adrianus, Pertinax, Severus, Baſſianus, Conſtantius Chlorus, Conſtantinus Magnus, Conſtantinus* II, *Clemens Maximus,* (by *Occo* and others *Flavius Magnus*

Maximus) Gratianus (Municeps) Conſtantinus III. which two laſt were fet up by the *Britiſh* Army, after the Death of *Maximus*.

From the laſt departure of the *Roman Legions, Anno Domini* CCCCXXXV. may be dated the final Period of the *Roman Empire* in this *Iſland*, which from the Conqueſt of it by *Claudius, Anno Domini* 44. had continued three hundred ninety one Years, tho' others accounting it from the firſt landing here of *Julius Cæſar*, in the fifty third Year before the Birth of *Chriſt*, make it four hundred and eighty eight.

What particular *Kings* or *Governors* the *Britains* had after they were fet free from the *Roman Empire*, is hard to determine, thro' the darkneſs and obſcurity of the Time, and fcarcity of Authors: Some Kings they had, among whom *Vortigern* is firſt named, who being preſt and overpower'd by the frequent and cruel Invaſions of *Scots* and *Picts*, call'd a Counfel, *Anno Domini* 449. in which it was agreed to call in the *Saxons* to their Aſſiſtance, who accepting of the Invitation came over in three Ships; *Tyrrell* fuppofeth them fifteen hundred, *Churchill* nine thoufand, under

B 2   the

But in the Year of our Lord 527, it was (together with their antient *Camulodunum*) [d] wrested out of their Hands,

the Command of two Captains, *Hengist* and *Horsa*, and landing at *Ypwinsfleet* in the Island of *Thanet*, they, by daily encreasing, became not only a Terror to, but even the Overthrowers and Destroyers of their Entertainers, driving them to seek Refuge among foreign Nations, and those that remain'd here to lead a miserable Life among Woods and Mountains: And having thus expell'd and subdu'd the native *Britains*, the *Saxons* set up Kingdoms of their own, *Hengist* being the first that erected *Kent* into a Kingdom for himself, *A. D.* 457. according to Mr. *Tyrrell's History of England*, Vol. I. Part I. *p.* 150. which seems more probable: Sir *Winston Churchill*, who in his *Div. Britannici*, *p.* 93. makes the Reign of *Vortigern* (the Inviter over of the *Saxons*) not to begin before *A. D.* 446. and yet *p.* 207. writes that *Hengist* made himself King of *Kent*, *A. D.* 445. therein making his History not reconcileable to itself.

Most of our *Antiquaries* do

allow this City to be in the Kingdom of the *Trinobants*, and within this County of *Essex*, tho' where the Situation of it was, is controverted among them; *Harrison* in *Hollingshed's* History of *England*, *Ed.* 2. affixeth it at *Colchester*; and is therein followed in the *new Map* of *Middlesex*, *Essex*, and *Hertfordshire* compil'd by *Warburton* and others; as also by Dr. *Stukeley*, in the Map to his *Itinerarium Curiosum*, *Cent.* I. *p.* 198. in which last mention'd *Map*, by as I presume a Mistake of the Graver, *Esterford* is call'd *Chesterford*. *Cambden* placeth it at *Maldon Brit. p.* 347. ed. 1695, and of the same Opinion is *Burton* in his *Antoninus*, *p.* 339. and *Tyrrell* in his *History*, Vol. I. *p.* 24. where he saith, that the *Britains* had a Temple for their Goddess *Andrasta* or *Andate*, who is suppos'd to be the Goddess of *Victory*, whose Representation is I presume stamp'd on the reverse of the Coin of *Cunobeline* aforemention'd. But how Mr. *Burton*

Hands, by the *Saxon Erthenwyn*, ^c and though but a small parcel of *Britain*, compared with the whole, yet had the Honour of being called the Kingdom of *East-Saxons*, which Denomination is preferved in the Name of this County at this Day, continuing about 280 Years under the Reign of fourteen Kings (of no great Power or Force, *Quorum Reges fere femper aliis pare-bant*

Burton came in his *Commentary upon Antoninus*, *p.* 238. to affirm, that *John Leland*, *Humphry Lhuyd*, and fuch as follow them do feek for *Camulodunum* at *Colchefter*, when no fuch thing is to be found in *Leland*, but the contrary, I cannot conceive. Dr. *Gale* carries it to *Walden* in his Commentary on *Antoninus*, *p.* III. as did before him that great Antiquary *Leland*, Vol. III. *p.* 123. which agrees with the *Chorograp. Brit.* of the *Anonymous* Author of *Ravenna* printed with the fame Author *p.* 145. *Pointer* alfo placeth it at the fame Place, *Brit. Rom. p.* 54. There is only one other Author which I fhall now mention, and that is *Salmon*, who believes *Caftle Camps* in *Cambridge-fhire* to be the Place, *Roman Stations, p.* 27. what the Reafons for the

feveral aforecited Opinions are, may be feen in their Works, to which I refer my Readers, they being too long for this Place.

^e *Erkenwin*, *Erchenwin*, or *Efcwin*, or in reality out of the Hands of the *Britains*, of whom *Arthur* was then *King*, of whom many fabulous Stories are reported by the Writers of that time, yet may he be juftly celebrated for many worthy Actions. See Dr. *Stillingfleet's Antiquities of the Britifh Churches, p.* 332. Whilft King *Arthur* was ingag'd againft *Cordic* King of the *Weft-Saxons*, and *Cenryc* his Son at a Place call'd *Cerdics-Leah*, this *Erthenwyn* landing with his Forces in *Norfolk*, and being affifted by the powerful King of *Kent*, made his way into *Effex*; and there erected the fourth *Saxon King-dom*.

bant Regibus, frequentius tamen ac diutius Regibus Mer-
ciorum. Ex Aurea Hiſt. MSS. penes Sil. Taylor *gen.*
Authorem horum collect.

ᶠ Till in the Year 808, King *Egbert* added it as
a Province to his Kingdom of the *Weſt-Saxons*, ſub-
duing *Cuthred* the laſt King thereof.

dom. King *Arthur* died *A. D.*
542. and was buried in the Monaſtery of *Glaſtenbury*, whoſe
Coffin was found in the Reign
of King *Henry* II. cover'd with
a large Stone, on which, on a leaden Croſs was ingraven the following Epitaph, *Hic jacet ſepul-*
tus inclytus Rex Arthurus in inſula
Avalonia. This being preſerv'd
until *Leland's* time he took a Copy
of it, the ſame which you have
in *Cambden, p. 65.*

ᶠ A ſhort Account of which I
ſhall tranſcribe from Sir *Winſton*
Churchill's Divi Brit. p. 116, 117.
adding the Names by which they
are call'd in other Authors, *viz.*

1. *Erthenwyn, Erchenwin, Er-*
kenwin or *Eſcwin*, the Son of *Offa*,
Great-grand-ſon of *Sneppa*, third
in deſcent from *Seaxnod*, third Son
of *Woden*, the common Progeni-
tor of the *Saxons*, began this Kingdom with the Happineſs of a long
Reign, which, however it be fel-

dom deſir'd, was certainly very
advantageous to his Succeſſor.

Mr. *Tyrrell* here mentions *Sige-*
bert and *Swithelm*, between *Er-*
thenwyn, and

2. *Sledda*, who thought the
readieſt way to what his Prede-
ceſſor got, was to add to it what
his Succeſſors were not like to
keep, namely, a Peace with the
Kings of *Kent*, his next Neighbours, confirm'd by an Alliance
with *Ethelbert* the Proto-Chriſti-
an, who converted his Son.

3. *Sigebert, Seabert, Sebert,* that
in honour to his Religion made
that League perpetual, which after his death was broken by his
three graceleſs Sons. This is
one of thoſe placed by *Tyrrell* before *Sledda.*

4. *Sered, Sexred, Seward, Sige-*
bert, who rul'd together like Brethren in Iniquity, perſecuting all
that were Chriſtians, till *Ingill*
the *Weſt-Saxon* (converted but a
little

little before) reveng'd the holy Caufe by putting a Period to their *Triumvirate*, upon which

5. *Sigebert*, Son of the middlemoſt, took Place, he was furnam'd *The Little*; (not from his Perfon, but his Credit) being fo deteſted by his People, that they put by his Son and Brother, to admit another of the fame Name, but of a different Temper.

6. *Sigebert*, the third Son of *Sigebald*, younger Brother of *Sigebert* the firſt, who declaring for Chriſtianity, was furnam'd the Good; and being murther'd, during the Minority of his Son, his Brother,

7. *Swithelm* fucceeded, as if to taſte of Royalty only, falling under the fame Fate, by the fame Hand, and for the fame Caufe; (this I take for the other Perfon mention'd by *Tyrrell*) by whofe Death,

8. *Sigehere*, *Sigher*, the Son of *Sigebert* the *Little*, affiſted by his Uncle *Sebba* got into the Throne; his Succeffor was

9. *Sebba* the Saint, to whom *Bede* afcribes that famous Miracle of lengthening the Marble Cheſt in which his Body was laid, which he fays, was too fhort by a Foot for the Corps, till the Body was put into it; which,

whofoever believes, muſt ſtretch his Faith to the Miracle.

Tyrrell makes this and the foregoing Coufins.

10. *Sigehere*, *Sigehard*, the fecond, one fitter to be a Monk than a Monarch, giving up his Scepter for a pair of Beads to his Brother

11. *Seafrid*, who if he rul'd not with him, rul'd very little after him.

Tyrrell makes this and the foregoing to reign together.

12. *Offa*, the Son of *Sigehere* fucceeded, who impoverifh'd himfelf by enriching the Church, and having quitted his Wife to perform a Pilgrimage to *Rome*, tempted her to retire from the World and become a Nun, whereby either loft the other, and both the Hopes of any Iſſue.

13. *Selred*, the Son of *Sigebert* the *Good*, whofe old Age was crown'd with an unexpected Succeffion, but he took not fo much Pleafure in it, as to furvive it.

14. *Suthred*, *Swithred*, *Cuthred*, fill'd up his Place, who being involv'd in the Fate of *Baldred* King of *Kent*, and attack'd by the *Weſt-Saxons*, loft this, as the other did that Kingdom, whereby it became a Province under the victorious *Egbert*. CHAP.

CHAP. I.

THEIR *Topographical* Concerns come firſt before
us: And of them *Harwich* firſt; becauſe honour'd with the Title of a *Borough*; and by that,
preceding *Dovercourt* in Denomination as well as
Power in all civil and judicial Affairs. *Harwich cum
Dovercourt.*

The higheſt Antiquity that as yet we have diſcover'd of it, is, what Mr. *Cambden* ᵍ p. 351. com-
memorates of a Sea-fight there, between the *Engliſh*
and the *Danes*; taking Notice of a Promontory, from
this Point (ſaith he) the Shore runs back a little to
the *Stour's Mouth*, famous for a Sea-fight between the
Saxons and the *Danes* in the Year 884. ʰ Here is
now

ᵍ *Brit. Ed.* 1696.

ʰ King *Ælfred* having now
(885) reinforc'd his Fleet, was
reſolv'd to fall upon the *Daniſh
Pyrates*, who then ſhelter'd a-
mong their Countrymen of *Eaſt-
England*; upon which he ſent his
Fleet, which he had got ready
in *Kent*, (being very well mann'd)
into the Mouth of the River
Stoure (not that in *Kent*, but an-

other which runs by *Harwich*)
where they were met by ſixteen
Daniſh Pyrates, who lay there
watching for a Prey; and immediately ſetting upon them,
after a ſharp Reſiſtance, the King's
Men boarding them, they were
all taken, together with great
Spoils, and moſt of the Men
kill'd. But as the King's Fleet
was returning home, they fell
among

now feated *Harwich* a very fafe Harbour as the Name
imports,

among another Fleet of *Danes*,
much ftronger, with whom
fighting again, the *Danes* obtain'd the Victory; tho' with
what Lofs to the *Englifh*, the
Annals do not fay. A different
Account of this fecond Engage-
ment is given by *Tyrrell* in·the
following Relation.

But the reft of the *Danes* of
Eaft England were fo much
incens'd at this Victory, as alfo
with the Slaughter of their
Countrymen, that fending out a
great Fleet very well mann'd,
they fail'd to the Mouth of
Thames; where fetting upon divers of the King's Ships, by
furprize in the Night, when all
the Men were afleep, they had
much the better of them, &c.
Tyrrell's Hift. Vol. I. *p.* 287.

Mr. *Lambard* gives an Account
likewife of this Sea-fight, with
fome Variation as follows. King
Alfred, having many times (and
that with much Lofs and more
Danger) encountered his Enemies the *Danes*, and finding that
by reafon of the fundry Swarms
of them arriving in divers Parts
of his Realm at once, he was

not able to repulfe them being
landed, he rigged up a Royal
Navy, and determin'd to keep
the High-Seas, hoping thereby
either to beat them upon the
Water, or to burn their Veffels if they fhould fortune to
arrive. Soon after this it for-
tun'd his Navy to meet with the
Danifh Fleet at the Mouth of
the River *Stoure*, where at the
firft Encounter the *Danes* loft
fixteen Sail of their Ships: But
(as many times it falleth out,
that Security followeth Victory) fo
the King's Army kept no watch,
by reafon whereof the *Danes*
having repair'd their Forces, came
frefhly upon the *Englifh* Mariners at unawares, and finding
them faft afleep gave them a
great and bloody Overthrow.

The Likenefs, or rather the
Agreement of the Names would
lead one to think, that the true
Place of this Conflict fhould be
Stoure Mouth in this Shire *(Kent)*,
the rather for that it is deriv'd
from the Mouth of the River
Stoure; and that by the Circum-
ftances of the Story it appeareth,
King *Alfred* was in *Kent* when

C   he

imports, for the *Saxon* hane-pic fignifies as much as an *Haven* or *Bay*, where an *Army* may lie[i].

This eafily reflecting or bending Shore from that Promontory (anciently nam'd Eaðulpheꝛ-neꝛꝛe now call'd the *Naze* or *Nafeland*, on which ftands *Walton on the Neffe*) tending Northwards, fhews near whereabouts the Mouth of *Stoure* anciently was; which River rifing in this County not far from a Place call'd *Sturmere*, running its Courfe by *Neyland*.and *Maningtree*, and fo by *Wrabnefs*, (where giving Name to a fair Wood, call'd *Stoure-Wood*, belonging to the worfhipful *William Whitemore*, Efq;) [k] a little below it, not only leaves, but at this prefent hath alfo loft its own

---

he made Determination of this Journey. (Voyage.) Howbeit, he that fhall advifedly read as it is fet down by *Afferus*, fhall confefs it to have been in *Eaft-Angle*, which contain'd *Northfolk* and *Suffolk*, &c. And for the more certainty, I take it to have chanced at the fame Place which we now call *Harwich* Haven. For that River divideth *Effex* from *Suffolk*; and not far from the Head thereof in *Effex*, there ftandeth a Town yet call'd *Sturmere*, which (in my Fantafy) fufficiently maintaineth the Knowledge of this

Matter, *Lambard's Perambulation, p.* 280, 281.

[i] Dr. *Skinner* delivers the *Etymology* of the Name of this Town in thefe Words 𝔥𝔞𝔯𝔢𝔴𝔦𝔠𝔥 *in Com. Eff.*AS. hanepic, *feu potiùs* hеnepic (i. e.) *Statio* 𝔲𝔢𝔩 𝔖𝔦𝔫𝔲𝔰 *Exercitûs Navale bello inter Anglos & Danos; nobilis, ab* AS. hеnе, *Exercitus* (an Hoft or Army) & Wic *Sinus,* (a Hollownefs of Water-banks) *Propugnaculum.* Skinner's *Etymologicon Onomafticon, Lit. H.* (a Blockhoufe, a Bulwark).

[k] Now 1727. to *Daniel Burr,* Efq;

Name

Name ₁ in the Salt Water of *Orwell* [*Gurgites* (are
certain fiſhing Wares) *in Aqua ſalſa de* Orwell (for
ſo

₁ The Riſe of this River *Stoure*
is from three Heads or Springs,
one of which ariſeth near *Bradley* in *Suffolk*, a ſecond is near
Haverill, a ſmall *Market Town*
in that County, (on the Edge
of *Eſſex* and *Cambridgeſhire*)
from whence having run about
a Mile, it with the firſt which
it there joins, forms a *Mere* of ſome
Acres of Ground, which giveth
the Name of *Stoure* or *Sturmere*
to the Pariſh in which it lyeth
or adjoineth ; dividing the two
Counties of *Eſſex* and *Suffolk*;
and having receiv'd the third
Head which ariſeth about *Helion
Bumpſtead* in *Eſſex*, maketh its
way under *Bathan - Bridge* to
Stoke-Clare, where formerly was
a College for ſecular Canons,
now the Habitation of Sir *Harvey Elways*, Baronet ; near which
on the *Eſſex* Side lyeth *Aſhen* alias
Eſſe; from hence the Courſe is
continued to *Clare*, (giving the
Title formerly to a Dukedom)
when it was a Town of great
Note, and had a famous Caſtle,
(the Ruins of which yet are to

be ſeen, in which one *Eluric*,
A. D. 1090. in the Reign of
Edward the *Confeſſor*, *Tanner*'s
Notit. Mon. 209. or rather 1060,
becauſe the Year 1090 was in
William the *Conqueror*'s Reign)
founded a *College* for ſeven *ſecular Canons*; it had alſo a Priory
(ſome Part of which is now a
Gentleman's Seat) of *Auguſtine
Friers*, ſuppos'd to be founded
by *Richard* Earl of *Clare*, *Weaver, p.* 742. and it is likely in
the ſame Place where the aforeſaid *College* ſtood, the Monks of
which were *Anno* 1123. remov'd
to *Stoke* aforeſaid, for the Priory
without doubt ſtood within the
Caſtle, the true River which
parts the two Counties being on
the *Eſſex* Side of it, and the preſent River, which ſeparates it
from the Site of the Caſtle,
being long ſince made for the
ſupplying of a Mill a little below it. There was alſo a Ram-
part of Earth, which fortified
the North - Weſt Side of the
Town, but now it is become a
poor Town, having a very ſmall
Market

C 2

fo in ancient Writings 'tis often call'd, *Chart. dat.* 19.
Ric. 2.] being betwixt *Harwich* and *Shotley*; a
Place

Market every *Friday*, retaining fome Shadow of a *Borough*, by the annual Choice of a *Bailiff*. From hence the *Stoure* paffing between *Cavendiſh* and *Pentlow*, continues its Courfe to *Milford*, vulgò *Long - Milford*, near the Church of which is a neat *Hoſpital* for   poor Men, and not far from it a magnificent *Houfe* built of Brick (as is likewife the *Hoſpital*) by Sir *William Cordwell*, Knight; being Speaker of the *Houfe of Commons* in the Reign of Queen *Mary*, and *Maſter* of the Rolls; and from hence to *Sudbury*, a *Borough Town* which fends Members to *Parliament*, being govern'd by a *Mayor* chofen annually out of feven *Aldermen:* It hath a good Market on *Saturdays*, and in it are now three *Churches*, in the Veftry of one of which, *viz.* St. *Gregory*'s,is kept the Head of *Symon* of *Sudbury* alias *Theobald*, (and not*Tibolds* or *Tibald*, as*Newcourt* and *Le Neve* write him) Archbifhop of *Canterbury*, who was beheaded by the Rebels

June 14. 1381. and buried in his own *Cathedral*, faith *Le Neve* in his *Fafti*, where indeed there is a handfom Monument or *Cenotaph*; but in the Church aforefaid, where they fhew a large Black Marble formerly much inlayed in a Chapel of his own Foundation, under which they fay his Body was buried: There are alfo the Remains of four *Religious Houfes*. From this Town the River is, by an Act of the fourth and fifth of Queen *Anne*, intitled, *An Act for making the River* Stower *navigable from the Town of* Maningtree *in the County of* Effex, *to the Town of* Sudbury *in the County of* Suffolk, made navigable to *Maningtree*, by the Help of Locks for Barges and Boats carrying and re-carrying Corn, Coal, *&c.* whereby the Country adjacent is fupplied; paffing by *Buers*, *Neyland*, and *Straetford* in its way to *Maningtree* aforefaid, to which and higher the Tide flows; it is there divided into three Streams: This laft Town is in *Effex*, and
has

Place where Ships may ride and find very good Anchorage ᵐ.

This is that *Orwell* noted for feveral paft Ages to be a Port of Trade ᵐ, and mention'd (relating to its Conveniency and excellent Situation for Merchandizing) by the famous *Jeoffrey Chaucer* in his *Merchant's Prologue,* viz.

has a Market on *Thurfdays*; here is a Salt-houfe at which they refine Salt; and near the Banks of the *Stoure* on the *Suffolk* Side ftand *Brentham, Sutton, Arwarton* the ancient Seat of Sir *Philip Parker* Member of Parliament for *Harwich* 1727, and *Shotley,* from which is a Ferry over to *Harwich.*

ᵐ *Orwell Haven* is properly that Part which reacheth to *Ipfwich,* where the River *Orwell* or *Gyping* emptieth itfelf, whofe Rife is from two Heads, one near *Wulpit,* and the other *Gipping*; and whatever this *Haven* was in *Chaucer's* Time, the Cafe is now alter'd; for tho' it is a broad Water even up to *Ipfwich* when the Tide is in, yet it is for fome Miles below that Town fo fill'd with Mud, that only fmall Veffels can come up to the Key; and when it is out,

it looks juft like a Haven without *Water,* as King *Charles* the fecond farcaftically faid of it.

Of the Name of this Haven was formerly a Family of fome Note in *Feverfham* in *Kent,* one *Simon Orwell* being Mayor thereof 16. *Hen.* VI. *Anno Domini* 1438. and in the Eaft Window of the North Chancel or Chantry of that Church, is a *Rebus* or *Name-device,* together with the Effigies of himfelf, Wife and Children kneeling, all painted in the Glafs, and under them is written, 𝖔𝖗𝖆𝖙𝖊 𝖕𝖗𝖔 𝖆𝖓𝖎𝖒𝖆𝖇𝖚𝖘 𝖲𝖎𝖒𝖔𝖓𝖎𝖘 𝖔𝖗𝖜𝖊𝖑𝖑 𝖖𝖚𝖎 𝖎𝖘𝖙𝖆𝖒 𝖋𝖊𝖓𝖊𝖘𝖙𝖗𝖆𝖒 𝖋𝖎𝖊𝖗𝖎 —— the reft is broken, *Lewis's Antiquities of Feverfham,* P. 2. *p.* 25. But whether the Name was taken from this Haven, or from a Parifh in *Cambridgefhire* I will not determine, tho' I rather believe the laft.

Þir peaꝛony he ꝛpake ꝼull ꝛolempnely
Sheping alpay þe eucpeaꝛe oꝼ hiꝛ pẏnnẏng
Þe polde þe See peꝛe kepte ꝼoꝛ any þhẏnȝe
Bẏꜩpẏxe ꝳẏddelboꝛouȝhe and Opeꝛell.

This is that *Orwell* upon whofe Shores the Town of *Harwich* is built, as by many authentick Teftimonies and Evidences is manifeft, among which a Deed with Seals, (*in Cifta Com. hujus Burgi*) of a Grant of a Meffuage in this Town. *Uno capite abut. fuper ftratum ducentem ufque ad portum Orwell, dat.* 1. Edw. 4.

It is generally believ'd that the *Stoure* did formerly in a ftreighter Current (than now it doth) difcharge itfelf into the Sea about *Hoafley-Bay*, under the Highlands of *Walton-Colenefs* and *Felixftow* (corruptè *Filftow*) in the County of *Suffolk*, betwixt which and *Landguard-Fort* are, as they are reputed, certain Remains of the old Channel, which the neighbouring Inhabitants ftill call *Fleets*, retaining at this Day the Tradition of the Courfe of the Water, and the Entrance into this Haven to have heretofore been by and through them; and confequently below them (North-Eaft) to have been that before mention'd *Oftium Stouri*[a].

The

---

[a] That there may be Truth in this Tradition from a natural Caufe, I am very much inclin'd to believe; daily Experience

The principal Officers of his Majefty's Ordinance in the *Tower* of *London,* do ftill (according to former Precedents)

rience manifefting, that by violent Floods great Quantities of Earth, Sand, and Gravel being wafhed down into Rivers, are carried towards the Sea and lodged at the Mouths of Havens and large Rivers, where they fo often change the Current of the Channels, that thereby the Navigation thro' them is made variable and difficult, and in many Places not to be attempted without a Pilot; and to fuch a Caufe as this may the firft Change of the Courfe of thefe Rivers be attributed: For thefe two great Rivers, *Stoure* and *Orwell,* bringing down much Sand and Gravel by the Floods, and by Degrees lodging it near their Mouths, firft make an Ifland in the Middle of the Haven; and then by frequent Additions on the *Suffolk* Side ftreighten the Paffage, until by Degrees it was fill'd up, and the wafhing away of the Clift on the *Effex* Side contribute to the building the Mouth of the Harbour more Southward than it was at firft;

and to me this feems a more probable Account than what an Author fometime fince affirm'd, and *that this Harbour or Channel is artificial and of no old Date, the Current having been formerly on the other Side of* Landguard-Fort, *which then ftood in* Effex. *And from this undoubtedly proceeds that Bed of Shells, that covers the Cliff at perhaps fifty Feet height, which muft be carried thither at the making of the Harbour, or clearing of it.* Thus far our Author; againft whofe Opinion, are divers Reafons urg'd in the *Philofophical Tranfactions* of the *Royal Society of* London. As that fo great a Work as this was, *viz.* the making a Channel two Miles wide (as it is in this Place) would not have been done without fome Record thereof in Hiftory: And then, that the Earth, *&c.* which would arife by this Work, muft confequently have made a much greater Hill than this Cliff ever was: Then, why the Workmen fhould bring all the Earth, *&c.* and lay it on this Side the Channel,

cedents) continue the Writing of *Landguard-Fort* in *Essex:* And although several now (1676.) living pretend to the Remembrance of the Building it, yet we find there was an ancienter Fort thereabouts, and call'd by the same Name as this; South West of which is the Entrance into Harbour °.   In the Commotion of

Dudley

Channel, and not some on the other, as it is plain they did not, because the Ground on which *Landguard-Fort* stands, as far as *Walton-Coleness* (which is about three Miles) is only a level of Beach or Shingle : Farther, that the same *Strata* of *Sand, Fossil-Shells,* and their *Fragments* which are in this Cliff, are to be found in other Cliffs some Miles distant from *Harwich,* as at *Walton-Ness* in *Essex,* and *Bawsey Cliff* in *Suffolk,* &c. *Philof. Tranf.* Vol. XXIV. N°. 291. *p.* 1574. To which may be added, that not only in this, but also in all the other Cliffs above mention'd, the Strata of Sand, Shells, &c. lie above the Clay and near the Surface of the Earth, which would have been either at the Bottom, or promiscuous with the Clay, had it been done by Workmen.

° The *Landguard-Fort* mention'd by our Author, was a handsome square *Fortification,* consisting of four *Bastions, viz.* at each Corner one mounted with divers Guns, those towards the Sea being the largest ; the Entrance into it was over a Draw-Bridge, thro' a Gate, over which was their Magazine ; fronting the Gate was a handsome Brick Building in which the *Governor,* when he was there, resided : Adjoining to the South End of which was a neat *Chapel,* in which the *Chaplain* read *Prayers* twice a Week, and preach'd a Sermon on the *Sunday.* On each Side of the *Parade* was a double Row of Brick *Barracks,* each containing eight, those on the right Hand, being for the Habitations of the *Deputy Governor, Master Gunner,* and the *Quarter Gunners;* and those

Dudley Duke of *Northumberland* in the firſt Year of *Queen Mary, A. D.* 1553. this Town of *Harwich* was furniſh'd with great Guns from thence [*in Lib. Maj. MSS. Burgi in Ciſta Eccleſiæ,* falſly there written *Layngay*] which *ancient Fort* was not far diſtant from this modern one; a little North of it: Where now is the common Burial for the Soldiers; and where are yet to be ſeen two Faces and Flankers of a *Baſtion;* the Remains doubtleſs of the ancient one; the reſt of it being eaten away by the Sea, but in its Place, hath left upon the Shore a long Row of *Sand-backs,* under which the *Dutch July* 1. 1667. landed about three thouſand Men at the Foot of *Felixſtow Cliff,* and with about two thouſand of them march'd near the *Fort,* under the Shelter of thoſe Banks or ſmall Hills, lodging them-ſelves within *Carbine Shot,* on two Sides of the *Fort:* Who after above an Hour's inceſſant firing their ſmall Arms, rather againſt the Firmament than the *Fort;* were put to Fright and Flight by two or three ſmall Guns out of a little *Galliot* firing amongſt the Shingle (which covered them from the Sight of the *Fort)* ſcattering

thoſe on the left for a *Sutling-Houſe,* and the reſt for Lodg-ings for the Garriſon; between theſe laſt and the Gate was the *Guard-Room,* for thoſe upon Duty. Freſh Water is brought in Pipes under Ground from *Walton* aforeſaid, about three Miles. About ſixty Men us'd to be here in Garriſon. This I am told hath been lately much di-miniſh'd, both in Buildings and Number of Men.

D the

the Pebbles amongſt them: Their great Guns from their Ships playing all that time upon the *Fort.* It was then defended by Captain *Dorrel,* ſince *Major* to his *Royal Highneſs* ᵖ his Regiment, and is at this Preſent (1676.) under the Command of the honourable Collonel, Sir *Charles Littleton,* Knight; Collonel of his *Royal Highneſs's* beforemention'd Regiment.

Over againſt this Fort and on the other Side of the Entrance into this Harbour, is a High-land call'd the *Cliff;* where

---

ᵖ *James* Duke of *York,* afterwards King *James* II.

ᑫ *Harwich Cliff* is a Sort of *Promontory,* which divides *Orwell Haven* from the *Æſtuarium,* contain'd between that and *Walton Naſe* or *Neſs;* it is ſituate on the Southern Part of the Town, about a Quarter of a Mile diſtant, on the Right of the Road from *Dovercourt,* and contains many Acres of Land. The Height of it from the Strand or Beach to the Top, where it is higheſt, is forty or fifty Foot. At the Bottom of this *Cliff,* there is a *Stratum* of Clay of a blueiſh Colour about a Foot thick, which is ſucceeded by another of *Stone* of much the ſame Colour for a Foot more; in this *Stratum* of *Stone* are imbedded *Shells* (tho' but ſparingly) as well of the *Turbinate,* as *Bivalve* Kinds, the *Shells* of which remain upon the incloſ'd *Stony Nucleus,* but not being ſupplied with that *Sparry* Subſtance, which thoſe imbedded in *Chalk* and *Quarries* of *Stone* moſtly are, they oftentimes moulder and crumble off, when they have for ſome time been expos'd to the Air; and alſo Pieces of *Wood* and *Sticks petrified.* Above this are divers *Strata* of the ſame bluiſh Clay about the Height of twenty Foot, or more; this *Clay* hath *Pyrites* or *Copperas Stones* ſticking in it, but no *Shells* that I could obſerve. *D. Plot* in his *Natural Hiſtory* *of*

Tab. 2. Page 18.

A. The greater Light-House. B. The lesser Light-House. C. Nacley Ferry-House. D. The River Stour which divides Essex and Suffolk. E. The Orwel which comes from Ipswich. F. The Haven. G. The Cliff where the Beacon stood. H. Bags gathering Copperas Stones. I. Cliff Stones. K. Arwarton in Suffolk.

R. Sheppard Sculp!

where ſtands a *Beacon*[r] near to which the *Relicks* of
an

of Oxfordſhire, p. 52. takes
Notice that it was common in
the blew Clays of that County
to have the *Pyrites aureus* or
Braſs-lumps (which are Sorts of
Copperas Stones) mixed with it:
And I have ſeen them among
Tile-Earth at *Bocking* in *Eſſex*;
without doubt it is ſo in other
Places.] Above this are divers
Strata, which reach to within a-
bout two Foot of the *Surface*,
ſome of which are only of fine
Sand, others have Stone and Gravel mixt with Fragments of *Shells*,
and others are mixt with ſmall
Pebbles; and it is in ſome of
theſe laſt mention'd *Strata*, that
the *Foſſil-Shells* are imbedded.
Theſe *Foſſils* lie promiſcuouſly
together, *Bivalve* and *Turbinate*,
neither do the *Strata* in which
they lie obſerve any order, being ſometimes higher and ſometimes lower in the *Cliff*; with
Strata of Sand, Gravel and Fragments of Shells between. Nor
do the *Shells* always lie ſeparate or diſtinct in the *Strata*,
but are oftentimes found in
Lumps or Maſſes, ſomething

friable, cemented together with
Sand and Fragments, of a ferruginous or ruſty Colour, of
which all theſe *Strata* are. O-
ver all is a covering of common
ſandy Earth, about the Thickneſs of two Foot, in which are
ſometimes to be ſeen Veins of a
White friable Subſtance reſembling *Oſteocolla*, tho' more tender than the *Oſteocolla Officinarum*, which being brought out
of *Germany*, this may not improperly be call'd *Oſteocolla Anglicana:* It doth incruſt about
ſmall Strings like the Fibres of
the Roots of Trees, and is of
divers Magnitudes, ſending forth
Branches here and there, but
ſo friable as not to be gotten
out of the Earth in any large
Pieces. Which made the late
Mr. *Edward Lhwyd* Keeper of
the *Aſhmolean Muſeum* at *Oxford*
conjecture it to be a Sort of
Lac Lunæ. What the aforemention'd *Foſſils* are I ſhall reſerve for the *Appendix.*

[r] The *Beacon* mention'd by our
Author is not now extant, for
as he afterwards obſerves, that

by

an ancient *Fortification* are ftill to be feen; which fhew not only Labour and Pains in the Greatnefs of the Work; but alfo the Marks and Tokens of no contemptible *Antiquity:* The Line runs Southerly from a little without the *Town-Gate* to the *Beacon-Hill-Field*; about the midft of which is a little artificial Hill (whereupon at this Time ftands a *Windmill*, belonging to the Fabrick of the *Chapel* of this Town) rais'd probably by the firft Fortifiers (whoever they were) for fome eminent Ufe, they had for fuch like, in thofe elder Times; perhaps for placing their *Standards*; or for a *Tumulus* over one of their deceas'd *Chiefs*, &c.   Many of which Sort are to be feen in many Places in *England:* But the encroaching Sea hath terminated our further Difquifition of the Camp in the *Beacon-Field*; except that on the Top of the Hill it is obfervable, another Work runs acrofs from the firft Eafterly: And is by the fame Means cut off near to the *Beacon*; as the other South Part of this Camp was faid to be ᶠ.   Not

by reafon of the falling down of the *Cliff*; it had been divers times remov'd, fo that Reafon hath at laft demolifh'd it, it having been down for many Years, and the Government not thinking them any longer needful, they have been fuffered to decay not only here, but in all (or at leaft) moft other Places. The Fortifications mention'd by Mr. *Taylors*'s *MSS.* are upon the *Cliff* on the *Harwich* Side of the Haven, and not at *Landguard-Fort*, as the Additions to *Cambden* would incline the Reader to believe.

    ᶠ When the Fortifications aforefaid

Not to queſtion Mr. *Cambden's* Derivation and Interpretation of the Name of this Town, out of the *Engliſh-Saxon Tongue* haɲe-pic, to betoken a *Station*

foreſaid had their Original, thoſe times of Confuſion and Obſcurity have left us no Record: Dr. *Skinner* in his forecited *Etymology* of this Town, ſeems to infer as if the Name came from the Action, in the *Orwell*, viz. the Sea-fight aforemention'd between the *Saxons*, (*not Angles*) and the *Danes*; for the *Danes* were then, as I take it, in Poſſeſſion of their Country, *viz.* the Counties of *Suffolk* and *Norfolk:* For *Hungar* the *Dane* having ſlain King *Edmund*, Anno 870. poſſeſs'd himſelf of the Kingdom of the *Eaſt - Angles*, and it was kept by that People many Years, between whom and the *Saxons* were great Conteſts; and they being ſuch near Neighbours to this Town of *Harwich*, might probably be the Occaſion, not only of the Camp laſt mention'd by Mr. *Taylor*, but alſo of the *Gates, Walls, Bulwarks*, and *Caſtle* of the Town itſelf.

'Tis ſtrong by Situation, writes a late Author, *and may be made more ſo by Art: But 'tis many Years ſince the Government of* England *have had any Occaſion to fortify Towns to the* Landward *;'tis enough that the Harbour or Road, which is one of the beſt and ſecureſt in* England, *is cover'd at the Entrance by a ſtrong Fort and a Battery of Guns to the Southward, juſt as at* Tilbury, *and which ſufficiently defend the Mouth of the River; and there is a particular Felicity in this Fortification, viz. That tho' the Entrance or Opening of the River into the Sea is very wide, eſpecially at High Water, at leaſt two Miles, if not three over, yet the Channel which is deep, and in which the Ships muſt keep and come to the Harbour, is narrow, and lies only on the Side of the* Fort; *ſo that all the Ships which come in, or go out, muſt come cloſe under the Guns of the* Fort; *that is to ſay, under the Command of their Shot.* Tour thro' *Great Britain*, Vol. I. Let. I. *p.* 47.

(or a *Creek*) where an Army encamp'd; although in all Extents and Circumstances it seems a little hard fully to comply with it; if it be granted that ꝩape doth signify an Army, then 𝖂𝖎𝖈𝖍, 𝖂𝖎𝖐𝖊, 𝖂𝖎𝖙𝖟, and 𝖂𝖎𝖈 may figuratively signify a Camp or Station for an Army; because if deriv'd from *Vicus* among the *Latins* (some Part of whose Language might have been as well among the *Germans*, as left among the *Britains*) signifying Houses conjoin'd in Rows on both Sides of a Street or Streets; in that Point (we say) the Manner of Soldiers, their encamping would very much resemble one; notwithstanding *Vicus* is taken genuinely to relate to Streets and Buildings unfortify'd; but to this Supposition, the Remains of the old Camp above the Town still extant may afford some probability: Again why the Name of it should signify a Safe-road or a Creek, as well as Station for an Army, we know not what to say to it ᵗ. Some make 𝖂𝖎𝖈𝖍 to signify

---

ᵗ 𝖂𝖎𝖈𝖍, *unde tot terminationes nominum Oppidorum & Pagorum,* ab Anglo-Saxon, 𝖂𝖎𝖈, 𝖂𝖎𝖈𝖊, 𝕭𝖊𝖑𝖌. 𝖂𝖎𝖈𝖍, Dan. 𝕯𝖎𝖈, *Sinus, Ripa seu Littus sinuosum, hoc à verbo* 𝖂𝖎𝖈𝖐𝖊𝖓, Teut. 𝖂𝖊𝖎𝖈𝖐𝖊𝖓, *Cedere, Recedere, Divertere, vel potiùs ab* Anglo-Saxon. 𝖂𝖎𝖈, Belg. 𝖂𝖎𝖈𝖐, *Castellum, Propugnaculum, Regio, Tractus, Ju-* *risdictio, Territorium, Vicus, Quadrivium,* Fr. Th. 𝖂𝖎𝖈𝖐 *Mansio vel Statio,* Anglo-Sax. 𝖂𝖎𝖈𝖎𝖆𝖓, *Habitare, Manere, Appellere, navem in Portum subducere,* Anglo-Sax. *autem* 𝖂𝖎𝖈, & Belg. & Fr. Th. 𝖂𝖎𝖈𝖐 *non incommodè declinari possent, à* Lat. *Vicus.* Fr. *Jun. tamen more suo deducit a* Gr. οἰϰΘ. Skinner's *Etymolog. Anglic.*

such

fuch Places where the Water is fo Salt, that falt is made
of it; fo the *Wiches* in *Chefhire,* and *Worcefter-
fhire* [u]. Some think that *Wich* fignifies fuch a Piece of
Land, about which the Waters almoft incircling make a
Peninfula: Which would well enough comply with the Situation of *Harwich:* Tho' not with all thofe Towns, who
have *Wich* in their Denominations. But from the
ancient *Saxon* Appellation of this Town we may obferve, that it had its being in thofe ancient *Saxon* times,
if not before.

Neither have we any certainty when it proceeded
to take a higher Degree of Honour, from *Vicus* an
unfortified *Wic* or *Wich* (which it ftill retains in its
Name) to *Burgus* a fortified Town; the Walls whereof
fhew fo much Antiquity, that it is probable it was a
fortified *Borough,* before it attain'd to be a *free Borough:*
The Remains of which *Muniments* or *Safeguards,* are
in many Places very obvious; tho' the precife Time
when thofe Walls, Towers, and Gates were firft built
is not difcover'd.

[u] Not only thofe which have
Salt Springs in them, have their
Names terminated with the
Word *Wich,* as thofe in the
Counties mention'd by our Author; but likewife many others,
which either have the Sea adjoyning, or the falt Water flowing
up to them: I might give many
Inftances hereof, but fhall only
name three, and they fhall be,
the Town we are treating of,
and *Ipfwich,* and *Dunwich* in
Suffolk.

A *Borough*

A *Borough* the Latins name *Burgus*, which fome derive from the *Greek* Word πυργὸς, a *fortified Place*, a *Caſtle-Fort*, or *Tower*; others from the *Saxon* Buᵽᵹ, and that denotes a Place covered or *ſheltered* with *Walls*: An analogical Uſe of which Word we ſtill preſerve in our Speech ; ſaying, to *Bury*, i. e. to *Cover* ʷ. And as *Urbs* relates to the Buildings of a *City*, and *Civitas* to that Body Politick, which inhabit thoſe Buildings: So *Burgus* not only comprehends the Coverings, Fortifications, and the Buildings of a Town : But alſo the *Burgeaſſes*, or *Burgeſſes*, the *Inhabitants* of thoſe Buildings ſo *inmur'd* or fortified, who had that Denomination anciently given to them, from their common Concern, to defend themſelves and their Habitations ˣ. To whom in a quite different way of living were the ancient *Pagani*; *qui in Pago habitant*

ʷ To 𝔅urp *ab* Anglo-Sax. Biᵽian, &c. *Sepelire,* Bӯ ɲᶾeꝺ *Sepultus, à nom.* Beoᵽᶾ, *Tumulus, Acervus,* Fr. Th. 𝔅erge, Dan. 𝔅ierg, Teut. 𝔅erg, *Mons:* vel inquit *Minſhew à* Teut. 𝔅ergen *Tegere,* vel q. d. 𝔅e-𝔈rꝺen, *hoc eſt terrâ condere. Nec tantùm* Anglo-Saxones *ſed & veteres* Romani *Lapidum moles & terræ aggeres in ſepultorum memoriam erexerunt. Skinner's* Etymol. Angl.

ˣ 𝔅orouth, *Municipium,* ab Anglo-Sax. Buᵽᶾ, Buɲᶾe, &c. *Urbs, Oppidum, Arx, hoc forte,* ab Beoᵽᶾ, *Collis, Tumulus, Acervus, Munimentum, verbo* Beoᵽᶾan, *Munire unde* Teut. 𝔅urger, Belg. 𝔅urgher, *Civis,* 𝔅orghermeeſter, *Prætor, Conſul,* Teut. 𝔅urg *Propugnaculum,* Fr. G. 𝔅ourg, *Urbs, Bourgeois, Civis, unde Nobis* a 𝔅urgeſs. Skinner, *ib.*

from

from the *Greek* πηγὴ *Fons* (as fome fay) a place com-
pos'd of feveral Streets ; whofe Inhabitants drew their
Water out of the fame *Fountain*, and being open (without defence) were not ingag'd to military Services in their
Original, as thofe our *Burgeffes* were after their Change
from *Vicus* into *Burgus* [r].

[r] *Paganus* is now generally tak-
en for a Countryman *quia in Pago
habitat*; or for one that doth not
believe the Chriftian Religion.
    Dr. *Brady* in his *Hiftorical
Treatife of Cities and Boroughs*,
quotes divers Authors in relation
to the Derivation of *Burgh* or
Borough.   As from *Cafaubon*,
that the *Greeks* made πύργ☉
and *Burgus* the fame, pronouncing it βύργ☉.   That *Cluverius*
afferts, 𝕭𝖚𝖗𝖌 to be of *German
Original*, fignifying the Situation
of many Houfes together, not
that every Street or Congrega-
tion of Houfes was a 𝕭𝖚𝖗𝖌,
but only fuch as were the Chief
of fome Country.   *Du Frefne*
thinks that it was rather *French*,
or *German*, than *Greek*.   *Wen-
delin* afferts, that 𝕭𝖚𝖗𝖌 fignifies
Receptaculum a Place of Receipt;
and in this Senfe he faith, that
𝕳𝖎𝖊𝖗𝖇𝖚𝖗𝖌 is now an Inn, or
Houfe of Receipt, which was
at firft a Place of Receipt of

Soldiers, from 𝕳𝖊𝖗𝖊 an Army;
and 𝕭𝖚𝖗𝖌, a Place of Receipt
and Security againft the Injury
of Weather ; from whence 𝕭𝖚𝖗=
𝖌𝖊𝖓 and 𝕭𝖊𝖗𝖌𝖊𝖓, fignify to cover
and defend.   And *Somner* in his
Saxon Dictionary, tells us : That
𝕭𝖚𝖗𝖌 fignifies a *City*, *Fort*, *For-
trefs*, *Tower*, *Caftle*, *Borough*, *Free
Borough* or *Town Corporate*; and
cites *Otfrid* for its Derivation
from the *Saxon* 𝕭𝖊𝖔𝖗𝖌𝖆𝖓 to preferve and keep in Safety.
    And whether 𝕭𝖚𝖗𝖌𝖍 *was taken
for a Place of* Strength, *or a Place
of* Trade, *as it was guarded with
the* Liberties *and* Privileges *granted by Princes, then (and perhaps
now) altogether neceffary to the Advantage of* Buying, Selling, *and*
Trading, *by which Tradefmen
quietly and without Difturbance
enjoy the Benefit of it ;* 𝕭𝖚𝖗𝖌𝖍𝖘
*might truly be call'd Places of
Safety, Protection and Privilege.*
Brady's Hift. of Cities, &c. v. 2.

E   Dr.

Dr. *Holland* in his additional Notes to his Tranflation of *Cambden,* gives this Defcription of *Harwich,*
viz. The Town is not great but well peopled: Fortified by Art and Nature, and made more fencible by Q.
Elizabeth. The Salt Water fo creeketh about it, that
it almoft infulateth it, but thereby maketh the
Springs fo brackifh, that there is a Defect of frefh Water, which they fetch fome good way off². This De-

² They have no frefh Water
in this Town; the nearnefs of
the Sea making all the Water
in the Wells of their Pumps fo
brackifh, that it is fit for nothing but to wafh their Houfes
with, to fupply which, they
make Conveniencies to catch
and keep Rain Water, for the
wafhing of their Clothes; but
for other Ufes they either have
it brought in *Water-Carts,* from
a Spring near a Mile from the
Town by the Road to *Dovercourt,* or it is brought in *Water-
Schoots* from a Spring in *Arwer-
ton* in the County of *Suffolk;*
which Privilege was granted
them by Sir *Philip Parker,* Baronet, one of their prefent Members of *Parliament* 1727, to prevent their being exacted upon
by thofe who are concern'd in
bringing it from the Well above
mention'd. About a Quarter
of a Mile from the Town on
the *London* Road is a Well, where
the Mafter of the Brew-Houfe
us'd to have his Water; but this
being overflow'd by a great Tide
three or four Years ago, the
Water was thereby fo fpoil'd,
that they have not fince thought
fit to make ufe of it; having
a better Conveniency by the a-
forefaid *Water - Schoots,* which
may be laid fo near the Brew-
Houfe, that they can pump
the Water out of the very Veffels into the Copper, &c. Befides the Price thereof is fo eafy,
as to be cheaper to them than by
fetching it in *Water-Carts,* from
the Well as they formerly us'd
to do.

fcription

fcription is indifferently true, but the Terms feem fome-what affected; in plain *Englifh*, the Air is clear and healthy, in *Summer* commonly affording refrefhing *Breezes* to allay and temper the uneafy and faintifh Heats, which are ufual when the *Dog-Star* reigns: And to check and affwage the Violence of the *Winter*'s Cold and Frofts, we have not only Store of Wood near the Shores of our Waters, but a great Conveniency alfo by the Situation of our *Port*, to purchafe *New-Caftle Coal* at indifferent Rates.

The chief Entrance into the Town upon the *Ifthmus*, is by the *Principal-Gate*, rather on the South End, than the South Side of it; a Relick of that ancient Induf-try, wherewith in part it was heretofore defended: The Accefs to which is at this prefent (1676.) thro' a late form'd *Ravelin* and over a *Draw-Bridge*. In a Room over the Gate there is a Light kept all Night, blown by a Fire of Sea-Coals, which anfwers to a lef-fer and lower Light upon the Town Green[a]. Thefe

two

[a] In which are every Night fet up fix great *Candles*, each weighing one Pound; the Charge of both were defrayed by Sir *Ifaac Rebow*, Knight; (but now 1727. by *Ifaac Leman Rebow*, Efq;) for which is paid by every Coafter one penny *per* Tun for Coals, and three half pence for other Goods.

This *Light-Houfe* doth not ftand upon the *Promontory*, which is call'd the *Beacon-Hill* as hath been lately publifhed by the *Anonymous Author* of the *Tour thro' Great Britain*, but on the

Green

Lights brought together by Ships from the Sea, con-duct them clear off the *Andrews* (a Sand ſtretching from *Landguard-Fort*, which makes as it were a Bar croſs the Entrance of this Harbour) into the *Rolin-grounds* where there is good Anchorage, from whence the Paſ-fage lies ſafely to *Orwell*, before the Town, where there is Room enough for a great Fleet of Ships, and to an-chor them [b].

From this principal Entrance Eaſtward, is the great *Baſtion* heretofore call'd, The *Queen's Bulwark* or *Bat-*

Green below, nearer to the *Town-Gate* than the ſaid Pro-montory or *Cliff*; and is call'd the *Town-Green*, according to Mr. *Taylor's* Account of it. To ſecure which *Light-Houſe*, the Shore about it is wharfed in, and there are likewiſe divers long *Water-Shies* of Timber, which run out towards the Sea to break the Violence of the Waves, and it is likewiſe ſupported with long Pieces of Timber ſet againſt the back Part of it to prevent its be-ing overturn'd by Storms, or high Tides.

[b] *This Harbour is of a vaſt Extent, for as the two Rivers empty themſelves here, viz.* Stour *from* Manington (Maningtree)

and the Orwell *from* Ipſwich, *the Channels of both are large and deep, and ſafe for all Wea-thers; ſo where they joyn they make a large Bay or Road, able to receive the biggeſt Ships: And the greateſt Number that ever the World ſaw together, I mean Ships of War. In the old* Dutch *War, great Uſe has been made of this Harbour, and I have known that there has been one hundred Sail of Men of War, and their Atten-dants; and between three and four hundred Sail of Collier Ships all in this Harbour at a Time, and yet none of them crowding or riding in Danger one of another.* Tour thro' *Great Britain,* Vol. I. Let. I. *p.* 48.

tery,

tery, and by fome the *Mount*; raifed by the Townfmen, *Anno* 1. *Mariæ Annoque Domini* 1553. and in Honour to her (and not from Queen *Elizabeth*, as Dr. *Holland* in his Tranflation of *Cambden* writes: It is likely fhe repair'd and refrefh'd thofe Works when fhe had Wars with *Spain:* But that and others to fecure to landward of the Town were firft built, 1. *Mariæ, as appears by a great MS. Book in the Church Cheft*) receiving its Name; they being very Zealous for her in that Commotion (as they call it) made by *John Dudley* Duke of *Northumberland* againft her; fhe was at that time retir'd to *Framingham* (*Framlingham*) Caftle in *Suffolk*, from whence fhe gave Orders to *Landguard-Fort*, to fupply this Town with Ordnance. In this *Baftion* is the Remains of an ancient *Tower* or *Tumet*, being in the Eaftermoft-Angle of the old Wall of the Town.

From thence keeping the *old Town Wall* upon your left Hand, we come to another ancient Entrance into the Town, heretofore call'd St. *Helen's Port*, within which are feveral *Alms-Houfes*[c], call'd the *Alms-End*, and by them a fmall Plat call'd St. *Helen's-Green*, from whence

[c] But what the *Original* of them was, is at this Day doubtful and in the dark: They were at firft built of *Cliff-Stones*, as yet appears by the Remains of fome Walls, &c. now ftanding *Anno* 1728. They feem to have been the Relicks of fome *Religious-Building* dedicated to St. *Helen*, becaufe the *Little Green* on which they ftand, is to this Day call'd St. *Helen's-Green*; and the

whence thro' St. *Helen's-Street*, we come to the South Side of St. *Nicholas's Church* [d]. Near to this Port was a

Tower

the *Town-Gate* near adjoyning was call'd St. *Helen's Port*, and the Street leading from thence to St. *Nicholas Chapel*, is call'd St. *Helen's-Street* : But whether this Houfe was an *Hofpital* of fome *Religious Fraternity*, *Hermitage*, *Chantrey* or *Chapel* diffolv'd or fuppreft before or about the *Reformation*, there is at prefent no Tradition : But whatever it was in former times, it at laft became the Habitation of the *Poor*, and divided into four Tenements, which being fallen much to Decay, for want of a Revenue to fupport them, they were repair'd with fifty Pounds left thereto by *Roger Coleman* of this *Borough Gentleman* and *Merchant*; as appears by the *Infcription* on his Tomb now ftanding in the *Chancel* of the *Chapel* of this Town : But *ftanding* within the intended *Line* of the *New Fortifications* defign'd in the Reign of Queen *Anne*, for the better Security of this *Port*, they were by Virtue of an *Act* of *Parliament* then made,

among divers other things purchafed by the *Government*, in whofe Hands they now are; and with the Purchafe-Money aforefaid, together with the Addition of fome other *Benefactions*, much better and larger have been built next the *Sea*, of which more hereafter.

[d] Or rather *Chapel* for fo (as Mr. *Taylor* afterwards calls it) it hath only been accounted ever fince its Foundation ; and tho' on divers of the Crofs-Beams of the *Roof* is carved a *Mullet*, which being part of the *Armorial Bearing* of the Family of *Vere*, formerly Lords of this Mannor, fome thereby might be induced to think it of their Foundation ; yet it was *Roger Bigod* Earl of *Norfolk*, Son of *Juliana*, Daughter of the younger *Aubrey de Vere*, that was the firft Founder of it, as appears by his Charter hereafter recited ; perhaps in Honour to his Mother and her Family, he might caufe that *Badge* thereof to be carv'd upon the Beams

I   aforefaid:

Tab. III. Page 67.

Harwich Church on the South Side.

R. Sheppard Sculp.

Tower of the Wall, which, becaufe the *Curtain* made to the *Outworks* in 1666. ranged too near to it, was taken down for the Conveniency of Paffage. Not far diftant from hence is the *Chapel* of *Harwich* dedicated to St. *Nicholas* , in whofe *Chancel* is a modern Memorial of

aforefaid: But what his Reafons for this Foundation were, fhall be mention'd when I come to *Dovercourt*. The Inhabitants here retain a Tradition, that the *Chancel* of this *Chapel* was built by the Daughter of a Taylor ; becaufe of the Portraiture of a Pair of Sciffars on divers Parts thereof.

ᵉ This Chapel confifts of a *Body* or *Nave*, with two fide *Ifles*, and a *Chancel* all cover'd with Lead; at the Weft End of the *Nave* ftands the *Steeple*, being a *Quadrangular Tower* of Stone, the Top whereof is an *Octangular* Wooden Frame embattled; in the Middle of which is a *Spire*, all which Wood Work is cover'd with Lead. In the *Steeple* are five Bells, a *Clock* and *Chimes*; and on the Outfide are three *Dials*, viz. on the North, South, and Weft Sides. The Infide of this

Chapel was new beautified, *An.* Mr. *Thomas Osborn*, and Mr. *Wildbore*, *Chapel Wardens*; (as it has been again this prefent Year 1728.) Againft the Eaft Window, (which is difannull'd) was then erected an *Altar-piece*, and the *Communion Table* then rail'd in. There was formerly a *Veftry - Room* on the North Side of the *Chancel*, but it hath been for fome time demolifh'd.

It is now annext to the Church of *Dovercourt*, and hath been fo almoft ever fince the Diffolution of *Monafteries*; before which, 'tis probable, it was a *Donative* or *Free Chapel* in the Gift of the *Prior* and *Convent of Colne*; who upon every Vacancy, did ufually beftow it upon one of the *Monks* of their own *Cell*, during his Life, by Indenture, which was confirm'd by the *Bifhop* of *London*, in whofe *Regiftry* under the Title *Braybroke*, 204. is

204. is recorded the *Inftrument* by which *Ralph de Pelham* was collated to this *Chapel, Anno* 1365. as follows.

Univerfi noverint per præfentes, quod nos Simon permiffione divina Londonienfis Epifcopus quafdam literas indentatas per partem dilectorum in Chrifto filiorum Prioris & Conventus Prioratus Beatæ Mariæ de Colne Ordinis S^ti Benedicti noftri Diœcefis, figillo fuo eorum ac fratris Radulphi de Pelham Monachi Prioratus ejufdem fignatas & nobis exhibitas receperimus, fub eo qui fequitur tenore verborum. Univerfis S^æ Matris Ecclefiæ filiis ad quos præfentes literæ pervenerint, Frater Rogerus Prior Monachus Beatæ Mariæ de Colne & ejufdem loci Conventus Salutem in Domino fempiternam. Noverit Univerfitas veftra nos confiderantes diuturnos labores quos Frater Radulphus de Pelham Confrater & Commonachus nofter pro negotiis Domus noftræ fuftinuit, & commoda quæ eidem procuravit, & confidentes de ejus induftria & laudabili vita, una cum confenfu totius capituli noftri dediffe & tenore præfentium conceffiffe Fratri Radulpho predicto Capellam noftram de Here-

vico cum omnibus juribus ab antiquo eidem Capellæ pertinentibus. Et quia obventiones ejufdem Capellæ non fufficiunt ad congruentem fuftentationem dicti Fratris Radulphi & onera dictæ Capellæ, & ejus cuftodi incumbentia fupportanda. Dedimus etiam & Conceffimus eidem tria quarteria & duos buffellos Frumenti una cum duabusCarectatis Straminis, quarum unam pro lecto fuo, & aliam pro dicta Capella ftraminanda, percipienda annuatim de Rectoria noftra de Dovercourt. Habendam & Tenendam dictam Capellam cum omnibus juribus ut prædictum eft, ac etiam dicta tria quarteria & duos buffellos Frumenti cum dictis duabus Carectatis Straminis eidem Fratri Radulpho ad terminum vitæ ejufdem, fine contradictione & revocatione noftra feu cujufcunque noftrûm vel fucceflorum noftrorum. Salvo cum fi contigerit dictum Fratrem Radulphum aliquod aliud Beneficium Ecclefiafticum acceptare, feu ftatum fuum quovis modo mutare: Quod tunc liceat nobis & fucceffaribus noftris dictam Capellam rehabere & eandem Capellam cum omnibus juribus & pertinentiis reingredi & in eadem Commonachum & Confratrem feu probum Conductivum libere

libere præficere, prout retroactis temporibus fine contradictione cujufcunque confuevimus. Datum apud Colne inCapitulo noftro ultimo die menfis Aprilis Anno Domini M°.CCC°.LX°.V°. *in cujus rei teftimonium figillum noftrum commune parti penes dictum Fratrem Radulphum remanenti eft appenfum, parti vero alteri penes nos remanenti figillum venerabilis Patris noftri Domini Simonis Dei gratia Londonienfis Epifcopi una cum figillo dicti Fratris Radulphi apponi procuravimus. Nos igitur Simon Epifcopus antedictus confideratis laudabilibus meritis Radulphi antedicti & plena conformatione per nos ex virorum teftimonio fide dignorum habita fuper contentis in literis memorabilibus donationem & conceffionem prædictas factas eidem Fratro Radulpho per Priorem & Conventum prædictos ratas habentes, & ratas fub forma & modo præmiffis approbamus & acceptamus eafdem & quatenus ad nos pertinent tenore præfentium confirmamus. Salvis in omnibus Epifcopalibus juribus & confuetudinibus ac noftræ Londonienfis Ecclefiæ dignitate. In cujus rei teftimonium figillum noftrum fecimus hic apponi. Datum apud Wytham penultimo*

die menfis Junii Anno Domini M°.CCC°.LX°.V°. *prædicto, & noftræ confecrationis Anno quarto.*

Thus far the *Record,* in which are two Words not commonly to be met with, the Explanation whereof will not, I prefume, be unacceptable, if I tranfcribe them from the *Gloffary* at the End of *Bifhop* Kennet's *Parochial Antiquities.*

1. *Buffellus.* 𝔄 𝔅uffel from *Buza, Butta, Buttis,* 𝔄 ftanding 𝔐eafure of Wine, from the old *French* Word *Bouts,* which were properly Leather Veffels to carry Wine, whence our Leather Boots, *&c. Buffellus* was firft us'd for a liquid Meafure of Wine (containing) eight Gallons, *&c.* The Word was foon after transferr'd to the dry Meafure of Corn of the fame Quantity.

2. *Carectata.* A Cart-load, or Waggon-load, *&c.* In the Inftrument of Ordaining a Vicar for *Oakle, Anno* 1344. The Prior and Canons of St. *Fridifwide* do grant by way of Augmentation to the new made Vicarage, *Duas Carectatas feoni, & duas Carectatas Straminis,* &c. Parochial Antiq. *p.* 455.

F   *For*

For the Entertainment of the Engliſh *Reader, I have annexed the following Tranſlation.*

Know all Men by theſe Preſents, that we *Simon* by divine Permiſſion Biſhop of *London,* have receiv'd certain Indentures on the Part of our beloved Sons in Chriſt, the Prior and Convent Priorate of the Bleſſed *Mary* of *Colne,* of the Order of St. *Benedict,* ſign'd with the Seal of our Dioceſs; and with that of them, and Brother *Ralph de Pelham,* Monk of the ſame Priorate, and delivered to us, in the ſame Tenour of Words which follows. To all the Sons of holy Mother Church to whom theſe Preſents ſhall come, Brother *Roger* Prior, Monk of the Bleſſed *Mary* of *Colne,* together with the Convent of the ſame Place with eternal Salvation in the Lord. Be it known to all of you, that we conſidering the daily Labours which Brother *Ralph de Pelham* our Confrater and Fellow-Monk has ſuſtain'd for the Service of our Houſe, and the Advantages which he has procured to the ſame, and in Confidence of his Induſtry and commendable Life, toge-

ther with the Conſent of our whole Chapter, have given, and by Virtue of theſe Preſents have granted to Brother *Ralph* aforeſaid, our Chapel of *Harwich,* with all Rights anciently belonging to the ſame Chapel. And becauſe the Revenue of the ſame Chapel is not ſufficient for a competent Maintenance of our ſaid Brother *Ralph,* and ſupporting the Burthens incumbent on the ſaid Chapel and its Curate, we have alſo given and granted to the ſame, three Quarters and two Buſhels of Corn, together with two Cart-loads of Straw, of which one is for his Bed, and the other for Strawing the ſaid Chapel, to be receiv'd annually from our Rectory of *Dovercourt.* To have and to hold the ſaid Chapel, with all its Rights as aforeſaid, and alſo the ſaid three Quarters and two Buſhels of Corn, with the ſaid two Cart-loads of Straw, to the ſaid Brother *Ralph* for the Term of his Life, without Contradiction or Revocation of us, or any one of us, or our Succeſſors. Saving that if our ſaid Brother *Ralph* ſhould accept any other Eccleſiaſtical Benefice, or any way change his Condition, that
then

of *Black Marble*, the *Tombstone* advanc'd upon open small Arches of Free-Stone with this inscription,

then it shall be lawful for us and our Successors to take the said Chapel again, and to re-enter the same Chapel with all its Rights and Appurtinances, and to put a Confrater or Fellow-Monk, or some honest Substitute freely into the same, as we have been accustom'd in times past, without being contradicted by any one. Given at *Colne* in our Chapter the last Day of the Month of *April, Anno Domini* MCCCLXV. In Testimony whereof our Common Seal has been affixed to that Part remaining in the Hands of our said Brother *Ralph*, but to the other Part remaining with us, we have procured the Seal of our Right Reverend Father SIMON by the Grace of God Lord Bishop of *London* to be affix'd, together with the Seal of our said Brother *Ralph*. We therefore, SIMON Bishop of *London* aforementi-oned, in Consideration of the great Merit of *Ralph* aforesaid, and in full Conformation on our Part from the Testimony of very reputable Persons to the Contents in the aforesaid Letter, we esteem the Donation and Grant aforesaid, made to the said Brother *Ralph*, by the Prior and Convent aforesaid ratified; and we approve and accept them being ratified under the Form and Manner aforemention'd; and we confirm the same as much as regards us by Virtue of these Presents. Saving in all things the Episcopal Rights and Customs, and the Dignity of our Church of *London*. In Testimony whereof, we have caused our Seal to be put hereunto. Given at *Wytham* the 29th Day of *June, A. D.* MCCCLXV. aforesaid, and in the fourth Year of our Consecration.

HIC

HIC REQVIESCIT ROGERVS
COLEMAN, HVIVS BVRGI GENEROSVS
ET MERCATOR, PAVPERIBVS BENEF⸗
ACT͂. CELEBERRIMVS VT IN PRAECLAR°:
EIVS DONO QVINQVAGINTA LIBRA^{RVM}
AD ROGATRIVM REPARANDVM PATET;
QVI CVM CHRISTIANVM SVVM CVRSVM
IMPLEVERAT; OPVM DIERVM ET FAMAE
SATVR TANDEM PLACIDE ET QVIETE
IN DOMINO OBDORMIVIT 6 DIE IVLII
A°: D͂M 1659 ETATIS SVAE 63.

Ingraved over this Infcription in the Marble is a
Coat of Arms, viz. *A. on a pale radiant rayonee or
a Lyon rampant* G. which were the Arms of the Family of the *Colemans* of *Burnt-Ely* in the County of
Suffolk, V. Gvillim's *Difplay of Heraldry*.

Upon the floaping Thicknefs of the Tomb-Stone is
fcatteringly written at the Head, the South Side, and
the Foot or Eaft of it [in Capital Letters] (*viz.* at the
Head or Weft End) VENIMVS (the South Side) VI-
DEMVS, REDIMVS ET (and the Foot of it, or Eaft
End) RESVRGIMVS.   Under the whole is a Vault and
near to the End of it, another Stone over the Entrance
into it; on which is engraven

THE

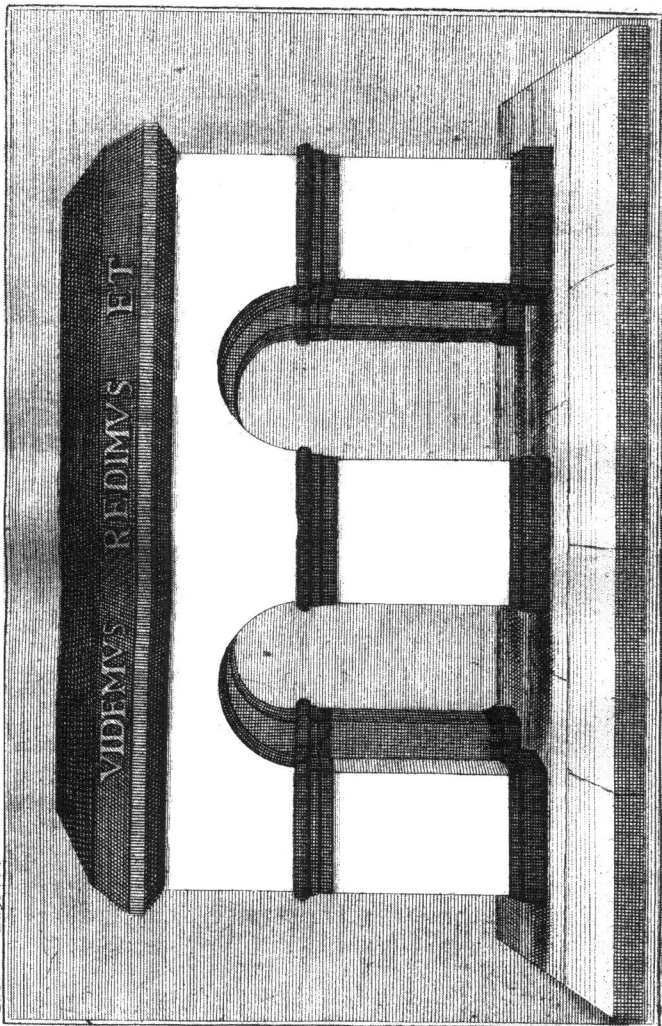

Tab. IV. Pag. 75.

VIDEMVS REDIMVS ET

THE COLEMANS VAVLT.

In it alfo lies the Body of *George Coleman* his *Nephew* and Heir, who leaving no Iffue of his own, died in his Mayoralty of this Borough in the Year of our Lord 1671 *f*.
Another

f Between the Monument of Mr. *Coleman,* and the North Wall of the *Chancel* lieth buried *Sylas Domvill* alias *Taylor*, Gent. the *Collector of thefe Memorials*; but without either Grave Stone or Infcription to preferve his Memory to Pofterity.

Eaftward of Mr. *Taylor's Grave*, between the Rails and the North-Wall lyeth a White Stone, with the following Infcription ;

HIC JACET
GEORGIVS TRENCHARD
FILIVS GVLIELMI TRENCHARD
DE CATTRIGE IN AGRO
WILTONIENSI ARMIG^{ERI}
SECVNDO GENITVS, NAVIS
REGIÆ PRÆFECTVS SVMMÆ
SPEI JVVENIS, FEBRE
CORREPTVS OBIIT ANNO
GRATIÆ 1696 ÆTATIS
SVÆ 23.

In the Middle of the Chancel lyeth a Black Marble Stone, on which is cut a Cheveron between fix Croffes Fitchè under which,

M^R. DANIEL SMITH
HIS VAVLT o—o

o—o The Colours of the Arms as printed in the new Map of *Effex*, &c. are *Sable a Cheveron between fix Croffes Fitchè Argent.*
Alfo

Alſo on a White Stone near the Paſſage into the Church,

M^R. William Kempster
his Vault.

Near the Door of the Chancel is a Black Marble Stone with
the following,

Abigale the davghter of Thomas
Langley & Thamer his wife de=
parted this life 22^d Septem^{br} 1670.
at the age of 7 years.
Here alſo
Lieth the Body of thomas Langley
Eſq; (Memorable to Posterity)
who was three times Mayor of this Burrough
of Harwich And one of his Majeſtys Juſtices of
the Peace of this County of Eſſex who depart^{ed}
this Life the 12th Day of June Anno Dom.
1717. Ætatis ſuæ 63.
Vivit post fvnera virtvs.

On the Eaſt End of the Chancel next the North is a Mural
Monument where on a Wooden Table is painted the following
Inſcription,

Underneath lyes the Body
of Robert Seaman gen^{ln}
who for his Stedfaſt love and reverence
To the Church of England
his Loyalty to the Goverment
his Charity to the poor
his Excellent Skill in Chyrurgery
his Service to this Burrough
in which he was born
and of which
he was Mayor three times
has left a bleſſed memory behind him
and deceaſed Aug^{ſt} 1^{ſt} 1695 aged 68 years.

Another

Tab. V. *Page 39*.

Sr. William Clarkes Monument

Another modern Memorial there is on the South Side of the Eaſt Window of the *Chancel* of Sir *William Clarke*, Knᵗ; where in a Table of White Marble this is to be read, *viz.*

HIC JACET
GVLIELMVS CLARKE, EQVES
AVRATVS SERENISSIMO CAROLO
II°. A BELLO SECRETARIVS, ILLVSTRISSIMO
GEORGIO DVCI ALBEMARLIÆ A SECRETIS
QVEM PLVS XII ANNIS PER OMNES CASVS SECVTVS
EI ETIAM IN RESTAVRATIONIS REGIS AC LEGVM INTER
PRIMAS ADFVIT : CVIQ; DVM TANDEM IN MEMORABILI PRELIO NAVALI
CVM FOED: PROVIN: CLASSE INITIO IVNII Aⁿ: Dⁱ MDCLXVI PER QVATVOR
DIES CONTINVOS COMʼISSO FORTITER ADSTITIT SECVNDO DIE GLOBO
FERREO PERCVSSVS CRVS DEXTRVM PERDIDIT QVARTO VITAM. NEQ;
AB EO INTEREA AVELLI SE PASSVS EST, AVT A PVGNÆ PERICVLO SVBDVCI
SED VVLNERATIS RELIQVIS IN LITTVS EXPOSITIS SOLVS IN ÆRVMNOSA
ET OBNOXIA NAVI, DVBIAM PRÆLII AC VITÆ SORTEM, CONSTANTI ANIMO
EXPECTAVIT. CORPVS LACERVM DEIN AC MORTVVM PER ALIQVOT DIES
MARI IACTATVM, HIC TANDEʼ PORTVM INVENIT, ANIMA AD COELVM EVOLAVIT
MANE VIATOR NONDVM INTELLEXTI VIRVM
QVI PVBLICIS MVNERIBVS DIV FVNCTVS PVBLICEʼ SEMPER PLACVIT
QVI OPES INDE ET HONORES ASSEQVTVS INFAMIAM & INVIDIAM VITAVIT
NON ARTE SED INTEGRITATE.
QVI EXEMPLO ERAT, AB AVLIS NON PENITVS ARCERE INNOCENTIAM
HIC SITVS EST
EQVES VERAX, FIDVS, GNARVS, IMPIGER, INDEFESSVS :
NEQ; LABORI PEPERCIT NEQ; INDVLSIT AVARITIÆ;
NEQ; DIVITES EMVNXIT NEQ; PAVPERES DESTITVIT
NEQ; VERBA DEDIT NEQ; VENDIDIT :
SIC VITâ INTEGER, MORTE FORTIS, VTRAQ; PROPTEREA FÆLIX :
TERTIVM DVNTAXAT SVPER QVADRAGESSIMVM ÆTATIS SVÆ ANNVM
LAVDVM VERO AC VIRTVTVM OMNIVM, PERFECTVM NVMERVM IMPLEVIT,
CONIVGEM RELIQVIT MOESTISSIMAM
FILIVM QVINQVENNEM, OPES MODICAS,
BONAM FAMAM,
MAGNVM SVI DESIDERIVM.
HÆC SVMPTIBVS SVIS POSVIT VXOR MOESTISSIMA, DVM
STVDET DILECTISSIMO MARITO IVSTA FACERE, ET CRESCEN⸗
TEM IN DIES DOLOREM FALLERE.

Over

Over this Memorial on a fmall Pedeftal betwixt two Scrowls of Alabafter, fuftain'd by two Pillars of Black Marble, is the Effigies of the faid Sir *William* from the Breaft upwards, and underneath the abovemention'd Table are thefe Arms without Colours, *viz.* Baron and Femme, *A Bend, three Swans between three Plates, a Canton Sinifter with a Bear's Claw erafed:* Impaled with a Coat of Arms, *viz. A Cheveron between three Mullets of five Points pierced.* The whole very workmanly done[s].

[s] Among the *Arms* on the Border of the new Map of *Middlefex, Effex* and *Hertfordfhire,* I find two Efcutcheons by the Name of *Clarke,* who bear *Argent a bend Gul. charged with three Swans of the firft between three Pellets fable,* and it is likely the Anceftors of this our Sir *William* did bear the fame, but upon what Account the *Canton* of *Augmentation* was granted I do not find. *Gvillim* ed. 1638. *p.* 395. mentions one Sir *John Clarke,* Knight; buried in the Church of *Tame Oxfordfhire,* who hath the fame bearing, only the Charge in the *Canton* is different: And there is or lately was a Baronet of this laft mention'd Family, as by the Arms in the Map to *Plot's Natural Hiftory of Oxfordfhire,* doth appear: And in the faid Map is likewife the Arms of *Clarke,* Efq; according to thofe mention'd in the firft Map, and in the Map to *Morton's Northamptonfhire* is the fame Arms to *Clarke,* Knight; all which evidently fhew the firft recited Arms to be thofe of the *Orignal* Family, and that the *Cantons* are *Augmentations* as a Reward for fome Services perform'd.

He lies buried under a Black Marble fix or feven
Feet within the South Door of the *Chancel*, whereon
thefe Words are cut,

DEPOSITVM GVLIELMI CLARKE EQVITIS AVRATI [h].

In

[h] In the middle Ifle of the Church on a Black Marble Stone,
is the following Infcription;

> Here lyes interr'd the Body of
> Mr Andrew Carr of this Town who
> departed this life the twentieth day of
> May in the Year of our Lord God one
> Thoufand fix hundred feventy & nine
> And was buried .the 24th day of the
> fame May he was aged 47 years
> And alfo his youngeft fon Godfry
> who departed this life in December
> 1678.

Alfo in the South Ifle near the Door lyeth another Black Marble on the Head of which is cut the following Efcutcheon, *viz.*
- - - . A Pallet - - - . between 4 Crefcents - - - Impailing - - - .
3 Bucks - - - .

> Under which is the following Epitaph;
>
> Sub hoc monumento repo-
> nuntur cineres Rogeri Reay, qui
> mare & terras gloriam que-
> ritans, tandem cecidit .fed forti-
> ter, nam & in Thalamis honoris
> obdormivit, obijt triceffimo die
> Septembris Anno 1673.
>
> Somnit
> Quid quæris lector quis hoc fub marmore?
> Hic gremio Martis virtus heroa jacet.

G

There

There are divers other Stones yet lying in this *Chapel* and *Chancel*, which have had *Effigies* and *Inscriptions* inlayed in Brass upon them; but they being gone, to whom they did belong is not now known.

In the Yard to this *Chapel* are divers *Altar-tombs*, the Inscriptions upon which are as follow.

On the South Side near the West End, on a Black Marble.

Here lyes Inter'd the Body of
IOHN ROLFE Gentleman who
Departed this Life on the 2ᵈ Day of
Octobʳ: 1717. in the 75 Year of
his Age who was married to his
Wife ELIZABETH 54. Years
And had issue by her six Sons
And Three Daughters
Here Lyeth also the Body of
Mˢ ELIZABETH ROLFE Wife to
Mʳ IOHN ROLFE who Departed
this Life the 23ᵈ Day of August
1721 Aged 76 Years.

Also Eastward of the foregoing on a Black Stone.

Here Lyes interred the Body of
Capᵗ: Robert Stevens
who departed this Life May the
15. 1715. Aged 58 Years he was
Honoured with A Medal and chain
of Gold by their late Majˢ
King William and Queen Mary
in the Year 1693.

More

More Eaftward than the laft on another Black Marble.

> HERE LIETH INTOMBED THE
> BODY OF CAP.ᵀ IOHN WESTBROWN
> WHO DEPARTED THIS LIFE
> SEPTEM:ᴿ THE 19 1691. AGED
> 49. YEARS.

> Here Alfo
> Lyeth Interr'd the Body of Capᵗ.
> MADDESON HVNT Who Departed
> this Life January the 9ᵗʰ 1720 Aged
> 49 Years

> Alfo the Body of Mʳˢ Elizabeth Weftbrown
> Wife of the faid Capᵗ Weftbrown
> who Dyed the 4 of January 1724.
> Aged 84 Years

Southward of this laft on a White Stone.

> Here Refteth the Body of
> Alexander Marfhal who was
> Surgeon to Her Ma:ᵗⁱᵉˢ Pacquet Boat
> the Marlborough He Departed
> this Life Auguft the 5ᵗʰ 1710
> Aged 41 Years

Eaftward

Eaftward on a Black Stone.

Here Lyeth the Body of Amy
A Former Wife of Iohn Lawne
She Departed this Life July 10th 1693.
Aged 34 Years

Alfo Ann Daughter to Iohn & Amy Lawne
Aged 2 Years.

Alfo 4 Children
of Iohn Lawne by
Mary his Wife viz
$\left.\begin{array}{l}\text{Hannah}\\\text{Iohn 1.}\\\text{Iohn 2.}\\\text{Ann}\end{array}\right\}$ who died in their
Infancy

And Alfo
Mary Daughter of Iohn & Mary Lawne
who Departed this Life Novr: ye 17th 1714
Aged 15 Years

Alfo Mary the wife of Iohn
Lawne She Departed this Life
November the 24th 1717 Aged 40 Years
and Alfo Lyeth the Body of Iohn
Lawne Hufband to the faid
Mary Lawne who Departed this Life
October the 16th 1720 in the 54
Yeare of his Age.

Southward of the laft on a White Stone.

Here Lieth ye Body of Mr Richard Ellis
of Hull Mafter and Mariner who Departed
this Life the 9th November 1717
Aged 33 Years

Near

Near the Chancel Door upon a Stone which lieth on the Ground.

> HERE LYETH THE BODY OF
> CAP.ᵀ IOHN DAVISON WHO
> DEPARTED THIS LIFE MAY
> Yᴱ 9ᵀᴴ 1723 AGED 51 YEARS

Againſt the ſaid Door a Black Stone with,

> HERE LYETH THE BODY OF
> HANNAH FOX WIFE OF ROBERT
> FOX WAS BORN THE   DAY
> OF MARCH A.° 1650 DEPARTED
> THIS LIFE THE FIRST DAY OF SEP=
> TEMBER A.° 1679. AND SIX OF
> HER CHILDREN, ONE SON
> AND FIVE DAVGHTERS

> Here Lyeth the Body of Henry Keabel
> who Departed this Life the 28 day of Oct.
> 1713. in the 76 year of his Age.

At the Eaſt End of the Chancel on a White Stone.

> Here Lyeth Interred the Body of
> SARAH HEBB daughter to RICHARD
> HEBB who Departed this Life yᵉ 13
> of October 1705 Aged 16 Years
> and Alſo her Father who Departed
> this Life yᵉ 15 of May 1706. Aged 62
> Years.

Next

Next the laſt on another White Stone.

HERE LYES INTERRED THE
BODY OF THEOPHYLVS WIMPLE
WHO DEPARTED THIS LIFE
THE 12TH DAY OF SEPTEMBER
ANNO DOM. 1687 AGED 27
YEARS. AS ALSO THE BODY
OF MARY HIS DAVGHTER WHO
DEPARTED THIS LIFE THE
20TH DAY OF IVLY 1684 AGED ONE YEAR.

Next another White Stone.

HERE LYETH INTOMBED THE
BODY OF ELIZABETH WOOD
LATE WIFE OF WILLIAM WOOD
AND SIX CHILDREN ISSVE OF
THE SAID WILLIAM AND
ELIZABETH SHE DEPARTED
THIS LIFE Ye 21 DECEMBER 1684
AGED 31 YEARS.

Next on another White Stone.

HERE LYE THE BODIES
OF MARK AND IOHN
COLE SONS OF HENRY
COLE and SVSANNA HIS
WIFE WHO DEPARTED THIS
LIFE THE one in MAY AND
THE OTHER IN IVNE A:NO
DOMINI 1678.

Next

Next towards the North on a White Stone.

> Here lieth intombed the
> body of William Rvdland
> who departed this life
> the first day of Avgust
> 1690. aged 81. years

On the North Side of the Chapel Eaftwards on a Black Stone.

> Here lieth the body
> of Henry Pordage who
> Departed this life
> the 8th of October Ano: dom: 1665.
> aged 39.

> Here Alfo Lieth the Body of
> Mrs Frances Seaman former
> wife of Mr Henry Pordage
> who Departed this Life the 24th day of May 1707.
> in the 82nd year of her Age.

Next on another Black Stone.

> Here Lyeth ye Body of Fran=
> ces Gray Davghter of Cap.t
> Richard Gray and Elizabeth
> his Wife who Departed This
> Life ye 6 Ivly 1701 Aged
> Twenty Years.

Here Lyeth Interred the Body of Captn
Richard Gray fometime Agent to her
Majties Packquet Boats of this Town who.
Departed this Life on the 27th Day of
September in the Year of Our Lord 1711.
and in the 55 Year of his Age.   *And*

And Alſo
three ſons of Geo: Rolfe & Martha his wife
viz.
John Rolfe who Departed this Life
June yᵉ 11 1709 Aged one Year.
George Rolfe who Departed this Life
Octobʳ: 16. 1709. Aged three Years
John Rolfe who Departed this Life
Mar. 16. 17¼¼ Aged fourteen Mon.ᵗʰˢ

Next on a Black Stone.

HERE LYETH THE BODY OF
FRANCIS DENNIS WHO DE=
PARTED THIS LIFE THE 21ᵀᴴ DAY
OF MAY ANNO DOM. 1645.

Next on a White Stone.

Here lyeth the Body of HANNAH
PHILLIPS wife of THOMAS PHILLIPS
Senioʳ who was the Mother of fourteen
children and left 12 of them behind
her Shee departed this life the 21ᵗʰ of
May 1704 in the 42ⁿᵈ Yeare of her age.

Next on another White Stone near the laſt.

Here lyeth the Body of Mʳ IOHN
Phillips who departed this life yᵉ 3ᵈ of
March 1693. in yᵉ 76 Year of his Age
Here lyeth alſo the Body of IOANE
his wife who departed this life yᵉ 6ᵗʰ
of March 1697. in yᵉ 77ᵗʰ yeare of her age
Here lyeth alſo 3 children of his Son
WILLIAM PHILLIPS who erected this tomb.

I   Next

In the Reign of King *Edward* VI. *(in lib. major. in Cifta Ecclefiæ) John Chapman* and *William Ollyffe* were Wardens of this *Chapel* of St. *Nicholas* for above fix Years together; in which time they fold from it above one hundred and eighty Ounces of *Silver Plate*, many *Veftments* and *Ornaments*, the very *Altar-Stone* and Organ-Cafe, and almoft all things they could make Money of[i]: So that in the Year 1553. Queen *Mary*

Next the North Porch on a Black Marble.

HERE LYETH MARY THE
WIFE OF M.[R] DANIEL RAVENS
SHE DEPARTED THIS LIFE Y[E]
11TH DAY OF APRIL 1716 AGED
66 YEARS
ALSO THE BODY OF M.[R]
DANIEL RAVENS DEPARTED
THIS LIFE THE 29TH OF APRIL
1719 AGED 64 YEARS.

Near this laft is another Black Stone, but at prefent nothing cut upon it.

There is likewife an Altar-tomb by the Steeple, on which there is no Infcription.

[i] In the Parliament holden at *Weftminfter Anno* 3. & 4. *Edw.* VI. cap. 10.   It was enacted that all the Books, call'd *Antiphoners, Miffales, Grailes, Portuaffes* and *Latin Primmers* ufed for Service in the Church, fhould be clearly abolifh'd; all *Images graven, painted* or *carved,* &c. fhould be defaced and openly burnt.   *Weaver.* 115.

H   coming

coming to the Crown; the *Church* was left so bare of Plate, that they paid for fashioning of a Silver Cup made out of fifteen Ounces of old Plate (heretofore belonging to the Town) for it: Which Change of hers brought a greater Charge upon them; notwithstanding the *Declaration* of her *Counsel*, August 13. 1553. in the *Tower* of *London* to the *Lord Mayor* and *Aldermen* of the *City* of *London* [è lib. MSS. Actor. Coutch. privat. ejusd. temp.] in these Words; *That although her* Grace's *Conscience is stayed in matter of Religion; yet she meaneth graciously not to compel or strain other Men's Consciences, otherwise than God shall (as she trusteth) put in their Hearts a Persuasion of the Truth that she is in; through the opening of the Word unto them by godly, virtuous, and learned Preachers,* &c. Yet they were obliged to make a new *Altar*, furnish the *Priest* not only with *new Vestments*, but also with a *Pax, Saint's-Bell, Mass-Books, Surplices, Candlesticks, Censers,* &c. pay for a new ᵏ *Crucifix*, and a *Mary* and *John.* And that nothing might be wanting to their

---

ᵏ She (i. e. Queen *Mary*) caus'd the like *Books* and *Images* to be bought, and brought into all Churches within her Dominions: *Holy-Water, Pax,* and *Censers* were commanded to be employed at the Celebration of *Masses* and *Mattins: Oil, Cream,* and *Spittle* used in the Administration of *Baptism; Altars* furnish'd with *Pictures,* costly *Coverings,* and the *Crucifix* thereon placed: Unto whom *Lights, Candles,* and *Tapers* were offer'd. *Weaver.* ib.

greater

greater Edification, one *John Swiverton* was fent thither with a Commiffion (as it is there recorded) for the Reformation of things wanting in Churches; in which he had thefe efpecial Words: *To Will and Command all Church-Wardens to fee him pleafed for his Pains-taking in that behalf.* Thither he goes and makes his Vifitation, the Wardens in Obedience to it give him of the *Towns Money,* 2 s. 2 d. and disburfed 2 s. more for painting the *Roods,* and making the St. *Nicholas* the *Patron* of the *Church,* purchafe a *Crofs-Staff* and get it painted, and are continually fupplying *Tapers* and *Candles:* Then buy they two *Portufes* [1] (*all their own Words*) the one to fay Service the one half Year, and the other the other half Year, (it may be *Summer Portufes* and *Winter Portufes*) two *Banner Cloths,* fet up the *Rood* or *Crucifix,* make the *Quier* in the *Chancel,* change another *Silver Goblet* belonging to the *Town* for a *Callice* (now in comes a parcel of hard Words) for *finging-Bread,* that was occupied about finging of *Mafs;* for *Hufling-Bread,* that ferved thofe that did receive at *Eafter* 1557, for *Oil* and *Cream;* for a *Lan-*

---

[1] By *Portufes* here Mr. *Taylor* feems to underftand *Garments,* for the *Prieft* to officiate in, when there were *Books* to *officiate* by, being likewife call'd *Breviaries,* thefe were according to the Conftitution of *Archbifhop Winchelfea, A. D.* 1305. to be found by the *Rector,* the ufual Price of one being five Marks. *Lewis's Hiftory and Antiquities,* &c. of *Feverfham* 64.

tern that ferved to be occupied in the *Chancel* or *Church*; (ftill the Words of their Record) for a Yard of *Cloth* to bind about the *Callice*; for a *Manual* and a *Prieft Chymar*; for *Broad Inkle* to make the *Prieft* a *Girdle* for the *Veftments* which coft three half pence: Then pay Sir *Chriftopher* (for fo their *Chaplain* is there named) after the Rate of 10 *l. per Annum*[m]. And becaufe this *Borough* had fhewed itfelf fo early and ready for the *Queen* before her *Coronation*, even then, when fhe was at *Framingham Caftle*, fhe and her *Council* out of a more than ordinary Care and Love for them, fent frequently Dr. *Wefton*[n], Mr. *Alablafter*, and feveral

[m] It is very probable that this Sir *Chriftopher* was *Chriftopher James*, Clerk, who during the Life of *John Roberts*, Vicar of *Dovercourt* might here officiate for the Service of the *Borough*, being thereto chofen or elected by themfelves, or fent by the *Queen* as *Patron* of the Living, after the Diffolution of *Coln Priory*, or appointed by the *Bifhop* of *London* before its being annex'd to *Dovercourt*; and that which confirms me in the Conjecture is the Prefentation of this *Chriftopher James*, Clerk, to the Church of *Dovercourt* with this

Chapel annex'd by King *Philip* and Queen *Mary* the 23[d] of *June* 1558.

[n] Dr. *Hugh Wefton* was Parfon of St. *Botholps* without *Bifhop*'s *Gate London*, Archdeacon of *Colchefter*, Dean of *Weftminfter*, and *Prolocutor* of the *Convocation*; and when St. *Peter*'s *Weftminfter* was by Queen *Mary* turn'd again into an *Abby*, he was put out thence to make room for *Fakenham* to be *Abbot* there, and had the Deanery of *Windfor* beftow'd upon him *An.* 1556. of which he was depriv'd by *Cardinal Pole Archbifhop of Canterbury*

ral other Minifters with Arguments and Perfuafions to them: And that no Means may be neglected that might feem but to tend to their Conviction and Reformation. There was one *William Bamford* alias *Butcher*, for Religion condemn'd at *Chelmsford* (with *Thomas Watts* and feveral others) fent hither to be burnt, and they with the Expence of 5 *s.* 6 *d.* for Wood obliged to fee him executed *June* 15ᵗʰ 1555°. But

Canterbury A. 1557. and afterwards put out of his *Archdeaconry* before *Oct.* 15. 1558. He died in the *Tower* of *London* in *December* 1558, and was buried in the *Savoy Church* in the *Strand. Newcourt's Rep.* Vol. I. 718.

Who Mr. *Alablafter* was I do not find, no fuch Perfon having had Ecclefiaftical Preferment within the Diocefs of *London.*

° *William Bamford* alias *Butcher*, was a Weaver of *Coggefhall* in *Effex*, being apprehended with five others of that Town by the Conftables, were on the firft of *May* 1555. carried before *John* Earl of *Oxford* at *Hedingham Caftle*, who that Day fent them to *Bonner Bifhop* of *London* with a Letter: And on the 17ᵗʰ of *May* only three of them were brought before the

faid *Bifhop*, and examin'd upon ten Articles ; to all which *William Bamford* gave his Anfwer, and fet his Hand, and was then difmift untill the Afternoon ; at which time they did again appear, and there were examin'd and travers'd with by fair and flattering Speeches, as well of the Bifhop as of others his Affiftants, to recant and revoke their Opinions, who notwithftanding remain'd conftant and firm ; and therefore after the Ufage of their *Ecclefiaftical Laws*, were fent away again until the nextDay being *Saturday* May 18ᵗʰ. Then in the Forenoon the Bifhop ufing his accuftomed manner of Proceeding, did likewife difmifs them; and at laft in the Afternoon condemn'd them as Hereticks, and fo delivered them

to

But Queen *Elizabeth* coming to the Crown the Scene altered, and the Charge run into another Current (as the aforefaid Record continues it) *viz.* To one *Hewet* for helping to carry the *Geare* out of the *Church* when it was burnt, and breaking the Refidue[p]. For a *new Service-Book*, a *Bible*, a *Paraphrafe* of *Erafmus*, the *Homilies*, &c. and pay Sir *John Gally* Parfon of *Wakes-Coln*[q], for the Pains he took the Space of

---

to the Sheriffs, (of *London*) in whofe Cuftody they remain'd until they were deliver'd to the Sheriff of *Effex*; (*William Harris* Efq;) and by him were executed. *Fox Acts and Monuments*, 1455.

[p] *Weaver* in his *Funeral Monuments, p.* 50. and 117. writes, that towards the latter End of the Reign of King *Henry* VIII, and throughout the whole Reign of King *Edward* VI, and in the Beginning of Queen *Elizabeth*'s, certain Perfons of every *County* were put in Authority to pull down and caft out of all Churches, *Roods, Graven Images, Shrines* with their *Relicks*; or any thing elfe which tended to *Idolatry* and *Superftition*. Thefe were in many Places burnt, together

2

with the *Copes, Veftments, Altarclothes, Amifes, Books, Banners* and *Rood-lofts*.

[q] On the 28th of *Feb. A.* 1547, one *John Colly* or *Calley*, Clerk, was prefented to the Living of *Wakes-Coln*, but deprived thereof in the Reign of Queen *Mary, viz.* 1554, and reftored upon the coming of Queen *Elizabeth* to the Crown *Anno* 1558, *Newcourt*'s *Rep.* Vol. II. 190. What the Caufes of his Deprivation were doth not appear in that Author, but it is likely for either being married, or a Proteftant. This muft have been the Perfon, who Mr. *Taylor* calls Sir *John Galley*, the Letter G. being through Mif-diftinction of Sound, or carelefsnefs in either Writer or Tranfcriber

of five Days in ferving thofe that would come to receive the *Communion* : Deface the *Images* call'd the *Feigned Miracles*, that ftood in the *Chancel Veftry*, and *Church Windows*[1]. And to ufe the greater Husbandry they fell the Boards which came off the *Rood-loft* when it was pulled down, and at laft the very Pewter and Brafs of their *Croffes* and *Candlefticks* to a Pewterer of *Ipfwich*.

Return we now to our Perambulation about the Town, and keeping by the Wall we pafs by a fmall piece of Ground adjoining on the North to the *Church-Yard*, where heretofore ftood the *Admiralty - Houfe* ; and where were kept the *Admiralty-Courts* of this *Liberty*. Near adjoyning to this is a fmall Out-let by a low Door which fome fay, was call'd the *Church* (or St. *Nicholas* his) *Poftern*; over againft which further out, is a *Plat-form* upon a modern *Demi-Baftion*[1 2].

Next

fcriber inferted inftead of C. He was likewife *Vicar* of *Roydon* in this County of which he was depriv'd at the fame time as of his Rectory of *Wakes-Coln*, and died *A.* 1565. *Newcourt* makes him Vicar of other Churches in this County; in which there feems fome Improbability, which being foreign to my prefent Defign I fhall omit.

[1] *Weaver*, l. c. complains of the aforemention'd *Commiffioners*, that under colour of this their *Commiffion*, and in their too forward Zeal they battered down *Croffes*, defaced the *Images* of *Kings*, *Princes*, and crackt in pieces *Glafs Windows*, &c.

[1 2] Between the faid *Demi-Baftion* and *Bartons*, and the *Water-gate* but facing the Town, ftand

ftand the forementioned new-erected *Alms-Houfes*, they are built of Brick, confifting of four dwellings, but with two Doors of Entrance, one Door ferving two Tenements, each of which containing one lower Room with a Chamber over it; behind is inclofed a piece of Ground with a Brick Wall for their Conveniency, at the Bottom of which towards the Sea is now 1728.

building with Brick a *Work-Houfe*, for the Ufe of the Town of *Harwich* wherein to imploy their *Poor*; towards the Charge of which their prefent Members of *Parliament* have given them 300 *l.* On the Middle of the Front of the aforefaid new-erected *Alms-Houfes*, is a White Stone on which is the following Infcription;

THE GIFT OF GEORGE
COLEMAN GENT.ᵀ 1673
REBVILT 1718. CAP.ᵀ
MAD:ˢᵒⁿ HVNT MAJOR
HEN: BICKERTON ⎫
GILES BAKER   ⎬ CHVRCH-WARDENS.

More to the South of the laft another fmall White Stone on which,   D. S. Senʳ.
                    dedit xxⁱ
                    1718.

Thefe *Houfes* have no Endowment, and only ferve as free Habitations for poor Perfons or Families.

A little further towards the *Water-gate* is another Brick building, about fixty Foot long, one half of which is a large Room defign'd for a *Charity School*, and the other half con-

fifting of two Rooms below Stairs and as many Chambers, for the Habitation of the *School-Mafter*: It was built at the Charge of *Humphry Parfons*, Efq; Member of Parliament for the Corporation, as appears by the following Infcription on a White Stone on the Front;

IVVENTVTI

IVVENTVTI HERVICENSI
Bonis moribus & literis
Et Religionis Sanctissimæ rudimentis
Secundum instituta EccLesiæ Anglicanæ
Imbuendæ
Has Ædes Sacrari voluit
Sumptibusq; suis extrui curavit
HVMPHRIDVS PARSONS ARM ᴿ.
Civis & Aldermannus Londinensis
Et
Ad Comitia Parliamentaria ab hoc Burgo delegatus
A. D. 1724.
Te DEVS OPTIME MAXIME
Patronum vult Fundator
Tu largitoris eximij munificentiæ
Felices des eventus
Te Favente Honori Succedant Tuo
Et Juventus & Ædes
Nullo peritura die.

Over the Inscription is an Escutcheon with the Arms of *Parsons*, viz. Quarterly of 4, 1, & 4. *Two Cheveronels ermin between* 3 *Eagles displayed*, 2, & 3. *two Cheveronels between* 3 *Goat's Heads eraced*, impailing *a Cheveron charged with a Star of many Points between two Roses*.

The Gift given by Mr. *Parsons* was 500 *l.* which being paid into the Hands of Mr. *Daniel Smith* then *Mayor*, was by him expended upon the Building with the Addition of 200 *l.* of his own, but having no Endowment it only serves for a School for Gentlemen's Children, and a House for their Master; and thereby the Donor's Design of a Charity School for poor Children of the Town defeated.

Between this and the Watergate stand divers Sheds for Store-Houses, &c. and here are built Hoys and other small Vessels for the Fishery.

I   Next

Next to this is *Barton*'s or *Water-gate*, over againſt
which on the Outſide are the *Cage* and *Pillory*; this
is now called the *Eaſt-gate*, and without towards the
Sea-ſhore near the *Angel-gate* is a Shelter from Rain,
call'd their *Exchange*[13].

A ſmall arched *Gate* is the next not large enough
to give Paſſage to Coach or Cart, call'd St. *Auſtin*'s-
Gate, within which is a Houſe formerly belonging to
the *Dukes* of *Norfolk* of an ancient Building: In the
Hall Window whereof, were very lately ſeveral Coats
of Arms of the *Lord Thomas de Brotherton*, Earl of *Norfolk*; but by the preſent Occupiers thereof all taken
away this Year 1676.   There are alſo within an inward Court to be ſeen ſeveral arched Paſſages, and (by
what we have heard) Vaults from the Cellar of this
Houſe as far as *Barton*'s-*Gate*.   The many great Foun-
dations that have been found in the Houſes near to it,
ſhew it was of a large Extent; but in moſt Places of
this Town in digging, they find Rubbiſh and Fragments

---

[13] The Exchange mention'd
by our Author, is now more than
a Shelter from Rain, being of late
Years handſomly rebuilt and ſet
facing the Sea, and on it is placed
a neat quadrangular Sun-Dial.
On the Bottom of the Eaſt Dial
is painted, 𝔚𝔞𝔱𝔠𝔥 𝔣𝔬𝔯 𝔶𝔢 𝔨𝔫𝔬𝔴
𝔫𝔬𝔱 𝔯𝔥𝔢 𝔥𝔬𝔲𝔯.   On the Top of
that of the South Lex dei lvx
diei.   At the Bottom of the
Weſt.   𝔏𝔢𝔱 𝔫𝔬𝔱 𝔱𝔥𝔢 𝔖𝔲𝔫 𝔤𝔬
𝔡𝔬𝔴𝔫 𝔲𝔭𝔬𝔫 𝔶𝔬𝔲𝔯 𝔚𝔯𝔞𝔱𝔥.   And
on the North at Top Non
ignavis lvceo.   Underneath
Capt Maddeſon Hunt, Mayor,
Mr. Tho. Oſborn Chambln.

of Walls of very great Antiquity; and moſt of them of that Sort of Stone, which at this preſent is taken up at the *Cliff*.

The next Gate in the Town-wall beyond this is now but a crowded Paſſage call'd the *Caſtle-Port*, from whence the Wall continued to the *Caſtle*; the principal Part whereof (as may be collected by its Relicks and Ruins) conſiſted in a *Tower*; which many now living remember, and aver that it equalled in Height, the *Steeple* of the *Church* (without the Spire.) The Walls were of a great Thickneſs, which at the Foot of it were waſhed with the Water of *Orwell*. In it heretofore were the *Town Priſon* and *Guild-Hall*; and hereabouts was a diſtinct *Pariſh*, call'd by the Name of the *Caſtle-Pariſh*, being a Liberty conſiſting of an Encloſure of Houſes belonging to the *Caſtle* when it flouriſh'd; which are ſuppoſed to have appertain'd to ſome ſmall *Church* or *Chapel* founded therein, (and) *in lib. maj. in Ciſta Eccleſiæ* (is) *an Account of Quit-Rents paid* the King 1603. *out of the Caſtle*

---

^f What was the Name of this *Pariſh*, or to what Saint it was dedicated, or who were the ſeveral Incumbents of the *Church* or *Chapel*, doth not appear in any *Hiſtory* I have yet met with.

Anno 1363. *King Edward* III. made one *John Rousbie* Parſon of *Harwich*, *Surveyor* and *Comptroller* of his *Majeſty's Works*,

Dan. Hiſt. 213. *Weaver* calls him *John Rouceby* Parſon of *Hardwicke*, page 72. which muſt be the ſame Perſon. In *Stow's Annals* it is put 1365. It is very probable that he was *Parſon* of this *Pariſh*, though the Silence of Authors doth not permit the Determination. Perhaps this our *John Rousbie* was the ſame Perſon,

I 2

Caſtle Pariſh^ſ. Further into the Water for the Security of the North-Weſt Part of the Town, were anciently ſeveral *Block-Houſes* remembred by ſeveral living (with the *Caſtle*) to have Guns in them; but now all gone and out of Sight; only thereabouts, the *Auguſtine* (heretofore a *Dutch Man* of *War*) is ſunk, being purpoſely there placed for the Preſervation of the *Graving Place* for his *Majeſty's* Ships of War, chiefly againſt the Weſtern Winds which come down the *Stour*^t.

Along the Shore Weſtward, above where the *Caſtle* was, is a landing Place of late, call'd *Cock and Pye Stairs*, from ſuch a Sign near them.

Above this again are ſeveral other *Keys* belonging to private Houſes, till we come to the King's Stairs heretofore call'd *Lambard*'s, and ſometimes *Evans*'s Stairs: (through a Gate leading to them, where ſeem to be ſome Remains of the old *Town-Wall* towards *Orwell*)

ſon, that upon the ſaid *King Edward*'s Letter of *Preſentation* dat. the 4th of *December* 1361. was on the *Kalends* of *January* following, collated to the Rectory of *Harlow* in *Eſſex*, by the Name of *John de Roucæby* or *Rozeby*, Clerk; which he again reſign'd *Anno* 1363. The ſame Year the aforeſaid *John Rousbie* was made the *King's Surveyor*.

^t This preſent Year 1728. there are no leſs than the *Hulks* of five Ships (one of which was a *French Man* of *War* call'd the *Trident)* which are there ſunk in two Rows, *viz.* three Hulks in one Row, and two in the other, upon the ſame Account that the *Auguſtine* mention'd by our Author was.

Near

Near to which is a Houfe belonging to his *Majefty's Navy*, now call'd the *King's Houfe*; which ftands at the lower End of the *High-Street*, at the upper End whereof betwixt it and the Church Street, the *Town-Markets* are kept in a *Street* not very convenient for them by reafon of its Narrownefs .

The next is a fair Street, call'd St. *Nicolas* or *Church-Street*, ftretching itfelf from the North-fide of the Church or Chapel to the Water-fide of *Orwell*.

And then the furthermoft Street from its Situation, call'd the *Weft-Street*; beyond which towards the *Town-Marfh* are *Ramparts* of Earth with a *Foffe*; but how this Side of the Town was anciently fortified doth not appear, no Remains of the *old Wall* being as yet difcover'd in the whole Length of this *Street*, except that towards the Point Weftward upon *Orwell*, there was lately found an ancient Foundation; which probably might have been fome *Tower* at the Angle. At the South End of this *Street*, ftands the *principal Gate* of this Town, from whence we began our Perambulation ʷ. There were anciently other *Gates* [*ex lib.*

ᵘ On the North-fide of this *Street* about the middle thereof is the *Market-place*, which is only a narrow *Shelter* tiled adjoining to a Houfe, fupported before by three round *Columns*.

ʷ This *Weft Street* is alfo a fair Street, ftretching from the faid Gate to the *Haven*, and is the longeft in the Town, this and the *Church Street* being much the faireft *Streets*.

maj.

maj. in Cifta Ecclefiæ] as *Savers*, and *Saulve-Gate*, *Burham's-Gate*, *Tilney's-Gate*, &c. whofe Names although we have found, yet their Places are loft to us.

Somewhat more than a Mile in Diftance South-Weft from *Harwich* is *Dovercourt*, which in Denomination in all *Ecclefiaftical* Concerns precedes *Harwich*, as being the Mother Church; and they are written *Dovercourt cum Harwich*.

Alberic de Vere (who is call'd *Albericus Senior*) founded a *Cell* for fome *Monks* taken out of the famous *Abby* of *Abendon*, to ferve God at *Coln* in this *County* (where were many coftly *Monuments* for feveral of this noble *Family* there inter'd, taking that Name from its Situation on the River *Coln* [x]: Which gives Denomination as well to *Coln-Engain*, *Coln-Wake*, and *White-Coln*, as to *Colchefter* itfelf, all in this County, *V. Dugdale's Bar.* Tom. I. 188.) and endow'd it (among feveral other Endowments and Gifts of Churches and Lands, &c.) with this Church of *Dovercourt* [y], and having fo great a liking

---

[x] This had afterwards the Addition of *Earls Coln* in Diftinction from the others, from the *Earls* of *Oxford*, Lords thereof.

[y] The *Foundation Charter* of this *Monaftry*, viz. of *Albericus Senior* is not in *Dugdale's Monafticon*, that I can find (and

therefore the Quotation from Vol. I. *p.* 436. of that *Author* inferted by *Newcourt* in his *Repertorium*, Vol. II. is from the *Charter* of *Confirmation* made by *Albericus Junior*, which doth appear by that Charter which hereafter follows) and therefore,

the

a liking Refpect and Love for this his Foundation, was at laft himfelf fhorn a *Monk* therein z. Whofe

the precife time of the faid *Foundation* is not to be known thereby; to me it feems probable that it was in the Reign of King *William* the firft, becaufe the faid *Founder* died *Anno* 1°. *Gul.* 2. *Annoq*; *Dom.* 1088.

Upon the Top of the Arch of one of the North Windows of the *Chancel* of *Dovercourt Church* is a *Lyon falient* cut in Stone, which being the Arms of fome of the *Bigods, Earls* of *Norfolk,* and Lords of this Manor, hath made it be conjectured that this Church was built by fome of them as well as the *Chapel* of *Harwich.* I grant that the latter of them was founded by *Roger Bigod* the fecond Earl of that Family, as appears by his Charter hereafter inferted; and it is likely fome of the later *Bigods* might repair if not rebuild the Chancel of *Dovercourt,* but that they were the Founders of the faid *Church,* I cannot allow; becaufe it appears by the Charter of *Alberic de Vere,* that there was a Church here at that time; and further, *Roger Bigod* Founder of *Harwich Chapel,* did not

according to *York,* page 204. give the Lion but a *plane Crofs* for his Arms as his Father *Hugh* did ; and the fame did alfo *Hugh* Son of the faid *Roger.* Nor was it a *Lion falient* as *Cambden* affirms, *Brit. Ed.* 1695. *p.* 387. but a *Lion rampant* according to *York* Union of Honour, *p.* 205. which the two laft *Roger Bigods* gave, the near likenefs to one another, may have occafioned the unattentive to take them one for the other. This Lion falient I could not find *Anno* 1728.

z Albricus Senior *ante fui obitus diem religionis habitum in eodem loco recepit & defunctus, fepulturæ traditur: Ubi &* Willielmus *filius ejus, fuorum junior fratrum parvo tempore fuperftes patri effectus, tumulatur. Pro cujus memoria Frater ejus* Albricus *fcilicet* junior, *terram duarum carrucarum in* Scaldulacon, *& Sancto Andreæ perpetua largitione contulit, præfente prædicto* Abbate Faritio. *Aderat enim ibidem & funeris defuncti exequias agebat. Horum itaque fepultorum epitafium hic anneximus.* Cedunt

Whofe Son *Alberic* ftiling himfelf, *Regis Camera-rius* confirm'd the Donation of the faid Church of *Dovercourt* to them, which his Father and Mother had formerly made [a].   King

> *Cedunt è vita votis animifq; cupita*
> *Barbarus & Scita, Gentilis & Ifraelita*
> *Has pariter metas habet omnis fexus & ætas*
> *En puer, en Senior, pater alter, filius alter*
> *Legem, fortunam, terram, venere fub unam*
> *Non juveni tote quas epotavit athene*
> *Non vetulo note vires vel opes valuere*
> *Sed valuere fides, & prædia quæ memoramus*
> *Ut valeant, valeant per fecula cuncta precamur.*
>   Dugd. Mon. I. 438.

Befides the foregoing *Weaver* in his *Funeral Monuments*, 614. affirms, that in a MS in the *Cotton Library* he found this *Infcription* to be engraven upon the *Monument* of *Aubrey de Vere*, and *Beatrice* his Wife in he Book of *Coln Priory*.

Here lyeth *Aulbery de Veer* the firft Erle of *Guifnes*, the Son of *Alphonfus de Veer*, whyche *Aulbery* was the Founder of this Place, and *Bettrys* his Wyf Syfter of *Kyng Wylliam* the *Conquerour*.

[a] *Albericus de Veer regis Camerarius omnibus hominibus fuis & amicis Francis & Anglis, prefentibus & futuris Salutem. Sciatis univerfi me conceffiffe & hac charta mea confirmaffe, in perpetuam eleemofinam, donationes pa-* tris mei & matris meæ & hominum meorum, quas fecerunt Deo & Beatæ Mariæ Monachis de Abendonia apud Coln Deo miniftrantibus; fcilicet in meo Coln ecclefiam S. Andreæ Apoftoli, & totam terram Randulphi presbiteri

2

teri in bofco, & plano & prato; & totam decimam de dominio, de villa & de parco, de omnibus rebus quæ decimari debent, & fexies viginti acras de dominio, & virgultum quod eft ultra vivarium cum vivario, molendinum de Coleford *cum omnibus pertinentiis, & ultra pontem de Coleford pafturam quandam quæ dicitur* Mers, *& unam acram prati, & unam rodam in* Brademede, *& pratum fuum quod habent in* Kinburne *& Linland, & fuperius ibi juxta dimidiam acram prati, & unam rodam, & duas filvas fcilicet* Dodefpollefho, *& Littleheia cum viginti acris terræ, & terram Godæ & terram Ælmari longi & terram Wuluricmucche, & terram Eadwini Brafiatoris & omnes alias tenuras ejufdem villæ quas prædicti Monachi, vel homines eorum, extra parcum habent in bofco & plano, & prato libere & quiete ab omni feculari fervicio mihi vel meis pertinente, falvo tantummodo regis fervicio; fcilicet quod Monachi cum omnibus fuis facere debent, quartam partem Regis fervitii quod villa de Coln Regi debet. Et ecclefiam de Bello campo & terras pertinentes cum tribus acris prati, & totam decimam de dominio, de virgulto,*

& de villa de omnibus rebus quæ decimari debent, & commutationem pafturæ pecoribus dominicis monachorum cum pecoribus meis libere & quiete in perpetuum, & ecclefiam de Duurecourt *& terras pertinentes & totam decimam de dominio & de villa, & de pifcaria, & de omnibus rebus quæ decimari debent, & centum ovium pafturam in marifco, & unum hominem cum quinque acris libere & quiete inperpetuum & ecclefias de* Campis *& de* Benecleia *cum omnibus pertinentiis fuis quas pater meus cum fupradictis ecclefiis in primis fundamentis ecclefiæ in liberam & perpetuam contulit eleemofinam, & in* Roinges *Grimbaldi totam decimam de dominio & ecclefiam cum omnibus pertinentiis & ecclefiam de* Coln Miblanc, *cum omnibus pertinentiis in Maneriis fcil. de* Haingham, Lanreham, Aldeham, Roinges, *duas partes decimæ de dominio de omnibus rebus quæ decimari debent. In* Walde *&* Wadoho, *medietatem decimæ de dominio de omnibus rebus quæ decimari debent, & apud* Haingham *tertiam partem decimæ de terra* Ranulphi Mengin *& de terra* Roberti Balci, *& de terra* Guinnamari, *& de terra* Willielmi Grofvaffal *de omnibus*

omnibus rebus quæ declinari debent; & Molendinum de Haingham *cum pertinentiis suis: Et apud* Burgate *decem solidatas terræ, & apud* Cripping *tres solidates terræ, & apud* Roinges *terram quam* Hargar *tenet unde debet annuatim monachis duos solidos & octo denarios. Et apud* Coleceſtriam *unum meſſuagium quod* Aſcetinus *tenet unde debet annuatim monachis ſexdecim denarios. Hæc omnia pro ſalute animæ meæ & patris mei & matris meæ & omnium parentum meorum vivorum & defunctorum cum omnimoda libertate quam pater meus, vel ego, melius habuimus, concedo & confirmo, in perpetuam eleemoſinam, Deo & Beatæ Mariæ & monachis præfatis, ita liberè & quietè ſicut eleemoſina debet eſſe & poteſt. His teſtibus,* Rogero de Veer,*&*Roberto deVeer *fratribus meis,* Bernardo *dapifero,* Lancelino *capellano;* Adam *filio* Warini, *&* Radulpho *filio ejus,* Roberto *de Marcheſhale,* Picoto *Prepoſito de Coln,* Pagano *Foreſtario,* Tedbaldo *clerico* Godwino Putiſan, *&* Ricardo *filio ejus,* Ricardo Pinet *& aliis multis.* Dugdale's Monaſt. Vol. I. *p.* 436.

Which I have endeavoured to render into Engliſh *as follows.*

Aubrey de Veer, Lord Chamberlain to his Majeſty, to all his Tenants and Friends *French* and *Engliſh,* preſent and future Greeting. Know all that I have granted and by this my Charter have confirm'd, as a perpetual Alms, the Donations of my Father and my Tenants, which they have made to God and the bleſſed *Mary,* to the Monks of *Abendon,* at *Coln* ſerving God, namely, in my *Coln* the Church of St. *Andrew* the Apoſtle, and all the Land of *Randulph* Preſbyter in Wood, Plain, and Meadows; and the whole Tithe of the Lordſhip, the Villa, and the Park, of all things which ought to be tithed, and ſix ſcore Acres of the Lordſhip, and the Coppice which is beyond the Park, with the Park, the Mill of *Coleford* with all its Appurtenances, and beyond the Bridge of *Coleford* a certain Paſture which is call'd *Mers,* and one Acre of Meadow and one Rode in *Brademede,* and their own Meadow which they have in *Kinburne* and *Linland,* and further thereabouts half an Acre of Meadow

Meadow and one Rode, and two Woods, *viz. Doddefpollefho* and *Littlehey* with twenty Acres of Land, and the Land of *Gode*, and the Land of *Ælmar* the long, and the Land of *Wuluricmucche*, and the Land of *Eadwin* the *Brewer*, and all the other Tenures of the fame Villa, which the Monks aforefaid, or their Tenants hold without the Park, in Wood, Plain, and Meadow ; freely and quietly from all fecular Service belonging to me or mine, fave only the Service of the King; Namely, that the Monks with all theirs ought to do a fourth Part of the King's Service, which the Village of *Coln* owes to the King. And the Church of *Bell-Champs*, and the Lands appertaining with three Acres of Meadow, and the whole Tithe of the Lordfhip of the Coppice, and of the Villa, of all things which ought to be tithed, and the Exchange of Pafture of the Monks Cattle with mine freely and quietly for ever, and the Church of *Duurecourt*, and the Lands belonging thereto; and the whole Tithe of the Lordfhip and the Villa, and of the Fifhery ; and of all things which

ought to be tithed, and the Pafture of an hundred Sheep in the Marfh, and one Man with five Acres freely and quietly for ever; and the Churches of *Champs* and of *Benecleia* with all their Appurtenances, which my Father gave with the aforefaid Churches in the firft Foundation of the Church as a free Gift for ever, and in *Roinges* the whole Tithe of the Lordfhip, and the Church with all its Appurtenances, and the Church of *Coln Miblanc* with all its Appurtenances, in the Manors fc. of *Haingham*, *Lanreham*, *Aldeham*, *Roinges*, two Parts of the Tithe of the Lordfhip of all things which ought to be tithed. In *Walde* and *Wadow*, the half of the Tithe of the Lordfhip of all things which ought to be tithed, and at *Haingham* the third Part of the Tith of the Land of *Ralph Mengin*, and of the Land of *Robert Balk*, and of the Land of *Guinamar*, and of the Land of *William Grofvaffal*, of all things which ought to be tithed; and the Mill of *Haingham* with its Appurtenances: And at *Burgate* ten dozen Acres of Land, and at *Cripping* three dozen Acres of Land, and at *Roinges*
the

K 2

King *Henry* the firſt in the eleventh Year of his Reign, *Anno7*; *D.* 1111. confirm'd the ſaid Grant [b].

Sometime

the Land which *Hargar* holds, of which he owes the Monks yearly two Shillings and eight Pence. And at *Colcheſter* one Meſſuage which *Aſcetine* holds out of which he owes the Monks ſixteen Pence yearly. All theſe for the Salvation of my own Soul, and of my Father's, and Mother's, and all my Relations living and dead; with all manner of Liberty which my Father or I have happily enjoy'd, I grant, and confirm as a perpetual Alms to God, and to the bleſſed *Mary* and the Monks aforeſaid, ſo freely and quietly as an Alms ought to be, and may be. Witneſs *Roger de Veer*, and *Robert de Veer* my Brothers, *Bernard* the Sewer, *Lanceline* the Chaplain; *Adam* the Son of *Warin*, and *Ralph* his Son, *Robert de Marcheſhale*, *Picote* the Provoſt of *Coln*, *Pagan* the Foreſter, *Tedbald*, Clerk; *Godwin Putiſan*, and *Richard* his Son, *Richard Pinet*, &c.

[b] Which Charter is as follows.

2

Omnibus Ecclesiæ Dei fidelibus ſub regimine meo, *Notum fieri volo*, *quod Ego Henricus Dei gratia Anglorum Rex*, *pro peccatorum meorum remiſſione*, *ac animæ meæ ſalute*, *Deo ac Beatæ Mariæ in Abbendonenſi ecclesia*, *& Sancto Andreæ in Colenſi ecclesia*, *quæ ut filia matri & membrum capiti ſubjecta*, *& coherens eſt ecclesiæ Abbendonenſi*, *concedo*, *& in æternum permanere auctorizo*, *omnes illas donationes quas Albericus de Ver & uxor ejus Beatrix*, *& eorum filius Albericus*, *cum fratribus ſuis*, *eorumque homines*, *jam fecerunt vel facturi ſunt*, *ſupradictæ ecclesiæ*, *tam in eccleſiis*, *quam in terris*, *hominibus & decimis*, *molendinis*, *ſilvis*, *& pratis*, *paſcuis & exitibus*, *quarum nomina rerum ſubnexa leguntur.* *Scilicet in Cola ecclesiam Sancti Andreæ cum terra Ranulfi preſbyteri.* *Et cum omnibus ad ecclesiam pertinentibus*, *& ſexies viginti acras de dominio & viridarium quod ultra aquam cum vivario*, *& terram quam Serlo habuit*, *ſicut melius & largius unquam*

*unquam habuit it se vel aliquis ante-
cessorum illius in pascuis & syl-
vis, & campis. Et duas sylvas
scilicet Dodepolisö, & Nodewde,
& terram Godæ decem solidorum
de Gablo, & terram Eadwini
quinque solidorum de Gablo, &
viginti acras de dominio quo cam-
bitæ fuerant pro terra Blache-
manni, & unum hominem cum
quinque acris terræ, & terram
Ælmari longi, & terram Wlfwini
foreftarii, & molendinum, gran-
gias & ecclefiam de Duvercurt
cum triginta acris terræ, & cum
omnibus sibi pertinentibus,& maneriis scil. Hethigaham, Belcheham,
Lanreham, Aldeham, Duvercurt,
Bonecleida, Bodingas, duas partes
decimæ de omnibus rebus, & unum
hominem cum quinque acris in
Walder & Waldanæ medietatem
decimæ, & unum hominem cum
quinque acris. In Hethingeham
duo molendina, quæ Aldwinus mo-
lendinarius tenebat, de terra Ad-
helelmi de Burgata decem solidatas. Dimidiam decimam de*
Miblanc *de* Cola, *& tertiam
partem decimæ* Rannulfi *magni.
Et ecclefiam de campis. Et Ecclefiam de Boneclera,* Ecclefiam
de Bello Campo *cum omnibus eis
pertinentibus, & sylvam de Litc-
haia, cum viginti acris terra.*

*Hæc Donationum concessio facta
eft a serenissimo Rege Anglorum
Henrico anno Dominicæ incarnationis* MCXI. *indictione quarta,
anno vero regni sui undeci-
mo, coram his teftibus,* Roberto Lincolnienfi *episcopo, &* Jo-
hanne de Bajocis, *&* Gilberto
capellano, & Goisfrido *de* Dina,
& Hamone *dapifero, &* Ranulfo
Mefchino, *&* Willielmo Peve-
rello, *de Notingeham,&* Hugone
de Bochelando *apud* Radingas.
Dugd. Monaft. I. 437.

In Englifh *as follows.*

To all the Faithful in the
Church of God under my Rule,
be it known, that I *Henry* by
the Grace of God King of *England*, for the Remiffion of my
Sins, and the Salvation of my
own Soul, to God and the bleffed *Mary* in *Abbendon* Church,
and to S. *Andrew* in *Coln* Church,
which as a Daughter is fubject
to the Mother and a Member
to the Head, and coherent to
the Church of *Abbendon*, do
grant and authorize to remain
for ever, all thofe Donations
which *Aubrey de Veer*, and his
Wife *Beatrice*, and their Son
Aubrey, with his Brothers, and
their

their Tenants have already made, or fhall make to the Church abovefaid, as well in Churches, as in Lands, Men and Tithes, Mills, Woods and Meadows, Pafture-Grounds and Strays, of which things the Names are fubjoin'd, *viz.* in *Coln* the Church of St. *Andrew*, with the Land of *Ralph* the Prefbyter. And with all things appertaining to the Church, and fix fcore Acres of Lordfhip, and the Green which is beyond the Water with the Park, and the Land which *Serlo* held as well and largely as ever he or any of his Predeceffors in Paftures, and Woods, and Fields. And two Woods, namely, *Dodepolifo* and *Nodewde*, and the Land of *Gode* of ten Shillings Gable, and the Land of *Eadwin* five Shillings Gable and twenty Acres of Lordfhip which were exchanged for the Land of *Blacheman*, and one Man and five Acres, and the Land of *Ælmare* the long, and the Land of *Wlfwine* the Forefter, and the Mill, Granges, and the Church of *Duvercurt* with thirty Acres of Land, and with all its Appurtenances, and

Mannors, *fc.* *Hethigaham*, *Belcheam*, *Lanreham*, *Aldeham*, *Duvercurt*, *Bonecleide*, *Bodings*, two Parts of the Tithe of all things, and one Man with five Acres in *Walder*, and at *Waldan* the half of the Tithe, and one Man with five Acres. In *Hethingeham* two Mills, which *Aldwin* the Miller held, of the Land of *Adhelelm de Burgate* ten dozen of Acres. Half the Tithe of *Miblanc* of *Coln*, and the third Part of the Tithes of great *Ranulph* and the Church of *Champs*, and the Church of *Boneclere*, and the Church of *Belchamps* with all their Appurtenances, and the Wood of *Littlehay*, with twenty Acres of Land. This Grant of the Donations was made by the moft ferene *Henry* King of *England* in the Year of our Lord MCXI. the fourth Indiction, but in the eleventh Year of his Reign, witnefs, *Robert* Bifhop of *Lincoln*, and *John de Bajocis*, and *Gilbert* Chaplain, and *Goiffrid*, *de Dina*, and *Hamon* the Sewer, and *Ralph Mefchin*, and *William Peverell* of *Nottingham*, and *Hugh de Bocheland* at *Redings*.

Sometime

Sometime after we find that *Roger Bigod* Earl of *Norfolk, Temp. Ric.* 1. grants to *Coln* and the *Monks* there, the *Church* of *Dovercourt, cum omnibus ad eam pertinentibus & cum Capella de* ϸɇɾɇⱲɨʧɇ, and taking no Notice at all of what the *Veres* had done in the aforemention'd Settlement, declares (but the Reasons thereof appear not plainly) that he had founded it *pro salute* Animæ suæ *& Comitis* Hugonis Fratris *ejus & Comitiffæ* Julianæ *matris ejus &* Idæ *uxoris ejus*c: And thus

---

c The Charter of *Roger Bigod* Earl of *Norfolk*, to the Monks of *Coln* of the Church of *Dovercourt* and Chapel of *Harwich*.

Sciant præfentes & futuri quod ego Rogerus Bigod Comes Norfolchiæ conceffi, & hac prefenti Chartâ meâ confirmavi Deo & Ecclefiæ Beatæ Mariæ de Colne, & monachis ibidem Deo fervientibus, Ecclefiam de Dovercourt cum omnibus ad eam pertinentibus; & cum Capellâ de Herewyche, quam ego affenfu eorum fundavi pro falute animæ meæ & Comitis Hugonis fratris mei, Comitiffæ Julianæ matris meæ & Ide uxoris meæ & omnium anteceforum meorum, & fuceforum meorum in 2

parochiâ de Dovercourt, &c. His *teftibus, Hugone Bigod filio meo, Euftachia de Braham, Rogero de Braham, Ricardo de Gosfeld, Willielmo & Bertramo de Verdon, Waltero de Cadomo, Galfrido de Bellomonte, & aliis.*

In Englifh *as follows.*

Know all Men that I *Roger Bigod,* Earl of *Norfolk* have granted, and by this Prefent Charter have confirm'd to God and the Church of the bleffed *Mary* of *Coln*, and to the Monks there serving God, the Church of *Dovercourt* with all things belonging to it, and with the Chapel of *Harwich*, which I with their affent, have founded for the

thus fetled upon *Coln* it continued until the Reign of *Henry* VIII, when it fuffered in the fatal *Crifis* of *Monafteries*, and after that continued in the Crown (where the Advowfon ftill refides) but the Glebe *&c.* King *James* alienated together with the Lordfhip of *Dovercourt*, to Sir *George Whitmore*, Knight; and is now in the Poffeffion of his Son the worfhipful *William Whitmore*, Efq; 1676 ^{c 2}.

the Salvation of my own Soul, and of Earl *Hugh* my Brother, and the Countefs *Juliana* my Mother, and *Ida* my Wife, and of all my Predeceffors and Succeffors in the Parifh of *Dovercourt*, &c. Witnefs, *Hugh Bigod* my Son, *Euftace de Braham*, *Roger de Braham*, *Richard de Gosfield*, *William* and *Bertram de Verdon*, *Walter de Cadome*, *Jeoffrey de Beaumont*, and others.

By the aforefaid *Charter* it appears that *Roger Bigod* Earl of *Norfolk*, with the Confent of the *Convent* of *Coln*, had founded the Chapel of *Harwich* for the Health of his Soul, and of Earl *Hugh* his Brother, Countefs *Juliana* his Mother, and of *Ida* his Wife, *&c.* which feems the plain Reafons of its Foundation, *viz.* of the Chapel of *Harwich*, and not of the Priory of *Coln*. But why he calls Earl *Hugh* his Brother I do not apprehend, when it fhould have been his Father, as I fhall prove when I come to treat of the feveral Lords of this Manor. Unlefs it was through fault of the Tranfcribers in writing it *Fratris* inftead of *Patris*, by inferting the Letters *Fr.* inftead of *P.* and being thus publifhed by Sir *William Dugdale*, our Author continued the Error, and from him *Newcourt* in his *Repertorium*, Vol. II. *p.* 216.

^{c 2} From whom it is now come *Anno* 1728. to the Poffeffion of *Daniel Burr*, Efq; of which more when we come to the *Defpotical* or *Dynaftical* Concerns of the Town.

This

Tab VI. Page 73.

Dovercourt Church on the South Side.

This Church of *Dovercourt* is dedicated to *All-Saints,* i. e. *Allhallows,* for in a Parchment Deed (*ex Autogr. in Cifta Com. Burgi Harw.*) dated 19. *Ric.* 2. one *Thomas Gowles* ftiles himfelf, *Perpetuus Vicarius Omnium Sanctorum de Dovercourt*[d].

In

---

[d] This *Church* confifteth of a *Body* and *Chancel* tiled, at the Weft End whereof is a *towred Steeple* embattled, on the South Side a *Dial-Plate,* and in the Steeple a *Clock* and *Bells.* It ftands on the North Side of the Road leading from *Ramfey* to *Harwich.*

Without all doubt this *Church* was originally a *Rectory,* but after the *Donation* thereof to the Monks of *Coln* by *Alberic* or *Aubrey de Vere,* they foon, according to the Ufage of thofe times, procured it to be made a *Vicarage,* though the time when, or Inftrument by which it was fo conftituted, doth not at prefent appear; but in the Reign of King *Edward* III. it was fo, and fo continues to be. The Names of fuch of the *Incumbents* as are to be found in the feveral *Regifters* of the *Bifhops* of *London,* with the times of their *Collations* have been publifhed by Mr. *Newcourt* in his *Repertorium,* Vol. II. *p.* 219. from whence I have extracted them with the Supplement of fuch as have been prefented thereto, fince the Publication of that *Book,* or were omitted by him.

I. *Such as were prefented by* the Prior *and* Convent *of* Coln.

Steven Abbot, Pr. 5. Kal. Sept. 1336.
Steven Balton,
Walter Legat, 14. Kal. Aug. 1367.
Thomas Gowles, 23. Mar. 1388.
John Arderne,
Thomas Savage, Pr. 14. Oct. 1433.
John Warham, Pr. 20. Sept. 1437.

L

Robert

In the Glaſs of a *North-window* in the *Chancel* is a very ancient *Coat* of *Arms,* viz. *Gul.* 3 *Lions paſſant gardant*

Robert Goodlake, Pr. 10. Nov. 1438.
John Oxenford,
John Abell, Pr. 26. June 1459.
John Mayskin, Pr. 20. Sepᵗ. 1459.
Martyn Wayte, 8. Mar. 1461.
Martin Aſslake,
John Mansfeld, Pr. 30. Apr. 1474.
Thomas Thornton, Pr. 18. June 1478.
Richard Strowgth, Cap. 17. Mar. 1508.
John Holland, Pr. 14. Dec. 1531.
John Roberts, Pr 24. Dec. 1533..

Upon the Diſſolution of the *Priory* of *Coln,* which being one of the *leſſer Monaſteries,* hapned about the Year 1536. the right of *Advowſon* of this *Vicarage* came to the *Crown,* but I do not find any *Vicar* preſented thereto, until

Richard Squyer, Clerk, *Anno* 1°. *Edwardi* VI. 1547.

After whom the next that was preſented, was through a Miſtake in the Hurry of Church Matters preſented thereto as a *Rectory.*

Chriſtopher James, Clerk, 23. June 1558.

II. Vicars *preſented* by the *Crown* to *Dovercourt with the* Chapel *of* Harwich *annext.*

William Burges, Clerk, 30. Oct. 1567.
Hugh Branham, Clerk, 7. Oct. 1574.
Thomas Drax, Clerk,
William Innes, A. M. 18. Mar. 1618.
Charles Bainbrigge, A. M. 6. Apr. 1639.

James

gardant Or *in chief a File of three Points Arg.* part of the Points upon the uppermoſt Lion. The *Arms* of the

> *James Fenton,* A. M. 20. June 1663.
> *Hippolitus de Luzency,* A. M. 18. Dec. 1678.
> *William Thompſon,* A. M.   1702.
> *George Ludgater,* A. M.   1706.
> *William Curtis,* A. M.   1706.

As to the State of the *Vicarage* of *Dovercourt* the moſt ancient Value thereof was but 12 *l. per Annum,* but upon the Deſtruction of the *Rood* there, the Oblations made by Perſons reſorting thereto ceaſing, the clear Value thereof was reduced to but *five Pounds* and eight Pence, as appears by the following *Tranſcript,* communicated by the Reverend Mr. *Robert Rich,* Rector of *Wrabneſs.*

Memorandum,

That whereas the Vicarage of *Dovercourt* in the County of *Eſſex,* at the firſt Taxation of all Spiritual Promotions, was taxed and certified by the Commiſſioners appointed for the ſame, to be of the clear Value of twelve Pounds, and was ſo return'd into our Sovereign Lord

the King's Court of Exchequer, as by the Records thereof now remaining in the Court of firſt Fruits and Tenths, it may, and doth appear: Which Vicarage is at this preſent time, and of long time paſs'd hath been void of any Incumbent, and no Clerk as yet inſtituted and inducted into the ſame. Whereupon one *Richard Squyer,* Clerk, thereunto preſented, came into the Court in the Term of *Eaſter* laſt paſt, to compound with the King's Majeſty for the firſt Fruits of the ſame, and there declared; that ſince the ſaid firſt Taxation the ſaid Vicarage was, and is greatly decayed, by reaſon that the Rood of *Dovercourt* aforeſaid, whereunto was wont to be recourſe of People there making their Oblations, was and is by the King's Majeſty's Commandment

the *Lord Thomas of Brotherton,* fifth Son of King *Edward* I. *Earl* of *Norfolk, Lord Marshall* of *England,* and

mandment there taken away, and the fame Pilgrimage difannulled, and commanded to be abolifh'd and withdrawn; and thereby the Incumbents of the fame Vicarage have been overcharged with the firft Fruits of the fame, fhould they become due. For Reformation whereof a Commiffion was awarded out of this Court to Sir *John Raynsford,* Knight; *John Lucas,* Efq; *John Chriftmas,* Efq; and *Richard Cornwallis,* and *George Sayer,* Gent. bearing date at *Weftminfter* the fourteenth Day of *May,* in the firft Year of our Sovereign Lord King *Edward* the fixth by the Grace of God, &c. commanding them to enquire by the fame of certain Articles to the fame Commiffion annexed, which *John Chriftmas, John Lucas* and *George Sayer,* by Vertue of the fame have enquired and certified to this Court, at the time of return aforefaid by the Oaths of certain Perfons thereupon fworn and examin'd: That they knew not nor ever did

know any Lands, Tenements, Rents, or Poffeffions belonging to the Vicarage of *Dovercourt* aforefaid, unlefs one fmall Houfe and two Acres of Pafture, worth by the Year fix Shillings and eight Pence. And as concerning Tithes and Oblations, they fay, that neither Tith-Hay, nor Tith-Corn belongeth to the faid Vicarage, but the fame belongeth to the Parfonage of *Dovercourt.* Neverthelefs they fay, that the four Offering-Days with the Tith-Lamb, Tith-Wool, Tith-Pig, Tith-Calf, Tith-Goofe, Tith-Apples, Tith-Nuts, Tith-Pears belong to the faid Vicarage. And becaufe there is no Tith-Cheefe payable in *Dovercourt,* therefore, for every Cow of the fecond Calf or more having a Calf is paid yearly three Pence, and for every Cow of the firft Calf, and for the Herbage of every Farrow-Cow, Heifer, Bullock or Steer, there is yearly paid to the faid Vicarage one penny half penny, and for every foul one penny; which

which Tithes and other yearly Commodities before rehears'd do belong to the faid Vicarage, and are worth in all to the Incumbent there [except Deductions hereafter fpecified] one hundred and ten Shillings, and no more. And alfo fay, that at the time of the faid firft Taxation, there was unto the Image in the Church of *Dovercourt* then call'd the Rood of *Dovercourt*, a yearly great Pilgrimage and Offering, which was yearly worth to the Vicar ten Pounds Sterling at the leaft, and now is not worth yearly, nor any Year thefe five or fix Years paft, hath been worth any penny; which is and hath been the Decay of the faid Vicarage. And that all the yearly Charges [except Taxations, and except the yearly Tenths payable to our Sovereign Lord the King] are only nine Shillings and four Pence, which is paid to the Archdeacon of *Effex* (it fhould be *Colchefter*) for Procurations and Synodals, and fo the clear Value of the fame Vicarage amounts not above the Sum of one hundred Shillings and eight Pence, as by the Certificates of the faid *John Chriftmas*, *John Lucas* and

George Sayer, more at large may and doth appear. Which faid Commiffion, with the Depofitions thereupon taken, and the whole Certificate and Examination thereof by the faid Commiffioners made, and into the faid Court certified and declared, the Chancellor and Council of this Court have diligently read, feen, and well underftand; and thereupon it is fully order'd, adjudged, and decreed by the Chancellor and Council of this Court, and by the Authority of the fame Court this prefent Term of the Holy Trinity in the firft Year of the Reign of our Sovereign Lord. That the faid former Certificates fhall be reformed, amended, and made conformable to the Certificates of the faid *John Chriftmas*, *John Lucas*, and *George Sayer*; and that as well the faid *Richard Squire* now incumbent of the faid Vicarage, and all others which fhall be Incumbents of the fame, fhall compound with the King's Majefty for the firft Fruits of the fame Vicarage, after the Rate of the faid Sum of one hundred Shillings and eight Pence, and after the like Rate for ever henceforth, yearly

yearly pay the Tenths and Subfidies as often as every Subfidy fhall hereafter chance, according to the Taxation of the fame latter Certificate, and none otherways. And furthermore, fhall be clearly acquitted for evermore, and difcharged of all Arrearages of every Tenth and Subfidy due before the making of this Decree, until fuch time as more effectual and better Matters and Caufe be found and fhewed on the behalf of our Sovereign Lord the King to charge the Incumbent. Thus far the Record.

As to the prefent State of the *Vicarage* of *Dovercourt cum Harwich*, the Value thereof was about thirty Pounds *per Annum*, after their Annexion, which being too fmall a *Premium* for fo great a Charge, and under the Value of fifty Pounds *per Annum*, was not only at firft releafed from the Payment of firft Fruits and Tenths, by Vertue of an Act made *Anno* 1º. & 2ᵈº. *Annæ*, entituled, *An Act for making more effectual her Majefty's gracious Intentions for the Augmentation of the Maintenance of the poor Clergy, by enabling her Majefty to grant in Perpetuity the* *Revenues of the firft Fruits and Tenths, and alfo for enabling any other Perfon to make Grants for the fame Purpofe.* But likewife was augmented by the Purchafe of a Farm in that *Parifh* of the Value of twenty Pounds *per Annum*, with the Sum of two hundred Pounds affign'd to that Purpofe, by the *Governors of the Bounty of the faid Queen* Anne, in conjunction with the like Benevolence given thereto by Dr. *John Robinfon* late *Lord Bifhop* of *London* ; but the Tithes of thofe Lands (purchafed by the *Government* for the Ufe of *Fortification*) in *Harwich* and *Dovercourt* being withheld by the *Leefors* from the *Crown*, it's now actually no better than *in Statu quo*. Ex MS. R. W. C.

According to the *Terrier* Aº. 1610. here did belong to the *Vicarage*, a *Vicarage* Houfe, befides the *Church-Yards*, a *Cottage* call'd the *Vicarage Houfe*, with an Orchard, and a Parcel of Land adjoining to the faid Houfe, all which contain together about two Acres; alfo all the Tithes of this Parifh (except Corn and Hay) likewife all Oblations and Obventions. *Newcourt*'s *Repert.* Vol. II. *p.* 219.

and

and *Lord* of this *Mannor* [d2]. There are several *Tomb-Stones* which have had *Brafs-Effigies* and *Infcriptions*, but robbed of all; as the *Chapel* of *Harwich* is [e].

This

[d2] *Anno* 1319. King *Edward* the fecond calls a great Council at *Northampton* on the firft of *Auguft*, wherein Commiffioners were appointed to treat with the Earl of *Lancafter* about the Honour and Welfare of the King and Realm; for performance of Ordinances by them agreed to, divers Perfons became Undertakers, the Earl of *Norfolk* Earl Marfhal, was one. *Tyrrell's* Hift. 3. 276. *Anno* 1327. This Earl was fent with a felect Detachment of Soldiers to *Newcaftle* upon *Tine* to prevent the Depredations of the *Scots*, ib. 351. He with others were commiffion'd to try the Rioters at *Bury St. Edmond* in *Suffolk*; where nineteen were hanged, and one preft for not pleading, and the Townfmen fined in 140000*l.* becaufe they did not prevent thofe Affaultsmadeupon the Abbey, *ib.* 349. *Anno* 2. *Edward* the third. He with the Earl of *Kent* and others raife Forces againft *Mortimer*, but

deferted that Caufe for Fear of the Queen Mother, and *Mortimer*, ib. *p.* 352. He alfo accompanied the King into *France*, when he did his Homage to that King, *ib. p.* 353. *Anno* 1330. The Peers as Judges in Parliament convict *Mortimer* and *Simon de Bereford* of Treafon, and this our Earl Marfhal commanded to fee the Execution done, *ib. p.* 364, 365.

[e] I have before taken Notice what Complaint *Weaver* made of the miftaken Zeal of the *Commiffioners*, appointed to demolifh Superftition and Idolatry; what remains for this Place is their violating of *Funeral Monuments*, *breaking* in Pieces of *Marble Tombs*, pulling up *Infcriptions* in *Brafs*, efpecially if they began with *Orate pro Anima*, or concluded with *cujus Animæ propitietur Deus:* To reftrain which Queen *Elizabeth* did iffue two feveral *Proclamations*, one in the fecond Year of her *Reign*, and the other in

her

2

This *Church* heretofore was famous for a *Rood* or *Crucifix*, whofe fuppofed Sanctity drew from far unto it many Votaries and devoted *Pilgrims* with their Offerings. The Generality verily believed, none without great Danger (even of *fudden Death*) to themfelves might attempt to fhut the *Church-Doors* upon it by Day or Night; upon which Confidence it became more eafily to be made the Sacrifice of three Men from *Dedham*, and a fourth from *Eaſt Bergholt*, Anno

her fourteenth, *vide Weaver*, 51. &c. *N. B.* Moft of the *Stones* in this *Church* and *Chancel* are very ancient, as appears by their Form, being much the *broadeſt* at the Head.

This defacing of *Monuments* is likewife taken Notice of by Sir *William Dugdale*, as follows. In the time of King *Edward* VI. and the Beginning of Queen *Elizabeth*, fuch Pretenders were fome to Zeal for a thorough *Reformation* in *Religion*, that under Colour of pulling down thofe *Images* here, as had been fuperftitioufly worfhip'd by the People, as then was faid, the beautiful and coftly *Portraitures* of *Brafs* fixed on feveral Marbles in fundry *Churches* of this

Realm efcaping not their facrilegious Hands, were torn away, and for a fmall Matter fold to *Copper-Smiths* and *Tinkers*: The Greedinefs of thofe who then hunted after Gain by that barbarous Means, being fuch, as that though the *Queen* by her *Proclamation* bearing date at *Windſor* 19. of *September* in the fecond Year of her *Reign*, taking Notice thereof, ftrictly prohibited any further Spoil in that kind; they ceafed not ftill to proceed therein, till that fhe iffued out another in the fourteenth Year of her faid *Reign*, charging the *Juſtices* of *Aſſiſe* to be fevere in the Punifhment of fuch Offenders. *Dugd. Hiſt. of St.* Paul's, *p.* 45.

1532.

1532. who in a frofty Night, together entring the fecure (yet always open) *Church*, took it down, and carrying it about a quarter of a Mile from thence, upon the Green, with its own Tapers, fir'd it to Afhes: For which three being apprehended, were hanged in feveral Places; one of whom *Nicholas Marfh* fuffered Death at *Dovercourt:* The fourth (*Robert Gardener*, out of whofe Letters Mr. *Fox* in his *Martyrology* collects the Story) of them efcaped; of which in the Parifh ftill remains a plentiful Tradition [f].

There

[f] Some Part of what Mr. *Fox* hath publifh'd concerning this *Rood* of *Dovercourt*, I fhall here tranfcribe for the further Dilucidation of what Mr. *Taylor* has here given, *viz.* That it was from the Town of *Dedham* to the Place where the *Rood* ftood ten Miles. Notwithftanding they were fo willing in that their Enterprife, that they went thefe ten Miles without Pain, and found the *Church-Doors* open, according to the blind Talk of the ignorant People: For there durft no unfaithful Perfon fhut it, which hapned well for their Purpofe; for they found the Idol which had as much Power to keep the Door fhut as to keep it open. And for Proof thereof they took the Idol from his Shrine, and carried him a quarter of a Mile from the Place where he ftood, without any Refiftance from the faid Idol. Whereupon they ftruck Fire with a Flint Stone, and fuddenly fet him on Fire, who burn'd out fo bright, that he lighted them homeward a good Mile of the ten.

This done, there went a great Talk abroad, that they fhould have great Riches in that Place: But it was very untrue; for it was not their Thought or Enterprize, as themfelves afterwards confeft; for there was nothing taken away but his Coat,

M

There was here a *Presbyter Gild* or *Fraternity* of St. *George* for the Maintenance whereof, there were fome Lands here and fome Houfes and a Garden at *Harwick*; it is fuppofed that the *George Inn* over againft the *Church* did firft take its Name from it, or either was it, or at leaft belonging to it: But what heretofore was appropriated to the Maintenance of it, was (among feveral other things) difpofed of by Sale by Queen *Elizabeth* (by her Deed at *Gorfham-Bury* dat. Mar. 8. *Regni fui* 14.) to *Richard Hill,* and others ᵍ.

This

Coat, his Shoes, and his Tapers. The Tapers did help to burn him, the Shoes they had again, and the Coat one Sir *Thomas Rofe* did burn, but they had neither Penny, Gold, Grote nor Jewel.

Notwithftanding three of them were afterwards indited of Felony, and hanged in Chains within half a Year after or thereabouts: *Robert King* was hanged in *Dedham* at *Burchet*: *Robert Debnam* was hanged at *Cartaway Caufey*: *Nicholas Marfh* was hanged at *Dovercourt*. Which three Perfons through the Spirit of God at their Death, did more edify the People in godly Learning, than all the

2

Sermons that had been preach'd there a long time before.

The fourth Man of this Company, named *Robert Gardener*, efcaped their Hands and fled. Albeit he was cruelly fought for to have had the like Death. *Fox Acts and Mon.* 940.

The three Perfons which fuffered were offered their Lives to have accufed the aforefaid *Thomas Rofe* (Minifter of *Hadley*) as of Counfel with them, which they refus'd to do, and therefore fuffered. The faid Mr. *Rofe* had the Coat of the faid *Rood* brought unto him afterwards, which he burned. *Fox Acts and Mon.* 1888.

ᵍ In *England* faith Mr. *Madox*

in

This Village hath yearly two *Fairs*; One of them is in *Lent*, even on *Good-Friday* before *Eaſter:* The other

in his *Firma Burgi*, page 23. the Word *Gild* is of *Anglo-Saxon* Birth; and ſignified a *Company, Society, Brotherhood,* and ſometimes the Privileges or Free-cuſtoms belonging to ſuch *Company. Skinner* in his *Etymologicon Angl. Cat. gen.* hath much to the ſame Purpoſe; for he writes that *Guild* is from the *Anglo-Saxon* Word ᴳⁱˡᵈ, *Belg.* ᴳⁱˡᵈᵉ, ᴳᵘⁱᵈᵉ, Teut. ᴳᵘⁱˡᵗᵉ, ᴳᵘⁱᵈᵘⁿᵍ, *Fraternitas, Sodalitium.* And in Biſhop *Kennet's Gloſſary,* under the Word *Geld,* you have Lat. *Gilda,* Engl. *Gild,* a *Fraternity* or *Society.* Some of theſe *Gilds* were *Religious* and others *Civil* or *Secular:* Theſe of the firſt Sort, where founded chiefly for *Devotion* and *Alms-Deeds,* and were commonly call'd *Brotherhoods* and *Fraternities*; and theſe being uſually founded in Superſtition, they were at the time of the *Reformation* of the *Church* of *England* in the Reigns of King *Henry* VIII. and *Edward* VI. aboliſh'd, by Vertue of a *Sta-*

tute made for that Purpoſe, in order to which an *Inquiſition* or *Survey* was taken in every County in *England,* by *Commiſſioners* thereunto appointed; who certified not only the Names of the *Founders,* but alſo the State and yearly Value of them. Theſe *Gilds* could not be erected without the *King's Licence,* thoſe who did were liable to be puniſhed as for a Trefpaſs. Without doubt this our *Gild* was one of the Religious, and therefore was ſuppreſt at the time, and for the Cauſe aforemention'd; but by whom founded, and for what ſpecial Uſe, and whether it confiſted of Men, or Women, or of both Sexes jointly, and how govern'd, I have not as yet ſeen.

Of theſe *Religious Gilds,* or *Fraternities,* Mr. *Madox* in his Book aforemention'd hath given ſome Examples, one of which founded to the Honour of St. *George* the *Martyr,* in the City of *Norwich,* confiſting of an *Alderman, Maſters, Brothers* and *Siſters,*

M 2

other on that *Munday* which follows next after *Holy-Rood*, or *Holy-Crofs-Day*; which falls on the 14ᵗʰ Day of

Sifters, erected in the Reign of King *Richard* II, and confirm'd by King *Henry* V; and the other at St. *Dunftan*'s in the *Eaft London*. I fhall for the better Information of my Readers, tranfcibe from the faid *Firma Burgi*, viz. *page* 24.

'*De Gilda & Fraternitate* Sᵗⁱ
' Georgij Norwici *fundata*.

'*Rex Omnibus ad quos*, &c. *fa-*
'*lutem. Sciatis quod cum, ut acce-*
'*pimus, quædam Fraternitas &*
'*Gilda gloriofiMartiris S*.Georgij
'*in Civitate noftri* Norwici *per*
'*triginta annos elapfos & amplius*
'*continue, bene & honefte gu-*
'*bernatæ fuerint & adhuc exif-*
'*tant: Nos* &c. *Fraternitatem*
'*& Gildam prædictas pro nobis*
'*& hæredibus noftris acceptamus,*
'*ratificamus & confirmamus; ac*
'*conceffimus quod prædicta Fra-*
'*ternitas & Gilda fratrum & fo-*
'*rorum prædictorum, & aliorum*
'*qui de eisdem Fraternitate &*
'*Gilda effe voluerint, fint per-*
'*petuæ, & Communitas perpetua*

'*temporibus fucceffivis in perpe-*
'*tuum; & quod Fraternitas &*
'*Gilda prædictæ habeant nomen*
'*Fraternitatis & Gildæ Sancti*
'*Georgij* Norwici *in perpetuum*
'*——; ac etiam quod præfati*
'*Aldermannus, Magiftri, Fratres*
'*& Sorores Fraternitatis & Gildæ*
'*prædictarum, & Succeffores fui,*
'*fint perfonæ habiles & capaces*
'*ad terras, tenementa, redditus*
'*& fervitia adquirenda, habenda*
'*recipienda, & tenenda, fibi &*
'*Succefforibus fuis, Aldermanno,*
'*Magiftris, Fratribus & Sorori-*
'*bus earundem Fraternitatis &*
'*Gildæ in perpetuum; & quod*
'*ipfi per nomen Aldermanni, Ma-*
'*giftrorum, Fratrum & Sororum*
'*Fraternitatis & Gildæ Sancti*
'*Georgij* Norwici, *in quibuf-*
'*cunque curijs & locis placitare*
'*& implacitari, refpondere &*
'*refponderi, ac lucrari & perdere,*
'*necnon Commune Sigillum, pro*
'*negotijs Fraternitatis & Gildæ*
'*prædictarum deferviendum ha-*
'*bere poffint in perpetuum. Et*
'*ulterius de uberiori gratia no-*
'*ftra conceffimus & licentiam de-*
'*dimus,*

of *September:* Neither of them are of any great Concernment; being chiefly frequented by the Country Neighbours,

' *dimus, pro nobis & hæredibus*
' *noſtris, quantum in nobis eſt,*
' *præfatis Aldermanno, Magiſtris*
' *Fratribus & Sororibus, quod ipſi*
' *& eorum Succeſſores, terras, te-*
' *nementa, redditus & ſervitia in-*
' *fra Civitatem prædictam, uſque*
' *ad valorem decem librarum per*
' *annum quæ de nobis tenentur in*
' *burgagio, adquirere poſſint &*
' *tenere ſibi & Succeſſoribus ſuis,*
' *tam pro ſuſtentatione unius Ca-*
' *pellani divina ſingulis diebus in*
' *Eccleſia prædicta pro ſalubri*
' *ſtatu noſtro celebraturi, quam*
' *pro ſuſtentatione Fraternitatis &*
' *Gildæ prædictarum, ac aliorum*
' *operum & pietatis onerum ——,*
' *Statuto de terris & tenementis*
' *ad manum mortuam non ponen-*
' *dis edito aut aliquo alio Statuto*
' *ſive Ordinatione incontrarium*
' *facta, ſeu eo quo terræ & tene-*
' *menta prædicta de nobis in bur-*
' *gagio tenentur non obſtantibus.*
' *Ac inſuper ad amovendum ma-*
' *nutenenciam, confœderationem*
' *& conſpirationem ——. In cujus*
' &c. *Teſte Rege apud Redyng* ix.
' *die Maij.* Pat. 5. Hen. 5. M. 8.

In Engliſh *as follows.*

Of the Gild and Fraternity of St. *George* founded at *Norwich.*

To all Perſons whom, *&c.* the King ſendeth Greeting. Know that ſince, as we have been informed, a certain Fraternity and Gild of the glorious Martyr St. *George* in our City of *Norwich* for thirty Years paſt and more, have been well and honeſtly govern'd and do ſtill exiſt. We *&c.* for us and our Heirs do accept, ratify, and confirm the foreſaid Fraternity and Gild, and have granted that the foreſaid Fraternity and Gild of Brothers and Siſters aforeſaid, and others, who ſhall be willing to be of the ſaid Fraternity and Gild, be perpetual, and a perpetual Community in ſucceeding times for ever; and that the Fraternity and Gild aforeſaid be call'd the Fraternity and Gild of St. *George* of *Norwich* for ever ——; and alſo that the foreſaid Alderman,

Neighbours, to eat a Mefs of *Frumenty*, fpend a Groat on *Cakes* and *Ale*, or a Penny with the *Pedler*.

In

Alderman, Mafters, Brothers and Sifters of the Fraternity and Gild aforefaid, and their Succeffors be Perfons able and capable of acquiring, having, receiving, and holding Lands, Tenements, Rents, Services, to themfelves and their Succeffors, the Alderman, Mafters, Brothers and Sifters of the fame Fraternity and Gild for ever; and that they by the Name of Alderman, Mafters, Brothers and Sifters of the Fraternity and Gild of St. *George* of *Norwich*, may in any Courts or Places plead and be impleaded, anfwer and be anfwered; and gain and lofe, and alfo have a common Seal to ferve for the Affairs of the faid Fraternity and Gild for ever. And farther of our good Grace we have granted and given Liberty for us and our Heirs, as much as in us lies, to the aforefaid Alderman, Mafters, Brothers and Sifters, that they and their Succeffors may acquire and hold for themfelves and Succeffors, Lands, Tenements, Rents, and Services with-

in the forefaid City to the Value of ten Pounds *per Annum*, which are held from us in Burgage as well for the Support of one Chaplain, who fhall officiate in holy things every Day in the Church aforefaid for our healthful State, as alfo for the fupporting the Fraternity and Gild aforefaid, and other Works and Offices of Piety —— Notwithftanding the Statute of *Mortmain*, or any other Statute or Order to the contrary, or that by which the Lands and Tenements aforefaid are held of us in Burgage. And moreover to remove Maintenance, Confederacy and Confpiracy. —— In whereof &c. Witnefs the King at *Redyng* ix. Day of *May*.

The other relating to St. *Dunftan's* in the *Eaft* you have in the fame Book, *page* 25. being taken out of the *Survey* and *Certificate* made by the *Commiffioners* for the City of *London* and *County* of *Middlefex*, remaining in the *Treafury of the late Court of Augmentations*. ' The

In this *Parish* grows a ftrong, knurly, and knotted and crooked fort of *Elms*, famous for their feveral

' The paroche of St *Dunftons*
   ' in *theaft*.

' The Fraternitie of our *Lady*
' founded of Devofyon within
' the fame Churche, That is
' to faye, *John Joye* by his will
' gave to the perfonne of the
' faide Churche and to the Ma-
' fter and Wardens of the faide
' Brotherhed, and to the War-
' dens of the faide Churche and
' their Succeffours, one tene-
' ment in Cofen lane in the pa-
' roche of *Allhallowes the much*
' in *London*, uppon condycyon
' that they fhuld repayre the
' fame tenement, and the Refy-
' deu of the profutes above re-
' parations fhuld be towardes the
' fyndinge of a *Chapleyne* to pray
' for the Soules of the brothren
' and Syftern of the faide Fra-
' ternytie, xx^s. Which was be-
' ftowed upon the Churche and
' reparacion of the tenement.

The Gild at *Dovercourt* was kept where the *George* Inn is now; there was about 28 *l. per*

Annum in Land and Houfes belonging to it, which ever fince the Diffolution thereof hath been apply'd in repairing and beautifying the *Church*. Ex *MSS. R. W. C.*

This *Parish* is one of thofe many which are intituled to the *Charitable Benevolence* of *Henry Smith*, Efq; who fettled all his Eftate both real and perfonal upon divers *Feoffees* for *charitable Ufes*, of which the quota fettled upon this Parifh, was fix Pounds fix Shillings and eight Pence *per Annum*, charged upon the Manor of *Strougton in Leicefterfhire*; but by the fall of Rents or other incidents they now receive but four Pounds fix Shillings and eight Pence, which is yearly difpos'd of by the *Church-Wardens* and *Overfeers* of the Poor in Clothing, *&c.* to the Poor: This feems to have been procured for this *Parish* by Sir *George Whitmore*, Knight, Lord of this Manor, who was one of thofe Gentlemen whom the faid Mr. *Smith* put in Truft with

ral ufes in Husbandry, which with ufing wear like Iron; it is faid (becaufe in vain often attempted) they will not grow out of this Place. Old *Tuffer* in the 9ᵗʰ Figure

with his whole Eftate; and tho' he put in and left out divers others, yet Sir *George* remain'd a conftant Feoffee.

Having an original Letter of the faid Sir *George Whitmore's* communicated to me by the Reverend Mr. *Robert Arch*, Rector of *Wrabnefs* not far diftant, which becaufe it relates to this *Charity*, I fhall here infert fo much thereof as concerns it.

'Freind *Richard Edwards* I re-
'feived yᵒʳ Letter by *Ireland*,
'&c. —— I allfoe refeived the
'Bond, &c. about *Smith's* lega-
'fie and the geivfte geiven is
'20ᵗⁱ Nobles A yeare to *Ram-*
'*fey*, & 20ᵗⁱ Nobles a Yeare unto
'the parrifh of *Dovercourt*,
'wheareof *Hardwitch* is a Mem-
'ber. So that yf you have not
'paid them fomutch I pray
'pay itt, for I refceived fo much
'for them as dewe at *Michell-*
'*mas*, and the 25ᵗʰ prefent ½ a

'22. March 1640.

2

'yeare more will be dewe to
'them, wᶜʰ will not bee paid
'eere *May*; but fo foon as I
'have itt will write to you to
'pay itt. I pay xiiᵈ. a peece
'acquittance monie wᶜʰ is to
'bee defallked: for 4 acquit-
'tances 4 fhillings, 2 s. a yeare
'a peece, and let them fend me
'theare acquittances for the
'next half yeare, and leave the
'date of the acquittances or
'bonds for me or *Robin Hurlock*
'to put in; theafe bonds fente
'are fallfe, for 3: 6: 8 is to
'bee paid to *Ramfey* halfe yearly,
'and 3: 6: 8 haulfe yearly to
'*Dovercourt* and *Hardwitch*, and
'the bonds are made butt for
'fo mutch yearly to bee bee-
'ftowed, let them bee paid
'and new bonds fent for 20ᵗⁱ
'Nobles a peece refeived by
'*Ramfey* and *Dovercourt cum*
'*Hardwitch* —— not ellfe but
'God keepe you and

Yᵒʳ loving freind *Geo. Whitmore.*

Here

Tab. VII. *Pag. 89.*

Mr. Smiths Monument

R. Sheppard Sculp.

9th Figure of his *husbandly Furniture* recommends them to his *Husbandman* for this Ufe in efpecial, *viz.* *A*

Here it may not be improper to give fome Account of the forefaid *Henry Smyth*, Efq; who lies interred in *Wandfworth* Church; at the upper End of the middle Ifle on a Brafs Plate inlaid in the Grave-ftone, is the following *Latin* Infcription;

Depofitum Henr: Smyth
Senatoris Londinenfis

Mole fub hac quæris, Quis conditur, Optime lector?
Cuias? Et Qualis? Quantus in orbe fuit?
A dextris muri ftatuam tu cernere poffis
Oranti fimilem marmore de pario,
Subter quam ftatuam cernatur tabula Sculpta
Auratis verbis quæ tibi cuncta notant.

And on the right Hand Side of the Communion Table under a large handfome Monument, is the following Epitaph;

Here Lyeth the Body of Henry Smyth Esqur. Sometime Citizen and Alderman of London, who Departed this Life the 3D Day of January Aº. Dñĩ. 1627. Being then neere the Age of 79 Yeeres who while He lived Gave unto the Several Towns in Surry Following one Thousand pounds a piece to buy lands for Perpetuity for yᵉ Releife and Setting the Poor People a Worke in the said Towns Viz̃. to the Towne of Croydon one Thousand Pounds; to the Towne of Kingston one Thousand Pounds; to the Towne of Guilford one Thousand Pounds. to the Towne of Darkin one Thousand Pounds. to the Towne of Farnham one Thousand Pounds; and by his last will and Testament Did Further give and Devise to Buy lands for Perpetuity for the Releife and Setting their poor a Work; unto the Towne of Rygate one Thousand Pounds; unto the Towne of Richmond one Especyaltye, or Debt of a Thousand Pounds and unto this Towne of Wandsworth wherein He was Borne, the Sum of Five Hundred pounds for the same Uses as before, and Did further will And Bequeath one Thousand to Buy Lands for Perpetuity to Redeeme Poor Captives and Prisoners from yᵉ Turkish Tyranie. And not Here stinting His Charity And bounty Did also give and Bequeath the Most part of His Estate Being to a Great Value For the Purchaseing Lands of Inheritance for ever For the releife of the Poor and Setting them a Woke a Patterne worthy the Imitation of those whom God hath Blessed with the Abundance of the Goods of this Life to Follow him Herein.

N   Befides

Besides the *Charities* mention'd in the *Epitaph* or *Monumental Inscription* for the said Mr. *Smyth*, there are divers others which I shall excerpt from Mr. *Aubrey's Natural History and Antiquities of Surrey*, viz.

Vol. I.	*per Annum*
P. 88. *Mortlock* - - -	3 : 0 : 0
144. *Wandsworth* for Clothing the Poor, of one Colour, with a Badge	4 : 0 : 0
158. *Clapham* An°. 1642. out of his Estate in *Sevenoke* in *Kent*	2 : 0 : 0
241. *Thames Ditton*	4 : 0 : 0
249. *Long Ditton* - -	2 : 16 : 0

Vol. II.

279 *Great Bookeham*	10 : 0 : 0

Vol. III.

20. *Limpsfeild* - -	2 : 0 : 0
56. *Lingfeild* out of the Mannor of *Worth* in *Sussex*	10 : 0 : 0
120. *Esher* certain Land	5 : 0 : 0
134. *Cobham* - - -	12 : 0 : 0
220. *Woking* - - -	10 : 0 : 0
Cramley - - -	8 : 0 : 0
Capol - - - -	4 : 0 : 0
Bramley - - -	6 : 0 : 0
Albury - - -	6 : 0 : 0
Awfold - - -	5 : 0 : 0
Shalford - - -	6 : 0 : 0
Dunsfold - - -	6 : 0 : 0
Hascomb - - -	3 : 0 : 0
Ognersh - - -	8 : 0 : 0
Stoke near *Guildford*	12 : 0 : 0
Meroe - - -	3 : 0 : 0
Send and *Ripley*	8 : 0 : 0
Malden - - -	1 : 10 : 0

Note; The Charity to all these 38 last Parishes do arise out of the Manor of *Warberton* in *Sussex*,

Vol. III.	*per Annum*
East Clandon -	3 : 0 : 0
East Horseley - -	2 : 0 : 0
West Horseley -	2 : 0 : 0
Purbright - -	1 : 0 : 0
Ashlie - - -	6 : 0 : 0
Occham - - -	2 : 0 : 0
Wistley - - -	1 : 0 : 0
Windlesham - -	8 : 0 : 0
Horshill - - -	2 : 0 : 0
Frimley - - -	2 : 0 : 0
Pepper Harrow -	1 : 0 : 0
Compton - - -	2 : 0 : 0
Puttenham - -	2 : 0 : 0
Hambledon - -	1 : 10 : 0
Witley - - -	4 : 0 : 0
Thursley - - -	4 : 0 : 0
Chiddingfold - -	5 : 0 : 0
Elsted - - -	2 : 0 : 0
Seale - - - -	3 : 0 : 0
Frencham - -	6 : 0 : 0
Harly - - -	1 : 0 : 0
Haselmore - -	3 : 0 : 0
Warplesdon - -	4 : 0 : 0

Vol. IV.

P. 15. *Godalming* - -	55 : 0 : 0
50 *l.* Of which from Lands in *Shalford*, and 5 from Cherry Gardens in *Kent*	
186. *Okeley* - - -	6 : 0 : 0
278. *Becksworth* - -	10 : 0 : 0

Vol. V.

P. 66. St. *Olaves* - -	30 : 0 : 0
138. *Newington* - -	10 : 0 : 0
184. St. *Saviours* - -	28 : 0 : 0

Mr. *Cambden*

Mr. *Cambden* faith that there are one hundred and forty Churches in the County of *Surry*, of which but about feventeen only are in Mr. *Aubrey's Natural Hiſtory*, &c. of that County faid to have any Remembrance publickly kept in their Churches of this Gentleman's Charity: And if *Micham* is the only Pariſh exempted from partaking thereof (as is faid in *Ockley* or *Okeley*,) then all the reſt muſt either be guilty of great Negligence or willful Ingratitude, to their Benefactor, in not publickly owning his Benevolence.

What was the Original of this Mr. *Henry Smyth* as to his Parentage I do not find, and though he was born according to his Epitaph in the Pariſh of *Wandſworth* in the County of *Surrey*, yet it feems he was not entered in their Pariſh Regiſter, becaufe his true Age could not be known. That his Parents were but mean, and his Condition low in his younger Years, I gather from his being whipped as a Vagrant by the Inhabitants of *Micham* a neighbouring Pariſh to that of his Birth, which Ufage he fo far refented, as to omit them from participating of

his Charity; which did diffufe to every other Pariſh in that County. To what Bufinefs or Occupation he firſt applied himſelf doth not appear; but becaufe he had an Habitation in *Silver-Street London*, among the working *Silver-Smiths*, he hath been thought by fome to have been of that Trade: by an Infcription in *Great Bookeham* Church in *Surrey*, he is call'd *Citizen* and *Salter* of *London*; and his Epitaph faith that he was *Alderman* thereof, but doth not fay of what *Ward:* Nor do I find that he ever ferved for *Sheriff* of that *City*. He amaſſed together a great Eſtate, fome particulars of which you have in his Epitaph, and fuch others which have come to my Knowledge ſhall be under inferted; notwithſtanding which, he feems to have been extremely Covetous, as appears from a Note in the faid Mr. *Aubrey's Hiſtory*, Vol. IV. page 186. *viz.* He had the nick Name of *Dog-Smith*, becaufe he kept no Houfe, but dined at Friends Houfes; and then defir'd a Bit for his Dog, which was to refect himſelf. He died as mention'd in his *Epitaph* on *January* 3d 1627. but on the

Tablet in *GreatBookcham*Church it is faid to be the 6ᵗʰ of that Month.

His Arms are made to be,

Sable on a Fefs Argᵗ. a Fleur de lis of the firft between three Saltiers of the 2ᵈ. Aubrey's Hift. Vol. II. page 279.

The Lands, &c. given by *Henry Smyth*, Efq; to charitable Ufes with the annual Values of fo many as have come to our Knowledge.

per Annum

The Manor of *Longftock Harrington* in the County of *Southampton* ——— ——— ——— ——— 159 : 00 : 00
The Manor of *Stroughton* in the County of *Leicefter* 200 : 00 : 00
The Manor of *Longney* in the County of *Gloucefter* 214 : 13 : 04
The Quit-rents of the fame ——— ——— ——— 056 : 00 : 00
The Manor of *Warberton* in the County of *Suffex* 160 : 00 : 00
The Farm in *Tollefhunt Darcy* in the County of *Effex* 140 : 00 : 00
Dudfey Meadows in *Deptford, Kent,* and *Surry* 040 : 00 : 00
Mefluage and Lands in *Shaldon* in the County of *Southampton* ——— ——— ——— 024 : 00 : 00
One Mefluage in St. *John*'s Parifh in the City of *Worcefter* ——— ——— ——— ——— 004 : 00 : 00
Manor of *Froddefwell* in the County of *Stafford*
Manor of *Worth* in *Suffex*
Lands in *Shalford* in Ditto
Mefluage in *Hartlepool* in *Durham*
Lands in *Sevenoke* in *Kent*
Cherry Gardens in the fame County
Land in *Efher* in *Surry*
Houfe in *Silver-Street, London*
Manors of *Southweck* and *Iwood* in *Suffex*

On a Table in *Ewell* Church.

CHARITY.

Virtus Invidiam fuperat.

The Church-Wardens and Overfeers of the Poor of every Parifh, are to difpofe of the Money they receive according to thefe Directions hereafter mention'd, which are fet down in Mr. Smyth's *Deed of charitable Ufes, an Abftract whereof is as followeth.*

To all Chriftian People to whom this prefent Writing fhall come, HENRY SMYTH of *London,* Efq; fendeth Greeting in our Lord God everlafting, &c.

Item, For the avoiding of Corruption in the Collection, Receiving, Diftribution, and Payment of the feveral Sums of Money heretofore given, limited, appointed, or affign'd, or hereafter to be given, limited, appointed or affigned, during his Life-time, or to be purchafed or conveyed by the faid Earl of *Effex,* Sir *Chriftopher Nevill,* Sir *Richard Lumley,* Sir *George Crook, George Whitmore, George Lowe, William Blake, William Rolfe, Richard Gurnard,* and *Henry Jackfon,* Executors, and Feoffees of the faid HENRY SMYTH; or the Survivors or Survivor of them, and to be yearly paid out of the Rents, Iffues, or Profits of the faid Manors, Meffuages, Lands, Tenements, and Hereditaments, hereafter to be purchafed according to the true Intent and Meaning of thefe Prefents, for the yearly Relief of the Poor of any Parifh, for the Marriage of poor Maids, or putting forth of poor Children to be Apprentices, fhall be yearly received as the faid Rents fhall grow due and payable, by the Church-Wardens and Overfeers of the Poor of each of the faid Parifhes, refpectively to receive the Rents of fo much Lands as is or fhall be given, limited, affigned or appointed to be employed as aforefaid, within the Parifh wherein they fhall be Church-Wardens and Overfeers as aforefaid.

Item,

Item, The faid Henry Smyth, for the better Security of the Performance of the faid charitable Gift, doth hereby limit, appoint, and declare his Intent and Meaning to be, That the Church-Wardens and Overfeers of the Poor of each of the faid Parifhes, for Relief of whofe Poor fuch Gift, Affignment, Limitation, or Appointment fhall be made as aforefaid, immediately after they fhall enter into the faid Office, and before they fhall meddle with the Receipt of the faid Rent, or any part thereof, fhall become bound in double the Value of fuch yearly Receipt, to the Parfon or Vicar of the faid Parifh, to collect and receive the faid Rent, and to imploy and beftow the fame according to the true Intent and Meaning of thefe Prefents; which faid Parfon or Vicar to whom fuch Security fhall be fo given, fhall, before the faid Church-Wardens or Overfeers of the Poor of the faid Parifh fhall intermeddle with the Receipt of the faid Rents, or any of them, certify the faid Obligation uncancelled to the Governors of *Chrift's-Hofpital* in

London. And in Default of fuch Security to be given, or Certificate made of the faid Obligation, that Parifh wherein fuch Default fhall be made, to lofe the Benefit of the faid Gift, Limitation, or Affignment fo made or to be made for that Year wherein fuch Default fhall be made as aforefaid.

Item, For the better Direction of the Church-Wardens and Overfeers of the faid feveral Parifhes in the Diftribution of fuch Sums of Money as are, or fhall be limited, given, affigned, or appointed to the faid Charitable Ufes aforementioned, the faid Henry Smyth doth hereby limit and declare, and doth think fit and appoint, that the faid Church-Wardens and Overfeers of the Poor of the faid feveral Parifhes refpectively, fhall give and diftribute the faid Money given, limited, affigned, or appointed to the faid Charitable Ufes, to, and for the Relief of aged, poor, or infirm People, married Perfons having more Children born in lawful Wedlock than their Labours can maintain, poor Orphans, fuch poor People as keep themfelves and Families to Work,

and

2

and put forth their Children to be Apprentices at the Age of fifteen Years, wherein each of the faid Church-Wardens and Overfeers of each of the faid Parifhes, are to obferve fuch Courfes in the difpofing of the faid Rents, as that a Stock may be provided, and always in Readinefs to fet fuch of the faid Perfons to work as are able to Labour and take Pains; and not to, or for the Relief of any Perfons who are given to exceffive Drinking, Whore-mongers, common Swearers, Pilferers, or otherwife notorioufly Scandalous, or to any Perfons that have been incorrigible, or difobedient to thofe whofe Servants they have been, or to any vagrant Perfons, or fuch as have no conftant Dwelling, or receive any Inmate or Inmates to dwell in the Houfe with them, or have not inhabited in that Parifh by the Space of five Years next before fuch Diftribution to be made, or, being able, refufe to work, labour, and take Pains.

Item, The faid H E N R Y S M Y T H, to the Intent and Purpofe aforefaid, doth farther limit, affign, appoint, and declare his Intent and Meaning to be, that for the better Ordering and Government of the Poor of the faid feveral Parifhes, and difpofing of the Sums of Money given to the Ufes aforefaid, the faid Church-Wardens of each of the faid Parifhes fhall, during the time they continue in the faid Office and Place, once in every Month at the leaft, on the Sabbath-Day after Evening Prayer, meet in the Church of the faid Parifh, to confider of the Eftate of the Poor thereof; and which of them have moft need of Relief. And alfo between the Feafts of *Eafter* and *Whitfuntide,* next after the End of every Year, wherein the faid Church-Wardens and Overfeers of the Poor of that Parifh, or any of them, fhall have continued in the faid Office and Place, openly and publickly in the Church of the faid Parifh after Evening Prayer, upon fome Sabbath-Day, upon Notice and Warning thereof given openly in that Parifh Church immediately after the End of Morning Prayer, make a true and perfect Account in a Book, to be fairly written and kept for that Purpofe, of all their Receipts and Difburfments for and during
the

the Year then next before, of all such Sums of Money as they, or any of them, shall receive of the said Money given to the Uses aforesaid; which said Account shall be openly read and publifhed in the Church of the faid Parish, on the Sabbath-Day next after the faid Account, immediately after the End of Morning Prayer there. And a Copy thereof fairly written and tranfcribed under the Hands of the faid Church-Wardens and Overfeers that did make the faid Account, fhall caufe to be affixed in a Table, to the Wall of the faid Church, there to remain by the Space of fourteen Days, to the Intent the fame may be publickly feen, read, and perufed, and Exceptions taken thereunto, if there be juft Caufe; and the fame Exceptions reformed and amended. And farther, that the faid Church-Wardens and Overfeers of the Poor, that fhall have fo paffed the faid Account, fhall within ten Days then next following after the End of the faid fourteen Days, fend or deliver, or caufe to be fent or delivered, under the Hands of the Parfon or Vicar of the faid Parish, and

2

of the faid Church-Wardens and Overfeers as fhall pafs the faid Account, and fuch others that fhall be prefent thereat, to the Governors of the faid *Hofpital* for the time being; and if the faid Church-Wardens and Overfeers of the Poor of any of the faid Parifhes, fhall fail in the Performance of any of the Premiffes, that then as a Penalty, Mulct, or Punifhment for fuch Neglect, the Poor of that Parifh fhall not have of the Gift of the faid HENRY SMYTH for one Year next enfuing after fuch Neglect; but the Benefit thereof to go for that time to the Poor of the faid *Hofpital.*

Item, The faid HENRY SMYTH doth farther, by thefe Prefents, limit, appoint and declare his Intent and Meaning to be, that the faid Sums of Money given, limited, affign'd, or appointed, to or for the Relief of the impotent and aged Poor of the faid Parifhes refpectively, fhall be diftributed, beftowed, and employed in Apparel of one Colour with fome Badge or other Mark, that the fame may be known to be the Gift of the faid HENRY SMYTH, or elfe in Bread, and Flefh or Fifh, upon each

each Sabbath-Day, publickly in the Parish-Churches of each of the said Parishes.

In witness whereof the said HENRY SMITH hath hereunto set his Hand and Seal, the six and twentieth Day of *January*, in the second Year of the Reign of our Sovereign Lord King *Charles*, by the Grace of God, King of *England, Scotland, France* and *Ireland*, Defender of the Faith, *&c.*

Aubrey's *Survey*, Vol. V. *p.* 364. HENRY SMITH.

The said *Henry Smith*, Esq; by his Indenture dat. 23. of *Oct. Anno* 17. *Jac.* I. did enfeoff *Robert* Earl of *Essex*, *Richard* Earl of *Dorset*, Sir *Edward Francis*, Knight, *John Middleton*, *William Wingfeild*, *George Whitmore, Richard Amherst*, Esq^{rs}; in all those his Manors of *Warbleton, Southweeke* and *Iwood* in the County of *Sussex*, and of his Dwelling-house in *Silver-Street*, *London*, to be applied to divers charitable Uses therein mention'd, with a Reservation of 500 *l. per Annum* for his own Subsistence, and likewise a Power of Revocation.

Also by another Indenture dated the same Day, he did give and grant unto the aforesaid *John Middleton, William Wingfeild, George Whitmore* and *Richard Amherst*, Esq^{rs}; all his personal Estate whatsoever, and all his *Houshold Goods* for the Uses aforesaid, (except 100 *l.*) and with the like Power of Revocation.

And by another Indenture dat. 20. *June A*°. 22. *Jac.* I. did confirm all his real Estate unto the aforesaid Earl of *Essex*, Sir *Edward Francis*, Knight ; *George Whitmore, Richard Amherst, John Middleton* and *William Wingfeild*, Esq^{rs}; without any Power of Revocation.

And on the same Day did revoke unto the said *George Whitmore, Richard Amherst, John Middleton* and *William Wingfeild*, Esq^{rs}; his Power of revoking his Settlement of his personal Estate.

And on the same Day he did by Indenture settle his whole Estate both real and personal upon the aforesaid Earl of *Essex*, Sir *Christopher Nevil*, Knight of

O

A Dovercourt *Beetle with Wedges of Steel,* &c [h].

of the *Bath*, Sir *Richard Lum-ley*, Sir *George Crooke*, Sir *Edward Francis*, Knights; *George Whitmore*, *Richard Amherst*, *John Middleton*, *William Wingfeild*, *George Lowe*, *William Blake*, *William Rolph* and *Richard Gurnet*, Efq[rs]; to the Ufes at firft declared.

And afterwards the aforefaid *Henry Smith*, notwithftanding his former Grants, obtained a *Decree* in *Chancery* dat. 20. *June* 2° *Car.* I. *A°. D.* 1626. to exclude *Richard Amherft* and *John Middleton*, Efq[rs]; the Truft he had repofed in them, and to affign their Intereft to *Robert* Earl of *Effex*, Sir *Chriftopher Nevill*, Sir *Richard Lumley*, Sir *George Crooke*, Knights; *George Whitmore*, *George Lowe*, *William Blake*, *William Rolfe*, *Richard Gurnet*, *Henry Henn*, Efq[rs]; and *Henry Jackfon*, Gent. And that notwithftanding his former Grants and Conveyances, he had Power and Liberty given

him during his Life, to receive the Rents, Iffues, and Profits of his whole Eftate; and to difpofe of the fame as he fhould think fit: And that after his Deceafe, the faid *Feoffees* or any feven of them fhould difpofe of the Eftate, not by him difpofed of in his Life-time, to and for divers charitable Ufes in the *Decree* mention'd; and to and for fuch other *charitable Ufes* as the faid *Henry Smith*, by his laft *Will* and *Teftament* in Writing, or any other Writing to be executed by him in the Prefence of three Witneffes, fhould nominate, declare, limit or appoint, or in default thereof to fuch charitable Ufes as the faid Feoffees, or any other feven of them fhould appoint.

[h] Naves made of this *Dovercourt* Elm, are much defir'd by *Wheelwrights* and others, as being very durable, and not fubject to fplit.

CHAP.

Tab. VIII. Page 146.

A. Land-guard Fort. B. The Andrews or Bar of Sand rising from the Fort. C. The South or Dover-Court Point of the Haven mouth. D D. The Strata of Sand, Gravel, Fossil-Shells, and their Fragments. E. The Stratum of Bluewish Clay above Feet deep. F. The heap of Gravel, Sand, & Shells, &c. which carrying down from the Top lye in the bottom of the Cliff. G. Cliff-Stones. H. Gushing Waters or Springs. I. A Scone or Stone of the Lime or Sorry Nodum. which lye upon the Shore before the Cliff.

R. Sheppard Sculp.

C H A P. II.

THE *natural* Accidents and *Productions* of a Place being fo near of kin to the *Topography* thereof, we will fubjoin by placing them next, and give an Account of thofe that are moft confiderable and remarkable: And begin with the *Beacon-hill*, which in the Memory of very many now living, hath very much decayed and ftill continues wafting, by the large Falls of the *Cliff*; which hath given occafion for feveral Removes of the *Beacon*, occafion'd either by the Springs within the Hill, or by the Sea its undermining of it from without; the firft of which doth fo foften the Subftance of it (being compofed of a mixt Clay and Gravel) that it renders it fubject and liable to that grand Injury and Lofs[i]. However, what remains of

---

[i] This I was an Eye-witnefs to in the *Summer* of 1698. when having with two *Gentlemen* been viewing the faid *Cliff*, we were but a little removed from the Place where we were, but a great quantity of Earth fell down: And within the Compafs of about forty Years, fince I firft viewed this *Cliff*, there have fome Acres of land fallen down; whereby not only the height, but likewife the Face of the *Cliff* is leffened, and much alter'd; fo that now it is rare to meet with any whole *Foffil-Shells* formerly fo frequent there: And the *Clayie Stratum* is nothing near fo deep as it was; nay, in fome Places not much feen.

this

this Hill is very much noted for the pleasant Prospect
it affords to Seawards; for, from thence we are often
delighted with the Sight of great Numbers of *Ships*,
and other Vessels sailing by us.   And in *July* 1666.
when the *Dutch* (then at Enmity with *England*) believing they had interpos'd between the main Body of his
Majesty's *Navy* at the *Buoy of the Nour*, and above
twenty Men of War (part of it) which were refitted in
this *Port*, after the memorable four Days Fight in the
Beginning of the Month before, and had spread about
one hundred of their Men of *War* in the *Seldway*,
and lower Part of the *Gun-Fleet* to hinder (as they
thought) the Conjunction of them, found themselves
under a great Mistake, when contrary to their Expectation, they saw *July* 22. 1666. about one hundred
Men of War of his *Majesty*'s, come down upon them
causing them in haste to weigh their Anchors, and (being pursued) stand for their own Coasts: This *Hill* then
giving us so plain a Prospect of two such potent *Fleets*
(and what is more *uno intuitu*) that the *Flags* of both
were easily discern'd without Glasses.

Between the *Beacon* and the *Town*, from the Side of
the *Cliff*, issues a *Spring* of excellent clear and delightful Water, very well approv'd of, by those who have
Judgment to distinguish Waters, and much us'd in
Drinks [k].   The

[k] This *Spring* mention'd by   derable thing above the level of
our Author is a small inconsi-   the *Sea,* and not subject to be
                                               overflown

The Wafhing of thefe *Cliffs* difcovers a blueifh *Clay*, which tumbling down upon the *Shore*, although wafhed by the Sea at High-water, within a fhort time turns into *Stone:* There they may be feen, fome that are new fallen as foft as the *Clay* in the *Cliff*, others that have lain there longer, crufted over and hard, but if opened or broke, the *Clay* ftill foft in the middle; others that have lain longer *petrified* to the Heart [1], and

overflown thereby; the Water is very pleafant to drink: I could not obferve that it did either *petrify* or *incruftate* either Pieces of Wood or Sticks. Nor doth Mr. *Taylor* attribute any fuch Property to this Spring. The R. R. Editor of *Cambden*'s *Britannia* in his firft Edition 359. takes Notice of this *Spring* on the Side of the *Cliff* between the *Beacon* and the Town, as being excellent clear Water.

[1] The *Anonymous Author* of the *Tour through Great Britain,* Vol. I. Let. I. *p.* 49. 'Speaking of ' *Harwich* faith, that they boaft ' that their *Town* is wall'd, and ' their Streets pav'd with *Clay*, ' and yet that one is as ftrong ' and the other as clean as thofe ' that are built and pav'd with ' Stone: The Fact is indeed ' true, for there is a Sort of ' *Clay* in the *Cliff* between the ' *Town* and the *Beacon-hill* (it is ' the very *Beacon-hill)* adjoining, ' which when it falls into the ' Sea, where it is beaten with ' the Waves and Weather turns ' gradually into Stone: But the ' chief Reafon affign'd is from ' the Water of a certain Spring ' or Well, which rifing in the ' faid Cliff runs down into the ' Sea, among thofe Pieces of ' Clay, and petrifies them as it ' runs; and the Force of the ' Sea often ftirring, and perhaps, ' turning thefe Lumps of Clay, ' when the Storms of Wind ' may give Force enough to ' the Water, caufes them to ' harden every where alike; o-therwife

and with thefe the *Walls* of the *Town* were for the moft part built, and the Streets generally are pitched; they

‘ therwife thofe which were not ‘ quite funk in the Water of ‘ the Spring, would be petrified ‘ but in part. Thefe Stones are ‘ gathered up to pave the Streets, ‘ and build the Houfes, and are ‘ indeed very hard: 'Tis alfo ‘ remarkable, that fome of them ‘ taken up before they are tho- ‘ roughly petrified, will upon ‘ breaking them appear to be ‘ hard as a Stone without, and ‘ foft as Clay in the middle; ‘ whereas, others that have lain ‘ a due time, fhall be thorough ‘ Stone to the Center, and as ‘ exceeding hard within as with- ‘ out. This Account feems chiefly to be copied from Mr. *Taylor*'s MS. But how far the Account there given by him is matter of Fact I will not determine; for though I have vifited the Place often, yet my Stay at *Harwich* hath always been much too fhort to make Obfervations fo criti- cal, as this *Phænomenon* doth re- quire, and deferve; nor could I ever yet fee any of the Clay that

I could fay, did fo much as be- gin to incruftate; and this pre- fent Year 1728, I obferved, that fome of the Clay of the *Cliff* which had lain fo long on the Shore, as to be fome Yards diftant from the *Cliff*, and there- fore to have long lain on the Shore, and by the frequent Tides fo imbedded with Sands as to look like a Pavement, yet cutting them with my Knife they proved to be nothing but a ftrong, ftiff and tenacious *Clay*: And on the other hand attempt- ing to break fome of the Stones upon the *Strode*, I found them too hard for me to penetrate, or make any Impreffion upon; and if I broke any part of them off, it was *Stone* to the very Center. What fhould any way incline me to Mr. *Taylor*'s Opinion, is the Probity of the Man; and his having lived long upon the Spot, one would think him not fo lia- ble to be prejudiced by an Opi- nion. There are fome things in- deed, which may induce one to favour his Affertion; as *firft*, Di-

I   vers

they by ancient Cuftom belonging to the Town as their Right^m. The

vers of the *Stones* have Cracks and Chops in them, as Clay and Earth will have by being expos'd to the Sun. *Secondly,* That *Anno* 1702, I found lying upon that Shore, a *Stone,* in which was imbedded a large *Pile,* fuch as was formerly made ufe of there to preferve the Cliff from the Injuries of the *Sea;* which to me feems to owe its Situation to no other Original, than by being preft into the Superficies of the Clay while foft, and petrifying with it, which being fquare, takes off an Objection, which fome might make had it been round, of its being lodged there in the general *Deluge.*

^m The *Production* of thefe Stones, *I referred to a Vitrioline juice in conjunction with the Loam, becaufe the common Copperas Stones are plentifully found on that Shore* (Harwich), *but whereas they lie thick where the Cliff is gravelly, where the Cliff was loamy, and the Shore floor'd with thefe Stones, I found no Copperas Stones: So that thefe Stones feem produced in the Loam, as the other (Coppe-*

ras Stones) in the Gravel, Nat. Hift. of Chalyb. and purging Waters, *p.* 106.

The Spring is faid to turn Wood into Iron: But this I take to be no more or lefs than the Quality which is found to be in much of the Stone, all along this Shore, viz. *of the* Copperas *kind; and 'tis certain, that the* Copperas Stone *(fo call'd) is found in all that Cliff, and even where the Water of this Spring has run; and I prefume that thofe who call the harden'd Pieces of Wood, which they take out of this Well by the Name of Iron, never tried the Quality of it, with the Fire or Hammer, if they had, perhaps they would have given fome other Account of it.* Tour, *&c.* ib.

That I might try whether *Vitriol* was the Caufe of this fuppos'd *Petrification,* I powdered not only fome of the *Clay* (fometime ago brought from thence) but likewife fome of the *Stonie Stratum,* and having feparately mixt them with *Rain Water,* let them ftand at leaft twelve Hours, that fo the Water might diffolve

The Water which diftilleth from under this *Cliff* doth petrify Wood as well as Clay; a large Piece fent from hence is referv'd in the *Repofitory* of the *Royal Society*[n].

Upon

diffolve any *Vitrioline* Salt, that might be lodged therein; but not obferving any fuch Tafte, I then tried whether the Powder of *Galls* put into the Liquors would difcover any change of Colour, but they gave neither Red, Blue, nor Black, though they ftood divers Hours together: Yet fome Water which ftood in a Place inclofed with a Row of loofe Stones at the hithermoft part of the *high Cliff*, did (1728.) tafte ftrong of *Vitriol*; but this as it was no Spring, nor did I fee any Water run from it, to me it feem'd only defign'd as a Place for laying their *Copperas Stones* in, when they are gather'd until they fell them; but either *Rain* had fallen upon them, or fome Spring Tide had overflowed the Place, and occafion'd that Collection of Water which by the *Copperas Stones* there laid had acquir'd that Tafte.

[n] Our Author here attributes the *petrifying* Faculty to the

Water which diftilleth from under the Cliff, whereby not only the *Clay* upon the Shore, but alfo *Wood* are turn'd into *Stone:* This the *Author* of the aforefaid *Tour* defcribes as a *Spring* or *Well*, which rifing in the *Cliff*, runs down into the Sea among the Pieces of *Clay* and *petrifies* them as it runs; which *Spring* is faid, faith he, to turn *Wood* into *Iron*. That there is any other *Spring* here than that I have before mention'd, I could never obferve; and the Water which Mr. *Taylor* thinks to diftil from under this *Cliff*, I could this Year 1728, difcern to be no other than fuch as the Tide had left (it having no other Tafte than that of Sea Water) draining down into the Sea, after the Tide was withdrawn. That petrified Wood and Sticks are often found imbedded in the Stones of this *Stratum*, I have already taken Notice in the Defcription of this *Cliff*: And about twenty Years ago I brought

I   from

from thence a large Piece of a *Spile*, which fo far as it was in the *Earth* was turn'd into *Stone*, what was above the *Earth* remain'd *Wood*: And that I might try how far the *Metamorphofis* had obtained upon it ; I committed fome part of it to the Fire, but it underwent no Alteration, though it retain'd the Grain of *Wood*, yet did not confume as *Wood*, the Fire having no power upon it: The like Experiment was made on fome of the Pieces of *Wood* imbedded in the *Stratum* of *Stone*.

I fhall now tranfcribe from the *Philofophical Tranfactions*, Nº. 291. *page* 1571. the Opinion of the late Reverend Mr. *John Morton Rector* of *Oxendon* in *Northamptonfhire*, Author of the *Natural Hiftory* of that *County*, which he was pleas'd to communicate to me in a Letter dat. *Auguft.* 4. 1699, as follows. ' At *Harwich* under the ' *Cliff* upon the Sea Shore there ' is a *Stratum* of a Clayie Stone, ' which is covered here and ' there with ragged Stones of a ' clofer Texture, which was for- ' merly (I conjecture) another ' intire *Stratum*, but is broken ' thus by the tearing of the

' Waves. The *Clayie - Stone-* ' *Stratum*, Mr. *D.* and Mr. *L.* ' my Companions were of Opi- ' nion had been formerly a ' fofter Subftance, but was daily ' *petrified* by the Sea Water. ' Having argued a little about ' it, then turning to the *Cliff*, ' I found a *Stratum* there of ' the very fame fort of *Clayie-* ' *Stone* with that upon the ' Shore ; yet the Sea Water very ' feldom comes up hither, un- ' lefs by Storms and at *Spring* ' *Tides* ; I broke a little Piece ' off, and fhew'd it to you, and ' then you was convinc'd (I ' think) it was not hardened or ' *petrified* by the Sea Water, ' but in its natural State. And ' I have often, I affure you, met ' with juft fuch a fort of *Stone* in ' many of our *Stone-pits* here ' in Inland Counties. It ap- ' pears to me, that the Water ' fhould have rather foftned ' than hardned the Stone upon ' the Shore ; though by wafhing ' away the loofer *Clayie* matter ' and other earthy Stuff, that ' is fometimes left upon it at the ' Ebb, it might feem to be a ' fort of *Petrifaction*, and occa- ' fion this Miftake.

P

Dr. *Plot*

Dr. *Plot* in his History of *Oxfordſhire*, *p.* 32, and 33. is inclin'd to believe *Petrifaction* proceeds in the main from the kindred of *Salts*, which ſublim'd and rarified in the Bowels of the *Earth* into an inviſible Steam, are received by the Waters as their moſt agreeable *Vehicle*, and brought hither to us at the riſing of *Springs*, as inviſibly as the Particles of *Silver* or *Gold*, when each is diſſolved in its proper Menſtruum : Where meeting perchance with an ambient Air, much colder and chilling than any under Ground, in all likelihood are precipitated, and thrown down on ſuch Subjects, as they caſually find at the Place of their Exit. If any aſk (ſaith he) what *Salts* are the apteſt to perform this Feat of Petrifaction; he inclines to refer it to that of *Vitriol:* To which he adds, that wherever he finds ſtrong *Vitriol Waters*, the petrifying ones are not far off. The Doctor diſtinguiſheth theſe *petrifying Waters* into three kinds, 1. Such as purely of themſelves are *petrified*, the very Body of Water being turn'd into Stone as it drops. from the Rocks, which are therefore call'd

Lapides Stillatitii. 2. Such as petrify only by *Incruſtation* and are only *ſuperficial.* 3. Such as petrify *per minima*, or *totum per totum*. Mr. *Morton Hiſt. North. p.* 271. obſerves as to his firſt: That the *Lapides Stillatitii*, and other Bodies of a like kind, are not as he conjectured form'd of the Water turn'd into Stone, as it drops from the Rocks, but of *ſparry Corpuſcles* convey'd by the Water into the *Figures*, or *Grotto's* of thoſe *Rocks*. His ſecond kind of petrifying Waters are ſuch as we ſo frequently meet with in this and ſome other *Inland Counties*. His third, that is ſuch as *petrify per minima*, converting, as I underſtand him, the very Subſtance of the Body into *Stone*, Mr. *Morton* avers, never yet to have met with either here or elſewhere. The ſaid Mr. *Morton* hath more largely diſcourſed of this in his ſaid *Nat. Hiſt.* but he having more compendiouſly delivered himſelf concerning *Petrification*, in his afore-quoted Letter to me, I ſhall tranſcribe his Thoughts from that, *viz.* ' As to *Petrifications*, ' I have only obſerved theſe ' three ſorts. 1. A *ſtony Incru-* ' *ſtation* upon Sticks and any ' thing

‘ thing that lies in the way, in
‘ the petrifying Springs; the
‘ Earth in thofe Waters is ufu-
‘ ally intermixt with particles of
‘ *Stone*, that trickle down into it
‘ with the Water, and are there
‘ detain'd; of this firft fort you
‘ have doubtlefs many Inftances
‘ in *Effex*. 2. The fecond fort
‘ is that which is perform'd by
‘ the *Permeation*, or *Infinuation*
‘ of the finer forts of *ftony Par-*
‘ *ticles*, as it is in the Cafe of
‘ fome of our petrifying Wa-
‘ ter, (I believe) particularly that
‘ at *Knaresborough* the *ftony Par-*
‘ *ticles* of which are very fine.
‘ And many of the *Foffil-Shells*
‘ have undergone the fameFate.
‘ The third, which is indeed a
‘ *Petrification* properly fo call'd,
‘ is often met with on the Sides
‘ of *Caves* and *Grotto's* as at
‘ *Pooly-hole* in the *Peak*, and in
‘ the *Fiffures*, and *Clefts* of
‘ Mines and Quarries. Of this
‘ kind are the feveral forts of
‘ *Fluors*, the *Lapides Stillatitii*
‘ *Stalagmitæ*, &c. that we meet
‘ with in the *Fiffures* and *Hia-*
‘ *tus's* of the *Earth*. Thefe are
‘ continually growing (as they
‘ vulgarly fay) that is are receiv-
‘ ing an additional Increafe of
‘ real and folid Stone, as is ob-

‘ ferv'd in many *Caves* in the
‘ *Peak*, &c. This I take to be
‘ perform'd in fuch manner
‘ as the *Incruftations* are, *viz.*
‘ the Particles of *Stone*, are
‘ brought along with the Water
‘ as their *Vehicle*, and are depo-
‘ fited at length upon the Sides
‘ of the *Cave* or *Fiffure*; for
‘ there is always a watery
‘ Stream, trickling down the
‘ Sides of thefe *Caves:* But here
‘ the Particles of *Stone* are ex-
‘ tremely minute and fine, and
‘ do thereby naturally concrete
‘ and join together very clofe.

Having given the Opinions
of divers Perfons in relation to
Petrification in general, and of
that in this Place in particular,
I fhall now give my own
Thoughts thereon, with fome
Obfervations about them: *Pe-*
trification vulgarly fo call'd, I
have obferv'd to be of three
forts, *viz. Incruftation, Adhæ-*
fion, and *Permeation* or *Infinua-*
tion: To begin with the firft,
tho' improperly call'd a *Petri-*
faction: This is frequently
to be met with in the Rivulets of this County of *Effex*,
in which *Shells* of *Water-Snails*,
Nuts, *Acron-Cups*, *Leaves*, *Sticks*
and *Grafs*, are to be found co-

ver'd

ver'd over with, some thicker and others thinner, a *friable* matter, retaining the Form of the thing incrusted; this is Dr. *Plot's* second *Species*, and is, I presume, perform'd by a *Vitrioline* Water mixing with a Gravelly, whereby the stony Particles of the latter are precipitated, and thereby incrustate the things they pass over; and in divers Places where I have found these, I have traced them to the *Spring-head*, and have observ'd, that after I had pass'd above the Place of the *Influx* of the *Gravelly-Water*, the other, *viz.* the *Vitrioline*, hath contain'd none of these *Incrustations*, but the Bottom and Sides not only of the Spring-head, but likewise of the *Channel* have been lined with a *ferruginous Slime*; and on the Surface of the Water a blue *oily Slime* or *Cremor*; and the Water itself had a *Vitrioline* or *Ironish Taste*: Not that they proceed from any *Iron Mine*, none such having as yet that I have heard of been found in this *County*, but from a *Pyrites* or *Copperas-Stone*, frequently occurring in the Clays, especially those us'd for *Tile-Earth:* And I am confirm'd in this Opinion, of

the Cause of these *Incrustations*, from the following Instance; there was for divers Years in the Parish of *White Notley* in *Essex*, on the Road leading from *Braintree* to *Witham*, a Trough set to receive a small *Cascade* of Water, which not only had in it such an abundance of *Incrustations* as required frequently emptying, but the said Trough was likewise strongly *coated* on the Outside with the same matter; of late Years this has ceas'd, occasion'd by the diverting the *Vitrioline-Water* another way, (whether intentionally, or accidental I know not) which thereby flows into an adjoining Ditch by the Road-side not many Yards distant from the said Trough: To these Incrustations Mr. *Morton, Nat. Hist. North. p.* 272. attributes a *Styptick* Property, and believes that were they prepar'd and administred as the *Osteocolla* of the *Shops*, they would prove as valuable an *Astrictive* as that is: And he likewise gives Instances of Waters in that County, which will *incrustate* though never any *Vitriolick Water* intermixes with them; but of these I have not yet met with any in this *County*; nor

2

nor have I obferv'd any of thefe *Incruftations* to confift of *fparry* Particles, as the faid Mr. *Morton* hath obferved thofe in that County to be, but of thofe that are gravelly.

The fecond fort of *Petrifactions* which I fhall take Notice of is that of *Adhefion*; and thefe are Dr. *Plot*'s firft kind, which he defcribes *as fuch as purely of themfelves are petrified, the very Body of Water being turn'd into Stone as it drops from the Rocks,* Hift. Oxf. *p.* 33. I am fully of Mr. *Morton*'s Opinion that thefe *Lapides Stillatitii* and *Stalagmitæ,* are not produced from the Petrifaction of the Water, into thofe *ftony Ificles,* as vulgarly call'd, but from the *Adhefion* of *fparry* and *earthy Particles,* which by the Water paffing through the *Fiffures* of the *Earth* are brought along with it, and left adhering there. But not having met with any of thofe either at this Place, nor in this *County,* I fhall fay no more of them, when I have obferved that thefe are occafion'd in the fame manner as the former, only in thefe, the Particles being finer, the Cohefion is the clofer.

The third fort is by Permea-tion, or as Dr. *Plot* terms them, fuch as *petrify per minima,* or *totum per totum.* This is like-wife the *Doctor*'s third, but the fecond in Mr. *Morton*'s aforefaid *Letter,* who avers, *Nat. Hift. North. p.* 271. that he never met with this fort of *Petrification,* neither in that County nor elfe-where, and that the Sample thereof, repofited by the Doctor in the *Afhmolean Mufeum,* for *Oaken-Wood petrified,* did appear to him not to be what it was reprefented to be in his *Nat. Hift. Oxfordfh. p.* 35. It being as he affirms a mere *Stone,* tho' it hath fome Refemblance of the Grain of *Wood.* What I fhall therefore add upon this Head is, that befides the Piece of *petrified Spile* aforemention'd, I have divers *Samples* of that which I believe was formerly *Wood,* im-bedded in the *Stratum* of Stone, which lieth near the Bottom of this *Cliff,* which to me feem to be as much *Stone,* as that in which it is imbedded, and un-dergoes as little Alteration by Fire as that doth; and though in one of the Samples I have, *Particles* of *Spar* may by the naked Eye be difcerned between the *Bark* and *Wood,* yet could I not

Upon this Shore alſo within the Flow of the Sea, are gathered as they are commonly call'd *Copperas-*

not even with a Glaſs perceive any of the aforeſaid *Particles,* intruded into the Spaces between the *Fibres.* Some, ſaith Mr. *Morton, p.* 263. have a Fancy that thoſe ſorts of *Foſſils* are the Roots of ſome *Trees,* which grew down thither from the Surface: And the Workmen generally call them *Roots;* but if we conſider the Depth of their lying here, and that in the ſame *Stone* with them is alſo imbedded ſeveral ſorts of *Shells,* the contrary will be manifeſt.

Dr. *Woodward* in his Attempt, *p.* 19. gives the following Account: ' This ſort of Wood is ' found moſt commonly in ' *Strata* of Gravel or Sand; and ' ſometimes in Stone, Clay or ' Marl. All that I have ever ' obſerved of it, was altered ' and increaſed in hardneſs and ' weight, either by Inſinuation ' of ſtony and mineral Matter, ' during the time that theſe and ' other Bodies were ſuſtain'd a- ' mong the diſſolv'd ſtony and ' mineral Matter, in the Water ' of the Deluge, or by a total ' Solution of the Vegetable Sub-

' ſtance; and a Succeſſion of ' Stony, Mineral, or Metallick ' in its Stead. What hath been ' imagin'd by ſome that this ' Alteration was made ſince, ' by petrifying Water, is with- ' out Reaſon, or good Obſer- ' vation to countenance it. ' Even that which is found in ' Lakes, and in Rivulets, was ' originally lodged in the Earth ' at the Bottom of them, and ' petrified before it was repo- ' ſited there: In particular, a ' more accurate Enquiry, and ' Trials, have ſhewn that what ' was formerly pretended of the ' petrifying Power of *Lake O-* ' *neagh* in *Ireland,* is not true: ' And the Water makes no ſuch ' Alteration upon any Wood ' that is put into it; the petri- ' fied Wood that is brought ' thence, being of that which ' was originally lodged in the ' Earth at the Bottom of the ' Lake: I inſtance in the Wood ' brought out of this Lake, ' becauſe it is frequently inſiſted ' on: And more Notice has ' been taken of it than any o- ' ther.

Stones,

Stones, and carried to certain *Copperas-Houses* not far distant from hence ⁰. Where being mixed with Earth and difpofed into light Beds, it diffolves by the Rain from the Sky, which Water being by Trunks guided into a great *Ciftern* made of *Lead,* from thence is conveyed into a *Boiler* of *Lead,* which having perform'd its Operation upon it, produceth *Copperas,* which is a fort of *Vitriol* ᵖ.

There

ⁿ Of which there are divers in this County, as at *Ramfey* three Miles from hence: Alfo at *Walton* Anno 1696 there were two, but one of them is I hear fince demolifhed by the *Sea.* There is alfo one at *Bricklefey.* The *Copperas - Stones* mention'd by our Author, are found upon all this Shore not only where the *Cliff* is gravelly, but likewife where it is *loamy* or *clayie*; and this Year 1728, I did not only gather fome there myfelf, but did likewife fee divers *Boys* gathering them even at the Place where the *Cliff* is higheft and moft loamy; and as every Tide wafheth away fome of the loofer Earth which falleth down from the Cavities of the *Cliff,* thofe Stones being moft ponderous are there left; and as foon as the

Tide permits they bufily gather them.

ᵖ The manner of making *Copperas* being much ∴ the fame, both at *Ramfey* and *Walton* in this County, with that at *Bricklefey* obferved by the late learned and ingenious Mr. *John Ray,* and publifhed in his *Collection of Englifh Words, p.* 198. I fhall tranfcribe it into this Place.

They lay the Stones upon a large *Bed* or *Floor* prepared in the open Air, underneath which there are Gutters or Troughs difpofed to receive and carry the Liquor impregnated with the *Mineral* to a *Ciftern* where it is referved. (For the Air and Weather diffolving the Stones, the Rain falling upon them carries away with it the Vitrioline Juice or Salt diffolved).

2

This

There are great Quantities of *Umber* (as some judge it to be) for Painters hereabouts.

Sometimes here (but more plentifully about *Land-guard-Fort*) are found *transparent Pebbles* of several Colours, but those that counterfeit *Diamonds* are most in request, which many cause to be cut and set in *Rings*.

Amber both fat and good is frequently found; and some affirm, that *Amber-greese* hath also been taken up there.

This Liquor they boil in large *Leaden Pans*, putting in a good Quantity of old *Iron:* When it is sufficiently evaporated they pour it out into large Troughs wherein it cools; the *Vitriol* crystallizing to the Sides of the Troughs, and to cross Bars put into them. The Liquor that remains after the *Vitriol* is crystallized they call the Mother, and reserve it to be again evaporated by boiling.

A larger Account of making *Vitriol* at *Deptford* in *Kent*, communicated by *Daniel Colwall*, Esq; was publish'd in the *Philosophical Transactions*, Nᵒ. 142. *p.* 1056. where any that desire it, may receive further Satisfaction.

Some Years ago some Persons did upon these Shores make *Pot-ashes*, by gathering and dry-

ing great Quantities of *Kali* and other *Sea-weeds*, of which either grow abundantly upon the Stones on the Shore, or are left there by the *Tide*; these they burned in little Holes made for that Purpose in the Sand into a *Blackish-grey* or *Ash-colour'd* Lump: But whether it did not answer their Expectation, or whatever else it was that prevented, they attempted it but one Year.

A sort of *Pot-ash* brought from *Woodbridge* in *Suffolk* is (as I am inform'd) used here to make *Lie* with for washing their *Linnen*. They are made of *Wood-ashes*, bought of the Country People, then burnt again in an *Oven* 'till they are very white, then they are quench'd with cold Water: They are sold at 12 *d. per* Peck. Ex MS. D. J.L.

Here

Here are feveral forts of Herbs for ufe, as *Beets, Sea-Coleworts, Sea Wormwood, Samphire* (efpecially that which is call'd *Marfh Samphire,* from the Place of its Growth) *Eringoes, Coltsfoot,* &c⁹. And for Delight the Sands afford not only variety of *Shells,* but many other ftrange things bred and nourifh'd in the Bowels of the Deep; which are many times caft up and expos'd to View.

In the *Winter-Seafon* our *Kitchen* Fires and *Ovens,* are commonly well provided with *Wild-Fowl,* and thofe in as great variety as abundance: From Sea the *Venifon* of Fowl: The *Road-goofe, Brent-goofe, Wild-geefe, Wild-fwans, Curlews, Plovers, Duck* and *Mallard, Eafterlings* or *Widgeons, Teal, Oxbirds,* &c. And from the Land plenty of *Pheafants, Partridges, Wood-pigeons, Larks, Wheat-ears,* &c.

For *Fifh* as we have good Store, fo we have feveral forts according to their Seafons, *Herrings, Mackarel, Mullets, Codlings, Whitings, Congers* and *Eels; Guard-fifh, Sea-bleaks,* and *Sprats; Sole, Plaife, Flounders, Butts, Scates, Maids,* &c. And from the *Fleets* on *Suffolk* Side, extraordinary well grown *Jacks,* &c. But for a Variety, a Difh of well-order'd *Harwich Sturgeon* is very acceptable ʳ. 　　　　　　　　　　 For

⁹ Befides thefe mention'd by Mr. *Taylor,* there fhall be added by way of *Appendix,* the many forts of the moft rare *Herbs,* &c. as well Sea as Land which I have collected there.

ʳ What the *Harwich Sturgeon* was, or how it was well-order'd

Q

For *Shell-Fish* we have plenty of *Lobsters* and *Crabs*, the best of which are taken in great abundance upon a Shelf of *Rocks* three Leagues off at Sea (and though lying S. E. from this *Town*, yet are call'd the *West-Rocks*) except some few that are taken upon the Ebb among the *Stones* on the *Shore:* The most noted of *Crabs* are those which are call'd the *Hammer-Crabs*, and are in greatest repute. Here are taken also excellent *Oysters*, *Cockles*, *Muscles*, *Perewincles*, *Pinpatches*, *Prawns*, *Shrimps*, &c[f].

der'd is not at this Day known there, enquiry having been made, though to no Purpose.

[f] Under the Title of *Shell-Fish*, Mr. *Taylor* begins and ends with those of *Lobsters*, *Crabs*, *Prawns* and *Shrimps*; which are by *Naturalists* ranked among the *cru-stacea*, and not *testacea*; these, as likewise the *Birds*, and *Fishes*, which are here to be found, or have been taken here and not mention'd by Mr. *Taylor*, I have reserved for the *Appendix.*

CHAP.

CHAP. III.

THE *Despotical* or *Dynastical* Concerns of these Towns, which relate to their particular *Lords* or *Owners* come next under our Inquiry.

The general Survey of *William* the *Conqueror*, that is *Dooms-Day-Book*, gives this Account.

TERRA Alberici de Uer.
hund. de Tendringa

Drunrecurt tenet A. in Dnio qd tenuit Ulluuinus p. Man.
7 p vi hid. Tc. viii Uill. m. vi Tc. vi Bor. m. xii Sep vi
Ser. 7 iii car. in dnio. 7 vi car hom. iii acr pti past.
cc. ov. 7 xl por Tc iii runc. xii an. cc ou. xl por. 7
in similit. Tc Ual vi lib m. xii. [t]

[t] *Terra Alberici de Ver*
Hundreda de Tendringa.

Drunrecurt tenet Albericus in Dominio quod tenuit Vluuinus pro Manerio & pro 6 *hides, tunc* 8 *Villani modo* 6 *tunc* 6 *Bordarii modo* 12 *semper* 6 *servi, &* 3 *carucæ dominio &* 6 *carucæ homines* 3 *acræ prati pastura pro* 200 *ovibus &* 40 *porcis tunc* 3 *Runcini,* 12 *Animalia* 200 *Oves* 40 *porci & modo similiter tunc totum valebat* 6 *lib. modo* 12.

The

The Land of *Alberic de Ver*
Hundreds of *Tendring.*

Alberic holds *Drunrecourt* (now *Dovercourt*) for a
Lordſhip, which *Ulvvin* held for a Manor, and ſix
Hides, then *(i. e.* in the time of King *Edward* the
Confeſſor) were eight Villains, now but ſix. Then
were ſix Borderers, now twelve. There were always
ſix Servants and three Ploughs in the Demeſn, and ſix
Ploughmen, three Acres of Meadow Paſture for two
hundred Sheep, and forty Swine: Then three Runcini,
twelve Animals, two hundred Sheep, and forty Swine,
and now in like manner, then it was ſix Pounds, now
twelve.

What *Hides, Villani, Bordarij, Servi,* &c. were, and
how they held ſeveral (among many See *Hiſtory of
Gavel-kind, p.* 168.) have plentifully wrote, to whom
the Reader is referr'd[u]; only be pleas'd to obſerve that
                                                Runcini

---

[u] For *Explanation* of divers
Words in the *Record* our *Author,*
refers you to ſeveral that have
plentifully wrote about them,
but names none except his own
Hiſtory of Gavel-kind: I ſhall
therefore for the Eaſe of my
Readers tranſcribe from ſome
Writers, what is generally meant
by thoſe Names. *Hide* according to *Skinner's Etymologicon* is
ſo much Land, as can maintain
one *Family,* or as one *Plough*
could *cultivate:* From the *Saxon*
Word hýd a Houſe or Habitation from hýðen to cover, the
                              Word

Runcini are (by the Ingenious Mr. *Edward Falconberge* one of the *Chamberlains* of his *Majefty's Exchequer*) judged

Word (as the *R. R. Bp. Kennet* obferves in his Ⓖⓛⓞⓕⓕⓐⓡⓟ) was fometimes taken for a Houfe, becaufe faith *Skinner* a Houfe hath a Portion of Land join'd to it. But what the Quantity of a *Hide* is, was never exprefly determin'd. *Gervafe* of *Tilbury* makes it one hundred Acres : The *Malmsbury* MS. cited by *Spelman* computes it at ninety fix Acres, accounting four *Virgates* in a *Hide*, and in every *Virgate* twenty four Acres. *Polydore Virgil* reduces a *Hide* to twenty Acres, fo that in truth a *Hide* contains no certain Number of Acres, but varied according to different Places. *Villain* or *Villane*, faith *Taylor's Hiftory of Gavel-kind, p.* 168. is a *Villager* or one that dwells in a *Village*, for the Name carried no fuch Odium and Reproach in elder times, as it hath done in later Days ; for what was *Villanus* more than a *Villager* to fuch a *Lord*, and their *Villanage*, but their *Duties* and *Cuftom-Services* belonging to a *Village* for the

Lord's Ufe ? Bifhop *Kennet* faith, that in *Dooms-Day* Inquifition thefe *Villanes* were recounted as an emolument and appendage of every *Manor :* They were of two forts, 1. *Villanes* in grofs, who as to their Perfons, their Iffue, and their Stock, were a fort of abfolute Slaves, the fole Property of their *Lord* ; moveable and alienated at Pleafure. 2. *Villanes regardant* or appendant to a Manor, who were afcrib'd as Members of fuch a Fee, and as a Pertinence of it, paft along to every new *Lord*. For their Service, they held fome fmall Portion of *Houfe* or *Land* in *Villanage*. Sir *Edward Coke* upon *Littleton* as quoted by *Taylor* faith, that *Villani* in *Dooms-Day* are not there taken for *Bond-Men* ; but had their Name *de Villis*, becaufe they had *Farms*, and did there Work of *Husbandry* for the *Lord* ; and they were ever before named *Bordarij*, and fuch as are *Bond-Men* are call'd *Servi*. *Bordarij* Bifhop *Kennet* in his *Gloffary* faith, that fome derive

judged to fignify *working* or *Mill-Horfes*; and the twelve *Animals* are commonly received in that Record to fignify *Horned-Beaft* [w].

derive it from the old *French* Word *Bords*, the Limits or extreme Parts of any Extent: As the *Borders* of a *Country*, and the *Borderers* or *Inhabitants* of thofe Parts, (and it is in this Senfe that Mr. *Taylor* in this Place hath taken it, though in his *Hiftory of Gavel-kind, p.* 172. he believes the *Bordarij* and *Bordmanni* to be the fame.) The *Bordarij* fo often mention'd in *Dooms-Day Inquifition*, were diftinct from the *Servi* and *Villani*, and feem to be thofe of a lefs fervile Condition, who had a Borio or *Cottage*, with a fmall parcel of Land allowed to them, on condition they fhould fupply the Lord with *Poultry* and *Eggs*, and other fmall Provifions for his *Board* and *Entertainment*, *Servi Servile-Tenants.* No Author, faith Bifhop *Kennet*, hath to his Knowledge fix'd the Diftinction between *Servus* and *Villanus*, though undoubtedly their Servitudes were different: For they are all along in *Dooms-*

Day-Book divided from one another. He fuppofeth the *Servi* were thofe whom our *Lawyers* have fince call'd *Pure-Villanes*, and *Villanes* in grofs, who without any determin'd Tenure of Land, were at the arbitrary Pleafure of the *Lord* appointed to fuch fervile Works, and receiv'd their Maintenance and Wages at the Difcretion of the *Lord.* The other were of a fuperiour Degree, and were call'd *Villani*, becaufe they were *villæ & glebæ adfcripti* held fome *Cottage* and *Lands*, for which they were burden'd with fuch ftated *fervile Offices*; and were convey'd as a Pertinence of the *Manor* to which they belong'd.

[w] The *Runcini* are by Mr. *Gouldman* interpreted *Nags*, and as for the *Animalia*, the *Inquifition* having already given the Number of the *Sheep* and *Hogs* upon the Lordfhip, it is very probable that *Black Cattle* are meant thereby.

It

It yielded in *Ulvvin*'s time fix pounds (which may be fuppofed to be by the Year) *Alberic de Vere* improved it to twelve, a double Improvement to what it was; yet but very fmall to what it yields at this Prefent.

We gather from the *Conqueror's Survey*, that in the Reign of King *Edward* the *Confeffor*, or very near it, they were the Poffeffions of a great Man by Name *Ulvvinus*; who (we fuppofe) loft them by ingaging with King *Harold* againft Duke *William* in the Battel of *Haftings*, that being in thofe Days the chiefeft Crime which caufed a Forfeiture; for many Men whofe Lands in that Hurry and Scramble were feized on, afterwards repoffeft them, upon their Plea and Proof that they were not at the Battel of *Haftings*.   Whatever the Caufe or Crime was, we find that the whole Inheritance of this *Ulvvin*, was by the *Conqueror*'s Bounty (*Dugdal*'s *Baron.* 188.) beftowed on *Alberic de Vere* [x], who not only poffeft himfelf of it; but alfo took from the Monks of *Ramfey* in *Huntington-fhire*, what the faid *Wulfewine* (for fo he is often call'd) had given to them before the *Norman-Conqueft* [y].

---

[x] From a Town of that Name in *Zeland*, *Camb. Brit. p.* 267. or a *Poffeffion of* theirs.   *Peerage of England*, 2. 270.

[y] This *Ulvvin* or *Wulfewine* doth not feem a Man of any great Note, becaufe none of the *Hiftorians* I have had the Sight of make any mention of him.

I. This

I. This *Alberic* was call'd *Senior* and married *Beatrice*, Niece and Heir to *Manaſſes* Earl of *Guiſnes* in *France* [z]. He founded (as is before ſaid) a Religious Houſe at *Coln* furniſhed with Monks from *Abindon*, to which it was a *Cell*; and was poſſeſſed of divers Lordſhips in *Middleſex* and the County of *Huntingdon*, nine in *Suffolk*, and fourteen in this *County*.

[z] He deriv'd his *Pedigree* according to *Cambden* from the Earls of *Guiſnes*, *Brit. p.* 267. *York* that he deſcended from them, *p.* 230. The Author of the *Peerage* of *England* writes, that *Miles*, who was createdCount of *Guiſnes* in *Normandy* by the Emperor *Charles the Great* his Uncle, was Anceſtor to this *Aubrey*, who came in with *William* the *Conqueror*, who may be accounted the Original of the Family, and had the Title of *Comes*; but it is not certain of what Place. *Peerage*, Vol. II. *p.* 270. His Grandſon *Aubrey* has the Title of Earl of *Guiſnes* in *Normandy* given him by *Miles*, *p.* 675. By *Beatrice* or *Beatrix* his Wife, he had five Sons and one Daughter, *viz. Godfrey*, who died in the Life-time of his Father and was buried in the Abby of *Abingdon. Aubrey*, who ſucceeded him, *Roger* and *Robert*, who outlived him, and *William* that was buried with him in *Coln Priory*; *Roſe* his Daughter was Wife firſt to *Pain*, Baron *Beaucamp* of *Bedford*, and ſecondly, to *Jeoffry de Mandevill*, Earl of *Eſſex*. This *Aubrey* died ſoon after he had finiſhed his Foundation aforeſaid, being there ſhorn a *Monk*, and was there buried *Anno Domini* 1088. as I have already ſhewed, as was likewiſe *Beatrix* his Wife whom *Weaver* from a MS. he affirms to have ſeen in the *Cotton Library* makes the Daughter of the *Conqueror*, which muſt be a Miſtake, no other Author that I have ſeen beſides him making mention of any ſuch Daughter the *Conqueror* had.

He bore for his Arms Quarterly *Gules* and *Or*, in the firſt a *Mullet Argent*.

II. *Alberic*

II. *Alberic* his Son and Heir call'd *Junior*, was made Lord *Great Chamberlain* of *England* by King *Henry* the firft, to hold the fame Office to himfelf and his Heirs in Fee, with all Dignities and Liberties thereto belonging, as honourably as *Robert Mallet* (Lord of the Honour of *Eye* in *Suffolk*) or any other before him held the fame. He in the fifth of King *Stephen* having executed the *Sheriff's Office* in feveral Counties, was killed (as was faid) in a Tumult in *London* [a], having in his Life-time confirm'd the Grants of his *Father* and *Mother* to the Monks of *Coln*. He by *Adeliza* Daughter of *Gilbert de Clare* had three Sons and two Daughters [b], the youngeft of which *Juliana* married to *Roger Bigod*

---

[a] He was, as faith *York, Portgrave* of *London*, and *Lord Chief Juftice* of *England*, and was flain by the Commons of *London, Anno* 1140. *York*, 230. In the Synod held by the *Pope's Legate* at *Winchefter, Anno* 1139. He in a long Speech makes the *King's* Defence againft the *Legate's* Charge, in which he aggravates the Caufe modeftly, and without reproachful Language againft *Roger Bifhop* of *Salisbury*, *Tyrrell's Hift*. 2. 222. In the fifth of King *Stephen*, in which Year he was kill'd, he executed the Office of *Sheriff*, for *Surry, Cambridge, Huntington, Effex, Hertford, Northampton, Leicefter, Norfolk, Suffolk, Bucks* and *Bedford*; and was a Benefactor to the Monks of *Abingdon* and *Thorney. Peerage*, Vol. II. *p.* 271.

His Arms the fame as his Father's.

[b] This *Adeliza* was Daughter of *Roger de Ivery* (who came in with the *Conqueror*, and to whom he was *Cup-bearer*) by *Adelina* his Wife, eldeft Daughter of *Hugh Grentifmaifnil* and *Adeliza*

R

Bigod Earl of *Norfolk*, and *Steward* to the *King's Houfhold*, whofe Father *Hugh* was advanced to thofe Titles by *Henry* II, being before that ftiled *Comes Eaft Anglorum*. She is frequently nam'd *Juliana Comitiffa*, without any other Addition. To whom (it feems probable) fhe brought with her thefe Lordfhips of

Dovercourt

Adeliza his Wife, and not of *Gilbert de Clare* (who had a Wife but no Daughter of that Name) as our Author has tranfcrib'd it from *Dugdale*. That this *Adeliza* was the Daughter of *Roger de Ivery* by *Adelina* his Wife appears from the following Inftance, *viz. Adelina* her Mother being dangeroufly fick gave to the Monks of *Abingdon*, to pray for her Recovery, one Hide of Land within the Village of *Fencot*, which Gift, this *Adeliza* her Daughter did confirm.

The Story of which is thus recorded in the Chartulary of *Abingdon*, *Nobilis quædam Matrona* Adelina de Hiverio (Iverio) *vocata apud locum qui* Faincote (Fencot) *dicitur, ubi diu irremediabiliter ægrotavit, hidam unam pro fuo remedio Abbatiæ de* Abbendun (Abingdon) *contulit,*
2

An. XI. *Hen.* I. *&* Adeliza *filia ejufdem* Adelinæ *dictum Donum maternum confirmavit. His teftibus.* Nigello de Oileio,&c. *Apud* Wudeftoc *in quadragefima.* As did alfo King *Henry* I, and it is likewife recited and confirm'd in a Bull of *Pope Eugene* III. All which are referved for the Appendix.

Another Inftance is in Dr. *Kennet's Paroch. Antiq. p.* 62. who faith, that *Roger de Iveri* died about this time, *viz. Anno* MLXXIX. 13, 14. *Will.* I, and left *Adeline* his Widow, who by Inheritance from her Father had Lands in *Charlton, Otendon* and *Iflip.* The two laft of which the fame Author mentions, *p.* 68. from Doomes-Day-Book. And fhe is again call'd *Adeline*, Widow of *Roger de Iveri*,ib.*p.*74. And a third Inftance is, that *Iflip* one of the Manors of which
Adeline

Dovercourt and *Harwich*, in *Frank Marriage* (as was much the Cuftom in thofe Days) for her Son *Roger*, who fucceeded

Adeline Widow of *Roger de Iveri* was poffeft at her Death, came thereby to *Adeliza* her Daughter, who bringing it in Frank Marriage to *Aubrey de Ver* her Hufband, he gave part thereof to the Monks of *Thorney*, for the Ufe hereunder to be mention'd, *viz.*

Terra uxoris Rogeri de Jberi in dimid Befentone Hund.
Tetelape Iflip Otendone Oddington.

But our Right Reverend Author did furely forget that he had *p.* 62. affirm'd, that this *Adeline*, as is aforemention'd, held Lands by Inheritance from her Father in *Charlton*, *Otendon* and *Iflip*, and *p.* 74. that at the general Survey fhe was poffeft, as by her Father's Gift, of the Manors of *Iflip* and *Oddington*, yet in *p.* 71. and 81. writes, that fhe held them in Dowry. By this *Adeliza*, he came into the Poffeffions in *Iflip*, *Hedington* and *Draton*; and gave to the Monks of *Thorney* ten Shillings *per Annum*, out of his own Part of the Tithe in *Iflip*, with as much other Tithe in *Draton* and *Hedington* as amounted to the Tithe of five *Carucates*, *Kennet*'s *Paroch. Antiq.* 82. He had three Sons *Alberic*, who fucceeding him - - - - - a Canon of St. *Ofiths*, and *Robert*, who confirm'd his Father's Grant juft mention'd to the Monks of *Thorney*; and two Daughters, *Adeliza* and *Juliana*. *Leland* doth not as I can find in his Itinerary make this *Adeliza* Wife of *Aubrey*, to be the Daughter of *Gilbert de Clare*, but faith, Vol. VI. *p.* 42. that the Wife of this *Aubrey* was *Alice* Daughter of *Jeffrey Mandevill* Earl of *Effex*, the contrary to which Error I have already fhewn.

A Copy

succeeded his Brother *Hugh* (dying without Iſſue) in theſe Lordſhips, as well as Earldom of *Norfolk*, regrants this

A Copy of the Grant of the Tithe of *Iſlip*.

Ego Albericus, *Regis Camerarius,* terram de Twiwell *quamdiu vixero de Domino Abbate* Guntero *&* monachis de Thorneya *per talem conventionem teneo ad firmam, ut per unumquemque annum eis* vj. *lib. pro ea reddam: ante Nativitatem* XL. s. *ante Paſcham* XL. s. *& ad vincula S.* Petri *extremos* XL. s. *Inſuper pro Remiſſione Peccatorum meorum, illis de una mea decima, ſcilicet de* Iſlip, *unoquoque anno, ad feſtivitatem S.* Michaelis x. s. *reddam. Totum vero ſurplus quod miſerim in eadem villa ultra quam recepi in extremo die vitæ meæ, pro Salvatione animæ meæ, Sanctæ* Mariæ, *fratribuſque meis, ſimul cum terra illorum, concedo ſolidum* [forte *ſolutum,*] *& quietum ab omni calumpnia. De alia terra quam pro dimidii Militis ſervitio in eadem Villa de* Willielmo *de* Bloſſavilla *teneo in feodo, & de dimidio unius Hidæ quam certo emi precio, ſanctam* Mariam, *meoſque*

2

Fratres poſt me concedo eſſe Hæredes, in quantum id eis concedere poſſum. Hujus conventionis ſunt Teſtes Hardwine *de* Eſcalers *&* Radulfus *dapifer,* Willielmus *dapifer,* Willielmus *de* Witleſige *& Simo, imo fratres illius loci & alii quamplures.* Dugd. Monaſt. I. *p.* 248.

In Engliſh *as follows.*

I *Aubrey,* Chamberlain to his Majeſty, hold in Farm as long as I ſhall live the Land of *Twiwel* of the Abbot *Gunter,* and the Monks of *Thorney* upon this Agreement, that I pay to them vj. lib. yearly for the ſame; before *Chriſtmas* XL. s. before *Eaſter* XL. s. and on St. *Peter's* the laſt XL. s. Moreover for the Remiſſion of my Sins, I will pay to them out of one of my Tithes; namely *Iſlip,* every Year on the Feaſt of St. *Michael,* x. s. But the whole Surplus which I ſhall leave in the ſame Villa more than I have receiv'd, I grant to St. *Mary* and my Brothers.

this *Church* and *Chapel* to the *Abingdon* Monks at *Coln*, as if he had been the *Original Founder*, taking ſmall Notice of what the elder *Alberic de Vere* had formerly done, as before hath been ſhewn ^c. III. This

thers together with their Land on the laſt Day of my Life, for the Salvation of my own Soul, free and quiet from all claim. Of the other Land which I hold in fee of *William de Bloſſaville*, in the ſame Village for the Service of half a Soldier, and of the half of one Hide which I bought for a certain Price, I grant St. *Mary* and my Brethren to be Heirs after me; as much as is in my Power to grant it to them. The Witneſſes of this Agreement are, *Hardwine de Eſcalers* and *Ralph* the Sewer, *William* the Sewer, *William de Wittleſige* and *Simon*, alſo the Brothers of that Place, and many others.

^c There are two Miſtakes in this latter Part of the *Paragraph*, which muſt be here rectified; as firſt, that *Juliana* youngeſt Daughter of the younger *Aubrey de Vere* was Wife to *Roger* the Son of *Hugh Bigod*, when ſhe was Wife to *Hugh Bigod Steward* of the *Houſhold* to King *Henry* I. Secondly, That ſhe had a Son

Hugh that died without Iſſue, who was poſſeſt of theſe Lordſhips as well as of the Earldom of *Norfolk*, whereas, I do not find by our *Antiquaries*, that ſhe had any Son of that Name. It is very likely that this laſt Error might be taken from an ancient Edition of *Cambden*, viz. *Anno* 1594. *p.* 370. where the *Hugh*, that was *Steward* to *Henry* I. is made different from *Hugh*, that took part with young King *Henry*, Son of King *Henry* II, whereas they were one and the ſame Perſon, as all our *Hiſtorians* and *Antiquaries* fully prove, of which I can give many Inſtances; but let *Brooks* only ſuffice, who affirms, that the firſt *Hugh*, and thoſe ſaid to ſucceed between from Father to Son to that *Hugh*, which is call'd (*i. e.* in *Cambden* aforeſaid) the Second, were all but one Perſon: For he that was *Steward* to King *Henry* the firſt, and was after made Earl of *Norfolk* by King *Stephen*, was the ſame Perſon that lived in.

in the time of King *Henry* II, and that took Part with the young *King* against his *Father*. *Brook's Errors*, 1. 54. The Truth of which, *Cambden* himself afterwards tacitly acknowledged, by correcting himself in the next Edition of his *Brit.* 1600. *p.* 429. and the same continues in the *English Edit. Anno* 1695. *p.* 393. But to proceed with this our *Hugh* Son of *Roger Bigod* Founder of the *Priory* of *Thetford*, A. D. 1103. by *Adeliza* his Wife, Daughter and Coheir to *Hugh Grentismaisnel*, *Grentmaisnil*, or *Grentmesnell* Lord *Steward* of *England*, *Brook*'s *Cat.* 152. which is transcrib'd in *Vincent*'s *Dis.* 338. but without Correction; whereas the Right Reverend *Bishop Kennet* hath authentically proved, as I have before quoted him, that the eldest Daughter of the said *Hugh Grentesmaisnell* by *Adeliza* or *Adelidis* his Wife, was *Adeline* the Wife of *Roger de Ivoris* or *Ivori*, whose Daughter *Adeliza* was Wife to *Alberic de Ver*, Junr. *Paroch. Antiq.* 57. 62. 71. 72. 74. 81. and 82. Which *Alberic* was Father of *Juliana* the Wife of *Hugh Bigot*, as I have already shew'd. He in Right of his said Wife I take to be the third *Lord* of this *Manor* after the *Conquest*. He proved by Oath before the *Archbishop* of *Canterbury*, that whilst the *King* (i. e. *Hen.* I.) was beyond the Seas, the King by his own Mouth, pronounced the Disinheritance of *Maud* the *Empress*, and appointed *Stephen* to succeed, *Mill's Cat.* 500. for which he by that *King* is made *Earl* of the *East-Angles*, and *Steward* of his *Houshold*, in the 6th Year of his *Reign*; was one of the Witnesses to that King's Laws in the tenth Year of that King; and in his eighteenth Year he held out the *Castle* of *Ipswich* for *Henry* Duke of *Normandy*, but not being reliev'd was oblig'd to surrender it to King *Stephen*, *Mills*'s *Cat.* 90. Upon that great Defection of *Jeoffry Magnaville Earl* of *Essex*, he was of his Party. *Peerage*, Vol. II. 231. Upon the Report that King *Stephen* was dead, he entred *Norwich Castle* and held it maugre the *King*, *Mills*'s *Cat.* 16. King *Henry* II. coming to the Crown, this *Hugh* rendred his *Castles* into the *King*'s Hands, who in the twelfth Year of his Reign, anew advanced him to the Dignity and Title of Earl of

Norfolk,

Norfolk, with a Grant of the Office of *Steward*, to hold as amply as *Roger* his Father did, *Peerage*, Vol. II. *p.* 231. King *Henry* having made his Son *Henry* Partner with him in the *Royal Title*, this Earl *Hugh*, notwithftanding all the Favours he had received from the old *King*, joined with *Robert* Earl of *Leicefter*, receiving him with his *Flemings* in his Caftle of *Framingham* in his rebellious Infurrection on the behalf of the young King, having (upon the Summons of *Lewis* King of *France)* fworn to affift him ; for which Service, faith *Mills*, he beftow'd upon him the Honour of *Eye* and Cuftody of the Caftle of *Norwich*, *Tyrrell's Hift*. 2. *p.* 380.

382. which according to *Cambden* he is thought to rebuild, and likewife joining the Forces brought over by *Ralph de la Haye*, they marched to *Norwich* which they fet on Fire; but the old King prevailing and befieging *Anno* 1174. *Framingham Caftle*, in which was this Earl *Hugh* with a ftrong Garrifon of *Flemings*, he upon the 25th of *Auguft* came out to the *King*, with whom he made his Peace, by delivering up his Caftles of *Framingham* and *Bungey* (having with much Difficulty obtain'd leave for the *Flemings* therein to return home) which laft he had fo ftrongly fortified, that he was wont to boaft:

Were J in my Caftle of Bungey
Upon the River of Wabeney
J would ne care for the King of Cockeney.

This Earl *Hugh* had two Wives, the firft of which (as I faid before) was *Juliana*, by whom he had only *Roger* which fucceeded him ; his fecond Wife was *Gunderd* by whom he had two Sons, *Hugh* and *William*, *Mill's Cat.* 501. *York.* 204. He died *Anno* 1177. and was buried in

the *Priory* of St. *Bennet's* in *Thetford*, which he founded according to *Cambden*, who is therein followed by *Weaver*, *p.* 828. and by the Editors of *Magna Britannia*, &c. Vol. III. *p.* 338. but according to *Ordericus Vitalis*, Lib. II. *Roger Bigod*, *Sewer* to King *Henry* I. the Father of
this

this *Hugh*, was the firſt Founder, whom *Dugdale Mon. Ang.* 1. *p.* 664. and *Stow* do follow; the Epitaph for the ſaid *Hugh* I ſhall here tranſcribe from *Weaver, p.* 829. Orate pro anima religiofiſſimi biri Hugonis Bigod Fundatoris hujus Mona-ſterij, Seneſchalli Hoſpitij Po-tentiſſimo Principi Henrico Conqueſtoris filio, Angliæ Regi, et Comes Norfolciæ, qui quidem Hugo obijt pridie Ka-lend. Martij anno mileſimo, centeſimo, ſeptuageſimo octavo. Propter miſericordiam Jeſu requieſcat in pace. The Foun-dation Charter of this *Monaſtery* is given by *Cambden* as follows, *Brit. p.* 384. *I* Hugh Bigod, *Steward to King* Henry, *by his Conſent and the Advice of* Her-bert *Biſhop of* Norwich, *placed Cluniac-Monks in the Church of St.* Mary, *lately the Epiſcopal See of* Thetford ; *which I gave them, and afterwards founded them an-other more convenient without the Village.* Cambden quotes no Au-thority for this *Charter,* nor doth *Weaver* for the Epitaph, which inclines me to think the *Charter* produced by *Dugdale* to be the moſt authentick, which *Charter* I ſhall reſerve for the

Appendix, to which I ſhall add the *Charter* of *Confirmation,* made by *William Bigot Sewer* to the *King,* whom from his large Conceſſions to this Mona-ſtery, I take to be eldeſt Son to *Roger ;* as likewiſe that of King *Henry* I. all which prove *Roger* the *Founder,* to which, let me add, that this Houſe being founded *Anno* 1103. as is teſti-fied by the Annals of *Norwich* in the *Cotton Library,* which was in the Life-time of *Roger,* if the ſaid *Hugh* founded it, he muſt be then a very young Man, he living to the Year 1177. which was ſeventy four Years after, nor could he be then poſ-ſeſs'd of theſe Lands his Father then being alive, as was like-wiſe *William* his Brother, who injoying his Father's Eſtate con-firm'd his *Donations:* To cor-roborate which, I ſhall tran-ſcribe from *Weaver* as follows, from *Ordericus Vitalis,* Eccleſiaſt. Hiſt. Lib. II. *Anno* 1107. *Opti-mates Angliæ* Richardus de Rad-varijs, *&* Rogerus *cognominato* Bigotus, *mortui ſunt, & in Mo-naſterijs Monachorum ſepulti ſunt, quæ in proprijs poſſeſſionibus ipſi condiderunt.* Rogerus *autem apud* Thetfordum *in* Anglia, Richar-dus

dus *vero tumulatus apud* Montis-
burgum *in* Normannia. *Super*

Rogerium Cluniacenfes Alonax
ditale fcripferunt Epitaphium;

Clauderis exiguo Rogere Bigote Sepulchro
Et rerum cedit portio parva tibi.
Divitiae, fanguis, facundia, gratia Regum
Intercunt, mortem fallere nemo poteff.
Divitiae mentes fubvertunt, erigat ergo
Te pietas, virtus, confiliumque Dei.
Soli moerebat virgo ter noxibus oxo,
Cum folvis morti debita morte tua.

All therefore that can be fuppofed to reconcile thefe contradictory Accounts feem only this,
that *Roger Bigot* founded this
Cluniac Monaftry in the *Church*
of St. *Mary*, which was confirm'd by *William* his eldeft Son,
after whofe Deceafe *Hugh* Earl
of *Eaft Anglia* his younger Son,
remov'd it to a more convenient Houfe without the Village,
which he founded for them;
and it is probable he likewife
then altered the *Dedication*, for
Tanner in his *Not. Mon.* 149.
writes, that it was built to the
Honour of St. *Mary* and St. *Andrew*, when in the *Charter* of
Roger Bigot, it is faid to be to
St. *Mary*, St. *Peter*, and St. *Paul*.

Weaver alfo mentions a *Priory*
of *Black Canons* dedicated to St.
Mary and St. *John*, to be found-

ed at *Thetford* by one of the *Bigots* Earls of *Norfolk*, but without mentioning which (valued
at the Suppreffion 49. 18. 1.) but
I rather think he is under a Miftake therein; for I find in *Tanner* 151. a *Priory* of *Canons regular* of the Order of the *Holy
Sepulcher*, founded by *William*
Earl of *Warren*, endowed with
the fame Sum according to *Speed*:
And I believe likewife to be the
fame with this laft mention'd,
another *Religious Houfe* in this
Town of *Thetford* for *Friers
Preachers*, founded by *Henry*
Duke of *Lancafter*, valued at
the Suppreffion at 39 : 6 : 9
which Sum wanting but one
Penny the laft mention'd *Canons* is
by *Dugdale* faid to be valued at.

Nor can I think the *Auguftine
Friers* of this Town mention'd
alfo

S

III. This *Roger* [d] had by *Ida* his Wife a Son nam'd *Hugh Bigod,* Earl of *Norfolk,* who in the Reign of *Henry*

alfo by *Weaver,* was different from that of the *Cluniac Monks* aforemention'd, their Values according to *Weaver* and *Dugdale,* differing but one Shilling. The Author of the *Peerage* faith, that he went into the *Holy Land* with the Earl of *Flanders,* and died there; whereupon the *King* feiz'd upon his Treafure, *Peerage,* 2. 130. *Baker* reckons him among the military Men of Note, 1. 82.

The Arms of this *Hugh Bigot* are according to *Cambd. Brit.* 387. *A Lion falient,* the fame is quoted by *Gibfon Introd.* 59. *Mills Gul. A Lion paffant Or, p.* 500. *Or a Crofs Gul.* 204. the fame doth *Brook, p.* 252. and *Vincent,* 134.

[d] *Roger* the Son of *Hugh* by *Juliana de Vere,* was after the Death of his *Father* the fecond Earl of *Norfolk,* and fourth Lord of this *Manor* after the *Conqueft.* He was by King *Richard* I. anew conftituted Earl of *Norfolk,* and *Steward* of his *Houfhold,* as likewife one of his *Ambaffadors* to *Philip* King of *France,* for obtaining

2

Aid towards Recovery of the *Holy Land:* In the third of the fame *King* he was one of the Sureties for *Richard* Bifhop of *Ely,* and *Prince John.* In the fixth of the faid *King,* he was at the great Council of *Nottingham;* and at the fecond *Coronation* of that *King,* was one of the four *Earls* that fupported the *Canopy. Peerage,* 2. 231. In the fecond Year of King *John,* he was fent with *Philip* Bifhop of *Durham,* with Letters of *fafe Conduct* for *William* King of *Scotland,* to come to *Lincoln* and do his Homage. In the fifteenth Year, he accompanied the *King* into *Poictou, Dugd. Bar.* 1. 133. He was one of the great Men who in *Eafter* Week 1215. met at *Stamford,* and afterwards at *Brackley* to demand a Reftitution of the *ancient Rights, Cuftoms* and *Privileges* of the *Kingdom,* upon which a *Treaty* was fet on foot in *Runnemead* between *Windfor* and *Stains,* where the *King* grants their Demands, and twenty five Perfons are appointed

Henry III. *married Magdalen* (or *Maud*) eldeſt Daughter, and one of the Heirs of *William Mareſhall*

pointed to ſee theſe *Laws* obſerv'd; but the *King* not obſerving them, and then procuring the *Pope* to *excommunicate* the *Barons*, was the Occaſion of much *Blood* and *Confuſion*, not only to the Country in general, but had like to have been ſo to the *Barons* themſelves, from *Lewis* the *Dauphin*, whom they had call'd in to their Aſſiſtance; had not the Deſign been diſcover'd by the *Viſcount Melon*, a *French Nobleman* upon his Death-bed; whence Mr. *Tyrrell* obſerves, that it may ſerve as a laſting Warning, how the *Engglifh* ever call in too great a Number of *Foreigners*; eſpecially *French*, let their Neceſſities be never ſo urgent, &c. *Tyrrell's Hiſt.* 2. 801. How this Town of *Harwich* fared in this time of general Waſte and Deſolation, doth not in particular appear in *Hiſtory*, yet it may reaſonably be ſuppoſed; that it could not be altogether exempt, when *Ipſwich* and *Colcheſter*

their Neighbours felt ſo much. But to return to our Earl *Roger* by his Wife *Iſabella* Daughter of *Hamclyn*, natural Son of *Jeoffrey Plantagenet* Earl of *Anjou*, &c. half Brother to King *Henry* II. (as *Mills, p.* 503. and *Yorke, p.* 204. call her) he had three Sons, viz. *William*, who was drowned with King *Henry's* Children, *Hugh* that ſucceeded him and *Thomas*; and three Daughters, *Margaret* married to *William de Haſtings* the King's *Steward*, *Adeliza* or *Alice* married to *Alberic de Vere* Earl of *Oxford*, and *Mary* to *Ranulph Fitz-Robert* Lord *Middleham*. This *Roger* died the fifth of *Henry* III. *Anno Domini* 1218. and was buried in the Abby of *Thetford*. *Weaver, p.* 829.

His Arms the ſame as his Fathers, *viz. Or a Croſs Gul. Brook,* 152. *Vincent,* 339. *York,* 204. *Gul. a Lion paſſant Or. Mills,* 502.

Earl

Earl of *Pembrook*, by whom the Title of *Lord Mar-shall* of *England* accrued to the Family [c].

IV. To

[c] I now come to *Hugh* the second (Son of the aforesaid *Roger* by *Ida* or *Isabel* his Wife) third Earl of *Norfolk* of the *Bigods*, and fifth Lord of this *Manor*; of whom I find little recorded in *History*, only that *Anno* 1223. he was with the King's *Army* in *Wales*. *Peerage*, 2. 232. It is likely he might accompany his Brother-in-law *William* Earl of *Pembroke* in that Expedition. He married *Maud* eldeſt Daughter to *William Mar-shall* the elder Earl of *Pembroke*, *Marshall* of *England*, by whom he had three Sons, *Roger*, *Hugh*, and *Ralph*; and dying of the Plague in *London* Anno 1225. was buried in the Abby of *Thet-ford*; upon whoſe Death King *Henry* III. committed the *Ward-ship* of his Children to *William* Earl of *Salisbury*, *Dodſw*. MS. Vol. XL. *p*. 239. His Arms *Or a Croſs Gul*. *Brook*, 153. *Vincent*, 339. *York*, 205. *Gules a Lion paſſant Or*. *Mills*, 504.

Mr. *Mills*, *p*. 504. affirms, *That he had ſeen a Charter of*

this Hugh*'s, ſign'd and ſealed, unto which was affix'd a Seal of a Lion paſſant upon the ſame, as proper to the Family of* Bigots. Which *Brook*, *p*. 153. contradicts, greatly marvelling at it, becauſe that both the ſaid *Hugh*, and *Roger* his Father did uſe to bear in their Shields and Seals, *a plain Croſs*, which is graven in Stone, and painted on the North-ſide of the Cathedral at *Weſtminſter*, in the time of *Henry* III. with many other Noblemens Arms who lived in that time. And further (adds he) I ſpeak of my own Know-ledge, that never any of this noble Family of *Bigots* did ever give other Coat of Arms, than *Gold a Croſs Gueulles*, before they married with the *Marſhal's* Daughter, and were *Marſhals* of *England*: This *Maud* accord-ing to *Tyrrell* did *Anno* 1246. bring the *Marſhalſhip* to this *Hugh* her *Husband*; but this muſt be a Miſtake, *Hugh* being dead above twenty Years before. She had for her ſecond Huſband *William*

IV. To *Hugh* fucceeded *Roger* his Son and Heir, Earl of *Norfolk*, and *Lord Marſhall*, he (9. *Hen*. III.) married *Iſabel* Sifter to *Alexander* King of *Scotland*. In thoſe unquiet times he was not conftant to any one Party; yet happen'd to be on the King's Part at the Battel of *Lewes*, where the King, Prince, and ſeveral Noblemen being taken he eſcap'd [f]. There

William Earl of *Warren* and *Surry*, by whom ſhe had one Son *John*, and a Daughter *Iſabel*, whom *York*, *p.* 205. makes to be Daughter to her firft Huſband *Hugh* Earl of *Norfolk*. She had for her third Huſband *Walter Dunſtanvile* Baron of *Caſtle-Cote*, and died *Anno* 1248. and was buried in the *Abby* of *Tintern* in *Wales*: Her four Sons carrying her to her Grave, *Dugd. Bar*. 1. 134. *Mills*, *p.* 505. faith, that ſhe died *Anno* 1248. and afterwards contradicts himſelf, *p.* 627. ſaying, that ſhe died *Anno* 1237. whether ſhe had *Dower* in this Manor doth not appear: She was call'd *Marſhaleſs* of *England*, and *Counteſs* of *Norfolk* and *Warren*.

[f] *Roger* Son of *Hugh Bigod*, by *Maud*, *Matilda* or *Magdalen*, was fourth Earl of *Norfolk* of this Family, and fixth Lord of

this *Manor*. He was Knighted by King *Henry* III. in the ſeventeenth Year of his Reign ; but ſoon after adhered to his Uncle *Richard Marſhall* Earl of *Pembroke* in his rebellious Actings. At a Tournement held at *Blyth* in the County of *Nottingham*, he behaved himſelf ſo bravely, that he was much taken Notice of 26. *Henry* III. He is reckon'd among thoſe Noblemen that behaved themſelves with Courage and Reſolution at the Battel of *Xaintes*. In the 28th of this King, he was one of the twelve choſen by Conſent of the *Clergy*, *Laity*, and *Barons* to conſider of what anſwer ſhould be given by the *Great Council* of the Nation, concerning the Aid then deſir'd by the *King*. *Tyrrell*'s *Hiſt.* 2. 926. In the 30th Year of King *Henry* III. he with other *Barons* repreſented to the *Pope* the Exactions

2

actions and Oppreffions of the *Romiſh Yoak* and required Remedy. Obtain'd the Office of *Marſhall* in right of *Maud* his Mother, ſhe being the eldeſt of the five Coheirs of *Walter* Earl of *Pembroke* (who died *Dec.* 4. *Anno* 1245.) ſhe firſt ſolemnly receiving the *Marſhall's Rod* from the *King*, deliver'd it to her Son: So that *Tyrrell*, as I ſaid before, did miſtake the *Perſon* of the *Bigod* Family firſt inveſted with the *Marſhall's Office*. In the thirty ſecond Year of this King he was preſent in *Weſtminſter Hall*, when the Violators of the *Two Charters* were ſolemnly *excommunicated* with *Bell, Book*, and *Candle. Tyrrell's Hiſt.* 2. 963. And *Anno* 38. *Hen.* III. was one of the *King's* two *Commiſſioners* from *Gaſcoigny* to declare his Deſires to the *Parliament* relating to an Aid, id. *p.* 966. The next Year apologizing for *Robert de Roſs* a Baron then charged with ſome Crime, the *King* gave him harſh Language and call'd him *Traytor*, whereat with a ſtern Aſpect he told him he lied, and that he never was nor would be ſo; adding, if you do nothing but what the Law warranteth, you can do no

harm; yes ſaith the *King*, I can threſh your Corn and ſell it; To which he replied, if you do, I will ſend you the Heads of the Threſhers: But this Heat was ſoon pacified, ſo that ſhortly after, he was with others ſent on an *Embaſſy* to the *King* of *France*. Peerage 232. This *Embaſſy* was to demand the Reſtitution of King *Henry's* Rights in *Normandy*, and other Parts of *France*, but return'd *re infecta. Tyrrell's Hiſt.* 2. 977. *Anno* 1258. he with his Brother *Hugh* were two of the twelve nominated by the *Barons*, that with twelve others nominated by the *King*, were to chooſe four Perſons who were to name the *King's Council*, of which four this Earl *Roger* and his Brother *Hugh* were two. *Tyrrell's Hiſt.* 2. 982. To perform which Duty the *King* commands them to proceed to their Nomination, *id.* 984. He was likewiſe with his *Brother* two of the eleven that ſign'd the Letter to the *Pope* againſt *Adomar Biſhop* elect of *Wincheſter*, and was afterwards a Witneſs to the *King's* Writ for electing four *Knights* to repreſent the *County* of *Huntington*, &c. *id.* 990. *Anno* 48. *Hen.* III.

was

There is a Record of the Pleas of the Crown at *Chemersford,* before *Gilbert de Preston,* &c. (Rot. 36. *penes Camerar. Scacc.*) 38. of *Henry* III. by way of Complaint: *Quod Homines Rogeri Comitis Marshall de Herewyz,* &c. *i. e.* That *Roger* Earl *Marshal* his Men of *Harwich,* bought by an old Meafure, and fold by a new one: Which being a Fault in them, yet fhews it was even in thofe elder-times a *Town* of *Trade.* This *Roger* was a Man of great Fame and Honour, and being at a Tournement 54. *Henry* III, (*Cambden* faith *Luxatis corporis articulis*) he died without Iffue, and was buried at *Thetford* ᵹ.   V. To

was one of thofe that undertook that the *King* fhould fubmit to the Determination of *Lewis* the *French King* concerning the Provifions of *Oxford:* And after the Battel of *Lewes* was conftituted Governor of *Oxford Caftle. Peerage* 2. 233. The Year after he was one of the *Peers* fummon'd to the *Parliament* at *London,* being in Arms againft the King, as faith Dr. *Brady, Anfwer to Petit. p.* 219. who being taken Prifoner at the Battel of *Lewes* aforemention'd, was committed to the Cuftody of the Earl of *Leicefter,* who carried him about with him at his Pleafure. *Tyr-*

rell's *Hift.* 2. 1025. He married *Ifabel* Sifter to *Alexander* King of *Scotland,* whom he put away, but receiv'd her again by Ecclefiaftical Cenfure. *Dugd.Bar.* 1. 135.

ᵹ *Wrefting* and *ftraining* his Joints in a *Tournement, Cambden*'s *Brit.* 393. *York* faith, that he died of a Bruife running at *Tilt. p.* 205. This *Roger* was according to *Weaver, p.* 829. likewife buried in the Monaftry of *Thetford,* if his laft Will and Teftament was perform'd, of which fo much as concerns that Purpofe, I fhall here tranfcribe from that Author.

In

In nomine Patris, & Filii, &
Spiritus Sancti, Amen. *Ego Ro-*
gerus Bigot · Comes Norfolcie
Marefchallus Anglie in bona pro-
fperitate conftitutus, condo Tefta-
mentum meum fub hac forma.
Imprimis, *commendo* animam
meam Chrifto, &c. *& corpus*
meum in Ecclefia beate Marie
Thetfordie fepeliendum, &c. *Da-*
tum apud Chefterford die Mercu-
rij proximo ante feftum Sancti
Bernabe Apoftoli, Anno Domini
Mcclviij.

He died, faith the fame Author,
about eleven Years after the making of his Will, without Iffue,
of a Bruife running at *Tilt, Anno*
1269.

His Arms *Party per pale Or*
and Vert a Lion rampant Gul.
Brook's Cat. 154. *Vincent's Difc.*
341. *York,* 205. *Kent's Banner,*
770. But by *Mills, p.* 506. *Gul.*
a Lion paffant Or, as is aforemention'd in his *Father's.*

Mr. *Brooks* having affirm'd,
p. 153. That upon this Family's
marrying with Marfhall's *Daugh-*
ter, and were Marfhalls *of* England, *they did affume a Coat us'd*

by William Marfhall *Earl of*
Pembroke, *and his Sons, (who*
were Marfhalls *of* England*) for*
the Office of Marfhall; *which*
was party per pale Or, and Vert,
a Lion rampant Gueulles: That
thefe laft mention'd Arms were
the Arms of the *Office of Mar-*
fhall of England, *Vincent, p.* 340.
thinks will hardly be prov'd.
Firft, *Unlefs it can be made ap-*
pear, that Arms have been appro-
priated anciently to Offices in this
Realm. Secondly, *Had it been*
the Arms of the Office of Marfhall,
the Seal thereof fhould only have
been us'd in matters concerning
the Office, or Marfhallfhip *and*
not in Donations, Covenants, *&c.*
Thirdly, Ifabel Marfhall *and the*
younger Daughters, could not have
us'd it as they did. Fourthly,
All who are defcended from the
Daughters of William Marfhall,
are not to bear it, if it was pecu-
liar to the Office. Fifthly, *Had*
it been appropriate to the Office,
the Marfhalls *of* England, *fuc-*
ceeding the Bigots, as the Mowbrays, Howards, *and others,*
would not have omitted it.

5. To

V. To him fucceeded *Roger le Bigod* (being then twenty five Years of Age) his Nephew Son to *Hugh Lord Chief Juſtice* of *England* [h].

[h] Made ſo according to *Baker's Chron.* 118. by publick Voice of *Parliament:* He was ſlain at the Battel of *Lewes, Camb. Brit.* 393. which is alſo affirm'd by *Mill's Cat.* 505. But the Editor of the *Peerage* of *England* ſaith, that he ſhamefully fled there, (the ſame alſo ſaith *Daniel's Hiſt. p.* 152. only he calls him *Marſhall*) and had his Lands ſeized by the Victorious *Barons,* till the *King* recovering all at the Battel of *Eveſham,* he return'd again *Peerage;* 2. 233. This ſeems confirm'd by *Tyrrel's Hiſt.* 2. 1024. But *Hugh Bigot,* ſaith he, with others he there mentions fled out of the *Battel* as far as *Pevenſey,* and thence paſſed over into *France;* and *p.* 1048. he ſaith, that *Hugh Bigot,* who a little before had landed in *Pembrokeſhire* with a ſtrong Party, joined him (Prince *Edward*). Now whether this *Hugh* was ſlain at the Battel of *Lewes,* or not, is no great matter ; but it plainly appears, that he died before his Brother *Ro-*

ger, becauſe upon his Death, his Son ſucceeded to the Title and Eſtate of his Uncle, and not, as the *Editor* of the *Peerage* hath(thro' Miſtake)affirm'd, that he ſucceeded his Father as Earl of *Norfolk* and Lord *Marſhall;* when it doth not appear that he ever had either of them.

This *Roger* eldeſt Son of *Hugh Bigot, Chief Juſtice of England* by *Joane* his Wife, Daughter of *Robert Burnell,* was, after the Death of his Uncle *Roger,* the fifth and laſt Earl of *Norfolk* of that Family, and ſeventh Lord of this *Mannor.* He married for his firſt Wife *Aliva* only Daughter and Heir of *Philip* Lord *Baſſet* Baron of *Wycomb,* and *Chief Juſtice* of *England,* and Widow of *Hugh le Spencer Chief Juſtice of England,* ſlain at the Battel of *Eveſham,* which *Philip* dying about St. *Andrew's* Day *Anno* 56. *Hen.* 3. 1271. the Mannors of *Kertlington, Chefield, Hunnington, Haſelee, Aſcot* and *Peryton,* moſt of which (if not all) in the County of *Oxford,*

T

King *Edward* I. intending a *War* upon *Gafcoign* propofed it to his *Lords*, but they refus'd unlefs the *King* went himfelf in Perfon, at which the *King* was offended, and urges this Earl of *Norfolk* in particular, who alfo refus'd ; and after fome hot Words between the King and him, he departed without Leave, and with the Earl of *Hereford* and feveral other *Barons* taking Arms; demanded the Confirmation of their *Grand-Charter*. The *King* who knew well how to make ufe of time, profecutes them not at prefent, but prudently yields to their Defires, and confirms (though with fome reluctancy) the two *Grand-Charters* of *Liberties* [i].

But

ford, paft to this Earl *Roger* in right of his faid Wife, *Kennet*'s *Antiquities, p.* 274. *Aliva* died in *April* Anno 9. *Edw.* I. and was buried in the *Abby* of *Thetford*. The following Year he was in the *Welch* Expedition, *Peerage* 2. 233. when *Leolin* and *David* his Brother made a Revolt from the *King*, which occafion'd the Death of thofe two *Princes*. In the twenty fecond of that King he obtain'd *Licenfe* to embattle his Houfe of *Bungey* in *Suffolk*, which whether it was diftinct from his *Caftle* there, Authors being filent, I rather think not.

[i] This Story about this Earl *Roger*'s Refufal to accompany the King into *Gafcoign*, being more fully fetforth by other Authors, I fhall here tranfcribe it, *Anno* 24. *Ed.* The *King* calls a *Parliament* at *Salisbury* (St. *Edmonds-bury* faith *Mills, p.* 508.) wherein he requires certain of the great *Lords* to go unto the Wars of *Gafcoign*: But they all making their Excufes, every Man for himfelf; the King in great Anger threatned they either fhould go, or he would give their Lands to others that fhould. To this *Humphry* Earl of *Hereford*, and this our Earl *Roger*

4

Roger made their Declaration, that if the *King* went in Perſon, they would attend him, otherwiſe not : But being urg'd again, This Earl *Roger* proteſted he would willingly go thither with the *King*, and march before him in the *Vantgard*, as by right of Inheritance he ought to do: But the King told him plainly, he ſhould go with any other, although himſelf went not in Perſon: I am not ſo bound, ſaid the Earl, neither ſhall I take that Journey without you: The King ſwore *by God, Sir Earl,* you ſhall go or hang: And I ſwear by the ſame Oath, I will neither go nor hang, ſaid the Earl; and ſo without taking his Leave departs. Soon after the two aforeſaid Earls aſſembled, many *Noblemen* and others their Friends, to the Number of thirty *Bannerets*, and with an Army of fifteen hundred Men, ſtand upon their own Guard. This Affair is more particularly related by *Tyrrell* from *Knyghton, Col.*2493. *viz.* That when each of the great Men or Barons of the Kingdom began to excuſe themſelves from Voyage, the King grew ſo very angry with them, that he plainly told them,

They either ſhould go, or elſe he would give their Lands to thoſe that would: At which Words many of them were provok'd. Then the Earl of *Norfolk*, Marſhal, and Earl of *Hereford*, Conſtable of *England*, excuſed themſelves, ſaying, *Their Offices obliged them by their Tenure only to attend the King when he went abroad in Perſon, which they were ready to do.* But when the King again urg'd the Earl Marſhal to go without him, he replied, *Sir, I am ready to attend your Perſon in the Front of the Army, as I am bound by Hereditary Right:* To which the King replied, *But you ſhall go with others, and that without me.* The Earl return'd, *I am not obliged to it, neither, Sir, will I go over without you.* The King thereupon (being put into a violent Paſſion) broke out into theſe Words, *By God, Sir Earl, you ſhall either go or hang:* To which he replied by the ſame Oath, *Sir King, I will neither go, nor will I hang ;* and ſo he departed without taking any Leave, and the Parliament was thereupon preſently broke up in Diſorder.

The Chronicle of *Norwich*, ſaith *Tyrrell*, is alſo very particular,

cular, in the Account of the Tranſactions of this Parliament, wherein it ſays, the Earl of *Norfolk*, Marſhal, and the Earl of *Hereford*, Conſtable, interpoſed themſelves, on the behalf of the *Community* or *general Body* of the *Realm* ; alledging, that neither they themſelves were obliged to perform their Offices at this time , nor were the King's Tenants *in Capite* bound by their Tenures to go over with the King, or perform any Service beyond Sea in that Expedition, for the following Reaſons. Firſt, *Becauſe it ſeems to the whole* Community, *that the Notice given by the King's Writs for this Expedition was not ſufficient, ſince they do not aſſign any Place whither they were to go, ſo as they might know how to make due Proviſion for this Voyage.* Secondly, *Becauſe it is commonly reported, that the King deſign'd to paſs over into* Flanders; *and if ſo, it ſeems to the whole* Community, *that they owe no Service to that Country; becauſe neither they themſelves, nor their Anceſtors or Predeceſſors, ever perform'd any military Service there.* Tyrrell's Hiſt. Vol. III. 107.

The ſaid two Earls when they return'd into their own Countries would not permit the King's Officers to take any *Wool, Leather*, or *Proviſions* contrary to Law, upon pain of their Lives. Theſe Noblemen were ſo incenſed at theſe and other Oppreſſions, that they reſolved to hold a ſeparate Aſſembly or Parliament in the Foreſt of *Wyre* in the Marches of *Wales*, to conſider how to prevent thoſe Extortions. *Tyrrell's Hiſt.* ib. 108.

When the King was ready to ſail, the *Archbiſhops, Biſhops, Earls, Barons* and *Commons* ſend him a Roll of the general Grievances of his Subjects: To which the King anſwered, that he could not alter any thing without the Advice of his *Council*, which were not then about him. *Dan. Hiſt.* 164, 165.

Anno 27. Edward I. The two Earls aforemention'd notwithſtanding their former Contempts attend the *King* into *Scotland*, and in the ſucceeding Year, in a *Parliament* held at *Weſtminſter*, the two Charters were confirm'd, *Dan. Hiſt.* 167. But adds *Tyrrell*, the Earls *Hereford* and *Norfolk* being diſcontented that

But in the thirtieth Year of his *Reign,* he reaſſumes his Reſentments (vid. *Baker's Chron. p.* 135.) of the ſtubborn Behaviour of his *Nobles* towards him in former times, and ſo terrified this *Earl,* that (as ſome write) to recover his Favour, he (*April* 12. 30. *Edward* I.) made the King his Heir in Poſſeſſion (*Dugd. Bar.* 1. 136.) And then in the *Abby* of St. *John* in *Colcheſter* deliver'd unto him the *Marſhall's Rod*; upon condition in caſe he ſhould have any Children it ſhould be reſtored to him again; as alſo to have one thouſand Pounds in Preſent, and one thouſand Pounds *per Annum* during Life [k]. He had two Wives, his firſt was
Alicia

that the King had done ſeveral things without their Privity, pretended their Horſes and Men were quite tired and worn out, took their Leaves at *Carliſle* and return'd home. *Tyrrell's Hiſt.* ib. 131.

[k] *Baker p.* 135. makes it the thirty ſecond, and *Daniel* the thirty third Year of King *Edward* I. *A. D.* 1346. when that King ſhewed his Reſentment, and the Surrender was made by this Earl *Roger.* Mr. *Cambden Brit. p.* 393. writes, that when the inſolent and ſtubborn Behaviour (of this *Roger*) had

thrown him under the Diſpleaſure of *Edward* I. he was forc'd to paſs over his Honours and almoſt his whole Eſtate to the *King,* for the Uſe of *Thomas de Brotherton,* the *King's* Son by *Margaret* Siſter to *Philip the Fair,* King of *France.* For ſo a Hiſtory has told us out of the *Library* of St. *Auguſtine's* in *Canterbury.* ' In the Year 1301. ' *Roger Bigod* Earl of *Norfolk,* ' made King *Edward* his Heir, ' and deliver'd up to him the ' *Marſhall's Rod,* upon this ' Condition, that if his Wife ' bore him any Children, all ' ſhould

4

Alicia [*Aliva* or *Adeliza*] Daughter and Heir to *Phi-lip Baſſet Juſtice* of *England:* And *Alicia* Daughter
to

' ſhould be return'd, and he
' ſhould hold it peaceably with-
' out any Contradiction on the
' *King*'s Part. And the *King*
' gave him one thouſand Pounds
' in Money, and a thouſand
' in Lands for Life, along with
' the Titles of *Marſhall* and
' *Earl*.' Sir *William Dugdale*,
Bar. 1. 136. faith, that upon the
aforeſaid Surrender, the *King*
regranted the *Earldom* and *Mar-ſhalſhip* to this *Roger* and the
Heirs of his Body, and paſſed
the Manors of *Dovercourt* in
Eſſex, &c. with divers other
Lands in *England* and *Wales*
unto him the ſaid *Roger* and
Alice his Wife, and to the Iſſue
of their Bodies lawfully begotten, and for lack of ſuch Iſſue
to remain to the *King* and his
Heirs. Some ſay, that this
Surrender was made through
Fear, his old Friend and *Alice*
the Earl of *Hereford* being dead,
and being thence unable to accompliſh his Purpoſes, *Peerage*
2. 233. Others, as the *Annals of*
St. *Auguſtin Canterbury*, That

he did not care for his Brother:
He was adjudged to deliver over
into the *King*'s Hands all his
Lands in *England*, *Wales*, and
Ireland; to receive them again
with increaſe of a thouſand
Pound a Year, *Anno* 34. *Edw.* I.
Mills's *Cat.* 508. But the *Chro-nicle* of *Abingdon* in the *Cam-bridge* and *Bodleian Library*,
gives a different Account of this
Tranſaction, *viz.* That this
Earl having much exhauſted his
Eſtate by his taking part with
the Barons againſt the King,
had borrowed a great Sum of
Money from his ſaid Brother
John a rich dignified Clergyman,
and Rector of many Churches,
who now demanded ſpeedy Payment of his Brother, without
giving him any time to raiſe it;
which ſo extremely provoked
him, that he went immediately
to the King, and made over to
him all his Honours and Eſtate
as aforemention'd: And not that
it was done, as Dr. *Brady* affirms,
(from the ſingle Authority of
Matth. Weſtminſter) for a Cauſe
ſo

to *John de Anesine* Earl of *Bayonne*; this laſt he married the eighteenth of *Edward* I. and endowed her among many other *Lordſhips* with this of *Dovercourt*, and died the thirty fifth of *Edward* I. leaving his Lady *Alicia* a Widow, and his Brother *John* then aged forty Years his next Heir, againſt whom ſome ſay he had taken ſo great an Offence, that it cauſed him to make the former Settlement; which depriv'd him of the Enjoyment of either his Honour or Eſtate[1].

ſo unworthy the Generoſity of the King, as his calling him to an Account for an Action done ſo long before, and for which he had already received his *Charter* of *Pardon* under the *Great Seal*, and that too confirm'd by an *Act* of *Parliament, Anno* 25. *Edward* I. *Chap.* v. as follows, 𝕿𝖍𝖆𝖙 𝖙𝖍𝖊 𝕶𝖎𝖓𝖌 𝖕𝖆𝖗𝖉𝖔𝖓𝖘 𝖙𝖍𝖊 Conſtable, 𝖆𝖓𝖉 Earl Marſhal 𝖔𝖋 England, 𝖆𝖓𝖉 𝖆𝖑𝖑 𝖔𝖙𝖍𝖊𝖗𝖘 𝖈𝖔𝖓= 𝖈𝖊𝖗𝖓𝖊𝖉 𝖜𝖎𝖙𝖍 𝖙𝖍𝖊𝖒, 𝖙𝖍𝖆𝖙 𝖗𝖊𝖋𝖚𝖘𝖊𝖉 𝖌𝖔𝖎𝖓𝖌 𝖆𝖑𝖔𝖓𝖌 𝖜𝖎𝖙𝖍 𝖍𝖎𝖒 𝖎𝖓𝖙𝖔 Flanders, 𝖆𝖑𝖑 𝕺𝖋𝖋𝖊𝖓𝖈𝖊𝖘 𝖙𝖍𝖊𝖞 𝖍𝖆𝖉 𝖉𝖔𝖓𝖊 𝖆𝖌𝖆𝖎𝖓ſ𝖙 𝖍𝖎𝖒, 𝖙𝖔 𝖙𝖍𝖊 𝖒𝖆= 𝖐𝖎𝖓𝖌 𝖔𝖋 𝖙𝖍𝖎𝖘 𝖕𝖗𝖊ſ𝖊𝖓𝖙 𝕮𝖍𝖆𝖗𝖙𝖊𝖗, Stat. de Tillagio non concedendo. *Tyrrell's Hiſt.* 3. 212.

[1] He died *Anno* 1306. and was buried in the *Abby* of *Thetford* with *Aliva*, (not *Alicia)* his firſt Wife, *Weaver* 830. *Brock* and *Vincent* both ſay, that it was *Anno* 1305. that he died; and by an Inquiſition taken the thirty fifth of *Edward* I. *John Bigot* was found to be his Brother and Heir.

His Arms the ſame with thoſe of his Uncle, *viz. Party per pale Or, and Vert a Lion rampant Gul.*

His ſecond Wife *Alice* was Daughter to *John de Avenne* Earl of *Haynault, Mill's Cat. p.* 509. *York,* 206. She upon his Death was Lady of this *Manor,* but when ſhe died doth not appear.

Whatever

Whatever was the Occasion of this Settlement, we find, that *Edward* II. in the sixth Year of his *Reign* grants them to his Brother *Thomas of Brotherton*, first Son of *Edward* I. surnamed from a small Village in *Yorkshire* call'd *Brotherton* ; he was the eldest Son by a second *Venter*, viz. *Margaret* eldest Daughter of *Philip the Hardy*, and Sister to *Philip the Fair*, successively *Kings* of *France :* She was married to him in the sixtieth Year of his Age, and the eighteenth of her own [m].   In which *Grant* (v. *Rot. Pat. penes Camer. Scacc.*

[m] This *Thomas* was the eighth Lord of this *Manor*, his Father King *Edward* I. upon his Death-bed signified to *Prince Edward*, that he design'd to give this *Thomas* the Title of *Marshall:* In fulfillment of which, King *Edward* II. did upon the 16th Day of *December Anno* 6to *Regni* by *Charter* grant him all the Honours, Manors, &c. of *Roger Bigod* in these Words, *Thomæ de Brotherton fratri nostro charissimo, totum jus & honorem & dominium quæ* Rogerus le Bygod, *quondam Comes* Norff. *& Marescallus Angliæ habuit, nomine Comitis in comitatu* Norff. *& quæ ad manus celebris memoriæ domini* Edwardi *; quondam regis Angliæ patris no-stri per concessionem, redditionem, remissionem & quietam clama-tionem ejusdem* Com. *devenerunt,* &c. *habendum eidem* Thomæ *& hæredibus suis de corpore suo,* &c. except what *Alice* his Widow had.   And on the 10th of *February* in the ninth Year of the same Reign, he made him another *Grant* of the foresaid E-state in special Tail.   *Dugd. Bar.* 2. 63. by which the said *Edward* II. gave him the *Mare-shall's* Office in these Words : *Dilecto & fideli nostro* Thomæ de Brotherton *Comiti* Norfolk, *fra-tri nostro charissimo* Marescalciam Angliæ, *cum omnibus ad* Ma-rescalciam *illam pertinentibus. Habendum & Tenendum sibi & hæredibus*

Scacc. ch. de An. 6. Edw. II.) it is related: That thoſe Lands, *&c.* were made over to the *King* his *Father*, *per conceſſionem, redditionem, remiſſionem & quietam clamationem Rogeri Comitis,* viz. *Norfolk;* yet excepts the *Dowry* aſſign'd by his Father to *Alice* the Wife of the aforeſaid *Earl,* and in particular mentions *Dover-court* to be part of that Aſſignation.

Within ſix or ſeven Years after, thoſe Lands in *Dower* to the *Counteſs Alice* fell alſo into his Hands; for in the thirteenth of *Edward* II. he obtain'd the *Charter of Immunities* for *Harwich;* in which it is ſaid, that his Men and Tenants of the ſaid *Town,* &c. were made Free, *&c* [n].

---

hæredibus maſculis de corpore ſuo legitime procreatis, &c. *faciendo inde nobis & hæredibus noſtris ſervicia quæ progenitoribus noſtris inde debebantur, antiquam eadem* Mareſcalcia *ad manus Domini* Edwardi *quondam Regis* Angliæ patris *noſtri, per donationem & remiſſionem* Rogeri le Bygod *quondam*Comitis Norff.*&* Mareſcalli Angliæ *devenit,* &c. *Dat. per manum noſtrûm apud* Lincoln. 10. *die* Febr. *anno regni noſtri nono.*

[n] He was three times in the Wars of *Scotland, viz.* eleventh of *Edward* II. and the firſt and ſeventh of *Edward* III. and in the thirteenth Year of *Edward* II. obtain'd a *Licence* for a *Tueſday* Market for *Harwich;* and when the *Queen* with her Son *Prince Edward* landed at *Harwich,* he adher'd to her againſt the *King* his half Brother; then ſaid to be ſeduc'd by evil Counſellors. And in the firſt Year of King *Edward* III. obtain'd two Confirmations of all the Lands, of *Roger Bigod;* which were granted him before, *Peerage* 2. 234.

U

In the Minority of *Edward* III. he was appointed one of the *Governors* of the Kingdom. He deceas'd during his *Nephew's* Reign, *viz.* in the twelfth of *Edward* III. and was buried in the Abby of St. *Edmonds-bury* in the County of *Suffolk, Dugd. Bar. p. 64.* leaving Iffue by his fecond Wife ---- the Daughter of ------ *Edward* Earl of *Norfolk* his Son and Heir, and by *Alice* his firft Wife Daughter to Sir *Roger Halys* of *Harwich*, Knight; two Daughters *Margaret* and *Alice.* This *Edward* married *Beatrix* Daughter of *Roger Mortimer* Earl of *March*, and deceafing without Iffue left his Sifter *Margaret* Heirefs of his Eftate and Honour ◦. She was call'd *Margaret Marſhall*

◦ Thefe *Governors* were in Number twelve, but the *Queen* and *Roger* Lord *Mortimer* ufurp'd this Charge, *Dan.* 185. He had three *Wives*, the firft of which was *Anne* Daughter to a certain Knight, who dwelt near *Bougan*, by whom he had *Edward* that married *Beatrix* feventh Daughter of *Roger Mortimer* Earl of *March*, which *Edward* died before his Father leaving no Iffue, *Mill's Cat.* 511. His fecond Wife was *Avis* Daughter to Sir *Roger Halys* of *Harwich*, Knight, *York*, 206. *Vin-*

cent, 343. (but *Mills* and *Brooks* call her *Katherine*,) and by her he had two Daughters *Margaret* and *Alice.* His third Wife was *Mary*, (but her Parents Names not recorded) Relict to *William de Brus* Lord of *Brembre* and *Gower*, by whom he had a Son named *John*, who became a *Monk* of *Ely Abby:* Of whom no more mention being made, it is probable that he died before his Father. And after the Death of this *Thomas de Brotherton*, his Widow *Mary* married to *Ralph Cobham*, by whom fhe had

2

shall Countess of *Norfolk*, as appears in several *Court Rolls (in Com. Cist. hujus Burgi de An. 5. 6. & 8. Rich. 2.) by*

had a Son (call'd *John* of *Cobham)* who was call'd the Son of *Mary* the *Countess, Mills's Cat.* ib. *Sanford Lancaster Herald* writes, that he was Earl of *Suffolk* as well as *Norfolk*, for which he produceth two Deeds or Grants, one *Anno* 6. *Edw.* III. and the other the seventh of *Edw.* III. in both which Inftruments he is fo ftiled. The fame Author makes him to have but two Wives, *viz. Alice* Daughter of Sir *Roger Halys*, by whom he had his Iffue, and *Mary* Daughter of *William Lord Roos*, and Widow to *William* Lord *Brewes* of *Bember* and *Gower*, and after his Deceafe to Sir *Ralph Cobham*, Knight. She died 36. *Edw.* 3. *Alice Plantagenet* youngeft Daughter to this *Thomas de Brotherton*, was married to *Edward Montague*, and had Iffue *Joane* her only Daughter and Heir, born at *Bungey* in *Suffolk*, (not *Norfolk* as erroneoufly writ) and there baptized *Anno* 23. *Edw.* 3. She was Wife to *William de Ufford* afterwards Earl

of *Suffolk*, but fhe dying without Iffue *Anno* 5. *Richard* 2. her Aunt *Margaret* became her Heir, *Geneal. Hift. p.* 205. 206. The Efcheators Inquifition taken the thirty fixth of *Edward* III, after the Death of his Wife *Mary*, make her but his fecond Wife, which mentioning among other matters the Donation of the Manor and Caftle of *Framelingham* by his Brother *Edward* II. I fhall here tranfcribe it, as I find it; *Juratores dicunt quod Dominus* Edwardus *Pater Regis nunc dedit* Thomæ de Brotherton *fratri fuo, & hæredibus de corpore fuo Manerium & Caftrum* de Framelingham *in Comitatu* Suffolciæ, *&c. qui quidem* Thomas *defponfavit quandam* Aliciam, *de quâ procreavit duas filias & hæredes,* Margaretam *&* Aliciam, *quæ quidem* Margareta *defponfata eft* Waltero de Manny *& prædicta* Alicia *filia prædicti* Thomæ, *defponfata fuit* Edwardo de Monteacuto, *de quibus* Edwardo *&* Alicia, *exivit quædam* Johanna *filia & hæres ejufdem* Aliciæ *filiæ prædicti*

U 2

2.) by which alfo we find, that then the Profits of the *Court Leets* of *Harwich* and *Dovercourt* were farm'd out to *Darly Martyn* and *John Kriftian*. She married to *John de Segrave*, whofe *Surname* was taken up by his Anceftors from a Town in *Leicefter-fhire* fo call'd (where his principal Seat was) a Family of great Renown in that Age both for Juftice and Knighthood, who by this Match received no fmall Addition of Wealth and Honour ᵖ. But he dying the twenty feventh of *Edward* III.

prædicti Thomæ, *& defponfata eft* Willimo de Ufford. *Et prædicta* Alicia Uxor *prædicti* Thomæ *obijt*, *poft cujus mortem dictus* Thomas *defponfavit* Mariam de Brewes, *fecundam uxorem fuam*, &c. Vincent*'s* Difc. 344. The Arms of this *Thomas de Brotherton* were *Gul. three Lions paffant Guardant Or*, (being the Arms of his Father *Edward* I.) *a File with three Labels Argᵗ*.

ᵖ This *Margaret de Brotherton* was the ninth Owner of this *Manor*, but whether ever fhe invefted her *Husband* therewith doth not appear, that I can find. This *John de Seagrave*, was Son of *Steven de Seagrave* the Son of *John*, who had Summons to

Parliament from the fourteenth of *Edward* I, to the eighteenth of *Edward* II, which *Steven* dying about a Year before his Father, the *Honour* defcended to this *John* the Grand-fon, who having been retain'd to ferve the *King* in his Wars, had Summons to *Parliament* from the tenth of *Edward* III. to the twenty fifth, *Peerage* 2. 169. By *Juliana* his Mother, Grand-Child to Sir *John de Sandwich*, the Manor of *Folkftone* in *Kent* was brought into this Family, *Camb. Brit.* 209. *Brooks error.* 1. 35. At the Coronation of King *Richard* II, this *Margaret* claim'd the *Office* of *Marfhal of England*, by her Petition to *John of Gaunt* Duke of *Lancafter*, High *Steward* of the

ward III. left Iſſue *Elizabeth* his ſole Daughter and Heir; at that time married to *John* the Son of *John Lord Mowbray*, of an honourable Family, anciently deſcended

the Court of Claims, *viz. A tres honorable Seigneur* le Roy de Caſtele *&* de Leon. *Duc de* Lancaſtre *&* Seneſchall d'Engleterre, *ſupplie* Margarete *file & heire* Thomas *de* Brotherton *nadgairs Counte de* Norff. *&* Mareſcall d'Engleterre, *d'eſtre acceptée al Office de* Mareſcalcie, *ore al coronement noſtre Seigneur* le Roy, *come a (on droit heritage apres la mort le dit* Thomas *ſon piere, faſante l'Office per ſon depute, Come* Gilbert Mareſchall *Counte de Strogoile, fiſt, al coronement le Roy* Henr. ſecon. *Ceſtaſſauoir de peſer debatz en me ſon le Roy, au jour de coronement, & a faire liverée des herbergages, & de garder les oeſſes del chamber le Roy, pernant de cheſcun Baron & Counte faitz Chivaler a cel jour, un Palfrey, oue une ſelle,* Vinc. Diſc. 345.

To which ſhe was thus anſwer'd. *Quod Officium illud in perſona domini Regis in feodo remanſit, ad aſſignandum & contulendum cuicunque ipſi Regi place-*
2

ret, & ſuper hoc auditis tam pro domino Rege, quam pro præfata Comitiſſa, pluribus rationibus, & allegationibus in hac parte, pro eo quod videbatur curiæ, quod finalis diſcuſſio negotij prædicti propter temporis brevitatem, ante coronationem prædictam fieri non potuit, Henricus de Purcy *ex aſſenſu & præcepto ipſius Regis aſſignatus fuit ad officium prædictum faciendum, percipiendo feoda debita & conſueta, Salvo jure cujuſlibet, & ſic idem* Henricus *Officium illud perfecit,* Vinc. Diſc. 374. but by Reaſon of the ſhortneſs of time her Claim could not be diſcuſs'd: And though ſhe was call'd *Lady Marſhall,* yet could ſhe not obtain that *Office,* it being given to her Grandſon *John Lord Mowbray,* and after him to his *Brother Thomas;* ſhe had two *Husbands* by the firſt, viz. *John Lord Segrave,* ſhe had *Anne Abbeſs* of *Barking* in *Eſſex,* and *Elizabeth* Wife of *John Lord Mowbray:* By her ſecond Sir *Walter Manny,* Knight of the Garter, defcended from *William de Albino Brito*; as he from *Robert de Todeni* Lord of *Belvoir*, a noble *Norman*, who came in with *William the Conqueror*.

This *John* was at full Age in *Anno* 1326. when his Father died, and in the forty fecond of *Edward* III.

Garter, fhe had *Thomas*, who at ten Years of Age was drowned in a Well at *Deptford* in *Kent*, buried at *Chefterfield*, and *Anne* married to *John* Lord *Haftings* Earl of *Pembroke*. Sometime before her Death fhe exchang'd with the Monaftry of *Leifton* in *Suffolk* the Advowfon of the Church of *Theberton*, for the Advowfon of the Church of *Kirkeby*, the Reafons of which Exchange are mention'd in the following Charter: *Domina Margareta Comitiffa Norff. Monafterio de Leifton in Suff. dedit advocationem Ecclefiæ de Theberton, in efcambium pro advocatione Ecclefiæ de Kirkeby, pro animabus Thomæ de Brotherton nuper Comitis Norff. & Marefcalli Angliæ, & Dominæ Aliciæ nuper confortis ejus patris & matris dictæ dominæ Margaretæ, & pro animabus nobilium Dominorum Johannis de Segrave, & Walteri Manny, dudum Baronum ejufdem*

Margaretæ, ac etiam pro falubri ftatu dominæ Annæ Comitiffæ Pembrochiæ, filiæ dictæ dominæ Margaretæ, ac etiam domini Johannis Haftinges Comitis Pembrochiæ, filij dicti Dominæ Annæ quoad vixerint, & pro Animabus eorum cum ab hac luce migraverint, &c. Dat. *Anno* 6° *Ric.* 2. Vincent'*s* Difc. 344. *Margaret* Dutchefs of *Norfolk* died *March* 24. 1399. and was buried in the *Minories* at *London, Brooks p.* 156. having outlived her Daughter the Lady *Mowbray* divers Years: Yet *Stow* in his *Survey* of *London*, faith, that fhe was buried with her laft Hufband in the *Charter Houfe London, Weaver*, 433. *Sandford. Genealog. Hift.* 208. makes *Anne Abbefs* of *Barking* her youngeft Daughter. Her Arms the fame as her Father's: Impailing *Segrave fab. a Lion rampant Arg*. *crown'd Or.* *Sandford*, 207.

taking

taking a Journey to the *Holy-Land*, had the hard Fate to be flain near *Conflantinople*, leaving Iffue *John* his Son and Heir about four Years of Age. In the forty eighth of *Edward* III. this laft mention'd *John* had Licenfe to travel beyond Sea, fhortly after his Mother died, and he returning home was created Earl of *Nottingham* on the *Coronation* Day of *Richard* II. and died at *London* being under Age q.

To him fucceeded *Thomas* his Brother then aged feventeen Years, who, the fixth of *Richard* II. was alfo created Earl of *Nottingham*; and the ninth of *Richard* II. was for term of Life conftituted *Earl Mar-fhal* of *England*, by reafon of his Defcent from *Thomas*

q This *John Lord Mowbray* of *Axholme*, the Hufband of *Eli-zabeth de Segrave* was flain on the Feaft of St. *Dennis, Dugd. Bar.* 1. 128. on the Feaft of St. *Botolph's*, *Sanford*, *p.* 208. by him fhe had two Sons, viz. *John* created Earl of *Notting-ham* at the Coronation of King *Richard* II. *Anno* 1377. he died the *Tuefday* before *Valentine*, viz. 10 *February*, 6 *Richard* II. and was buried with the *Car-melite Friers* near *Fleet-ftreet*, *London*, Anno 1398. *Stow's Sur-vey* 438. Anno 1383. according to *Mills*, *p.* 512. and *Vinc. Difc.*

whofe Account is right. Whe-ther this *Earl* of *Nottingham*, or his Father, or Mother had ever Poffeffion of this *Manor* doth not appear; but on the contrary, *Margaret de Brother-ton* his *Grandmother* not only outliving them all, but as Mr. *Taylor* hath fhew'd was Lady of this *Manor*, in the fifth, fixth, and eighth of *Richard* II. which was about the time and after the Deceafe of her Daughter *Eliza-beth*, and Grandfon *John*. The Arms of *John* Earl of *Notting-ham*, *Gul. a Lion rampant Arg*. armed and languid *Or*.

of

of Brotherton, but in the twentieth of the fame *King*, he had a *Charter* of *Confirmation* of the Office of *Earl Marfhal* of *England* to the Heirs Male of his Body, *&c.* and for the *Enfigns* of their *Office*, that they might bare a golden *Truncheon* enamelled with *Black* at both Ends, having at the upper End of it, graven, the King's *Arms*, and at the lower End his own [r].

[r] This *Thomas Baron Mowbray* of *Axholme, Broafe, Bower* and *Seagrave*, Earl of *Nottingham* and *Marfhal*, was after the Death of his Grandmother *Margaret* the tenth *Lord* or Owner of this *Manor* from the *Conqueft*: He was afterwards made *Knight* of the *Garter*. He in his younger Years was in many Actions, as entring *Scotland* in a hoftile manner with the Earl of *Northumberland*; being at Sea with *Richard* Earl of *Arundel*, then *Admiral* when they took *Breft*: Made Governor of *Berwick* upon *Tweed*, and of the *Caftle* of *Merk* in *France*; Captain of *Calais* for Life, and afterwards the King's *Lieutenant* at *Calais, Picardy, Flanders* and *Artois, Peerage* 2. 268. He had two Wives, the first of which was *Elizabeth* Daughter and Heir to *John le Strange* of *Blackmore* in *Effex*, from his Manor Houfe there; which ftanding near a large Mere, from the blacknefs of the Water was call'd *Blackmere. Collins's Peerage*, Vol. II. Part II. *p.* 164. *Brook, p.* 156. and *Vincent*, 346. call him Lord *Strange: Ralph* his Father being fummon'd to Parliament from the fecond *Edw.* II. to the feventeenth inclufive, and with this *John* ended the Male Line, *Peerage*, ib. who died without Iffue on the 23[d] of *Auguft* A. D. 1383. *Dugd. Bar.* 1. 130. by reafon whereof all her Inheritance fell to *Ancharet Strange* her Aunt. *Sandford, p.* 211. But of her no mention is made either by *Mills* or *York*.

The

The next Year after (21 *Richard* II.) on *September* the 29th he created *Margaret* Daughter and Heir to *Thomas de Brotherton, Duchefs* of *Norfolk* for term of Life, her Grandfon *Thomas* (*Mowbray*) being the fame Day advanced to the Title of *Duke* of *Norfolk*, who out of Refpect to the Memory of this Match, forbore his own paternal Arms (*Afhmole's Order of the Garter, p. 718.*) which were *Gul. a Lion rampant Arg. arm'd and languid Az.* and gave the Arms of *Thomas of Brotherton* aforemention'd. He had no Iffue by his firft Wife *Elizabeth* Daughter and Heir to *John le Strange* of *Blackmere*; but by his fecond Wife *Elizabeth* alfo, Daughter of *Richard Fitz Allen* Earl of *Arundel*, Widow of *William Montacute* eldeft Son to *William* Earl of *Salisbury*, he had two Sons and two Daughters, *Thomas* and *John, Margaret* and *Ifabel.* What in Reafon could be more defir'd, than what he had already acquir'd; but fee, faith my Author, *Dugd. Bar.* 1. *p.* 130. how flippery all earthly Greatnefs is, whofe Foundation is laid in *Blood*; for being thus fet up with Honour and Riches he foon irrecoverably fell; and having run through many Changes and Troubles, fometimes out of the *King's* Favour, and other times immoderately in it; one while being *indicted* and *arrefted* for Treafon; and not long after we find him affifting, even at the Execution of his *Father-in-law* (the aforemention'd *Richard* Earl of

X *Arundel*[r];

Arundel^f; but the worſt is ſtill behind. *Richard* II. looking upon his Uncle *Thomas* of *Woodſtock* Duke of *Glouceſter* (a *Prince* of great Repute for his Valour and Wiſdom) to be too ſevere an Inſpector into and Obſerver of his Actions, cauſed him to be arreſted by this our *Duke* (as being *Earl Marſhal*) and hurried away

---

^f *Mills, p.* 514. names another Daughter of *Thomas* Duke of *Norfolk*, by *Elizabeth Fitz Allen* his Wife elder than either of the aforemention'd, *viz. Elizabeth* married to *Michael de la Pool* the younger Earl of *Norfolk:* But neither *Brook*, *Vincent*, nor *Sandford* make any mention of her here, but among the Earls of *Suffolk*, *Vincent, p.* 502. takes Notice of her, and of her three Daughters, viz. *Katharine, Elizabeth* and *Iſabel. Sandford* makes no mention of her. *Dugdale*, and from him Mr. *Taylor*, gives the Priority of Birth to *Iſabel*, but *Mills*, *Sandford* and *York* to *Margaret.*

The Earl of *Arundel* being apprehended by the Earls of *Rutland* and *Kent*, for ſuch Crimes as had before been pardon'd, which being revok'd by *Parliament*, though contrary to the Opinion of the *Judges* and *Lawyers*, is condemn'd by his *Peers*, of which this *Thomas* Earl of *Nottingham* his Son-inlaw was one, and on the *Towerhill* beheaded; at which this our Earl being preſent, his *Father-in-law* ſaid, *That truly it would have beſeemed you to be rather abſent, than here at this Buſineſs; but the time will come e're long, that as many ſhall marvel at your Misfortune, as they do now at mine, Baker*, 2. 19. He was buried in the *Auguſtine Friers* at *London*, *Mills*'s *Cat.* 652. He accompliſhed the Deſtruction of the Earl of *Arundel* his Father-in-law, and was one of the Chief that guarded him to his *Execution*; nay, ſome affirm, that he bound up his *Eyes* and *beheaded* him himſelf. *Peerage* 2. 268.

to *Calais,* where after fome fmall time, the *Duke of Gloucefter* was made away (and as fome fay) by *fmothering* t.
The

t The manner of this *Duke* of *Gloucefter's* Apprehenfion and Death, being more fully related by divers Authors, I fhall therefore here infert it. The Duke being at *Plefhey* in *Effex*, King *Richard* confulted with our Duke of *Norfolk*, then only Earl of *Nottingham*, how he might take him out of the way; the Plot being contriv'd, the *King* with our Earl rid into *Effex* as tho' they went on hunting, when they were in the Forreft, the Earl with a felected Troop ftayed behind, while the King with a fmall Train came to *Plefhey*, and was kindly entertain'd by the *Duke*, but pretending occafion of prefent Return, defir'd the Duke to accompany him to *London*; to which he confenting, they pleafantly rode together untill they came near the Place of the Earl's Ambufh, when the *King* fuddenly fetting Spurs to his Horfe galloped away; but the Duke following eafily was fuddenly intercepted, and with Violence hurried to

the *Thames* Side; and being blindfolded, was fhipped and carried to *Calais*, Truffel's Hift. 21. The Duke finding himfelf betray'd, call'd in vain for the *King's* Help. It was about eleven at Night, *Peerage* 2. 142. *Baker* 2. 18. faith, that the *Duke* was in Bed when the *King* came, but being inform'd of it caft his Cloak above his Shoulders, and came down with all Reverence to bid the *King* welcome, who requefted him to make himfelf ready, and ride with him a little way to confer on fome Bufinefs; which the Duke readily obey'd, and was arrefted by the *Earl Marfhal*. At *Calais* he was by the King's Order fmothered under a Feather-Bed *September* 8. *A. D.* 1397. by *William Serle,* - - - - *Franceis*, and others; who having declar'd to him the *King's* Command, that he fhould die, anfwer'd, *That if it were his* Soveraign's *Pleafure, he willingly fubmitted thereunto:* This appears upon the Examination of *John Hall*,

X 2
taken

The next Year after (in *Anno* 1398.) the Duke of *Hereford* charges our Duke of *Norfolk* for speaking disgraceful Words of the King, and before the King challenges him to the Combat ᵘ. The Day being come and the

taken in *Parliament* Anᵒ. 1. Hen. 4. who being privy to, though not active in the said Murther, was sentenced to be executed at *Tiburn*, and his Head sent to *Calais* where the Fact was done. The Body of the Duke of *Gloucester* was convey'd to *Pleshey*, and there buried with all Funeral Pomp in the College of *Canons Regular* by him there founded, in a goodly Sepulchre provided in his Life-time, but was afterwards remov'd to *Westminster* Abby, and there laid under a Marble inlaid with Brass, on the Floor, on the South Side of the Tomb of S. *Edward. Sandford's Geneal. Hist.* 231. In whose time, *viz.* A. D. 1677. part of the Epitaph in old *French* was to be seen, but, I presume, now gone, because in the Antiquities of St. *Peter's* Anno 1711. it is omitted. *Sandford* writes, that this *Thomas* Duke of *Gloucester* was ap-

prehended in the base Court of *Pleshey*, *p.* 217.

ᵘ Most of our *Historians* and Antiquaries following *Polydore Virgil*, make the accused the Accuser, contrary to what Mr. *Taylor* in this Place, and the Editor of the *Peerage* 2. 235. have affirm'd, which being sum'd up in a narrow Compass by *Mills* and some others, I shall here give it, *viz. Henry* Duke of *Hereford*, Son of *John* of *Gaunt* great Duke of *Lancaster*, one Day by chance conferring with *Thomas* Duke of *Norfolk*, made many Complaints to him of the King, all which the said *Thomas* misunderstanding, and watching Opportunity (as commonly Flatterers do) discover'd the matter to King *Richard* (*Martyn, p.* 154. writes, that he related what the Duke of *Hereford* had said, in the rudest and most uncivil manner he could devise; adding many Untruths never spoken: And

the Lifts prepared upon *Gosford-Green* at *Coventry*, comes our Duke on a barb'd Horfe covered with Crimfon Velvet, embroider'd with Lions of Silver and Mulberry-trees, *&c.* (He made ufe of Silver Lions as properly belonging to the Arms of the *Mowbrays*, and the *Mulberry-trees* as alluding to his Name) Both the Dukes in great Pomp having entred the *Lifts*, and both with their Spears in their Refts ready to fet forward, the *King* prohibits the Combat u ²; banifhing
Henry

And *Truffel, p.* 24. That to exaggerate the matter, he intermixed with fome Truths many Lies, thereby making the Truth feem worfe than it was.) The *King* being thereat moved call'd Duke *Henry* before him, who ftiffly denied theAccufation, pronouncing himfelf not guilty, and that by Arms he would retort the Fault upon the Accufer's Head, if his Majefty would grant him leave. On the contrary *Norfolk* maintain'd whathe had before affirm'd: In the Heat of this Contention the Day was affign'd, wherein the Combat fhould be tried, *Mills's Cat.* 513.
  u ² The Account of this intended Battel given by Mr. *Taylor* being very fhort, as is like-

wife the Record thereof as aforecited, it may not be unpleafant to the Reader if I in this Place infert the chief Circumftances of this Combat, fince it will fhew the great State and Formality that was us'd in that ancient way of *Trial by Battel*.
  The King and all the Lords being arrived at *Coventry*, each of the Lords who were to be the Combatants, being attended with a fplendid and numerous Retinue, appear'd on the Day appointed; the Duke of *Albemarl* was *pro Tempore* made *High Conftable*, and the Duke of *Surry Lord Marfhal*, who came to the Lifts moft honourably waited on by many Followers in rich Liveries, fuitable to the Greatnefs

Henry Duke of *Hereford* (afterwards King *Henry* IV.) for ten Years, and this our Duke during Life, forbidding

nefs of their Quality, each of their Servants carrying Tipftaves for clearing the Field.

There the Duke of *Hereford* as Challenger, firft mounted on a *White Courfer*, (in Caparifons of *green* and *blue Velvet*, embroider'd thick with *Swans* and *Antelopes*,) arm'd *Cap-a-pee* with his Sword drawn approach'd the *Lifts*, of whom the *Marfhal*, demanding *who he was*, receiv'd this Anfwer. *I am* Henry *of* Lancafter *Duke of* Hereford, *that am come hither to my* Devoir, *againft* Thomas Mowbray *Duke of* Norfolk, *as a falfe Traitor to God, the King, the Realm, and me*; and then taking his Oath that this Quarrel was true and juft, defired Leave to enter the *Lifts*; which being granted, he put up his Sword, pulled down his *Beaver*, fign'd himfelf on the Forehead with the Crofs, took his Spear, and paffing the Barriers, difmounted, and fat down in a Chair of *green Velvet*, plac'd in *Travers* of *green* and *blue Velvet* at one End of the *Lifts*.

Then King *Richard* enter'd the Field with great Pomp, accompanied with the Earl of St. *Paül*, (who came out of *France* on purpofe to be a Spectator of this Combat;) and attended with moft of the Nobles of *England*, and a Guard of ten thoufand Men in Arms, to prevent any fudden Tumult or Diforder. His Majefty being feated in a Chair of State, one of the King's at Arms made Proclamation, that none but fuch as were appointed to marfhal the Field, fhould touch any part of the Lifts upon pain of Death; which being ended, another Herald proclaim'd; *Behold here*, Henry *of* Lancafter *Duke of* Hereford, Appellant, *who is enter'd into the Lifts, to do his* Devoir *againft* Thomas Mowbray *Duke of* Norfolk, *upon pain of being counted falfe and recreant.*

Immediately upon this, appear'd the Duke of *Norfolk*, bravely mounted, his Horfe barb'd with *Crimfon Velvet*, embroider'd with *Lions of Silver*, and

2

and *Mulberry Trees* proper, and having taken the like Oath before the *Conftable* and *Marfhal*, that his Quarrel was right and juft, he enter'd the Field, crying aloud, *God aid the right*; and then lighted from his Horfe, plac'd himfelf in a Chair of *Crimfon Velvet*, oppofite to his Antagonift, at the other End of the *Lifts*; the *Marfhal* view'd their Spears, to fee that they were of equal length, and then he delivered one of them to the Duke of *Hereford*, and fent the other by a Knight to the Duke of *Norfolk*. This done, *Proclamation* was made for them to prepare for the Combat. Upon which, the Dukes inftantly mounted their Horfes, clofed their *Beavers*, cafting their Spears into their Refts, and then the Trumpets founding, the Duke of *Hereford* fpur'd his Horfe forward, but before he of *Norfolk* could advance, the King caft down his *Warder*, and the Heralds cried *ftay, ftay*. Then the King caufing their Spears to be taken from them, they return'd to their Chairs, whilft he retir'd to Council, to debate what was fit to be done in fo weighty a Caufe. Where after two

Hours Debate, their Doom was agreed upon without Fighting; and one Sir *John Bouray*, by the King's Command, after Silence was made, read their Sentence, which was thus. *That forafmuch as the Dukes* Appellant *and* Defendant *had honourably appear'd in the* Lift-Royal, *and were not only ready, but forward to entertain the Combat; therefore it being an Affair of great Confequence, for avoiding the effufion of* Chriftian Blood, *the King by the Advice of his Council had decreed, that* Henry *Duke of* Hereford *fhould within fifteen Days depart the Realm, not to return within the Space of ten Years, on pain of Death, without the King's fpecial Licenfe.* And after a fecond Proclamation, *Sentence of* Banifhment *was alfo read againft the Duke of* Norfolk, *but with thefe* feveral Aggravations. Firft, *That the fame was for Life*; Secondly, *That the Caufe thereof was exprefs'd to be, for having uttered feditiousWords, whereof he could not clear himfelf*; and Thirdly, it was added, as part of his further Punifhment, *That the King fhould receive the Revenues of his Lands, untill he was fatisfied all fuch Sums*

of

ding any Perfon whatfoever, under grievous Penalties, to intercede for either of them *w*.   It was believed our Duke

of Money, as the faid Duke had taken out of the King's Coffers, on pretence of paying the Garrifon of Calais.

Then another Proclamation was made, that no Perfon from thenceforth fhould prefume to petition or intercede, with the King on the behalf of either of the faid Dukes, to alter this Sentence, on pain of his Majefty's high Difpleafure; which being fo declared, the King call'd them before him, and took of them a folemn Oath, that they fhould never converfe together beyond the Seas, nor willingly come into each other's Company. *Tyrrell's Hift.* Vol. III. Part. II. *p.* 985.

w Mills faith, that the *King* confidering that it was only Words (if any fuch had been fpoken) was advifed by his Council to forbid the Combat, and feeing there was no certain Proof in whom the Fault refted, and that neither might be held free, were both *banifh'd:* but *Martyn* writes, that the Secre-

tary pronounc'd the Decree of Banifhment againft the Duke of *Norfolk,* for that he had us'd feditious Words, of which he could produce no Proof. He travelling into *Italy,* and thence to *Venice,* died there with Grief, and was buried in the Abby of St. *George* in that City, *Sandford,* 210.

A different Account from the foregoing is related by Mr. *Tyrrell,* which being taken from the *Pleas of the Crown in Parliament* Anno 21. *Ric.* 2. I fhall, as being the moft authentick, here tranfcribe, *viz.* That on *Wednefday* the 30th of *January* (being the Day before the Parliament ended) *Henry* of *Lancafter* Duke of *Hereford* came before the King with the *Schedule* in his Hand, and faid thus: That he had already come by his Command into his Prefence at *Haywode,* where he had inform'd him that *Thomas Mowbray* Duke of *Norfolk* had fpoken many difhoneft Words in Slander of his Royal Perfon, and that they were

2

Duke had a Hand in that execrable Murther of *Thomas* Duke of *Gloucefter*, and obferv'd, that this Sentence paffed

were fpoken to him the Duke, and then the King charged him upon his Allegiance, that he fhould truly repeat the Words as they were fpoken. Upon this, the Duke of *Hereford*, not through Malice, or any other Caufe, but only to obey the King's Command, as he was bound, had now fet down in Writing the Words which the Duke of *Norfolk* fpake to him, as before he had conceived and born them in his Memory, and were in this *Schedule*, which he deliver'd to the King with *Proteftation* to add or to diminifh therefrom at all times, and when he pleafed, as it fhall be needful, *faving* always the Subftance of the prefent *Schedule*, which was to this Effect.

That the Month of December, *in the twenty firft Year of your Reign, the Duke of* Hereford *travelling between* Brainford *and* London, *met the Duke of* Norfolk *with a great Train, and difcourfed with him of divers matters; amongft which he told him,*

they were all ready to be undone; and the Duke of Hereford *demanded why? He anfwer'd, for the Fact at* Radoot-Bridge [That was when the Duke of *Ireland* was routed and ran away] *The Duke of* Hereford *faid, how can that be? For the King hath fhewn us Favour, and declared us in Parliament to have been good and loyal towards him. The Duke of* Norfolk *anfwer'd, notwithftanding that, it will be done to us as it has been done to others before, for he will vacuate this Record. The Duke of* Hereford *replied, this would be a great Wonder, fince the King had faid it before all the People, that he fhould afterwards make it to be annulled. And further, the Duke of* Norfolk *faid, this was a marvellous World, and unfafe; for I know well, faid he, that if my Lord your* Father *and you had been taken, or kill'd, when you came to* Windfor *after the Parliament was up, that the Dukes of* Albemarle, *and* Exeter, *the Earl of* Worcefter, *and himfelf were agreed, never to undo any*

Y

Lord

paſſed upon him that very Day twelve Month after, whereon he cauſed the Duke to be ſmother'd at *Calais*.

He

Lord without juſt and reaſonable Cauſe, and that the Malice of this Fact was in the Duke of Surrey, *with the Earls of* Wiltſhire *and* Saliſbury, *drawing to them the Earl of* Glouceſter, *who had ſworn to undo ſix other Lords, that is to ſay, the Dukes of* Lancaſter, Hereford, Albermarle, *and* Exeter; *with the Marquiſs of* Dorſet, *and himſelf. He alſo ſaid, they propoſed to reverſe the Judgment of Earl* Thomas *of* Lancaſter, *and hereby we and many others ſhould be diſinherited. The Duke of* Hereford *ſaid, God forbid, for it would be a great Wonder if the King ſhould aſſent to this, for it was with a chearful Countenance, that he promis'd to be a good Lord to them, and others; and alſo that he knew he had ſworn it by St.* Edward; *and the Duke of* Norfolk *anſwer'd, He had done the ſame to him many times, and ſworn by the* Body *of* God, *and that for all this he was never the more to be truſted; and further ſaid to the Duke of* Hereford, *that the King was about to*

draw the Earl of Marche *and others to the ſame Agreement and Purpoſe of the ſaid four Lords to deſtroy the reſt aforeſaid. The Duke of* Hereford *replied, if he be ſo, we can never truſt them. The Duke of* Norfolk *return'd, for certain not; for although they cannot accompliſh their Deſign at preſent, yet they will be contriving ten Years from this to deſtroy us in our Houſes.*

The *Schedule* being read before the King and Lords on *Thurſday* the thirty firſt of *January* (and laſt Day of the Parliament) it was then ordain'd by him, with the Aſſent of all the Eſtates in Parliament, that the matters therein compriz'd ſhould be determin'd and ended by the good Advice and Diſcretion of the King, and the Commiſſioners already aſſign'd by *Authority of Parliament*, to wit, the Dukes of *Lancaſter, York, Albemarle, Surrey* and *Exeter*; the Marquiſs of *Dorſet*, the Earls of *Marche, Sarum, Northumberland*, and *Glouceſter*,

or

He was firft committed Prifoner to *Windfor Caftle*
Feb. [September] 26. A°. 21 *Richard* II. and in *Octo-*
ber

or any fix of them, with the
Earls of *Worcefter* and *Wiltfhire*
as Procurators of the Clergy,
or one of them: *John Buffy*,
Henry Grene, *John Ruffel*, *Ro-*
bert *Tey*, *Richard Chelmefwyck*,
and *John Golofree*, Knights of
the Parliament, or any four or
three of them.

After the Parliament was ended, both the Dukes appear'd
before the King at *Ofwaldftrie*
on the twenty fecond of *Febru-*
ary, when a further Day was
affign'd to meet them at *Wind-*
for, viz. on *Sunday* the twenty
eighth of *April*. In the mean
while, it was advis'd and agreed
by the King, and all the Lords
and Knights abovefaid, on the
nineteenth of *March*, that the
Determination of this Difference
fhould be according to the Law
of *Chivalry*, if other fufficient
Evidence or Proofs could not be
found for the ending of it by
ordinary courfe of Law; but no
further Proofs being produc'd by
either of the Parties, who now
appear'd on the Day prefixed at

the place laft mention'd, to receive the King's Judgment therein; hereupon, according to the
late Refolution at *Ofwaldftrie*, he
ordain'd, that fince other fufficient Proofs could not be found
for determining this Difference,
&c. it fhould be decided by fingle Combat at *Coventry*. So on
Monday the twenty ninth of the
faid Month of *April*, they both
appearing again before the King,
Battel or Duel was appointed
between them, according to the
Advice and Opinion of the
Dukes, Earls, Barons, Bannerets, *&c.* there in great Numbers affembled for this Caufe,
together with all thofe that had
the *Authority of Parliament* committed to them, where the former Judgment of the King, and
his Council, was again confirmed.

But the King of his fpecial
Grace, and as rightful and fovereign Lord, took the Battel
into his own Hands, and by
full Advice, Authority, and Affent of Parliament, ordain'd and
adjudged

ber following was fent away to his *Banifhment*, having Liberty to tranfport himfelf with forty Perfons of his

adjudged for the Peace and Tranquillity of him, his Kingdom, and Subjects, and to efchew Debates and Troubles, particularly between the faid Dukes, their Friends, and Well-willers, that the Duke of *Hereford* fhould leave the Kingdom for ten Years, and be gone within eight Days after the Feaft of St. *Edward* the *Confeffor*, or thirteenth of *October*, upon pain of incurring Treafon by *Authority of Parliament*. It was alfo ordain'd by the fame Authority, that the Duke of *Hereford* fhould not come into the Company of *Thomas* Duke of *Norfolk*, nor of *Thomas Arundel* late *Archbifhop*, nor fend, nor caufe to be fent, nor receive, nor caufe to be receiv'd, any Meffage, or other thing to or from either of them.

And it was declared to the Duke of *Norfolk*, that forafmuch as on the twenty ninth of *April*, at *Windfor*, in the twenty firft Year of the King, he had confefs'd certain Points of the *Appeal* or *Schedule* abovefaid, which

he had denied at *Ofwaldftrie* on the twenty third of *February* before, which were very likely to have bred great Troubles in the Realm, therefore the King defiring as a juft and rightful Lord, to punifh all fuch as were the Authors of fuch Troubles and Debates, and alfo willing to avoid the Occafions of them, adjudged and ordain'd by the fame *Advice, Authority, and Affent of Parliament*, that *Thomas Mowbray* Duke of *Norfolk* fhould avoid his Realm for term of Life, and that he fhould depart out of the Kingdom by the twentieth of *October* next coming, and remain either in *Bohemia, Germany, Hungary*, or in fome other Parts of Chriftendom, upon pain to incur Treafon by Authority aforefaid. And likewife upon the fame Penalty not to come into the Company of the Duke of *Hereford* or of *Thomas Arundel* (late Archbifhop of *Canterbury*) nor hold any Correfpondence with him.

And

his Retinue, from any Haven between *Orwell* and *Scardeburg* [*Scarborough*] &c. after which he never more return'd into *England*, but died (as it is said) of the Pestilence at *Venice*, in his Return from *Jerufalem*, *September* 30. 1° *Henry* IV. being seized of vast Possessions, both in *England* and *Wales* ᵂ ².

Elizabeth his second Wife before mention'd (Daughter to *Richard*, and Sister and Coheir to *Thomas Fitz*-

---

And it was further ordain'd by *Authority of Parliament* as abovefaid, that if either of the Dukes, or any other, do procure any thing to be done against the least Point of the Ordinance, or what was done on the sixteenth of *September*, shall incur the Pain of Treafon, as if it had been done against any Ordinance of the Parliament begun at *Westminster*, and adjourn'd to *Shrewsbury*; or if they, or any other for them, shall seek for any manner of Pardon, or Licence to return home, they were to incur the same Pain. *Tyrrell's Hist.* Vol. III. Part II.

ᵂ ² *Et portoit Gueulles au Lion rampant d'argent, armé & lampasse d'azur* Brook's *Cat.* 157. *Vincent's Disc.* 346. Gul. a Lion

rampant *Arg*ᵗ. *Mills* 513. *York* 207. He bare in his Seal by Grant from King *Richard* II. *per pale one of St.* Edward *the Confessor*, and the other of *Thomas of Brotherton Marshal* of *England*, and in Place of a Crest *a Lion paffant guardant gorged with a Ducal Coronet upon a Chapeau*, Sandford 210. whose Family leaving off the *Lion rampant Argent, in a Field Gules* their paternal Coat of Arms, assum'd the Coat-Armour of *Thomas of Brotherton*, Duke of *Norfolk*, fifth Son of King *Edward* I. from whom by Heirs general they were descended, viz. *Gules* 3 *Lyons paffant guardant Or, a Label of three Points Argent*, id. *p.* 393.

Alan

Alan Earl of *Arundel*) furviving him had (among many other Lordfhips) *Dovercourt* affign'd to her for Dowry, bringing this unfortunate Duke the four Children before mention'd[x].

The eldeft Son *Thomas,* fourteen Years of Age at his Father's Death, had not the Title of Duke, or any other but *Earl Marfhal,* and taking part againft the King with *Richard Scroop Archbifhop* of *York* was the fixth of *Henry* IV. beheaded at *York*[y]

John

---

[x] This *Elizabeth* had three Husbands, the firft was *William Mountacute* of which before; her fecond was this *Thomas Mowbray,* who was Earl of *Surrey* in her right, of whom alfo before. Her third was Sir *Robert Gowfel,* Knight; by whom fhe had two Daughters and Coheirs, viz. *Joan,* Wife of *Thomas* Lord *Stanley,* and *Elizabeth* Wife of Sir *Robert Wingfield, Mills's Cat.* 653. and 880. which Author *p.* 514. doth vary from the foregoing, calling her third Hufband Sir *Robert Gonfhill,* Knight; after whom he faith, fhe married to Sir *Gerard Ufflete* Knight, her third Hufband, when, according to that Account, it fhould have been her fourth. She died the eighth of *July* in the third Year of King *Henry* VI.

[y] *Cambden Brit. p.* 394. *Mills p.* 514. and *York p.* 207. do all aver this *Thomas* to have the Title of Earl of *Nottingham,* as well as *Earl Marfhal.* Sandford *p.* 211. faith, that the Inquifition taken *An.* 6 & 8 *Henry* IV. was by the Name of *Tho. Comitis Marefcalli.* And that the fame taken *Anno* 16 *Henry* VI. after the Death of his Wife, fhe was ftiled *Conftancia nuper Comitiffa Marfhal.* This Office of *Earl Marfhal* feems to be executed by a *Deputy,* during the Minority of *Thomas;* for *Mills p.* 991. faith, that *Ralph Nevill* Earl of *Weftmoreland* was

I   by

John his Brother fucceeded him, aged feventeen Years, the eighth of *Henry* IV. He at a *Parliament* held at *Weftminfter*, the third of *Henry* VI. was reftored to the Title and Dignity of Duke of *Norfolk*, ufing before no other than *Earl Marfhal* and *Nottingham* z. He departed this Life *October* the nineteenth, the

by King *Henry* IV, made *Earl Marfhal* of *England*. Nor doth it appear, that he was ever poffeft of this Manor ; becaufe his Mother outlived him. He married *Conftance* Daughter of *John Holland* Duke of *Exeter*, who outlived her Hufband (but had no Iffue by him) and dying *A*⁰. 16. *Henry* VI. was buried at St. *Katharine*'s near the *Tower*. This *Thomas* joining with *Richard Scroop Archbifhop* of *York*, in a Confpiracy againft King *Henry*, was by Stratagem taken by the Earl of *Weftmoreland*; and being beheaded at *York*, his Head was fet upon the Walls of that *City*, and his Body buried in the *Cathedral*, Anno 1404. *Truffel* 87. *York* 1405. *p.* 20. He bore the Arms of *Mowbray*, *Gules a Lion rampant Argent*.

z By *Brook*, *York*, Herald *p.* 157. he is faid to be reftored to

the Dukedom of *Norfolk*, *Anno* 4ᵗᵒ *Hen.* V. but his Error therein was corrected by *Vincent p.* 347. it being not before *Anno* 3⁰. *Hen.* VI. for which he produceth the *Parliament Roll* of that Year, in which the Petition of this *John Mowbray*; with the Proceedings thereon, are recorded; which Petition, although long, yet to fhew the different Dialect between thofe times and this, I fhall here tranfcribe:

𝕺ur 𝖘𝖔𝖛𝖊𝖗𝖆𝖎𝖓 𝕷𝖔𝖗𝖉, 𝖑𝖎𝖐𝖊 𝖎𝖙 𝖞𝖔𝖚𝖗 𝖓𝖔𝖇𝖑𝖊 𝖌𝖗𝖆𝖈𝖊 𝖙𝖔 𝖇𝖊 𝖗𝖊𝖒𝖊𝖒𝖇𝖗𝖊𝖉, 𝖍𝖔𝖜𝖊 𝕴 John 𝕮𝖗𝖑𝖊 Marefcall, 𝖍𝖆𝖛𝖊 𝖘𝖚𝖊𝖉 𝖎𝖓 𝖉𝖎𝖛𝖊𝖗𝖘𝖊𝖘 𝖞𝖔𝖚𝖗 𝕻𝖆𝖗𝖑𝖊𝖒𝖊𝖓𝖙𝖘, 𝖎𝖓 𝖙𝖞𝖒𝖊 𝖔𝖋 𝖞𝖔𝖚𝖗 𝖌𝖗𝖆𝖈𝖎𝖔𝖚𝖘𝖊 𝖗𝖊𝖌𝖓𝖊, 𝖉𝖊𝖘𝖎𝖗𝖞𝖓𝖌 𝖙𝖔 𝖍𝖆𝖛𝖊 𝖉𝖊𝖈𝖑𝖆𝖗𝖆𝖈𝖎𝖔𝖓 𝖒𝖆𝖉𝖊 𝖋𝖔𝖗 𝖒𝖞 𝖕𝖑𝖆𝖈𝖊, 𝖎𝖓 𝖕𝖎𝖘 𝖞𝖔𝖚𝖗 𝖍𝖎𝖊 𝖈𝖔𝖚𝖗𝖙 𝖔𝖋 𝕻𝖆𝖗𝖑𝖊𝖒𝖊𝖓𝖙, 𝖆𝖇𝖔𝖛𝖊 𝖒𝖞 𝕮𝖔𝖚𝖘𝖞𝖓 𝖔𝖋 Warwyk, 𝖆𝖘 𝕴 𝖆𝖓𝖉 𝖆𝖑𝖑 𝖒𝖞 𝖆𝖚𝖓𝖈𝖊𝖘𝖙𝖗𝖊𝖘, 𝖆𝖓𝖉 𝖕𝖗𝖊𝖉𝖊𝖈𝖊𝖘𝖘𝖔𝖚𝖗𝖘

the eleventh of *Henry* VI. and was buried in the *Char-ter-House* in the *Isle* of *Axholm.*   He left his Widow
Katherine,

fours have had at all tymes, of which no mind ys ye contrarie, as Erles of Northfolk, as well for ye blode riall, and arms riallp pat I am come fro and bere, as for the said Erldome, as by diverses evidences, wryptinges, and recordes in yis pour present Parlement declared, fully in my conseit, is proved, which proves notwithstandyng par hie and myghti prince my Lord of Glouc. pour Bealuncle and pour oper Lords, by pour hic auctoritie in pour Parlement assembled, for diverses Causes hem moeuping, will not take upon hem declaracion for my saide place; whereupon the Comunalte of pour realme at yis tyme, by pour commaundement callid to yis pour rial court of Parlement; saping, yis delay, of which were like to growe uncase and unfrendly love, betwene me and my said Cousyn of Warwyck, hau in all humble wise, instaunced pour In-

nocent and benygne Soveraine Lordship, consyderyng howe pei herefey by common laugage, pat I shuld be born to be Duc of Norffolk, which if so were, pour said Comunaltie supposeth shold make finall conclusion of ye determination of my seid place, above my said Cousyn of Warwyck, at ye reverence cf which Comunalte, as well as for ye defire pat I love to have peas, rest, and tranquillite with my seide Cousyn of Warwyck, and in especial, to fave ye right and inheritance of me, and my heires pat God of his Grace hath suffered me to be borne unto, clepme to be Duc of Norfolke; declarpng to pour noble grace, to pat hic and myghtie prince pour Bealuncle my Lord of Glouc. and to all ye oper Lordes in pour present Parlement assembled, howe pat yt liked to It. Rychard ye seconde after the conquest, pour worthi predecessour, for diverses notables causes him moeupng

I

Katharine, Daughter to *Ralph Nevill* Earl of *West-moreland*, among many other *Lordships* assign'd to her for

moeupng in his Parlement holden at Westm. the xxix day of Septembre pe pere of his regne xxi bp his letters paten-tes, to erce Thomas that tpme Erell of Notyngham, and Mare-scall of Ingeland, into Duc of Norffolk,, with pe stile, title, name, and worship to pe same Duche appendant; to have the said stile, title, name, and worship to pe said Duc, and to his heires males of his body compng for evermore. And over pat pe said Kyng Rychard pat same tpme, bp his letters patents granted to the said Duc, and his heires males of his bodie compng, for pe better sustentacion of the said stile, title, name, and worship xl. marcs perlie to be take in his Escheequier, at pe Festes of Pasque and Seint Michell. Which Thomas Duc hadde issue Thomas and me, and of pis stile, title, name, worship and annuel rent of xl marc; pe said Thomas Duc dyed seised in pe

tyme of pe saide Kynge Rychard, after whos decesse, pe said stile, title, name, worship and an-nuell rent of xl. marc descended to the said Thomas pe sonne, as sonne and heir, which Tho-mas pe sonne died perof seised within age, and without issue of his Body compng, after whos decesse, pe said stile, ti-tle, name, worship, and annu-ell rent of xl. marc, descended to me as broper and heir, be force of pe said creacion and graunt. And so I clayme to be Duc of Norfolke, and to have pe stile, title, name, wor-ship and annuell rent of xl. marc aforesaid, And I may bp pou our Soverain Lord, mp saide worthi Lord pour beal-uncle, and all pour oper Lordes be so reputed, holde and de-clared, in pis pour riall court, and to have and enjoie mp place thereto accordant; sauyng al-weis, pe title, right and pos-session of mee and mpn heirs of mpn body compng, as Crels of Norfolk,

Z

for *Dowry*, the Burrough of *Harwich*, and the Lordſhip of *Dovercourt*, and by her had Iſſue ꝫ ²

John

Norfolk, to my place in his hie court aboue my ſaide conſyn of Warwyk, and his heirs, by cauſe ye name of Duc of Norfolk is tailled to me ; and to my heirs males of my body comyng. And the name of Erel of Norfolk is tailled to me, and to my heires of my body coming generaly. Beſechyng mekely unto your hie and noble grace, yat yis my ſupplicacion, and all oyer matteres into yis your ſaid Parlement, by mee and myn counſell notifi ed, mynyſtred and declared in proef of my place for to be hadde as Erell of Norfolk, aboue my ſaid conſyn of Warwyk, may be in yis your Parlement entred, and of recorde enacte.

After the reading and conſidering the aforeſaid Petition by the King his, Lords, Judges, the King's Serjeants and Counſells at Law; *declaratum fuit, & unanimiter concordatum, quod præfatus* Johannes *Comes* Mareſcal-

4

lus, *ut filius prædicti* Thomæ *ducis, & frater, & hæres prædicti* Thomæ *filii* Thomæ *virtute cartæ & ſucceſſionis prædictarum, de cetero Dux* Norff. *reputetur & teneatur, ac ſtilo, titulo, nomine & honore Ducis* Norff. *gaudeat, ut utatur, juxta tenorem Cartæ ſupradictæ. Quam quidem declarationem, & concordiam, præfatus dominus Cancellarius authoritate regia, poſtmodum, viz.* xiiij *die* Julij, *ultimo die hujus Parliamenti, de aviſamento dominorum ſpiritualium & temporalium prædictorum, in pleno Parliamento prædicto, in preſentia Domini noſtri Regis, publice declaravit. Super quo, præfatus* Johannes *ut Dux* Norff. *homagium ligeum eidem Domino noſtro Regi tunc ibidem immediate fecit, (quo facto) idem Dominus noſter Rex, de aviſamento & aſſenſu prædictis, ipſum Ducem inter pares Parliamenti prædicti in loco competenti ſedere demandavit, quod idem Dux gratanter fecit tunc ibidem,* Vinc. Diſc. 350.

ꝫ 2 This *John* Duke of *Norfolk*

folk was after the Death of his *Mother* the *eleventh* Lord of this *Manor*, who in the third of *Henry* V. was with the King at the Siege of *Harfleu*, where growing fick of the Flux by eating of Fruit, he was obliged to return before the Battel of *Agincourt*, *Peerage* 2. 235. But *Goodwin* names him among the Nobles at that famous Battel, *p*. 84. *Anno* 5 *Henry* V. He was at the Siege of *Caru* in *Normandy*, and continued in thofe parts until the Death of the King, *Peerage* 2. 235. In the Month of *Auguſt* that Year, he accompanied the Duke of *Bedford*, who with a Fleet of two hundred *Ships* fail'd from *Rye* to the Mouth of the River *Sien*, where ingaging the *French*, the *Engliſh* got the Victory, and relieved the *Town* of *Harfleu*; then ftraitly befieged by the *French* Anno 1416. The *Archbiſhop* of *Canterbury* call'd a *Synod* to meet on the ninth of *November*, at which the *Earl Marſhal* and others fo prevalently urged the Neceffity of a Supply, that a tenth were by the Clergy given for the Support of the War. The fame Year, the Nobility powerfully affifted the King with Men, the *Earl Marſhal* raifing one hundred Launces, and three hundred Archers at his own Coft, and imbarking on the twenty third of *July* at *Portſmouth*, failed with the King into *France*; and landed on the firft of *Auguſt* at *Beville* in *Normandy*, in the Face of the *French Army*, *Goodwin*, 154, 155. At the Siege of *Roan*, he commanded the Attack againft the *Caſtlegate*, id. 186. He was made *Knight* of the *Garter* by King *Henry* V. He was in the *King's* Wars *A⁰.* 1 & 8 *Hen.* VI. He died *Anno* 1432. 11° *Hen.* VI. at his Manor of *Epleworth*, and was buried in the *Abby* of the *Carthuſians*, within the Ifle of *Axholme*, to which place he likewife order'd his Father's Bones to be remov'd from *Venice*. He married *Katharine* Daughter to *Ralfe* Lord *Nevill* firft Earl of *Weſtmoreland*, by her he had one Son *John*, and two Daughters, *Anne* married to *William Berkley*, and *Katharine* married to *Thomas Grey* of *Banoick*; by her fecond Hufband *John* Vifcount *Beaumont*, fhe had alfo two Daughters, *Jane* and *Katherine*, *Mills's Cat.* 516. In relation to this *Katharine*

Wife

John his Son and Heir, at his Father's Death aged seventeen Years.   In the twenty third *Henry* VI.

Wife to *John* Duke of *Norfolk*, it is somewhat difficult to reconcile our *Genealogical* Authors; *Mills* notwithstanding what he had before asserted, yet *p.* 993. affirms, that there was no Issue remaining of this *Katherine* by *John Mowbray* Duke of *Norfolk*. He likewise, as afore quoted, makes her second Husband to be *John* Viscount *Beaumont*, and that by him she had two Daughters *Jane* and *Katherine*, of which marriage, neither *Brooke*, *Vincent*, *York* nor *Sandford* take any Notice. *Collins* in his *Peerage* saith, that she was second Wife to *John* Viscount *Beaumont*, but that by him she had no Issue, Vol. II. Part I. *p.* 454. *Vincent* saith, that after the Death of the Duke of *Norfolk*, she was married to Sir *John Widevile*, Knight, (or *Woodvile*) Brother of *Anthony* Earl *Rivers, p.* 347. He was the fourth Son of *Richard Woodvile* Earl *Rivers*, with whom he was slain at *Edgecotefield* near *Banbury* against *Robin* of *Riddisdale*; that upon loss of the Day he fled, and

being taken in the Forest of *Dean*, was brought to *Northampton*, and suffer'd there by Command of *George* Duke of *Clarence*, and *Nevill* Earl of *Warwick, Peerage* 2. 2. *p.* 305. Others, that they were taken out of the Manor of *Grafton* by *Robin* of *Riddisdale*, Captain of the lewd People of *Northampton-shire*, and carried to *Northampton*, and there beheaded without any legal Proceeding *Anno* 1469. *Brooks's Cat.* 193. who hath both the Stories. Whether it was this *Katharine* of *Woodvile*, or her last Husband which died *Anno* 9 *Edw.* IV. is to me uncertain: As likewise where buried unless in the Cathedral of *Lincoln* with her Mother and Grandmother. The Arms of this Duke *John* are, *Il portoit les Armes de son pere Brooks's Cat.* 157. *Vincent Disc.* 347. *Gules a Lion rampant Argent, Mills* 515. *York* 208. His Seal is charged with the Arms of *Brotherton* between *two Escocheons* of *Mowbray, Sandford* 211.

upon

upon the Confirmation of the Title of Duke of *Nor-folk* upon him, (which was formerly conferr'd upon *Thomas* his Grandfather) he had a Grant alfo of a Place and Seat in *Parliament* and elfewhere, next to the Duke of *Exeter.* He died the firft of *Edward* IV, and was buried in *Thetford Abby.* He by *Eleanor* Daughter to *William* Lord *Boucher* left Iffue [a]

John

---

[a] This *John* was after the Deceafe of *Katharine* his Mother the twelfth Lord of this *Manor.* He fucceeded his Father as Duke of *Norfolk,* Earl *Marſhal* and *Nottingham,* Baron *Mowbray, Seagrave,* and *Bruce* of *Gower, York* 208. was made *Knight* of the *Garter* by King *Henry* VI, in the fourteenth Year of that *King* he was fent *Ambaſſador* into *Picardy* to treat of Peace between *England* and *France;* the *Peerage* faith, it was the feventeenth Year, *Vide* Vol. II. 236. *An°.* 25 *Henry* VI. Our Duke went on *Pilgrimage* to *Rome,* and in the thirty fifth of that Reign had *Licenſe* to *viſit* other *Holy Places* in *Ireland, Scotland, Britanny, Picardy* and *Cologne,* and to the *Blood* of *our Saviour* at *Windiſmark,*

as alfo a fecond time to *Rôme* and *Jeruſalem* ; having vowed to do it for Recovery of the *King's Health,* *Peerage* ib. To our Duke was likewife committed the *Cuſtody* of King *Henry,* when he was taken at the firft Battel of St. *Albans, Baker* 2. 85. He join'd with the Earl of *March* againft the *King, Churchill's Div. Brit.* 269. He with the Earl of *Warwick* commanded the Army againft Queen *Margaret* at the 2[d] *Battel* of St. *Albans, Truſſel* 177. 1 *Edward* IV. was made *Judge Itinerant* of all the *Foreſt* South of *Trent.* He died 1461. *An°.* 1 *Edward* IV, and was buried before the High Altar in *Thetford Abby.* He married one of the Daughters of *William de Burgo Caro* or *Bourchier,* created Earl of *Ewe* in *Normandy* by King

John his Son and Heir. In his Father's Life-time, *viz. March* the twenty fourth, in the twenty ninth of *Henry* VI, he was created Earl of *Warren* in *Surrey.* After his Father's Deceafe in the eighth of *Edward* IV. he had by *Charter (ex exemplif. confirm.* Eliz. Regin. *in Cifta Burgi)* granted unto him certain *Royal Jurifdictions* and great *Privileges* in moft of his *Manors* (being very highly in that *King's* Favour) among which *Harwich* and *Dovercourt* are particulariz'd. In the fifteenth of *Edward* IV. he died and was buried in the *Abby* of *Thetford,* leaving by *Elizabeth* his Wife, Daughter of *John Talbot* Earl of *Shrewsbury,* an only Daughter and Heir [b]   *Anne,*

King *Henry* V. by *Anne* his Wife, Daughter of *Thomas* of *Woodstock* Duke of *Gloucefter:* She is by *York* call'd *Elizabeth, p.* 208, but by *Mills Eleanor, p.* 517. fhe was buried in the *Abby* at *Thetford, Weaver* 130. by her he had Iffue *John* who fucceeded him.

Mr. *Taylor* was under a Miftake when he writ, that it was this *John* that was confirm'd Duke of *Norfolk, Anno* 23 *Hen.* VI. and had then a Place and Seat in Parliament and elfewhere, next to the Duke of *Exeter,* as likewife was the Author of the *Peerage* Vol. II. *p.* 236. when it was his Father that was fo confirm'd, and that was *Anno* 3 *Hen* VI, as I have before fhewn.

His Arms, *Il portoit Gueulles au Lion rampant d'argent arme & Lampaffe d'azur* Brook's Cat. 157. Vincent Difc. 351. *Gules a Lion rampant Argent,* Mills 517. *York* 208. *Gules three Lions paffant guardant Or, Label three Points Argent,* Sandford 212.

[b] This *John Mowbray* was the thirteenth *Lord* of this *Manor,* and fucceeded his Father in his Titles of Duke of *Norfolk, Earl Marfhal,*

Anne, of the Age of four Years, married the seventeenth of *Edward* IV. to *Richard* Duke of *York*, youngeft Son to King *Edward* IV, who with his Brother King *Edward* V, were unhappily made away in their younger Years in the *Tower* of *London*. She died alfo without Iffue and was *buried* in the *Chapel* of St. *Eraf-mus* in the *Abby Church* of *Weftminfter*. This great Inheritance by this Means returns to the Female Offspring of the beforemention'd unfortunate *Thomas* firft Duke of *Norfolk*, and paffed out of the Name of *Mowbray* ᶜ.

John

Marfhal, &c. having been by King *Henry* VI. created Earl of *Warren* and *Surrey*; he was by King *Edward* IV. made *Knight of the Garter*. Without doubt he was on the Part of King *Edward* at the Battel of *Tewkesbury* in *Glouceflerfhire*, which was fought on the 4ᵗʰ of *May* *A*ᵒ. *Domini* 1471. for on the 6ᵗʰ of the fame Month *Richard Plantagenet* Duke of *Gloucefter High Conftable*, with this our Duke as *Earl Marfhal*, fat in Judgment upon *Edmond* Duke of *Somerfet*, *John Longftrother Prior of St.* John's, Sir *Thomas Trefham* and others, who being found guilty were all beheaded the next Day, *Baker* 2. 105.

He ferved in the *King's* Wars in *France* A°. Domini 1475. he died the fifteenth of *Edward* IV. at his *Caftle* of *Framingham*, and was buried in the *Abby* of *Thetford*, *Weaver* 830. who faith, he died without Iffue, but by *Elizabeth* his Wife Daughter of *John Talbot* the great Earl of *Shrewsbury*, where it appears that he had a Daughter named *Anne*, Mills*'s* Cat. 519.

By the Death of this *John* all his Honours as being entailed on the Male Heir reverted to the Crown.

His Arms the fame as his Father's.

ᶜ This *Richard Plantagenet* of *Shrewsbury*, was fecond Son to King

King *Edward* IV. made *Knight of the Garter* in the seventh of *Edward* IV. was upon the 28ᵗʰ Day 1474. created Duke of *York*, and the following Year upon the Death of *John Mowbray* (*Sandford* calls him firſt *Thomas*, afterwards *John, p.* 393. Duke of *Norfolk*, whoſe Honours for want of Male Iſſue fell to the King, who on the twelfth of *January* in the ſixteenth of *Edward* IV. created him Earl of *Nottingham* and *Earl Marſhal*, and on the ſeventh of *February* following Duke of *Norfolk*; on the 15ᵗʰ of *January* 1477. he was married to *Anne* the Daughter of *John Mowbray* aforeſaid, in St. *Steven's Chapel Weſtminſter*; and in her Right he injoyed the Inheritance of the Family, and thereby became the fourteenth *Lord* of this *Manor*. On the fifth of *May, Anno* 19 *Edward* IV. this Duke *Richard* had granted to him the Office of Lieutenant of *Ireland* for two Years; to which two Days after, by reaſon of his Minority, he deputed *Robert Preſton* Lord of *Gormaneſton* under theſe Titles, *Ricardus ſecundus filius Illuſtriſſimi Principis Edwardi quarti, &c. Dux Ebor. & Norff. Comes*

Warren, Surr. & Nottingham. Comes Mareſcallus & Mareſcallus Angliæ, ac Dominus de Segrave, de Mowbray & de Gower, omnibus, &c. cum idem Excellencellentiſſimus Princeps Pater & Dominus meus, &c. per Litteras ſuas Patentes, dat. apud Wyndſoram 5 Maij, Anno Regni ſui 19. *Ordinavit nos præfatum Ricardum, Locum-tenentem ſuum Terræ ſuæ Hiberniæ, Habend. pro termino* 2. *An. &c. Sciatis nos deputâſſe Dilectum noſtrum Robertum Preſton Dominum de Gormaneſton Deputatum noſtrum, &c. dat.* 7 *Maij Anno ſupradicto.*

Not three Years after, this *Richard* (being yet a Child) with his Brother King *Edward* V. were by the Command of their unnatural Uncle and Protector *Richard* Duke of *Gloucester*, ſecretly murther'd in the Tower of *London*, upon the 9ᵗʰ of the Kalends of *June* 1483. *Sandford* 394, 395. and eleventh Year of his Age, was ſmother'd by two Villains, *Miles Foreſt* and *John Dighton*, (procur'd by Sir *James Tyrrell*) and by them buried at the Foot of the Stairs of the *Bloody Tower* (ſo call'd from their being murther'd therein) but King *Richard* III.

being

being told in what an obscure Place they were laid, gave Order for their better Interment, which was performed by a *Priest* belonging to Sir *Robert Brackenbury*; who dying soon after, the Place where was unknown, *Sandford Geneal.* 402. But the Continuator of *John Harding*, as publish'd by *Speed*, *Hist.* 919. tells us from the Report of others, that *King Richard* III. caused Sir *Robert Brackenbury's* Priest to close their dead Bodies in Lead, and so put them in a Coffin full of Holes, and hooked at the End with two Hooks of Iron, and so to cast them into a Place call'd the *Black-deepes* at the *Thames* Mouth, whereby they should never rise up or be any more seen. But the probable Place of their Interment was after one hundred and ninety Years Obscurity discover'd upon the 17th Day of *July* Aᵒ. Domini 1674. to be under the *Stairs* which led from the *King's*

Lodgings to the *Chapel* in the *White Tower*; for digging down the said *Stairs* about ten Foot in the Ground, were found the Bones of *two Striplings* in (as it seem'd) a wooden Chest; which upon the Survey were found proportionable to the Ages of those two *Brothers*, the Scull of the one being entire, the other broken, as were indeed many of the other Bones, as also the Chest, by the Violence of the Labourers, who not being sensible of what they had in Hand, cast the Rubbish and them away together; but by sifting the said Rubbish afterwards all were preserved. This being reported to King *Charles* II. he commanded that the Bones should be put into a Marble *Urn*, and deposited among the *Reliques* of the *Royal Family* in the *Chapel* of King *Henry* VII. in *Westminster Abby*, with the following monumental Inscription:

H. S. S.

RELIQVIÆ
EDWARDI Vᵗⁱ REG. ANGLIÆ ET RICARDI DUCIS
EBORACENSIS.
HOS FRATRES GERMANOS TURRE LONDINˢᵗ: CONCLVSOS
INIECTISQ CULCITRIS SUFFOCATOS,
ABDITE ET INHONESTE TUMULARI IUSSIT
PATRUUS RICARDUS PERFIDUS REGNI PRÆDO ;
OSSA DESIDERATORVM, DIU ET MULTUM QVÆSITA,
POST ANNOS CXC &c.
SCALARUM IN RUDERIBUS (SCALÆ ISTÆ AD SACELLUM
TURRIS ALBÆ NUPER DUCEBANT)
ALTE DEFOSSA, INDICIIS CERTISSIMIS SUNT REPERTA
XVII DIE IULII Aᵒ. Dʳ. MDCLXXIIII.
CAROLUS II REX CLEMENTISSIMUS ACERBAM SORTEM MISERATUS
INTER AVITA MONUMENTA PRINCIPIBUS INFELICISSIMIS
IUSTA PERCOLVIT
ANNO DOMᴵ. 1678 ANNOQ REGNI SVI 30.

In *Brook's Cat.* 158. it is. faid, that this *Richard* was Duke of *Norfolk,* and *Earl Marfhal* of *England* in Right of *Anne* his Wife, which Titles fhe could not be invefted with as of Inheritance from her Anceftors; becaufe the Grant thereof from King *Richard* II. to *Thomas Mowbray* as *Vincent* clearly proves, was *Habendum & poffidendum ftilum, titulum, nomen, honorem*

prædicta (i. e. Norff.) *præfato Duci & hæredibus fuis mafculis de corpore fuo exeuntibus imperpetuum:* Which being a Limitation to Heirs Males, this *Anne* is thereby barred from all colour of Title, and therefore this *Richard* could not injoy it as of her Right, but from a new Inveftiture from his Father, as appears from the Words of this Patent: *Edwardus Dei gratia Rex*

Rex Angliæ & Franciæ & Dominus Hiberniæ, Archiepiſcopis, &c. and after reciting his creating this *Richard* of *Salop* Duke of *York*, and his Inveſtiture therewith, proceeds: *Nos tamen ipſum filium noſtrum, ulterius & uberius decorari & exaltari volentes, de abundantiori gratia noſtra, ipſum filium noſtrum in Ducem Norfolc. & Comitem Warranæ, erigimus, creamus, præficimus, & ordinamus, ac nomen, ſtilum, ſtatum, titulum & honorem, tam Ducis Norff.* &c. *præfato filio noſtro & hæredibus ſuis prædictis imperpetuum,* &c. *His teſtibus,* &c. *Dat. per Manum noſtram apud Palatium noſtrum Weſtm. Septimo die Februarij Anno regni noſtri Sexto decimo.* To which may be added, that the Marriage of this *Richard* and *Anne* was not perform'd untill the fifteenth of *January* following, which was above eleven Months after; ſo that by this Marriage this *Richard* enjoyed only the Inheritance of the Eſtate, but not the Honour.

The Arms of this Duke *Richard, Portoit, France eſcartelle d'Engletterre, au l'ambell d'argent chargée de neuf torteaux,* Brook's Cat. 158. but *Vincent*

faith, that the File ſhould have only on the firſt *Label* a *Canton Gules*, the other being the Arms of *Richard* Duke of *York*, Son of *Richard* of *Conisburg, p.* 362. *France and England a Label of three Arg*ᵗ. *charged with a Canton in the firſt File*, York 209. but the Type of this doth not belong to this Duke *Richard*, but to *Lionel* of *Antwerpe* Duke of *Clarence* third · Son of King *Edward* III. as by comparing them, *p.* 110. will appear. *France and England, a Label of three Points Argent, the firſt charged with a Canton Gules*, for ſo it is on this *Duke*'s Stall at *Windſor*, Sandford 393.

This *Ducheſs Anne* is likewiſe ſaid to be murther'd in her Childhood by *Richard* III. but when or how our Hiſtorians are ſilent, only it could not be long after that of her Huſband, but ſome time in *June* 1483. *viz.* between the ſecond and the twenty eighth, on which Day Sir *John Howard* Knight, *Lord Howard* was by King *Richard* III. created Duke of *Norfolk* and *Earl Marſhal,* &c. in which Patent he was ſaid to be one of her Heirs, and next of Blood to her; which muſt

A a 2   conſequently

John the Son of Sir *Robert Howard* by *Margaret* eldeſt Daughter of the aforeſaid *Thomas* Duke of *Norfolk*, being next Couſin in Blood, and one of the Heirs of the aforeſaid *Anne Ducheſs* of *York* and *Norfolk*, was the firſt of *Richard* III. againſt his Coronation, made *Duke* of *Norfolk*, and *Earl Marſhal* of *England*; at which Solemnity he carried the *Crown* betwixt his Hands; and his Son Sir *Thomas Howard* being alſo made *Earl* of *Surrey*, carried the fourth *Sword* before him in a rich Scabbard. They ſtuck firmly to him, and notwithſtanding that diſcouraging *Rythm* made known to him the Night before the Battel near *Boſworth*, viz.

𝕵𝖆𝖈𝖐 𝖔𝖋 𝔑𝖔𝖗𝖋𝖔𝖑𝖐 𝖇𝖊 𝖓𝖔𝖙 𝖙𝖔𝖔 𝖇𝖔𝖚𝖑𝖉
𝕱𝖔𝖗 𝕯𝖎𝖈𝖐𝖊𝖓 𝖙𝖍𝖞 𝔐𝖆𝖘𝖙𝖊𝖗 𝖎𝖘 𝖇𝖔𝖚𝖌𝖍𝖙 𝖆𝖓𝖉 𝖘𝖔𝖑𝖉.

Yet led he the *Vanguard* of King *Richard's* Army, where valiantly fighting with the *King* he loſt his Life [d]. In

conſequently be after her Deceaſe. She was buried in the Chapel of St. *John the Baptiſt* (not that of St. *Eraſmus*) *Weſtminſter*, but there is neither Grave-ſtone nor Tomb erected for her.

Her Arms *Gules, three Lions paſſant guardant Or, a Label of three Points Argent.* Sandford 393.

[d] This *John* Duke of *Norfolk* was the fifteenth *Lord* of this *Manor*, and firſt *Duke* of *Norfolk* of the Family of *Howard*: He was Knighted by King *Henry*

Henry VI. in the thirty firſt Year of his Reign, and march'd with *John* Earl of *Shrewsbury* to the Relief of *Caſtileon* beſieged by the *French*, Dugd. Bar. 3. 265. and in this *King's* Reign was made *BaronHoward* by Summons to Parliament, *Dale's Cat. p.* 10. but the time not afſerted. He was in the firſt of *Edward* IV. *Sheriff* of *Norfolk* and *Suffolk*, and *Conſtable* of *Norwich Caſtle.* In the ſecond of *Edward* IV, he kept the Seas with ten thouſand Men, and landing them in *Britanny* took *Couquet :* And in the eighth of that *King* was made *Treaſurer* of the *King's Houſhold*, and had a Grant of the *King's Coinage* through *England.* He attended the *Lady Margaret* the *King's* Siſter into *Flanders* to be married to the Duke of *Burgundy.* In the tenth of this *King* having the Title of *Lord Howard*, was made *Captain General* of the *King's Forces* againſt the Duke of *Clarence*, Brother to the *King* and others, *Dugd. Bar.* 3. 265. he had Summons to *Parliament* Oct. 15. 1470. as he had alſo *Auguſt* 19. 1472. *Dale's Cat.* 16. *Comines* notes, that the *King* of *France* beſtowing Preſents upon

I

the *Ambaſſadors* gave this Lord four thouſand Crowns more than his Part with the reſt, *Dugd. id. ib.* He was conſtituted *Deputy Governor* of *Calais* and the *Marches* with the *Lord Haſtings*; the eighteenth of this *King* was made *Conſtable* of the *Tower* of *London*, and the Year following was *Captain General* of the *King's Fleet* againſt the *Scots*, and inſtalled *Knight of the Garter, Peerage* 1. 45. He was on the twenty eighth of *June*, in the firſt of *Richard* III, created *Earl Marſhal* and *Duke* of *Norfolk*, as likewiſe *High Steward* for the *Coronation*, *Dugd. id. ib.* He was ſlain on the 22[d] of *Auguſt* 1485. *Mills* 1489. but that is an Error. He was buried at *Thetford*, *Weaver* 830. Our *Duke* had two Wives, the firſt of which was *Katharine* Daughter of *William* Lord *Molins*, by whom he had one Son, *Thomas*, and four Daughters, *Anne, Iſabel, Jane* and *Margaret.* She died according to her Epitaph recorded by *Weaver*, p. 774. A[o]. 1452. and was buried in the Church of *Stoke* by *Nayland* in the County of *Suffolk*; her Tomb yet remains on the North-ſide next the Eaſt of the *Chantry* or Chapel

Chapel belonging to *Tendring Hall* (formerly the Eftate of this our Duke.) It is a large Stone raifed about a Foot above the Floor, and on it inlayed in *Brafs* the *Effigies* of a *Woman*, as figured by *Weaver*; under her Feet was a Plate with an Infcription, which is now gone, and near the four Corners of the Stone four Efcutcheons, three of which now *(viz. Apr. 25. 1724.)* remain, but the dexter Chief gone. The Infcription as I find it in *Weaver* is as follows:

Under this Stone is buried the body of the right honorable Woman and Ladie, fometime wife unto the right high and mighty Prince Lord John Howard Duke of Norfolke, and mother unto the right noble and puiffant Prince, Lord Thomas Howard, Duke alfo of Norfolke which Lady departed this prefent Life, Ann. Dom. 1452.

If this Monument was erected for this Lady foon after her Deceafe, yet the Infcription could not be thereon ingraven until the fourth of *King Henry* VIII. (which was at leaft fixty Years after) before which her Son thereon mention'd was not Duke of *Norfolk*.

The fecond Wife of our Duke *John* was *Margaret* the Daughter of Sir *John Chedworth*, Knight; by whom he had only one Daughter nam'd *Katharine, Mills* 521. This *Margaret* outlived her Hufband, and dying the fifth of *Henry* VII. bequeathed her Body to be buried in the *Choir* of the Church of our *Lady* at *Stoke* 1490. *Dugd. Bar.* 3. 265. in the Chancel of which Church lieth now, i. e. 1724. Stone on which was the *Effigies* of a Woman, with an Infcription at her Feet, and at the Corners four *Efcutcheons*; what remains is only the *Effigies*, and that *Efcutcheon* on the finifter Chief, on which is a Cheveron between three Wolves Heads erafed, which being the Coat Armour of *Chedworth, Mills* 521. is together with the Place where it lieth a ftrong Prefumption, that this Stone was laid for the faid *Margaret Duchefs Dowager* of *Norfolk*.

This Stone feems to be one of thofe which *Weaver* complains was impioufly robb'd of their Braffes before his time, 773.

According

In the firſt *Parliament* of *Henry* VII. both the deceaſed Father, and the ſurviving Son, *Thomas* Earl of
Surrey (with many others who aſſiſted *Richard* III. in
that Battel) were *attainted*; but ſhortly after not only
pardon'd, but reſtored alſo to their Lands and Dignities
(ſay our Authors); however we find not that the *Earl*
of *Surrey* was admitted to the *Dukedom,* though to
the Eſtate.   In this *King's* Reign, he was much in the
Guard of the *Scottiſh Borders*; and about the Year 1496.
was challenged to a ſingle Combat by the King of *Scots* c.

After

According to *Weaver* this
Margaret Ducheſs of *Norfolk*
had another Daughter nam'd
Joan, who was buried in this
Church near her Mother, for
whom he gives the following
Epitaph 772.

..... Domina Johanna Redmeld quondam ſponſa UUillielmi Redmeld militis, ac filia recolenda memorie Domine Margarete Howard
Duciſſe Norfolcie hic ſuperius tumulate obijt ..... xx Feb. MD .....

It is probable that a Stone
now lying in the Chancel on
which remains only the *Effigies*
of a Woman inlaid in Braſs,
may be that of this Lady *Joan
Redmeld,* it having been robb'd
of the Plate on which was the
Inſcription.

The Arms of this *John* Duke
of *Norfolk, Portoit de Gueulles a
la bende entre ſix croix recroiſet-*
tées au pied Fitche de Argent,
Brook's Cat. 159. Vincent's
Diſc. 354. *Gul. a bend between
ſix Croſs Croſlets Fitche Argent,*
Mills 520. *Gul. a bend inter ſix
Croſlets Fitche,* York 210.

c This *Thomas Howard* Son of
John the firſt *Duke* of *Norfolk*
of that Family, was by King
Henry VII. pardoned the *High
Treaſon* of which he was at-
tainted

After this he was made *Lord Treafurer* of *England*, and King *Henry* VII. dying *April* 22. 1508. he left him by Will one of his *Executors.* Whilft *Henry* VIII. was at the Siege of *Tournay*, having left him *Lieutenant* of the North, King *James* IV. of *Scotland* (notwithftanding he had married *Margaret* the *King*'s eldeft *Sifter*) entred *England* with a great Army, and was by this *Earl* overthrown in Battel; and flain in *Flodden-field* September 9. 1513. Upon the Return of *Henry* VIII, he was created *Duke* of *Norfolk*; and in

tainted by *Parliament*, and reftored to the Eftate of his Father, whereby he became the fixteenth *Lord* of this *Manor*; but at what time this Reftoration was made I have not yet feen, perhaps not before he was by that *King* confirm'd *Earl* of *Surrey* (*viz.* 3. Nov. 1492. 8 *Henry* VII. *Dale's Cat. p.* 10.) moft likely *A*°. 1489. when he was fent with an Army into the North to fupprefs a Rebellion there headed by *John a Chamber*, *Baker* 2. 144. being then deliver'd out of Prifon, and receiv'd into the *King*'s Favour, *Martyn*'s *Hift.* 334. At his being at *Hayton* the *King* of *Scots* fent to him *Marchemont*, and an-

other *Herald* requiring him at his Election, either to fight with him with their whole Armies, or elfe they two to fight in fingle Combat; upon condition that if the Victory fell to the *Scottifh King*, the *Earl* fhould deliver him the Town of *Berwick*. To which the *Earl* anfwer'd, that the Town of *Berwick* was the *King* his Mafter's, and therefore not for him to difpofe of, but for his Offer of fingle Combat he willingly accepted it, and thought himfelf highly honoured by fuch a Match: But King *James* had no mind to perform either, and therefore in the Night retired into *Scotland*, *Baker p.* 150.

Memorial

Memorial of the Victory had *granted to him, and his Heirs Male for ever, that they should bare in the midst of the Bend of the Arms of Howard: The whole half part of a Lion Gules, pierced through the Mouth with an Arrow, in the due Colours of the Arms of the King of Scots,* as it was (faith *Cambden Itin. Norf.*) tranflated *verbatim* from the *Patent.* He died the fixteenth of *Henry* VIII. *Anno* 1524. of the Age of eighty Years, and was interr'd in *Thetford Abby,* with a large Memorial printed by Mr. *Weaver (Funeral Monuments p.* 834.) of the moft remarkable Paffages of his Life f.

To

---

f He was made *Knight of the Garter,* and Aº. 6. *Henry* VIII. conducted the *Lady Mary* Sifter to the *King* into *France,* in order to be married to the *French King;* the thirteenth of the fame *King* was *Lord High Steward* at the Trial of *Edward* Duke of *Buckingham, Dugd. Bar.* 3. 267. having attended the King the precedent Year at the famous Interview between the *Kings* of *France* and *England* on the 7th of *June* 1520. between *Andres* and *Guifnes* call'd the *Golden Campe, Godwins Annals* 41. He died at *Framingham Caftle* 21.

May 1524. He married two *Wives,* the firft was *Elizabeth* Daughter and Heir of Sir *Frederick Tilney,* Knight, and Relict of *Humphrey Bouchier* Lord *Berners,* by whom he had Iffue three Sons and two Daughters, *viz. Thomas, Edward, Edmund, Elizabeth* and *Murella,* and two of his Grandchildren were Wives to King *Henry* VIII. *viz.* his fecond and fifth, and both had the fame Fate to lofe their *Heads.* When this Wife died or where buried, I have not yet met with any Account.

B b

In

In the Chancel of *Lambeth* Church on a Braſs Plate was this
Inſcription.

Here lieth the Lady Elizabeth Howard,
ſometime Counteſs of Wiltſhire.

This Lady *Wiltſhire* was Daughter to *Thomas* Duke of *Norfolk*, by his firſt Lady *Elizabeth Tilney*, and Mother to *Anne* of *Bollein* Wife to King *Henry* VIII. His ſecond Wife was *Agnes* Daughter of *Philip Tilney*, Eſq; by whom he had likewiſe divers Children, *viz.* three Sons, *William*, *Richard* and *Thomas*, as likewiſe four Daughters, *Anne*, *Dorothy*, *Elizabeth*, and *Katharine*. She was buried at *Lambeth*, but when I do find not, *Mills*'s *Cat.* 523. as were likewiſe *two* of her Children on which were formerly the following Epitaphs ; as alſo on the firſt Wife of *William* Lord *Effingham* another of her Sons ; but the Braſſes on which they were, are now gone, many ſoon after the Reformation (as is obſerv'd by Mr. *Aubrey*) when Queen *Elizabeth* was obliged to publiſh a Proclamation againſt the Violators of Tombs and Monuments. *Survey*, Vol. V. *p.* 231.

In *Howard*'s Chapel on a Braſs Plate.

Hic jacet Johannes Howard Arm. filius Comitis Surr. et Agnetis matris ejus, qui obijt Viceſſimo tertio die Menſis Martij An. D'ni Mccccciij Cujus anime propicietur Deus Amen.

Upon another Stone on a Braſs Plate.

Hic jacet D'nus Ricardus Howard unus filiorum nobiliſſimi Principis Thome Ducis Norfolcie et Agnetis conjugis ſue, qui obijt 22 die Menſis Martij Anno D'ni 1517. Cujus anime propicietur Deus. Amen.

4

Upon

Upon another in the fame Chapel.

Here lyeth the Lady Elizabeth Fitzwalter,
lately Wife to Henry Lord Fitzwalter
Son and Heir of the Lord Robert Earl of
Suffex, and one of the Daughters of the Right
Noble Prince Lord Thomas late Duke of
Norfolk, and the Lady Agnes his wife which
Lady Elizabeth deceffyd the xviij Day of Septemb.
in the Yeare of our Lord God Mcccccxxxiv.
on whofe Soule Jefu have Mercy.

In the Chancel on a Brafs Plate fix'd in Stone.

Here lyeth Katharine Howard
one of the Sifters and Heires of John
Broughton Efq; Son and Heire of John Broughton Efq;
and late Wife of the Lord William Howard,
one of the Sonnes of the Right High and Mighty
Prince Lord Thomas late Duke of
Norfolk, High Treafurer and Earl
Marfhall of England; which Lord William and Lady
Catherine left Iffue between them
laufully begotten, Agnes Howard the only
Daughter and Heir; which faid Lady Catharine
deceafed the xxiij Day of Aprill
Anno D'ni Mcccccxxxv. whofe Soule Jefu pardon.

The

To him fucceeded *Thomas* his Son and Heir, who in the Year 1 5 3 3. at the famous Congrefs at *Bulloign*, attended the *King* there, and was by the *French King* Honoured with the *Order of St. Michael.* But fee the Inftability and Uncertainty of human Affairs, efpeci-ally with thofe in high Dignity and Place. In the thirty eighth of *Henry* VIII. *Annoq*; 1 5 47. the laft Year of his Reign, this *Thomas Duke* of *Norfolk*, and *Henry Earl* of *Surrey* his Son and Heir, upon certain

The three following Epitaphs in the fame Chapel, are for three others of the faid Duke's Children ; but whether by his firft or fecond Lady doth not appear.

Upon a fmall Marble on Brafs is the following.

Ꝑic jacet Johannes Ꝩoward Arm. filius Comitis de Surr. qui obijt ii die Ԑenfis Februarij Anno Ꝺ ni Mccccci. Cujus Anime propicietur Deus. Amen.

Upon another was this Infcription.

Ꝑic jacet Carolus Ꝩoward unus filiorum Ꝅhome Ꝩoward Comitis Surrie, qui quidem Carolus obijt iij die Ԑaij Anno Ꝺ ni Mcccccxij. Cujus Anime propicietur Deus. Amen.

Upon another was this Infcription.

Ꝑic jacet Ꝺ nus Ꝩenricus Ꝩoward filius Sereniffimi Ducis Ꝉorfolcie, qui obijt 22 Febr. Anno Ꝺ ni Mcccccxiij Cujus Anime propicietur Deus. Amen.

Surmifes

Surmifes were committed to the *Tower* of *London*, and the *Earl* tried by a *Common Jury*, becaufe (as it was then alledg'd) he was no *Lord* of *Parliament*, and was fentenced and beheaded on *Tower Hill*. The Crime wherewith he was charged was for bearing certain Arms, that were faid did belong to the *King* and *Prince*. The *Earl* juftified the bearing of them, as belonging to divers of his *Anceftors*; affirming, that he had alfo with him the Opinion of the *Heralds* therein. The Duke was attainted by *Parliament* and kept in Prifon till the firft of *Queen Mary*, when the *Attainder* was revers'd; and he again in much Efteem. He fat *Lord High Steward* of *England*, when *John Dudley* of *Northumberland* was tried and fentenced to die; and accordingly afterwards executed, for endeavouring to fet up *Jane* Daughter to the *Duke* of *Suffolk*, faid to be appointed by *Edward* VI. to fucceed him in the Crown. But having attained through fo many Viciffitudes of Fortune to a very great Age, dying left his Honours to his Grandfon [g].   *Thomas*

[g] This *Thomas Howard* Son of *Thomas* Duke of *Norfolk* by *Elizabeth* his firft Wife, was after the Death of his faid Father *Duke* of *Norfolk*, *Earl Marfhal*, Lord *High Treafurer* of *England*, and the feventeenth *Lord* of this *Manor*, being before created *Earl* of *Surrey*, February 1. 1515. *York p.* 212. and *Knight of the Garter*, and in 1519. was made the *King's Deputy* in *Ireland*, where he fuppreffed the *O-Neals* and *O-Carols*, *Peerage* 1. 44. and afterwards *Admiral* of *England*, *Mills's p.* 524.

4

524. and in 1522. He landed in *Bretagne*, forced the Town of *Morleys* and burned it; and having wasted the Country went into *Picardy* to joyn the *Emperor*, *Godwin's Annals* 56. *Cardinal Woolsey* deliver'd the *Great Seal* to this our *Duke* Oct. 18. 1522. *Godwin's Ann.* 105. & *An°.* 25 *Henry* VIII. was upon the Surrender of the *Duke* of *Suffolk* made *Earl Marshal*, and assisted in suppressing that memorable Insurrection in the North call'd the *Pilgrimage* of *Grace*, *Peerage* 1. 49. *May* 2. 1536. *Queen Anne* being arrested was by our *Duke* conveyed to the *Tower*, and on the 15th he sat as *High Steward* on the Arraignment and Trial in the *Hall* of the *Tower*; and passed Sentence upon her either to be burned or beheaded on the Green in the *Tower* as the *King* should think fit, *Godwin's An.* 139. He was after one of the *Godfathers* of *King Edward* VI. who was born *October* 12. 1537. And in 1542. commanded an Army against the *Scots*, whom he overthrew, *Godwin's An.* 183. But *Anno* 1547. he was *attainted* by *Parliament*, and condemn'd to perpetual *Imprisonment*, *January* 20th, and

was excepted out of the *Pardon*, *A°.* 1°. *Edward* VI. and so continued *Prisoner* in the *Tower* until *Queen Mary* came to the Crown, when he was discharg'd and pardon'd, and rode before her in the Procession from the *Tower* to *Westminster*, *Baker* 3. 93. and upon the eighteenth of *August* 1553. he sat as *High Steward* of *England*, when *John Dudley Duke* of *Northumberland*, and others, were at *Westminster* convicted and condemned of High-treason. He died in *September* 1554. *Godwin's An.* 311. at *Kenningale* in *Norfolk*, and was buried at *Framingham* in *Suffolk* (as is suppofed) near his first Wife; there being in the *Chancel* of that *Church* an Alter-tomb for a *Duke* of *Norfolk* and his Wife (their *Effigies* in full Proportion lying thereon) but without any Inscription; at each Corner of which is a *Lion* supporting the Arms of *Howard* with four Quarterings, and on the Bend the Demy-Lion within the *Scotch* Tressure, that *Augmentation* being first granted to his *Father*, who was buried at *Thetford* (as is before mention'd) and this our *Duke* having here buried his first Wife, it is most probable that this

this Monument was erected for him and her: To which may be added (as an Argument to support the aforegoing suppofition) the ufing a *Lion* (one of the Supporters of the *Arms* of *King Edward* IV. whofe Daughter this *Lady* was) to fupport the Arms of *Howard*. He had two Wives, the firft of which was *Anne* third Daughter to *King Edward* IV.

fhe dying without Iffue, was buried at *Framingham*, but the time when, I have not yet met with: By her he had two Sons, both of which died before their Mother without Iffue; whereof one of them nam'd *Thomas* died the third of *Auguft* 1508. and was buried at *Lambeth*, *Sandford Geneal.* 396. *Weftminfter*, *Mills* 525.

On him was the following Epitaph on a Brafs Plate.

Hic jacet D͞nus Thomas filius Thome D͞ni Howard et Uxoris fue, filie Edwardi Regis Anglie Quarti, qui quidem Thomas D͞nus Howard, erat filius et heres Thome Comitis Surrie magni Chefaurarij Anglie, Et obijt iii die menfis Augufti Anno Mccccviij.

Aubrey's Survey Vol. V. 237.

His fecond Wife was *Elizabeth*, Daughter of *Edward Stafford* Duke of *Buckingham*, beheaded the feventeenth of *May* 1521. and by her he had two Sons, *Henry* Earl of *Surrey*, and *Thomas* Vifcount *Bindon*, and one Daughter married to *Henry Fitz-roy* Duke of *Richmond*.

She died according to an Inſcription on a Table in *Howard*'s Chapel at *Lambeth* on the thirtieth of *November*, but in what Year is not ſaid, and was there buried; on which Table was the following Inſcription:

> Good Dutcheſſe of Norfolke
> the Lord have Mercy upon the;
> who dyed at Lambeth
> the laſt of November

> Farewell good Lady and Siſter deare
> In Earth we ſhall never meet heare;
> But yet I truſt with Godis Grace
> In Heaven we ſhall deſerve a Place;
> Yet thy Kyndneſſe ſhall never depart,
> During my Life, out of my Heart:
> Thou waſt to me both fare and neare,
> A Mother, a Siſter, a Friend moſt deare,
> And to all thy Friends moſt ſure and faſt,
> When Fortune had founded his froward Blaſt:
> And to the Poore a very Mother,
> More than was known to any other;
> Which is thy Treaſure now at this Day,
> And for thy Soule they heartily pray:
> So ſhall I doe that here remayne,
> God thy Soule preſerve from Payne.

> By this moſt bounded Brother,
> Henry Lord Stafford.

Aubrey's Survey, Vol. V. 236.

Henry

Henry Howard Earl of *Surrey* (made *Knight of the Garter* by *King Henry* VIII.) eldeſt Son to the aforeſaid *Duke Thomas* by *Elizabeth* his ſecond Wife was, as our Author hath obſerv'd, committed to the *Tower* with his *Father*, and being tried in *Guild-Hall London* by a *Common Jury* January 13. 1546. was by them found guilty, and beheaded on *Tower-Hill* the nineteenth following: What the Reaſons of his Death were, are variouſly reported, our *Author* as aforeſaid gives one, and *Biſhop Godwyn, p.* 203. makes his Popularity, and near Affinity to the Throne the occaſions of the King's Jealouſy; but be they what they will, the *King's Ambaſſadors* abroad notified, to the Courts of their Reſidence, that the *Duke* and his *Son* had conſpired to take upon them the Government during his Life, and after his Death to get the *Prince* into their Hands, *Peerage* 1. 45. This *Henry*, ſaith *Cambden Brit.* 394. was the firſt of our *Engliſh Nobility*, that graced his high Birth with the Ornaments of Learning. *Baker* ſaith, that he wrote divers Treatiſes in *Engliſh Metre, p.* 69. He was firſt buried at *Allhallows Barking*, and thence remov'd to *Framingham*, where in the *Chancel* he is buried together with his Wife, both whoſe *Effigies* lie upon an *Altar-tomb* in full proportion; he with his Coronet by him, and on the Side the following Inſcription.

Henrico Howardo Thomæ ſecundi Ducis Norfolciæ filio primogenito, Thomæ tertij Patri, Comiti Surriæ & Georgiani Ordinis Equiti aurato immaturè anno ſalutis MDXLVI *abrepto: & Franciſcæ uxori ejus filiæ Joannis Comitis Oxoniæ.*
Henricus Howardus Comes Northamptoniæ filius ſecundo genitus hoc ſupremum pietatis in Parentes Monumentum poſuit. Anno Dom. 1614.

By *Frances* Daughter of *John* Earl of *Oxford* he had five Children, *viz. Thomas, Henry, Jane, Margaret* and *Katharine*; whoſe *Effigies* are upon the Ends of the Tomb.

His Arms are the ſame of his Father's.

C c   *Thomas*

Thomas by his Son *Henry* who was beheaded in the time of King *Henry* VIII. as we have before related. When *Charles* IX. of *France* sent *Monsieur Rambolet* his *Ambassador* into *England*, with the Robes and Ornaments of the *Order of St. Michael*, to be bestowed upon which two of the *English* Nobility *Queen Elizabeth* pleas'd; she made choice of this *Duke* of *Norfolk* and the *Earl* of *Leicester*, who were by the said *Rambolet* invested with them.

Mary Queen of *Scots* being made *Prisoner* in *England*, notwithstanding his several Promises and Engagements to the contrary; yet he sollicited her Love, and maintained a Commerce by Letters with the *Bishop* of *Ross* and others sent to and fro in Bottles: And too much inclining to the Persuasions of one *Higford*, who waited on him in his Bed-chamber, and the Insinuations of one *Ridolphus* a Stranger, by the Miscarriage of a Pacquet of Letters the Continuation of his Affections was discover'd; and the *Duke* thereupon committed to the *Tower*. *Higford* being examin'd confess'd the whole matter, as also a Commentary which the *Queen* of *Scots* had caus'd to be written, a Copy whereof the *Duke* had, and having perus'd it order'd *Higford* to burn it, which he neglecting to do, but hiding it under a Bed-mat in the *Duke's Bed-chamber*, it was found and produced as an Evidence against him; so that upon the sixteenth of *January*

and

and fifteenth of *Elizabeth* Annoq; **1573.** the *Duke* was brought to his Trial in *Westminster-Hall, George Talbot* Earl of *Shrewsbury* sitting *Lord High-Steward* for that Day, with twenty six *Lords Commissioners,* this foremention'd Miscarriage, with several other Articles were brought in against him; upon which he was found guilty and condemn'd [h].

[h] This *Thomas* the Son of *Henry,* succeeded his *Grandfather,* and was the eighteenth and last *Lord* of these *Towns* of the *Norfolk* Family in which it had been above four hundred Years. In the first Year of *Queen Mary* the Attainder against him was taken off, and in *January* following he was sent to suppress the Rebellion of Sir *Thomas Wyat* in *Kent,* but upon the Revolt of *Alexander Brett* with his five hundred *Londoners,* our *Duke* and those that accompanied him were so terrified that they betook themselves to flight, *Godwyn's Ann.* 291. In the first Year of *Queen Elizabeth* he was made *Knight of the Garter,* which *Queen* had not sat long on the *Throne* before there was a Design to raise a terrible Rebellion against her, to which our *Duke* was excited, being promis'd by *Robert Rolf* a *Florentine* a Marriage with the *Queen* of *Scots. Bishop of Chichester's Thankful Remembrance, p.* 13. This Proposition being repeated to him by the *Bishop* of *Ross,* and the *Earl* of *Murray,* he advised with the *Earl* of *Arundel* and others of his Friends about it, who all advis'd to acquaint the *Queen* of *Scots* with it, which was done by the said *Earl* of *Arundel* and others, as she was also by the *Duke* himself, who wrote to her. Which coming to *Queen Elizabeth's* Ear, she sharply rebuk'd him, commanding him to desist, which he promised to do, and retired into *Norfolk;* but the *Duke's* Correspondence being discover'd, he upon Examination own'd it, and was sent to the *Tower;* and upon his Acknowledgment was afterwards releas'd,

Thus (faith *Speed*) *Thomas Duke* of *Norfolk* for pro-poſing a *Marriage*, &c. proceeded ſo far as the Letter of the Law took Advantage of his Life, to the great Sorrow and Laments of many. He was a Perſon favoured of his *Prince*, and beloved of the People. *Queen Elizabeth* reſpited his Execution till *June* 2. 1574. when about eight of the Clock in the Morning being brought out of the *Tower* to the ordinary *Scaffold* upon the *Hill*, he penitently there ſuffered Death, by the Loſs of his Head, and in him the Dominion of the *Dukes* of *Norfolk* over this *Town* ceaſed[i].

Queen

leas'd, *Baker* 4. 23. 26. But the Continuance of his Affections and Correſpondence being again diſcovered by the Miſcarriage of a Pacquet of Letters ſent from *Ridolph* to the *Biſhop* of *Roſs*, he was again committed to the *Tower*, and at his Trial charged with a Conſpiracy to dethrone *Queen Elizabeth*, and bring in foreign Forces. And that whereas he knew, that the *Queen* of *Scots* had quartered the Arms of *England*, and aſpired at the Crown, he had without conſulting *Queen Elizabeth* gone about to marry her, and lent her great Sums of Money con-

trary to his Promiſe and own Hand writing: That he had ſupplied the *Earls* of *Northumberland* and *Weſtmoreland* with Moneys, who having broke out into open Rebellion were fled into *Scotland*: That he had ſought for auxiliary Forces from the *Pope*, *Spain*, &c. for ſetting the *Queen* of *Scots* at Liberty ; and reſtoring the Romiſh Religion, &c. *Dugd. Bar.* 3. 276.

[i] He had three *Wives*, the firſt was *Mary* Daughter and Coheir of *Henry Fitz-Alan* Earl of *Arundel*, by whom he had Iſſue only *Philip*, who was afterwards *Earl* of *Arundel* in

4   Right

Queen *Elizabeth* kept thefe Lordfhips of *Harwich* and *Dovercourt* in the Crown during her Life [k].

King

Right of his Mother. She died *Auguft* 25. 1557. and was buried at St. *Clement Danes, Dugd. Bar.* 3. 276. His fecond Wife was *Margaret*, the Daughter and only Heir of *Thomas Audley*, *Baron Audley* of *Waldon* in *Effez*, *Chancellor* of *England*; and Widow of *Henry Dudley* (*Audley* faith *Mills* 527.) that was flain at St. *Quintins*. She died in Childbed the ninth of *January* 1563. and lies buried at *Framingham*, where her Effigy in full Proportion lies upon an *Altar-tomb* in the *Chancel*: By her he had four Children, *viz. Thomas*, *William*, *Elizabeth* and *Margaret*. His third Wife was *Elizabeth* Daughter of Sir *Francis Leiborne*, Knight; and Widow of *Thomas Lord Dacre Baron* of *Gilfeland* and of *Grey Stock*, *Mills*'s *Cat.* 527. By her I find no Iffue recorded, nor when fhe died, nor where buried; perhaps it was at *Framingham*, there being the Effigy of another Wife of this *Duke* on the fame *Tomb* with

the foregoing; but *Peter Le Neve*, Efq; *Norroy* thinks it was for the firft Wife, which Opinion of his feems probable, from the Arms of *Fitz-Alan* being on the faid *Tomb*; and then as the *Effigies* is fo, that if that of the *Duke* had been thereon placed, that of hers had lain on his Right Hand in token of precedency of the other, and fhe being according to *Dugdale* buried at St. *Clement Danes London*, this then can be only her *Cenotaph*. Between the two Effigies aforefaid was room referv'd for that of the *Duke*, whereby is fhewed it was his Defign to be himfelf there buried; but he was firft buried in the *Chapel* of the *Tower*, and after that remov'd, but to what Place I have not yet met with; probably it was to *Framingham*, when the Remains of his Father was removed from *Allhallows Barking London* thither.

[k] Queen *Elizabeth*, after her being poffeft of this Mannor by the Attainder of the Duke of *Norfolk*,

Norfolk, did by Patent dat. in the Year of her Reign *Annoque Domini* grant the Marſh lying on the Weſt-ſide of *Harwich* to Hill, and *James* who ſold it out by Cow-walks to ſuch Perſons as would pur-chaſe of them.

The long Reign of this Queen, even after ſhe became Proprie-tor of theſe Towns, and the great variety of Events therein tranſacted, afford a long Field for Hiſtory, and they having been copiouſly treated of by o-thers, all that I ſhall mention in this Place, are, *Firſt,* A Mar-riage propounded between the Queen and the Duke of *Alanſon* or *Anjou,* which is earneſtly ſo-licited by the Queen Mother of *France, Delegates* are here-upon appointed on both Sides, and *Articles* at laſt agreed on, after which the Duke came over, and ſtays here three Months, is kindly received by the Queen, and admitted to many private Conferences with her; but being thwarted by the Earl of *Leiceſter* and the *Court Ladies,* for fear of re-introducing Popery, it came to nothing. A ſecond Thing is the Accuſation, Ar-

4

raignment, Condemnation, and Execution of *Mary* Queen of *Scots;* four *Articles* are alledged againſt her, as her uſurping the Title of *England:* Endeavour-ing without the Queen's Con-ſent a Marriage with the Duke of *Norfolk:* Imploring Aid from foreign *Princes:* And practiſing her own *Enlargement,* all which Queen *Mary* either denied or fairly extenuated. Her Trial was in *Foderinghey Caſtle* in *Nor-thamptonſhire,* where being found guilty ſhe was ſentenced, and on the firſt of *Auguſt* 1586. be-headed on a Scaffold erected. in the great Hall of the Caſtle. A third was her aſſiſting the States of *Holland* againſt the King of *Spain,* with one thou-ſand Horſe, and five thouſand Foot, under the Command of the Earl of *Leiceſter* as General; who landing at *Fluſhing* in *De-cember* 1584. was well received by Sir *Philip Sidney* Governour of that Place. A fourth was the *Spaniſh* intended Invaſion in 1588. in which they had about one hundred and thirty Ships, with nineteen thouſand two hundred and ninety Soldiers, eight thouſand three hundred and fifty Mariners, two thouſand and

and eighty Galley-flaves, and two thoufand fix hundred and thirty great Ordnance: The *Queen* fets forth her Navy, under the Command of the Lord *Charles Howard* Admiral, Sir *Francis Drake* Vice-Admiral, *Hawkins, Forbiſher* and others; who fetting Sail from *Plymouth* on *July* the twenty firſt bore up to them, and upon Signal given the head Ships on each fide engaged, until Night parted them; on the twenty third and twenty fifth they renewed the fight with great Refolution, wherein the *Engliſh* had the better; when on the twenty feventh of *July*, the *Spaniſh Armada* came to an Anchor near *Calais*, where the *Engliſh Admiral* having on the twenty eighth converted eight of his worſt Ships into Fireſhips, fent them in the Night before the Wind towards the *Spaniſh* Fleet, who feeing them all on fire made the beſt way they could flying towards *Flanders*, where before *Graveling* being encountered by the *Engliſh*,

affifted by the *Dutch*, the Remains of them were forced home by the North Paffage round *Scotland:* Queen *Elizabeth* herfelf came with a confiderable Army to the Camp at *Tilbury* in *Effex* to prevent the defigned Invafion. Fifthly, The Queen *Anno* 1591. fent the Earl of *Effex* with four thoufand Men to affift the King of *Navarre* in gaining the Crown of *France* left him by *Henry* III, which was afterwards effected. And laftly, Her Death which happened at *Richmond* on the 24th of *March* 1602. of her Reign the forty fifth, and Age the feventieth, and buried at *Weſtminſter* on the North fide of King *Henry* the feventh's Chapel, on the twenty eighth of the following *April*, attended by fixteen hundred Mourners, over whom King *James* erected a fumptuous Monument, on which is her Effigies royally attired cut in white Marble, with the following Epitaphs.

I. On a Tablature over the Cornish at the Head of the Tomb.

MEMORIÆ ÆTERNÆ

ELIZABETHÆ ANGLIÆ, FRANCIÆ, ET HIBERNIÆ
REGINÆ, R. HENRICI VIII. FILIÆ, R. HEN. VII. NEPTI, R.
ED. IIII. PRONEPTI, PATRIÆ PARENTI, RELIGIONIS
ET BONARVM ARTIVM ALTRICI, PLVRIMARVM
LINGVARVM PERITIA, PRÆCLARIS TVM ANIMI
TVM CORPORIS DOTIBVS REGIIS Q. VIRTVTIBVS

SVPRA SEXVM PRINCIPI
INCOMPARABILI.

IACOBVS MAGNÆ BRITANNIÆ FRANCIÆ ET
HIBERNIÆ REX, VIRTVTVM ET REGNORVM
HÆRES, BENE MERENTI PIE
POSVIT.

On the Basement at the Head.

REGNO CONSORTES ⎱⎰ ET MARIA SORORES,
ET VRNA, HIC OBDOR ⎰⎱ IN SPE RESVRREC-
MIMVS, ELIZABETHA ⎱⎰ TIONIS.

On another Tablature over the Cornish at the Foot.

MEMORIÆ SACRVM

RELIGIONE AD PRIMÆVAM SINCERITATEM RESTAVRATA,
PACE FUNDATA, MONETA AD IUSTVM VALOREM REDVGTA,
REBELLIONE DOMESTICA VINDICATA, GALLIA MALIS
INTESTINIS PRÆCIPITI SUBLEVATA, BELGIO SUSTENTATO,
HISPANICA CLASSE PROFLIGATA, HIBERNIA PULSIS
HISPANIS, ET REBELLIBUS AD DEDITIONEM COACTIS
PACATA, REDDITIBUS UTRIUSQ. ACADEMIÆ LEGE
ANNONARIA PLVRIMUM ADAVCTIS, TOTA DENIQ. ANGLIA
DITATA, PRUDENTISSIMEQ. ANNOS XLV. ADMINISTRATA
ELIZABETHA REGINA VICTRIX TRIUMPHATRIX, PIETATIS
STVDIOSISSIMA, FÆLICISSIMA, PLACIDA MORTE SEPTVAGENARIA
SOLUTA, MORTALES RELIQVIAS DUM CHRISTO IVBENTE
RESURGANT IMMORTALES, IN HAC ECCLESIA CELEBERRIMA
AB IPSA CONSERVATA, ET DENVO FUNDATA DEPOSUIT.

On the Basement at the Foot.

OBIIT XXIIII. MARTII ⎫ ⎧REGNI XLV
ANNO SALUTIS ⎬ ⎨ÆTATIS LXX.
M.DC.II. ⎭ ⎩

For

For the Benefit of the *English* Reader, I have here tranfcribed this Epitaph, as *Englifhed* by Mr. *Speed* in his Chronicle of the Kings of *England, p.*

For an eternal Memorial.

Unto Elizabeth, *Queen of* England, France *and* Ireland; *Daughter of King* Henry VIII, *Grandchild to King* Henry VII, *Great-Grandchild to King* Edward IV. *The Mother of this her Country; the Nurfe of Religion and Learning; for perfect Skill of very many Languages, for glorious Endowments as well of Mind as Body, and for her regal Vertues beyond her Sex.*

A Prince incomparable.

James *of* Great Britain, France *and* Ireland, *King, Inheritor both of her Vertues and Kingdoms, to her fo well deferving, pioufly hath this erected.*

Conforts both in Throne and in Grave, here reft we two Sifters, Elizabeth *and* Mary, *in hope of our Refurrection.*

Sacred unto Memory.

Religion to its primitive Sincerity reftored, Peace thoroughly fetled, Coin to the true Value refined; Rebellion at home extinguifhed; France *near Ruin by inteftine Mifchiefs relieved;* Netherlands *fupported;* Spain's Armado *vanquifhed;* Ireland, *with* Spaniards *Expulfion, and Traitors Coercion, quieted; both* Univerfities *Revenues, by a Law of Provifion, exceedingly augmented: Finally, all* England *enriched, and* XLV Years *moft prudently governed,* Elizabeth *a Queen, a Conquerefs, a Triumpher, the moft devoted to Piety, the moft happy, after* lxx *Years of her Life, quietly by Death departed, hath left here (in this moft famous collegiate Church, which by her was eftablifhed and refounded) thefe Remains of her Mortality, until at* Chrift's Call *they fhall again rife immortal.*

She died xxiiii. *March, the Year of* Salvation MDCII. *of her Reign* XLV, *of her Age* LXX.

King

King *James* continued them feveral Years as he found them, but in the Year   of his Reign, difpofes not only of what remained of them,   but alfo of feveral other Lordfhips and Lands in this Hundred (of *Tendring*)[1] unto Sir *George Whitmore*, Knight; from whom they

[1] Upon the Succeffion of King *James* I. to the Crown he became Lord of this Manor, which he kept for fome time in his Hands. Upon the Death of Queen *Elizabeth*, he was proclaimed King of *England, Scotland, France* and *Ireland*; and having confirmed the Privy Council of *England* with fome Additions, he fet forward for *England* the 5th of *April* 1603, and by eafy Journeys came to *Theobalds* in *Hertfordfhire* on the third of *May*, and on the feventh came to *London*, being followed by the *Queen*, Prince *Henry*, and Lady *Elizabeth*, who arrived on the twenty feventh of *June*. In 1603, he granted to the Corporation of *Harwich*, that ample Charter by which they are now governed, of which a fuller Account will be afterwards inferted. The fame Year a Confpiracy was difcovered for

furprifing his Majefty and Council, and fetting up the Lady *Arbella*, for which the Lords *Cobham* and *Grey*, Sir *Walter Raleigh* and others are apprehended in *July*, and fent to the Tower; and in *November* arraigned at *Winchefter* and condemned, and fome executed. On the twenty fifth of *July* the fame Year being the Feaft of St. *James*, the King and Queen were crown'd at *Weftminfter* by *John Whitgift*, Archbifhop of *Canterbury*, Anno 1605. was the memorable Difcovery of the *Powder Plot*, which was a Defign of Blowing up the King and Houfe of Lords by Gun-powder, thirty fix Barrels of which were found in thofe Cellars, depofited there by *Robert Catisby* and others; the Difcovery of which being made on the fifth Day of *November*, that Day was therefore fet apart for a Memorial of

Thankf-

Thankſgiving: The Manner of diſcovering which, as well as the ſecret Conſpiracy for carrying on the Deſign, is more fully and at large related by Dr. *Carlton* Biſhop of *Chicheſter*, in his *thankful Remembrance of God's Mercy*, cap. 17. contained in thirty four Pages, to which I refer thoſe that deſire to ſee more of this Matter, and only take Notice that *Guido Faux* and others were arraigned, condemned and executed for it.

The next Year, *viz.* 1606. *Chriſtian* King of *Denmark*, Brother to Queen *Anne*, did *July* 17. with eight Ships come to Anchor in the River *Thames* overagainſt *Graveſend*, where he was met the next Day by King *James* and Prince *Henry* attended with many Lords, who conducted him thro' *London* to *Somerſet-Houſe* in the *Strand*, where being royally entertained until the twelfth of *Auguſt*, he departed for his own Country.

Hugh Earl of *Tyr-Oen* Anno 1608. notwithſtanding he had been but newly pardoned, fled beyond Sea, where with the Earl of *Tyrconnel* and others, he ſollicited Aid from foreign Princes in Order to a new Rebellion, offering the Kingdom of *Ireland* to the Pope for his Aſſiſtance.

The *New-Exchange* in the *Strand* was *Anno Domini* 1609. finiſhed by *Robert* Earl of *Saliſbury*, to which the King on *April* the eleventh gave the Name of *Britain's Burſe*. And upon making Prince *Henry* a Knight, the King had an Aid of his Subjects. This Year the King by his *Letters Patents* dat. the twenty fourth of *September*, granted the *Rectory* of the Church of *Dovercourt* to *Francis Morris* and *Francis Phillips*.

Prince *Henry* the following Year was created *Prince of Wales* with great Solemnity upon the 30th of *May* 1610. And by *Letters Patents* bearing date the fourteenth Day of *March Anno* 8º. *Jac.* The King granted the Manor of *Dovercourt* to *George Whitmore*, Eſq; and *Thomas Whitmore*, and to the Heirs of the ſaid *George* in Fee Simple, who thereby became Lord of this Manor.

they

they defcended to his Son and Heir, the worfhipful *William Whitmore*, Efq; [m].   CHAP.

[m] This *George Whitmore*, Efq; was fecond Son of *William Whitmore* Merchant of *London*, the Son of *Richard Whitmore*, of *Charley* in the County of *Salop*, Efq;. He was one of the Aldermen of *London*, being chofen for *Langbourn* Ward, and by *Henry Smith*, Efq; made one of the Truftees to whom he conveyed all his Eftate both real and perfonal for charitable Ufes; as is before related *Anno* 1621. He was chofen one of the Sheriffs of *London*, and *Lord-Mayor* Anno 1631. and *Knighted* by King *Charles* I. at *Greenwich* the 27th of *May* 1632. He lived moftly at his Manfion Houfe call'd *Barnes*, between *Hoxton* and *Kingfland* in the County of *Middlefex*, and Parifh of *Hackney* (which Houfe ftill bears his Name) where he died the 12th of *December* 1654. and was buried at *London*, *January* the eleventh following: He married _____ Daughter and Heir of _____ *Cafcot* of _____ by whom he had five Children ; *William* , *Charles* , *George*, *Mary*, *Elizabeth*, MS. P. Le *Neve*, Efq; *Norroy*, *Anne* Wife of Sir *John Robinfon*, Bart. appears to have been another of his Daughters, as an *Epitaph* in *Newnham* Church in the County of ----- doth feem to prove, which *Epitaph* is as follows,

H. S. E.

GVLIELMVS ROBINSON *Eques auratus* JOHANNIS ROBINSON *Baronetti filius natu maximus, quem delicias humani Generis uno ore prædicabant quotquot Illuftres ejus natales, morum fuavitatem, lumen Juventæ, & egregij vultûs amabiles honores æquo animo contemplantur ; fed ut magis, Viator, mireris, magifq; plores, vix in ullo unquam Juvene vel dulciùs emicuit, vel benigniùs confpiravit chariffimum illud & numerofum animi Corporifq; Decus.*

4   *Spacium*

Spacium annorum quinque (& proh dolor ! seipsum) con-
sumpserat, Galliam, Italiam, Ægyptum, Palæstinam *aliasq; cele-*
briores Turcici Imperij *partes peragrando ; o quid in exteras Re-*
giones avidè transvolamus ! num sit mortalis vel etiam Domi
transacta. Natus est Decem. 16. 1654. *Denatus* Febru. 16. 1678.

Monumentum hoc Mater ejus mœstissima ANNA ROBINSON,
GEORGIJ WHITMORE *Equitis Aurati filia & ipsa eximia Fœmina*
dilectissimo filio è proprijs sumptibus erigendum instravit.

Le Neve Mon Angl. V. 2. 193.

William Whitmore the Father of this Sir *George* was likewise an *Alderman* of *London*, as appears from the following *Epitaph* in the Church of St. *Peter* in the City of *Bath*.

ANN BABER Widow of FRAN.
BABER of Chew magna in Com.
Somerset Esq; who was Daughter
of WILLIAM WHITMORE of London
Alderman Obijt ult Dec. 1651.

Le Neve's Mon. Angl. 2. 10.

This *William* I take to be the same Person who *Anno* 1600. gave two hundred Pounds to the Hospital of *Bridewell London, Review of London, p.* 734. See an Inscription on the Wall: Also Mrs. *Ann Whitmore* gave one hundred and fifty Pounds to this Hospital *Anno* 1615. See the Inscription on the Wall without, ib. It is probable she was likewise related to our Sir *George*.

He was succeeded in the Lordship of this Mannor by *William Whitmore*, Esq; his eldest Son and Heir, who upon the Death of his Father, left *Ramsey*, where he had sometime resided, and went and lived at his Father's late House at *Barnes*; where he kept open House for some Years, and in his advanced Years he married one of his menial Servants with whom he lived happily, and had

had by her one Son. He died at *Barnes*, and was buried at *Ramfey Auguft* 9. 1678. in the Paffage between the Pews of the Chancel at the Entrance thereof out of the Church, over whom is laid a Black Marble Stone with the following Infcription:

Here lyeth the Body of,
William Whitmore Esq; dyed
in the Year of our Lord God 1678.
Aged 64 Years.

On the North-fide of this, but covered by Mr. *Burr's* Pew, is another Black Marble Stone with the following fhort Infcription:

And also the Body of Penelope
his Wife.

Over which is cut the following *Efcutcheon,* viz. Quarterly of 4 1 and 4 *Fretty,* 2 and 3 *Barry of* 8. Creft a *Bird perching.*

By his laft Will and Teftament, he fettled his Eftate (provided his Son died without Iffue) upon divers *Truftees,* who were to fell the Eftate and divide it among about twenty five *Legatees* therein named.

William his only Son and Heir held this Manor, he was about the eighth or ninth Year of his Age, and in the Life-time of his Father contracted in Marriage with the Daughter of Sir *William Whitmore* of *Shropfhire,* which Marriage he confummated fometime after his Father's Death; he was unfortunately killed by his Piftol which lay by him in his own Chariot, as he was returning from *Epfom,* dying under Age and without Iffue; and was buried under his own Pew in the Chancel of *Ramfey* clofe to his Father, over whom is laid a Black Marble Stone.

Sir *Thomas Davall,* Knight, was the next Lord of this Manor, which he purchafed among others

others (in the Month of *March* 168⅘. The Truftees who fold were *William* Lord Marquis of *Powis*, *William* Earl of *Craven*, and *Charles* Lord *North* and *Grey*) of the Truftees aforefaid. He was knighted at *Whitehall* by King *Charles* II. on the twenty firft of *February* 1682, was made *Recorder* of *Harwich*, and reprefented that Corporation in *Parliament* divers times, a Juftice of the Peace for the County of *Effex*, and *Anno* 1707. one of the Lieutenancy of the *City* of *London*. He died *November Anno* 1712. and was buried at *Ramfey* the feventh of *December* following in a Vault he had made in the Chancel; but there is no Monument nor Infcription for him, only on the South - fide are his *Gauntlets*, *Spurs*, *Helmet* with his Creft (a *Hand proper holding a Flower de lys Arg.) Surcoate, Buckler* and *Sword*, over which hand three *pendants,* viz. one with the *Union Crofs*, the fecond with the Arms of *Davall,* viz. *Gul. a Lion rampant between eight Flower de lys Argt.* third the Arms of *Davall Imp. Burr.* viz. *Ermin on a Chief indented fab. two Lionels Or.* He married *Rebecca* Daugh-

ter of *Daniel Burr* of *Amfterdam* in *Holland* Merchant, fhe was buried in the fame Vault with him on *January* 13. 1714. By her he had three Children, *viz. Daniel* buried in the fame Vault *September* 29. *Anno* 1711. *Thomas* who fucceeded his Father, and *Mary* who dying at *London* at about eight Years old was there buried ; but upon the Death of her Brother *Daniel* brought down to *Ramfey* and depofited with him, in the fame Vault.

Thomas Davall, Efq; only furviving Child was upon the Death of his Father Lord of this Manor, he was knighted by Queen *Anne* at *Kenfington* upon the 19th of *June* 1713, and dying before his Mother in *April* 1714. was likewife buried at *Ramfey* the fixth Day of *May* following, for whom on the North-fide of the Chancel are againft the Wall the fame Trophies as for his Father, with the Addition of two Pendants, *viz.* one with the *Union Crofs*, one with *Davall* only as afore, and the other *Davall* Impailing *Van Hatton* quarterly of 4 *viz.* 1 and 4 *Gul. a Cheveron Argt.* between three Sea Pies (as I take them)

them) *Or*. 2 and 3 *Argt. two Quills in Saltier Or*. He married *Lydia Katharine* Daughter of *John Van Hattam*, Efq; by *Lydia* his Aunt, who furvived him: By her he had two Sons, *Thomas* and *John*, which laft not long furviving his Father, was buried in the Vault at *Ramfey*, *Feb.* 8. 1715. On the fame North-fide of the Chancel, but Weft of his Father's are likewife two Pendants for him, *viz.* the Arms of his Father with a *Crefcent* of Diftinction *Or*.

Thomas Davall, Efq; the eldeft Son of the laft Sir *Thomas* was Lord of this Manor, but did not long enjoy it, for dying in his Infancy was buried alfo in the Vault at *Ramfey* on *June* 23. 1718. and with him ended the Family of the Surname of *Davall*. On the South-fide of the Chancel are his *Helmet*, on which his Creft lieth along, and under it his *Surcoat, Buckler* and *Sword*, over which are two Pendants with *Daval* as before.

Upon the Death of this laft Child, a Conteft arofe about the Title to this Eftate, between *Daniel Burr*, Efq; who claimed by Vertue of the Will of Sir *Thomas Davall* the younger,

made in *April Anno Dom.* 1714. and *Lydia Van Hattam, Elizabeth Davall*, and *Mary Davall*, three of the Sifters, and *Kathathrine Bovey* (Daughter and Heir of a fourth Sifter deceafed of Sir *Thomas Davall*, Senr.) who claimed as Co-heirs to the *Davall* Family, which Suit continued until the 30th of *May* 1722. when upon an Iffue directed out of *Chancery*, at a Trial at Bar in the Court of *King's Bench*, (of which Sir *John Pratt* was then Lord *Chief Juftice*) a Verdict was found for Mr. *Burr*: After which the Co-heirs conveyed the Eftate to Mr. *Burr* and his Heirs. The Controverfy arofe upon this Cafe. The Younger Sir *Thomas* having by his Will aforementioned, given this Manor of *Dovercourt*, with other Eftates in *Effex*, to his eldeft Son *Thomas* and the Heirs of his Body, and an Eftate in *Middlefex*, to his younger Son *John* and the Heirs of his Body, and if either of his Sons died without Iffue, what was devifed to him in Tail, to go to the other Son and the Heirs of his Body; (then follows the controverted Claufe) *And if both my faid Sons fhall*

E e *depart*

depart this Life with *(inftead of* without) *Iffue of either of their Bodies,* then *I give all the Pre-mifes in the Counties of* Effex *and* Middlefex *unto my Coufin* Daniel Burr *and his Heirs.*

Daniel Burr, Efq; the Pre-fent Lord of this Manor, mar-ried *Elizabeth* Daughter of *Fre-derick Danchert* of *Amfterdam,* and *Petronella* his Wife, by whom he hath at prefent only three Children, *viz.* two Sons *Frederick* and *Daniel,* and one Daughter *Sophia-Rebecca.* His Arms are *Ermin, on a Chief in-dentate fab. two Lionels ram-pant Or,* and on a Wreath *Argt. and fab. a Cockatrice Gul. Fredrik Dancherts fcheper der ftadt Am-fterdam.*

C H A P. IV.

THE *Municipal, Political, Civil-Conftitution* and *Publick Concern,* exacts our next Difquifition: From its Name is to be gathered, that it was a Town before it was a *Borough,* and a *Borough* before a *Free-Borough,* to which from the Conveniency of its Situa-tion it in procefs of Time attained. And it yet re-tains its ancient Name, *Harvicus,* 𝔥𝔢𝔯𝔢𝔴𝔦𝔷, 𝔥𝔞𝔯-𝔴𝔦𝔠𝔥, &c.

The firft Knowledge we have of its being made a *Free Borough* in the Acceptation of *a Corporation* or *Body-Politique,* was by the Procurement of *Thomas de Brotherton* Earl of *Norfolk,* Lord Marfhal of *England,* and Lord of thefe Towns; who obtained it from his
Brother

Brother King *Edward* II. in the twelfth Year of his Reign, firſt at *York July* the twenty ninth, as he was upon his March with his Army, for regaining the Town of *Berwick* upon *Tweed*; which had been perfidiouſly betrayed about three Years before to the King of *Scots*, by one *Peter Spalding* the Governor thereof, whom juſtly he rewarded for his Treaſon by hanging him [n].

And

[n] The *Scots Anno* 1315. in vain attempted the Surpriſe of *Berwick*, by means of certain Veſſels from the River, which being diſcover'd they were repulſed with Loſs, *Tyrrell's Hiſt.* 3. 264. but on *April* the ſecond *Anno Domini* 1318. the Town was betrayed to them by *Peter Spalding* for a conſiderable Sum of Money, permitting them to Scale the Walls in the Night at a Place where he and his Men kept Guard, as ſaith the Chronicle of *Lanercoſt*; but, *Thomas de la More*, *Polydore Virgil* and others relate, that the Town was taken by Force from the *Engliſh* by King *Robert Bruce*, *Tyrrell's Hiſt.* 3. 272. but be it as it will, King *Edward* Anno 1319. Having raiſed an Army and left the *Queen* at *York*, went and beſieged it, but without effect, tho', as ſaith the foreſaid Chronicle, the *Engliſh* at the firſt Aſſault mounted the Walls, and had they been timely ſeconded, might have taken the Town. *Spalding*, ſaith Mr. *Taylor*, was hanged for his Treachery, but how he came into the King's Hands doth not appear, ſeeing the Attempt the King made to retake the Town, proved ineffectual: For the King upon the News of the Defeat, which the *Scots* on the twenty firſt of *September* gave to the *Yorkſhire* Army under the Command of *William de Melton* Archbiſhop of *York*, preſently raiſed the Siege of *Berwick*, and made haſte with his Army to have intercepted their Return, *Tyrrell* Vol. III. *p.* 274.

E e 2

But

And then Secondly, at the Siege of 𝕭𝖊𝖗𝖜𝖎𝖈𝖐 on the fixteenth of *September* following, wherein the King by his Charters grants to his moft dear Brother, *That the Town of* 𝕳𝖆𝖗𝖜𝖎𝖈 *be a Free-Borough, and that the faid Earls Men and Tenants of the faid Town, and their Heirs and Succeffors be Free-Burgeffes; and that they ufe and injoy the Liberties and Free-Cuftoms appertaining to a Free-Borough, with a Market every Week on* 𝕿𝖚𝖊𝖋𝖉𝖆𝖕, *and Free-Cuftoms belonging to the like Markets,* &c.

How it was governed by thefe firft *Charters* we are much to feek: Some fay, they refer'd to a then known Ufage and Practice, or elfe were left very much at large to themfelves, to order their Government as near as they could to fome one *Specimen* or Example of any one particular *Free-Borough* in *England:* For our firft *Charters* never prefcribe, or order any fet Form of *Government* to the Town: And we find at this Day in feveral Corporations, feveral different Reliques and Remains of their ancient Ufages.   Some being governed

---

But Sir *Richard Baker* hath cleared this Matter, that it was not King *Edward*, but the King of *Scots* that hanged *Spalding*, for he thus writes, *Not long after the Town of* Berwick *was betrayed to the* Scots, *through the Treafon of* Peter Spalding *the Governor, and other* Englifhmen, *whom the King of* Scots, *to make them an Example, caufed to be hanged for being Traitors to their Country*, Chron. I. 145.

by

by *Port-Reeves* or *Port-Men*, fome by an *Alderman*, others by *Bailiffs*, fome by *Conftables*, aad fome inter-mixt *Bailiffs* and *Conftables*; and thus we find it was here, in the thirty fecond of *Henry* VI. in a *Court Roll*, where a Letter is entred from the Reverend Prince their Lord the Duke of *Norfolk* (as he is there intitled) [*in Cifta Burgi*] to the *Bailiff*, *Conftables* and *Tenants* of *Harwich*, wherein he defires and prays them to admit one *Clayfon* to the Freedom of their Corpo-ration to practife the Law, and begins his Letter in thefe Words; Rých tpuytý anð pelbelovýð ye ʒnete yoy pell Anð yoyaymuch ay Jon Clayyone a tenant oy Ouyýy, &c.

In the Reign of King *Edward* VI, and after him of *Philip* and *Mary*, we find [*in lib. major. in Cifta Ecclefiæ*] the *Church-Wardens* were the *Chamberlains* and *Treafurers* of this Borough.

In Queen *Elizabeth*'s Reign it was govern'd by twelve *Burgeffes*, out of which every Year one was elected to *prefide*, who was fometimes call'd *Capitalis Burgenfis*, and other whiles *Capitalis Burgenfis*, *five Præpofitus villæ Herewici:* But they always acted with the Con-fent of the *Community*. There is [*in Cifta Burgi*] an indented Deed dated *apud Herwic Septembris quarti primo* Edwardi IV. *by which* Henry Broke, John Bufh, *&c. cum tota Communitate Villæ, Burgi five Libertatis* Herwici *in Com.* Effex, *unanimis affenfu & voluntate dant, concedant & confirmant,* Johannæ *uxori* Johan-

I

nis

nis Clayſon *de* Herwico *prædiƈto, &c.* a certain Parcel of their *Common Key,* founded lately by the *Caſtle* near the *Neſs,* &c. which proves not only the Government of the Town anciently incorporated, but alſo the being of the *Caſtle* two hundred Years ago.

The former *Charters* of Incorporation of King *Edward* II, were confirmed in the *Tower* of *London* on the twelfth of *Auguſt* 16. *Edward* III. over *England,* and third of *France.* Then again the twentieth of *March* 1°. *Richard* II. and afterwards ſucceſſively by the three *Henry*'s IV. V. and VI. the laſt of which in the firſt Year of his Reign confirms (as it is there ſaid) *Their Liberties and Franchiſes not in the leaſt revoked; by the Adviſement and the Aſſent of the Lords Spiritual and Temporal in his Parliament held, and being at* Weſtminſter*;* and again *May* the twenty firſt *Regni ſui* 16°. at *Weſtminſter accepts of, approves of, ratifies and confirms to the Burgeſſes of the aforeſaid Town,* &c.

Theſe were again confirmed and renewed by the Charters of *Edward* VI, King *Philip* and Queen *Mary* in the firſt Years of their Reigns, and by Queen *Elizabeth* in the ſecond of hers.

April the eighteenth *Anno* 2°. *Jacobi Regis,* Sir *Edward Coke,* Knight, at that Time *Attorney-General* to King *James* obtained of him that noble *Charter,* whereby the former Governments of this Corporation were

were altered and fixed upon a *Mayor* °, annually to
be

° The Election of whom is upon St. *Andrew's* Day *November* the
thirtieth, and he is to be sworn into his Office upon the twenty
first of *December* following, *viz.* the Feast of St. *Thomas:* The
first *Mayor* appointed by this *Charter* was *John Hankin,* Gent.
who served for the Year 1603. The Persons who succeeded
him in that Office, until the present Time, with the several
Years that they served in, are contained in the following List.

1604 Mr. *Edmund Seaman*	1634 Mr. *Walter Stanley*
1605 Mr. *James Burker*	1635 Mr. *John Peck*
1606 Mr. *Robert Bence*	1636 Mr. *John Rolfe*
1607 Mr. *Robert Smarte*	1638 Mr. *Richard Hankin*
1609 Mr. *Henry Hankin*	1639 Mr. *Roger Coleman*
1610 Mr. *John Hankin* 2.	1640 Mr. *Arthur Hawkes*
1611 Mr. *Robert Goodwin*	1641 Mr. *John Mace*
1612 Mr. *Thomas Shrive*	1642 Mr. *Edward Seaman*
Mr. *Robert Offley*	1643 Mr. *John Rolfe* 2.
Mr. *Edward Rafe*	1644 Mr *Richard Hankin* 2.
Mr. *William Wye*	1647 Mr. *Robert Pashall*
Mr. *Edmond Seaman* 2.	1648 Mr. *Thomas Crispe*
Mr. *William King*	1649 Mr. *Richard Hankin* 3.
Mr. *Robert Ruffel*	1651 Mr. *Thomas King*
1620 Mr. *Richard Smart*	1652 Mr. *Arthur Hawkes* 2.
Mr. *Robert Lee*	1653 Mr. *James Sacks*
Mr. *Thomas Shrive* 2.	1654 Mr. *Richard Hurlock*
Mr. *Robert Seaman*	1655 Mr. *Richard Hankin* 4.
Mr. *John Allen*	1656 Mr. *John Hunter*
1627 Mr. *Richard Smart* 2.	1657 Mr. *Daniel Cole*
Mr. *Hugh Branham*	2658 Mr. *Richard Smart*
1632 Mr. *John Hearde*	1660 Mr. *Milo Hubbard*
1633 Mr. *Richard Smart* 3.	1661 Mr. *Arthur Hawkes* 3.
2	1662 Mr.

1662 Mr. *Thomas Keys*
1663 Mr. *George Coleman*
1664 Mr. *James Sacks* 2.
1665 Mr. *Arthur Hawkes* 4.
1666 Mr. *Edward Robinson*
1667 Mr. *John Hunter* 2.
1668 Mr. *William Garrard*
1669 Mr. *Henry Munt*
1670 Mr. *Thomas Keyes* 2.
1671 { Mr. *George Coleman*
      { Mr. *Thomas Langley*
1672 Mr. *John Brown*
1673 Mr. *Robert Seaman*
1674 Mr. *John Rolfe*
1675 Mr. *Thomas Langley* 2.
1676 Sir *Anthony Dean* K^t.
1677 Mr. *Samuel Newton*
1678 Mr. *Thomas Langley* Senr.3.
1679 Mr. *Edward Robinson*
1680 Mr. *John Brown* 2.
1681 Mr. *Robert Seaman* 2.
1682 Sir *Anthony Dean* K^t. 2.
1683 Mr. *Daniel Smyth*
1684 Mr. *William Garrard*
1685 Mr. *John Rolfe* 2.
1686 Mr. *Simon Sandford*
1687 Mr. *John Brown* 3.
1688 Mr. *Charles Smith*
1689 Mr. *Thomas Langley*
1690 Mr. *Robert Seaman* 3.
1691 Mr. *Daniel Smith* 2.
1692 Mr. *Richard Tye*
1693 Mr. *Simon Sandford* 2.
1694 Mr. *Thomas Langley* 4.
1695 Mr. *Charles Smyth* 2.

1696 Mr. *Daniel Smyth* 3.
1697 Mr. *Thomas Langley* Junr.2.
1698 Mr. *William Rudland*
1699 Mr. *Richard Tye* 2.
1700 Mr. *Richard Grey*
1701 Mr. *Simon Sandford* 3.
1702 Mr. *Phillip Deane*
1703 Mr. *Charles Smyth* 3.
1704 Mr. *Daniel Smyth* 4.
1705 Mr. *Thomas Langley* 3.
1706 Mr. *Richard Tye* 3.
1707 Capt. *Richard Grey* 2.
1708 Mr. *John Phillipson*
1709 Mr. *Simon Sandford* 4.
1710 Mr. *Phillip Deane* 2.
1711 Mr. *Madison Hunt*
1712 Mr. *Daniel Smyth* 5.
1713 Mr. *Thomas Langley* 4.
1714 Mr. *Madison Hunt* 2.
1715 Mr. *Samuel Lucas*
1716 Mr. *Thomas Osbourn*
1717 Mr. *Richard Tye* 4.
1718 Mr. *Madison Hunt* 3.
1719 Mr. *Milo Rudland*
1720 Mr. *Samuel Lucas* 2.
1721 Mr. *John Phillipson* 2.
1722 Mr. *Thomas Phillips*
1723 Mr. *Daniel Smyth* 6.
1724 Mr. *Samuel Lucas* 3.
1725 Mr. *John Phillipson* 3.
1727 { Mr. *Thomas Phillips* 2.
      { Mr. *Thomas Osborn* 2.
1728 Mr. *George Rolf*
     Mr. *Giles Baker*
1729 Mr. *Samuel Lucas* 4.

be

be chofen out of eight *Aldermen*ᵖ, who with twenty four *capital Burgeffes* conftituted the *Corporation* and *Government* of this *Borough*, Sir *Edward* himfelf being the firft *Recorder* for his Life q, which alfo gives them
the

ᵖ Which were nominated in the *Charter*, and were the following Perfons.

John Handkin, Ambrofe Gilbert, *James Burkery*, *Robert Smart*, *Henry Handkin, Edmund Seaman*, *Thomas Shrive* and *Thomas Grey*, Gentlemen; of thefe neither Mr. *Ambrofe Gilbert*, nor Mr. *Thomas Grey*, lived to be *Mayors*.

The Election of the *Mayor Alderman* and *capital Burgeffes* are in the faid *capital Burgeffes* only.

q This Sir *Edward Coke* was only Son of *Robert Coke* of *Milleham (Mileham)* in the County of *Norfolk*, Efq; by *Winefred* his Wife, Daughter of *William Knightly*; as appears by the Infcription on the Monument of the faid *Robert*, which was for-

merly on a Wall of the Chancel of St. *Andrews Holbourn, London*, as follows.

Monumentum Roberti Coke *de* Milleham *(Mileham) in Comitatu* Norfolciæ *Armig. Illuftriffimi Hofpitii* Lincolnienfis *quondam Socii Primarii. Qui ex* Winefrida *uxore fua*, Gulielmi Knightly *filia, hos fufcepit Liberos* Edwardum Coke, *filium, Majeftatis Regiæ* Attornatum Generalem, Winefridam, Miloni Mingay, *Generof.* Dorotheam, Gulielmo Francklyn, *Generof.* Elizabetham, Richardo Ofborne, *Generof.* Urfulam, Georgio Ledys, *Generof.* Annam, Francifco Stubbe, *Generof.* Margaretam, Roberto Barker, *Armig.* Ethelredam, Nicholao Bohun, *Armig. nuptas.*

Obiit in Hofpitio Prædicto, 15. *die* Novemb. Anno { Domini 1561. Elizab. ——4. Ætat. fuæ 48.

The

The said *Edward Coke*'s birth, saith Sir *Henry Spelman*, might presage his wonderful Excellency, his Mother being delivered of him so suddenly by the Fireside, that she could not be soon enough carried up to her Bed, which stood in the Room above. *New Survey of Great Brit.* Vol. III. *p.* 301. He was educated in Grammatical Learning at *Norwich School*, from thence removed to *Trinity-College* in *Cambridge*; where having studied four Years, he was admitted at *Cliffords-Inn*, and soon after in the *Temple*, where for his remarkable Proficiency, he was called to the Bar in six Years, and upon that chosen Reader of *Lyons-Inn* for three Years. Here his learned Lectures begat him such a Reputation, that crowds of Clients flocked after him; which rendered him acceptable to *Bridget Pafton*, Daughter and Coheir of *John Pafton*, Esq; worth thirty thousand Pounds, and recommended him to *Norwich* for their *Recorder*, and to *Norfolk* for their *Knight* of the *Shire* to sit in Parliament, where he was chosen *Speaker*; after which he was successively the *Queen's Sollicitor* and *Attorney*.

King *James* honoured him with Knighthood, and made him *chief Justice*, first of the *Common-Pleas*, and then of the *King's-Bench*. He did many good and charitable Works, and wrote many excellent Things, among which his Reports will ever be esteemed by all those who value or understand our Constitution. At last, however, this good *Judge*, for Non-compliance with some Court Measures, which he thought unlawful, was removed from his Offices; after which he retired to his Seat at *Goodwick* in *Norfolk*, triumphing in his own Innocency, that he had done nothing illegally, and calling to mind his Motto, when made *Serjeant*, *Lex est tutissima Cassis*. 'Tis remarkable, that Sir *Edward* after he had been a Judge himself was obliged to attend upon others, being forced to serve *High-Sheriff* of *Bucks*, to prevent his being chosen a Member of Parliament, *Kent's Guillim abridged, p.* 773, 774. Which by another Author is thus delivered, that he acted so contrary to the *Court Party* while in *Parliament*, that to prevent his being elected (*again*) as a Member, he he was chofen *Sheriff* of *Buck-ingham-fhire*, and no Excufe would ferve to exempt him from that Office, though he had him-felf been a *chief Juftice*. He was a Man of admirable Parts and of a comely Countenance, de-lighting in good Cloaths, fay-ing, *The Neatnefs of the Body might denote the Purity of the Soul*. He died worth ten thou-fand Pounds a Year, fo that tho' he had many Children, they might be faid to be all Heirs, *New Survey of Great Brit.* Vol. III. 301. He was a great Be-nefactor for fupporting the Free-School at *Thetford* in *Norfolk*, *New Survey of Great Britain*, Vol. III. *p.* 339. He alfo found-ed a *School* at his own Charges in *Goodwick*. He had when he was a private Lawyer fecured fome Lands to the Church of *Norwich*, which had like to have been loft ; and when he was re-tired, hearing that a Peer had called the fame Lands in quefti-on, and was labouring to get

them, he went to him, and de-fired him to defift from that At-tempt, telling him, that if he did not, he would put on his Gown and Cap, and plead in any Court at *Weftminfter-Hall* in Juftification of what he had done. He had many Benefices in his Gift, and freely gave them to fuch Men as he thought wor-thy of them, faying in his Law-Language, *Church-Livings fhould always pafs by Livery and Seifin, and not by Bargain and Sale*, ib. 299. His Arms *Party per Pale Gul. and Az. three Eaglets dif-played Arg.* He was buried at *Tattlefhall (Titlefhall)* in *Norfolk*, for whom was erected a ftately Monument of Marble, on the Top are placed his Coat of *Arms*, with the four Cardinal Virtues to fupport it at each Corner ; his *Effigies* is of Mar-ble laid out in full length, above this Motto is ingraved PRUDENS QVI PATIENS, and underneath in Golden Characters, this fol-lowing Infcription.

Brome's Travels, 139.

Deo Optimo Maximo
Hæ Exuviæ humanæ expectant Resurrectionem Piorum
Hic Situs Est
Non perituri nominis Edvardus Coke Eques auratus
Legum Anima, interpres, Oraculum non Dubium,
Arcanorum promicondus Mysteriorum,
Cujus fere unius beneficio
Jurisperiti nostri sunt Jurisperiti
Eloquentiæ flumen, torrens, fulmen,
Soadæ Sacerdos Unicus,
Divinus Hæros
Pro rostris ita dixit
Ut literis insudasse crederes non nisi humanis
Ita vixit ut non nisi Divinis,
Sacerrimus intimæ pietatis Indagator,
Integritas ipsa:
Veræ semper causæ constantissimus assertor
Nec favore nec Muneribus violandus.
Eximie misericors,
Charior erat huic Reus quam sibi,
(miraculi instar est)
Siccoculus sæpe ille avdiit sententiam in se prolatam,
Nunquam hic nisi madidoculus protulit.
Scientiæ Oceanus:
Quique dum vixit Bibliotheca viva
Mortuus dici meruit Bibliothecæ Parens.
Duodecim Liberorum, Tredecim Librorum Pater.
Facessant hinc Monvmenta,
Facessant Marmora,
(Nisi quod pios fuisse denotarunt posteros)
Ipse sibi suum est Monumentum
Marmore perennius,
Ipse sibi sva est Æternitas.

I   Dedicated

DEDICATED TO THE MEMORY OF
Sᴿ. EDWARD COKE KNIGHT A LATE REVEREND IUDGE
BORN AT MILEHAM IN THIS COVNTY OF NORFOLKE,
EXCELLENT IN ALL LEARNING DIVINE AND HUMANE;
THAT FOR HIS OWN,
THIS FOR HIS COVNTRYS GOOD, ESPECIALLY IN THE KNOWLEDGE
AND PRACTICE OF THE MUNICIPAL LAWS OF THIS KINGDOM
A FAMOVS PLEADER A SOVND COVNCELLOR
IN HIS YOVNGER YEARS RECORDER OF THE CITIES OF NORWICH
AND LONDON, NEXT SOLICITOR GENERAL TO QUEEN
ELIZABETH AND SPEAKER OF THE PARLIAMENT IN THE 35ᵀᴴ
YEAR OF HER REIGNE. AFTERWARDS ATTORNEY GENERAL TO THE SAME
QUEEN AS ALSO TO HER SUCCESSOR KING IAMES
TO BOTH A FAITHFULL SERVANT
FOR THEIR MA͠TIES, FOR THEIR SAFETYES.
BY KING IAMES CONSTITUTED CHIEF IUSTICE OF BOTH BENCHES
SUCCESSIVELY, IN BOTH A IUST IN BOTH AN EXEMPLARY IUDGE,
ONE OF HIS MAJESTIES MOST HON͠BLE PRIVY COVNCELL
AS ALSO OF COVNCELL TO QUENE ANNE & JUSTICE IN EYER
OF ALL HER FORESTS CHASES & PARKS
RECORDER OF THE CITY OF COVENTRY AND HIGH STEWARD
OF THE UNIVERSITY OF CAMBRIDGE WHEREOF HE WAS SOMETIME
A MEMBER IN TRINITYE COLLEDGE
HE HAD TWO WIVES
BY BRIDGETT HIS FIRST WIFE (ONE OF THE
DAVGHTERS AND COHEIRS OF IOHN PASTON ESQ;)
HE HAD ISSUE SEVEN SONS AND THREE DAVGHTERS.
AND BY THE LADY ELIZABETH HIS SECOND
WIFE ONE OF THE DAVGHTERS OF THE RIGHT HON͠BLE THOMAS LATE EARLE
OF EXETER) HE HAD ISSUE TWO DAVGHTERS.
A CHAST HUSBAND A PROVIDENT FATHER
HE CROWNED HIS PIOVS LIFE WITH AS PIOVS AND
CHRISTIAN DEPARTURE AT STOKE POGES IN THE
COVNTY OF BUCHINGHAM ON WENSDAY
THE 3ᴰ DAY OF SEPTEMBER IN THE YEAR OF
OUR LORD MDCXXXIV AND OF HIS AGE LXXXIII
HIS LAST WORDS
THY KINGDOM COME, THY WILL BE DONE.
LEARN READER TO LIVE SO
THAT THOU MAYST SO DYE

This

This is the *Epitaph* for this great Man, which was given me by *Peter Le Neve*, Esq; *Norroy*, which he believes was the Original from whence the Infcriptions on his Monument were cut. The *Latin* Part of this Epitaph publifhed by Mr. *Brome* in his *Travels*, differs but little from the foregoing, but the *Englifh* is fo different that I could not omit tranfcribing it.

The Monument of Sir Edward Cook, *Knight, born at* Mileham *in* Norfolk, *Recorder of* Norwich *and* London, *Sollicitor to Queen* Elizabeth, *and Speaker to the Parliament; afterwards Attorney-General to her and King* James, *Chief Juftice of both Benches, a Privy-Counfellor, alfo of Counfel to Queen* Anne, *and Chief Juftice in Eyre of all her Forefts, Chafes and Parks; Recorder of* Coventry, *and High-Steward of* Cambridge, *of which he was a Member in* Trinity-College. *He died in the eighty third Year of his Age, his laft Words being thefe,* Thy Kingdom come, thy Will be done.

Next to Sir *Edward* ftands likewife a Marble Monument of his firft Wife *Bridget*, with eight of her Children, fix Sons and two Daughters, *Brome's Travels*, 140.

The next *Recorder* which I find was Sir *Harbottle Grimfton*, Bart. he was Son and Heir of Sir *Harbottle Grimfton* of *Bradfield* in the County of *Effex* Knight: created *Baronet* by *Patent dat.* 25. *November Anno* 10. *Jac.* I. 1612. He ftudied fometime the Common Law, became a learned Man in that Profeffion, then married - - - - - - - Daughter of Sir *George Croke*, Knight, one of the Juftices of the Court of *Common-Pleas*, whofe Reports he publifhed, and by her he had Iffue *George*, who died without Iffue, and *Samuel* who fucceeded him in the *Baronetfhip*; and two Daughters *Mary* and *Elizabeth*: His fecond Wife was *Anne* the Daughter of Sir *Nathaniel Bacon* of *Culford-Hall* in the County of *Suffolk*, Knight, and Relict of *Thomas Meautys* of *Gorham-bury* in *Hertfordfhire*, Knight; by her he had only one Daughter *Anne*, which died in her Minority. He ferved in feveral Parliaments for the Borough of *Colchefter*, and in the Parliament held *Anno* 12. *Charles* II. was chofen *Speaker*, where he was very active and inftrumental

mental in reftoring that King to his Throne, and whom he entertained at Dinner at his Houfe in *Lincolns-Inn-Fields*, *June* 25. 1660. and was on the third Day of *November* following made *Mafter* of the *Rolls* in *Chancery*, which Office he executed for the Space of fix and twenty Years: And likewife in the fame Year was made *Chief Steward* of St. *Albans*. He had a lively Fancy, a quick Apprehenfion, a rare Memory, an eloquent Tongue, and a found Judgment; was a Perfon of free Accefs, fociable in Company, fincere to his Friend, hofpitable in his Houfe, charitable to the Poor, and an excellent Mafter to his Servants. He died ---- *January* Anno 1683. Where he was buried I do not find, but it is probable it was in the Chancel of St. *Michael*'s Church in St. *Albans*, for there was buried his eldeft Son *George*, as likewife was the Mother of his firft Lady, *Chancy*'s *Hartfordfhire*, *p.* 465.

The next *Recorder* of this *Corporation*, which I meet with, was *Chriftopher* Duke of *Albemarle*, only Son and Heir of *George Monk* Duke of *Albemarle*, by *Anne* his Wife, whom he fucceeded in Title *Anno Domini* 1669. and in the Year 1671. was made Knight of the *Garter* by King *Charles* II, and fworn of his Privy Council, as he was alfo in the Reign of King *James* II, Lord Lieutenant of the Counties of *Devon* and *Effex*, Chancellor of the Univerfity of *Cambridge*, and being fent Governor of the Ifland of *Jamaica*, he there died of a *Dropfy*, Anno 1686. and being brought over to *England* to be buried, was depofited in

The next that I meet with as *Recorder* of *Harwich* was Duke *Schomberg*, of whom further Notice will be taken.

Sir *Thomas Daval*, Knight, did probably fucceed him, of whom there is fome Account among the *Lords* of this Manor.

Henry Lord Vifcount *Bolingbrook*, fo created by Queen *Anne*, and Secretary of State to her Majefty even to her Death, and of her moft honourable Privy Council, was likewife *Recorder* of this *Borough*, but whether he immediately fucceeded Sir *Thomas Daval* or not, I am not informed: He was Son of Sir *Henry*

Henry St. *John* created by King *George* I. on the fecond of *July* 1716. Vifcount St. *John* and *Baron of Batterfea* by *Mary* the fecond Daughter and Coheir to *Robert Rich*, Earl of *Warwick:* He ferved in divers Parliaments for feveral Corporations.

His Arms the fame with his Father, viz. *Argt. on a Chief Gul. two Mullets Or with a Label with three Points, for diftinction.*

The next *Recorder* was *Edward* Earl of *Orford*, Son of *Edward Ruffel*, fourth Son of *Francis* Earl of *Bedford.* This noble Lord was one of the Number of Nobility and Gentry, that upon the fatal Appearance of the Extirpation of Religion and Liberty in this Kingdom, quitted the fame, and went over to the then Prince of *Orange* in *Holland*; with whom he returned the fame Year 1688. And upon his Advancement to the Throne was fworn of his *Privy-Council, An.* 1690. he was made Admiral of the *Blue-Squadron* of his Majefty's *Navy*; and the next Year, (upon the removal of the Earl of *Torrington*) Commander in chief of the whole Navy, and Treafurer of the fame.

In the Year 1692. he gave a total Overthrow to the *French Fleet* [at *La Hoge*] under the Command of *Monf. Tourville*, for which he had the Thanks of the Houfe of Commons; yet was next Year (for what Reafon is hardly known) difplaced, and the Command of the Fleet given jointly to *Henry Killegrew*, Efq; Sir *Ralph Delaval*, and Sir *Cloudefley Shovel*; but his Majefty thought fit, upon his juft Refentment of the Mifmanagement of the Navy that Summer, to appoint him the Year following again *Admiral* and Commander in chief of the whole Fleet, with which he failed for the Mediterranean, and at that time prevented the Defign of the *French* againft *Barcelona.*

The next Year, having again the fole Command of the Fleet, by his Diligence, he prevented the defigned Invafion of King *James*, who lay with a *French* Army ready to embark near *Diepe*; for failing over to the Coaft of *France* with the *Englifh* Fleet under his Command, he ftruck fuch a Terror into the Enemy, that that Expedition was laid afide. For which, and other his fignal Services, he was
Anno

the Privilege of electing two *Burgeſſes* for *Parliament*ᵗ, with

Anno 1697. (being then appointed one of the *Lords-Juſtices* of *England*) created [by King *William* III.] Baron of *Shingey*, Viſcount *Barfleur* and Earl of *Orford*.

In the Year 1701. he was impeached by the *Houſe* of *Commons*, concerning the Treaty of *Partition*, and other Matters; but honourably acquitted. And in the Year 1710. appointed firſt Commiſſioner for executing the Office of Lord High *Admiral* of *England*. This noble Lord

married the Lady *Mary*, third Daughter to *William* late Duke of *Bedford*, his near Couſin by whom he hath no Iſſue. He died *Anno* 1727.

His Arms the ſame as the Duke of *Bedford*, viz. *Argent, a Lion rampant Gul. on a Chief Sab. three Eſcallops of the firſt.*

John Lord Viſcount *Percival* of the Kingdom of *Ireland* is the preſent Recorder, and one of the preſent Members of Parliament to repreſent this Borough.

ᵗ The following is a Liſt of the Perſons, which have repreſented this Corporation in *Parliament* (i. e. ſo far as I could obtain them) from the time of their *Charter*, with the reſpective Years of their Election, but who they were that were choſen for the four Parliaments of King *James* I, nor the three firſt Parliaments of King *Charles* I, I have not yet ſeen.

1640 { Sir *Harbottle Grimſton*, Knight and Baronet Sir *Thomas Cheek*, Kt.

1640

1660

1661 { Sir *Henry Wright*, Knight and Baronet Sir *Capel Luckin* *Thomas King*, Eſq;

1678 { Sir *Anthony Deane*, Kt. *Samuel Pepys*, Eſq;

1678 { Sir *Philip Parker*, Bart. Sir *Thomas Middleton*, Kt.

1680 { Sir *Philip Parker*, Bart. Sir *Thomas Middleton*, Kt.

1685 { Sir *Anthony Deane*, Kt. *Samuel Pepys*, Eſq;

G g

with the Grant of a fecond *Market* weekly on the *Friday*, and two *Fairs* yearly, each to endure for three Days; the one at the Feaft of St. *Philip* and *Jacob*, the other on the Feaft of St. *Luke* the *Evangelift*, with *Pye-powder-Courts*, &c.

Thefe and all other their Franchifes and Immunities were lately confirmed *April* the twenty fourth, 17°. *Car.* II. obtained by Sir *Harbottle Grimftone*, Bart. Mafter of the Rolls, and Recorder of this Borough[f].

Heretofore

1688 { Sir *Thomas Middleton*, Kt. { *John Eldred*, Efq;	1705 { Sir *Thomas Daval*, Kt. { *John Ellis*, Efq;
1689 { *Charles Lord Cheney*, { Sir *Thomas Middleton*, Kt.	1708 { Sir *John Leake*, Kt. { *Thomas Franklin*, Efq;
1695 { Sir *Thomas Daval*, Kt. { Sir *Thomas Middleton*, Kt.	1710 { *Kendrick Edisbury*, Efq; { *Thomas Franklin*, Efq;
1698 { Sir *Thomas Daval*, Kt. { *Samuel Atkinfon*, Efq;	1714 { *Benedict Leonard Calvert*, Efq; { *Thomas Heath*, Efq; { Sir *Philip Parker*, Bart.
1700 { Sir *Thomas Daval*, Kt. { *Dennis Lyddall*, Efq;	1721 { Sir *Philip Parker*, Bart. { *Humphrey Parfons*, Efq;
1701 { Sir *Thomas Daval*, Kt. { *Dennis Lyddall*, Efq;	1727 { Sir *Philip Parker*, Bart. { *John Lord Percival*
1702 { Sir *Thomas Daval*, Kt. { *John Ellis*, Efq;	

[f] Which he was made for Life, and after his Deceafe the Election of another, was to be in the *Mayor*, *Aldermen*, and *capital Burgeffes*, as was alfo the Election of the *High Steward*.

King *James* II. when he was regulating Corporations fent a *Quo Warranto* to *Harwich*, and the Charter being delivered up, He granted them a new one, in which divers Perfons were named

2

Heretofore the Dukes of *Norfolk* had Royal Jurifdictions, and great Privileges granted to them (as before is hinted) in *Harwich* and *Dovercourt*. There was adjoyning to the Church-yard an *Admiralty-Houfe*, where their *Admiralty-Courts* were kept, having not only Jurifdiction here; but alfo the full Return of all *Writs* as well of the *Affizes* of *new Defeifin*, *Mort-d'anceftre* and of *Perfons attainted*, as of all other *Writs*, *Mandates*, *Precepts*, *Bills of the King* his Heir and Succeffors; and their *Juftices* and *Commiffioners*, &c. All *Fines*, *Fines pro licentia Concordandi*, *Iffues*, *Amerciaments*, *Redemptions*, *Penalties*, *Waives*, *Strayes*, *Felons-goods*, *Power to appoint Coroners*, *Clarkes* of the *Market*, and feveral other *Officers;* and the *Cognifance* of all things (Treafon excepted) with the *Profits* of all to themfelves, without Account into the *Exchequer*, firft granted unto *John* Duke of *Norfolk*, 8°. of King *Edward* IV, and again confirmed by *Queen Elizabeth* to *Thomas* Duke of *Norfolk*, *July* the fourth, in the firft Year of her Reign, who forfeiting them together with his Life *Anno* 1574. they remained in

named for *Mayor*, *Aldermen*, and capital *Burgeffes*, who could not qualify themfelves as the Law directed, and upon the News of the great Preparations in *Holland*, for the Prince of *Orange*'s Expedition into *England*, their old Charter as well as others was by Proclamation reftored, and their new one fuperfeded.

the

the Crown until fhe regranted them, together with the appointing divers *Officers* for the executing them, to *Edward Coke*, Efq; her *Attorney-General*; who by one *Deed* under his Hand and Seal, dated *February* the fecond *Anno* 40 *Eliz.* 1597, grants them to the Magiftrates of the Borough at that time.   And afterwards by another *Deed* dated *December* 1. *Anno* 12. *Jac.* 1. 1614, (the *Government* of the *Town* being before altered) regrants them to the *Mayor* for the time being (who at thefe *Seffions* hath had a *Silver Oar* carried before him, ftill preferved in the Town Cheft) and the precedent *Mayor* of the Year next before paft, and eleven others; any one of which with the *Mayor* might put thefe in Execution.   And in this Deed he nominates himfelf, Sir *Edward Coke*, Knight, *Chief Juftice of our Sovereign Lord the King of his Pleas, before his Highnefs to be holden and affigned, and one of his Majefty's Honourable Privy Council.*

The Extent of this *Borough* or *Corporation* is not yet very large: King *James* in his aforementioned *Charter* makes the *Burgeffes of the Borough of* Harwich, *and the Tenants, Refidents, and Inhabitants of the Village of* Dovercourt *in the County of* Effex, *near adjacent and adjoyning to the fame Borough of* Harwich, *into one Body Corporate and Politique*; *by the Name of the Mayor and Burgeffes of the Borough of* Harwich *in the County of* Effex.   Which Incorporation is alfo confirmed by the

gracious

gracious *Charter* of King *Charles* II, under the fame Denominations, but how far they reach in the Water is not afcertained, only in their *Records* of their *Admiralty-Courts*, they have amerced certain Perfons for unlawful Fifhing near *Shotley*.

They give for their Arms a *Port-cullis*, and for their Creft and Badge an *ancient one-mafted Ship, with Sail furled, the Stem and Stern much higher than the midft-Ship*, the Colours forgot.

The ancient *Town-Hall* and *Goal* (as is already faid) were heretofore in the *Caftle*, but that Convenience is loft by its ruin: They were afterwards removed into the narrow Street within St. *Auftin's-Gate*, where they remained 'till the Year 1673, being then excited by the Council and Bounty of *Anthony Deane*, Efq; fince Sir *Anthony Deane*, Knight, one of their *Aldermen*, the *Common-Council* fell their old *Hall* and fome of their Houfes, and purchafed a better in St. *Nicholas* or the *Church-ftreet*, where they have not only their *Goal* and *Houfe* of *Correction*, but alfo a neat (though a fmall) *Guild-Hall* adorned with Pillars, Rails and Ballifters, and his Majefty's Arms carved over the Mayor's Seat (the Gift of Mr. *Ifaac Betts* one of the *capital Burgeffes*) very richly gilded; who hath built upon thefe Shores, feveral excellent Ships and Veffels of fundry forts for feveral Merchants and Mafters, and is now (1676) building feveral Doggers for the *Royal-Fifhery*.

2   Overagainft

Overagainſt the *Mayor's Seat* in the *Hall* on the embowing over the Pillars, is a Memorial of their famous Benefactor; *a Shield Gul. three Lions of England Or in Chief a file of three Points Argt.* over which is written: *Memoriæ perenni,* and on both Sides the ſaid Shield: *Inclytiſſimi & Illuſtriſſimi Thomæ de Brotherton, Edwardi* 1ᵐⁱ *filii quinti Comitis Norfolciæ, Angliæ Mareſchalli ac hujus ville Herewici cum Dovercourt inſignis & liberalis D̄ni. Qui a fratre ſuo Edwardo* 2ᵈᵒ *apud Eboracum Julij* 29° *in progreſſu ejus ad re-acquiſitionem Berevici ſuper Twedam ; ac etiam Sep*ᵗ. 16ᵗᵒ *in obſidione ejuſdem Anno* 1320. *& regni ſui* 13° *huic municipio emancipationis & immunitatum prima diplomata impetravit*ᵗ.

On both Sides below the *King's-Arms* (yet over the Bench) are two Memorials. On the one Side is this; *In memoriam digniſſimæ beneficentiæ huic Aulæ publicæ Antonii Deane Arm. unius Alderm. hujus Burgi,* &c.

ᵗ Mr. *Tyrrell* makes it to be *Anno* 1319. when King *Edward* II. did beſiege *Berwick,* Hiſt. Vol. III. *p.* 274. *Daniel* likewiſe ſaith the ſame ; his Account of which is as followeth. *The next Year after* (i. e. Anno 12° Edw. II. 1319.) *upon the rendring up of* Berwick *to the* Scots *by the Treaſon of* Peter Spalding, *who had the Cuſtody thereof; the King of* England *raiſes an Army and Beleaguers it : The* Scots *to divert his Forces, enter upon* England *by other ways, and were like to have ſurpriſed the Perſon of the* Queen *lying near York. The Siege notwithſtanding is eagerly continued, and the* King *in great probability to have regained the* Town, *had not the* Earl *of* Lancaſter *and his Followers withdrawn upon Diſcontent,* &c. Hiſt. *p.* 178.

Anno

Anno 1674°. He gave in Money, Timber, &c. about fixty Pound, he was one of the *Commiffioners* of his *Majefty's Navy* (King *Charles* II.) and is *Mayor* of this *Borough,* for this prefent Year of our Lord 1676. On the other fide is this; *Monumentum meritiffimi impendii Richardi Ratford nautæ unius capitalium Burgenfium hujus Oppidi maritimi,* &c. *Anno* 1674°. He gave about nine Pounds, which Hall was *finifhed* and beautified that very Year, Mr. *John Rolfe* being *Mayor.*

It is a Cuftom here that whoever are made free of this Corporation (efpecially thofe that have not ferved an *Apprenticefhip* for it) fhould prefent a *Leather Bucket* to hang up in the *Hall* to be in readinefs in cafe of Fire. The aforefaid Sir *Anthony Dean,* Knight, gave twelve, upon which were expreffed an Account of this his Gift, and the taking up his Freedom in the Mayoralty of Mr. *Robert Seaman,* 1673.

There is one upon which is the Arms of his Grace the Duke of *Albemarle, Gules a Cheveron between three Lions Heads eraced Argt.* with his Garter, Supporters, ducal Coronet, and Creft underneath this Motto, *eo non dubio.* The Town Arms on both Sides under which is written *Harwich,* with this Infcription: *The Memorial of his Grace Chriftopher Duke of Albemarle, Earl of Torrington, Baron Monk of Poutheridge and Tayes, accepting the Freedom of a Free-Burgefs of this Borough on the twenty firft of May* 1674. Mr. *John Rolfe, Mayor,* all in capital Letters of Gold.
Another

Another upon which in large Letters is painted *Harwich*, and on an Efcutcheon *Arg. a Cheveron between three Efcallop Shells fab.* and under Sir *Charles Littleton made free April* 7. 1671. *Mr.* Thomas Langley *then Mayor.* This is the Bucket of the Honourable *Collonel* Sir *Charles Littleton*, Knight, *Collonel* of the Regiment of his *Royal Highnefs* the Duke of *York*, and Governor of *Landguard-Fort.*

In the fame Form alfo is another with *Harwich* above written, and on a Shield *Az. a Lion rampant Argt. coloured Gul. a Canton of the fecond*, with this underwritten, *Sylas Domville alias Taylor made free, Dec.* 21. 1672. *Mr.* John Brown, *and Mr.* Robert Seaman *that Day Mayors*, (that is, it was on that Day the one *Mayor* went out, and the other fucceeded) fince then one of the *capital Burgeffes* u.

This

---

u The *Buckets* mention'd by Mr. *Taylor*, are now *Anno* 1728, not to be feen, but are plentifully fupplied by others; divers of which have Coats of Arms upon them, fome the Arms of *Harwich* only, and others of a particular *Company* or *Society.* Thofe which were in being this prefent Year, are as follow.

1. On one *Bucket* is *Checkie Or and Az. a Fefs Gul. Fretty Ermin*, on which is a *Vifcount's Coronet*, the Supporters a *Lion* and *Griffin*, this feems the Gift of *Charles* Lord *Cheney*, Vifcount *Newhaven*, who was chofen to reprefent this Corporation *Anno* 1689.

2. On another Bucket, *Sab. gutte d'eau Argt. on a Fefs of the*
2ᵈ 3

2ᵈ 3 *Jackdaws of the firſt armed Gul.* over which a Baron's Coronet, the Supporters two *white Harts* attired *Or,* collared with *Laurel vert.* The Motto *Virtus vincit invidiam,* 1720.

3. Another hath *Argt. two Feſſes ſab. on the firſt two Plates, and on* 2ᵈ *one, in Chiefe* 3 *Bucks Heads caboſſed ſab. in the middle between the two Feſſes a Lion paſſant Gul.* in the middle *Gul.* an *Eſcutcheon of the Arms of Ulſter,* 1714. Q. whether the Arms of Sir *Philip Parker,* Bart. choſen Parliament Man for this Borough that Year.

4. Another Bucket hath *Ermin, a Croſs quarter pierced Argt. four Fer-de Moulins ſab.* 1694. This I take to be the Gift of Sir *Edward Turner,* Knight, frequently Member of Parliament for *Orford* in *Suffolk,* he was Son of Sir *Edward Turner,* Knight; Speaker of the *Houſe* of *Commons,* Anno Domini 1664.

5. On another *ſab. a Cheveron between* 6 *Croſſets Fitche Or. Charles Smith,* 1683. twice *Mayor* of this *Borough,* viz. *An.* 1688, & 1695.

6. Another hath *Gul. a Lion rampant between* 8 *Fleurs de Lis Argt. Daniel Daval,* Eſq; 1697.

(alſo the Arms of *Harwich)* he was eldeſt Son of Sir *Thomas Daval,* Recorder of *Harwich,* and Repreſentative of this *Borough* in divers Parliaments.

7. On another *Az.* 6 *Garbs Or. Timothy Hurlock,* 1699.

8. Another had *Argent a Croſs ſab. in the dexter quarter, a Fleur de Lis of the* 2ᵈ. The Gift of Capt. *Richard Hadcook.*

9. On another *Or a Croſs ſab.* charged with five *Creſſents Argt.* J. E. 1702. This ſeems to be the Armorial Bearing of *John Ellis,* Eſq; twice choſen to repreſent this *Borough* in Parliament, *viz. An.* 1702. & 1705.

10. Another *parted per Feſs Crenelle Gul. and Ermin in chief three Lions Heads erazed Or.* B. T. 1704. This is the Arms of *Timewell* according to *Kent's Banner, p.* 767. and it ſeems probable, that this *Bucket* was given by one of that Name by the initial Letters thereon.

11. Another hath the Name in a *Cypher,* over which is a Creſt, *a Garb Or, between two Eagles proper,* 1707.

12. On another Bucket is *Az. a Dolphin naiant imbowed Argt.* on a *Chief Or,* 2 *Saltiers Gul.* 1709. This I take to be the Armorial

H h   Bearing

Bearing of *Thomas Frankland,* Efq; one of the *Commiffioners* of the *Poſt Office,* who twice reprefented this *Borough* in Parliament, *viz.* in the Years 1708, & 1710.

13. Another *quarterly* 1 *and* 4th *Az. three Lionels rampant Or, with a Crefcent of Diſtinɛtion Argt. within a Bordure Ermin.* 2 *and* 3 *Argt. a Cheveron between* 6 *Mullets Gul.* under *Henry Troiver,* 1709.

14. On another *a Goat,* under which *Don.* Mr. *Kendrick Edisbury.* He was chofen to reprefent this *Borough* in the Parliament *Anno* 1710.

15. Another hath *Az. a Cheveron between three Efcallops within a Bordure engrailed Or. Thomas Colby,* Efq; 28 *November* 1715. He feems the fame Perfon who was *Store-Keeper* and *Clerk of the Check* in the *King's Yard* here.

16. On another is *Argt. a Cheveron fab. charged with three Efcallops Or, between three Pellets each charged with a Martlet of the firſt, all within a Bordure ingrailed vert. Anthony Hammond* 1717.

17. On fix *Buckets* are *parted per Cheveron embattled fab. and Argt. in Chief two Stars pierced Gul. in Bafe a Heathcock fab. an Efcutcheon of Pretence Argt. on a Fefs Gul. charged with three Plates, between three Martlets of the fecond* 1720. Thefe were the Gift of *Thomas Heath,* Efq; one of their Reprefentatives in Parliament *Anno* 1714.

18. On twelve other *Buckets* are painted *quarterly of four Coats, whereof* 1 *and* 4th *Gul. two Cheveronels Ermin between three Eaglets difplayed Or,* 2d *and* 3d *Az. two Cheveronels Or, between three Goats heads erazed Argt. Imp. Vert. on a Cheveron Or a Star of Points between two Rofes Gul.* H. P. S. Thefe were the Gift of *Humphrey Parfons,* Efq; *Alderman* of *London,* upon his being elected a *Burgefs* to ferve in Parliament for this Borough *Anno* 1721.

19. On another fix *Buckets* are *fab. a Cheveron Ermin between three Batts Argent* Imp. *fab. Cheveron Or, between three Owls Argt. crowned of the fecond.*

Befides

Besides the foregoing there are divers other *Buckets* which hang up in the *Town-Hall*, some of which have no other Arms upon them but that of the *Borough*, viz. *Gul. a Portcluse Or.* Of these are the following.

1. *Thomas Osborn*, 1684. he hath twice been *Mayor*, viz. in the Year 1716, and again in 1727, upon the Death of Mr. *Thomas Phillips*, who died in his Mayoralty.

2. *T. R.* 1694.
3. *W. M.* 1694.
4. *John Life*, 1696.
5. *J. B.* 1711.
6. *Richard Hunt*, Junᵣ. 1719.
7. *R. J.* 1720.

The following have the Arms of some Company painted upon them.

First, The *Coopers Arms,* of which there are three, these are *Girony of eight Sable and Gules, a Cheveron Or, charged with a Croze between two Axes of the first between three Annulets of the third, on a Chief vert three Lilies Argt.*
1. *Joseph Fred*, 1700.
2. *Andrew Carter*, 1700. this hath also the Arms of *Harwich.*
3. *Henry Verrin*, 1710.
Secondly, *Cordwainers* of which there is only one, The Arms according to *Kent, Gules a Cheveron between three Goats Heads erazed Argt. attired Or. p.* 337. but according to the new View of *London, p.* 600. the Field is *Az.*

1. *Samuel Narbrow*, 1695.
Thirdly, *Butchers,* viz. *Azure two Axes salterwise Or, headed proper, between two Bulls Heads couped Argent armed Or, on a Chief of the fourth a Boar's Head erazed Gules* between two *Garbes.*
1. *John Buckell*, 1702.
Fourthly, There remains only two *Buckets,* which have only the initial Letters of their Names.
1. *J. C.* 1724.
2. *A. C.* 1726.
N. B. The *Hall* being now well replenished with *Buckets,* this Custom is changed into a *Pecuniary Mulct* of the Value of a *Bucket.*

H h 2   This

This *Borough* had a *Common-Key*[w], but they have thought fit to leafe it out as they have done their Marfh; This *Key* was between the *Caftle* and the *Nefs*[x].

The *Nefs* where anciently was a *Bulwark*, with *Guns* mounted and called *Harwich-Nefs*, is now laid plain, and is part of that Ground which was taken in for the *King's Building-Yard* for *Ships*, for which the Town do receive a Rent from the Right-honourable the principal *Officers* and *Commiffioners* of his *Majefty's Navy*; much more Ground than what at firft was found there, hath been fince by *Wharfs* recovered out of the Sea. The chief Entrance whereof is through the *Great-Gate*, over which are placed his *Majefty's Arms* carved and in Colours; and above them on the Outfide as well as on the Infide two *Dials* governed by an excellent *Pendulum-Clock*; over which in the *Turret* hangs the *Bell*, on which the *Clock* not only ftrikes the Hours of

---

[w] A *Key* for *Ships* à Belg. Kaeÿe, Teut. Kay: French *Quay* *Littus navale, Cothon,* ναύςαθμ☉, ϸεώϱιον, ναύλοχον, *Jof. Scal.* in Gloffis *Ifidori* invenit Lat. *Caï, Cancelli, Caiare, Cohibere, à Cohibendo mare. Ego tamen mallem* (fcribit Dr. *Skinner) à Lat. Cavea defleĉtere,* q. d. *navium Cavea,*

i. e. *Receptaculum,* Etymol. Angl.

[x] *Terminatio Nominum multorum locorum frequens eft* ab A S. Næϼe, Neϼe, *Promontorium boc ab alt.* Neϼe, *Nafus,* q. d. *Nafus Terræ; qui a fc. inftar Nafi prominet. Skinner's* Etymol. Angl. It is a Prominence or ftanding out like a Nofe.

the

the *Day*; but it is alfo ufed by ringing it, to give Notice to the *Workmen* and *Artificers* there imployed, of
the fitteft Seafons for their Labour or Reft. In this
Yard are the Conveniencies of *Store-houfes* and *Strong
Cranes*, whereof one is of late Years rendered ufelefs
by the *Eddy* of the *Ebb*, which lodgeth the Sand by
working againft the *Wharf* of it, fince the gaining of
the *North-Angle* of this Yard wholly out of the Sea,
&c. There are alfo *Lanches*, the biggeft of which is
excellently approved of; whereupon the *Ships* there
built refting upon *Bily-ways*, by a very eafy Motion,
without any probable Hazard or Danger, forfake the
firm Land and betake themfelves to their watery Refi-
dence into four Fathom at low Water at the End of
the *Ways.*

In and about the Year **1666.** during that *Dutch
War* were many *Ship-wrights*, *Calkers*, &c. kept here
in conftant Pay, not only for building of Ships, but to
be alfo in Readinefs always without delay to refit any
of his Majefty's Ships that came in any ways difabled;
and for their greater Difpatch, there was a *Hulk* for
the unburthening them of their Artillery and Stores,
to make them more fit for cleaning, calking, tallow-
ing, *&c.* either by careening or coming afhore; and
then alfo were employed feveral *Officers* by his Majefty; as a *Commiffioner* for the *Port*, a *Keeper* of the
Stores, a *Mafter-builder*, a *Clerk* of the *Check*, a *Ma-*

2   *fter*

fter of *Attendance,* a *Clerk* of the *Survey,* a *Boatfwain* of the *Yard,* and a *Porter* of the *Gate* ; the chiefeſt of thefe *Officers* had their convenient (tho' ſmall) Offices in the Yard. But after the *Hollanders* had made Peace with his Majeſty, this Yard in 1667 was laid aſide, only the *Store-keeper* was continued to take Care of his Majeſty's Concerns left there; who was in the next *Dutch War* 1672, in a manner ſolely concerned in this Port, not only in his Majeſty's Affairs of the Navy, but alfo by the *Office* of *Ordnance*; *Agency* of *Prizes* brought in thither; the charge of ſuch Seamen as were from time to time ſent by the neighbouring Counties to his Majeſty's Navy; and ſeveral other Truſts and Concerns. And by a *Commiſſion* dated *May* 14, 1672, under his Majeſty's *Royal Hand* and Seal, received Command to form a *Company* there for the Security of this *Town* and *Port:* Since the Death of the aforeſaid Mr. *Taylor,* the *Collector of thefe Notes,* there have been divers Perſons who have been *Store-keepers* of the King's.

Thefe *Ships* following were here built for his Majeſty, by that excellent and ingenious Artiſt the aforeſaid Sir *Anthony Deane,* one of the *Commiſſioners* of his *Majeſty's Navy,* reſiding of late Years, for the moſt part, at his Majeſty's Yard at *Portfmouth,* but lately removed to *London.* The *Rupert* a third rate Ship was launched from the great Launch, on the 26*th*

2 of

of *February* 1 665. Prefently after the *Frances* and the *Roebuck*, two fix Rates, were built upon the fame Launch at one and the fame time. The *Refolution*, another third Rate, was launched from the fame Launch *December* the 6*th* 1667. The *Swiftfure* of the fame Rate, and from the fame Launch, with Balconies and Galleries, *April* the 8*th* 1673. The *Harwich*, a very beautiful Ship and fwift Sailer of the fame Rate, built likewife with Balconies and Galleries, partly imitating the fetting off of fome of the *French* Men of War; fhe was launched from the fame place, *April* the 12*th* 1674. upon whom in her Name his Majefty was gracioufly pleafed to honour this *Borough*ʳ.

About the Year 1666 his Majefty was pleafed to caufe the building of two Sloops here of a fmall Draught of Water, to clear the Sands before this Harbour, then much infefted with fmall *Dutch Pickaroons*; the one was named the *Spy*, and the other the *Fan-fan*; of

ʳ To the Account given by Mr. *Taylor* of Ships built here in the King's building Yard may be added:

The *Sandwich*, a fecond Rate Ship.
The *Ipfwich*, }
The *Yarmouth*, } both third Rate Ships.
The *Seafare*, a fifth Rate Ship.

Thefe were all built during the Reign of King *William* III, but the precife time: when, I am not informed of; fince which I do not hear of any other Ships built at this place upon the Government's Account.

this

this laſt Prince *Rupert*, and his Grace *George* Duke of *Albemarle*, in their Letter from Sea to his Majeſty dated *July* 27, 1666, gave this Account: *That on* Thurſday *Morning* (July 26) *it being very calm, and the Enemy to* Windward *of them, the* Fan-fan, *a ſmall new* Sloop *of two Guns, built the other Day at* Harwich, *made up with his Oars towards the* Dutch Fleet, *and drawing both his Guns to one ſide, very formally attacked* De Ruyter, (*in the* Admiral's *Ship of* Holland) *and continued this honourable Fight ſo long, till ſhe had received two or three Shots from him between Wind and Water; to the great Laughter and Delight of our Fleet, and the Indignation and Reproach of the Enemy.*

There was during the late War, *viz.* (in 1672, and 1673.) by his Majeſty's Command an every *Day Poſt* from hence to *London*, and from thence hither, appointed for the Conveyance of Pacquets and Orders to and from the Fleet; this Port being judged the moſt convenient Station for that Purpoſe in that War ʏ².

Here

ʏ² And for ſecuring and collecting his Majeſty's Duties on *Goods* and *Merchandizes* exported or imported, here is a *Cuſtom-houſe,* called the *King's Houſe,* with proper *Officers,* as a *Collector, Comptroller, Land-Surveyor, Tide-Surveyor, Land-Waiters,* and *Tide-Waiters;* with whom entries are made, and the *Duties* either paid or ſecured, *&c.* The preſent *Collector,* 1729. is Mr. *David Ruſhton, Comptrollor;* Mr. *James Langley,* Deputy *Land Surveyor;* Mr. *Griffith Davis, Tide-Surveyor;* Mr. *John*

Here are alfo the *Pacquet-boats*, which on every *Wednefday* and *Saturday* carry over the publick Mails, with foreign Letters and Paffengers alfo, not only for *Holland*, but for all *Germany* and other Parts; and obferve the fame Days for their Return from the *Briel*, which heretofore was from *Helvoet-Sluice*. Of thefe Boats there are at prefent three, wherein Paffengers find good Accommodation, the Paffage fhort moft commonly; and many times furthered by the two contrary Tides which they encounter in the Voyage [z].

Such

Mr. *John Coleman*. *Land-Waiters* are *two*, one at *Harwich*, Mr. *Ralph St. John*; and one at *Manningtree*, Mr. *Richard Bully*. As to *Tide-Waiters*, their *Boatmen*, which are four, are made ufe of for that Purpofe.

[z] *Harwich* is known (faith the Author of the *Tour* aforementioned) for being thePortwherethe *Pacquet-Boats* between *England* and *Holland* go out and come in: The Inhabitants are far from being famed for good Ufage to Strangers, but on the contrary, are blamed for being extravagant in their Reckonings in the publick Houfes, which has not a little encouraged the fetting up of *Sloops*, which they now

call *Paffage-Boats* to *Holland*, to go directly from the River *Thames*; this, though it may be fomething the longer Paffage, yet as they are faid to be more obliging to Paffengers, and more reafonable in the Expence; and as fome fay alfo, the Veffels are better *Sea-Boats*, has been the Reafon why fo many Paffengers do not go or come by the way of *Harwich* as formerly were wont to do; infomuch, that the Stage Coaches between this Place and *London*, which ordinarily went twice or three times a week, are now entirely laid down, and the Paffengers are left to hire Coaches on purpofe; take Poft Horfes, or hire Horfes to *Colchefter*,

Such was the Importance of this Port in former Times, that in the Reign of Queen *Elizabeth*, there refided here one (fome fay four) in the nature of *Mafters* of *Attendance*; one of them in feveral publick Writings in this Town is often nominated. *John Hankin* of *Harwich*, one of the Mafters of her Majefty's *Navy Royal*, firft Mayor of this *Borough*.

Colchefter, as they find moft convenient, *Tour through Great Brit.* Vol. I. Let. 1. 49. The Reafons of the Decreafe of Paffengers going and returning from *Holland* by way of *Harwich*, are chiefly the ceafing of the War in *Flanders*, whereby fewer People are obliged to go or return to or from thofe Countries; it is true, fome Perfons whofe Bufinefs doth not require Expedition, may make ufe of the other way of Paffage, which perhaps may be rather cheaper than this, tho' not altogether fo commodious, nor more obliging; and whatever might formerly have been the Ufage of fome Perfons towards Strangers, yet the whole are not to be condemned for their Extravagancies; having my felf received no civiler Entertainment than I have had there.

The *Pacquet-Boats* at prefent are four, *viz. The Prince*, Captain *Robert Lucas* Commander: *The Difpatch*, in which Prince *Frederick* came over; it was then cammanded by Captain *John Demerit*, who is fince made Captain of the *Boneto* Man of War; and Captain *John Fuller*, who was then the *Mate* is made Commander of her: *The Eagle*, commanded by Captain *Thomas Wimple*; and *The Dolphin*, by Captain *Henry Stevens*.

During the War with *France* here was a fifth *Pacquet-Boat*, but the War ceafing, that was laid afide.

CHAP.

CHAP. V.

TO give a probable Account of the *Historical* Concerns of this *Town*, we are as much to seek, as we are, who were the ancient Fortifiers of the Hill above the Town, or the first Raisers of the Stone *Walls* and *Turrets* about the Town.

King *Edward* II, who first (as is aforesaid) incorporated and infranchised this Borough, bestowed such extraordinary Favours on the two *Spencers*, that disgusted not only the Nobility but the Queen also, who taking her Son with her, deserted the Kingdom and retired into *France*[a]. Where meeting with *Edmund* Earl

[a] This Account of the *Queen*'s deserting the *Kingdom*, and retiring with her Son into *France*, is differently reported by *Tyrrell* (and other Historians) who writes to this effect: That she was sent over by the *King* in order to prevail with the King of *France* her Brother to abate some of his Rigour towards her Husband, that she passed over to *Calais* in the beginning of *July Anno* 1325, where she was kindly received by her Brother, who at her Intercession came to this Agreement: *That King* Edward *should make over his Right in the Duchy of* Aquitain *and Earldom of* Ponthieu *to his Son* Edward, *upon his doing Homage to him, he would give him Seisin of both.* This being agreed to on both sides, and confirmed by *Charter*, with the Advice of the Prelates and other Noblemen at *Dover* on the seventh of *September*

ber

Earl of *Kent,* *Roger Mortimer* Earl of *March,* and many others of the *English* Nobility *(Dugd. Bar.* Tom. I. p. 393.) were all in danger of being betrayed by the King of *France,* and sent Captives into *England* [b]. But they privately getting from thence to *William* Earl of *Henault,* (*Haynault*) with whom the Queen had con-

ber in the eighteenth Year of the King, the Prince is accordingly sent over attended by the Bishop of *Exeter,* and several Noblemen, *Tyrrell's Hist.* 3. 300. Sir *Richard Baker* writes, That it was thought fit, that the Queen should go to accommodate the Difference with the King of *France,* which she did so well, as that all Quarrels were ended, *&c.* and the Prince is sent over by the King, *Baker's Chron.* 150.

[b] Sir *Richard Baker* writes, that upon the Queen's solliciting her Brother the King of *France,* he aided her with Men and Money; but others, that he refused to aid her, as being wrought underhand by the *Spencers* against her, *Chron.* 150. Sir *Winston Churchill,* That the King of *France* not owning the Design (of returning to *England* with Forces) so as to give any ready

Assistance to it, they withdrew into *Holland* (*Haynault*) *Div. Brit.* 237. As the time of Queen *Isabel's* leaving the Court of *France* is uncertain, so is likewise the Cause, saith *Tyrrell;* for some, saith he, relate, that King *Charles,* either not willing to join with her in a new Quarrel, or else not approving her Conduct, would not permit her to stay longer in his Dominions; occasioned either by that King and his Council being bought off by presents from *England,* or from his being threatned by the *Pope* with *Excommunication,* if he any longer entertained her: Others relate, that she stole from thence, either for fear she should be delivered up to her Enemies, or for fear of being killed with her Son by the Procurement of the *Despensers, Tyrrell's Hist.* 3. 312.

tracted

tracted a Marriage between her Son *Edward* and *Philippa* his Daughter, and from whom fhe received all the Aid he could give; they failed for *England*, and landed at *Harwich*, where they were met and welcomed by the difcontented Nobility [c], who at laft forced the King to flight with the two *Spencers* into the mountainous part of *Glamorganfhire* in *Wales* [d]. *Edward*

[c] The *Queen* being accompanied by Prince *Edward* her Son, *Edmund* of *Woodftock*, Earl of. *Kent*, Sir *John* of *Haynault*, (Lord *John* of *Haynault*, Brother to the Duke of *Haynault*, Tyrrell) and the Lord *Roger Mortimer* of *Wigmore*, with divers others, as alfo two thoufand feven hundred and fifty feven Souldiers well appointed, fhe landed at a Haven in *Suffolk* near to *Harwich*, called *Orwell*, on the twenty fifth of *September* 1326. No fooner was fhe and the Prince landed, but it was wonderful to behold how faft the People on all fides flocked to them. The Earl Marfhal *(Thomas* of *Brotherton)* in whofe Lands fhe came on fhore was the firft that came to her, *Mill's Cat.* 155. Mr. *Tyrrell* writes, That the Queen, *&c.* took Ship at *Dort*, and

landed at the *Haven* of *Orwell* near *Harwich*, and was met by *Henry* Earl of *Lancafter*, and other Barons and Knights, with almoft all the Prelates, but efpecially with the Bifhops, *Lincoln*, *Hereford*, *Dublin* and *Ely*; notwithftanding the King's Proclamation, commanding all Men to be ready to refift them at their Landing, *Hift.* 3. 213, 214, and 215.

[d] As to the two *Spencers* whom the Queen looked upon as her greateft Enemies, *Hugh Spencer* the Elder, Earl of *Winchefter*, was taken in the Caftle of *Briftol*, of which he was Governour, and was drawn and hanged in his Coat of Arms upon the common Gallows of the Town. *Hugh Spencer* the Son (being taken with King *Edward* in *Glamorganfhire*) was drawn

2

and

Edward III. *Anno* 1340. being ready to repaſs the Seas, had certain Intelligence, that the *French* lay in wait about *Sluice* in *Flanders*, to intercept him with a mighty Navy of four hundred Ships, [*Dugd. Bar.* Tom. I. p. 218, & 231. *etiam Speed in vita Edw.* III.] who therefore accordingly prepared, reſolving to open his way by Force; he ſet Sail from *Harwich* upon St. *John Baptiſt*'s Eve towards the Coaſts, where his Enemies attended, having joined the Northern Navy of *England*, which the Lord *Morley* brought unto him; ſo that he had in all about two or three hundred Sail. He ſet on the *French* with incredible Fury in the very Mouth of the Haven of *Sluice*, who loſt about half of their Ships, and near upon thirty thouſand of their Men; and as our Authors conclude, that greater Glory than this, the *Engliſh* are ſcarce found to have atchieved in any Battel at Sea[c].   They

and hanged upon a Gallows fifty foot high, and being quartered, his Head was fixed upon *London-Bridge*. But a more particular Account of the manner of his Arraignment and Condemnation are to be found in *Henry de Knighton*'s *Col.* 2547, and 2548. And of his Execution by *Froiſ-ſart*, *Tyrrell*'s *Hiſt.* 3. 322.

[c] Hiſtorians mentioning ſome things relating to this Place in the Reign of King *Edward* III, which are prior to the Story here recited by Mr. *Taylor*, I ſhall therefore here give an Account of them, before I ſay any thing of what the ſaid Mr. *Taylor* hath here related.

The Preſence of King *Edward* III. in *Flanders*, being earneſtly deſired by *Jacob Van Artefeld*, and his Party, he reſolved to go over thither, and

2   on

on the fixteenth of *July* 1338. he took Shipping at the Port of *Orwell* near *Harwich* in *Suffolk (Effex)* with a Royal Navy of five hundred Sail, with many Earls and Barons of *England* in his Company; thefe with their Retinue made a formidable Body of Horfe, befides whom the King had a great Multitude of *Archers* and *Welfhmen*, with all which he arrived at *Antwerp* on the two and twentieth of *July*, *Tyrrell*'s *Hift.* 3. 403. *Anno* 1339. Eleven of the *French* Gallies failling upon the Coaft of *Effex*, endeavoured to fire the Town of *Harwich*, but without Succefs, *Tyrrell*'s *Hift.* 3. 312. By what means the *French* were obliged to fteer off, and this Town preferved, our Hiftorian doth not mention; tho' perhaps it might be by the *Militia* of the Country, as in other places that Year, *Anno* 1340. This Year King *Edward* III. took upon himfelf the *Title* and *Arms* of *France*, quartering the *Arms* of *England* before that of *France*; tho' afterwards, perhaps the more to ingratiate himfelf with the *French Nation*, he placed the *French* Arms in the firft Quarter, and placed the *French Motto* upon

his Shield, *Dieu & mon Droit*, i. e. God and my Right. No fooner had the King fettled his matters in *Flanders*, and changed his Seals, but taking Shipping at *Sluice*, he landed at *Orwell* near *Harwich* on the twenty firft of *February:* Where as foon as he arrived, he caufed Writs to be iffued, fealed with his *new* Seal, for fummoning a Parliament to meet on the nine and twentieth of *March* next enfuing; thefe were dated at *Harwich* on the Day of his Landing, *Tyrrell*'s *Hift.* 3. 420. This Parliament met at *London, Sandford*'s *Genealog.* 161.

I now come to the Story given us by Mr. *Taylor*, in which I fhall take notice of fome Paffages omitted in that. *May* the 30th 1340. the King iffues out Writs for calling another Parliament to meet after his Departure beyond Sea, in which he declares his Intentions of going fpeedily beyond Sea, for the Defence and Safety of his Kingdom, and Recovery of his Own, and the Rights of his Crown, &c. And he publickly declared his Intention of going over, and would pafs from *Orwell* into *Flanders* on the thirteenth of *June*, and

for

for that End had prepared a Fleet of about forty Sail of Ships, that lay ready there to attend him. Upon this, the Archbishop of *Canterbury* informs him, that he was waylaid by the *French*, and therefore advises him not to go over; but the King not believing him, answered, *That he would go whatever come of it*; but upon further Information, and thinking better of the matter, he reinforces his Fleet to two hundred and sixty Sail, and on the two and twentieth of *June*, he took Shipping at *Orwell*, attended by his Navy and a sufficient Number of Land-Soldiers, and arriving on the Coast of *Flanders*, they discovered the *French-Fleet*; whereupon the King sent a Boat on Shore privately with the Lord *Cobham*, &c. to view their Number and Strength, who being returned made their Report; That they consisted of about four hundred Sail, and were riding in the Harbour of *Sluice*, divided into three Squadrons.

The King being resolved to fight, commanded himself in Person, ordering his best Ships, that were well manned with *Archers* and other Soldiers, to be set for-

most in the Line of Battle, then having tacked about to get the Weathergage of Wind and Sun, they boldly received the first Onset; for the *French* Admirals seeing the *Banner Royal* of *England* displayed on the Main-topmast of one of the biggest Ships, they were satisfied, that the King was there in Person; they therefore resolved to do their utmost to rout his Fleet and take him Prisoner: So falling boldly upon the *English*, there began a bloody Fight, first by Showers of Arrows, and then by boarding each other, making use of their Grapling Irons for that Purpose; The Men at *Arms* leaping into each other's Ships fell to Handy-Strokes, whereby a most desperate Slaughter was made, and the *English* gained the Advantage. This Fight continued from ten in the Morning untill seven at Night, when the *French* Ships were put to Flight, their first Squadron being entirely defeated, and the second so much shattered, that they could not get away. So that of their whole Fleet there did not escape above thirty Vessels, which made all the Sail they could for the Coast of *France*

Some

King *Henry* VIII. came to this Town *June* 8. 1543. (*lib. maj. in cifta Ecclefiæ*) which was towards the latter part of his Reign, but what caufed this Vifit here appears not.

Whether *Philip* King of *Spain*, who married Queen *Mary* of *England* was here or no we cannot determine: But we find the Town provided for his Reception in the Months of *March* or *April* Anno 1558. a little before the *Queen* died.

But *Auguft* 12. 1561. Queen *Elizabeth* came hither and accepted of an Entertainment from the Borough, lodging, as it is faid, for feveral Days at a Houfe about the middle of the High-Street, and being attended by the Magiftrates at her Departure as far as the Windmill out of Town, fhe gracioufly demanded of them,

---

Some of the *French Hiftorians* tell us, that King *Edward* was then wounded in the Thigh with a Spear, but if he was, it was fo inconfiderable, as that he himfelf does not fo much as mention it in his Letters, nor did it any way hinder him in his Affairs, *Tyrrell's Hift.* 3. 422, 423.

Moft of the *French*, rather than endure the Arrows, or be taken, defperately leapt into the Sea. None would willingly acquaint the King of *France* with the ill News of this Overthrow; whereupon the *French* King's *Jefter* is fet on to give him Notice thereof, who oftentimes repeating in the King's Hearing; *Cowardly Englifhmen, daftardly Englifhmen, faint-hearted Englifhmen!* The King at length afking him why? He anfwered, That they durft not leap out of their Ships into the Sea as our brave *Frenchmen* did, *Baker's Chron.* 160.

K k   what

what they had to requeſt of her, from whom ſhe received this Anſwer, *Nothing,* *but* *to* *wiſh* *her* *Majeſty* *a* *good* *Journey:* Upon which ſhe turning her Horſe about, and looking upon the Town ſaid, *A* *pretty* *Town* *and* *wants* *nothing,* and ſo bad them *farewel.* And indeed, the State and Condition of this Town at this preſent is not much unlike what it was at that time, not having any Inhabitants, who may paſs in repute of being very rich Men, nor any ſo poor and indigent as to beg an Alms from Door to Door, it being in no wiſe guilty of begging or beggary [f].

The Works or Ramparts of Earth were ſomewhat reſtored and altered in the Year 1666. by the Command of his moſt excellent Majeſty King *Charles* II, againſt any Surprize intended them by the *Dutch.* After this, *viz.* *October* the third and fourth, his Majeſty was pleaſed in his own Royal Perſon to honour this

---

[f] *Harwich* is a Town of Hurry and Buſineſs, not much of Gaiety and Pleaſure; yet the Inhabitants ſeem warm in their Neſts, and ſome of them very wealthy: There are not many (if any) Gentlemen or Families of Note, either in the Town or very near it, *Tour* *thro'* *Great* *Brit.* Vol. I. Let. 1. 51.

The chief Trade of this Town is the *Fiſhery,* about twenty four well-built *Scoots,* are imployed therein, and ſupply *London* with *Codfiſh* in Winter, and *Lobſters* from *Norway* in the Summer: They complain, that this Trade hath of late been much prejudiced by Foreigners ſupplying the Markets with the Prime of the Fiſh; which they keep in their own Hands, and return with ready Money and no Exports.

Town

Town with his Prefence⁵; he came from *New-Market*
to *Land-guard-fort,* and fo by his Yachts over hither:
The

⁵ King *William* III. was twice
at *Harwich* in his Paffage to and
from *Holland* during the *French
War,* one of which times was
on the firft of *May* 1691. when
his Majefty lay at Mr. *Thomas
Langley*'s in the *Church-ftreet.*
Where the Corporation waited
upon his Majefty in a Body,
were gracioufly received by him,
and had the Honour to kifs his
Royal Hand.

During the War with *France*
in the Reign of Queen *Anne,*
two Acts of Parliament were
paffed for the better fortifying
of *Portfmouth, Chatham* and *Harwich,* one in the feventh and the
other in the eighth Year of her
Reign, by which divers Lands,
&c. at *Harwich* were purchafed
for that ufe; as the Marfh on
the Weft-fide of the Town, as
likewife the Farm on the Cliff on
the South-fide, but that War
ceafing, that Project hath for the
prefent been laid afide.

The *Marquis* of *Caermarthen*
was at *Harwich* during this
Queen's Reign, where he treated

the Corporation, among whom
was Captain *Robert Stevens,* having in his Medal given him by
King *William* and Queen *Mary,*
as is aforementioned in his
Epitaph.   The *Captain* was
Commander of the *Vine-Pac-
quet-Boat* of twelve or fourteen
Guns, which being attacked by
a *French Privateer* of twenty
four Guns, vigoroufly defended
itfelf, until being fhot through
and though, it funk; by which
divers Perfons were drowned.
The Seamen in the Action behaved themfelves very bravely,
encouraged thereto by the Valour of Mr. *John Fofter* the Mafter.

On the third of *December*
1728, about four in the Afternoon, his *Royal Highnefs Frederick Prince of Wales,* eldeft Son
to his Majefty *King George* II,
landed here from *Hanover* at the
King's *Stairs* near the Cuftom-
Houfe, coming over from *Holland* in *The Difpatch Pacquet-
Boat incognito,* with a fmall Retinue.   He ftayed about one
Hour

K k 2

The fourth Day being *Sunday,* he heard *Divine Service,* and a *Sermon* preached in this Church by Dr. *Tully* one of

Hour at the three Cups, when he went to *Colchester* in a Coach and eight Horses, and lay there that Night at the *White Hart* ; from whence next Day proceeding for *London,* he arrived at St. *James*'s in the Evening. His *Royal Highness* ordered Mr. *John Fuller*   Mate of the said *Pacquet-Boat* one hundred Guineas, and a Gold Medal for his Care, and recommended him for Preferment, and also ordered five Guineas to each of the Sailors.

As soon as the landing of his *Royal Highness* was confirmed, Mr. *David Rushton* his Majesty's *Collector* of the *Customs* here, caused a Bonfire to be erected at the Place the Prince landed, illuminated the Custom-house, and treated the Officers.

This Town hath been erected into a *Marquisate,* in Honour to that illustrious Family of *Schombergh* or *Schonbergh* in *Germany,* one of which, *Frederick* Count *Schonbergh,* who landed with the Prince of *Orange,* afterwards King *William* III,

2

of glorious Memory, was created Baron of *Teys,* Earl of *Brentford* , Marquis of *Harwich* and Duke of *Schonbergh,* by Patent Dat. 9°. *May Anno* 1°. *Gul. & Mariæ Annoque Domini* 1689. and elected one of the Knights Companions of the honourable Order of the *Garter,* on the third Day of the preceding *April.* He went that Year over into *Ireland* Commander of their Majesty's Forces, sent to prevent the late King *James* from making himself Master of that Kingdom. And in 1690. at that famous Battle of the *Boyne,* on the twelfth Day of *July,* (at which the said King *James*'s Army was totally routed) he being without his Coat of Armour, was unfortunately killed by a Pistol-shot and the Thrust of a Sword, being generally lamented. He was buried in the Cathedral Church of St. *Patrick* in *Ireland.*

This Duke *Frederick* was Son of Count *Schonberg,* who was killed at the Battel of *Prague* in

of his Majefty's *Chaplains.* He was accompanied by his Royal Highnefs *James* Duke of York. And at the fame time came alfo hither, their Graces the Dukes of *Monmouth, Richmond* and *Buckingham,* the Earl of *Oxford,* Lord *Conwallis,* Marquis *Blancford* (fince created *Baron Duras* of *Holdenby*) and feveral others. And towards the Evening departing in their Yachts, they landed at *Aldborough,* and went thence to *Ipfwich.*

Finis Collect-Sylvæ Domville alias Taylor.

in *Bohemia, Anno* 1620. by Daughter of Lord *Dudley,* he had two Wives, the firft was his CoufinGerman, by whom he had nine Sons moft killed in Battel; three only furvived him, *viz. Frederick, Meinhardt* and *Charles.* His fecond Wife was *Sufanna Domel,* of an ancient Family in *Picardy,* but by her he had no Iffue.

The Importance and Succefs of his Services in divers Countries, did occafion his being dignified with fundry Titles and Dignities: As in *England* befides thofe above mentioned, he was *Mafter* of the *Ordnance:* In *France* (notwithftanding his being a Proteftant) he had the *Batoon* of *Marfhal* and Duke. In *Portu-*

gal he was *Grandee* and Count of *Mertola,* with a Penfion of 5000 *l. per Annum* to him and his Heirs, fo fignal were his Services to that Crown. In *Germany* Count of the facred *Roman* Empire, Stateholder of *Pruffia,* Minifter of State and *Generaliffimo* to the Elector of *Brandenberg.*

When the Proteftant Religion was fuppreft in *France* Anno 1685. he having no Inclination to change his Religion, was fuffered to depart that Kingdom and retire into *Germany.*

He was fucceeded in his Honours (by fpecial Entail in the *Patent*) by his youngeft Son *Charles,* who died in *Italy* of the Wounds he received at the Battle

tle of *Marfaglia* againſt the *French* Anno Domini 1693. he left no Iſſue, and was buried at *Laufane*, for whom the follow-ing Epitaph, or Cenotaph on a Table is erected near the Altar of the *French* Church in the *Savoy Weſtminſter*.

LAVSANNA CORPUS
ANIMAM BEATAE SEDES
QUOD
PUGNANDO FORTITER PRO SABAVDIAE PRINCIPE
PULSARE DESIIT
CAROLI DUCIS A SCHOMBERG
IMPAVIDUM COR
SABAVDA BASILICA POSSIDET
SED DUM ID DETULIT
MORIENTI PIE QUI CLVSERAT LUMINA
ET VIVENS INTULIT SUUM
I DUBOURDIEV A SAC. CASTR.
KAL. IUN. A. AE. DION. CIƆIƆCIIIIC.

Upon the Death of Duke *Charles*, theſe Honours came to his eldeſt and only Brother *Meinherdt Count Schomberg*, Ba-ron of *Tarragh*, Earl of *Bangor*, and Duke of *Leinſter* in *Ireland*, ſo created by Patent Dat. 3°. *Martii Anno* 4°. *Gul. & Mariæ* 1691. who was *Lieutenant-General,* and Commander in chief of all his Majeſty's (*i. e.* King *William*) Land Forces, within the Kingdom of *England*, Dominion of *Wales*, and Town of *Berwick* upon *Tweed*; and one of the Lords of his Majeſty's moſt honourable Privy-Council; elec-ted Knight Companion of the noble Order of the *Garter* by Queen *Anne*, and inſtalled *Sep-tember* 2ᵈ 1703. He married the Lady *Charlotte*, eldeſt Daugh-ter of *Charles-Lewis* Elector *Pa-latine*, by *Lovifa Degenfelt*, Wi-dow of *Chriſtopher* Baron of *De-genfelt*: She died at *Kenfington*

Tab. IX . *P . 254 .*

D. Shombergs Monument

in *July* 1696, and was buried in *Weſtminſter Abby.*

by whom he had Iſſue one Son *Charles* Lord *Marquis* of *Harwich* born *December* 15. 1683. (He was *Colonel* of a *Regiment* of *Horſe*, and on his Return from *Ireland* died in *September* or *October* 1713. without Iſſue, and was buried on the 14th of *October* in *Weſtminſter Abby.*) Alſo three Daughters, *viz.* Lady *Carolina* the eldeſt, ſhe died unmarried and was buried likewiſe in *Weſtminſter Abby June* 18. 1710. 2dly, Lady *Frederica*, firſt married to *Robert d'Arcy* Earl of *Holderneſs*, and after his Deceaſe to the honourable *Benjamin Mildmay*, Eſq; now Lord *Fitz-walter.* 3dly, Lady *Mary* married to *Chriſtopher* Count *Dagenfelt*, Count of the *German* Empire.

This Duke *Meinherdt* died in *July* 1718, and was alſo buried in *Weſtminſter Abby* with his Lady and Children, and leaving no Male Iſſue, the Title is now extinct.

His Arms *Argt. Eſcutcheon ſab. over all a Carbuncle of* 8 *Rays Or. with a Creſcent for difference.* Dale's Cat. 23.

This Town is ſometimes overflown by great Tides, the laſt of which was about the Year 1723. when the Water ran thro' the *Weſt Street*, and was ſo high at that End next the *Gate*, that Boats rowed in thereat as high as the *Spread-Eagle* Ale-houſe, at which Door ſome Men ſat in their Boat, and drank divers Pots of Beer.

On *Wedneſday June* 26. 1728. there was a violent Storm of Thunder, Lightning and Rain, the Dint of which fell upon the *Windmill* near the Town, where it ſplit the main Poſt on which the Mill ſtands, much ſhattered the Weather-boards before, broke one of the Sails, and much damaged the inner Part of the Mill. By good Providence there was no Perſon in the Mill at the time, (the Miller himſelf being but juſt gone into the Houſe) ſo that no Perſon received any bodily hurt, as they muſt undoubtedly have done had any hapned to have been therein: The Miller's Dog which lay aſleep under the Mill was killed, but no outward Marks of harm appeared upon him.

THE

THE

APPENDIX,

CONTAINING

Additions and Emendations.

P*AGE* 1. *Col.* 1. *Lin.* 1. *r.* hundred. *p.* 2. *c.* 2. *l.* 19. after *Cuno* add, the *Britiſh Coins* figured and deſcribed in *Cambden's Britannia*, are by Mr. *Salmon* conjectured not to be *Britiſh*, but brought in by the *Romans* and *Saxons*. See his *Examination of the Britiſh Coins* at the End of his *Survey of England*, Part V. *p.* 387.

Having in the fourth and fifth Pages of the foregoing Hiſtory, given the Opinions of divers *Antiquaries* concerning the Situation of the ancient *Camulodunum*, I intend here for the Satisfaction of my Readers, who perhaps may not have all the Authors there cited, to tranſcribe their Reaſons at large, but leave every one to follow his own Judgment therein. And I ſhall begin with the late learned Mr. *William Baxter's* excellent *Gloſſarium Antiquitatum Britannicarum*, whoſe Opinion I indeed did not quote in the Place aforementioned, becauſe I then had not that Book by me.

CAMULODUNUM *Antonino ſimpliciter* Colonia *dicitur*, Ravennati *etiam vitiosè & ſexto caſu*, Camulodulo Coloniâ, *& in* Vaticano, Monulodulo Coloniâ. *Etiam in veteri Lapide* Colonia *eſt* Victricenfis ; *quod Veterani* XIV. *Legionis Geminæ Martiæ Victricis, quos* Tacitus *Domitores Britanniæ dicit, hic agebant. In Inſcriptione quadam ſatis luculentâ* Camalodunum *legitur, & in* Ptolemæo Κα-μχλόδχνον. *Equidem non video cur* Camdenus *majorem fidem habeat*

L l   *imperito*

imperito marmorario quàm ipfius Cunobelini *nummo, in quo plane fignatum eft* CAMV. *Quin &* Antoninus *& nofter* Ravennas *eodem modo fcripfére.* Verum *voluit vir magnus* Coloniam Camulodunum *effe* Waldon, *parùm advertens* Othonam, *validiffimam ftationem, effe ferè in confpectu tantæ urbis à fe ipfo pofitam ; quod fanè inutile foret & fupervacaneum.* Redeat *igitur* Camulodunum *quò &* Talbottus *& magnus* Stillingfleta *illud pofuêre,* Coleceftriam *fcilicet ; cujus vel ipfum nomen, cum cognomine fluvio* Colne, Coloniam *fibi vendicat.* Sunt *etiam ingentia Caftrorum veftigia in vico vel hodie de Legione vocato* Lexdon, *circa duo millia Paffuum citra* Coleceftriam ; *parte tamen maximâ in egregio Ericeto dicto* Stanp-way Heath, *five Lapideæ viæ Ericeto, ubi & ingens Puteus, vulgò dictus* Coili Regis Culina. *Etymon hujus urbis planè Britannicum eft : nam fi folutè fcribatur,* cam a laün üi dun. *Civitas erit ad Alauni five pleni amnis curvaturam, atque hoc confirmant cognomina loca, &* Camalan *in* Oftidamniis, *&* Camalon *apud* Damnios *in* Valentiâ. *Atque hinc quidem conftat fluvium hodie dictum de loco* Coloniam, *olim fuiffe* Alaunum. *Spectabat hæc urbs ad* Trinovantes *Ptolemæi ævo ; cùm olim fedes fuerit* Cunobelini *Icenorum Imperatoris.* Baxter's Gloffar. 63.

Which for the Entertainment of the Englifh *Reader, I fhall tranflate as follows.*

Camulodunum is by *Antoninus* fimply called *Colonia,* and by *Ravennas* falfly and in the Ablative Cafe *Camulodulo Colonia,* and in the *Vatican* MS. *Monulodulo Colonia.* In like manner on an old Stone it is *Colonia Victricenfis,* becaufe the *Veterans* of the fourteenth Legion of the *Gemina martia victrix,* whom *Tacitus* calls the Conquerors of *Britain,* quartered here. In a certain Infcription which is pretty fair it is writ *Camalodunum,* but in *Ptolomy* Καμυλόδυνον. Indeed I fee no Reafon why *Camden* fhould give greater credit to an ignorant Statuary than to a Coin of *Cunobeline* himfelf, upon which CAMV is very plainly expreffed. Befides both *Antoninus* and *Ravennas* wrote it after this manner. But this great Man was willing to have *Colonia Camulodunum* to be *Maldon,* not.

considering

considering that he had placed *Othona,* a very considerable Station almost in Sight of that great City; which would indeed be useless and unnecessary. Therefore let *Camulodunum* return whither both *Talbot* and the great *Stillingfleet* have placed it, namely to *Colchester*; of which the very Name, with the additional Name of the River *Colne* claims *Colonia* to itself. There are likewise large Remains of a Camp in a Village called even at this Day *Lexdon* from a Legion, about two Miles on this side *Colchester*; for the most part however in a remarkable Heath call'd *Stany-way Heath,* where there is also a large well, commonly call'd King *Coilus*'s Kitchen. The Etymology of this City is plainly *British:* for if it be writ distinctly, *Cam a laün üi dun:* it will be a City situated at the Bending of *Alaunus* or a full River. And this is confirmed by several Places, whose Names have an affinity with this, and particularly *Camalan* among the *Ostidamnii,* and *Camalon* among the *Damnii* in *Valencia.* And from hence it is evident that the River now call'd *Colne* was formerly *Alaunus.* This City belonged to the *Trinobantes* in *Ptolomy*'s Time, and was anciently the Seat of *Cunobelinus* King of the *Iceni.*

CAMULODUNUM. M. P. VI. *Before fifteen hundred Years this was a noble Town of Britain among the* Trinobantes. *There make mention of it besides an ancient Stone, whose Inscription* Onuphrius *first published, ancient Coins and Authors too,* Plinie. &c. *It was of old the Palace of King* Cunobelinus, &c. *But for the present Situation of* Camulodunum, *where I mean the Place of it stood of old; then I must not dissemble, that some great Antiquaries, as* John Leland, Humphry Lhuyd, *and such as follow them, do seek for* Camulodunum *in* Colchester, Hanc credo, faith Lhuyd, fuisse Coloniam illam Claudii Cæsaris Templo celebrem, quam nunc Colchestriam vocant. Hector Boëtius placed it in Scotland, and faith, Regiam Pictorum fuisse olim ad Caronæ flu. ripam; which George Buchanan his Countryman says, is, vanissimum mendacium. Polydor. Virgil seeks it in Yorkshire: Puto Camulodunum (quando de eâ re ambigitur) eo loci olim situm, ubi nunc est Doncastrium, quia vel Castrorum memoria*

videtur

videtur retinere nomen loci ad belli præfidium elati : aut Pontifractum, quod paulò propius, & etiam extra Eboracum *eft, circiter millia paffuum* xviii. *loco magis amœno quam munito. Extat caftellum, & in eo aliqua veftigia Templi, quod ibidem* Claudio Cæfari. *In a Word,* Hector *and* Polydorus, *are in very Deed alike, and according to the* Greek *faying,* χρηςὶς ἀκίνδυν⊙- εἰσὶν ἀδελφοὶ. *But others alfo will have it to have flood among the* Brigantes, *or in* Yorkfhire, *perfuaded thence, becaufe in* Ptolemy *there goes next before it* λεγίων ςʹ νικηφό-μι⊙-, *or* Legio fexta Victrix; *as if the Title thereof* Victrix *had explained that which erewhile we brought out of the Stone,* Colonia Camulodunum Victricenfis : *when as it is plain enough, that that* Legio fexta Victrix, *is to be meant of* Eboracum, *accordingly as it is put, and to be referred; which alfo is retained in a* Coin *of* Severus: *which fee there. There have been fome alfo who have fought it at* Chefter, *the Seat of the* Viceffima Victrix *in* Ptolemy. *But what fays the old* Greek *Proverb ?*

Χωρὶς τὰ μυσῶν ὁρίσματα.

Let us hear our great Antiquary Camden *inftead of all: It was verily no other then* Maldon *in* Effex. Maxima, *faith he,* dictionis parte etiamnum integra, & fuperftite. Nec hoc folummodo expreffum nominis veftigium perfuafit, verum etiam diftantia à Mona apud Plinium, à Vanonio apud Antoninum & ipfe fitus in antiqua Tabula Itineraria probationem præftant vel apertiffimam. *But what is the Complaint of the Poet ?* Nec fe cognofcunt terræ vertentibus annis. *In fpace of Time the Lands themfelves not know.* Burton on Antonin. à p. 231. ad. 339.

Now the Chelmer *(with the Confluence of other Waters, being divided by a River* Ifland, *and lofing its old Name for that of* Blackwater *or* Pant) *falutes the old Colony of the* Romans, Camalodunum, *which has made this Shore famous, call'd by* Ptolemy Camulodanum, *by* Antoninus Camulodunum, *and* Camoludunum : *but that the true Name is* Camalodunum *we have the Authority of* Pliny, Dio, *and of an ancient Marble to evince. In the Search of this* City, *how ftrangely have fome Perfons loft themfelves ! Though the very Name*

*Name points it out, and difcovers it plainly to them be they never fo
blind. Many have fought for it in the Weft of* England, *as that notable Man, who thought he carried the Sun of Antiquities about with
him ; others in* Scotland *; others have with* Leland, *affirm'd* Colchefter *to be the Place ; when all this while the Name is very little alter'd,
and inftead of* Camalodunum, *'tis called at prefent* Maldon, *in* Saxon
Malevune *and* Mealvune *the greateft part of the Word ftill remaining whole and entire. Nor are the plain* Reliques *of the Name the
only Argument for this Affertion ; but the Diftance too of the* Mona
of Pliny, *and the very Situation in an ancient Itinerary Table are as
plain Proofs as any in the World. I fcarce dare be fo bold as conjecture
that this Place was fo call'd from the* God Camulus, *yet is there fome
Grounds for fuch a Fancy from* Mars's *being worfhip'd under this
Name, and from an old Stone at* Rome *in the Houfe of the* Collo-
tians; *and from Altars that have been found with this* Infcription,
CAMULO DEO SANCTO ET FORTISSIMO. *And upon an old Coin of*
Cunobeline, *whofe chief Seat this was, as I have before obferved ; I
have feen a Figure with a Helmet and a Spear, which might probably
be defigned for that of* Mars, *with the Letters* CAMV. *&c. which feem
to relate to this* Camalodunum. Cambden's Brit. Ed. 1695. p. 347,
348.*

Going along with this River (Chelmer) *towards the Sea, we find
Maldon, without all doubt the ancient* Camalodunum, *(tho' as our
Author obferves) feveral Men have fought it in feveral Places. It has
been fo largely treated upon by Authors, that little more can be faid.
Only as to the Original of the Name, concerning which moft of them
feem to be at a Lofs, a late Writer* (Samme's Brit. p. 67.) *has advanced a new one in favour of his own* Hypothefis ; *that it comes
from* Camol, *which in the* Phœnician *fignifies a* Prince *and Governor, and the old* Dun *a Hill: So that this may be call'd the* King's-
hill ; *as* Mons Capitolinus *at* Rome, *fignifies* Jupiter's-hill. *It being*
Cunobeline's Regia *(as our Author calls it) or Palace, feems to give
fome Strength to the Conjecture; but then how it will fuit with the
old Altar Infcription, which mentions* Camulus Deus, *and the* Coins
*which confirm it, I very much doubt ; and thefe muft be looked upon as
the beft Authorities.* Ib. p. 358. CAMULO-

CAMULODUNUM. *In nummis abreviatè* CAMV. *Fluvius oritur, ut diximus, in confiniis* Effexiæ, *cui nomen* Camus, *Cam Britannis;* Collem *five* Dunum *præterlabitur, cujus à vertice urbis* Romanæ *reliquiæ regias fedes,* Audley-end, *defpectant, fed ad primum ab hodierno oppido* Walden *lapidem, & occidentem verfus. A Fluvio ifto & Duno* Camulodunum *formârunt Romani fuum,* Saxonibus *fuit* Waldenburgh. *Dunum hoc ab incolis jam vocatur* Sterbury-Hill, *ubi & aureus* Claudii Cæfaris *nummus, & argentea patera, operis, ponderis, & formæ antiquæ detecta fuit.*

Multa funt quæ fuadent, hìc fuiffe celebrem illam Romanorum Coloniam. *Sedet ad vias militares, quarum illa, ad Boream, altera ad Eurum &* Icenos *flexit. Multa & manifefta fefe ingerunt circumquaque Romanorum monumenta:* Coloniæ *termini, vel ager* arcifinius ad Arcden; *fepulchra &* tumuli *ad* Barklow, *ciftæ lapideæ, offibus aduftis plenæ, quales defcripfimus ad* PRÆTORIUM, *in campis vicinis erutæ;* nummi *plurimi,* pavimenta; *præfidia & caftra ad utramque* Chefterford; *ad* Caftle-Camps, *&* Shedy-Camps, *[fortè* Sidii *Getæ, qui cum* Vefpatiano *meruit imperante* Claudio; Dio l. 60.] *Caftella, qualia circa* Coloniam *Camulodunum pofita recenfet* Tacitus. *Fœminâ duce inquit, exurere* Coloniam, *expugnare caftra potuere. Et fumpfere univerfi bellum, ac fparfos per Caftella milites confectati, expugnatis præfidiis, ipfam* Coloniam *invafere. Quid nifi Caftra & Caftella fupra nominata, hic innuit Hiftoricus? Quid nifi præfidia illa quæ inter* Icenos *&* Camulodunum *recta interjacebant, & quæ expugnari, antequam ipfam coloniam, neceffitas rei poftulabat? quænam alia poteft effe* Colonia *ab* Icenis, *&* Trinobantibus, *ad rebellionem commotis excifa, quam ad* Camulodunum *hoc; quam illuc præfago fatis timore, validâ veteranorum manu deduxerat* Oftorius, *cum* Silurum *genti, longè ab his oris remotæ, bellum inferret, ut fubfidium effet adverfus rebelles, & imbuendis Sociis ad officia legum? Quinam Socii nifi* Londinates *&* Verolamienfes, *qui deleto hoc Camuloduni fubfidio, ab hofte ftatim oppreffi funt, cum internecione Septuaginta millium civium & fociorum?*

His adde fitum loci adeo falubrem effe, & amœnum, ut nihil fuprà facilè videas, unde & hic Amœnitati priùs quam ufui confulebatur à ducibus Romanis. Tacitus. Campi lætiffimâ fegete ubique arrident, id eft quod Cunobelini *nummus per fpicam repræfentavit, hic enim Regiam fuam habuit. Alia ex parte valles blandiffimo croco (unde nomen hodiernum* Saffron Walden) *fpirant, qui licet in hanc Infulam longè poft Romanorum tempora primùm advectus fuerit, & feri cœperit, folum tamen arguit fœcundiffimum, cum alium planè fpernat. Inde montes fylvis corufcant comantibus, hinc campeftres planities in immenfum diffunduntur, ad venationes & equitandi voluptates comparatæ, quod ipfum* Cunobelini *in nummis equus non obfcurè indicat. Ad hanc igitur* Walden, *Reges* Trinobantum, *loci jucunditate allecti, fuum condidere Palatium, Romanique* Coloniam *deduxere. Qui verò volunt* Coloniam *hanc ad* Maldon *(ob tenuem vocabuli fonum) figere, oftendant vel volam vel vefligium Romanæ ibidem elegantiæ: cætera non confero quæ circa* Walden *attuli; unum dico, Cererem adeo odiffe* Maldonenfes *ut plerumque neceffe habeant frumentum è longinquo devehere.*

Alii interim Coloniam *hanc* Colne-Ceftriæ *fufpicantur confediffe. His repugnant quod* Antoninus Camalodunum *&* Coloniam *non pro diverfis locis habeat, quod tamen hi admittunt, licet in diverfis itineribus ponat ut fupra monui; &* Ravennas *ex veritate* Camaloduno *jungit* Colonia, *ita enim fcribendum eft pro* Camalodulo. *Denique, ne quid dicam de infanabili numerorum difcrepantiâ, fi eos ad* Colne Ceftriam *referre, oportet ex illo nomine* Britannicum *aliquod vocabulum erui, quod fono* Camalodunum *repræfentet, nam Britannicum fervârunt Romani.*

Non nego ftationem, vel oppidum Romanum aliquando fuiffe Colne-Ceftriæ, *id nummi retecti probant, fed nomen loco* Colaneam *contendo, ut eft aliis ad Boream, (de quâ* Ptolemæus) *non* Coloniam *fuiffe. Quæ res non obfervata aliquos hic in errorem impulit. Appellationem illam à fluvio* Colne *fumpfit,* Colne-Ceftria, *quemadmodum & illa alia* Colonia *(pro quâ corruptè poft* Camalodunum Ravennati *eft* Calunio) *inter confinia* Lancaftrenfis *&* Eboracenfis *agri. Emergit ex monte* Colne-hill *dicto fluvius ille non procul ab oppido, ubi plurimæ Romanorum reliquiæ (inter quas patera nummis* Gordiani *&* Volufiani *referta) funt inventæ.* Gale Antonin. p. 111. &c.

I

This

This is likewise in Englifh *as follows.*

Camulodunum. Upon Coins it is abbreviated into CAMV. There arifes a River in the Confines of *Effex* which is call'd *Camus, Cam* by the *Britains*; it runs by an Hill or *Dunum*, from the Top of which the Remains of a *Roman* City look towards a Royal Palace call'd *Audley* End, but about a Mile from a modern Town called *Walden*, and towards the Weft. From that River and the Word *Dunum* the *Romans* formed their *Camalodunum.* This was the *Waldenburgh* of the *Saxons.* This *Dunum* is call'd by the prefent Inhabitants *Sterbury-Hill*, and there have been found there a Gold Coin of *Claudius Cæfar*, and a Silver *Patera* of antique Workmanfhip, Weight and Fafhion. There are many Reafons to believe that here was the celebrated *Colonia* of the *Romans.* It is fituated by two military Ways, of which one turned towards the North, the other to the Weft and the *Iceni.* There are every where hereabouts many and remarkable Monuments of the *Romans:* Particularly the Boundaries of *Colonia*, or the *ager arcifinius* at *Arcden*; Sepulchres and Tombs at *Barklow*; Stone Veffels, filled with burnt Bones, fuch as we have defcribed at PRÆTORIUM dug up in the adjacent Fields, many Coins and Pavements; Garrifons and Camps at both *Chefterfords*, at *Caftle-camps*, and *Shedy-camps* [perhaps of *Sidius Geta* who ferved with *Vefpafian* under the Emperor *Claudius. Dio*, Lib. LX.] Forts fuch as *Tacitus* mentions to have been placed about *Colonia Camulodunum.* Under the Conduct of a Woman, they were able, fays he, to burn up *Colonia*, and ftorm their Camps. And they undertook a general War, and having attacked the Soldiers who were difperfed thro' the Caftles and ftormed their Garrifons, they invaded *Colonia* itfelf. What can the Hiftorian mean here, but the Camps and Caftles abovementioned? What but thofe Garrifons which were placed directly between the *Iceni* and *Camulodunum*, and which muft neceffarily be deftroyed before *Colonia* could be taken. What other *Colonia* could there be cut off by the *Iceni* and the *Trino-*
bantes

bantes who had rebelled, than at this *Camulodunum*, which *Oſtorius* by a provident kind of Dread had carried thither with a ſtrong Body of *Veterans*, when he made War upon the *Silures*, who were very remote from theſe Parts, that he might oppoſe the Rebels and inſtruct the Allies in the Laws? *Who were theſe Allies* but the *Londoners* and the People of *Verulam*, who when *Camulodunum* was deſtroyed were immediately oppreſſed by the Enemy, with the Deſtruction of ſeventy thouſand Citizens and Allies?

To this add the wholſome and pleaſant Situation of the Place, than which nothing could be more ſo, wherefore the *Roman* Generals conſulted here rather their Pleaſure than their Advantage. *Tacitus.* The Fields every where ſmile with the plenteous Harveſt, which is repreſented by a Wheat-Sheaf upon a Coin of *Cunobeline*, who had a Palace at this Place. On one ſide the Vallies breathe the fragrant Saffron, (whence is derived the modern Name of Saffron *Walden)* which tho' it was firſt brought and cultivated in this Iſland long after the Time of the *Romans*, it however argues the Soil to be very fertile, ſince no other agrees with it. On that ſide Mountains loaded with thick Woods; on this champain Plains are extended to a great Length, well adapted for hunting and the Pleaſures of Riding, which is pretty clearly indicated by the Horſe on the Coins of *Cunobeline*. At this *Walden* therefore the Kings of the *Trinobantes*, being invited by the Pleaſantneſs of the Place, built their Palace, and the *Romans* planted a Colony. But thoſe Perſons who will have this Colony to have been at *Maldon* (by reaſon of ſome Reſemblance in the Sound) let them ſhew ſome Trace of the *Roman* Elegance in it. I ſhall only mention one thing, that *Ceres* is ſo averſe to the Inhabitants of *Maldon*, that for the moſt part they are under a Neceſſity of fetching their Corn from a great Diſtance; others in the mean Time imagine that this Colony was planted at *Colne-Cheſter*. This however is refuted by *Antoninus*, who makes *Camulodunum* and *Colonia* the ſame Place, which yet they admit, tho' he places it in different *Itinera*, as I have before obſerved; and *Ravennas* rightly joins *Colonia* to *Camulodunum*; for thus muſt it be writ inſtead of *Camulo-*

dulc.

dulo.   Laftly, not to fay any thing of the irreconcilable Difference of the Numbers, if you refer them to *Colne-Chefter*, fome *Britifh* Word muft be derived from that Name, which reprefents *Camulodunum* in found, for the *Romans* preferved the *Britifh* Word.

I do not deny but that there has been a Station or *Roman* Town at *Colne-Chefter*, that is proved by the Coins which are digged up there; but then I contend for the Places being call'd *Colanea,* as fome would have it to the Northward (of which *Ptolemy)* and not *Colonia:* Which thing not having been obferved has drawn feveral into this Error. *Colne-Chefter* received that Name from the River *Colne,* as likewife the other *Colonia,* (which *Ravennas* corruptly calls *Calunio)* fituated between *Lancafhire* and *Yorkfhire.* That River arifes from *Colne-hill* a little diftant from the Town, where feveral Remains of *Roman* Antiquity have been found, and particularly an earthen Veffel full of Coins of the Emperors *Gordian* and *Volufius.*

COLONIA, Numeri xxiv. *huic* Coloniæ *à* Cæfaromago, *(five fit illa ftatio* Witham, *five* Writtle*) affixæ, cum veris adeo ad amuffim, & cum illis qui in alio itinere* Camuloduno *opponuntur, adeò benè, licet non omninò congruunt, ut quod unus idemque fint* Colonia *&* Camulodunum *locus facile crediderim.   Quamquam autem ad fluvium* Colne *non negem Caftrum fuiffe Romanorum, non tamen hanc* Coloniam *ibi deductam fuiffe exiftimo, quia nec* Camulodunum *ibi ftetit.   Sint igitur* Colonia, *&* Camulodunum *una eademque urbs, & hæc apud* Walden, *cui pulchre convenit diftantia à* Cæfaromago *ex hac parte, quemadmodum & ex altera à villa* Fauftini, *fi cum plurimis* MS. *legas* M. P. xxv. loco xxxv. Id. p. 91.

In Englifh *as follows.*

Colonia. Since the Number xxiv. affixed to this *Colony* from *Cæfaromagus,* whether that Station be *Witham* or *Writtle,* agrees fo well, tho' not entirely with the true Numbers, as well as thofe which are placed to *Camulodunum* in another *Iter,* I am eafily induced

duced to believe that *Colonia* and *Camulodunum* were one and the same Places. But altho' I cannot deny that there was a *Roman* Camp at the River *Colne*, yet I do not think that this Colony was fixed there, since even *Camulodunum* itself was not situated in that Place; for this Reason *Colonia* and *Camulodunum* must be one and the same City, and this at *Walden*, which exactly agrees with the Distance from *Cæsaromagus* on one side, and from *Villa Faustina* on the other, if you read according to several MS. M. P. XXV. instead of XXXV.

Near little **Canfield** in *Essex*, within a Mile of **Dunmow** are two ancient Fortifications, &c. Also near **Walden** (the ancient *Camalodunum*, and consequently *Colonia*, (a) standing upon two *Military-ways*, and where Coins of *Claudius Cæsar* have been found) are Forts, &c. *Pointer's Britannia Rom.* p. 54. In *Essex* (saith the same Author) we find a *Military-way*, running from *Epping-Street*, thro' part of *Hartfordshire* to **Walden**, and then cross from **Dunmow** to **Colchester** (*Colonia*) call'd to this Day **The Street**, the very Word *Strata*, used by our Countryman *Bede* to signify a *Roman Road*, ib. p. 51. Now if **Walden** was *Colonia* as in *p.* 54. why is **Colchester** likewise *Colonia*, p. 51.

Hence we pass (that is from **Cullow Wratting**) to **Castlecamps** at six Miles Distance, the *Camulodunum*, I take it of *Antonine*. On the way from **Wratting** at two Miles End we enter the West End of **Haverill**, which stands upon the Bordering of *Suffolk, Essex,* and *Cambridgeshire*. Here we fall into the *Ikening*, which with the *Ermin*, at this Place makes a *Saltire*, as will appear by the settling the fifth *Iter*, which shall be done in its Place. We keep our *Ermin* and *Ikening* about two Miles to the House of Mr. *Bridge*. The *Ikening* hath its Course by *Linton*, &c. Our *Ermin* to which we keep for this ninth *Iter*, near Mr. *Bridges's* House deflects a little to the Left. And after two or three short serpentine Turnings, which the boggy Ground occasions, goes in a direct Line to *Castle-camps*, six Miles from *Ad Ansam*. This seems to me the famous *Camulodunum* call'd

by

by fome *Colonia*, by others *Colonia Camuloduni*. The Ground, which at prefent we can fee has been fortified, contains no more than fix or feven Acres, including the *Church* and *Church-yard*, &c. This I take to be the Royal Seat of *Cinobeline*, who was defeated by *Aulus Plautius* and *Claudius* in Perfon. He placed here a Colony of *Veterans*, according to the *Roman* Accounts, and invefted them with the Right of Poffeffion. The Objection to this Scheme; that the Place lies too far from the *Thames*, which *Claudius* paffed, engaged the *Britains*, and having defeated them, marched to *Camulodunum*, has no great Force in it.

A further Proof this is the Place, moves upon *Boadicea*'s defeating the *Veterans* fo eafily. The brave *Virago* drawing the *Trinobantes* alfo into a Revolt, fell boldly on the *Veterans* at *Camulodunum*, fhe put them to the Sword. This Place too has the Air of a *Britifh* Town enclofed with Woods at fome Diftance on every fide, which was the Situation they chofe. *Salmon*'s *Roman Stations*, p. 20, &c.

One thing muft be remembred by the way, that *Ptolomy* places his *Camulodanum*, which others call *Camulodunum*, in the Country of the *Trinobantes*; which contradicts what I have advanced, for then it fhould be looked for in *Effex*, not in *Cambridgefhire*.

This I own a Difficulty, but with as little Pains got over as many other things that pafs Mufter. The Place ftands juft within *Cambridgefhire*, upon the very Borders of *Effex*, in a fort of Indenture, where the firft mentioned County thrufts itfelf into *Effex*, between *Barklow* and *Haverill*. The Divifion of Counties was *Saxon*; and they were perhaps not fo very nice and exact in following the *Roman* Defcriptions as we imagine them. One County might in their Wars gain upon another, and make thefe trivial Alterations. The Place lies plainly in the Line from *Canonium* to *Ad Anfam*, and thence to *Cambretonium*. As an Inftance, *Ptolomy*'s *Cantium* took in *Southwark*, now reckoned to *Surry*. And *Languard-Fort*, on the *Suffolk* Side the *Haven* from *Harwich*, is yet efteemed in *Effex*. *Salmon*'s *New Survey of* England *in* Effex, *p.* 129.

Let

Let *Camulodunum* be where it will, if in or about *Effex*, it muft be out of the way to *Lincoln*, whither the fame Journey carries us. Therefore more time need not be fpent to fhew the direct way is not conftantly meant in the Itinerary. *Ib. p.* 131.

Camulodunum is the next *Cambridgefhire* Station I propofe: And this may be done without fo much Hardinefs as at firft Sight appears. *Caftle-camps* is the Place, I humbly prefume, of itfelf ignoble, any farther than *Norman* Honour has made it otherwife, nor of extent enough to be thought a *Colony*. So that the Charge would be to bring a Situation *ex fœce Romuli*, and to exalt it to the higheft *Roman* Honour.

Firft let the adverfary Opinions appear, making it *Malden*, *Colchefter* and *Walden*. The Firft took its Title from Similitude of Sound, and from that only, as was obferved upon *Effex* in our fecond Part. The Second had the great *Stillingfleet* and *Talbot* to fupport it; but all they have attempted is to prove it *Roman*, which *no-body can deny*. The Third hath its chief Evidence from Sound, and that *Roman* Remains are in the Neighbourhood. To all which let this be added, that not one of the three Schemes pretends to keep *Antonine*'s Numbers facred, or indeed to treat them with any Refpect.

Having faid enough already upon this Place, I only fhew here the way of coming at it, and the juft Diftance in which it ftands from *Cannonium* 𝕽ing-𝕳ill, and *Ad Anfam* 𝕮allow 𝕽ratting, from the firft nine Miles, from the other fix, in a Line as direct as the Ground will bear from *London* to *Yarmouth*.

Our Road to *Caftle-camps* from 𝕽ing-𝕳ill *Cannonium*, is thro' the Ground upon which *Audley Inn* now ftands, thro' the Park by *Magnaville*'s Caftle to St. *Aylots*, a Farm belonging to the Earls of *Suffolk*. There the broad Military-way is loft, which points to *Caftle-camps*. *Hale*'s Wood ftops it up; and the Fields beyond the Wood thro' which it feems anciently to have gone, fhew no Traces of a Road till we come to the Place. Thence again our *Ermin*, as we take the Liberty to call it, moves towards *Haveril*; and two Miles before it arrives there, falls into the *Ikening* from *Linton,*

2

ton,

ton, and keeps it Company to *Haveril*, parting there in a Saltire as hath been said in the former Part upon *Essex*.

We are now to account for the Smallness of the Garrison, and its Pretence to claim the Honour of a *Roman* Colony against *Colchester*, or any other considerable Place, an Honour which *London* at that time did not enjoy, as appears from what is related of *Suetonius Paulinus*. *Tacitus* makes *Camulodunum* a Place without Forts and Castles, and accuses the Officers of consulting Ease and Plenty above Security. Here seems to have been the *Prætorium*, and the Temple of *Claudius* near it, but the *Veterans* had dispersed themselves about the Country, enjoying the Fruits of Husbandry, without imagining their Tenure so precarious as it was. They might probably have some Fortifications on the Verge of their Colony, but these so weak, or so weakly guarded, that *Boadicea* made no difficulty of surprizing them. The above mentioned Author saith as much: *Fœmina duce exurere Coloniam, expugnare Castra potuere. Et sumpsere universi bellum, & sparsos per Castella milites consectati, expugnatis præsidiis, ipsam Coloniam invasere.* These *Castella* might be as far off as *Chesterford* on one side, as *Heveningham* on the other, or as *Haveril.* At this last mentioned Place are Coins now found in abundance. And there is a sort of Proof the Colony was continued hither, if we will depend upon the Exactness of the *Itinerary:* And that a Part, if not the chief Part of the Colony, was three Miles farther from *London*, than *Castle-camps* entended from thence. This appears from the different Number of Miles the fifth Journey gives from the ninth. In the fifth from *Cæsaromagus* to *Colonia*, we find twenty four Miles. In the ninth we find from *Cæsaromagus* to *Cannonium* twelve, and nine more to *Camulodunum*; in the whole twenty one.

The Ground we see at present is not more than six or seven Acres fortified; and the Works seem to be *Norman*, whatever there might have been in elder Times. This, however, may have been the Residence of *Cynobelin*. His *Prætorium*, or something equivalent to it, might be within this Compass, and the exterior Defence of his *Oppidum* at a greater Distance. This Defence

2   consisting

confisting of Ditches and Trees without, might be totally defaced by *Roman* Induſtry upon Improvement of the Lands. There is not at preſent any Traces of ſuch Works. *Aulus Plautius*, and *Claudius* in Perſon are ſaid to have been here; and here was a Temple built to the Honour of that Emperor, and according to *Tacitus* an Altar inſcribed, *The Altar of eternal Dominion*. Here the conquered *Britons* adored him as a God.

This may give ſome Light to the Inſcription *Camden* mentions *Camulo Deo ſanċto & fortiſſimo*. He labours from this, and an old Stone found at *Rome* in the Palace of *Colloti*, to prove *Camulus* another Name for *Mars* by which he was worſhipped. As *Claudius* was deified and had a Temple here; and was according to *Seneca*'s Relation, worſhipped by theſe *Barbarians*, this Temple, and this Adoration might be at *Camulodunum*. Thus *Camulo* may ſtand for *Camuloduni* according to the *Roman* Praċtice of cutting Words ſhort. *Claudius* may be the *Deus ſanċtus & fortiſſimus*, whoſe Altar was at this Place. The *Camu.* which is on ſome Coins attributed to *Cynobelin*, is ſtill a ſhorter way of Writing the Place than *Camulo*. It is more probable theſe very Coins were *Roman*, in Memory of Viċtory over *Cynobelin*. *Cæſar* expreſly denied the *Britons* had any Coins; and theſe, tho' ſomething later, have no great Evidence on their ſide.

Camulodunum, wherever it ſtood, was the Quarters of the fourteenth Legion, the *Gemina Martia Viċtrix*, called by *Tacitus* the Conquerors of *Britain :* The ſame that in the Inſcription of *Cuæus Munatius*, correċted by the Dean of *York*, is ſaid to be, *Colonia viċtricenſis quæ eſt in Britanniâ Camuloduni*. The Hiſtory of *Claudius* ſaith, he actually came to *Britain* and reinforced *Aulus Plautius*, that he defeated the *Britons*, who diſputed his Paſſage over the *Thames*; that he took *Camulodunum*, upon which his Son was ſtiled *Britannicus*; and that the Prieſts who officiated in the Temple built to his Honour, were call'd *Sodales Auguſtales*. Salmon's Survey, &c. Cambridgeſhire, *p.* 209, &c.

This long Account of Mr. *Salmon*'s relating to *Camulodunum*, being taken from three ſeveral Books, I have endeavoured to
avoid

avoid Repetition, as much as I could, without breaking in upon the Argument.

As for Goddeſſes, they (the *Britains*) worſhipped *Diana* under the Name of *Camma*, another Goddeſs the *Britains* had, who is call'd by *Dion*, *Andraſte* or *Andrate*, and is ſuppoſed to have been the *Goddeſs of Victory*; ſhe had a Temple at *Camalodunum* now Malden in *Eſſex*. *Tyrrell's Hiſt.* Vol. I. p. 24.

Thus having tranſcribed what is ſaid about the Situation of *Camulodunum*, by thoſe Authors I have before quoted; thoſe which remain are *Harriſon*, *Leland* and the *Anonymous Author* of *Ravennas*, which conſiſting only of the *Iters* of *Antoninus*, with the Addition of the Names of the *Towns* which they did ſuppoſe them to be, I have nothing more to add about them; but only take Notice that in the *Chorographia Britanniæ Anonymi Ravennatis* aforemention'd, *p.* 303. *Camulodunum*, is written *Camulodulum Colonia*: And in the *Codex Vaticanus*, *Camulodunum*, *Monulodulum Colonia*. I ſhall now here add a Note from another by me omitted.

Camulodunum, Malden, a Town in *Eſſex*, written by *Ptolomy Camulodanum*; *Antoninus* and *Dio Caſſius*, *Camulodunum*, *Pliny* and *Tacitus* more exactly *Camalodunum*; *Dio Caſſius*, calls it the Court of *Cunobelin*; *Camol* ſignifies a Prince and Governor in the *Phœnician* Tongue, and Dun a *Hill*, ſo that this may be call'd the *King's Hill*, as *Mons Capitolinus* at *Rome*, *Jupiter's Hill*, and in favour of this Interpretation we may find the Court of *Arthur* call'd *Camalot*. Samme's Britan. Antiq. illuſ. p. 67.

Dr. *Stillingfleet* is mentioned by *Baxter*, as making *Colcheſter* to be *Camulodunum*, what I find of that Author relating thereto is as follows. The learned Primate (Archbiſhop *Uſher*) thinks it (i. e. *Civitas Colonia Londinenſium*) to be Colcheſter; that being call'd by *Antoninus Colonia*. Stillingfleet's Orig. Brit. p. 75.

Baxter likewiſe mentions *Talbot* as being of the ſame Opinion, but not having that Author's MS. Book by me, I cannot direct to the Page, but only obſerve, that in *Harriſon's Antoninus* printed by *Burton* before his *Antoninus*, in the *Iter à venta Icenorum Londinio*, *Talbot* makes *Cambritorium* Ipſwich, *Ad Anſam* Catwarbridge, *Camolodunum*, Colnceſter, and *Canonium* Colne, &c. *Page*

Page 5. Col. 1. *l.* 20, *and* 21. *r.* Caftle.   *p.* 8. *c.* 1. *l.* 1. *r.* 1695.
p. 12. *c.* 1. *l.* 9. *after the Word* for *add* 12.   *p.* 16. *c.* 1. *l.* 13, *and*
14. *r.* Bawdfey.

The Foffils mentioned *Page* 19. of which fome Account was
there promifed, may be reduced to two Heads, *viz.*

I. *Such as are real and natural.*
II. *Such as are extraneous.*

I. Thofe I have obferved in this Cliff, that are *real* and *natural,*
are
   1. *Belemnites Pyramidalis bafi foratâ niger minor,* Langii Hift. Lap.
Helv. 131. Tab 37. N°. 4.
   2. *Ofteocollâ Anglicana.* This I have taken Notice of and defcribed in the foregoing *Hiftory,* p. 19. Dr. *Woodward* affirms
one of our River Incruftations, found in a Rivulet near
Norleach in *Gloucefterfhire,* to be the *Ofteocolla* or *Bone-binder* of the
Shops. *Attempt.* Tom. I. p. 151. f. 5.   Mr. *Morton* alfo writes,
that the *Ofteocolla* of the Shops appears to him, both by the conftituent Matter, and the Figure of it, to have the very fame Origin
with the River Incruftations, *Nat. Hift. Northampt.* p. 272.   How
they may agree in Vertue, (not having ever tried them) I know
not; but as to their place and manner of Produ&ion, I am fure
they are much different; for thofe of Dr. *Woodward* and Mr. *Morton* are found in *Rivulets,* but this in the Sandy-ground near the
Top of the *Cliff,* where no Water but Rain can come: And ours
agrees with that of *Wormius,* who thus writes of it : *Lapis eft
mollis, albo & cinereo colore, figuram offis exhibens, concavus, quandoque in fe medullam habens friabilem, linguæ adherentem, & facile in
liquore folubilem, quandoque vero nullam.   Nafcitur in locis arenofis,
crefcit per arenam formâ Coralli,* Muf. Worm. *p.* 53.
   3. *Stalagmites mammillaris verrucofus,* Lhuyd Lithop. *p.* 4. N°.
60. *Stalagmites Bullatus major,* Morton Nat. Hift. North. *p.* 146.
§. 116. *Stalagmites,* Plot's Staffordfh. *p.* 182. 8. 10. Tab. II. Fig. II.

N n   only

only his was purely white, and ours inclines more to a rusty Colour.

4. A *yellow Spar*, very near the Colour of Bees Wax, but rather paler, a *Stalagmites electrinus*, Lhuyd Lithop. *p.* 3. This I take to be what Dr. *Woodward* calls *Spar, flat with a cast of yellow*, Vol. I. p. 153. f. 36. This is to be found infinuated into the Cracks of the Stones which lie on the Shore. The Doctor describes his to consist of numerous thin *Incrustations* fuceffively cast by Water each on other, very much like the Spar that compofes the *Septa* or *Partitions* of the *Ludus Helmontii*, that is found in *Sheppey Island*. My Sample is of the Colour of the aforefaid *Septa*, but is, where thickest, about one Inch; yet there I can discern but three feveral Partitions. Whether it is the *Spar* or the inclofed *Tali* that hath the *Vertue*, ascribed by *Van Helmont* to his *Ludus*, viz. in diffolving the *Dualech* or *Lapis Spongiofus* (as Dr. *Plot* terms it) generated in human Bodies, of a middle Nature, between a *Tartar* and the ordinary *Calculus Humanus*, Hist. of Staffordsh. p. 188. I do not find.

Ludus Helmontii. The Waxen Vein, *Grew*'s *Muf. Reg. Soc.* p. 311. It is a Sort of compact Stone, of a fine Grain, and brown Colour, diftinguished into *Tali* (as Dr. *Woodward* terms them) of various and irregular Bigneffes, by means of certain *Septa* or Partitions of a yellowish or *wax coloured Spar*, which like Veins or Plates run thro' it every way. *Van Helmont* took this for the *Ludus Paracelfi*, attributing the fame Vertues to it; the like doth Dr. *Grew*, l. c. p. 312. but therein they were greatly mistaken, as Dr. *Woodward* obferves; the Chymist and Mineralist of *Germany* agreeing that the true *Ludus* of *Paracelfus is a teffulated Pyrites quod tala teffaræ aut cubi formâ femper eruatur*, as the aforefaid *Helmont* himfelf defcribes it, *de Lithiafi* cap. 7. n. 22, 23. So that the *Ludus* of *Helmont* ought not to be confounded with that of *Paracelfus*; neither can the *Vertues* of one be reasonably attributed to the other. That this Body is the *Ludus* of *Helmont* is evident from the Sample thereof found in the Place, *viz.* on the Banks of the River *Scheld* near *Antwerp*, mentioned by that Author, *Lib. de Lithiafi*, p. 700.

and

and brought from thence into *England* by his Son *Fr. Merc. Van Helmont*, and is now to be feen among Dr.*Woodward*'s Collections, *Attempt.* Tom. II. Part. I. pag. 8. Dr. *Grew* writes, that both of thefe Bodies make an *Effervefcence* with *Spirit of Nitre*, but the *Tali* or afh-coloured the greater.

5. An hexangular Sprig of *Selenites* or *mock Cryftal*. It is about two Inches in length, ¼ of an Inch in Diameter near the Bafe. It is a little foiled on the outfide. *Selenites longiufculus lamellam hexagonam conftituens*, Lhuyd. Lithop. Brit. p. 5. N°. 81. *Hexagonal Prifm. Selenites growing gradually fmaller*, Mort. Nat. Hift. North. *p.* 177. *Selenites* 3. Plot Hift. Oxford. *p.* 83. As the *Selenites* or *mock Cryftal* is compofed of the fame Matter as *Talc*, its Effects in Medicine muft needs be as great; and therefore we may fitly make ufe of it inftead of the foreign *Talc*. 'Tis eafily reduced into a foft, fine, and impalpable Powder; and recommendable in thofe Diftempers wherein *Alkalies* are of ufe. 'Tis ufed in fome Places in ftopping exceffive *Bleeding* with Succefs; on which Account it is by fome call'd *Stanch. Mort.* Ibid. p. 178. The finding of the *Selenites* frequently near the *Purging Wells* hath induced, faith Dr.*Woodward*, fome to believe that thefe impart the purging Power to thofe Waters, *&c.* But all our Trials inform us, that its Properties are the fame with *common Talc*, it being a pretty ftrong Exficcant and Abforbent; and is very powerfully binding, inftead of purging. *Woodward*'s *Attempt.* 74. The Powder of this, faith Mr. *Lawrence*, is found good to cicatrize green Wounds, *Mercur. Central.* p. 10.

6. *Succinum, Electrum.* 𝔄𝔪𝔟𝔢𝔯. *Succinum citrinum Officinarum*, Pharm. noft. 56. This is fometimes found on this Shore, but more frequently on the oppofite about *Landguard-Fort*. The Original of this is much controverted among the Writers of *Natural Hiftory*; fome rank it among the *Foffils*, and of this Opinion was the late Dr. *Woodward*, having fo placed it in his *Attempt towards a Natural Hiftory of Foffils:* Where he faith, that a Perfon (at *Whitby*) who had been long enquiring into the Nature of this Body, is very pofitive, that all *Amber* is originally lodged in the Cliffs and

N n 2 Strata,

Strata, and beat thence by the Agitation of the Sea ; and that it is all, when firſt beat out, covered with a Cruſt, after the Manner of *Flints*, and ſome other *Foſſils*.   And all that is found naked, and uncovered, has had the Cruſt worn off by the ſucceſſive Agitation of it upon the Shores by the Sea, *Attempt.* Tom. I. Part I. p. 169.   And in his Catalogue of *foreign Foſſils*, Part. I. p. 19. he mentions ſeveral *Nodules* of *Amber*, found in great Numbers upon the Shores near *Tangier* ; and Sir *Henry Sheers* told him, that at the demoliſhing the *Mole* there ſeveral Rocks were torn and blown up, in which Pieces of *Amber* were lodged ; of which one Mr. *Robert Ball* had a Piece.   This, ſaith the Doctor, is an additional Proof, that *Amber* is as much a real *Foſſil* as *Flints*, &c. and that the Sea ſerves by its Agitation, only to fetch it forth of the Cliffs and uncover it, *Attempt.* Tom. II. *Boccone* brings many Arguments to prove that *Amber* is nothing elſe but *Naphtha*, or *Oleum Petroleum* coagulated or condenſed, *Muſeo di Fiſica & di Eſperienze*, p. 32. *Hartman* thinks it of *Foſſil Original*, and of the Gemm kind, *Succincta Succini Pruſſici Hiſtoria*, &c. Philoſ. Tranſact. Nº. 248. p. 24.   The late Dr. *Hook* judges it the Juice (or *Roſin*) of a certain Tree, upon which Account he read three *Diſcourſes* before the *Royal Society*, which being very long, I ſhall only give you the Sum of them, drawn up by Mr. *Waller*, and publiſhed by Mr. *Derham*, as follows.   " That *Amber* being found " almoſt all over *Pruſſia*, as well in the Inland Parts, as in the " Sea ; on the Shore, as well as in the Caverns, Cliffs, and under the " Hills by digging, and this in a Sort of *Minera Arenaria* ; which " by the Subſtances found in it, ſuch as Shells petrified and the " like, Dr. *Hook* judges to be a certain Layer or Bed of Sea-Sand, " the Remains of the Bottom of ſome Sea, that formerly covered " the whole Country, which, in proceſs of Time, has been raiſed " above the Level of the preſent Sea ; but at a certain Depth, all " that ſandy Bottom yet remains, containing ſuch Subſtances as " were there depoſited, whilſt it was in that State, at leaſt, ſuch " of them as have not been rotted and conſumed by Time, ſuch " as petrified *Shells*, *Wood*, *Bones*, with *Vitriol*, *Alum*, *Nitre* and
" *Sea-Salt*,

" *Sea-Salt*, together with Lumps of *Amber*, are frequently now
" found in digging into this Sand for Wells, or the like.   Here
" he has recourfe to his Hypothefis, formerly difcourfed of, for
" the Solution of the Appearances, *viz.* that not only the Vales
" and lower Parts of the Land have been fometime the Bottom
" of the Sea, but even the Tops of Hills and Mountains; as the
" feveral Subftances now found thereon make evident.   *Amber*
" then being thus found, either at the Bottom of the Sea adjoin-
" ing, or in thefe Layers of Sand, the Queftion is, How it came
" there?   To anfwer this Inquiry, tho' the Author of the *Treatife*
" is of another Opinion, yet from feveral Obfervations therein
" mentioned, Dr. *Hook* judges it to have been the *Gum* of a cer-
" tain *Tree* petrified, and altered to the prefent State and Appear-
" ance it has, *Philofophical Experiments,* &c. p. 315."   *Thomas
Bartholinus* is of the fame Opinion, *Acta Medica Hafn.* Vol. I. *Obf.*
57. and Vol. XI. *Obf.* 122. both which Dr. *Hook* makes the Subject of his third *Difcourfe concerning Amber,* Ib. p. 329.   To which
p. 336, 337. he adds fix *Arguments* of his own, the firft of which,
viz. That *Amber* is not to be found in larger Lumps or Pieces,
then may be fuppofed the Exudation of a Gum out of one or two
Vents of the fame Tree; whereas *Hector Boetius* writes, that a
Piece bigger than a Horfe hath been found in the Northern Parts
of *Scotland.*   And another is, that there are Inftances enough to
be found of the *Petrifaction* of *vegetable* Subftances; and fo this
cannot be looked on as a Singularity in thofe Parts.   That *Woods,*
and perhaps fome other Parts of *Vegetables* have been found fo far
petrified, as to fuffer no Diffolution by Fire, is eafily granted, but
I have never yet met with any Inftance of any *Gum* that could
undergo that Trial; and the contrary is to be found in the Subject here treated of; for *Amber* will, like other bituminous Subftances, be confumed to Afhes by the Fire.   There is another
Opinion concerning the Original of *Amber, viz.* That it is either
the Fat or Spawn of *Whales,* but as this wants no refuting I fhall
fay no more about it.

7. *Pyrites*

7. *Pyrites.* 𝕮𝖔𝖕𝖕𝖊𝖗𝖆𝖘-𝕾𝖙𝖔𝖓𝖊𝖘. Thefe are abundantly found on this Shore, where they are gathered by Children, and fold to the *Copperas Houfes*, as I have already taken Notice. Thefe are beat out of the Cliffs by the Agitation of the Sea. The *Pyritæ* of *Effex*, *Kent*, &c. yield upon Trial a fmall quantity of *Gold* and *Silver*, and fome of them a little *Copper*. As to *Iron*, faith Dr. *Woodward*, I have found fome few that have yielded one eighth of that Metal. He adds, that he could never perceive any *Arfenic* in the *Pyritæ*; in which they differ from the *Marcafites*, moft of which contain more or lefs of that Mineral. The *Arabian Naturalifts* exprefs this Body in their Language by the Word *Marcafit*, but for Diftinction fake the Doctor hath call'd thofe that are independent, in form of *Nodules*, and lodged in *Strata*, *Piritæ*; and thofe that are found run in the Veins perpendicular Fiffures, *Marcafits*, *Woodward*'s *Attempt*. Tom. I. Part I. p. 172.

8. *Geodes.* Thefe are frequently to be found here, and of feveral Forms and Shapes: The outward Cafe is ferruginous and hard, containing a friable Matter within of a darker Colour than the outward Cruft.

9. *Bezoar-Mineral.* Thefe likewife are frequently to be met with. They are of different Sizes and Shapes, many of them are of the Bignefs and Shape of a *Pigeon*'s Egg and ponderous: Their outfide is near the Colour of the *Oriental Bezoar*, very fmooth as if polifhed, having divers irregular *Septa* or Cracks, being broken, the outward Cruft is about ¼ of an Inch thick, confifting of *Striæ* like the *Belemnites*. The inward Crufts are more of an *Ochreous* Colour, and twice the Thicknefs of the outward. That which I broke upon this Shore did not exactly agree with Dr. *Woodward*'s Bezoar Mineral +₀ 19. which was found at this Cliff, *Attempt*. Tom. I. Part I. p. 238.

10. *An oval Stone of a brown or Chefnut Colour, but lighter than the Mineral Bezoar aforegoing.* This weighed two Ounces Averdupoife, and filled with a ferruginous Matter, very ponderous and hath irregular Cracks in the Surface, and is probably the fame with that which Dr. *Woodward* thus mentions; *A Stone of a dark brown*

2 *Colour,*

Colour, and environed with a thin Cruſt of lighter brown, found under Harwich Cliff *by Mr.* Groome, *who fancies this of the Size and Form of a Magpye's or Crow's Egg. There were more found there of the like Size and Form: And he will have it, that theſe were antediluvian Eggs filled with ſtony Matter; obſerving that theſe Eggs are frequent in* Spring Seaſon, *when the Deluge began,* Attempt. Tom. II. p. 70. c. 64.

II. Such Fossils as are extraneous; *That is the Parts of Vegetables, or Animals found in and at this Cliff, and the ſtony Bodies formed in them.*

1. PEtrified Wood, *ſuch as lies looſe in the Strata, or Layers of the Cliff:* Of which here are two Sorts ; one is of a *ferruginous* or ruſty Colour, being four or five Inches long, about three broad, and 1¼ of an Inch thick where thickeſt; one Side of it is convex, and the other flat, as if ſawn off from a round Body of a much larger Circumference. The other is as long, but not above an Inch and Quarter wide; this is of a ſhining dark brown Colour, as if poliſhed on the out-ſide, but paler within.

2. *Petrified Wood incloſed in a Stratum of Stone.* It is of a brown Colour, and of divers Bigneſſes ; one Piece I have yet imbedded in the *Stone,* about one Inch in Diameter; the *Bark* is of a deeper Colour, being ſeparated from the Wood by a darker *Spar.* Which of theſe it is that is intended in Dr. *Woodward's Attempt,* Tom. I. Part II. p. 20. n. 6. 49. I cannot at preſent inform myſelf: " The *Doctor* mentions *petrified Wood,* of a " deep brown Colour near black ; and having a Vein of a very pale " or yellowiſh brown talky Spar running length-ways of it. This " Body is very hard, and ponderous ; but has much of the Grain " of *Wood.* 'Twas given him by *Monſieur Miſſon,* who broke it " off the Trunk of a *Tree,* petrified, and of the ſame Conſtitution " and Colour throughout ; in length about fourteen Feet, in *Dia-* " *meter* about a Foot, at one End tapering, and ſomewhat leſs at " the other, where there were ſome ſmall Remains of *Branches.*
" It

" It lay on the Shore near *Harwich* underneath the *Cliff*, out of
" which doubtlefs it had been beaten by the Agitation of the Sea.
" Sir *Anthony Dean* alfo faw the Tree under the *Cliff*, and attefts
" this Account. When he faw it, it was yet actually lying in the
" *Cliff*; but a great Part of it uncovered and bare. He judged
" by the Shape that 'twas a *Tree*. This was in the Year 1666.
" *Attempt.* Tom II. p. 57." Whether this was of the fame as the
laft abovementioned, I cannot at prefent determine? The faid *petrified Tree* being gone before I ever was at *Harwich*.

3. *A Piece of a Stick ponderous, of the Conftitution of the common
vitriolic Pyrites*, Woodward's Attempt. Tom. I. Part II. p. 20.
This is to be found on the Shore under the *Cliff* among the *Cop-
peras-Stones*. The Sample I have hath loft its Bark, but hath
apparently the Grain, Texture and Knots of Wood, that were thus
altered by the Infinuation of the mineral Matter of the *Pyrites*.
And it is to this Infinuation of the conftituent Matter of the *Pyrites*,
faturating or filling the Pores of the *Oaken-Spike* aforementioned,
p. 105. that the Alteration made thereon is principally to be attributed; for I obferve, that divers efflorefcences of a *Vitrioline*
Salt do this Year 1729. appear upon it.

Having pag. 105. taken notice of the *Incombuftiblenefs of the Foffil Wood* of this *Cliff*, I fhall here add the Experiments made on
fome *Foffil Wood* by Dr. *Hooke* then *Curator* to the *Royal Society*, as
I find it publifhed by himfelf in his *Mocrographia*, p. 108. As it
is likewife by *John Evelin* Efq; in his *Sylva*, p. 206.

This petrified *Subftance refembled* Wood, in *that Firft*, all the
Parts of it feemed not at all *diflocated* or altered from their natural Pofition whilft they were Wood, but the whole Piece retained the exact Shape of Wood, having many of the confpicuous
Pores of Wood ftill remaining Pores, and fhewing a manifeft Difference, vifible enough, between the Grain of the Wood and that
of the Bark, efpecially when any fide of it was fmooth and polite;
for then it appeared to have a very lovely Grain, like that of
fome curious clofe Wood.

Next

Next (it refembled Wood) in that all the fmaller and (if I may fo call thofe which are only vifible with a good magnifying Glafs) *Microfcopical Pores* of it appear (both when the Subftance is cut and polifhed *tranfverfly* and *parallel* to the Pores of it) perfectly like the *Microfcopical Pores* of feveral kinds of Wood, efpecially like and equal to thofe of feveral Sorts of rotten Wood which I have fince obferved, retaining both the Shape, Pofition and Magnitude of fuch Pores.

It was differing from Wood. *Firft*, In *Weight*, being to common Water as $3\frac{1}{4}$ to 1. whereas there are few of our *Englifh* Woods, that when very dry are found to be full as heavy as Water.

Secondly in *hardnefs*, being very near as hard as a Flint; and in fome Places of it alfo refembling the Grain of a Flint: And like that, it would very readily cut Glafs, and would not without difficulty, efpecially in fome Parts of it, be fcratched by a black hard Flint: It would alfo as readily ftrike fire againft a Steel, or againft a Flint, as any common Flint.

Thirdly, In the *Clofenefs* of it; for though all the *Microfcopical Pores* of this *petrified* Subftance were very confpicuous in one Pofition, yet by altering that Pofition of the polifhed Surface to the Light, it was alfo manifeft, that thofe Pores appeared darker than the reft of the Body, only becaufe they were filled up with a more dufky Subftance, and not becaufe they were hollow.

Fourthly, In its *Incombuftiblenefs*, in that it would not burn in the Fire; nay, though I kept it a good while red hot in the Flame of a Lamp, made very *intenfe* by the Blaft of a very fmall *Pipe*, and a large *Charcoal*, yet it feemed not at all to have diminifhed its Extenfion; but only I found it to have changed its Colour, and to appear of a more dark and dufky brown Colour; nor could I perceive that thofe Parts which feemed to be Wood at firft, were any thing wafted, but the Parts appeared as folid and clofe as before. It was further obfervable alfo, that as it did not confume like Wood, fo neither did it crack and fly like a Flint, or fuch like hard Stone; nor was it long before it appeared red hot.

O ●

Fifthly,

Fifthly, In its *Diſſolubleneſs*; for putting ſome Drops of diſtilled *Vinegar* upon the Stone, I found it preſently to yield very many Bubbles, juſt like thoſe which may be obſerved in Spirit of *Vinegar* when it corrodes *Corals*, though perhaps many of thoſe ſmall Bubbles might proceed from ſmall Parcels of Air which were driven out of the Pores of this *petrified* Subſtance by the inſinuating liquid *Menſtruum*.

Sixthly, In its *Rigidneſs* and *Friability*, being not at all flexible but brittle like a Flint, infomuch that I could with one Knock of a Hammer break off a Piece of it, and with a few more, reduce that into a pretty fine Powder.

Seventhly, It ſeemed alſo very differing from Wood to the *Touch*, *feeling* more cold than Wood uſually does, and much like other cloſe Stones and Minerals.

The Reaſons of all which *Phænomena* ſeem to be;

That this *petrified Wood* having lain in ſome Place where it was well ſoaked with *petrifying Water* (that is ſuch Water as is well *impregnated* with ſtony and earthy Particles) did by degrees ſeparate, either by *Straining* and *Filtration*, or perhaps by *Præcipitation*, *Coheſion*, or *Coagulation*, abundance of ſtony Particles from the permeating Water; which ſtony Particles, being by means of the fluid *Vehicle* conveyed, not only into the *Microſcopical* Pores, and ſo perfectly ſtoping them up, but alſo into the Pores or *Interſtitia*, which may, perhaps, be even in the Texture or *Schematiſm* of that Part of the Wood, which, through the *Microſcope*, appears moſt ſolid, do thereby ſo augment the Weight of the Wood, as to make it above three times heavier than Water, and perhaps ſix times as heavy as it was when Wood.

Next, they thereby ſo lock up and fetter the Parts of the Wood, that the Fire cannot eaſily make them fly away: But the Action of the Fire upon them is only able to *char* thoſe Parts, as it were like a Piece of Wood; if it be cloſed very faſt up in Clay, and kept a good while red hot in the Fire, it will by the Heat of the Fire be *charred* and not conſumed, which may, perhaps, alſo be ſomewhat of the Cauſe, why the *petrified* Subſtance appeared of a dark-brown Colour after it had been burnt.   By

By this *Intrufion* of the *petrifying Particles*, this Subftance alfo becomes *hard* and *friable*; for the fmaller Pores of the Wood being perfectly wedged, and ftuft up with thofe ftony Particles, the fmall Parts of the Wood have no Places or Pores into which they may flide upon bending, and confequently little or no flection or yielding at all can be caufed in fuch a Subftance.

The remaining Particles likewife of the Wood among the ftony Particles may keep them from cracking and flying when put into the Fire, as they are very apt to do in a Flint.

ANIMALIUM PARTES EX TELLURE EFFOSSÆ.

I. *Conchylia univalvia.*

1. *Tubulofa.*

A *Congeries of Vermiculi, fome greater, fome fmaller*, Tab. XIII. fig. 1. It is bigger than a Man's Fift, being Part of a much larger Body, compofed of a coarfe, lax, *coraline* Matter: It feems to have been the *Thecæ*, or Cafes of fome Infects. *An Lapis Spongiæ? Woodward's Attempt.* Tom. II. Part I. p. 49. Who thus defcribes it. " 'Tis light, porous and friable: As to " its Form, 'tis commonly hollow or *fiftulofe*. It has a brackifh " falt *Tafte*, manifeftly of *Marine Origin*, and compofed of a " coarfe, lax, *coralline* Matter. The *Septiments* in this Collection, " and all the reft of it that I have feen, appear to have been the " *Thecæ, Latibula,*or *Cafes* of fome *Infects*, made in the Manner " of thofe of the *Phryganium* or *Cad-worm*, or rather the *Thecæ* " of the *Penicilli marini*. 'Tis common to find on the Sea-Shore " *Infects* thus involved in Cafes compofed of Sand, very fmall " Bits of Shells, Sticks, or the like; as well as of *coralloid* Matter." This Defcription fo well anfwers to our *Specimen*, that I cannot but judge it to be the fame. Mr. *Morton* writes, that the wreathed Sorts of the *Tubuli Vermiculares* are fmall, hollow, Pipe-like *Shells*, that in Bignefs, in external Form, and in the Inconftancy of their Convolutions, do refemble *Worms:* And he mentions three Sorts of them, the laft of which, *viz.* the fmalleft Size, fcarce

bigger

bigger than a *Crow's Quill:* which is the *Vermicularis Minus tortilis, denſe Stipata,* Lhuyd. Lithog. Angl. Nº. 1213. *Morton Nat. Hiſt. North.* p. 228.

A Congeries of ſmall Vermiculi, Woodward's Attempt. Tom. I. Part II. p. 23. Nº. 22. but whether theſe leſſer *Congeries* are of the ſame kind with this, I cannot determine.

2. *Diſcoidea.*

PAtella exigua alba, cancellata, Fiſſura notabili in margine, *Liſt. Hiſt. Conchyl.* Lib. IV. Fig. 28. A ſmall *Patella* mentioned by Dr. *Liſter. Woodward's Attempt.* Tom. I. Part. II. p. 24. who ſaith it was found in *Harwich* Cliff.

3. *Cochleata.*

1. COchlea clavicula brevi, Nº. 38. *Harwich* Cliff, *Woodward's Attempt.* Tom. I. Part II. p. 33. Buccinum bilingue ſtriatum, labro propatulo digitato, *Liſt. Hiſt. Conchyl.* Lib. IV. Sect. 12. Fig. 20. Turbo Pentidactilus alteri &c. *Bonan. Recreat. Ment. & Ocul.* p. 132. Nº. 87. This and the foregoing it was not my hap to meet with at *Harwich,* tho' the Doctor ſaith they were both found there.

2. Cochlea clavicula brevi, 33. from *Harwich* Cliff, *Woodward's Attempt.* Tom. I. Part II. p. 33. Nerita edentula lævis, *Liſt. Hiſt. Conchyl.* Lib. IV. Sect. 6. Nº. 39. Nerita ex fuſco virideſcens, &c. *ejuſd. Hiſt. Animal. Angl.* p. 164. Nerita parva flaveſcens, *Aldrov. de Teſt.* p. 364. Nerita Æliani, *Rond. Teſt.* p. 94. *Geſn. Aquat.* 626. This is figured Tab. x. Nº. 1.

The Shells of this, as well with as without the Animal, are to be found frequently on the Sea-Coaſt all about *England,* they being of divers Colours. This our Foſſil is of a whitiſh ruſty Colour: It weighed about eighteen Grains, the ſame did the native Shell.

3. Buccinum

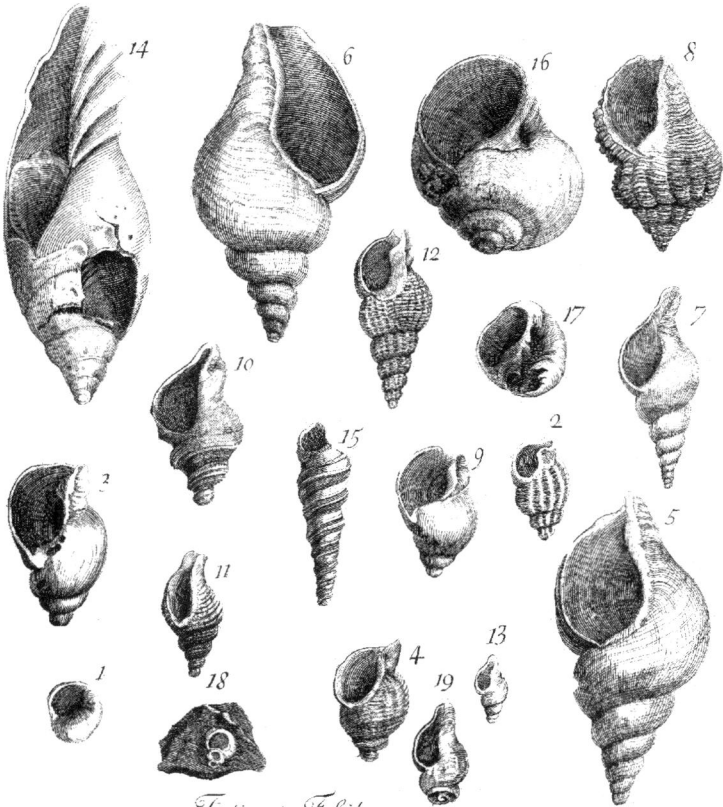

Tab. X. *Page.284*.

Turbinated Fossils.

3. Buccinum brevi roftro ftriatum denfe finuofum, Tab. x. Fig.

2. Buccinum brevi roftro cancellatum, denfe finuofum labro dentato, *Lift. Hift. Conchyl.* Lib. IV. Sect. 15. N°. 21. which Shell, tho' common to be found on our Coaft, yet not being found on the Northern Shores, was not taken Notice of by Dr. *Lifter* in his *Hift. Animal. Angl.* The Foffil Shell is very frequent in this Cliff, but rarely to be met with whole; the *Sulci* are larger than in the other, it hath commonly five Twirls, three Quarters of an Inch long, and three Eighths wide.

4. Buccinum brevi roftro magnum, tenue leviter ftriatum, *Lift. Hift. Conchyl.* Lib. IV. Sect. 15. N°. 15. Buccinum tenue, leve, ftriatum et undatum, *Ejufd. Hift. Animal. Angl.* p. 157. Cochlea clavicula productiore, 107. *Woodward's Attempt.* Tom. I. Part. II. p. 36. Buccina fenis orbibus finita, minutiffimis filis tranfverfe ductis afpera, colore tophaceo in parte externa, interna verò albo, *Bonan. Recreat. Mentis & Ocul.* p. 137. N°. 190. The Figure of this is in Tab. x. Fig. 3. The *Striæ* of this are all worn out by the Fluxion of the Water, fo that it appears to be fmooth. My Sample is but a fmall Shell of five turnings, in length one Inch three Quarters, and in breadth an Inch, in Colour white tinged with a rufty Colour, and but light for its Bignefs.

5. Buccinum Foffile tenue confragofum, *Philof. Tranf.* 291. p. 1577. Tab. x. Fig. 9. This is like the laft, only fmaller, of four Turns, ftriated very fine, the length of the Foffil one Inch ¼, and the Breadth three Quarters: It is very light, weighing but half a Dram Troy.

6. Buccinum Foffile tenue minus ponderofum, ftriatum et undatum, *Philof. Tranfact.* N°. 291. p. 1577. Tab. x. Fig. 8. Buccinum craffum rubefcens ftriatum & undatum, *Lift. Hift. Animal. Angl.* p. 156. Buccinum brevi-roftrum tenuiter ftriatum, pluribus undatis finubus diftinctum, *Ejufd. Hift. Conch.* Lib. IV. Sect. 15. N°. 14. Buccina extrinfecus livida, intrinfecus terrea, *Bonan. Recreat. Ment. & Ocul.* p. 136. N°. 189. The Figure of this is good, but the Defcription thereof very imperfect and doubtful, only the Author faith, that he had it out of the *Britifh* Seas.

7. Buccinum

7. Buccinum Foſſile ſtriis prominulis marginalibus inſignitum, *Philoſ. Tranſ.* N°. 291. p. 1577. Buccinum brevi roſtro album denticulo unico ad imam columellam, *Liſt. Hiſt. Conchyl.* Lib. IV. Sect. 15. N°. 19. Cochlea clavicula productiore, 108 *. *Woodward's Attempt.* Buccinum minus albidum, aſperum, intra quinas ſpiras finitum, *Liſt. Hiſt. Animal. Angl.* 158. Turbo, N°. 52. *Bonan. Recreat. Mentis & Oc.* p. 119. Vide Tab. x. Fig. 10. This differs from the Shell of the Fiſh, in that the Mouth is wider and longer, the Twirls are flatter than in that, each having a *Stria* which terminates it.

8. Buccinum Foſſile minus ore dentato, Tab. x. Fig. 10. Buccinum brevi roſtro ſupra modum craſſum ventrioſius labro denticulato, *Liſt. Hiſt. Conchyl.* Lib. IV. Sect. 15. N°. 18. Buccinum minus, ex albo ſubviride, ore dentato, eoque ex flavo leviter rubeſcente, *Ejuſd. Hiſt. Animal. Angl.* p. 159. This and the foregoing are by Dr. *Liſter* termed *Purpuræ Anglicanæ*, from that famous Crimſon Colour, which their Juice doth impart to Linen or Silk tinged with it like that of the *Purpura* of the Ancients ; the Diſcovery of which is in part owing to Mr. *William Cole* of *Briſtol*; but whether that Juice is to be found in both theſe Fiſhes or not, is to me a doubt, becauſe it is only the Figure of the firſt of them; *viz.* N°. 7. which was communicated to the *Philoſophical Society* of *Oxford*, and publiſhed in the *Philoſ. Tranſ.* N°. 178. Tab. III. N°. 3, 4, 5, 6, and 7. which Fiſh being to be found on our own Coaſt, I ſhall thence tranſcribe the Manner how it is performed, and in what part of the Fiſh that fine Juice is to be found. *Theſe Shells being harder than moſt of other Kinds, are to be broken with a ſmart Stroak of a Hammer, on a Plate of Iron, or firm Piece of Timber (with their Mouths downwards) ſo as not to cruſh the Body of the Fiſh within: The broken Pieces being picked off, there will appear a white Vein, lying tranſverſly in a little Furrow or Cleft, next to the Head of the Fiſh, which muſt be digged out with the ſtiff Point of a Horſe-Hair Pencil, made ſhort and tapering ; which muſt be ſo formed, by reaſon of the viſcous Clammineſs of that white Liquor in the Vein, that ſo by its Stiffneſs it may drive the Matter into the fine Linen or Silk.* The

The Letters, Figures, or what elſe ſhall be ſo made, will preſently appear of a pleaſant Light Green Colour; *and if placed in the* Sun, *will change into the following Colours;* firſt *a* Deep Green, *then a full* Sea Green, *after into a* Watchet Blew, *then into a* Purpliſh Red, *and laſtly, into a very deep* Purple Red, *beyond which the* Sun *can do no more. But then the laſt and moſt beautiful Colour, after waſhing in ſcalding Water and Sope,* and *dried in the* Sun, *will be of a fair bright* Crimſon, *or near the* Prince's Colour, *which will continue, though there is no uſe of any Stiptic to bind it.*

Nº. 1. *That the Changes of Colours are made faſter or ſlower, according to the Degree of the* Sun's *Heat.*

2. *While the Cloth ſo writ upon, lies in the* Sun, *it will yield a very ſtrong fetid Smell, like* Garlick *or* Aſſa-fœtida.

For what uſe Nature hath deſigned this *Vein* of colouring Juice in this *Animal,* Mr. *Cole* thinks will be difficult to find out: He ſuppoſeth it either a *Spermatick* Matter to propagate the Kind, or by its vital Energy to ſupply the Spring of Life and Motion inſtead of *Heart, Liver, Blood,* &c. as in other *exſanguinous Animals.*

9. Buccinum Foſſile roſtratum maximum Liſteri referens, *Philoſ. Tranſ.* Nº. 291. p. 1577. Tab. x. Fig. 5. Buccinum album leve, maximum, ſeptem minimùm ſpirarum, *Liſt. Hiſt. Animal. Angl.* p. 155. Buccinum roſtratum, majus, craſſum, orbibus paululum pulvinatis, *Ejuſd. Hiſt. Conchyl.* Lib. IV. Sect. 14. Nº. 4. An Buccinum roſtratum, ſee 115. out of *Harwich* Cliff, *Woodward*'s *Attempt.* Tom. I. Part. II. p 37. This is the moſt common ſmooth Wilk of theſe Seas.

10. Buccinum Foſſile heteroſtrophum roſtratum lævum maximum Liſteri referens, *Philoſ. Tranſ.* Nº. 291. p. 1577. Tab. x. Fig. 6. Buccinum roſtratum, heteroſtrophum, ſee 132. *Woodward*'s *Attempt.* Tom. I. Part II. p. 37. Theſe were found plentifully in this Cliff formerly, but now more ſcarcely: They are like the precedent in all things excepting in the wrong Turn. I have been told that the natural Fiſh are found in the Sea before *Walton* in this County, but I have not ſeen them myſelf.

2 11. Buccinum

11. Buccinum Foffile leve minus, Tab. x. Fig. 18. This being embedded in the *Stratum* of *Stone*, and thereby the Mouth thereof hid, what Species it is of cannot be fo well difcovered: It feems to have but three Turns, and the *Shell* to be but thin by the Remains thereof; perhaps it is one of the *frefh Water-tribe.* The *Buccinitæ læves Tab.* 32. N°. 4 *Lang. Hift. Lap. Fig.* that well refembles this.

In a Piece of the fame *Stone Stratum* of this *Cliff* (which I have now by me) there are many fmall *Buccinitæ* of divers Bigneffes imbedded, fome of which feem very fmall, but whether of the fame *Species* with the laft mentioned, or of any other I cannot determine, but only add, that this agrees with the Obfervation of Mr. *Lhuyd* on the fame Head, *Lithophil. Brit.* p. 135. which I fhall hereafter quote.

12. Buccinum Foffile tenue reticulatum feptem fpirarum, Tab. x. Fig. 12. Cochlea clavicula productiore 105. *Woodward's Attempt.* Tom. I. Part II. p. 36. Turbo veluti malleo frequenter compreffus, *Bonan. Recreat. Ment. & Oc.* p. 119. N°. 48. This fomething refembles N°. 3. only it is a thinner Shell. The *Sulci* much fmaller, and confift of feven Turns, whether the Lip of mine was dentate or not cannot be made out by my Sample, being but one, and the Mouth a little broken.

13. Buccinum roftratum gracilius, *Lift. Hift. Conchyl.* Lib. VI. Sect. 14. N°. 5. Buccinum roftratum 116. *Woodward's Attempt.* Tom. I. Part II. p. 37. Buccinum anguftius, tenuiter admodum ftriatum, Octo minimùm fpirarum, *Lift. Hift. Animal. Angl.* p. 157. Turbo feptem fpirarum anfractibus finitus, ore valde longo, levis ubique, colore lapidis Tibertini, interdum ex helvo fubniger, *Bonan. Recreat. Ment. & Oc.* p. 119. N°. 53. An Buccinum lapideum leve *Colum. Aquatil. & Terreft. Obf. liv.* vide Tab. x. Fig. 7.

14. Buccino-turben Foffile reticulatum minus, *Philof. Tranf.* N°. 291. p. 1577. Tab. x. Fig. 11. This is but a fmall Shell, both ftriated and fulcated fo finely, as to make it feem reticulated. By the Appearance this fhould be a-kin to N°. 7. and 8. aforegoing, only this is lighter and produced at both Ends.

I

15. Buccino-

15. Buccino-turben Foffile fulcatum, *Philof. Tranf.* N°. 291. p·
1577. Tab. x. Fig. 19. This hath very deep *Sulci*, with very
fmall *Striæ*, being produced at both Ends. I do not find either
this or the foregoing in Dr. *Lifter*'s Collection.
16. Buccino-turben Foffile roftratum, *Philof. Tranf.* N°. 291.
p. 1577. Tab. x. Fig. 13. This is alfo a fmall Shell, but emi-
nently ribb'd, and likewife not among thofe of Dr. *Lifter*, the Weight
of it not exceeding Grains.
17. Buccino-turben maximum roftratum Foffile fpiris intus ftriis
elatis infignitis, *Philof. Tranf.* N°. 291. p. 1577. Tab. x. Fig. 14.
This *Foffil* is about four Inches in length, and might be when
whole about two Inches thick where thickeft; it confifts of five
or fix fmooth Circumvolutions. I do not find it figured by either
Lifter or *Bonanus:* It fomething refembles the fixth *Buccinitis*
of Dr. *Lifter*'s *Appendix ad Hiftor. Conchyl.* which he found in the
fandy Grounds about *Paris,* only that is ribb'd and this fmooth.
Or more exactly the *Cochlites cylindroides minor turbine productiore,* Lhuidii Lythoph. Brit. p. 23. N°. 420. Tab. 6. A different
Sample of which Mr. *Morton* names the larger Cylindroids, with
a more produced Clavicle, *Nat. Hift. North.* p. 221. *Langius* feems
to give the *Nucleus* of this Shell by the Name of Cochlites Cylin-
droideus feu Pyramidalis, lævis, mediocris, fubcinereus, quatuor fpirarum turbine productiore, *Hift. Lapid. Fig.* p. 112. Tab. xxxiii.
Fig. 3. The *Buccinum Ampullaceum, variegatum, fafciatum, clavicula
leviter nodofa,* Lift. Hift. Conchyl. Lib. IV. Sect. 13. N°. 5. doth
fomething refemble this in its Form. This is much broken by
lying fo long in the Cliff. The Body which appears within is one
of the fmaller Shells of the *Pectunculus,* &c. *valvis per ginglymon
connexis* among the Bivalves following, N°. 3.
18. Turbo Foffilis fpiris duabus ftriis eminentibus infignitis,
Philof. Tranf. N°. 291. p. 1577. Tab. x. Fig. 15. Cochlea alba
medio quoque orbe latè excavato, *Lift. Hift. Conchyl.* Lib. IV. Sect.
5. N°. 58. Buccinum craffum duobus acutis & inæqualiter altis
ftriis in fingulis 12. mininum fpiris donatum, *Lift. Hift. Animal.
Angl.* p. 160. Tab. iii. Fig. 7. Turbo eburneus fulco admodum
P p profundo

profundo excavatus, quem duo veluti cingula simul unita comitantur, *Bonan. Recreat. Ment. & Oc.* p. 126. N°. 113. The Figure of a *Nucleus* is given us by *Langius Hist. Lap. Fig.* Tab. xxxii. Fig. 4. of the *Turbinitæ Striati,* which he names *Turbinites striatus striis secundum spiras sitis,* &c. p. 111. the same is likewise figured embedded in its *Matrix.* The like appears to me to be figured by *Helwing. Lithog. Angerb.* Tab. viii. Fig. 10. On this are three Balani parvi striati, *List. Hist. Conchyl.* Lib. III. Sect. 3. N. 287. Balanus cinereus, velut è senis laminis striatis compositus, ipso vertice alterâ testâ, bifidâ rhomboide occluso, *Ejusd. Hist. Animal. Angl.* 196. Balanus *Rond.* II. p. 28. *Aldrov. Test.* 522. *Bonan.* p. 92. Clas. I. N. 14.

19. Cochlea Fossilis maxima umbilicata quinque spirarum, *Philos. Transf.* N. 291. p. 1577. Tab. x. Fig. 16. Cochlea rubescens, fascis maculatis, maximè ad imos orbes distincta, *List. Hist. Animal. Angl.* p. 163. Cochlea sublivida oro fusco ad basin cujusque orbis velut funiculus depingitur, *Ejusd. Hist. Conchyl.* Lib. IV. Sect. 5. N. 19. Strombites primus, *Aldrov. Mus. Metal.* p. 841. Cochlea clavicula brevi, e. 42 *. *Woodward's Attempt.* Tom. I. Part II. page 33. Cochlites umbilicatus lævis major cinereus quatuor spirarum, umbone parum eminente, *Lang. Hist. Lap. Fig.* p. 106. Tab. xxxi. 1. This seems the *Nucleus* of my Fossil: As doth likewise the fourth Figure of *De Laet.* p. 291.

20. Cochlea Fossilis umbilicata mucrone obtuso, *Philos. Transf.* N. 291. p. 1577. Tab. x. Fig. 17. Cochlea albida crebris lineis subruffis transversim & undatim ductis depicta, *List. Hist. Conchyl.* Lib. IV. Sect. 5. N. 1. My Sample resembles this, only the Lines are defaced by time, *Lachmund's* Fig. 9. p. 47. seems the *Nucleus* of this, only larger.

II. Conchylia Bivalvia.

1. PEcten minor Fossilis unica aurita, *Philos. Transf.* N. 291. p. 1577. Tab. xi. Fig. 1. Pecten tenuis, subruffus, maculosus circiter viginti striis majoribus, at levibus donatus, *List. Hist. Animal. Angl.* p. 185. Pecten Mediocris latus ex ruffo variegatus, circiter

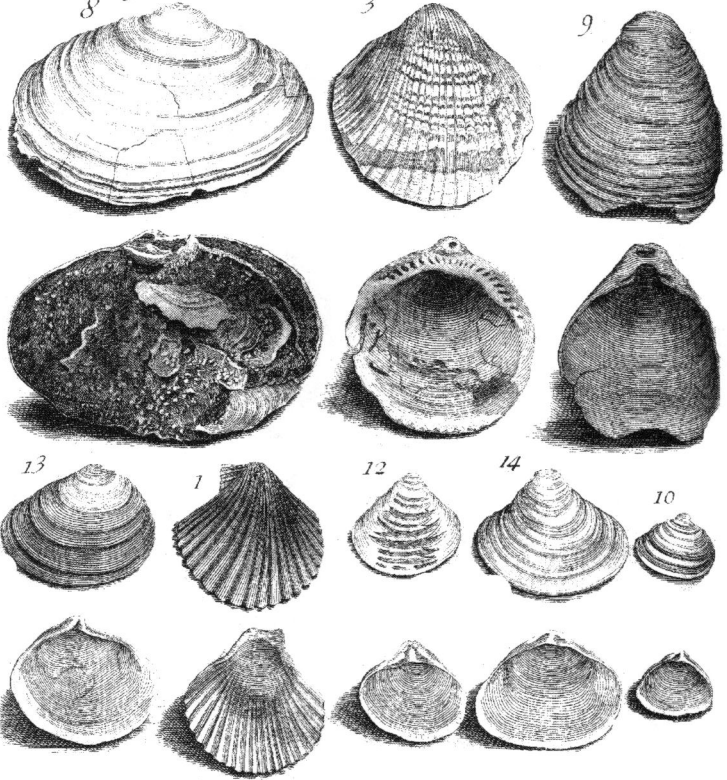

Tab. XI. P. 291

Bivalve Fossils.

citer viginti ſtriis tenuiter admodum ſtriatis diſtinctus, *Ejuſd. Hiſt. Conchyl.* Lib. III. Sect. 1. N. 27*. A ſmall Pecten very fair, *Harwich Cliff, Woodward's Attempt.* Tom. I. Part. II. p. 39. N. 37*. An Pecten omnium longiſſimus, levibus rugis ſtriatus. *Bonan. Recreat Ment. & Ocul.* p. 99. N. 15. An Pecten quintus, *Aldrov. de Teſtat.* p. 502. Pectunculus, *Rond.* Part II. p. 18. This in Stone is by *Scheuchzer* call'd Pectinites denſe ſtriatus, *Specim. Lithog.* p. 23. An Pecten, *J. B. Bahn. Bol.* Lib. IV. p. 28.

2. Auricularia maxima, *Philoſ. Tranſ.* N. 291. p. 1577. Tab. XI. Fig. 2. This belongs to the *Oyſter* kind being the upper Valve of the Shell, the Name is taken from Dr. *Plot*, who from the Shape of it, reſembling an *human Ear*, calling ſome of this Species by the Name of *Otites* or *Auriculares*, in his *Natural Hiſtory of Ox-fordſhire*, p. 130. Tab. VII. Fig. 12. might occaſion Mr. *Lhuyd* not only to continue it in his *Lithoph. Britan.* p. 28. but likewiſe to impoſe that Name upon this. An Lapis aurem humanam re-ferens, *Lang. Hiſt. Lap. Fig.* Tab. 51 ? Dr. *Plot* calls his a Stone, tho', as Mr. *Morton* obſerves, it is really a *Shell*, (as likewiſe is this of ours) who adds, " that the ſureſt and moſt material Diſtinction of " this Species is, That on that ſide of it which anſwers to the " thickeſt Part or *Ala*, of the *human Ear*, the upper *Laminæ* reach " very near as far as the lower; whereas in the other Sorts of *Oy-* " *ſter-ſhells*, the upper Parts of the Shell are much ſhorter than " the lower, *Hiſt North.* p. 193.

3. Pectunculus Foſſilis fere circinnatus, ſtriis tenuibus, valvis per ginglymon connexis, *Philoſ. Tranſ.* N. 291. p. 1577. Tab. XI. Fig. 3. Conchylium bivalvium Leptopolyginglymum, ſee 420. *Woodward's Attempt.* Tom. I. Part. II. p. 52. f. 420. Pectunculus ingens variegatus ex ruffo, *Liſt. Hiſt. Conchyl.* Lib. III. N. 82. Chama nigra ſive Glycimeris, *Bellon. Aquat.* p. 408. *Aldrov. Teſtac.* 471. There is a ſmaller one of this found in this Cliff, which ſeems to be figured by Dr. *Liſter* by the Name of Pectunculus exiguus al-bus admodum tenuiter ſtriatus, *Liſt. Hiſt. Conchyl.* Lib. III. N. 69.

4. Pectunculus Foſſilis craſſus roſtro acuto ſtriis majoribus, *Phi-loſ. Tranſ.* N. 291. p. 1578. Tab. XIII. Fig. 4. An Pectunculus

ex

ex ruffo variegatus ftriis craffiufculis donatus, *Lift. Hift. Conchyl.*
Lib. III. N. 148. This is a thick Shell, but much rubb'd by the
Agitation of the Sea, having lain for fome time on the Shore.

5. Pectunculus vulgaris Foffilis, *Philof. Tranf.* N. 291. p. 1578.
Tab. XII. Fig. 5. Pectunculus figura fubrotunda, ftriatus a cardine
ad Marginem 526. *Woodward's Attempt.* Tab. I. Part II. p. 57.
Pectunculus capite minore, rotundiore & magis æquali margine,
Lift. Hift. Conchyl. Lib. III. 171. Pectunculus vulgaris albidus,
rotundus, circiter 26. ftriis majufculis & planioribus donatus, *Ejufd.
Hift. Animal. Angl.* p. 189. Concha ftriata prima *Rond.* de Pifc.
pars alt. p. 21. Concha ftriata prior Rondeletii, *Aldrov. Teft.* 448.
Concha ftriata Rondeletii, *Gefn. Aquat.* 263. Pectunculus, *Belon.
Aquat.* 410. *Lachmund's* Fig. 1. p. 45. feems the figure of our
Foffil; this he names *Conchites cinereus ftriatus*, p. 41. Alfo *Langius* hath likewife figured this as imbedded in Stone, but hath referred it to a *Terebratula*, calling it Matrix Terebratularum ftria-
tarum ftriis majoribus cinerea, *Hift. Lap. Fig.* p. 158. Tab. XLIX.
Fig. 4. but wrongly in my Judgment, becaufe that Tribe hath
unequal Bottoms, but this equal.

6. Pectunculus Foffilis ftriis majoribus & elatioribus, *Philof.
Tranf.* N. 291. p. 1578. Tab. XII. Fig. 6. Pectunculus echinites,
Lift. Hift. Animal. Angl. 188. Pectunculus orbicularis, fufcus ftriis
mediis muricatis, *Ejufd. Hift. Conchyl.* Lib. III. N. 161. Concha
echinata, *Rond.* de *Pifcib.* pars alt. p. 22. Concha ftrigis femicir-
cularibus fulcata, *Bonan. Recreat. Ment. & Oc.* p. 110. N. 90.

7. Pectunculites maximus ftriis latis, *Philof. Tranf.* N. 291. p.
1578. Tab. XII. Fig. 7. This was bedded in the *Stratum* of *Stone*
at the Bottom of the *Cliff*; the Shell when firft taken out was
whole, but hath fince crumbled off, being in Subftance like one
calcin'd. This perhaps is the fame with Dr. *Woodward's, f.* 523.
Attempt. Tom. I. Part. II. p. 54. only mine is filled with Stone,
and if the Shell had been quite off, it might well have been accounted one of the Species of *Bucarditæ.* The *Doctor's* two fucceeding Numbers, *f.* 524, 525. feem the fame as this, but are perhaps lefs. An Conchites bivalvis ftriatus, *J. B. Baln. Bol.* Lib. IV.
p. 24?

8. Pectunculus

Tab. XII. *P. 293.*

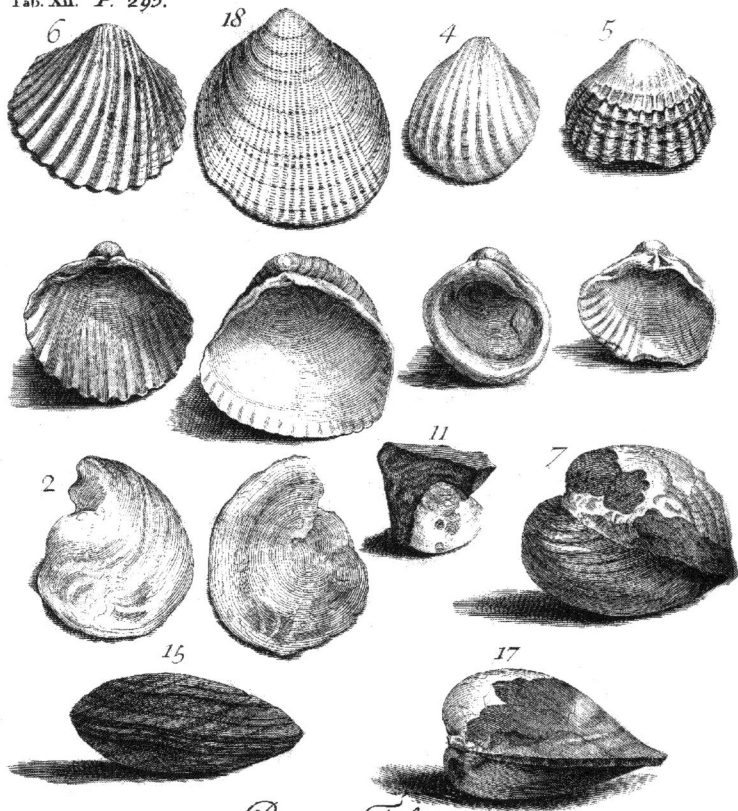

Bivalve Fossils.

8. Pectunculus maximus Fossilis Listerianum maximum referens, *Philos. Trans.* N. 291. p. 1578. Tab. XII. Fig. 18. Pectunculus maximus, at minus concavus, plurimis minutioribus & parum eminentibus striis donatus, rostro acuto minusque incurvato, *List. Hist. Animal. Angl.* p. 187. Pectunculus subfuscus striis leviter tantum incisis, *Ejusd. Hist. Conchyl.* Lib. III. N. 169. Concha striata tertia, *Rond. de Pisc.* pars alt. p. 22.

9. Pectunculus Fossilis fasciis transversis undantibus notatis, *Philos. Trans.* N. 291. p. 1578. Tab. XI. Fig. 8. Pectunculus gravis subfuscus radiatus, *List. Hist. Conchyl.* Lib. III. N. 105. Pectunculus longa lataque, in mediis cardinibus cavitate quadam pyriformi insignita, *Ejusd. Hist. Animal. Angl.* p. 170. Concha lævis, *Rond. Test.* p. 33. *Belon. Aquat.* p. 405. *Gesn. Aquat.* 272. The Figure of the Chama-glycymeris of *Rond. Test.* p. 13. *Aldrov. Test.* p. 472. *Gesn. Aquat.* 271. *Johns. Exang. Aquat.* Tab. XIV. doth seem to be the same with our Fossil; Dr. *Lister* likewise was doubtful whether it was not the same. The Inside of our *Fossil* is filled with Sand and Fragments of *Shells*, cemented together by a Vitrioline Juice of a ferruginous or rusty Colour.

10. Conchites lævis maxima, *Philos. Trans.* N. 291. p. 1578. Tab. XII. Fig. 17. This was bedded in that *Stratum* of *Stone* which lieth near the Bottom of the *Cliff*, the Shell of this is mostly broken off, those Parts that remain are smooth and shining. This I take to be Dr. *Woodward*'s, *f.* 448. which he saith is in Stone; with some also moulded in it. *Attempt.* Tom. I. Part II. p. 54. It seems as if he accounted it one of the *Bucardites*, by placing it next to them, among his *Pectunculi læves.* Chamites lævis major cinereus, rugosus, ventre crassiore, & ad imam oram sensim attenuato, *Lang. Hist. Lap. Fig.* p. 138. Tab. 38. Fig. 5. agrees in its Figure well with our Fossil.

11. Concha Fossilis tenuiter fasciata & striata Chama dicta, Tab. XI. Fig. 13. Chama fusca striis tenuissimis donata, *List. Hist. Cochyl.* Lib. III. N. 271. The Figure at the Bottom of *p.* 192. *de Laet. de Gemm. & Lap.* seems the same with this our Fossil, only ours is a Shell, and that a Stone.

12. Conchites parva fasciata, *Philof. Tranf.* N. 291. p. 1578. Tab. xii. Fig. 11. An Pectunculus fasciatus, f. 489 *. *Woodward's Attempt.* Tom. I. Part II. p. 56? The *fasciæ* in this, saith the Doctor, are very small and fine. This which I found in *Harwich Cliff* was likewise imbedded in the *Stratum* of Stone as the foregoing, some Part of which *Stone* yet adheres to the *Shell*, as in the Figure thereof.

13. Concha longa Fossilis fasciata, *Philof. Tranf.* N. 291. p. 1578. Tab. xi. Fig. 9. I have not observed either in *Aldrovandus, Rondeletius, Belonius, Gefner, Johnfon, Lifter,* or *Bonanus,* any Shell that resembles this our Fossil, unless it is one of those figured by *Lachmund.* p. 43. N. 6, and 7. the inward part resembling our Fossil.

14. Concha parva Fossilis fasciis transversis insignis, *Philof. Tranf.* N. 291. p. 1578. Tab. xi. Fig. 12. Pectunculus planus crassus ex ruffo radiatus, *Lift. Hift. Conchyl.* Lib. III. N. 136.

15. Concha Fossilis crassiuscula albida, Tab. xi. Fig. 14. Pectunculus crassiusculus albidus, *Lift. Hift. Conchyl.* Lib. III. N. 87. Concha crassa, ex alterâ parte compressa, ex alterâ subrotunda, *Ejufd. Hift. Animal. Angl.* p. 174. Concha crassa testa, *Rond. Teft.* p. 32. *Aldrov. Teft.* p. 463. *Gefn. Aquat.* p. 269. Dr. *Lifter* hath figured this among his Fossils, *Append.* Lib. III. N. 62. Concha à Rondeletio rugata dicta, *Bonan. Recreat. Ment. & Oc.* p. 105. N. 54. quoad Fig.

16. Trigonella minor sive vulgatior Anglica, *Lhuidii Lithop. Brit.* p. 816. *Philof. Tranf.* N. 291. p 1578. Tab. xi. Fig. 10. Pectunculus lævis, 447. *Harwich* Cliff, *Woodward's Attempt.* Tom. I. Part II. Concha crassa, ex alterâ parte compressa, ex alterâ rotunda, *Lift. Hift. Animal. Angl.* p. 174. Pectunculus gravis subfuscus radiatus, *Ejufd. Hift. Conchyl.* Lib. III. N. 105.

17. Musculites rugosus litoralis seu vulgatior Anglicus, *Lhuidii Lithop. Brit.* p. 38. N. 771. Conchites, N. 76. *Lift. Hift. Conchyl.* Lib. III. Append. Vide Tab. xii. Fig. 15.

18. Concha candida dupliciter striata & veluti aculeata, *Lift. Hift. Animal. Angl.* p. 193. Concha altera longa, *Rond. Hift. Pif.* Pars II. p. 23. Concha longa altera Rondeletii, *Aldrov. Teftac.* p. 453. Concha longa

Tab.XIII. *P. 295.*

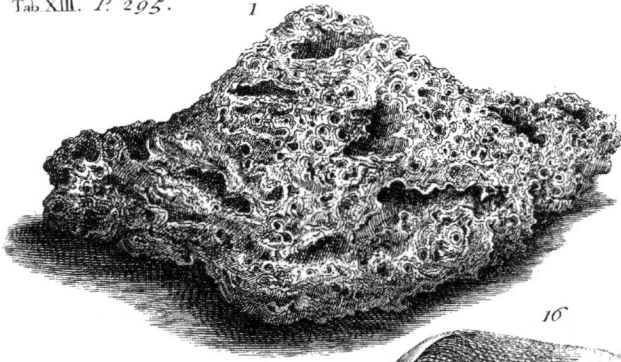

1

16

3

4

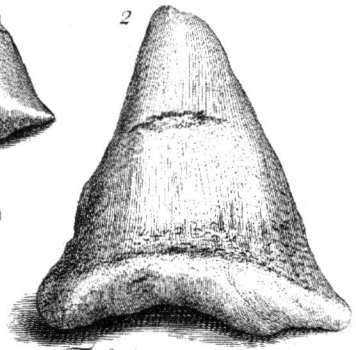

2

Miscellaneous Fossils.

longa prima, *Aldrov. Teſtac.* p. 455. This Dr. *Woodward* found in *Harwich* Cliff. Vide Tab. xiii. Fig. 16. Pholas longus acuminatus & rugatus, *Lang. Meth. Teſt. Mar.* p. 76. Balanus, *Bonan.* p. 101. *Claſ.* 11. N. 25, 26. Pholas noſter five concha inter lapidem quondam cretaceum degens, *Liſt.* Pholas ſtriatus ſinuatus, *Liſt. Hiſt. Conchyl.* Lib. III. N. 276. *Woodward's Attempt.* Tom. I. Part II. p. 63.

On this Shore are many Stones to be found perforated by the Pholas, a Cut of which is given by *Liſter*, who calls it *Saxum Pholadibus foratum*; the like is to be ſeen in *Rondeletius*, but both theſe Perforations are much larger than ours.

III. Animaliorum Partes.

1. **O**Dontopetra maxima ſpadicea lævis, mucrone obtuſo, Tab. xiii. Fig. 2. This ſeems only to differ in Bigneſs and Colour from the Gloſſopetra maxima cuneata Cantianorum : five anthracina lævis, quatuor unciarum latitudine; mucrone obtuſo, *Lhuidii Lithophyl. Brit.* p. 64. N. 1259. Gloſſo ſeu Odontopetra cuſpidata major livida, *Lang. Hiſt. Lap. Fig.* p. 49.

2. Odontopetra media latiuſcula, Tab. xiii. Fig. 3. Gloſſopetra 2. *de Laet.* p. 104. Gloſſopetra latiuſcula fine radice, *Geſn. de figuris lapidum,* 162. N. 2. Dens Lamiæ Piſcis, *Steno. Canis Carchariæ caput.* Tab. iv. Vide Tab. xiii. Fig. 3. When Mr. *Ray* wrote his *Topographical Obſervations,* he had never heard of any of the *Gloſſopetræ* being found in *England:* How he miſt them in the Chalk-pits of *Cherry-Hinton* (a Place ſo well ſearched by him while he lived at *Cambridge* is to be admired) from whence this very Year 1729. I was ſhewn divers there found, tho' none very large, they being moſtly of that ſort which Mr. *Lhuyd* calls *Acanthinæ,* p. 65. perhaps the ſame with Dr. *Woodward's Attempt.* Tom. I. Part II. p. 84. N. 11. 72. They are by *Langius* ſaid to be Alcalies and Sweetners, being Alexipharmic Anti-epileptic, provoking Urine, and therefore helpful in Dropfies : One Scruple

of

of the Powder given inwardly drives out the Small-Pox and Meaſles, and reſiſteth the Malignity of Fevers, *Hiſt. Lap. Fig.* p. 50.

3. A Piece of a Bone; being part of the *Os Ileum* of ſome Animal. This I took out of the *Stratum* of Clay in the Cliff, Tab. XIII. Fig. 4.

Dr. *Woodward* mentions five Pieces of large Bones, ſeeming to be of Sea-Fiſhes, which were found upon the Shore near *Harwich* Cliffs, by the late Reverend Mr. *Adam Buddle, Attempt.* Tom. I. Part II. p. 82. N. 2. &c. of theſe I have not met with any there; but not far diſtant from thence, *viz.* at *Wrabneſs* ſome Years ago, divers Bones of an extraordinary Bigneſs were found in digging for Gravel to mend the Road, about fifteen or ſixteen Foot beneath the Surface of the Earth, two Pieces of which were given me by my learned and ingenious Friend, the late Reverend Mr. *Rich,* Rector of the Place: Theſe ſeemed to be the cribrous Parts of large Bones. Mr. *John Lufkin* in his Account of theſe *Bones* publiſhed in the *Philoſ. Tranſ.* N. 274. p. 924. believes them to be the *Bones* of ſome *Elephant,* for ſome Reaſons he there gives. To me they ſeemed rather of ſome Fiſh of the *Cataceous Kind*; which I was induced to believe, from the Thickneſs, Shortneſs, and Largeneſs of them.

Theſe are all the *Foſſils* of this *Cliff,* which I have either met with there my ſelf, or that have been obſerved by Dr. *Woodward,* or his Friends. I have likewiſe endeavoured to reduce to mine the Doctor's Names or Numbers mentioned in his Book call'd *An Attempt,* to which he hath aſſigned this *Cliff* as the Place of their *Invention*; and that I might not multiply Species needleſly by dividing Synonyms, I did endeavour to procure a Sight of the Doctor's *Collections,* that by comparing theſe *Foſſils* with my own, I might have been more certain in my References: But the Doctor ordered in his *Will,* when he bequeathed his two Cabinets of *Engliſh* Foſſils to the Univerſity of *Cambridge,* that they ſhould not be opened, till his Executors had appointed a Profeſſor.

There

There are two things controverted among the *Learned* in Relation to thefe *Foffil* Bodies; as

I. *What their Original is.*
II. *How they came to be depofited in the Earth.*

As to the Firft of thefe, *viz. Their Original.* Here the Inquiry hath been much controverted, and of late bufied the Heads, and exercifed the Thoughts and Pens of fome of our greateft *Theorifts,* to conceive, and give the World a fatisfactory Solution: About which the Learned vaftly differ. Their Sentiments may be reduced to the following Heads, *viz.* Firft, *That they are the Effects of fome plaftick Power in the Earth:* Or Secondly, *That they are the Exuviæ of Animals* ; or Laftly, *Of Seminal Production.*

Firft, *That they are the Effects of fome* plaftick *Power in the Earth,* being the regular Workings of Nature, wherein fhe fometimes feems to fport, and play, and make little Flourifhes and Imitations of things, to fet off and embellifh her more ufeful Structures; and that they have been form'd after the Manner of *Diamonds* and other precious *Stones,* or the *Chryftals* of coagulated *Salts,* by fhooting into fuch Figures. Of the Maintainers of this *Opinion,* the *firft* which I fhall mention is the late Ingenious Dr. *Martin Lifter,* who in his Letter publifhed in the *Philof. Tranf.* N. 76. p. 2282. upon the reading of *Steno*'s *Prodromus,* writes as follows.

" Concerning *petrified Shells*; I mean fuch *Shells* as I have ob-
" ferved in our *Englifh* Stone-quarries: You will eafily believe,
" that in fome Countries, and particularly along the Shores of the
" *Mediterranean Sea,* there may all Manner of *Sea-Shells* be found
" promifcuoufly included in *Rocks* or *Earth,* and at a good Di-
" ftance too from the *Sea.* But for our *Englifh* Inland *Quarries,*
" which alfo abound with infinite Numbers and great Variety of
" *Shells,* I am apt to think there is no fuch Matter, as *petrifying*
" of *Shells* in the Bufinefs; or, as *Steno* explains himfelf, *p.* 84. &

" *alibi,*

" *alibi*, in the *Englifh Verfion*, [*Where the penetrating Force of Juice hath diffolved the Subftance of the Shell, the fame Juices being either drunk up by the Earth hath left the Spaces of Shells void (which he calls* Aereal Shells,) *or being altered by new adventitious Matter, have, according to the Variety of that Matter, filled up the Spaces of Shells, either with* Chryftal, *or* Marble, *or* Stone: *Whence comes that very pretty kind of* Marble *called* Nephiri, *which is nothing elfe but a Sediment of the Sea full of all Sorts of Shells, where the Subftance of the Shells being wafted, a ftony Subftance is come into the Place thereof.*] " but that thefe *Cockle* like *Stones* ever were, as they are at
" prefent, *Lapides fui generis*, and never any part of an *Animal*.
" That they are fo at prefent is in effect confeft by *Steno* in the
" above cited Page; and it is moft certain that our *Englifh Quarry*
" *Shells* (to continue that abufive Name) have no Parts of a diffe-
" rent Texture from the *Rock* or *Quarry* they are taken, that is,
" that there is no fuch thing as *Shell* in thefe Refemblances of
" *Shells*, but that the *Iron-ftone Cockles* are all *Iron-ftone*, *Lime* or
" *Marble*, all *Lime-ftone* and *Marble*; *Spar* or *Chryftalline-Shells*,
" all *Spar*, &c. and that they never were any Part of an *Animal*.
" My Reafon is: That *Quarries* of different *Stone* yield us quite
" different Sorts or Species of *Shells*, not only one from another
" (as thofe *Cockles-ftones* of the *Iron-ftone Quarries* of *Adderton* in
" *Yorkfhire* differ from thofe found in the *Lead-Mines* of the
" neighbouring Mountains, and both thefe from that *Cockle-Quarry*
" of *Wansford-bridge* in *Northamptonfhire*; and all three from thofe
" to be found in the *Quarries* about *Gunthorpe* and *Beavoir-Caftle*,
" &c.) but I dare boldly fay, from any thing in Nature befides,
" that either the Land, Salt, or frefh Water doth yield us. 'Tis
" true that I have picked out of that one *Quarry* of *Wansford* very
" Refemblances of *Murices*, *Telinæ*, *Turbines*, *Cochleæ*, &c. and
" yet I am not convinced, when I particularly examined fome of
" our *Englifh* Shores for *Shells*, alfo the Frefh-waters and the Fields,
" that I did ever meet with *(N. B.)* any one of thofe *Species* of
" *Shells* any where elfe, but in their refpective *Quarries*, whence
" I conclude them *Lapides fui generis*, and that they were not caft
" in

" in any *Animal* mould, whofe *Species* were or is yet to be found
" in being at this Day.

" This *Argument* perhaps will not fo readily take place with thofe
" Perfons that think it not worth the while exactly and minute-
" ly to diftinguifh the feveral Species of the things of Nature, but
" are content to acquiefce in Figure, Refemblance, Kind, and fuch
" general Notions; but when they fhall pleafe to condefcend to
" heedful and accurate Defcriptions, they will, I doubt not, be
" of that Opinion, which an attentive View of thefe things led
" me into fome Years ago. Tho' I make no doubt, but the *Re-*
" *pofitory* of the *Royal Society* is amply furnifhed with things of
" this Nature; yet if you fhall command them, I will fend you
" up two or three Sorts of our *Englifh Cockle-ftones* of different
" *Quarries*, nearly refembling one the other, and all of them very
" like a common Sort of *Sea-fhell*; and yet if there fhould not be
" enough fpecifically to diftinguifh them, and hinder them from
" being fampled by any thing of the *Spoils* of the *Sea*, or *Frefh-*
" *Waters*, or the *Land-fnails*, my Argument will fall, and I fhall
" be happily convinced of an Error.

Thus far Dr. *Lifter*'s Account, the greateft Part of which Mr.
Ray hath tranfcribed into his *Obfervations Topographical*, &c. p. 128.
and in the following Page hath added: The like Argument alfo
Goropius Becanus ufes, to prove that thefe Bodies are not *petrified
Shells*; but Mr. *Ray* not mentioning the Title of this laft mentioned Book of *Becanus*, I am not able to fatisfy my Reader any further about it.

Dr. *Plot* is another Advocate for this Opinion, in his *Natural
Hiftory of Oxfordfhire*, where Page 3. after having ftated the Quefti-
on, whether the *Stones* we find in the Forms of *Shell-fifh*, be *Lapides fui generis*, naturally produced by fome extraordinary plaftic
Virtue latent in the Earth or Quarries where they are found? Or
whether they rather owe their Form and Figuration to the *Shells*
of the *Fifhes* they reprefent, &c. brought to the Places where they
are now found by a *Deluge*, *Earthquake*, or fome other fuch
Means, &c.

In

In handling whereof the *Doctor* declares, that he doth not intend any peremptory Decision, but a friendly Debate. And upon mature Deliberation, he inclines to the Opinion of Dr. *Lister*, that they are *Lapides sui generis*, which, he saith, may be strongly suspected from the following Reasons.

" *First*, Because some of them resemble *Shell-fish*, that always
" stick to *Rocks*, and cannot well be presumed to have come away
" with the greatest *Flood*, unless so violent as to have brought the
" *Rocks* too. *Secondly*, Because there are many *Shells*, and other
" *testaceous* and *bony Substances* belonging to *Fish*, that must also
" have been left behind upon the Ebb of the *Deluge*, as well as
" the rest, of which we have no *Stones*, that resemble them at all.
" *Thirdly*, Because there are many *Stones* formed indeed in the
" Manner of *Bivalves*, &c. which yet resemble no Species of
" *Shell-fish* now to be found. And this is ingenuously confessed
" by *Fabius Columna*, tho' one of the Adversaries of this present
" Opinion. *Aquatil. & Terrestr. Observationes* cap. xxi. p. 11. *Ad-*
" *demus etiam nunc Pectunculi cujusdam lapidei cum notas, tum*
" *iconem, aliarumque rerum etiam maritimarum rariorum tantùm,*
" *quarum quasdam non nisi lapideas vidimus,* of which that he calls
" his *Mytulo-pectunculus auritus rarior Berberoïdes,* Tab. p. LII. is
" one. *Fourthly*, Because there are several formed *Stones*, that no
" Body pretends to know whither to refer, as representing neither
" *Animals* or *Plants*, either in the whole or parts; such as the
" *Astroites,* and *Belemnites;* which if thus tacitly confest to be
" *Lapides sui generis,* and formed by some latent *plastick* Power of
" the Earth, why might it not as well produce all the rest? Espe-
" cially since scarce any of them are reduced to *Animals* or *Plants*
" without great Inconvenience. *Fifthly*, Because that even those
" *Stones,* which so exactly represent some Sort of *Shell-fish,* as
" *Oysters, Cockles,* &c. that there can be no Exception upon the
" Account of Figure, but that they might formerly have been
" Shells indeed; in some Places are found with only one *Shell,* and
" not the other: Which had they been once the *Shells* of *Oysters*
" and *Cockles,* in all probability had scarce been thus parted. *Sixthly,*

I   " Because

" Becaufe I can by no Means fatisfy myfelf, how it fhould come
" to pafs, that in cafe thefe *Stones* had once been moulded in
" *Shells*, fome of the fame kind fhould be found in Beds. Nor
" how it fhould fall out, that fome of thefe *Bivalvulars* fhould
" always be found with their *Shells* apart; and others always
" clofed together. *Laftly*, Becaufe, many of thefe formed *Stones*
" feem now to be *in fieri*; for within a Clay *Cockle* I found a
" little one of *Stone*, not exceeding a *Vetch* in Bignefs; which had
" they been formed heretofore by *Cockle-fhells*, in all likelyhood
" would both have been either *Stone* or *Clay*. Nor can it be faid
" they were brought hither by different Floods, becaufe they were
" both found in the fame Bed, one included in the other." Thefe
are Dr. *Plot*'s Reafons why he believes them to be *Lapides fui ge-*
neris, and not of *Animal* Production.

The Second Opinion of the *Original* of thefe *Bodies* is, that they
are the *Exuviæ* of *Animals*; this hath many Patrons, whofe Affer-
tions, and the Reafons thereof, I fhall as compendioufly give as
I can. And *Firft*, I fhall begin with *Fabius Columna*, who hath
publifhed a *Differtation* to prove that the *Gloffopetræ*, which in
Malta go by the Name of *Serpents Tongues*, &c. are not really *ftony*
as fome affirm, but the *Teeth of Fifhes* of the *Dog-kind*, commonly
known by the Name of *Sharks*. *Firft*, Becaufe thofe things which
have a *woody*, *bony* or *flefhy* Nature, by burning are changed firft
into a Coal, before they go into Afhes: But thofe which are of a
tophaceous or *ftony* Subftance, go not firft into a Coal, but burn
immediately into a *Calx* or Lime, unlefs by fome *Vitreous* or *Me-*
tallick Mixture they be melted. Now thefe *Teeth* being burnt,
pafs prefently into a Coal, but the *tophous* Subftance adhering to
them, doth not fo; whence it is clear, that they are of an *offeous*,
and not *ftony* Nature. *Secondly*, Becaufe they do not fhoot into
this Form, after the Manner of *Salts* or *Cryftal*. *Thirdly*, Becaufe
of that *Axiom, natura nihil facit fruftrà*, i. e. Nature makes nothing in vain. But thefe *Teeth*, were they thus formed in the Earth,
would be in vain; for they could not have any ufe of *Teeth*; Nature
never made *Teeth* without a *Jaw*, nor *Shells* without an *Animal*
Inhabitant.

Inhabitant. *Fourthly*, Becaufe of the Difficulty or Impoffibility of the Generation of *Gloffopetræ* in fuch Places; becaufe among *Tophi* and Stones in thofe dry Places, there could not be found Matter fit to make them of. But fuppofing there were, then he afketh whether they were generated at Firft all of a fudden, or Secondly, grew by little and little from fmall to great, as *Animals Teeth* do. Thirdly, Whether the *Tophus* out of which they were extracted was generated before, or after the *Teeth* are perfected? Fourthly, Whether there was a Place in it of the Figure and Magnitude of the *Tooth*, or did the *Tooth* make itfelf a Place? Fifthly, If the *Tophus* was concrete before, and without a Cavity, the vegetative Power of the *Stone* now in Birth, could not by Force make itfelf a Place in the hard and folid *Tophus:* And if it could and did, the *Tophus* muft needs be rent. If there were a Place before ready made in the *Tophus*, then was not that Figure excavated in the *Tophus*, by the vegetative Nature of the *Tooth* itfelf; but the *Tophus*, by its own Nature and precedent Cavity, gave the Form to the *Tooth*. If it be objected that the *Stone* by its *vegetative* Power grew by Degrees; it may be anfwered, that could not be; becaufe the Hardnefs of the *Tophus* could not have yielded to the *vegetative* Force of the *Tooth*, but would rather have been rent or divided by it; or rather the *Tophus* itfelf muft have been *vegetated* with a Cavity or *Uterus* of the Shape of the *Tooth*, into which an *offeous* Humour, penetrating through the Pores, and filling the Cavity of the *Uterus*, muft there have coagulated, and taken the Form thereof, as is obferved in *Stones* that have their Original from a *Fluor*. Sixthly, That both *Tooth* and *Cafe* might *vegetate* together he denied, becaufe in all the *Teeth* which he had feen, the *Bafis* or *Root* was found broken, and that not with an uniform *Fracture*, but different in every one. Which *Argument* is not to be flighted, for that it fhews or proves, that there was no *Vegetation* in the Cafe; becaufe in all other figured *Foffils* it is obferved, that they are never found *mutilous*, broken or imperfect. Neither can it reafonably be faid or believed, that thefe *Roots* or *Teeth* were by fome chance broken within the *Tophi*, but rather that when they were cafually overwhelmed and buried in that *tophous*

phous Earth, they were broken off from the *Jaws* of the *Animal* in thofe *Volutations*, and fo in that Manner *mutilated*. The laſt *Argument* to prove them to be true *Teeth* and no *Stones*, he brings from their various Parts and Figures, which muſt elſe have been fo wrought and formed in vain. The *Tooth* being not one *homogeneous* Body, but compounded of *Parts* of a different Conſtitution, there muſt in the Formation of it be made a various Election of Humours, one for the *Root*, one for the *inner Part*, one for the *Superficies* of it. Then for the Figures, Magnitude, Situation or Poſture, and fitting of them; fome are great, and broad, and almoſt *triangular*; others narrower and fmaller, others very fmall and narrow, of a *pyramidal* Figure, fome ſtreight, fome crooked, bending downwards, or towards the nether ſide; fome inclining towards the Left-ſide, others towards the Right-ſide, fome ferrate, with very fmall *Teeth*, others with greater, which is obſerved in the leſſer *triangular*, and inward *Teeth*, fome fmooth in the narrow *pyramidal* ones. All which Things are obſerved in *Sharks-Teeth*, not only by the learned Naturaliſts, but alſo by Fiſhermen and Mariners. The firſt Row of Teeth in theſe Animals hanging out of the Mouth, bend forward and downward; the fecond Row are ſtreight, eſpecially towards the Sides of the Mouth, where they are *triangular* and broad, the other Rows bend downwards towards the inner Part of the Mouth. Thus much concerning the Opinion of *Columna*, and his Arguments to fupport it. Thofe that defire to fee more of it, let them conſult the Author's *Diſſertatio de Gloſſopetris* at the End of his *Purpura*, viz. p. 31, &c.

Secondly, *Agoſtino Scilla* a famous Painter of *Meſſina* in *Sicily*, is of the fame Opinion the *Proceſſes*, faith he, in the *Gloſſopetræ*; demonſtrate their Original, were there nothing elſe; fince they exactly anſwer to thofe in *Sharks Teeth*, whereby every *Tooth* is inſerted into its Neighbour in the living *Animal*, with thofe Parts porous, and thofe fpongious, that are fo in the *Tooth* of the *Fiſh*. Nay, whereas *Sharks Teeth* are mortiſed into one another in fuch a Manner, that a Man may eaſily tell which belongs to which ſide, which lie near the *Throat*, which near the *Snout*, which lie to the Right, which to the Left. And whereas in a *Shark's Jaw*, the Teeth on the Left-fide will not fit on the Right, nor thofe above ferve below; fo that upon feeing a *Tooth*, one may know which fide and what *Jaw* it belongs to. He hath obferved every one of thefe things (faith Dr. *Wotton*) in his *Gloffopetræ*, which punctually anfwer in every Part to the feveral Ranks of the *Teeth* of living *Sharks*, *Philof. Tranf.* N°. 219. p. 190. He alfo appeals to all that ever compared *Shark's Teeth*, and thefe *Gloffopetræ* together if they be not exactly alike. In anfwer to that Objection, that the *Gloffopetræ* are natural Chryftallizations of Salts; *Scilla* demonftrates, that Salt is Salt, as well within as without; A *Granate* and a *Topaz* is a *Granate*, and a *Topaz* throughout; *Diamonds* and *Rubies* are *Diamonds* and *Rubies* all over; they are *Aggregates* of *fimilar* Particles which compofe the whole Mafs, be it greater or be it lefs: Whereas *Gloffopetræ*, for Example, like all other vegetating Subftances, are made of various and diffimilar Corpufcles, put together in fuch a Manner as is peculiarly fubfervient to the End for which they are made: Accordingly the *Cortex* is of one Subftance, the *Medulla* of another, and that lodged in proper Cells, the *Root* diftinct from them both. Befides Nature fometimes produces monftrous and defective Things. An *Animal* fometimes wants a *Limb*, a Tree is without fome principal Branches, a Fruit may want fome of its chiefeft Parts, yet ftill we may obferve, that Nature fupplies and covers that Defect with a Skin or Bark, or Rind, fo that it never appears torn off or rent to the naked Eye, as it would if it were torn off by a Hand, or cut with a Knife. This is *Nature*'s conftant Courfe: Which evidently fhews, that the *Lufus Naturæ*, as thefe are erroneoufly call'd, were never produced in the Earth; fince all the Bruifes and *Fractures* which they have met with, are apparent without any Difguife to hide them, which *Nature* always puts on to hide the Effects of her own irregular Productions. He concludes at laft with taking Notice, that all the *Echini*, or other *Land-fhells* that he had found bruifed upon the *Calabrian* or *Meffinefe Hills*, or had been brought him from *Malta*, were bruifed by a perpendicular Preffure: This he explains thus;

the

the Cruft of all *Echini* has two Centers, one directly oppofite to the other; fo that if they happen to lie in the liquid Mud in fuch a Manner, as that the loweft Center was perpendicular to the *Horizon*, they were bruifed fo as not to lofe their circular Figure; only they were much compreffed. If they lay on one Side, they were fqueezed out of that Shape, and the Membranes of the *Ligatures* parted from each other varioufly, according to the Situation of thefe *Shells* in the Mud at that Time. All which plainly fhews, that as the Mud dried, the fuperincumbent Weight preffed perpendicularly upon the inclofed Bodies, which were then compreft together in that Pofture they then happened to lie in: And were more or lefs compreffed, according as the Mud got into their Cavities in greater or leffer Quantities, and as it dried, propped them up on the Infide againft the Preffure of the Matter in which they lay. Thus far *Scilla*, the Quotations from whom are taken from the *Philofophical Tranfactions* afore quoted: which contains an Abftract, or Abridgment of *La vana Speculatione difignannata dal fenfo: Lettera Rifponfiva circa i corpi marini, che Petrificati fi trovano in varii Luoghi Terreftri. Di Agoftino Scilla Pittore Academico della Fucina*, In Napoli 1670. 4to.

The third Patron of this *Opinion*, which I fhall mention, is Dr. *Robert Hook*, who thus difcourfes concerning thefe Bodies, " Examining fome of thefe very curioufly figured Bodies (found about " *Keinfham*, which are commonly thought to be Stones formed by " fome extraordinary *plaftick* Vertue latent in the Earth itfelf) " I took Notice, faith he, of thefe particulars. *Firft*, That thefe " figured Bodies, or *Stones* were of very differing Subftances, as " to hardnefs: Some of Clay, fome Marle, fome foft Stone, al- " moft of the hardnefs of thofe Stones which *Mafons* call *Fire- " ftone*, others as hard as *Portland-ftone*, others as hard as *Marble*, " and fome as hard as a *Flint* or *Cryftal*.

" *Secondly*, That they were of very differing Subftances as to " Tranfparency and Colour; fome white, fome almoft black, fome " brown, fome *Metalline* or like *Marcafites*; fome tranfparent like " white *Marble*, others like flowed Cryftal, fome grey, fome of

R r " divers

" divers Colours; fome radiated like thofe long petrified Drops
" which are commonly found at the *Peak*, and in other fubter-
" raneous *Caverns*, which have a kind of Pith in the Middle.

" *Thirdly*, That they were very different as to the Manner of
" their outward Figuration; for fome of them feemed to have
" been the Subftance that had fill'd the *Shell* of fome kind of
" *Shell-fifh*; others to have been the Subftance that had contained
" or enwrapped one of thofe *Shells*, on both which, the perfect
" Impreffion either of the Infide or Outfide of fuch *Shells* feemed
" to be left, but for the moft Part, thofe Impreffions feemed to
" be made by an imperfect or broken *Shell*, the great End or
" Mouth of the *Shell* being always wanting, and oftentimes the
" little End, and fometimes half; and in fome there were Impref-
" fions, juft as if there had been Holes, broken in the figurating,
" imprinting or moulding *Shell*; fome of them feemed to be made
" by fuch a *Shell* very much bruifed or flawed, infomuch that one
" would verily have thought that very figured *Stone* had been
" broken or bruifed whilft a Jelly, as 'twere, and fo hardened;
" but within in the Grain of the *Stone* there appeared not the
" leaft Sign of any fuch Bruife or Breaking, but only on the very
" uttermoft fuperficies.

" *Fourthly*, They were very different, as to their outward co-
" vering, fome having the perfect *Shell*, both in Figure, Colour,
" and Subftance, fticking on upon its Surface, and adhering to it,
" but might very eafily be feparated from it, and like other com-
" mon *Cockle* and *Scollop-Shells*, which fome of them moft accu-
" rately refembled, were very diffoluble in common *Vinegar*; others
" of them, efpecially thofe *ferpentine*, or *helical Stones* were cover-
" ed or retained the fhining or *pearl-coloured* Subftance of the In-
" fide of a *Shell*, which Subftance, on fome Parts of them, was
" exceeding thin, and might very eafily be rubbed off; on other
" Parts it was pretty thick, and retained a white Coat, or flaky
" Subftance on the Top, juft like the Outfides of fuch *Shells*;
" fome of them had very large Pieces of the *Shell* very plainly
" fticking on to them, which were eafily to be broken or flaked

4   " off

" off by degrees: They likewise, some of them, retained all along
" the Surface of them very pretty kinds of *Sutures*, such as are
" obferved in the *Skulls* of feveral kinds of living Creatures, which
" *Sutures* were moft curioufly fhap'd in the Manner of leaves, and
" every one of them in the fame *Shell*, exactly one like another,
" which I was able to difcover plainly enough with my naked
" Eye, but more perfectly and diftinctly with my *Microfcope*; all
" thefe *Sutures*, by breaking fome of thefe Stones, I found to be
" the *Termini* or Boundings of certain *Diaphragms* or *Partitions*,
" which feemed to divide the Cavity of the *Shell* into a Multitude
" of very proportionate and regular *Cells* or *Caverns*, thefe *Dia-*
" *phragms* in many of them, I found very perfect and complete,
" of a very diftinct Subftance from that which filled the *Cavities*,
" and exactly with the fame kind with that which covered the
" Outfide, being for the moft part whitifh, or *Mother of Pearl*
" coloured.   As for the *Cavities* between thefe *Diaphragms*, I
" found fome of them filled with Marle, and others with feveral
" kinds of *Stones*, others for the moft Part hollow, only the whole
" Cavity was ufually covered over with a kind of *Tartareous* pe-
" trified Subftance, which ftuck about the Sides, and was there
" fhot into very curious regular *Figures*, juft as *Tartar*, or other
" diffolved *Salts* are obferved to ftick and cryftallize about the
" Sides of the containing Veffels; or like thofe little *Diamonds*
" which I before obferved to have covered the vaulted Cavity of
" a Flint; others had thefe *Cavities* all lined with a kind of
" *Metalline* or *Marchafite* like Subftance, which with a *Microfcope*
" I could as plainly fee moft curioufly and regularly figured, as I
" had done thofe in a Flint.

    " From all which, and feveral other Particulars which I ob-
" ferved, I cannot but think, that all thefe, and moft other kinds
" of *Stony-bodies* which are found thus ftrangely figured, do owe
" their Formation and Figuration, not to any kind of *plaftick*
" Vertue inherent in the Earth, but to the *Shells* of certain *Shell-*
" *Fifhes*, which either by fome *Deluge, Inundation, Earthquake*, or
' fome fuch other Means, came to be thrown to that Place, and

" there to be filled with fome kind of Mud or Clay, or *petrifying*
" Water, or fome other Subftance, which in Tract of Time has
" been fettled together and hardned in thofe *Shelly-Moulds* into
" thofe fhaped Subftances we now find them; that the great and
" thin End of thefe *Shells*, by that *Earthquake*, or whatever ex-
" traordinary Caufe it was that brought them thither, was broken
" off; and that many others were otherwife broken, bruifed and
" disfigured; that thefe *Shells* which are thus *fpirallied* and fepa-
" rated with *Diaphragms*, were fome kind of *Nautili* or *Porcelane-
" Shells*; and that others were *Shells* of *Cockles, Mufcles, Periwin-
" cles, Scollops*, &c. of various forts; that thefe *Shells* in many,
" from the particular Nature of the containing or enclofed Earth,
" or fome other Caufe, have in Tract of Time rotted and moul-
" dred away, and only left their Impreffions, both on the con-
" taining and contained Subftances; and fo left them pretty loofe
" one within another, fo that they may be eafily feparated by a
" Knock or two of a Hammer. That others of thefe *Shells*, ac-
" cording to the Nature of the Subftances adjacent to them, have
" by a long Continuance in that Pofture been *petrified*, and turned
" into the Nature of *Stone*. That oftentimes the *Shell* may be
" found with one kind of Subftance within, and quite another
" without, having perhaps, been filled in one Place, and after-
" wards tranflated to another, which I have very frequently ob-
" ferved in *Cockle, Mufcle, Periwincle*, and other *Shells* which I
" have found by the *Sea-fide*. Nay further, that fome Parts of
" the fame *Shell* may be filled in one Place, and fome other *Ca-
" verns* in another, and others in a third, or a fourth, or a fifth
" Place; for fo many differing Subftances have I found in one of
" thefe *petrified Shells*, and perhaps all thefe differing from the en-
" compaffing Earth or *Stone:* The Means how all which Varie-
" ties may be caufed, I think will not be difficult to conceive, to
" any one that has taken Notice of thofe *Shells*, which are com-
" monly found on the *Sea* Shore: And he that fhall throughly
" examine feveral kinds of fuch curioufly formed *Stones*, will (I
" am very apt to think) find reafon to fuppofe their Generation
" or

" or Formation to be afcribable to fome fuch Accidents as I have
" mentioned, and not to any *plaftick Vertue:* For it feems to me
" quite contrary to the infinite Prudence of Nature, which is ob-
" fervable in all its Works and Productions, to defign every thing
" to a determinate End; and for the attaining of that End, make
" ufe of fuch ways as are (as far as the Knowledge of Man has
" been yet able to reach) altogether confonant and moft agreeable
" to Man's Reafon, and of no Ways or Means that does contra-
" dict or is contrary to human *Ratiocination*; whence it has a
" long Time been a general Obfervation and *Maxim*, that *Nature*
" *does nothing in vain*; It feems, I fay, contrary to that great Wif-
" dom of Nature, that thefe prettily fhaped Bodies fhould have
" all thofe curious Figures, and Contrivances (which many of them
" are adorned and contrived with) generated or wrought by a
" *plaftick Vertue*, for no higher End than only to exhibit fuch a
" Form; which he that fhall throughly confider all the Circum-
" ftances of fuch kind of figured Bodies, will, I think, have
" Reafon to believe; though, I confefs, one cannot prefently be
" able to find out what *Nature*'s Defigns are." Thus far Dr.
Hooke's *Micrographia*, p. 110, 111, 112. who hath in his fourth
Obfervation afore tranfcribed, accurately defcribed moft of the
Forms thefe *Bodies* have been found in; but there is one fort omitted, and they are *real Shells*, fuch are thofe in the gravelly *Strata*,
which are imbedded near the Top of this *Cliff*; fome of which
retain their real Texture, though others of them are by length
of time rotted, fo as eafily to break and crumble to Pieces.

The Fourth *Advocate* to be produced is *Nicholas Steno* an *Italian*, who reduceth the *Shells* that lie under Ground into three
Sorts. " The Firft, he faith, is thofe *That are fo like the true*
" *ones, as an Egg is to an Egg*; forafmuch as the *Shells* them-
" felves are refolved into little *Shells*, and the fame little
" *Shells* into Threads, and there is the fame Difference in the
" Threads, as alfo the fame Pofition or Site. That thefe *Shells*
" were once the Parts of *Animals* living in a Fluid; though there
" never had been feen any *teftaceous marine Creatures*, the very

4   " View

" View of the *Shell* itſelf evinceth, as may be made evident by the
" Inſtance of *Bivalve Cockle Shells.* The ſecond ſort is of thoſe
" Shells *which in the reſt are like to the lately deſcribed ones, but dif-*
" *fer from them only in Colour and Weight*; *in regard that ſome of*
" *them are found too light, others too heavy:* Foraſmuch as theſe have
" Pores filled up with an adventitious Juice, but the Pores of thoſe
" are widened by the Expulſion of the lighter Parts; which I ſhall
" ſay no more of, they being nothing elſe but either *petrified* or
" *calcined Shells* of *Animals.* The third Sort is of ſuch *as in their*
" *Figure alone reſemble thoſe that were newly diſcourſed of, but for*
" *the reſt totally differ from them,* ſeeing that in them are to be
" found neither the little *Shells,* nor the Threads, much leſs the
" Diverſity of the Threads. Of theſe, ſome are *aereal,* ſome *la-*
" *pideous,* others *Marbly,* others *Cryſtalline,* others of other Mat-
" ter. The Production of all which I explain in manner follow-
" ing. Where the penetrating Force of Juices hath diſſolved the
" Subſtance of the *Shell,* the ſame Juices being either drank up
" by the Earth, have left the Spaces of *Shells* void (which I call
" *aereal Shells)* or being altered by new adventitious Matter, have,
" according to the Variety of that Matter, filled up the ſame
" Spaces of *Shells* either with *Cryſtal,* with *Marble,* or with *Stone:*
" Whence comes that very pretty kind of *Marble* call'd *Nephiri,*
" which is nothing elſe but a Sediment of the *Sea* full of all Sorts
" of *Shells,* where the Subſtance of the *Shells* being waſted, a
" ſtony Subſtance is come into the Place thereof." Thus far *Steno*
in his *Prodromus, Engliſh* Edit. p. 81. &c. To which I ſhall add
from another *Tract* of the ſame Author, another *Argument* againſt
theſe Bodies being produced by the ſame Concretion of *Salts,*
which he thus urges; who can deny that the *hexedrical Figure*
of *Cryſtal,* the *Cubes* of *Marcaſites,* and the *Cryſtals* of *Salts*
in *Chymical Operations,* and infinite other Bodies coagulating and
cryſtallizing in a Fluid, have Figures much more ordinate, than
are thoſe of *Scollops,* and other *Bivalves,* and alſo *Turbens;* yet we
ſee in theſe ſimple Bodies, ſometimes the Top of a ſolid Angle cut off, ſometimes many of them, without any Order, ſticking

ⁱng one to another; fometimes their Planes differing among
themfelves in Magnitude and Situation; and many other ways
receding from their ufual Figure: Which being fo, how much
greater and more notable *Defects* muft there needs have been in
Bodies that have a far more compound Figure, fuch as are thofe
which imitate the Forms of *Animals*, if they were in like manner
generated? Seeing therefore in thefe Bodies, which are very much
compounded, thefe Defects do feldom occur, which in thofe other
moft fimple Bodies are very frequent, the like whereto are not
in like Manner feen in the Bodies of *Animals*; and feeing that
wherefoever they are found, they are exceeding like both among
themfelves, and to the Parts of *Animals*, it is very unlikely they
fhould fhoot into thofe *Figures* after the Manner of *Salts*; but on
the contrary, highly probable that they were originally the *Parts*
of *Animals*; the Similitude of Conformation in their *Pores*, *Striæ*,
Hinges, *Teeth*, *Prominences*, *Threads*, &c. almoft neceffarily infer-
ring a Similitude of *Original*; which is an Argument of the Government of fome Principle, fuperior to matter figured and moved
in their Formations. Thus far from *Steno's Canis Carchariæ diffectum Caput*, p. 131. in which I have made ufe of the late Reverend and Learned Mr. *John Ray's* Tranflation, as I find it in his
Three Phifico-Theological Difcourfes, p. 141, 142.

The fifth *Advocate* for this *Opinion* which I fhall produce is
John Woodward, M. D. Profeffor of Phyfick in *Grefham College*,
Fellow of the *Royal Society*, and of the *College* of *Phyficians London*. He hopes clearly to make out, *Firft*, That the *Sea* gave Birth
to thefe *Bodies*: That they are far from being formed in the
Earth, or in the *Places* where they are now found. *Secondly*,
That though thefe *Bodies*, which confift of *Stone*, *Spar*, *Flint* and
the like, and yet carry a Refemblance of *Cockles*, *Mufcles*, and
other *Shells*, were originally formed in the Cavities of *Shells* of
thofe kinds which they fo refemble, thefe *Shells* having ferved
as *Matrices* or *Moulds* to them; the Sand, fparry and flinty Matter
being then foft, and fo fufceptible of any Form, when it was thus
introduced into thefe *Shelly-Moulds*; and that it confolidated, or
became

became hard afterwards. *Thirdly*, That for the *Metallick* and *Mineral* Matter, which sometimes adheres to the Surfaces of these *Shells*, or is intruded into their *Pores*, and lodged in the *Interstices* of their *Fibres*, 'tis all manifestly adventitious; the *mineral* Particles being plainly to be distinguished from the *testaceous* ones, or the Texture and Substance of the *Shell*, by good Glasses, if not by the naked Eye. There being besides such vast Multitudes of *Shells* contained in Stone, *&c.* which are to be matched by others at this Day found upon our *Shores*, and which do not differ in. any Respect from them: Being of the same Size that those are of, and the same Shape precisely, of the same Substance and Texture, as consisting of the same peculiar Matter, and this constituted and disposed in the same Manner, as is that of their respective fellow-kinds at *Sea:* The Tendency of the *Fibres* and *Striæ* the same: The Composition of the *Lamellæ* constituted by these *Fibres* alike in both: The same *Vestigia* of *Tendons* (by Means whereof the *Animal* is fastned and joined to the *Shell*) in each the same *Papillæ;* the same *Sutures,* and every thing else, whether within or without the *Shell,* in its Cavity or upon its Convexity, in the Substance or upon the Surface of it. Besides, these *Fossil-shells* are attended with the ordinary Accidents of the *Marine* ones; as for Example, they sometimes grow to one another, the lesser Shells being fixed to the larger; they have *Balani, Tubuli Vermiculares, Pearls, Coral,* and the like, still actually growing upon them. And which is very considerable, they are most exactly of the same *Specifick* Gravity with their Fellow-kinds now upon the Shores. Nay further, they answer all *Chymical* Trials in like Manner as the *Sea-shells* do: Their Parts when dissolved have the same Appearance to View, the same Smell and Taste: They have the same Vertues and Effects in Medicine, when inwardly administred to *animal* Bodies. In one Word, so exactly conformable to the *marine* ones are these *Shells, Teeth* and *Bones,* that there is no doubting whether they are really the very *Exuviæ* of Sea Fishes or not, *Woodward's Essay,* &c. p. 20.

I shall

I fhall now clofe this *Head* with the Sentiments of the learned and ingenious Mr. *John Ray* thereon; his Arguments being, *Firft*, Becaufe it feems contrary to that great Wifdom of *Nature*, which is obfervable in all its Works and Productions, to define every thing to a determinate End; and, for the attaining that End, make ufe of fuch ways as are moft agreeable to *Man's Reafon*; that thefe prettily fhaped Bodies fhould have all thofe curious *Figures* (which many of them are formed and adorned with) generated or wrought for no other higher End, but only to exhibit fuch a Form. *Ray's three Phyfico-Theol. Difc.* p. 124.

For that *Nature* fhould form real *Shells* without any Defign of covering an *Animal* is indeed fo contrary to that innate *Prolepfis* we have of the Prudence of Nature, (that is, the Author of Nature) that without doing fome Violence to our *Faculties*, we can hardly prevail with ourfelves to believe it; and gives great Countenance to the Atheift's Affertion: That Things were made or did exift by Chance, without Counfel or Direction to any End. *Ib.* 132.

Secondly, There are found in the Earth at great Diftance from the Sea, real *Shells* unpetrified and uncorrupted, of the exact Figure and Confiftency of the prefent natural *Sea-fhells*, and in all their Parts like them, and that not only in the lower Grounds and Hillocks near the Sea, but in Mountains of a confiderable Height, and diftant from the Sea, *Ib.* p. 126.

Thirdly, That there are other Bodies befides *Shells* found in the Earth, refembling the *Teeth* and *Bones* of *Fifhes*, which are fo manifeftly the very things they are thought only to refemble, that it might be efteemed Obftinacy in any Man, that hath viewed and confidered them, to deny it. Such are the *Gloffopetræ*, and the *Vertebras* of *Thornbacks* and other *Cartilaginous Fifhes*; which have no greater Diffimilitude to the *Teeth* of a living *Shark*, and *Vertebras* of a *Thornback*, than lying fo long in the Earth, as they muft needs have done, will neceffarily induce. *Ib.* p. 132.

Fourthly, If thefe formed *Stones* be indeed original Productions of Nature, in Imitation of *Shells* and *Bones*, how comes it to pafs,

S f   that

that there fhould be none found that refemble any other natural
Body, but the Shells and Bones of Fifhes only? Why fhould not
Nature as well imitate the Horns, Hoofs, Teeth or Bones of Land
Animals, or the Fruits, Nuts, and Seeds of Plants? Ib. 139.

My learned Friend Mr. Edward Lhuyd, who has been moft diligent in collecting, and curious in obferving thefe Bodies of any
Man I know, or ever heard of, tells me, that he never found himfelf, or had feen in any Cabinet, or Collection, any one Stone, that
he could compare to any Part of a Land Animal. Ib.

Since Mr. Ray wrote the laft recited Paragraphs, or fourth Argument, large Horns and Bones of a fort of Deer, fuppofed to be
a Moofe, have been found buried in the Earth in Ireland, Vide
Philof. Tranf. No. 227. p. 489. Alfo in Mr. Morton's Northamptonfhire, p. 252. &c. mention is made of the Tusk and Tooth of an
Elephant, found in Bowdon parva, likewife Stag's Horns at Bough-
ton in digging the Canal at the Duke of Montague's Seat.

Fifthly, Thofe that deny thefe Bodies to have been the Shells
and Bones of Fifhes, have given us no fatisfactory Account of the
Manner of their Production.   For that they do not fhoot into that
Form after the Manner of Salts, may be proved by many Arguments. Firft, All Salts, that fhoot their Cryftals or Concretions,
are of one uniform Subftance. Secondly, Did thefe Bodies fhoot
into thefe Figures, after the Manner of Salts, it feems ftrange to
me, that two Shells fhould be fo adapted together at the Heel, as
to fhoot out to the fame Extenfion round, and the upper and nether Valve be of different Figure, as in natural Shells. Thirdly,
Were thefe Bodies produced in the Manner of faline Concretions,
it is ftrange there fhould be fuch Varieties of them and their Shapes
fo regular, and exactly circumfcribed: So great a Diverfity of Figures, arguing a greater Variety of Salts, or of their Modifications
and Mixtures, than are likely to be found in Nature; and the
Concretions of Salts never, that I have yet feen, appearing in that
Regularity of Figure, and due Circumfcription, as in thefe Bodies.
Fourthly, Were thefe Bodies nothing but Concretions of Salts, or
faline Mixtures, it feems no lefs ftrange, that fo many Liquors impregnated

pregnated with all Sorts of *Salts* and *mineral Juices* in all Proportions, having been at one Time or other induftrioufly, or accidentally expofed to *cryftallize*, and let ftand long in Veffels, there fhould never have been found in them any fuch Concretions. For if they had happened we fhould, doubtlefs, have heard of them, and the Obfervers would have improved fuch an Experiment in the Production of the like Bodies at their Pleafure, *Ib.* 140, *&c.* Thus far Mr. *Ray*, and fo I have done with the Arguments of thofe Gentlemen who are for thefe figured Bodies being the *Parts* and *Exuviæ* of *Animals.*

The third Notion or Opinion of the Original of thefe Foffil-Bodies is, that they are of feminal Production from marine Animals.

One of the Maintainers of this *Hypothefis* was the late Learned and Ingenious Mr. *Edward Lhuyd* in his *Lithop. Brit. Ichnogr.* p. 134. *Hoc ut paucis expediam,* &c. which being tranflated by himfelf, I fhall here tranfcribe his Thoughts and Reafons in his own Words: " I humbly offer to your (i. e. Mr. *Ray)* Confideration, " fome Conjectures I have of late Years entertained concerning " the Caufes, Origine and Ufe of thefe furprifing *Phænomena.* I " have, in fhort, imagined they might be partly owing to *Fifh-* " *fpawn* received into the *Clinks* and other *Meatus's* of the Earth " in the Water of the *Deluge,* and fo be derived (as the Water " could make way) amongft the *Shelves* or *Layers* of Stone, Earth, " *&c.* and have farther thought it worth our Enquiry, whether " the *Exhalations* which are raifed out of the *Sea,* and falling " down in *Rains, Fogs,* &c. do water the Earth to the Depth here " required, may not from the *Seminium* or *Spawn* of marine *Ani-* " *mals,* be fo far impregnated with, as to the naked Eye invifible, " *Animalcula,* (and alfo with feparate or diftinct Parts of them) as " to produce thefe *marine Bodies,* which have fo much excited " our Admiration, and indeed baffled our Reafoning, throughout " the Globe of the Earth, *&c.*

" I am

" I am not fo fond of this *Hypothefis*, as not to be fenfible my
" felf that it lies open to a great many Objections; and in all
" probability, will foon difcover more Difficulties than I fhall be
" able to remove: However, thofe *Arguments* that firft led me to
" it, fhall be here laid before you.

" *Firft*, Becaufe I obferved, that of all thefe *extraneous Figures*
" or Reprefentations dug out of the Earth, there is fcarce one in
" a Thoufand, but is reducible to fuch natural *Bodies* as expofe
" their *Seeds* either to the open Air or the Water: Namely,
" *Plants, Infects*, or *Fifh.*

" *Secondly*, I am abundantly fatisfied, that thefe *Bodies* do in
" Tract of Time quite lofe their Forms, and become fuch fhape-
" lefs Lumps as to be diftinguifhed for *marine* by none but
" fuch as are very converfant in Obfervations of this Kind, nor even
" at laft by them neither. Now feeing that in Tract of Time
" fome of them lofe their Subftance and Form, degenerating into
" other *Bodies*, may we not fufpect that others (confidering the In-
" tirenefs of many of them, and their vaft Plenty) might be in the
" interim produced?

" *Thirdly*, If this *Hypothefis* may be admitted, fome Account
" might probably be given of the *Foffil Nautili*, and other ftrange
" *Shells*, by fuppofing, *Firft*, That many of thofe *Clouds* which
" fall here in Rains, *&c.* have been exhaled in very remote Parts:
" And *Secondly*, That fuch a *Generation* as is here fuppofed muft
" be much more liable to monftrous Productions than the Com-
" mon. For as *Agricola* fays, appofitely to this Purpofe, *Quanto*,
" &c. *As much as the* Earth *is thicker than the* Water, *fo far it pro-*
" *duceth imperfect* Forms, *and which want Animals.*

" *Fourthly*, I have often in one and the fame *Quarry* gathered
" twenty or thirty different *Magnitudes* of the fame Species of
" *Shell-ftones*; whence I began to fufpect, that they might have
" a certain *vegetative* Growth, and that they had therefore their
" *Generation* and *Corruption* in the very Place we find them: And
" that hence it is, that we find fome *Nautili, Lapides Judaici*,
" *Gloffopetræ*, and *Aftropodia*, of fuch monftrous Largenefs, that
" no

" no Seas, as far as our curious Naturalists have difcovered, afford
" any thing comparable to them.

" *Fifthly*, To comprife the reft in few Words: The vaft Quan-
" tity of thefe *marine Bodies*; the incredible Variety of *exotick* and
" unknown *Shells, Sea-ftars,* &c. in fo narrow a Compafs as this
" *Ifland*; their fo frequently diftorted and uneven *Surfaces*; that
" they fhould be found at all Depths, from the Top of the higheft
" *Rocks* to the Bottom; that they fhould be not rarely found ad-
" hering to the *Roofs*, and to the *Walls*, or fides of *Caves*, as well as
" perpendicular *Clefts* of *Rocks*; and be alfo fometimes difcovered in
" *animal Bodies* at *Land*; and that there fhould be *Sea-fhells* dug at
" Land, containing living *Animals*: I fay, all thefe confidered to-
" gether, feem inconfiftent with the *Effects* of a *Deluge.*" *Ray's*
Three Phyfico-Difcourfes, p. 190. & feq.

To thefe Mr. *Lhuyd* hath added divers *Objections* and *Anfwers*,
as may be feen in the laft quoted Book, which for Brevity fake I
fhall here omit, referring the curious Reader to the Book itfelf
for further Satisfaction.

For my part, faith Mr. *Ray*, (if my Opinion be confiderable) I
think that my learned Friend hath fufficiently proved, that thefe
Foffil-fhells were not brought in by the *univerfal Deluge*. He hath
made it highly probable, that they might be originally formed in
the Places where they are now found by a *fpermatick Principle*,
in like Manner as he fuppofes. Why do I fay probable? It is neceffary that at leaft thofe which are found in the *Vifcera* and *Glands*
of *Animals* be thus formed; and if thefe, why not thofe found
in the Earth? I fhall fay no more, but that thofe who are not fatisfied with his *Proofs*, I wifh they would but anfwer them."
Ray's Three Phyfico-Theological Difcourfes, p. 203.

Something *analogous* unto Mr. *Lhuyd*'s is that Opinion which
I find in a Book intitled, *An Account of the Origin and Formation
of Foffil-fhells*, &c. which is this: " That all *Foffil-fhells, Bones,*
" &c. digged up and found entomb'd in *Slate, Stone, Chalk, Mar-*
" *ble*, &c. all the Parts and Contents of them, however wreath-
" ed, marked and ftriated, are on the one fide fo much the *Pro-*
" *ductions*

" *ductions* of *Nature*, that they were originally formed and figur-
" ed in thofe very Places from whence they are taken up; and
" yet are alfo on the other fide fo much the Remains of the Parts
" of thofe *Fifhes* they do imitate, that they are the Productions
" of the fame *univocal Sperms*, which thofe Parts of *Animals* they
" refemble are derived from." He conceives *page* 50, &c. " That
" the *Principle* to produce thefe Effects can be no other than a
" powerful *Seed* or *Sperm*, and that thefe furprifing Effects may
" be the Products of *feminal Parents*, as their like are in other
" Circumftances: For thefe *offeous* and *teftaceous* Remains taken
" out of the Earth, are the Products of, and owe their Forma-
" tion and Exiftence to what we call *Seeds* or *fpermatical Ener-*
" *gies:* For there are certain Portions of Matter of extraordinary
" Finenefs and Activity call'd *Seeds* or *Sperm*, indued with a Power
" of unfolding and augmenting themfelves unto determinate Shapes
" and Meafures of Extenfion; which contain in them the Body
" or Bodies they produce with all the Parts thereof. The *Crea-*
" *tion* of thefe *feminal Powers* or *Vehicles* of Life were at firft pre-
" pared, modified, and produced into Being in a *primogenial chao-*
" *tick Fluid*, on, or before the firft Day of the *Mofaick Creation*,
" and is there fymbolically expreffed by *Light* and *Darknefs*; and
" that from that time thefe *original Seeds* of things, gradually one
" after another, arrived unto their full Dimenfions, Habitations
" and Perfections, in the Space of fix Days; in which time, efpe-
" cially the third and fourth Day, when the *Coagulum* of the
" *Earth*, newly feparated from the *Water*, was very raw, foft and
" yielding, and the hardeft *Rocks* and *Strata* of it were yet in their
" *Gellies:* Then it is not unreafonable to conclude that thefe men-
" tioned *Sperms*, left included in the various Juices of the concre-
" ted Earth, might very well perform thofe *Feas* we now behold
" with Wonder; and as a Proof and Confirmation that *Shells* may
" be produced, and perfectly formed in a much groffer Subftance
" than the hardeft *Rocks* can be fuppofed to have been before their
" acquiring *Solidity* and *Hardnefs*, that is, when the Parts were
" yet loofe and in a Sort of *Fufion* and *Fluidity*, he hath often
" obferved

" obferved Multitudes of fmall very perfect *Shells* lying fcattered
" in all Pofitions, and of all Sizes, from the Bignefs of a fmall
" Pin's Head, to that of an ordinary *Periwincle*, in the midft and
" throughout the Pulp and Subftance of a very thick Clay or
" Marle; neither is there any Caufe to fufpect their having funk,
" or in any manner made their way into thefe thick Beds of
" *Clay*: there appearing not the leaft Token of fuch a Paffage:
" So that it muft be concluded they were generated there. Now
" if thofe *Shells* found in *Clay* and *Marle* may not pretend to any
" other *Origin* than a *feminal Production* in thofe very *Clays* in
" which they are found enclofed, whether the very fame Reafon
" will not oblige us to make the fame Account of the *Origin* of
" thofe other *Shells*, found in the fame manner in *Rocks* and *Stones*?
" For fince the *Origin* of thefe two Subjects, *Clays* and *Stones*, was
" the fame, why may we not afcribe the Production of thefe
" *Foffil-fhells* to one uniform Caufe, in both thefe Subjects? that
" is, to thofe *original Seeds*, difperfed in the engroffed earthy Mat-
" ter; part whereof by the Concurrence of certain Caufes came
" to be congealed and petrified into a *Stony* Hardnefs; and the
" other Part, for want of fuch Caufes, ftill continuing in their
" *Clayey* State and Condition." Thus far I have excerpted from
this Author, as fuitable to my purpofe: He lays down many *Reafons*,
Arguments and *Poftulata* to confirm what he delivers, which are
too long to be inferted here; but who the *Anonymous* Author of
this Difcourfe is hath by fome been doubted; tho' others have
not fcrupled to affirm, that it was written by one Mr. *Henry Row-
land*.

The laft Opinion which I fhall mention is, that of M. *Tournefort*, whofe Opinion was, that *Stones* like *Plants* did *germinate*; for
Confirmation of which, he read a *Difcourfe* in the *Academy of
Sciences* of *Paris* Anno 1702. fome parts of which I fhall here
tranfcribe: *Stones* perhaps, faith he, multiply like *Plants*, and have
a *Germ* from whence they fpring. The *Stones* we call the *Cornes
d'Amon (Cornua Ammonis)* may ferve for a Proof of this. We
may fuppofe this *Germ* to be of the Nature of thofe of *Mufhrooms*,

2 and

and other *Plants*, whofe *Seed* we know not: For there is no probability that the different Sorts of *Stones* are formed in *Moulds*, fince notwithftanding all the Enquiries made, he could not find any fuch fort of *Moulds*. Moreover, he cannot conceive how a *Mould* alone can form a *Stone*, fuch as they call'd *Corne d'Amon*, which is turned fpirally, and whofe *Joynts* are connected by a *Suture* like that of the *Bones* of the *Skull*. The *Jewifh Stones (Lapis Judaicus)* which cut obliquely, and are of the Nature of *Talk*, are no more like to come out of a *Mould*. He fays the fame of the *Toadftone*, &c. which, he fays, have their particular *Germ*.

Another Inftance he gives is *Rock Cryftal*, which he likewife thinks may be formed of a *Germ*. There are feveral Sorts of them, fome are cut into three Panes, others into five, and others fix or feven: This is not the Effect, he faith, of a *Cryftallization*; becaufe they are of all Sizes. There being fome that weigh 60 *l.* can we think they were *cryftallized*? If it were fo, the matter which formed them abounding fo much would fhed itfelf all at once, and rather produce a Piece like *Ice*, than a Piece of *Cryftal* cut into *Panes*.

He likewife inftanced in *Flints*, which cover the Plain of *Salon* in *Provence*, in fuch great Numbers, that there could not be fuch vaft Quantities there, if new ones were not daily produced, and probably by the Affiftance of *Germs*, which abound in this Plain. [*The like great Quantities of* Flints *I have obferved in fome Fields near* Dover *in* Kent.] He confirms this by an Obfervation formerly made by M. *Peirefc*, who wafhing himfelf one Day in the *Rhone* near *Avignon*, felt at the Bottom of the Water rugged, flabby Bodies of the Confiftence of hard Eggs, which afterwards became *Flints*, both thofe that remained in the *River*, and thofe he brought away with him. He thought they were caft out of the Earth in that Condition by fome *Earthquake*. As for the *Flints* that are loofe upon the Earth, M. *Tournefort* thinks they are with refpect to other Stones as *Mufhrooms* are to other Plants.

According to M. *Tournefort's* Obfervation, the *Stones* of the *Labyrinth* of *Candia* grow infenfibly, from whence he draws the

I   Proofs

Proofs of his *Syftem*, that *Stones* have a *vegetative Life* as well as *Plants.* He obferved, that the Names which have been engraved on fome Places of the Walls of that Cavern, inftead of remaining hollow, are filled up with a Sort of Embroidery of two or three Lines thick, and make fo many *Bas-reliefs.* The Matter is a whitifh Scale, though the Stone be grey. This *Cavern,* he faith, is extreme dry and there is no Place to be feen where the Water *filtrates* thro' the Stones, as we fee in moft *Caverns.* He compares this Matter with thofe *Callofities* which grow between *Bones,* and the *Barks* of Trees. He fays, it is nothing elfe but the *nutritious Juice* of the *Stone* extravafated and congealed on the Surface: And he proves his *Opinion* by Examples taken from feveral Sorts of *Stones.* Thofe *ftony Plants* that abound fo in the *Indies,* and of which they make Lime, grow like *Cockles* by the Help of the *nourifhing Juice.* He thinks, there is no more difficulty in comprehending that a *Rock* was at firft contained in *Miniature* in a *Germ,* then in conceiving, that the *Whale* fo great a *Fifh* could be included in a *Germ,* or *Seed. Works of the Learned* A°. 1703. p. 601, &c.

   M. *Tournefort* hath likewife taken Notice of this *Phænomenon* in his *Travels,* for he obferved, that among the Writings of this *Labyrinth,* there are fome really wonderful: Which corroborates the *Syftem* propofed by him fome Years paft, concerning the *Vegetation* of *Stones,* which he faith, do there increafe and grow infenfibly, without being fufpected to receive the leaft adventitious Matter from without. *Voyages* Tom. 1. p. 52. *Engl. Edit.*

   The late learned *Georgius Baglivius* in his Treatife, *De Vegetatione Lapidum,* was of Opinion, That Stones did grow and were nourifhed after the Manner of Plants. This *Hypothefis* is much doubted by *Langius,* who obferves, that Plants have Roots in which the *nutritious Juice* is elaborated, from whence proceed Veffels, by which it is diftributed to all the Parts of the Plants, the Subftance of which in all its Dimenfions, may be expanded to receive it, which the concrete and hard Subftance of the Stone will refift; neither are Stones furnifhed with Roots or Veffels,

T t   fels,

fels, by which to convey the nutritious Juice, *Lang. Hift. Lap.*
Fig. p. 11.

I now come to anfwer the II. Queftion, *viz.*

HOW THESE Bodies CAME TO BE DEPOSITED IN THE EARTH.

About this there are divers Opinions, moft of which having
been mentioned among the foregoing, I fhall be the more brief in
the Account I fhall give of them, to prevent repeating what hath
been before recited.

Firft, Thofe that affirm them to be *Lapides fui generis:* from
hence infer, that they exift from a *plaftick* Principle in the
Earth, and are thence produced in the very Places where they are
found.

Secondly, Others who alledge their being Parts of *Sea animals*,
do believe them the Effects either of fome great *Inundation*; or
of *a general Deluge:* The latter of which was the Sentiment of
Steno, who faith, that 'tis certain, that the Production of many
Shells we meet with in our Days, is to be referred to the general
Deluge, *Prod.* p. 90. And after him Dr. *Woodward*, writes that
thefe *marine Bodies* were borne forth of the *Sea* by the *Univerfal
Deluge*; and that upon the Return of the Water back again from
off the Earth, they were left behind at Land.   This is a Propo-
fition of fome Weight (faith the *Doctor)* and Confequence; upon
which Account I fhall be fomewhat prolix and particular in the
Eftablifhment of it; careful and exact in conferring every Circum-
ftance of thefe marine Bodies, to fee how they fquare with it,
Effay, p. 72.   He further affirms; That during the Time of the
Deluge, whilft the Water was out upon, and covered the *terref-
trial Globe*, all the *Stone* and *Marble* of the *Antediluvian* Earth; all
the *Metals* of it; all *mineral Concretions*; and in a Word, all *Foffils*
whatever, that had before obtained any *Solidity*, were totally diffolved, and their conftituent *Corpufcles* all disjoined, their *Cohæfion*
perfectly ceafing.   That the faid *Corpufcles* of thefe folid *Foffils*,
together with the Corpufcles of thofe which were not before folid,

lid, such as Sand, Earth, and the like; as also all *animal Bodies*, and the Parts of *Animals, Bones, Teeth, Shells; Vegetables* and Parts of *Vegetables, Trees, Shrubs, Herbs*; and to be short, all *Bodies* whatsoever that were either upon the Earth, or that constituted the Mass of it, if not quite down to the *Abyss*, yet at least to the greatest Depth we ever dig; were assumed up promiscuously into the Water, and sustained in it, in such manner that the Water, and Bodies in it, together made up one common confused *Mass*. That at length all the *Mass*, that was thus borne up in the Water, was again precipitated and subsided towards the Bottom. That this Subsidence happened generally, according to the *Laws* of *Gravity*: That Matter, Body, or Bodies, which had the greatest Quantity, or degree of *Gravity*, subsiding first in order, and falling lowest: that which had a still lesser Degree of *Gravity*, subsiding next after, and settling upon the precedent, and so on in their several Courses; that which had the least *Gravity* sinking not down till last of all, settling at the Surface of the Sediment and covering all the rest. That the *Shells* of those *Cockle, Escallops, Periwincles,* and the rest which have a greater Degree of Gravity, were enclosed and lodged in the *Strata* of *Stone, Marble* and the heavier Kinds of *terrestrial Matter*: The lighter *Shells* not sinking down till afterwards, fell among the lighter Matter, such as *Chalk*, &c. That the *Shells* of Sea *Shell-fish*, Trees, Shrubs, &c. being lighter than *Sand, Marle, Chalk,* or the other ordinary Matter of the *Globe*, were not precipitated till the last, and so lay above all the former, constituting the supreme or outmost *Stratum* of the *Globe, Ib. p.* 74, &c.

The late Reverend Mr. *Morton* was likewise of this Opinion: He having (as he saith) considered the Number and Variety of these *marine Bodies*, with the Depth they are found at, and other Circumstances of them, thought it might be expected he should shew by what Means they became thus lodged in the Earth. This Subject he intended to have handled at large; but upon further Considerations concluded to do no more at present, than refer the Reader to the Account given of it in Dr. *Woodward's Natural History of the Earth*, which being in the Hands of all who are

curious

curious in this Part of Learning, he needed not tranfcribe them, *Northamptonfhire*; p. 251.

N. B. In this *Cliff* the *Foffils* may be obferved not exactly fub-fiding according to the *Doctor's* Rule, for in the *Stratum* of *Stone* at the Bottom, are Sticks and Pieces of Wood imbedded, together with *Cockles, Clams* and *Periwincles*; and in the *Stratum* of *Sand* and *Gravel* near the Surface, are to be found the *Heteroftrophus Wilks*, together with *Cockles,* and lighter *Shells,* but no Wood that I could obferve.

I have little more to add upon this Subject, becaufe thofe two learned Perfons, who make thefe *Foffils* of *feminal Production* have themfelves demonftrated how thofe *Seeds* or *Sperms* came to be depofited in the Earth; but herein they differ from each other. Mr. *Lhuyd* conjectures them to be conveyed in Part by the *General Deluge*; yet he thinks, that they may be likewife the Effects of *Exhalations* from the *Sea,* which being dropt upon the Earth, are thence by Rains wafhed into the *Fiffures* of it, and there generated. The other, that their Generation is by *Univocal Sperms,* thefe being the Work of the firft *Creation,* and therefore antecedent to the *Noarchal Deluge,* muft be before Rocks, &c. had acquired Solidity and Hardnefs, being yet as in their Gellies (as the Author of the aforementioned Tract expreffeth it) then thefe *original Seeds* obtained their full Dimenfions, and were depofited in the Places in which we now find them.

Mr. *Thomas Lawrence* in his *Mercurius Centralis,* p. 19. imagineth that *Stones* in the Shape of *Oyfters, Mufcle* and *Cockle-fhells,* were made by lying in fuch Places, where they have been caft out by *Men,* cafually receiving the *fuccus Lapidefcens,* or unconcrete Matter of *Stones,* which hath become a Bed or Matrix to it, fo that Stone hath been fhapen according to the Mould, as *Gourds* while young put into Glaffes grow not according to their ufual natural Form, but according to the Shape and Proportion of the *Glaffes.* If they were really *Mufcle* and *Cockle-fhells,* that (the Earth) could not be the Place of their *Generation,* but they muft be by fome Violence and Impetuofity hurried thither. If

4　　　　　　　　　　　　　　　　　　they

they are brought from the *Sea* to the Place they are found in under the Earth, it muſt be either by a *natural* or by a *ſuperna-tural* Impellent or Mover, by Spirits, or by a natural Vehicle. And *Paracelſus* would have us believe that there are innumerable ſuch *Spirits* or *Genii* that Inhabit the Earth, and to impute all to them, muſt needs be an *aſylum ignorantiæ*, and a *Remora* to all Ingenious and *Philoſophical* Diſquiſitions, of the Nature and Cauſes of all things, and Actions in the Bowels of the Earth. So that he takes it for granted, that ſome natural ordinary Vehicle there is under the Earth, that brings ſuch *Heterogeneous* Bodies from their native and *genial Seat*, and proper Place to ſuch *Vaults, Hills, Veins*, and *Caverns* where they are found. Now the moſt likely Movers of all others to carry Bodies of Weight under the Earth are two ; either *Exhalations* or *Waters* ; for as for Vapours, he looked not on them as capable of carrying any thing of Weight, eſpecially ſo low in the Earth, where they cannot be ſo much rarefied by Reaſon of the natural Coldneſs of that *Element*. So that it muſt be concluded, that Vapours cannot be ſerviceable to our Purpoſe, ſo as to force whole Veins of Shells or other Bodies to Places ſo far diſtant from the Sea, and there to ram them in. As for *Exhalations*, their Force is ſuch, they can impetuouſly move Bodies of the greateſt Weight. Their Strength under Ground appears by *Earth-quakes*. And therefore Exhalations may be grant-ed to remove *Stones*, and *Sands*, and with them ſuch *Heterogeneous* Bodies as lie on them, from one Place to another, from the *Sea* to the *Hills*, and from a Coaſt far into the Country. But they are moſt likely to be hurried thither by the Force of Waters paſſing from the *Sea* through the *Caverns* of the Earth. Thus far the Reverend Mr. *Lawrence's* Letter to Sir *Thomas Brown*.

There remains yet another Opinion, and that is of my Neigh-bour Mr. *Benjamin Allen*, M. B. in his *Natural Hiſtory of Chaly-beat and purging Waters of* England, Edit. 1699. p. 107. in which after mentioning the preceding Page, The *Stones* that lie plen-tifully on the Shore at *Harwich*, and ſtuck in the *Bank* (as he terms it) at the Bottom of the *Cliff*: He adds, that this Bed of *Stones*

Stones was the Foundation of the *Loamy Cliff*, where the *Cliff* has been waſhed away or cut: For the *Harbour* or *Channel* there is artificial, and of no old Date. The not underſtanding this made the Gentleman in *Cambden* to mention them as *Petrifactions* made by the Sea. And from this undoubtedly proceeds that *Bed* of *Shells* that covers the *Cliff* at perhaps fifty Feet high, which muſt be carried thither at the making the *Harbour*, or clearing it; how elſe could the petrified clay-bed, which contains the *Shells*, lie at top, and no Petrifaction lower till you come again to the Bottom? Thus far Mr. *Allen*, whoſe Opinion is that the *Shells* were here layed; but having mentioned ſome part of this before, *viz.* page 15. what I have here recited is ſufficient for my purpoſe.

Page 2. *Col.* 2. *l.* 8. after the Word *Fort*, dele *and a Battery of Guns to the Southward, juſt as at* Tilbury. There being no ſuch Platform there. *Page* 29. *l.* 15. for *Tumet* read *Turret*, *p.* 31. *c.* 2. *l.* 2. fill up the Blank with 1699. *l.* 3. *r.* Mr. *Mark Wildbore*, *l.* 12. after demoliſhed, add ſince the printing of the foregoing Paragraph; in a Letter received from *Brown Willis*, Eſq; I have the following Account of this Chapel: *It is a neat handſome compact Building tho' plain; the Body is ſixty Foot long, and as many broad excluſive of the Steeple; ſupported by ten Pillars, the Pewing is regular, and* at the Weſt End one *large Gallery; the Chancel is thirty ſix Foot long, and thirty broad. There is in it a Library of three hundred Books, given by ſeveral Gentlemen of the Corporation and others.* What Mr. *Willis* adds more relating to this Chapel, which having been already taken Notice of in the Hiſtory, I ſhall omit to prevent Tautology.

I ſhould here add the mentioning of (which was omitted in its proper Place) a Charity of 50 *l. per Annum* given to the Poor of this Borough by a Gentlewoman payable out of a Houſe in *Fleet-ſtreet*, but having miſlaid the Letter, in which the Account of it was ſent me by the Reverend Mr. *William Curtiſe*, and not having Time to retrieve it, I can ſay no more about it here, nor how it is to be diſpoſed nor by whom. *Page* 36. *l.* 11. add the ſame in *Engliſh* as follows:

4 *Here*

Here refteth Roger Coleman, of this Borough Gentleman and Mer-
chant. He was a good Benefactor to the Poor, as appears by his
noble Gift of fifty Pounds for the Reparation of their Alms-houfes;
who when he had filled up his Chriftian Courfe, at length full of Days
and Fame he calmly and quietly flept in the Lord on the 6th *Day of*
July 1659. *and* 63d. *Year of his Age.*

Line 13. *r.* Azure, *l.* 16. after Heraldry, add *p.* 197. ed. 1638.
p. 37. after *fuæ* 23. add the fame in *Englifh* :

Here lyeth George Trenchard fecond Son of William
Trenchard of Cattrige in the County of Wilts Efquire,
A Captain of a Man of War, and a Young-man of
Great Hopes, he died of a Fever in the Year 1696. *and of*
His Age the 23d.

Line penult and antepenult dele this Mark o——o, *p.* 39. *l.* 10.
for Reftaurationis *leg.* Reftauratione, and *l.* 11. for primas *leg.*
primos. *Page* 39. *l.* ult. add, This Epitaph for the Benefit of the
Englifh Reader is rendered as follows.

Here lies Sir *William Clarke*, Knight, and Secretary at War to
the moft ferene King *Charles* II; and Secretary to the moft noble
George Duke of *Albermarle*, whofe Fortune he followed through
all Emergencies for more than twelve Years; and whofe Efforts
in reftoring our Monarchy and Laws he ftrenuoufly affifted. In
the famous Sea-fight with the *Dutch* Fleet in the Beginning of
June 1666, which continued for four Days fucceffively, as he
fought by the Admiral's Side, on the fecond Day he loft his right
Leg by a Cannon Ball, on the Fourth his Life; yet in fpight of
this Wound he would not fuffer himfelf to be removed from the
danger of the Battle, but while the reft of the wounded were carried on Shore, he remained alone in the Ship which was fhattered
and expofed to the Fire of the Enemy, and with furprifing Con-
ftancy waited the doubtful Event of the Battel and his own
Life. His wounded Body having for feveral Days been toft on
the Sea, was at length caft into this Haven, while his Soul retired
to its native Heaven. Stay Reader a Moment, you do not yet
know

know the Character of this great Man, who having long executed
the greateft publick Employments had always the Happinefs of
the publick Approbation: Who though he attained to Riches and
Honours, yet efcaped Infamy and Envy, not by Artifice but the
Force of his Integrity; and in fhort was a fhining Inftance that
Innocence does not always forbid a Man to engage in the Affairs
of a Court. You have here the Remains of a Gentleman of Integrity, Honour, Knowledge, Abilities and Application; who fur-
mounted Labours and fuppreffed Avarice, who neither defrauded
the Rich, nor neglected the Poor, and obferved the ftricteft Sincerity in word and Action. His Life was crowned with Integrity,
his Death with Fortitude; in both he was equally happy. The
Period of his Life contained but three and forty Years, yet even
in that fhort Space were exerted all the Virtues and Graces of
Life. He left a forrowful Widow, and a Son five Years old, a
moderate Eftate, and excellent Character, and a deep Regret for
the Lofs of him; his forrowful Widow raifed this Monument in
order to do Juftice to his Memory, and alleviate in fome meafure
her own Sorrow.

Page 41. *l.* ult. The *Englifh* of the foregoing Epitaph is as follows:

> *Under this Marble are layed the Afhes of Roger Reay, who*
> *Seeking Glory by Sea and Land, at length died a valiant Death,*
> *And fleeps in the Bed of Honour, he died the* 30th *of September* 1673.
> *Reader do you enquire who fleeps under this Marble? Here Heroick*
> *Virtue lies in the Bed of Honour.*

Page 57. *l.* 19. The *Englifh* of the Infcription on the *School-
houfe. This Edifice for the Inftructing the Youth of Harwich in good
Manners, Literature, and the Doctrine of the Church of England,
was founded and built at the proper Charge of Humphrey Parfons,
Efq; Citizen and Alderman of London, and Member of Parliament
for this Borough, A. D. 1724. The Founder begs thee, O Almighty
God, to take it into thy Protection; do thou profper the Munificence of
this illuftrious Benefactor, and under thy Favour may both the Youth
and the Building fucceed to thy Honour for ever.*   Page

Page 65. *Col.* 1. *Line* 7. add, Although the Donation Charter
is not in the *Monafticon*, as I have before obferved, yet the Inftrument whereby *Faritius*, or *Farecius* Abbot of *Abingdon* was infti-
tuted, and had feizing of the *Priory* of *Coln*, is there recorded,
Vol. I. p. 438. as follows: *Omnium verò rerum quæ per cartam
iftam notantur*, *Abbas* Faritius *apud* Colas, *quadragefimali tempore
et die Fefta Sancti* Cuthberti *conftitutus inveftituram, id eft, faifitio-
nem accepit, per manum* Picoti *dapiferi* Albrici, *jubente eodem* Albrico
juniore *& uxore ejus* Beatrice, *concedentibus id* Albrico juniore, *&
cæteris eorum filiis, cum fuis univerfis militibus qui huic donationi in-
terfuerunt idem videntes & annuentes. Quorum nomina hæc fuerunt
filiorum*; *jam nominatus* Albricus, Rogerus, Robertus, Willielmus.
Militum vero Alfredus *Vicecomes*, Goisfredus *filius* Haimonis, Haimon *de* Lamara, *& multi alii.*

The fame englifhed for the Benefit of the Englifh *Reader.*

Of all things fpecified in that Charter, *Faricius* appointed Abbot of *Coln* in the time of *Lent*, and on the Feaft of St. *Cuthbert*,
received the Inveftiture, *i. e.* the Seizure, by the Hand of *Picot*
Senefchal to *Aubrey*, at the Command of the fame *Aubrey* and
his Wife *Beatrice*, and with the Confent of *Aubrey* the Younger,
and their other Children, together with all their Knights, who
were prefent at this Donation, and confented to it. The Names
of the Children are as follows, *Aubrey* aforementioned, *Roger*,
Robert and *William*. But of the Knights, Vifcount *Alfred*, *Gof-
fred* the Son of *Haimon*, *Haimon de Lamara* and many others.

Here is fome Fault either in the writing, tranfcribing or printing of this laft mentioned Record, which runs thus, *jubente eodem*
Albrico *juniore*, which fhould have been *feniore*, for *Beatrix* was
not the Wife of the Younger, but of the Elder *Alberic*, and therefore Mother of the Younger, his Wife being *Adeliza* as I have
fully fhewn, *p.* 121. of the foregoing Hiftory.

U u   By

By the aforecited Record it is proved that *Faritius* was Abbot of *Abingdon*, at the time of the Donation of *Coln Priory* to that Abby ; and that he was perfonally prefent at the Delivery and feizing thereof, by *Picote* Sewer to the Elder *Alberic*, which confequently muft be before the Death of the faid *Alberic*, who as I before p. 63. fhewed died *Anno* 1088. But *Wharton* in his *Angl. Sacr.* Vol. I. p. 168. writes that *Fariceus* (as he calls him) was not made Abbot until *Anno* 1100. how then to reconcile thefe two contradictory Accounts I know not.   *Leland* writes, that this *Farecius* (for fo he names him) was a Stranger and Phyfician, a very wife, grave and learned Man.   *Iter.* Vol. VII. p. 63.

Ib. c. 2. l. ult. the afore recited Account is in *Englifh* as follows : *Alberic* the Elder the Day before his Death did in this Place take the Habit of a Monk, and when dead was there buried: As was alfo *William* his youngeft Son, who outlived his Father but a little while.   In Memory of whom his Brother *Alberic* the Younger gave two *Carrucuts* of Land in *Scaldulican* for ever to the Monks aforefaid, in the Prefence of *Faritius* the Abbot, who came thither to perform the funeral Rites.

Page 64. *l.* 14. The following is the Tranflation of the foregoing Epitaph.   The Epitaph here follows:

The Barbarian, Scythian, *Bond and Freeman, however defirous of Life, muft quit it ; Death is the common Lot of every Sex and Age: The fame Law, Fortune and Grave, befall the Aged and the Young, the Father and the Son; neither the great Learning of the Son, or the Strength and Riches of the Father, availed them any thing ; but Faith, and the Donations we have mentioned avail them ; and we pray that they may do fo for ever.*

Ib. c. 2. *l.* 3. *r.* the p. 73. *c.* 1. *l.* 6. *r.* and four Bells, *Page* 88. *c.* 1. *l.* 8. *r. Robert Rich, p.* 89. The Tranflation of the foregoing Infcription is:

If Reader you fhould be Inquifitive to know what Countryman, and how great a Perfonage lies under this Tomb ?   On the right Side of the Wall, you may obferve a Marble Statue in a praying Pofture: Under which Statue, you will find his whole Hiftory in Golden Letters.

2   The

The Monument for this Mr. *Smith* you have engraven on the adjoining Plate, in which under a Nich (adorned with Rofes) between two Marble Pillars of the *Corinthian Order*, he is figured in his *Alderman's Gown*, with a Ruff about his Neck, kneeling upon a Cufhion before a reading Defk, on which is an open Book: He holding a Death's Head between his Hands; upon the Plancher over his Head is between two Genii his Coat of *Arms*, viz. *Quarterly firft and fourth fable, a Fefs between three Salters Or, fecond and third Argent, three Bars Gul. in Chief three Wolves Heads erafed of the fecond.*

And underneath on a Black Table is the foregoing Infcription in Gold Letters.

By the above Blazonry it appears, that the Arms inferted *p.* 92. from *Aubrey's Hiftory* is not right. Alfo by the quartering of the faid *Arms*, it is more than probable, that his Parents were not fo mean, nor his Condition fo low in his younger Years as is there conjectured; and as to the Occafion of his being fo roughly treated at *Micham*, we are ftill in the Dark.

N. B. The following Account from this *page* to *p.* 98. relating to Mr. *Smith* and his Charities, are not fo methodically printed as they ought to be by Reafon divers of them, were not communicated until the Copy was out of the Publifher's Hands; and his Diftance from the Prefs prevented the more correct placing them.

Page 97. read *Aubrey's Surry, p.* 98. *c.* 2. *l.* 21. *dele* other, *p.* 104. *c.* 2. Although I could not *Anno* 1728. difcern any other than *Sea Water* to drain down from the Bottom of this *Cliff*, yet in the Year 1729. near that End of the *High Cliff*, which is next the *Town*, I obferved a Water to run down from under the *Cliff*; what Tafte it had, or what Colour it would ftrike with *Galls*, I did not examine, being then not provided with any thing to make any Experiments in or with. My not finding any fuch *Spring* there the preceding Year makes me fufpect, that it is not a conftant *Spring*, but only temporary, and runs in wet Years; nor was this Water of any Breadth, being no more than what a Man could ftep over, nor fo deep as to wet above the Thicknefs of the Sole of an ordinary Shoe; nor to iſſue but only at one Place: What other or wetter Years may produce, I cannot tell.

Having mentioned the *Temporary Spring* at the Bottom of this *Cliff*, it may be expected that I ſhould ſay ſomething about the *Origine* of *Springs*; which being a Subject of great Extent and much controverted among the *Literati*, each Opinion having many *Patrons*, I ſhall not give the whole of the Controverſy, but only Extract ſome few Heads, to give my Readers ſome little Taſte thereof, I mean ſuch as are not yet acquainted with the Subject. This may be compriſed under *three Heads*. *Firſt*, That *Springs* are cauſed by the *Percolation* of the Sea Water; and of this Opinion are divers learned Men, both ancient and modern, ſome of which laſt are our Countrymen as Mr. *Lydiat*, Mr. *Carpenter*, Dr. *Jorden* and Dr. *French*: Their Arguments as I find them in Dr. *Wittie's Scarborough Spaw*, p. 56. are *Firſt*, There is nothing but the vaſt *Ocean*, that can afford ſuch Abundance of Waters as do *Spring* from the *Earth*. *Secondly*, Becauſe the *Sea* is not encreaſed by the Multitude of *Waters* which flow into it daily, as it muſt of Neceſſity be, if they had not by *ſubterraneal Channels* a Recourſe to their *Fountains*. There are ſome Arguments given to back theſe, as the Opinion of *Solomon, Eccleſ.* i. 7. Then that the *Sea* is higher than the *Earth*, being depreſſed only upon the Shore; but theſe Authors not agreeing among themſelves, about the Manner of Conveyance of the *Water* to the ſeveral *Springs*, I ſhall only direct thoſe that deſire further Information to read Dr. *Wittie's* Anſwer to them. Dr. *Plot*, although he makes the greateſt Part of *Rivers* to derive their *Water* from the *Sea*, yet he allows *temporary Springs*, and likewiſe ſuch *Perennial* ones as are near the Tops of Hills to depend upon *Rains* and *Dews*. *Hiſtory* of *Staffordſhire*, p. 51. Mr. *Derham* is alſo of the Opinion, that the *Origin* of *Springs* is from the Sea, *Phyſ. Theol.* p. 50. A ſecond Opinion is, the *Tranſmutation* of *Air* within the Bowels of the *Earth*, or as others expreſs it, the Condenſation of *Vapours* in the *Caverns* of the *Earth* into Water. *Seneca*, as ſaith Dr. *Wittie*, would have the *Earth* itſelf thus *Tranſmuted*: Which Opinion *Lydiat de Origin. Font.* rejects

jects as a thing void of Reason, and needs no Arguments to disprove. Others allow of a *Transmutation*, but it is of *Air* into *Water*, performed in the *Caverns* of the *Earth* by *Cold*; and of this Opinion was Dr. *Fulk* on Meteors, and *Hen. ab Heer Spadecrene*. Mr. *Morton* in his *Nat. Hist. Northampt.* p. 302. thinks, that *Springs* proceed also from *Vapours* within the *Earth*, not condensed by *Cold*, but the contrary *Quality*; for he saith, that there is a sufficient Quantity of *Heat* in the *Earth*, not only to raise, but also to bear up Water in Form of *Vapours*; Dr. *Woodward* faith, *Essay*, p. 121. That it is this Heat which evaporates and elevates the Water of the *Abyss*, buoying it up indifferently on every Side, and towards all Parts of the *Surface* of the *Globe*: Which *subterranean Magazine* of the *Abyss* with its Partner the *Ocean*, is the standing Fund and Promptuary, which supplies with Water *Springs* and *Rivers*. The third *Opinion* is, that Springs are caused by *Rains* and *Dews*; I might mention many learned Persons ancient and modern, for the Maintainers thereof, but shall instance in those that are modern, as many of the *French Vertuoso's*, and my late learned Friend Mr. *John Ray*, writes, that he doth not peremptorily affirm, that all *Fountains* do proceed from *Rain*; but only contends that *Rain* may suffice to feed them, and that probably it doth feed ordinary *Springs*, *Phys. Theol. Disc.* 89. And as an Instance of this, our Wells about *Braintree* in the Years 1724, and 1725. being dry Years, the Generality of the *Pumps* failed of their Water, so that many were constrained to sink their Wells deeper, that they might be supplied; but the Years 1728, and 1729. being much more wet, such a Quantity of Water was produced in the last of them, as that many were obliged to take up the Trees of their *Pumps*, and cleanse their Wells from Sand, which the Current of the *Spring* brought along with it. The like is taken notice of by Dr. *Wittie*, (p. 97.) where he writes: *That in the Year* 1654-5, *and* 6. *when our Climate was drier than ever it had been mentioned to be in any Stories, so as we had very little* Rain *in Summer, or* Snow *in Winter, most of our* Springs *were dried up, such as in the Memory of the oldest Man living had never wanted*

I   *Water,*

Water, but were of thofe Springs we call Fontes Perennes, *or at leaft were fo efteemed. He inftances alfo a* Parallel *Story out of* Heylin's Geography *in the Defcription of* Cyprus. And Dr. *Wittie* doth p. 84. give an Inftance of the breaking out of *Springs* in the *Wolds* of *Yorkfhire,* after great *Rains:* The like it did in *Kent* as quoted by Mr. *Ray* from Dr. *Childrey's Britannia Baconica* as follows: *Sometimes there breaks out Water in the Manner of a fudden* Land Flood, *out of certain* Stones, *that are like* Rocks *ftanding aloft in the open Fields near the Rifing of the River* Kynet, *which is reputed by the common People a forerunner of* Dearth. *That the fudden Eruption of Springs in Places where they ufe not always to run, fhould be a Sign of Dearth is no Wonder. For thefe unufual Eruptions (which in* Kent *we call* Nailbourns) *are caufed by extreme* Gluts *of* Rain, *or lafting* wet Weather, *and never happen but in* wet Years: *And in the Year* 1654. *feveral* Springs *and* Rivulets *were quite dried up, by Reafon of the precedent* Drought, *which raged moft in* 1651-2, *and* 3. *At the Head of the* Stour, *that rifes near* Eltham *in* Kent, *and runs through* Canterbury, *it was dry for fome miles Space: And the like happened to the* Stream, *that croffeth the Roadway at* Ofpring *near* Feverfham; *which at other times ran with a plentiful Current, but then wholly failed.* To thefe I fhall add the Sentiment of Dr. *Behrens,* who after mentioning the *Hypothefis* of Springs being caufed by Rain and Snow-water, as likewife that other of Sea-water, either fucked up by the Earth like a *Sponge,* or conveyed through it by *Tubes* and *Pipes* as the Blood in *animal Bodies,* thinks that the moft plaufible Opinion is, *That the Water, being rarefied by the* fubterranean Heat, *rifes in the Nature of a Vapour till it gets to the* Summit *of the Mount, where the external* Air *condenfes it into* Water, *as* Vapours *do in* Diftillation. And he adds, That though this *Syftem* may be applied to moft *Springs* upon *Mountains,* yet the chief Caufe of that upon 𝕭𝖑𝖔𝖈𝖐'𝖘𝖇𝖊𝖗𝖌 is the Snow, which lies there almoft all the Year round, and the frequent *Rains* and *Mifts* that fall there, *Nat. Hift. of Hartz-Foreft,* p. 65.

Dr. *Plot*

Dr. *Plot* in his *Nat. Hist. of Staffordshire*, p. 52. ranges Dr. *Hook* among thofe that make the *Original* of *Springs* to arife from *Rain* and *Dews*.   Mr. *Ray* quotes as Dr. *Hook*'s Opinion, *That the Preponderancy of the Salt-water above the Frefh, raifes up the Frefh-water above the Level of the Salt, as high as the Springs and Fountain Heads, and Forces it out there*, Phyf. Theol. Difc. *p.* 89.   But not having yet feen any of the Doctor's Works which relate to the *Origin* of *Springs*, I cannot fay any thing farther about it. Againft the *Hypothefis* that *Rain* is the *Original* of *Springs* and *Rivers*, is this *Objection*; That the *Rain* never finks above ten Foot deep at moft into the Earth, and therefore it cannot fupply them: Againft this Objection, Mr. *Ray* gives feveral Reafons, *viz.* that in *Pool's Hole* in *Derbyshire*, there are in fome Places conftant Droppings and Diftillations of Water from the *Roof,* which muft make its way through a great Thicknefs of Earth: And that out of the Mouth of the fame *Hole*, after great and continuing Rains a great Stream of Water did ufually iffue forth. Likewife the late Lord *Middleton* did acquaint him from the Report he had from his Colliers; *That if there be Springs lie before they come at the* Coal *they carry the Water away*; *but if there be none, it falls into the Works, in greater or lefs Quantity, according as the Rains fall*, Phyf. Theol. Difc. 91, *&c.* This Inundation from Rain is token notice of by Dr. *Wittie*, Lib. cit. *p.* 105. Dr. *Halley* is of Opinion, that *Springs* and *Rivers* owe their *Original* to *Vapours* condenfed on the Sides of *Mountains*, by the coldnefs of the Air in the Night, *Philof. Tranf.* N°. 192. *p.* 468.

Dr. *Merret* mentions *Salt-Springs* to be found near *Harwich* in *Effex: Pin.* p. 221. I never did hear of any there unlefs he means thereby the Brackifhnefs of the Water of their *Pumps* in the *Town*; but that doth not arife from any fuch *Spring*, but is occafioned by the Percolation of the *Sea-water* into their Wells.

Page 111. *c.* 1. *l.* 20, and 21. *r.* by the Cavings, *p.* 112. *l.* 8. *r. Amber-greafe* which our Author from the Obfervations of others, mentions to be taken up upon this Shore, but that being of *animal* and not of *mineral* Production; I fhall refer what I have further
ther

ther to fay about it, unto the *Catalogue of Fifhes* to which
Tribe it properly belongs.

Ib. c. 2. l. 2. dele of *l. 6. r.* on little Hearths, *l. 12.* add. Mr.
Ray obferved about *Whitby* in *Yorkfhire* the People very bufy in
making *Kelp*, which they do in this manner. They gather the
Sea-wreck and lay it on Heaps; and when 'tis dry, they burn it.
While it is burning, they ftir it to and fro with an *Iron-rake:* So
it condenfes and cakes together into fuch a Body as we fee *Kelp*
(i. e. *Pot-Afhes*) to be. If they fhould not ftir it, it would burn
to afhes as other combuftible Bodies ufe to do. *Cambd. Brit.*
p. 766. For what Ufe the *Pot-Afhes* here made were defigned I
cannot learn, perhaps for making of *Soap* or *Glafs;* thofe at *Whitby*
are for making of *Allum.*

Page 113. *c. 2. l. 2.* add, The following is a *Fafciculus* of the
more rare Plants, which I have either obferved growing wild
about *Harwich,* or to have been caft up there by the Sea.

Thefe I have rather chofe to put into a *Synoptical* Order, than
into that of the Alphabet; but for the readier finding them the
Index at the End of the Book will direct. And if it be objected,
that there are many more to be found there, than thofe which I
herein mention, I anfwer; that my Defign was not to publifh all
the Plants that grew here, but fuch as are rare, *viz.* fuch as are
found but in few Places, and therefore in a more large Senfe,
may be call'd *Topical;* among which number may be reckoned
thofe which are maritime: of thefe I have endeavoured to give as
full an Account as I could, referring to the Authors that have
written of them, for the Information of Botanifts, whether Ty-
rones or Adepts, that fo many of them as fhall refort hither, may
know what to expect, and be encouraged to make further Difcoveries.
To thefe I have added thofe mentioned by our Author Mr. *Tayler,*
though fome of them are very common and frequently to be met
with: As to the moft common Plants of all, they are fo numerous as to exceed my intended Defign, requiring rather a Book by
themfelves than a fhort Place in an Appendix; befides I was not
there at all Seafons of the Year to obferve them, neither had I
time,

time, nor Conveniencies, when there, to collect so enormous a Quantity as they would amount to; if every Plant there growing were to be collected.

I. PLANTÆ SUBMARINÆ.

I. *Spongia.*

1. SPongia ramosa *C. B. Pin.* 368. *Pluk. Almag.* 356. *Chab.* 579. *Ger. emac.* 1577. *Tournef. Inst.* 576. *Boerh. Ind.A.* 8. *Raij Hist.* I. 81. *Ejusd. Synop.* III. 29. Spongia ramosa Britannica *Park. Theat.* 1304. *Raij Fasc. Stirp.* 20. *Hist. Oxon.* III. 653. Spongia diforma arborea *Imp.* 638. Confervæ marinæ genus *Lob. icon.* 2. 257. Confervæ marinæ genus Lobelio *Ludg.* 1372. Corallina Britannica Penæ, *Ejusd.* 1371. ꛃranched ſponge. This is sometimes found cast upon this Shore. The Figures in *Johnson's* Edition of *Gerard,* and in *Parkinson's Theatrum Bot.* are taken from *Lobel's Icons,* but do not so well represent the Plant as could be desired: The Figure in *Imperatus* is rather too specious for our Plant. Dr. *Dillenius* in his Edition of *Ray's Synopsis* takes notice of two Varieties of this Plant; in one of which the Branches are longish and round, the Tops flat and broad, but the Stalks or Branches are narrow; in the other the Tops end in a Point, and the Stalks broad with many Branches like Horns coming out of the Sides thereof. In the *Historia Lugdunensis,* there are two Figures of this Plant, which seem to be taken from the two Varieties thereof, though that Author hath erroneously put one under the Title of a *Corallina:* The same you have likewise in the *French* Edition of that Book, Vol. II. *p.* 256, 257.

2. Spongia dichotomos teretifolia viridis *Raij Synop.* III. 29. Fucus teretifolius spongiosus parvus *Ejusd.* I. 3. *Item.* II. 4. Fucus spongiosus teres ramosior viridis erectus D. *Steven's Hist. Oxon.* III. *p.* 647. *Tournef. Inst.* 567.

X x II. *Corallina.*

II. *Corallina.*

1. COrallina *J. B.* III. 810. *Raij Hift.* I. 45. *Chab.* 577. *Dale Pharm.* 112. *Tourn. Inft.* 570. *Elem. Bot.* 444. Corallina Anglica *Ger.* 1379. *emac.* 1571. Corallina pennata longior *Phyt. Brit.* 31. *Johnf. Merc. Bot.* 30. *Ejufd. Itin. Cant.* II. *p.* 3. *Mer. Pin.* 30. Mufcus maritimus five Corallina Officinarum, *C. B. Pin.* 363. *Hift. Oxon.* III. 651. Mufcus marinus, five Corallina alba Officinarum *Park. Theat.* 1295. 𝕾𝖊𝖆=𝖈𝖔𝖗𝖆𝖑𝖑𝖎𝖓𝖊, 𝖜𝖍𝖎𝖙𝖊 𝖂𝖔𝖗𝖒=𝕾𝖊𝖊𝖉. It grows frequently on the Sea Rocks, as likewife on Stones and Shells, and frequently to be found wafhed up upon the Shore. It varies in its Colour, being befides white, found purple, yellow and green. The Powder given in Wine, Milk, or any other proper Vehicle kills Worms in either old or young; one Dram to a grown Perfon, and half that Quantity to a Child. There is great Confufion among Botanick Authors about the Figure of this Plant, and tho' it is not well defigned by any, yet the Figures in *Gerard* and *Tabernæmontanus* feem to me the beft.

2. Corallina marina Abietis forma, *Tourn. Inft.* 571. *Raij Synop.* III. 35. Corallinæ affinis Abies marina dicta *Pluk. Almag.* 119. Mufcus marinus major argutè denticulatus *Raij Hift.* I. 78. *Pluk. Phytog.* Tab. 48. f. 5. *Hift. Oxon* III. 650. Mufcus marinus fcrupofus five Coralloides Abietis facie, *Ejufd.* Mufcus Coralloides albus alter, *Lob. Icon.* II. 250. Mufcus Coralloides marinus denticulatus major *Raij Synop.* I. 5. *Ejufd.* II. 8. Mufci marini genus foliolis pennatis, & Abies Clufii Belgica *J. B.* III. 799. Abies marina Belgica *Cluf. Hifp.* 27. *Hift.* 35. *Raij Hift.* I. 76. *Ger. emac.* 1574. Abies marina *Park. Theat.* 1301. Abieti fimilis maritima *C. B. Pin.* 365. 𝕿𝖍𝖊 𝖌𝖗𝖊𝖆𝖙𝖊𝖗 𝖙𝖔𝖔𝖙𝖍𝖊𝖉 𝕮𝖔𝖗𝖆𝖑𝖑𝖎𝖓𝖊. This I have feen caft up by the Tide on the Shores. The Figures of this given by *Clufius, Lobel, Johnfon* and *Parkinfon,* are but of fmall Plants growing upon Oyfter-Shells; Dr. *Plukenet* hath in his *Phytographia* given a much better and larger, with toothed Stalks, tho' otherwife mentioned in Mr. *Ray's Synopfis*; but the beft Figure is in the

I   *Oxford*

Oxford Hiftory; however Mr. *Bobart* came to refer it to the *Mufcus maritimus filicis foliis C. B. Pin.* 363. which is the *Myrophyllum Pelagium Cortufi Cluf. Hift.* ccli. with which this our Plant hath a refemblance, as will appear by comparing their Figures.

3. Corallina mufcofa pennata, ramulis & capillamentis falcatis *Pluk. Almag.* 119. *Phytog.* Tab. XLVII. *f.* 12. *Tourn. Inft.* 570. *Raij Synop.* III. 36. Mufcus pennatus, ramulis & capillamentis falcatis, *Ejufd.* II. 9. *Hift.* I. 79. *Hift. Oxon.* III. 650. Tab. IX. *f.* 2. Mufcus marinus fpiralis pennatus, nec defcribitur necdepingitur, *Johnf. Mer. Bot.* II. 26. *Phyt. Brit.* 78. Mufcus marinus fpiralis pennatus N. D. *Mer. Pin.* 81. 𝕾𝕚𝕔𝕜𝕝𝕖 𝕗𝕖𝕒𝕥𝕙𝕖𝕣𝕖𝕕 𝕾𝕖𝕒-𝕸𝕠𝕤𝕤. Mr. *Johnfon* found this on the Coaft of *Anglefey*; and in his *Itinerary*, p. 10. calls it *Mufcus marinus elegantiffimus.* We have obferved it on thefe Shores.

4. Corallina mufcofa denticulis bijugis unum latus fpectantibus, *Pluk. Almag.* 119. *Raij Synop.* III. 35. *Tourn. Inft.* 570. Mufcus marinus denticulatus, denticulis bijugis unum latus fpectantibus, *Raij Hift.* I. 79. *Synop.* II. 8. *Hift. Oxon.* III. 650.

5. Corallina mufcofa, alterna vice denticulata, ramulis in creberrima capillamenta fparfis, *Pluk. Almag.* 119. *Phytog.* Tab. XLVIII. *Tourn. Inft.* 570. *Raij Synop.* III. 36. Mufcus marinus erectior, ramulis in innumera & tenuiffima capillamenta divifis, *Raij Hift.* I. 79. *Synop.* II. 9. Mufcus marinus argenteus Coralloides ramofus erectus *Boc.Muf.*I.259. 𝕱𝕚𝕟𝕖 𝕝𝕖𝕒𝕧𝕖𝕕 𝕥𝕠𝕠𝕥𝕙𝕖𝕕 𝕮𝕠𝕣𝕒𝕝𝕝𝕚𝕟𝕖. This is likewife found on this Shore. D. *Dillen.* here joins the afore-cited Synonims of D. *Plukenet* and Mr. *Ray*, but D. *Plukenet* makes them diftinct, joining to his the *Mufcus marinus denticulatus minor denticulis alternis*, of Mr. *Ray*'s *Hiftory* and *Synopfis* inftead thereof; and in this he is followed by *Tournefort* in his *Inftitutions* afore-quoted, as likewife by Mr. *Bobart* in his *Hift. Oxon.* who calls it *Mufcus marinus minor denticulis alternis*, III. 650. This Plant is well figured by *Plukenet*, *Boccone* and *Bobart* in the Tables abovementioned. Why D. *Plukenet* fhould fuppofe this to be the *Myriophyllum Pelagium Cortufi* which *C. Bauhin.* names *Mufcus maritimus filicis folio* Pin. p. 363. I cannot conceive, fince neither their Defcriptions nor Figures agree.   X x 2   6. Coral-

6. Corallina capillaceo multifido folio albido *Tourn. Inst. 571.*
Raij Synop. III. 34. Corallinæ affinis, feu Mufcus marinus tenui
capillo *J. B.* III. 811. *Chab.* 578. Corallinæ affinis candida multifido capillaceo folio Palmites *Pluk. Almag.* 119. *Phytog.* Tab. xlvir.
f. 10. Mufcus capillaceus multifido folio albidus *C. B.* 363. Mufcus marinus five Corallina rubra *Ger.* 1379. Mufcus marinus albidus *Ger. emac.* 1571. Mufcus marinus candidus Coralloides *Hist.*
Oxon. III. 651. Mufcus marinus rubens five Corallina rubens *Park.*
Theat. 1296. **Fine leaved Coralline Mofs.** It is found of divers
Colours, but moft commonly white and greenifh. It is beft reprefented by the Figures in *J. Bauhine, Johnfon,* and *Plukenet.* It
is faid by *Chabræus* to have the fame Vertue of killing Worms as
the Coralline.

7. Corallina confervoides albicans. An Fucus minimus capillaceus ramofiffimus, per ficcitatem albicans *Raij Synop.* II. 8.
Corallina capillaceo folio tenerior, candidiffima & nodulis afperfa
Ejufd. III. 34. **Long leaved Coralline Mofs.** This is alfo to be
found on thefe Shores, being frequently of a fandy Colour. The
Figure of the *Mufcus marinus five Corallina alba* Ger. emac. 1571.
doth well reprefent this Plant. The fame Figure *Parkinfon* alfo
gives for the *Coralline* of the Shops *Theat.* 1295, but erroneoufly.

8. Corallina confervoides gelatinofa rubens, ramulis & geniculis
peranguftis *Raij Synop.* III. 34. Mufcus marinus capillaris rubens
non ramofus D. *Dale*: *Muf. Pet.* 274. **Reddifh flender Coralline**
Mofs. It grows upon the Stones which the Tide overflows;
D. *Dillenius* hath obferved it to be flightly ramofe.

III *Fucoides.*

1. FUcoides rubens variè diffectum *Raij Synop.* III. 37. Mufcus
marinus foliis multifidis *Johnf. Merc. Bot.* II. *p.* 27. *Phyt.*
Brit. 78. Mufcus marinus rubens pennatus noftras *Raij Hift.* I. 78.
Syn. II. 8. Mufcus maritimus tenuiffimè diffectus ruber *C. B. Pin*
363. *Mer. Pin.* 80. Mufcus pelagicus pennatus rubens, ramulis
numerofis mollibus latiùs fe fpargentibus *Pluk. Almag.* 258. *Phyt.*
Tab.

Tab. xlviii. *Hift. Oxon.* III. 650. Mufcus marinus purpureus parvus, foliis oblongis millefolii fere divifura *Raij Hift.* I. 79. *Synop.*
II. 9. Mufcus maritimus Neapolitanus *Park. Theat.* 1289. *Raij*
Synop. II. 9. Mufcus marinus *Cluf. Hift.* ccl. Mufcus marinus Clu-
fio *Ger. emac.* 1573. Corallina rubens millefolii ferè divifura *Tourn.*
Inft. 571. 𝔯𝔢𝔡 𝔣𝔢𝔞𝔱𝔥𝔢𝔯𝔢𝔡 𝔖𝔢𝔞=𝔐𝔬𝔰𝔰.. This is likewife fometimes
found upon this Shore. Mr. *Ray* hath this twice over in his *Hi-*
ftory, and thrice in his firft and fecond Edition of his *Synopfis*, which
Error he might be led into, by Names fent him from his Friends,
as may be demonftrated by the *Appendix* to the firft *Synop.* p. 241.
in the Mufcus maritimus Neapolitanus *Park.* fent him by Dr. *Pluke-*
net, which he there likewife erroneoufly makes the Mufcus Coralloides lenta fœniculacea *J. B.* Fucus Fœniculaceus colore livido
Almag. 160. The Figures of this Plant in *Clufius* and *Johnfon* are
very good.

IV. *Fucus.*

1. FUCUS folio fingulari, longiffimo, lato, in medio rugofo,
qui balteiformis dici poteft, *Raij Synop.* II. 6. III. 39. Fucus
folio fingulari, longiffimo, lato, in medio rugofo *Ejufd. Hift.* I. 74.
Hift. Oxon. III. 646. *Tourn. Inft.* Fucus baltei-formis *Raij Cat.*
Angl. I. 119. II. 114. *Threlk. Synop. Hybern.* Fucus phafganoides
foliis indivifis *Mer. Pin.* 40. Fucus marinus craffus latifolius *Park.*
Theat. 1292. Fucus longiffimo, latiffimo, craffoque folio *C. B. Prod.*
154. Alga longiffimo, lato, craffoque folio *Ejufd. Pin.* 364. *J. B.*
801. 𝔖𝔢𝔞=𝔟𝔢𝔩𝔱. This is fometimes caft up here. The Footftalk
of this is fhort and not thick. The Fucus latiffimus & longiffimus, oris crifpis *Hift. Oxon.* III. 646 *Threlk. Synop. Hybern.* is another Variety of this; as is likewife according to D. *Dillen.* the
Fucus Phyllitidis folio D. *Lhuyd.* Synop. III. 40. The *Welch* call
this laft *Mor-dowys*; the poor People eat the fmall Leaves and
Clufters, as they do *Delefh.*

2. Fucus chordam referens teres prælongus *Raij Hift.* I. 75.
Synop. I. 5. II. 6. III. 40. *Hift. Oxon.* III. 647. *Pluk. Almag.* 160.

I Fucus

Fucus marinus rotundis tenuibus longiffimifque loris *Raij. Cat. Angl.* I. 119. II. 114. Fucus marinus rotundus (quem à forma *Guil-Broad* nominavit) ligula marina *Johnf. Mer. Bot.* 36. *Phyt. Brit.* 43. Fucus marinus rotundus *Mer. Pin.* 40. Fucus five Filum maritimum Germanicum *Boc. Muf.* 271. Tab. VII. Fig. 9. Fucus fetaceus niger longiffimus non ramofus *Hift. Oxon.* III. 649. Filum maritimum Germanicum *C. B. Pred.* 155. Alga nigro capillaceo folio *Ejufd. Pin.* 364. Ligula marina alba Suffexiana *Pet. Gaz.* Tab. XCI. f. 5. Alcyonium vermiculatum Anglicum *Tourn. Inft.* 577. Sea-laces. I gathered thefe by the Dock-Gates of the *King's Yard.* They are round, at firft tender, afterwards more firm, within hollow, divided by fome films: They are about a Yard long, and flender at both Ends. In Colour brown, and when dried black; but if they lie long upon the Shore they turn whitifh. Mr. *Bobart* hath this twice in his Hiftory.

3. Fucus five Alga marina latifolia vulgatiffima *Raij Synop.* II. 2. III. 40. Fucus maritimus vel Quercus maritima veficulas habens *C. B. Pin.* 365. *Raij Hift.* I. 70. *Cat. Angl.* II. 115. *Pluk. Al. mag.* 161. *Tourn. Inft.* 566. *Boerh. Ind.* A. 9. Fucus marinus vulgatiffimus, latifolius, foliis Quercinis, veficulis donatis *Hift. Oxon.* III. 647. Quercus marina *Ger.* 1378. *emac.* 1567. Quercus marina herbacea *Park. Theat.* 1293. Fucus minor alias fimilis *Raij Synop.* II. 2. The moft common broad-leaved Sea-wrack. This is the moft common Sea-wrack, not only of this Shore, but of moft if not of all others which I have been at. This Plant often varying in its Form, hath according to D. *Dillen.* occafioned a Multiplication thereof; what therefore he makes Varieties of this as differing in the length and breadth of the Leaves, or in the Manner or Confiftence of the Bladders and Tubercles, or by Reafon of Age or Place, I fhall add as follows. I. *Fucus five Quercus marina latifolia humilis fine veficulis* Raij Synop. II. p. 328. *Fucus maritimus vel Quercus maritima, foliorum extremis tumidis, quam aliqui glandiferam vocant,* C. B. Pin. 365. *Fucus palmaris latioribus foliis in binas ternafve veficulas verrucofas terminatis* Hift. Oxon. III. 647. 2. *Quercus marina humilior, crebris veficulis & tuberculis feminalibus fere*

fere rotundis dotata Raij Synop. II. 327. 3. *Quercus maritima barbata* C. B. Prod. 154. *Fucus maritimus foliis tumidis barbatis* Ejufd. Pin. 365. *Quercus marina foliis inferioribus fimbriatis fœniculaceis* Mer. Pin. 100. 4. *Quercus marina angustiori folio raro veficulas habens* Synop. II. 327. *Fucus palmaris angustifolius ad extrema veficulis rugosis bifurcatus* Hist. Oxon. III. 647. 5. *Fucus feu Quercus marina minima angustifolia* Raij Synop. II. 328. 6. *Quercus marina longiore & latiore folio* Mer. Pin. 100. 7. *Quercus marina angustifolia in extremitate referens Chelas Cancrorum* Mer. Pin. 100. There may be other Varieties in this Plant, besides these seven I have here noted, which I shall leave to the Obfervation of the Curious.

4. Fucus fpiralis maritimus major *Tourn. Inst.* 568. *Boerh. Ind.* A. 9. *Raij Synop.* III. 41. Fucus maritimus noftras foliis in modum fpiræ convolutis *Pluk. Almag.* 161. Fucus marinus fpiralis major *Raij Hist.* III. 9. Alga fpiralis maritima major *Raij Synop.* II. 5. *Hist. Oxon.* III. 646. Alga fpiralis Bocconi *Raij Synop.* I. 7. 𝕮𝖙𝖎𝖎𝖘𝖙𝖊𝖉 𝔚𝖗𝖆𝖈𝖐. This is fometimes to be found on this Shore but not in plenty. D. *Dillen.* refers to this as being but a Variety thereof, *Alga fpiralis ramofa maritima minor Petiverii* Raij Synop. II. 321.

5. Fucus five Alga latifolia major dentata *Raij Synop.* II. 3. III. 42. *Hist. Oxon.* III. 648. *Tourn. Inst.* 566. *Raij Hist.* I. 71. *Pluk. Almag.* 161. Quercus marina foliis ferratis *Johnf. Itin. Cant.* II. p. 3. 𝔅𝖗𝖔𝖆𝖉-𝖑𝖊𝖆𝖛𝖊𝖉 𝖎𝖓𝖉𝖊𝖓𝖙𝖊𝖉 𝔖𝖊𝖆-𝔚𝖗𝖆𝖈𝖐. It grows upon the Stones where the Tide overflows before the Cliff. There is a good Figure of this in the third Volume of *Morrifon's Herbal* Sect. 15. Tab. ix. Fig. 1.

6. Fucus telam lineam fericeamve textura fua æmulans, *Raij Synop.* II. 5. III. 42. *Tourn. Inst.* 568. Tab. cccxxxiv. *Raij. Hist.* I. 71. Fucus marinus fcrupofus albidus telam fericeam textura fua æmulans *Hist. Oxon.* III. 646. *Boerh. Ind.* A. 9. Alga marina platyceros porofa *J. B.* III. 809. Porus cervinus Imperati *C. B. Pin.* 367. 𝔅𝖗𝖔𝖆𝖉-𝖑𝖊𝖆𝖛𝖊𝖉 ℌ𝖔𝖗𝖓-𝔚𝖗𝖆𝖈𝖐. This is found caft up by the Tide upon this Shore. Mr. *Bobart* hath given a good Figure

gure of this, Sect. 15. Tab. VIII. Mr. *Ray* in his *Cat. Angl.* I. 12.
II. 11. gave this for the *Alga marina platyceros porosa* J. B. but
that being of a stony Substance, which this is not, he changed his
Thoughts although the Figure which is given of that by *Imperatus* and *J. Bauhine* doth well expres this.

7. Fucus angusti-folius ligulas referens *C. B. Pin.* 364. *Tourn.
Inst.* 567. Fucus longo, angusto, crassoque folio *Raij Synop.* III.
43. *Ejusd. Hist.* I. 72. Fucus marinus secundus *Dod. Pempt.* 479.
Park. 1293. Quercus marina 2. *Ger. emac.* **Sea-Thongs.** This
is not generally to be found but when the Tide is out, growing on
the Stones below the Cliff. There is some Confusion among Bo-
tanists about this Plant: For Mr. *Ray* in his *Synopsis* and *History*
took the *Fucus marinus secundus of Dodonæus's Pemptades* for the
Fucus longo, angusto crassoque folio of *C. Bauhine's Prodromus* and *Pinax*; whereas *Bauhine* after describing his Plant adds, *Hic ad Fucum
maritimum secundum Dodonæi editionis Belgicæ referri posse videtur,
cujus species altera breviore & angustiore folio dici poterit* Prod. 155.
n. v. and the same Author in his *Pinax* gives it the same Name
as in his *Prodromus,* and affirms it to be the said fifth in that Book;
and likewise adds as a *Synonim* thereof *Fuci maritimi* 2. *species
Dod. Belg.* but refers the *Fucus maritimus secundus Dod. Belg.* as a
Synonim to his *Fucus angustifolius ligulas referens.* Nor is *Tournefort* blamelefs in making the *Fucus longo angusto crassoque folio* of
Bauhine's Prodromus and *Pinax,* the *Fucus marinus* 1. of *Dodonæus's
Pemptades,* which is by *C. Bauhine* made a Synonim of his *Fucus
maritimus vel Quercus maritima vesiculas habens* Pin. 365. and is
there rightly referred, being no other than the *Fucus sive Alga
marina latifolia vulgatissima* of *Ray's Synopsis* by me afore given N°.
3. as they who will read the Description thereof in *Dodonæus* may
observe; indeed that Author gives but a bad Figure thereof, *viz,*
a narrow-leaved Variety of that Plant. I do not find that either
D. *Plukenet* in his *Almagestum* or Mr. *Bobart* in the *Hist. Oxon.* have
taken any Notice of this Plant. *Dodonæus's* Figure of this Plant in
his *Pemptades* is good, as is likewise that of *Johnson* in his *Gerard,*
and *Parkinson* in his *Theater;* only this last Author hath crowded it
with Pieces of the third and fourth *fuci* of *Dodonæus.* 6. Fucus

8. Fucus maritimus Gallo-pavonis pennas referens *C. B. Prod.* 155. *Hift. Oxon.* III. 645. *Raij Hift.* I. 75. *Ejufd. Fafc. Stirp.* 6. *Synop.* III. 43. *Pluk. Almag.* 162. *Tourn. Inft.* 569. Alga maritima Gallo-pavonis plumas referens *C. B. Pin.* 364. Auricula marina *Raij Hift.* I. 77. Fungus auricularis Cæs. *C. B. Pin.* 568. 𝕿urkep'ſ=𝕱eatḥer.. This grows plentifully upon the Stones that lie before the Cliff, but fo far down as not to be feen but when the Tide is loweft. Both Mr. *Ray* and *C. Bauhine* have this twice over. There is a good Figure of this Plant given by Mr. *Bobart*.

9. Fucus membranaceus ceranoides variè diffectus *Raij Synop.* III. 44. Fucus five Alga membranacea purpurea parva *Raij. Hift.* I. 71. *Synop.* I. 3. II, 3. *Tourn. Inft.* 567. 𝕾mall purple mem= branaceouſ 𝕾ea=𝕎rack. Among the Recrements caft up by the Sea. D. *Dillen.* refers to this, as a Variety thereof the Fucus humilis dichotomus membranaceus ceranoides, latifolius, foliis ut plurimum verrucofis *Hift. Oxon.* III. 646. Tab. viii. *f.* 13. There are alfo divers other Varieties of this Plant varying in Breadth, Colour, Figure and Divifion of the Leaves, whereby *Botanifts* are often led to multiply *Species*, of which two or three have been obferved by the faid *Doctor*, among the dried Plants of Mr. *Adam Buddle*, in his *Hortus Siccus*, now in the Poffeffion of Sir *Hans Sloane* Bart. *viz.* 1. *Fucus membranaceus fegmentis in multa cornicula acutiora divifis.* 2. *Alga membranacea purpurea parva fegmentis latis multum laciniatis & crifpatis.* 3. *Alga membranacea purpurea parva fegmentis latis verrucofis,* which laft feems to be the fame as the firft Variety mentioned from the *Hift. Oxon.* as above.

10. Fucus parvus fegmentis prælongis teretibus acutis *Raij Hift.* I. 71. *Synop.* II. 4. III. 45 *Hift. Oxon.* III. 648. Tab. ix. *f.* 4. *Tourn. Inft.* 567. *Pluk. Almag.* 160. Fucus marinus πολυρίδης *Flor. Prufc.* 77. Tab. xv. Forcellata *Imp.* 601. Fucus forcellata lumbricalis fpecies *C. B. Pin.* 366. Fucus marinus forcellata, lumbricariæ fpecies *J. B.* III. 800. 𝕾mall brancḥed 𝕾ea=𝕎rack. This is likewife caft up and left by the Tide on the fandy Shores. Mr. *Bobart* hath referred the *Fucus forcellata of Imperatus* to this,

which I see no Reason to separate; *Gottsched's Fucus* I have likewise brought to this as better pertaining to it, than to the following.

11. Fucus five Alga exigua dichotomos foliorum segmentis longiusculis crassis & subrotundis *Raij Hist.* I. 71. *Synop.* III. 45. Fucus palmaris tenuis in orbem expansus, in segmenta bifida vel trifida breviora teretia divisus, *Hist. Oxon.* III. 649. Fucus parvus in orbem expansus, in segmenta bifida vel trifida breviora teretia divisus, *Ib.* Tab. ix. *f.* 9. Fucus parvus plurimus ab eadem radice cauliculis, segmentis teretibus in summo apice bifidis vel trifidis *Pluk. Almag.* 160. Fucus parvus teres dichotomos pauciflimis divisuris, obscurè viridis & per siccitatem nigricans *Raij Hist.* III. 9. Small branched Sea-Wrack with forked tops. This is likewise to be found with the former, from which it differs in having shorter and blunter segments. Mr. *Bobart* received this from *Barbados,* and hath given a good Figure of it.

12. Fucus trichoides nostras aurei coloris ramulorum apicibus furcatis *Pluk. Almag.* 160. *Phytog.* Tab. clxxxiv. *Raij Synop.* III. 45. Fucus five Alga exigua dichotomos arenacei coloris *Pluk. Almag.* 160. Alga exigua dichotomos arenacei coloris *Ejusd. Hist.* I. 71. *Synop.* II. 4. Fucus exiguus dichotomos arenacei coloris *Fasc. Stirp.* 7. Fucus ceranoides ramofus tenuissimè divisus Dodonæi *Raij Synop.* II. 329. Small branched sandy-coloured Sea-Wrack. This is also to be found with the others but not so frequent. Mr. *Bobart* doubts whether this is his *Fucus five Alga lenta capillacea pallida flagellis ramosis chordas musicas minores referentibus* Hist. Oxon. III. 649. Dr. *Plukenet's* Figure doth not well express this Plant: He hath this twice in his *Almagestum*; who there queries whether it is not the *Coralloides tenuifolia obsequiosa minima* J. B. III. 798. 13. Fucus teretifolius spongiosus pilosissimus D. *Harrison, Raij Synop.* II. 4. III. 46. Fucus teres villis quaquaversum obductus *Ejusd. Synop.* II. 330. Muscus marinus hirsutus, flagellis longis ramosis subviridibus *Hist. Oxon.* III. 650. Tab. ix. *f.* 6. Green hairy Sea-Wrack. This is to be found sometimes among the Stones before the Cliff. Mr. *Bobart* hath figured this.

14. Fucus

14. Fucus arboreus polyfchides edulis *C. B. Prod.* 154. *Ejufd. Pin.* 364. *Raij Synop.* III. 46. *Hift. Oxon.* III. 647. *Tourn. Inft.* 567. Fucus arboreus polyfchides *Ejufd. Hift.* I. 75. Fucus poly-ichides *Johnf. Itin. Cant.* II. 3. Fucus Phafganoïdes & polyfchides *Ger. emac.* 1570. *Phyt. Brit.* 44. *Threlk. Synop. Hybern.* Fucus po-lyfchides *Mer. Pin.* 40. Fucus maxima polyfchides *Park.* 1292. Fucus latiffimo folio coriaceus polyfchides ex Harvich *Boc. Muf. di Fif.* 272. **Sea-girdle and Hangers.** This is to be found on this Shore. D. *Dillen.* thinks the *Fucus membranaceus polyphyllos major Doody* Synop. II. 329. to be either a Variety or a younger Plant of this. That in *Scotland*, where it is at fome time efculent, is fold together with the *Duls.*

15. Fucus Dealenfis pedicularis rubrifolio *Muf. Pet.* p. 39. Nᵒ. 405. *Raij. Hift.* XII. 111. *Ejufd. Synop.* III. 48. Alga cervi cornu divifura *J. B.* III. 797. **Sea-wreck with the Leaves of Red-rattle.** This was found at *Harwich* by my late friend Mr. *John Lufkin*, an ingenious Apothecary of *Colchefter*, as Mr. *Ray* in his Hiftory hath rightly obferved; and not at *Deal* in *Kent* as men-tioned in the *Synopfis* by error from Mr. *Petiver.*

16. Fucus anguftifolius veficulis longis filiquarum æmulis *Raij Synop.* II. 5. *Ejufd.* III. 48. *Ejufd. Hift.* I. 73. *Tourn. Inft.* 566. *Hift. Oxon.* III. 647. *Pluk. Almag.* 161. *Boerh. Ind.* A. 9. Fucus marinus quartus *Dod. Pemp.* 480. *Park. Theat.* 1293. *Johnf. Iter. Cant.* II. 3. quoad *Icon.* Quercus marina quarta *Ger. emac.* 1596. Fucus maritimus alter tuberculis pauciffimis *C. B. Pin.* 368. *Boerh. Ind.* A. 9. *Comm. Cat. Holl.* 37. Fucus cum filiquis longis minor D. *Dale, Raij Hift.* III. 11. **Narrow-leaved Wrack with long Pods.** This grows upon the Stones before the Cliff, and is not to be found, but when the Tide is out. The different Face that is to be obferved between young and old in this Plant, hath oc-cafioned the dividing it into two or three forts. *Dodonæus*'s Figure well reprefents this Plant while young.

17. Fucus maritimus nodofus *C. B. Pin.* 365. *Raij Synop.* III. 48. *Pluk. Almag.* 161. *Tourn. Inft.* 566. *Boerh. Ind.* A. 9. *Comm. Cat. Holland.* 37. Fucus five Alga marina anguftifolia veficulas ha-

bent

bens *Raij Hift.* I. 70. *Ejufd. Synop.* II. 3. Fucus marinus tertius Dodonæi, *Park. Theat.* 1293. Fucus marinus veficulis majoribus fingularibus per intervalla difpofitis *Hift. Oxon.* III. 647. Quercus marina tertia *Ger. emac.* 1568. 𝕷𝕠𝕟𝕘=𝕟𝕒𝕣𝕣𝕠𝕨=𝕝𝕖𝕒𝕧𝕖𝕕 𝕾𝕖𝕒=𝕨𝕣𝕒𝕔𝕜. This grows frequently on the Stones before the Cliff. In this the Leaves and Bladders are fometimes greater and fometimes lefs; and therefore to this may belong the *Fuci maritimi nodofi Species major Doody*, Raij Synop. II. 328.

18. Fucus fpongiofus nodofus *Johnf. Iter. Cant.* 3. *f.* 3. *Ejufd. Mer. Bot.* I. 36. *Ger. emac.* 1570. *Raij Hift.* I. 76. *Ejufd. Synop.* III. 49. *Phyt. Brit.* 44. *Mer. Pin.* 40. Spongia ramofa altera Anglica *Park. Theat.* 1304. 𝕾𝕖𝕒=𝕨𝕣𝕒𝕘𝕘𝕖𝕕 𝕾𝕥𝕒𝕗𝕗. This is often caft up on thefe Shores. Dr. *Dillen.* well obferves, that this ought not to be called *Spongiofus* but *Gelatinofus,* for it confifts of a clear gellied Subftance. It is but rarely found of the Figure which *Johnfon* gives it.

V. ALGA.

ALGA *Ger. emac.* 1560. *Raij Synop.* III. 52. Alga anguftifolia vitriariorum *Ejufd. Hift.* I. 75. *J. B.* III. 794. *C.B. Pin.* 364. *Tourn. Inft.* 569. *Comm. Cat. Holl.* 3. Alga marina *Lob. Icon.* 248. *Gotts. Flor. Pruff.* 7. Fucus marinus five Alga marina graminea *Park. Theat.* 1242. *Hift. Oxon.* III. 647. Potamogeiton gramineum marinum imo caule geniculatum *Pluk. Mant.* 155. 𝕲𝕣𝕒𝕗𝕤=𝕨𝕣𝕒𝕔𝕜. This is driven up by the Sea here and on all Shores. The Figure of this Plant in Authors is not good. It is fometimes found with fibrous Roots.

2. Alga marina graminea minor *Raij Hift.* III. 8. Fucus marinus feu Alga marina graminea *Ejufd. Synop.* II. 7. *Ejufd.* III. 52. Fucus marinus five Alga marina graminea D. *Dale, Hift. Oxon.* III. 647. Potamogeiton marinum in utriculis epiphyllofpermon minus *Raij Synop.* II. 346. *Ejufd.* III. 53. Potamogeiton gramineum marinum imo caule geniculatum minus *Pluk. Mant.* 155. 𝕿𝕙𝕖 𝕝𝕖𝕗𝕗𝕖𝕣 𝕲𝕣𝕒𝕗𝕤=𝕨𝕣𝕒𝕔𝕜.. This grows on this Shore. It is much lefs than the former, and hath narrow Leaves. II. MUSCI.

II. M u s c i.

I. *Conferva.*

1. COnferva marina capillacea longa, ramofiffima mollis *Raij* *Synop.* III. 59. Corallina viridis tenuiffima & ramofiffima mollis Doody *Ejufd. Synop.* II. 330. 𝔊𝔯𝔢𝔢𝔫 𝔥𝔞𝔦𝔯𝔭 𝔖𝔢𝔞-𝔚𝔢𝔢𝔡 : In the Ditches belonging to the Sea Marfhes on the Weft-fide of the Town.

2. Conferva marina trichoides feu Mufcus marinus virens tenuifolius *Pluk. Mant.* 53. *Ejufd. Phytog.* 182. *Raij Synop.* III. 60. 𝔉𝔦𝔫𝔢 𝔤𝔯𝔢𝔢𝔫 𝔥𝔞𝔦𝔯𝔭 𝔖𝔢𝔞-𝔚𝔢𝔢𝔡 : On the Stones before the Cliff when the Tide is out.

3. Conferva paluftris bombycina *Raij Synop.* III. 60. Alga bombycina *C. B. Prod.* 155. *Ejufd. Pin.* 363. Mufcus aquaticus bombycinus tenuiffimis filamentis *Gottf. Flor. Pruf.* 173. Tab. LV. 𝔖𝔦𝔩𝔨𝔢𝔫-𝔴𝔯𝔞𝔠𝔨. In the Marfh Ditches. Mr. *Bobart* refers to this the *Mufcus capillaceus multifidus niger* C. B. Pin. 363. but not rightly.

4. Conferva marina multifida niger. Mufcus capillaceus multifidus niger *C. B. Pin.* 363. Mufcus marinus capillaceus multifidus niger *Hift. Oxon.* III. 649. Mufcus marinus niger capillaceus ramofiffimus *Raij Synop.* II. 330. 𝔅𝔩𝔞𝔠𝔨 𝔖𝔢𝔞-𝔴𝔢𝔢𝔡. This grows on the Stones before the Cliff, and may be found when the Tide is out.

II. *Ulva.*

1. ULVA marina lactucæ fimilis *Raij Synop.* III. 62. Lichen marinus *Johnf. Mer. Bot.* 47. *Phyt. Brit.* 68. *Mer. Pin.* 72. *Ger.* 1377. *emac.* 1566. *Raij Hift.* I. 77. Lichen marinus platyphyllos *Pluk. Almag.* 216. Fucus lactucæ folio *Tourn. Inft.* 568. *Boerh. Ind.* A. 9. Fucus marinus, lactuca marina dictus *Park. Theat.* 1293. Lactuca marina five intybacea *J. B.* III. 801. Lactuca

tuca marina: Bryon Theophrafti, Diofcoridis & Plinii *Chab.* 572. Mufcus marinus lactucæ folio *C. B. Pin.* 364. *Hift. Oxon.* III. 645. *Bot. Monfp.* 180. **Oyſter-green.** This is found every where caſt up on this Shore.

2. Ulva marina tubulofa, inteſtinorum figuram referens *Raij Synop.* III. 62. Lichen marinus tubulofus in cellulas divifus *Ejufd. Synop.* II. 10. Lichen five lactuca marina tubulofa *Ejufd. Faſc. Stirp.* 14. Lichen longiſſimus fluitans tubulofus *Pluk. Almag.* 216. Lactuca marina tubulofa *Ejuſd. Hiſt.* I. 77. Fucus tubulofus inteſtinorum forma *Tourn. Inſt.* 568. Fucus five Lactuca marina tubulofa *Hiſt. Oxon.* III. 645. Fucus cavus *C. B. Pin.* 364. *J. B.* III. 803. **Sea-thitterling:** It is often found caſt by the Tide on this Shore. It is moſt commonly found not branched, but fometimes branched, to which variety may be referred *Fucus herbaceus cavus fluitans ramofus, calami anferini fere craſſitudine Doody* Raij Synop. II. 340.

III. HERBÆ FLORE IMPERFECTO SEU APETALO.

I. *Salicornia.*

SAlicornia geniculata annua *Tourn. Corol.* 51. Salicornia *Raij Synop.* III. 136. *Ger.* 429. *Boerh. Ind.* A. II. 94. Salicornia five Kali geniculatum *Ger. emac.* 535. *Park. Theat.* 280. *Mer. Pin.* 68. Kali geniculatum five Salicornia *J. B.* III. 704. *Chab.* 543. Kali majus geniculatum five Salicornia *Johnf. Mer. Bot.* I. 45. *Phyt. Brit.* 64. Kali geniculatum noſtras vulgatiſſimum minus non ramofum *Pluk. Almag.* 202. Kali geniculatum majus *Raij Hiſt.* I. 211. *Hiſt. Oxon.* II. 611. *Comm. Cat. Holl.* 59. Kali geniculatum majus annuum *C. B.* 289. **Jointed Glaſswort** or **Marſh-Samphire:** In the Marſhes plentifully. Some pickle this as they do *Samphire* to be uſed with Meat. It provokes Urine, and the *Menfes* powerfully, and expells the dead Child *J. B.* It is therefore no proper Sauce for Women with Child.

II. *Urtica.*

II. *Urtica.*

URtica pilulifera folio profundius Urticæ majoris in modum ferrato, femine magno Lini *Raij Synop.* III. 140. *Ejufd.* II. 54. *Pluk. Almag.* 393. Urtica Romana *Raij Hift.* I. 161. *Phyt. Brit.* 131. *Ger.* 570. *emac.* 706. *Park. Theat.* 440. Urtica Romana feu mas cum globulis *J. B.* III. 445. *Chab.* 478. Urtica urens pilulas ferens, prima Diofcoridis, femine Lini *C. B. Pin.* 232. *Tourn. Inft.* 531. *Boerh. Ind.* A. II. 105. Urtica pilulifera facie Urticæ vulgaris, femine Lini *Hift. Oxon.* III. 435. Urtica urens pilulas ferens *Bot. Monfp.* 281. **Roman Nettle**: On the North-fide of the Church near the Steeple, and a Meadow on the Weft-fide of the Gate, plentifully; I alfo faw it in the Street facing the Marfh. A Syrup made of it, is here ufed againft the Convulfive Cough in Children.

III. *Atriplex.*

1. ATriplex anguftifolia maritima dentata *Raij Hift.* I. 123. *Ejufd. Fafc. Stirp.* 2. *Synop.* II. 62. *Ejufd.* III. 152. *Tourn. Inft.* 505. Atriplex maritima anguftifolia *C. B. Prod.* 58. *Ejufd. Pin.* 120. Atriplex anguftifolia dentata *Pet. Herb. Brit.* Tab. VII. *f.* 4. **Narrow leaved indented Sea-Orach.**: On the Sea Bank on the Weft-fide of the Town. Mr. *Ray* queftions whether this is the *Atriplex anguftifolia laciniata minor* J. B. II. 972. *Hift. Oxon.* II. 607. Atriplex fylveftris anguftifolia laciniata minor *Chab.* 305. and that not without Reafon; there being no Defcription extant in any Author that I have yet feen, except that of Dr. *Morrifon* in the Place above quoted, where he makes it a true *Atriplex,* faying, that it differs from none of his foregoing, neither in Stalks, jagged Leaves, Flowers nor Seed-veffels, except in its glaucous Colour, like other Sea Plants: As to *J. Bauhine,* he hath given a Figure of his Plant, which well enough reprefents this, except in that he hath added the Flower of a *Chenopodium* or **Blite** to it;

2   but

but the Figure itself is only upon suppofition. As to his *synoni*
mous Names, the firft is *Atriplex Sylveftris* II. Tab. *Icon.* 427.
(which he faith, is not defcribed in that Author's Hiftory) this
C. Bauhine takes no Notice of in his *Pinax;* nor doth he of his
fecond, which is the *Atriplex Sylveftris* III. Cap. Epit. 243. as I
prefume (for he hath it not in his *Hortus)* the Figure of which is
the *Chenopodium foliis integris racemofum* Raij Synop. III. 155. and
hath adapted the Defcription of *Matthiolus* to his own Figure by
altering fome Words as may be feen by comparing it with that
of the Quarto *Edit.* p. 220. The laft *Synonim* mentioned by *J. B.*
and that with a doubt is the *Atriplex fimetaria minor* Thal. 8.
which is the *Atriplex Sylveftris minor* C. B. Phytopin. 195. *Atri-*
plex Sylveftris altera C. B. Pin. 119. As to the *Atriplex Sylveftris* II.
Tab. aforementioned, the Figure feems to belong to the *Blitum*
Quercus folio Pet. Herb. Brit. Tab. VIII. *f.* 1. *Blitum procumbens*
folio botryoide fubtus incano D. Rand Buddl. Hort. fic. Vol. IV. fol.
43. *Chenopodium angustifolium laciniatum minus* Tourn. Inft. 506.
Herb. Parif. 316. Vaill. Bot. Par. 35. and is the very fame with
that of the *Atriplex Sylveftris* II. C. B. Matth. 362. *Tournefort* and
Vaillant make *J. B.* plant *Synonimous* to their *Chenopodium* laft
mentioned.

2. Atriplex maritima noftras *Cat. Angl.* I. 35. II. 32. Atriplex
maritima folio deltoide *Pet. Herb. Brit.* Tab. VII. *f.* 2. **Small**
Sea-Orach on the Marfh Banks plentifully. Mr. *Ray* in his *Cat.*
Angl. refers to this *Atriplicis marinæ fpecies Valerandi* J. B. II.
974. *i. e. Atriplicis marinæ fpecies alia Valerandi* Chab. 306. but
not rightly; he himfelf making a Doubt of it in his *Hift.* I. 193.
10. as likewife in his firft and fecond Edition of his *Synopfis,* it
being a *Chenopodium.* This Plant of *J. Bauhine,* I obferved on
the Marfh Banks, and communicated it to Dr. *Sherard;* and therefore did diftinguifh it from, and not refer it to the **Small Sea-**
Orach above; as the feparating my Name from the Place where it
was found in the laft Edition of the *Synopfis,* p. 152. would lead
fome to think. In the two laft mentioned Books of Mr. *Ray,* he
added as a *Synonim* to his *Atriplex maritima noftras,* the *Atriplex*
maritima

maritima perennis folio deltoide feu triangulari minus incano Hift.
Oxon. II. 607. which if the Doctor did not miftake in, cannot be
our Plant, for I have never yet found it *perennial*; but its being annual
makes fome fufpect it to be no other than the *Atriplex Sylveftris
folio haftato feu deltoide* Synop. III. 151. only altered by growing on
fandy Banks near the Sea. Neither is our Plant at any time near fo
large as Dr. *Morrifon* defcribes his to be; nor doth *Commeline* in
his *Dutch* Catalogue mention any perennial *Atriplex*, the *Halimus*
excepted.

3. Atriplex maritima *J. B.* II. 974. *Chab.* 306. *Pluk. Almag.*
60. *Raij Hift.* I. 193. *Fafc. Stirp.* 3. *Synop.* III. 152. Atriplex maritima laciniata *C. B. Pin.* 120. *Tourn. Inft.* 505. *Boerh. Ind.* A. H. 89.
Comm. Cat. Holl. 12. *Bot. Monfp.* 35. *Hift. Oxon.* II. 607. Atriplex
marina *Ger.* 257. *emac.* 325. Atriplex marina repens *Park. Theat.*
758. *Johnf. Mer. Bot.* 22. *Phyt. Brit.* 13. **Jagged Sea-Orach:**
On the fandy Shore between the Town and the Cliff. *Parkinfon* following *Lobel*, calls this Plant repent, whereas its an annual
Plant, and is only procumbent. There is no good Figure of this
Plant in any Author, they expreffing the Seed as growing in Spikes
like a *Chenopodium*, whereas the Seeds grow among the Leaves;
each covered with two large *triangular Valves.*

4. Atriplex maritima fruticofa, Halimus & Portulaca marina
dicta anguftifolia *Raij Synop.* II. 63. III. 153. Atriplex maritima
anguftiffimo folio *Hift. Oxon.* II. 608. *Tourn. Inft.* 505. Atriplex
maritima Halimus dicta furrectior & vulgaris *Pluk. Almag.* 61.
Halimus feu Portulaca marina *C. B. Pin.* 120. *Raij Hift.* I. 195.
Cat. Angl. II. 154. *Comm. Cat. Holl.* 54. *Bot. Monfp.* 124. Halimus vulgaris five Portulaca marina *Ger. emac.* 523. *Johnf. Mer.
Bot.* I. 41. *Phyt. Brit.* 56. *Mer. Pin.* 60. Portulaca marina noftras
Park. Theat. 724. Portulaca marina fruticofa, quæ Halimus 2.
Clufii *J. B.* I. Part 2. p. 228 **Common Sea-Purflane:** On the
Marfh Banks plentifully. *J. Bauhine* as Mr. *Ray* well obferves,
confounds it with the *Halimus* 2. *Cluf. Hift.* 54. which Error he
might perhaps be led into by *Clufius* himfelf, who gives the Figure
of our Plant entitling the Figure *Halimus* II. when it fhould have
Z z   been

been *Halimus* III. as he hath put it in his Margin againſt the Deſcription.

IV. *Chenopodium.*

1. CHenopodium ſedi folio minimo, ſemine ſplendente annuum *Boer. Index* A. II. 91. Blitum Kali minus album dictum *Raij Synop.* II. 64. III. 156. Blitum marinum teretifolium, Kali minus album dictum *Ejuſd. Hiſt.* I. 198. Kali minus *Ger. emac.* 535. *Mer. Pin.* 68. Kali minus album *Park. Theat.* 279. Kali minus five Kali album *Johnſ. Mer. Bot.* I. 45. *Phyt. Brit.* 64. Kali minus album ſemine ſplendente *C. B. Pin.* 289. *Hiſt. Oxon.* II. 610. Kali minus five ſedum minus arboreſcens vermiculatum *J. B.* III. 703. quoad deſcript. **Sea-Blite, white Glaſswort :** In the Marſhes next the River plentifully. Some account it an excellent boiled Sallet. The Figure in *J. Bauhine* is of the *Salicornia.*

2. Chenopodium, ſedi folio minimo, fruteſcens perenne *Boerh. Ind.* A. II. 91. Blitum fruticoſum maritimum, Vermicularis Frutex dictum *Raij Synop.* III. 156. Kali Species ſeu Vermicularis marina arboreſcens *J. B.* III. 704. *Bot. Monſp.* 147. Kali fruticoſum minus flore minore *Hiſt. Oxon.* II. 611. Sedum minus fruticoſum *C. B. Pin.* 284. *Raij Hiſt.* I. 199. Vermicularis Frutex minor *Ger. emac.* 523. Vermicularis fruticoſa altera *Park. Theat.* 731. **Shrub Stone-crop** or **Blite.** On the Weſtern-end of the Marſh Bank plentifully. It flowers in *June,* and ripens its Seed in *Auguſt.*

V. *Beta.*

BETA ſylveſtris maritima *C. B. Pin.* 118. *Park. Theat.* 750. *Raij Hiſt.* I. 204. *Synop.* III. 157. *Tourn. Inſt.* 502. *Threlk. Synop. Hib.* Beta ſpontanea maritima communis viridis *Hiſt. Oxon.* II. 596. *Hort. Lugd. Bat.* 87. Beta ſylveſtris ſpontanea maritima *Johnſ. Iter. Cant.* II. 15. Beta communis viridis *Park. Parad.* 489. **Sea-Beet.** In the Sea Marſhes on the Weſt plentifully. Dr. *Johnſon* in his *Merc. Bot.* and *Gerard's Herbal,* as alſo Dr. *Merret*

in his *Pinax* and *Phyt. Brit.* make the *Beta alba* to be our 𝕾𝖊𝖆=
𝖂𝖊𝖊𝖙; but therein they are miftaken, the 𝕾𝖊𝖆=𝖂𝖊𝖊𝖙 being *perennial,* and the other *annual* as Mr. *Ray* well obferves. *Beta
communis five viridis* C. B. Pin. 118. is by *Magnol Hort. Monfp.* 32.
made a Variety only of the white, and fo it really ought to be,
if it is an annual, as *Herman* hath it in his *Hort. Lugd. Bat.* 87.
and I obferve, he faith the fame of the Sea-Beet. Mr. *Ray* thinks the
Common-green-Beet of *Bauhine* is the fame with the *Sea-Beet*; and
of the fame Opinion is *Morrifon* Hift. Oxon. and *Magnol* in his *Bot.
Monfp.* 37. which Plant of *C. B.* having only one *Synonim,* and
that the *Beta agreftis* Trag. 708. who calls it alfo *nigra,* and thus
defcribes it: *Quæ nigricantia profert folia, omnium eft vulgatiffima,
eam nos agreftem five erraticam Betam cenfemus.* This is the *Beta
nigra* C. B. Phytog. 190. *J. B.* II. 961. who cenfures *Tragus* for
making it a wild Plant; and defcribes it of a darker green than
the white, but it being fomething like, might be the Occafion of
the naming it white by fome as above. It is not always found
growing by the Sea, or in Salt Places for Mr. *Ja. Sherard* found it
plentifully near *Nottingham,* Dr. *Magnol* in the ways about *Montpelier,* and Dr. *Johnfon* between *Gillingham* and *Sheppy Ifle* in *Kent,
Iter. Cant.* Anno 1629. Edit. This is one of the Plants taken Notice of by Mr. *Tayler.* It is ufed as a boiled Sallet, and in Broths
and Soups.

N. B. It is not this Plant that Nature feems to play and fport
itfelf with: Nor was it Dr. *Johnfon* that affirmed it, as it is by
Dr. *Threlkeld* cited, but what is publifhed, was firft by Mr. *Gerard*
himfelf; and the Plant mentioned for the Production of fuch Ra-
rities is the *Beta rubra Romana* Ger. p. 251. though the fame is continued by Dr. *Johnfon.*

VI. *Parietaria.*

PArietaria Ger. 261. emac. 331. *J. B.* II. 976. *Chab.* 307. *Raij
Hift.* I. 206. *Synop.* III. 158. *Threlk. Synop. Hib. Mer. Pin.* 90.
Parietaria vulgaris *Park. Theat.* 437. *Johnf. Mer. Bot.* I. 57. *Phyt.*

Brit. 88. Parietaria Officinarum & Diofcoridis *C. B. Pin.* 121·
Hift. Oxon. II. 600. *Tourn. Inft.* 509. *Boerh. Ind.* A. II. 92. *Magnol.*
Bot. Monfp. 199. 𝔓𝔢𝔩𝔩𝔦𝔱𝔬𝔯𝔶 𝔬𝔣 𝔱𝔥𝔢 𝔚𝔞𝔩𝔩. Upon the Town Wall
near the King's-Yard. It is opening and cleanfing, good againft
the Stone, Gravel, and Stoppage of Urine, either taken by the
Mouth or in Clyfters; it eafeth Pains in the Belly. The Powder
taken either in Honey, Beer, or Poffet-drink, cures old Coughs and
Confumptions. *Magnol* commends the Herb bruifed and mixed
with Hog's Lard to help the Gout, if applied to the Feet. The
Figure in *Johnfon's Gerard* is good.

VII. *Kali.*

TRagus feu Tragum Matthioli *Park. Theat.* 1034. Tragon Mat-
thioli *Ger.* 960. *Johnf. Iter. Cant.* 1629. Tragon improbus
Ejufd. Iter. Cant. II. 3. Tragon Matthioli feu potius Tragus im-
probus Matthioli *Ger. emac.* 1117. Tragus five Tragum Matthioli
Park. Theat. 1034. Tragus fpinofus Matthioli feu Kali fpinofum
J. B. III. 706. Kali fpinofum cochleatum *C. B. Pin.* 289. *Raij*
Hift. I. 212. *Synop.* III. 159. *Threlk. Synop. Hib.* Kali fpinofum
Johnf. Mer. Bot. I. 45. *Phyt. Brit.* 64. *Mer. Pin.* 68. Kali fpinofum
foliis longioribus & anguftioribus *Tourn. Inft.* 247. *Boerh. Ind.* A. II.
93. Kali fpinofo affinis *C. B. Pin.* 289. Kali fpinofa affinis planta
Hift. Oxon. II. 611. Kali fpinofum longioribus & anguftis foliis
Pluk. Almag. 202. Kali fpinofum foliis craffioribus & brevioribus
Ejufd. Kali fpinofum, Tragus Difcoridis quibufdam *Chab.* 544.
𝔓𝔯𝔦𝔠𝔨𝔩𝔶-𝔊𝔩𝔞𝔰𝔴𝔬𝔯𝔱. On the fandy Shore going to the Cliff. It
is fomething Difficult to reconcile Authors about this Plant; for
C. Bauhine having as it feems to me made two of one, he hath
been therein followed by divers others. The beft way I think
to untie this Knot, will be to examine the Vouchers he produces
which I fhall do fo far as any of them are in my Cuftody. To
begin with his firft, *viz. Kali fpinofum cochleatum,* of which he
mentions only three Authors, 1. Drypis Theophrafti *Tab. Icon.*
144. which hath no Refemblance to our Plant. His fecond is

2   Kali

Kali five Alkali *Dod. Belg.* which not having, I confulted that Author's *Pemptades* (as the Tranflation of the other) p. 81. where Kali is defcribed and figured, both which defcribe our Plant as it appears in the Spring when young. His third and laft is only a dubious Plant in *Lugd.* 1486. which no way agrees with ours. I now come to his fecond *viz. Kali fpinofo affinis,* and here he is more numerous in his *Synonims. Firft,* Tragum *Matth.* 1035. *Ejufd.* 4to 698. the Figures of both feem taken from a Plant paft Perfection, *Cafter* 460. His Figure bad, *Lon.* 60. His Defcription taken from *Diofcorides,* but his Figure is of the Sedum minus flore albo, *Tab. Icon.* 702. His Figure from *Matthiolus. Secondly,* Tragus & Kali fecundum genus *Dod. gal.* which Book I have not; but in the *Englifh* Edition thereof by *Lyte,* p. 116. the Figure of *Kali* is from a young Plant. *Thirdly,* Tragon improbus Matth. *Adverf.* 355. Our Plant is defcribed, but not figured. *Fourthly,* Tragon Matthioli *Lob. Obf.* 463. *Lob. Icon.* 797. the Figure of both which is the fame as *Lyte's.* The *Lugd.* p. 1388. hath two Figures, but neither right, the Defcription I take to be of this Plant, *Ger.* 960. his Figure is copied from *Matthiolus.* I have now done with *C. Bauhine* and do believe, that both his Species of Tragum are but one ; and he himfelf was of that Opinion in his *Matthiolus,* p. 731. where having given *Matth.* Figure he adds, *Quæ pro Trago proponitur* Matthiolo, *Kali fpinofum dicitur, & in Figura folia minus recte expreffa; hæc quidem foliis eft aliquando longioribus (ut Figura* Lob. &c.) *aliquando brevioribus, latioribus & anguftioribus variat;* the Difference being occafioned chiefly by obferving the Plant in two States; nor do *J. Bauhine,* Mr. *Ray,* Dr. *Morrifon, Herman* or *Johnfon* divide them: and *Parkinfon* is of that Opinion in his Chapter of *Tragum Matthioli,* blaming *Bauhine* for dividing them, and gives *Lobel's* Figure for it; yet in his Chapter of *Kali* he gives another Plant with a different Figure taken from *Donatus,* p. 94. who calls it Tragon Diofcoridis quorundam, for the Kali fpinofum of *C.B.* making it different from his former becaufe this had Leaves, and the other not; and this Difference about the Leaves mentioned as above by *Bauhine* hath occafioned as I believe *Plukenet, Tournefort,*

fort and *Magnol* in his *Hortus* to divide it, making thereof two Plants.

IV. HERBÆ FLORE COMPOSITO, NATURA PLENO.

I. *Lactuca.*

LActuca fylveftris major odore Opii *Ger. emac.* 309. *Raij Hift.* I. 219. *Synop.* III. 161 Lactuca fylveftris lato folio, fucco virofo *J. B.* II. 1002. *Chab.* 314. Lactuca fylveftris odore virofo *C. B. Pin.* 123. *Tourn. Inft.* 473. *Elem. Bot.* 376. *Boerh. Ind* A. 81. Lactuca fylveftris Opii odore vehementi foporifero & virofo *Hift. Oxon.* III. 58. Lactuca Endiviæ foliis odore virofo *Park. Theat.* 813. **The greater ſtrong ſcented Wild=Lettuce.** On the Bank going from the Town to the Cliff.

V. HERBÆ FLORE DISCOIDE.

I. *Tuſſilago.*

TUffilago *Ger.* 666. *emac.* 811. *Raij Hift.* I. 259. *Synop.* III. 173. *J. B.* III. 563. *Chab.* 513. *Park. Theat.* 1220. *Hift. Oxon.* III. 130. Tuffilago vulgaris *C. B. Pin.* 197. *Tourn. Inft.* 487. *Boerh. Ind.* A. 101. Chamæluce Plinii *Bod. à Stapel. in Theoph. Hift.* 877. Bechion five Farfara *Dod.* 596. **Colts=foot.** On the Banks between the Town and the Cliff. This is fo common a Plant that I fhould not have here mentioned it, had it not been named by Mr. *Tayler:* A Syrup, Conferve, &c. are prepared of the Leaves or Flowers, which are good in Coughs, and other Difeafes of the Breaft and Lungs.

II. *After.*

The APPENDIX.

II. *After.*

ASTER maritimus cœruleus Tripolium dictus *Raij Synop.* III. 175. After maritimus purpureus Tripolium dictus *Ejuſd. Hiſt.* I. 170. *Boerh. Ind.* A. 95. *Pluk. Almag.* 56. After cœruleus glaber, littoreus pinguis Tripolium dictus *Hiſt. Oxon.* III. 121. After maritimus paluſtris, cœruleus, ſalicis folio *Tourn. Inſt.* 481. Tripolium majus *J. B.* 1064. Tripolium vulgare majus *Ger.* 333. *emac.* 413. Tripolium majus cœruleum *C. B. Pin.* 267. Tripolium majus ſive vulgare *Park. Theat.* 673. 𝕾𝖊𝖆-𝖋𝖙𝖆𝖗𝖙𝖜𝖔𝖗𝖙. In the Marſh Ditches plentifully.

VI. HERBÆ CORYMBIFERÆ.

Abſinthium.

1. ABſinthium marinum album *Ger.* 940. *emac.* 1099. *Boerh. Ind.* A. 126. *Raij Synop.* III. 188. Abſinthium maritimum album *Ejuſd. Hiſt.* I. 370. Abſinthium marinum ſive ſeriphium *Johnſ. Mer. Bot.* I. 16. *Phyt. Brit.* 1. Abſinthium ſeriphium Belgicum *J. B.* III. 178. *C. B. Pin.* 139. *Comm. Cat. Holl.* 1. *Tourn. Inſt.* 458. *Hiſt. Oxon.* III. 9. Abſinthium ſeriphium ſive marinum Anglicum *Park. Theat.* 102. Artemiſia maritima incana, lanuginoſa, Rutæ minoris folio *Vaill. Mem. Academ. Par.* Anno 1719. p. 377. 𝕰𝖓𝖌𝖑𝖎𝖘𝖍 𝕾𝖊𝖆-𝖜𝖔𝖗𝖒𝖜𝖔𝖔𝖉. On the Marſh Bank on the Weſtſide of the Town plentifully.

2. Abſinthium maritimum ſeriphio Belgico ſimile, latiore folio odoris grati D. *Plukenet, Raij Synop.* II. 94. III. 188. *Tourn. Inſt.* 458. Abſinthium maritimum ſeriphio Belgico ſimile latiore folio odoris grati *Threlk. Synop. Hib.* Artemiſia incana lanuginoſa, tenuiſſimè laciniata, ramis quaſi expanſis & quaſi pendulis, *Vaill. Mem. Acad. Par.* Anno 1719. p. 377. 𝕾𝖊𝖆-𝖜𝖔𝖗𝖒𝖜𝖔𝖔𝖉 𝖜𝖎𝖙𝖍 𝖋𝖕𝖗𝖊𝖆𝖉𝖎𝖓𝖌 𝕭𝖗𝖆𝖓𝖈𝖍𝖊𝖘. This grows likewiſe with the former of which Mr. *Ray* takes it for a Variety: It is different in that the Branches of this are hanging down, and much more ſpread about. 3. Ab-

3. Abſinthium ſeriphium tenuifolium marinum Narbonenſe *J. B.* III. 177. *Chab.* 373. *Raij Synop*. III. 189. Abſinthium ſeriphium Narbonenſe *Park. Theat.* 102. *Raij Hiſt.* I. 307. Abſinthium ſeriphium Gallicum *C. B. Pin.* 139. *Tourn. Inſt.* 458. *Magnol. Bot. Monſp.* 1. *Hiſt. Oxon.* III. 9. Abſinthium ſeriphium Gallicum five primum *C. B. Phytog.* 236. Abſinthium minus tenuifolium altè inciſis foliis, ſalſum Hiſpanicum *Bar. Obſ.* 1008. *Icon.* 460. Abſinthium ſeriphium vulgò dictum *Cam. Epit.* 458. Artemiſia maritima cinerea, Sophiæ foliis *Vaill. Mem. Acad. Par.* Anno 1719. 𝔉𝔯𝔢𝔫𝔠𝔥 𝔖𝔢𝔞=𝔴𝔬𝔯𝔪𝔴𝔬𝔬𝔡. It is to be found with the foregoing flowering in *Auguſt*. It is good to warm the Stomach, create an Appetite and kill Worms. *Matthiolus* commends it in the Dropſy and others in the Jaundice, and continual Fevers. *Magnol* thinks it warmer than the Common; a Conſerve thereof is more uſed, becauſe it is more grateful to the Stomach. *C. Bauhine* refers the *Abſinthium ſeriphium vulgo dictum* of *Camerarius* to this, and I think rightly; becauſe that Author ſaith it grows about *Marſeilles*; and *Magnol* that it grows upon all their Sea Coaſt; he never finding any other but this and the *Santonicum Gallicum* there; but *Tournefort* joins it to our firſt.

VII. HERBÆ SEMINE NUDO SOLITARIO.

I. *Limonium.*

Limonium *Ger.* 332. *emac.* 411. *Mer. Pin.* 72. *Chab.* 501. *Raij Hiſt.* I. 395. *Synop.* III. 201. Limonium majus vulgatius *Park. Theat.* 1234. *Threlk. Synop. Hib.* Limonium vulgare *Johnſ. Mer. Bot.* 47. *Phyt. Brit.* 68. Limonium maritimum majus *C. B. Pin.* 192. *Hiſt. Oxon.* III. 600. *Tourn. Inſt.* 341. *Boerh. Ind.* A. 76. Limonium majus multis; aliis Behen rubum *J. B.* III. 876. 𝔖𝔢𝔞= 𝔏𝔞𝔳𝔢𝔫𝔡𝔢𝔯. In the Marſh Ditches. It flowers in *July*. The Seed drank in Wine ſtops all Fluxes of the Belly.

II. *Statice.*

II. *Statice.*

STatice montana minor *Tourn. Inſt.* 341. *Raij Synop.* III. 203. Caryophyllus marinus minimus Lobelii *Ger.* 482. *emac.* 602. *Johnſ. Mer. Bot.* 27. *Phyt. Brit.* 23. *Mer. Pin.* 22. Caryophyllus marinus minimus, ſtatice montana minor *Threlk. Synop. Hib.* Caryophyllus montanus minor *C. B. Pin.* 211. *Raij Hiſt.*II. 1037. Caryophyllus flos aphyllocaulos vel Junceus minor *J. B.* III. 336. Caryophyllus flos junceus ſive aphyllocaulos minor *Chab.* 442. Limonium minimum vulgatius flore globoſo *Hiſt. Oxon.* III. 601. Scabioſa montana ſive maritima minima foliis anguſtiſſimis *Pluk. Almag.* 336. Scabioſa montana globoſo flore, gramineis foliis anguſtioribus *Hort. Lugd. Bat.* 540. Gramen marinus minus *Park. Theat.* 1279 Thrift, Sea-Julpflower. In the Marſhes plentifully. It is much uſed in Borders of Gardens.

VIII. HERBÆ UMBELLIFERÆ.

I. *Smyrnium.*

SMyrnium *Matth.* 773. *Ejuſd.* 4to 475. *Cam. Epit.* 530. *Raij Synop.* III. 208. *Tourn. Inſt.* 316. *Boerh. Ind.* A. 54. Smyrnium majus *Mor. Umb.* II. Smyrnium Dioſcoridis *Magnol. Bot. Monſp.* 242. Hippoſelinum *Ger.* 866. *emac.* 1019. *Raij Hiſt.* I. 437. *Phyt. Brit.* 59. *Mer. Pin.* 63. Hippoſelinum ſive Smyrnium vulgare *Park. Theat.* 930. *Hiſt. Oxon.* III. 277. Hippoſelinum Theophraſti, vel Smyrnium Dioſcoridis *C. B. Pin.* 154. Hippoſelinum, ſeu Smyrnium vulgare *Threlk. Synop. Hib.* Macerone quibuſdam Smyrnium ſemine magno nigro *J. B.* III. 126. Macerone *Chab.* 399. Alexanders. Upon the Bank leading from the Town to the Cliff, and in the Hedge on the Right-Hand of the Road from *Dovercourt.* Not only the tender Stalks and Leaves, but alſo the Roots ſliced, are uſed in Sallads both raw and boiled, as likewiſe in Broths and Soups; eſpecially in the Spring to cleanſe the Blood.

The

The Figure of this Plant in *Johnson* upon *Gerard,* is good; but that in the firſt Edition is of a *Sphondylium* or *Cow-Parſnep.* *J.* *Bauhine*'s Figure is only of ſome lower Leaves.

II. *Apium.*

APium paluſtre & officinarum *C. B. Pin.* 154. *Raij Hiſt. I.* 447. *Synop.* III. 214. *Tourn. Inſt.* 305. *Boerh. Ind. A.* 58. *Hiſt. Oxon.* III. 293. *Magnol. Bot. Monſp.* 25. Apium offic. five Paludapium *Johnſ. Mer. Bot.* I. 20. *Phyt. Brit.* 9. Apium paluſtre ſeu Paludapium *Threlk. Synop. Hib.* Apium vulgare five paluſtre *Park. Theat.* 926. *Mer. Pin.* 9. Apium vulgare ingratius *J. B.* III. 100. Apium paluſtre heloſelinum *Chab.* 196. Apium paluſtre Paludapium dictum *Mor. Umb.* 21. Eleoſelinum ſeu Paludapium *Ger.* 862. *emac.* 1014. **Smallage.** By the Marſh-Ditches. The Root of this Plant is one of the five opening Roots of the Shops; and the Seeds one of the four leſſer warm Seeds. The Roots provoke Urine and the Menſes, expel the Stone, and are uſeful in the Jaundice and Dropſies, by opening the Obſtructions of the Liver and Spleen; and diſcuſſeth Wind. The Seeds are accounted more efficacious than the Roots, but neither ſo convenient to be uſed by ſuch as are ſubject to the Epilepſy. It is believed to be warmer than the *Sallery,* the culture and blanching of which making it more mild, though otherwiſe but the ſame Plant; and is called *Selinum five Apium dulce* Park. Theat. 926. *Apium paluſtre Seleri dictum* Mor. Umb. 21. *Apium dulce Celeri Italorum* Hort. Reg. Par. 22. Tourn. Inſt. 305. Boerh. Ind. A. 58. Hort. Lugd. Bat. 50.

III. *Fœniculum.*

FOeniculum vulgare *Ger.* 877. *emac.* 1032. *Park. Theat.* 884. *Raij Hiſt.* I. 457. *Synop.* III. 217. Fœniculum vulgare minus acutiori & nigriori ſemine *J. B.* III. 2. *Tourn. Inſt.* 311. Fœniculum vulgare Italicum, ſemine oblongo, guſtu acuto *C. B. Pin.* 147. *Hiſt. Oxon.* III. 270. *Boerh. Ind.* A. 48. Fœniculum vulgare

2   Germanicum

Germanicum *Mor.Umb.* 3. Marathrum five Fœniculum *Chab.* 381. ꝼ**ennel or ꝼinckle.** On the Bank between the Town and the Cliff. The Roots are one of the five opening Roots of the Shops, and the Seeds of the four greater warm Seeds. The Roots provoke Urine, open Obſtructions of the Liver and Spleen, and are helpful in the Jaundice, and expel the Stone and Gravel. The Leaves increaſe Milk in Nurſes, the Seeds ſtrengthen the Stomach, diſcuſs Wind, and are good for Aſthmaticks, and quicken the Sight; ſo doth alſo the diſtilled water or Juice of the Leaves. The whole Plant uſed in Food prevents being over fat.

IV. *Eryngium*

ERyngium marinum *Ger.* 999. *emac.* 1162. *Park. Theat.* 986. *J. B.* III. 86. *Chab.* 355. *Raij Synop.* III. 222. *Ejuſd. Hiſt.* I. 384. *Mer. Pin.* 36. *Threlk. Synop. Hib.* Eryngium maritimum *C. B. Pin.* 386. *Hiſt. Oxon.* III. 165. *Tourn. Inſt.* 327. *Boerh. Ind.* A. 134. *Magnol. Bot. Monſp.* 92. Eryngium marinum vulgare *Johnſ. Mer. Bot.* I. 34. *Phyt. Brit.* 39. **Sea-Holly or Eryngo.** Upon the ſandy Shore between the Town and the Cliff. The candied Roots provoke Venery, and are eaten in a Morning to prevent the Plague and Contagion of the Air, it is helpful to conſumptive People (being a Reſtorative) in the Lues and Jaundice; but eſpecially in Obſtructions of the Urine, Liver, and Gall-bladder.

IX. HERBÆ FLORE MONOPETALO.

GLaux maritima *C. B. Pin.* 215. *Raij Synop.* III. 285. Glaux maritima minor *Park. Theat.* 1283. Glaux exigua maritima *J. B.* III. 373. *Ger.* 448. *emac.* 562. *Raij Hiſt.* II. 1102. *Hiſt. Oxon.* III. 607. *Tourn. Inſt.* 88. *Boerh. Ind.* A. 206. *Johnſ. Mer. Bot.* I. 38. *Phyt. Brit.* 48. *Mer. Pin.* 46. *Threlk. Synop. Hib.* **Sea-Milkwort or Black Saltwort.** In the Salt Marſhes; it flowers in *July*.

X. HERBÆ

X. Herbæ flore Tetrapetalo.

I. *Napus.*

NApus fylveſtris *J. B.* II. 843. *Chab.* 272. *C. B. Pin.* 95. *Hiſt.*
Oxon. II. 215. *Raij Hiſt.* I. 802. *Synop.* III. 295. *Tourn.*
Inſt. 229. *Boerh. Ind.* A. II. 13. Bunias ſeu Napus fylveſtris noſtras
Park. Theat. 865. *Threlk. Synop. Hib.* Bunias fylveſtris Lobelii *Ger.*
181. *emac.* Napus Bunias *Johnſ. Mer. Bot.* I. 52. *Phyt. Brit.* 79.
Bunias five Napus fylveſtris *Mer. Pin.* 17. 𝖂𝖎𝖑𝖉 𝕹𝖆𝖛𝖊𝖜. On
the Bank going from the Town to the Cliff. The Figure in
Parkinſon anſwers well unto this Plant, the upper Leaves upon
the Stalks almoſt incompaſſing them at their Baſe, ſo that they
much reſemble a perfoliate Plant; this is the Plant I ſhewed Mr.
Ray, who then took it for the *Braſſica perfoliata.* It is not the
Seeds of this, but of the *Napus dulcis* or *Napus* J. B. II. 842. that
are to be uſed in the Compoſition of *Venice Treacle.* Not only
Mr. *Ray*, but alſo *J. Bauhine, Dodone,* and *Gerard* do affirm, that
it is of the Seeds of this Plant that *Rape Oil* is made. *Parkinſon,*
that it is of the *Rapum fylveſtre, non bulboſum,* p. 862. but *Lyte*
in his *Dodone's Herbal,* p. 553. the Editor of *Tournefort's Herbal,*
p. 431. and Dr. *Threlkeld* do ſay, that the *Braſſica arvenſis* C. B.
Pin. 112. is the Plant from whoſe Seeds this Oil is expreſt: Now
whether *Dodone* was of this Opinion when he publiſhed his *Dutch
Herbal,* or whether it was added by *Cluſius* when he tranſlated it
into *French,* or put in by *Lyte* when he publiſhed it in *Engliſh,*
I cannot now diſcover, not having either the *Dutch* or *French*
Editions. The Editor of *Tournefort* aforeſaid, *p.* 431. complains
of the Confuſion of Botaniſts about this Plant, as if they did not
clearly underſtand what they write; this *Threlkeld* ſhould have ſet
to rights before he tranſcrib'd that Complaint; all the Plants which
occaſioned it growing in the Neighbourhood of *Dublin,* as he himſelf has publiſhed; which demonſtrates, that it is eaſier to find
Fault than to mend.

II. *Cochlearia.*

II. *Cochlearia.*

1. COchlearia folio finuato *C. B. Pin.* 110. *Raij Hiſt.* I. 823. *Synop.* III. 303. *Tourn. Inſt.* 215. *Boerh. Ind.* A. II. 10. *Threlk. Synop. Hib.* Cochlearia Britanica folio finuato *Hiſt. Oxon.* II. 308. *Pluk. Almag.* III. *Hort. Lugd. Bot.* Cochlearia vulgaris longo & finuato folio *Johnſ. Mer. Bot.* I. 29. *Phyt. Brit.* 29. Cochlearia vulgaris *Park Theat.* 285. *Mer. Pin.* 27. Cochlearia Britannica *Ger.* 324. *emac.* 401. **Engliſh** or **common Sea-Scurby-grafs.** In the Salt Marſhes. It flowereth in *May.* It is of great uſe in curing the Scurvy, a Diſtemper the *Engliſh* are very ſubject to, and from that Diſeaſe takes its Name; the volatile Parts it abounds with make unfit for Decoctions; thoſe therefore that boil it looſe its Vertues; its Infuſion in new Wort, Ale or Wine is beſt. In the Shops are to be had the Conſerve and Spirits of the *Garden* Sort, which abounds more with a volatile Salt than the *Sea-kind.* The Juice of the Herb with the bruiſed Leaves applied to the Face in Six Hours takes away Freckles; but it muſt be waſhed off by a Decoction of Bran, Dr. *Palmer* from *Herman's* Prelections; but it doth not ſay whether the *Garden* or *Sea* Sort is to be uſed. The Cochlearia vulgaris ſive Britannica vera Plinii, *Phyt. Brit.* Cochlearia longiori & finuato folio *Mer. Pin.* Cochlearia major Batavica erecta, folio oblongo, *Hort. Lugd. Bat. Boerh. Ind.* A. *Tourn. Inſt.* are perhaps only a Variety or Varieties of this.

2. Cochlearia marina folio anguloſo parvo D. *Lawſon, Raij Faſc. Stirp.* 4. *Synop.* III. 303. *Threlk. Synop. Hib.* Cochlearia Hederæ folio *Hiſt. Oxon.* II. 309. *Boerh. Ind.* A. II. 10. Cochlearia major Portlandica, Chelidonii minoris folio *Pluk. Almag.* III. Cochlearia Aremorica *Hort. R. Par.* 54. *Tourn. Inſt.* 215. Thlaſpi hederaceum *Ger. emac.* 271. *Park. Theat.* 848. *J. B.* II. 933. *Chab.* 293. *Phyt. Brit.* 120. *Mer. Pin.* 111. Thlaſpi repens Hederæ folio *C. B. Pin.* 108. **Small Sea-Scurby-Grafs with cornered Leaves.** This grows not that I know of at *Harwich*, but finding

finding it plentifully in a Journey thither *Anno* 1729. on a Bank by the Sea-fide about two Miles beyond *Manningtree* in *Effex* on the Right-Hand of the Road; I could not omit here inferting it. *C. Bauhine* terms it *repens* ; Plants being often fo call'd when they are only *procumbent.*

III. *Nafturtium.*

NAfturtium fylveftre Ofyridis folio *C. B. Pin.* 105. *Park. Theat.* 829. *Boerh. Ind.* A. II. 8. *Threlk. Synop. Hib. Raij Synop.* III. 303. Nafturtium fylveftre Ofyridis folio capfulis minimis *Hift. Oxon.* II. 301. Thlafpi minus *Ger.* 204. *emac.* 262. *Phyt. Brit.* 121. *Mer. Pin.* 118. Thlafpi anguftifolium Fuchfii Nafturtium fylveftre *J. B.* II. 914. Nafturtium fylveftre *Chab.* 289. Nafturtium fylveftre J. Bauhini *Raij Hift.* I. 825. 𝕭𝖔𝖜𝖕𝖊𝖗'𝖘 𝕸𝖚𝖋𝖋𝖆𝖗𝖉 or 𝕭𝖆𝖋𝖋𝖆𝖗𝖉 𝕮𝖗𝖊𝖋𝖘. On the Weft-fide near the River.

IV. *Lepidium.*

LEpidium latifolium *C. B. Pin.* 97. *Raij Hift.* I. 828. *Synop.* III. 304. *Tourn. Inft.* 216. Lepidium latifolium ferratum *Hift. Oxon.* II. 312. *Boerh. Ind.* A. II. 9. *Pluk. Almag.* 212. Lepidium Pauli *J. B.* II. 940. Lepidium Pauli & Plinii *Chab.* 296. Lepidium five Piperitis *Johnf. Mer. Bot.* II. 25. *Phyt. Brit.* 67. Lepidium Æginetæ *Mer. Pin.* 71. Piperitis feu Lepidium vulgare *Park. Theat.* 855. Raphanus fylveftris Officinarum, Lepidium Æginetæ Lobelio *Ger.* 187. *emac.* 240. 𝕯𝖎𝖙𝖙𝖆𝖓𝖉𝖊𝖗 𝕻𝖊𝖕𝖕𝖊𝖗𝖜𝖔𝖗𝖙. This I think I have feen in the Marfh here, but not noting it down, am not certain; but it being fo frequently found in Salt Marfhes, makes it probable. It is a hot Herb, being chewed provokes fpitting, and is ufeful in the Scrophula or King's-Evil. *Parkinfon* writes, that the Women at *Bury St. Edmond* in *Suffolk* boil it in Beer to help the Birth ; outwardly applied with Hog's-greafe, it eafeth the Gout and Hip-Gout.

V. *Cakile*

V. *Cakile*.

CAkile maritima ampliore folio *Tourn. Cor.* 49. Cakile feu Eruca marina latifolia *J. B.* II. 868. *Boerh. Ind.* II. 21. Crambe maritima foliis Erucæ latioribus fructu haftiformi *Tourn. Inft.* 212. Eruca maritima latifolia Italica filiqua haftæ cufpidi fimili *C. B. Pin.* 99 Eruca maritima Anglica, filiquâ torofâ fungofâ, rotundifoliis craffioribus latioribus *Hift. Oxon.* II. 231. Eruca 5. *Ger. Defc.* 191, 192. Eruca marina *emac.* 248. *Raij Hift.* I. 840. *Syn.* III. 307. *Johnf. Mer. Bot.* 34. *Phyt. Brit.* 38. *Mer. Pin.* 36. Eruca marina, Cakile quibufdam *Threlk. Synop. Hib.* Eruca marina Anglica *Park. Theat.* 820. Erucago maritima *Magnol. Hort. Monfp.* 74. Raphaniftrum filiquofum, monofpermum, maritimum, Anglicum, foliis craffioribus *Hort. Lugd. Bat.* 520. **Sea-Rocket.** On the fandy Shore between the Town and the Cliff. The diftilled Water hereof is much commended againft cholick and nephritick Pains *Magnol.* Some Authors confound this with the *Eruca maritima Italica*, others divide them: I was fhewn them both growing together in Mr. *James Sherard's* curious Garden at *Eltham*, being manifeftly different; and as a further Proof thereof, this hath but one Seed in a *Capfula*, the other two as *Herman* obferved.

VI. *Crambe*.

CRambe maritima Braffica folio *Tourn. Inft.* 211. *Boerh. Ind.* A. H. 1. *Raij Synop.* III. 307. Braffica maritima *Raij Hift.* I. 838. Braffica marina Anglica *Ger.* 248. *emac.* 315. *Mer. Pin.* 16. Braffica marina monofpermos *Johnf. Mer. Bot.* 24. *Phyt. Brit.* 16. *Park. Theat.* 270. Braffica maritima major, repens alba monofpermos *Hift. Oxon.* II. 209. Brafficæ affinis maritima monofpermos *Magnol. Hort. Monfp.* 34. An Braffica marina *Threlk. Synop. Hib?* **Sea-Colewort.** On the fandy Shore between the Town and the Cliff. This I take to be the *Sea-Colewort*, which Mr. *Tayler* reckons among his ufeful Herbs. *N. B.* This and all Herbs which
grow

grow near the Sea, require being boiled in two Waters to take away their Bitterneſs before they are fit to be eaten.

VII. *Glaucium.*

GLaucium flore luteo *Tourn. Inſt.* 254. *Boerh. Ind.* A. 305. Papaver corniculatum luteum *Park. Theat.* 261. *J. B.* III. 398. *Raij Hiſt.* I. 857. *Synop.* III. 309. *Threlk. Synop. Hib.* Papaver corniculatum *Chab.* 460. Papaver corniculatum flore luteo *Johnſ. Mer. Bot.* I. 56. *Phyt. Brit.* 87. Papaver corniculatum luteum κερατίτης Dioſcor, & Theoph. ſylveſtre, ceratites Plinio *C. B. Pin.* 171. *Hiſt. Oxon.* II. 273. Papaver cornutum flore luteo *Ger.* 294. *emac.* 367. 𝔜𝔢𝔩𝔩𝔬𝔴 𝔥𝔬𝔯𝔫𝔢𝔡-𝔓𝔬𝔭𝔭𝔶. On the ſandy Shores. In ſome Places this is called *Bruiſe-Root*, and it is uſed there for Bruiſes; the deleterious Qualities it hath, make it unſafe to be uſed inwardly; a remarkable Inſtance of which effect is related in the *Philoſophical Tranſactions* N°. 242. p. 263.

VIII. *Tithymalus.*

TIthymalus paralius *J. B.* III. 674. *Chab.* 534. *Ger.* 401. *emac.* 498. *Raij Hiſt.* I. 865. *Synop.* III. 312. *Johnſ. Mer. Bot.* I. 72. *Phyt. Brit.* 121. *Mer. Pin.* 118. Tithymalus paralius five maritimus *Park. Theat.* 184. *Threlk. Synop. Hib.* Tithymalus maritimus *C. B. Pin.* 291. *Hiſt. Oxon.* III. 337. *Tourn. Inſt.* 87. Tithymalus arboreſcens folio glauco, anguſto, acuto denſè congeſto *Boerh. Ind.* A. 256. 𝔖𝔢𝔞-𝔖𝔭𝔲𝔯𝔤𝔢. On the ſandy Shores between the Town and the Cliff.

IX. *Coronopus.*

1. COronopus maritima noſtras *J. B.* III. 511. *Chab.* 500. Coronopus maritima major *C. B. Pin.* 190. *Boerh. Ind.* A. II. 105. *Hiſt. Oxon.* III. 261. Plantago marina *Ger.* 343. *emac.* 423. *Raij Synop.* III. 315. *Hiſt.* I. 880. *Johnſ. Mer. Bot.* I. 59. *Phyt.*

2   *Brit.*

Brit. 95. *Mer. Pin.* 95. *Threlk. Synop. Hib.* Plantago marina vulgaris *Park. Theat.* 498. Plantago maritima major tenuifolia *Tourn. Inſt.* 127. **Sea-Plantain.** On the Sides of the Marſh Banks plentifully. It is thought to have the Vertues of *Plantain.*

2. Coronopus ſylveſtris hirſutior *C. B. Pin.* 190. Coronopus vulgaris ſive cornu cervinum *Park. Theat.* 502. *Raij Hiſt.* I. 879. *Threlk. Synop. Hib.* Coronopus, ſtella Herba, *&c. Chab.* 500. Cornu cervinum *Ger.* 340. *emac.* 427. *Mer. Pin.* 30. Cornu cervinum Offic. *Johnſ. Mer. Bot.* I. 30. *Phyt. Brit.* 31. Plantago foliis laciniatis Coronopus dicta *Raij Synop.* III. 315. **Buckhorn-Plantain.** On the ſandy Shores. It is generally believed, that the *Coronopus hortenſis* C. B. Pin. 190. Boerh. Ind. A. II. 101. Hiſt. Oxon. III. 261. *Plantago Coronopus dicta ſativa in Acetariis utilis,* Pluk. Almag. 298. differs from this only in Culture; that which grows by the Sea-ſide and in ſandy Grounds, being ſmaller and more hairy than that which is cultivated in Gardens. This is the **Star of the Earth,** mentioned in that famous Receipt for the Cure of Mad-Dogs, *Philoſ. Tranſ.* N°. 187. p. 298. and not that Sort of *Lychnis,* which is there ſuppoſed to be it. The Tribe of *Plantains* having that Vertue attributed to them.

XI. HERBÆ FLORE PAPILIONACEO.

I. *Trifolium.*

1. TRifolium flore viridi foliaceo elegans *Phyt. Brit.* 124. Trifolium album umbellâ ſiliquoſâ *Mer. Pin.* 120. *Pluk. Almag.* 375. **Trefoil with green Heads.** On the Sides of the Bank beyond the *High-Cliff* plentifully. I do not take this for a new or diſtinct Plant from the *Trifolium pratenſe album* C. B. Pin. 327. Raij Synop. III. 327. but only as a luxuriant Variety which I never before had ſeen proliferous as this is, but often have obſerved that Variety mentioned by Dr. *Merret;* where the *Siliquæ* or Pods ſtand on long Foot-ſtalks.

2. Trifolium

2. Trifolium ftellatum glabrum *Ger. emac.* 1208. *Pluk. Almag.* 376. *Phytog.* Tab. CXIII. *Johnf. Mer. Bot.* I. 74. *Phyt. Brit.* 125. *Mer. Pin.* 121. *Raij Synop.* III. 329. *Hift.* I. **Ccafel-headed Cre-foil.** Although I never found this myfelf about *Harwich,* yet I doubt not, but it is there to be found in its Seafon being an early Plant; Mr. *Ray* obferved it at *Holland,* a Parifh not far diftant. It feems to delight near Salt-Water : I have found it abundantly in the Parifh of *Hartey* in the *Ifle* of *Sheppey Kent.*

3. Lagopus perpufillus fupinus elegantiffimus Anglicus *Lob. Il-luftr.* 158. Lagopus perpufillus fupinus perelegans maritimus *Phyt. Brit.* 65. *Raij Synop.* III. 330. Tab. XIV. Fig. 2. **Small or Sea-Haresfoot Trefoil.** On the fandy Shore between the Town and the Cliff.

II. *Medica.*

1. **M** Edica echinata minima *J. B.* II. 386. *Chab.* 166. *Pluk. Almag.* 245. *Raij Hift.* I. 965. *Synop.* III. 333. *Tourn. Inft.* 410. *Hift. Par.* 492. *Vaill. Bot. Par.* 124. Medica fpinofa globofa *Mer. Pin.* 76. Medica echinata parva recta *Park. Theat.* 1115. Medica cochleata πολύκαρπ☉ annua capfula minima rotunda *Hift. Oxon.* II. 154. Trifolium echinatum arvenfe fructu minore *C. B. Pin.* 330. **The fmalleft Hedgehog-Trefoil.** On the fandy Shore.

2. Medica echinata glabra cum maculis nigricantibus *J. B.* II. 384. *Raij Hift.* I. 963. *Tourn. Inft.* 410. *Boerh. Ind.* A. II. 36. Medica cochleata minor πολύκαρπ☉ annua capfula majore alba, folio cordato macula fufca notato *Hift. Oxon.* II. 154. Medica Arabica Camerarii, five Trifolium cordatum *Park. Theat.* 1115. Trifolium cordatum *Ger.* 1021. *emac.* 1190. *Mer. Pin.* 120. Trifolium cochleatum folio cordato maculato *C. B. Pin.* 329. *Raij Synop.* III. 333. *Johnf. Mer. Bot.* I. 74. *Phyt. Brit.* 123. **Heart-Trefoil** or **Claver.** On the Bank between the Town and the Cliff abundantly.

XII. HERBÆ

XII. HERBÆ PENTAPETALÆ VASCULIFERÆ.

I. Lychnis.

LYchnis maritima repens *C. B. Pin.* 205. *Raij Hift.* II. 998. *Synop.* III. 337. *Threlk. Synop. Hib. Tourn. Inft.* 335. *Pluk. Almag.* 232. Lychnis marina repens alba *Park. Theat.* 638. Lychnis marina Anglica *Ger.* 382. *emac.* 469. *Johnf. Mer. Bot.* 48. *Phyt. Brit.* 70. *Mer. Pin.* 74. Lychnis marina Anglicana *J. B.* III. 357. *Chab.* 445. Lychnis perennis anguftifolia marina Anglica procumbens *Hift. Oxon.* II. 535. Lychnis fylveftris; quæ Been album vulgo Anglicana procumbens *Boerh. Ind* A. 212. **English Sea-Campion.** On the fandy Shore.

II. Spergula.

1. SPergula marina noftras *J. B.* III. 772. *Chab.* 549. *Raij Hift.* II. 1034. *Threlk. Synop. Hib.* Spergula marina *Johnf. Mer. Bot.* 171. *Phyt. Brit.* 118. Spergula marina Dalechampij *Ger. emac.* 1125. *Mer. Pin.* 116. Saginæ fpergula minor *Park. Theat.* 561. Alfine fpergulæ facie media *C. B. Pin.* 251. *Raij Synop.* III. 351. *Tourn. Inft.* 244. *Boerh. Ind.* A. 209. Alfine fpergula major maritima perennis flore violaceo *Hift. Oxon.* II. 551. **Sea-Spurry.** In the Salt Marfhes. There is another Species of this, which I do not remember to have feen here; which I firft obferved growing with the above mentioned *Anno* 1722. at *Ramfgate* in *Thanet Ifle Kent*; and have fince feen it in other Places, this Dr. *Dillen.* calls *Spergula maritima flore parvo cæruleo, femine vario* Cat. Giff. App. 30. *Raij Synop.* 351. where it is well diftinguifhed from others.

2. Alfine littoralis foliis Portulacæ *C. B. Pin.* 251. *Tourn. Inft.* 242. Alfine marina foliis Portulacæ *Got. Flor. Pruf.* 12. *Raij Synop.* III. 351. Alfine pelagica & littoralis *Boerh. Ind.* A. 209. Anthyllis maritima lentifolia *C. B. Pin.* 282. *Park. Theat.* 282. Anthyllis lentifolia Peplios effigie maritima *J. B.* III. 374. Anthyllis lenti-

folia

folia feu Alfine cruciata marina *Ger. emac.* 622. Rubiæ affinis maritima Portulacæ foliis *Hort. Lugd. Bat.* 530. Polygonum maritimum lentifolium *Hift. Oxon.* II. 594. **Sea-Chicklweed.** On the fandy Shores. It flowereth in *June.* The Figures in *Lobel, Gerard, J. Bauhine,* and *Morrifon* are not good; but *Gotfcheld* hath given a much better, *Icon.* Nº. 2.

XIII. HERBÆ GRAMINIFOLIÆ CULMIFERÆ.

I. *Gramen.*

1. **G** Ramen caninum maritimum fpicâ triticeâ noftras, *Raij Synop.* II. 247. III. 390. *Raij Hift.* II. 1256. *Sch. Agroft.* 6. *Ejufd. Meth. Gram.* 2. Gramen loliaceum maritimum, fpicâ magis albicante *Monti Prod.* 41. Gramen caninum marinum fpica filigineâ *Johnf. Mer. Bot.* I. 39. *Phyt. Brit.* 51. *Mer. Pin.* 50. Gramen loliaceum, radice repente maritimum *Tourn. Inft.* 516. Gramen caninum marinum *Ger. emac.* 25. Gramen caninum maritimum fpicatum *C. B. Pin.* 1. *Theat.* 14. *J. B.* II. 467. *Boerh. Inft.* A. II. 156. Gramen caninum maritimum fpicatum foliis anguftis longioribus *Hift. Oxon.* III. 178. **Sea Dog's-grafs.** On the fandy Banks. The Roots of this are of the fame Ufe as the common *Quick-grafs.* The Figure of this Grafs was firft given by *Lobel,* but is not good as Dr. *Johnfon* complains, yet divers Botanifts copy after him.

2. Gramen caninum maritimum fpicis rarioribus craffis *Pet. Concord. Gram.* p. 1. Nº. 17. Gramen loliaceum maritimum fupinum fpicâ craffiore *Tourn. Inft.* 516. **Thicker fpiked Sea Dog's-grafs.** On the fandy Shore at *Harwich,* where I found it about twenty Years ago, and then named it *Gramen caninum maritimum fpicis fpicam totalem componentibus craffioribus & rarioribus* about *Harwich,* Hort. noft. fic. Mr. *Buddle* found it in *Suffolk* near *Yarmouth.* The Figure which *Lobel* gives for the foregoing, would better anfwer this had the *Spike* been better expreft.

3 Gramen fecalinum paluftre & maritimum *Raij Synop.* III. 392. *Hift.* II. 1257. Gramen fecalinum maritimum glaucifolium, fpicis

ſpicis brevioribus *Hiſt. Oxon.* III. 179. Gramen ſpicatum, ſecalinum maritimum minus *Tourn. Inſt.* 518. *Sch. Agroſt.* 18. *Meth. Gram.* 4. *Mont. Prod.* 60. Gramen hordeaceum δίςιχον, majus ciliaribus glumis durius *Bar. Icon.* 112. *Obſ.* 1171. 𝔚𝔞𝔯𝔰𝔥 𝔉𝔦𝔢-𝔤𝔯𝔞𝔰𝔰. On the Marſh Bank plentifully.

4. Gramen ſparteum ſpicatum foliis mucronatis longioribus vel ſpica ſecalina *C. B. Pin.* 5. *Theat.* 67. *Raij Hiſt.* II. 1259. *Synop.* III. 393. *Hiſt. Oxon.* III. 180. Gramen ſpicatum ſecalinum maritimum maximum ſpica longiore *Tourn. Inſt.* 518. *Boerh. Ind.* A. II. 156. *Sch. Agroſt.* 138. *Mont. Prod.* 60. Gramen maritimum ſpicâ loliacea, foliis pungentibus noſtras *Pluk. Phytog.* Tab. xxxiii. *Almag.* 173. Spartum Anglicanum *Ger.* 38. *emac.* 42. *Mer. Pin.* 115. Spartum ſpica Secalina vel Spartum Anglicanum *Johnſ. Mer. Bot.* I. 71. *Phyt. Brit.* 117. Spartum marinum noſtras *Park.* 1198. Spartum ſpicatum pungens Oceanicum *J. B.* II. 511. 𝔈𝔫𝔤𝔩𝔦𝔰𝔥 𝔖𝔢𝔞-𝔐𝔞𝔱𝔴𝔢𝔢𝔡, or 𝔐𝔞𝔯𝔯𝔞𝔪, or 𝔥𝔢𝔩𝔪. On the ſandy Banks by the Sea.

5. Gramen parvum marinum ſpicâ loliaceâ *Ger. emac.* 30. *Johnſ. Iter. Cant.* II. 37. *Raij Hiſt.* 1263. *Synop.* III. 395. Gramen parvum marinum panicula loliacea *Johnſ. Mer. Bot.* 40. *Phyt. Brit.* 54. *Mer. Pin.* 56. Gramen loliaceum maritimum, ſpicis gracilibus articulatis recurvis *Hiſt. Oxon.* III. 182. Gramen loliaceum ſpicis articuloſis erectis *Tourn. Inſt.* 517. *Mont. Prod.* 43. *Sch. Meth. Gram.* 9. *Ejuſd. Agroſt.* 43. Gramen loliaceum junceum minus, *Bar. Icon.* 6. *Obſ.* 1163. Gramen parvum ſpicarum loco ferens caules erumpentibus alternatim acutis glumis veluti dentatos *Trium-fett. Obſ.* 64. Gramen pumilum arundinaceum Myuros erectum non ramoſum minimum *Boe. Muſ. di Piant.* 70. Tab. lix. Phœnix aceroſa aculeata *Park. Theat.* 1145. An Gramen loliaceum minus ſpica ſimplici *C. B. Prod.* 19. *Pin.* 9. *Theat.* 130. Phœnix maritima ſpica aculeata *Pet. Conc. Gram.* 28. 𝔇𝔴𝔞𝔯𝔣, or 𝔯𝔲𝔰𝔥 𝔖𝔢𝔞-𝔇𝔞𝔯𝔫𝔢𝔩-𝔊𝔯𝔞𝔰𝔰. On the Sea Bank. *Barreliere,* and *Scheuchzer* make two of this, *viz.* a greater and leſs, but *Monti* makes the Difference to be in the *Gluma;* which he ſaith in one is ſingle, and in the other double; perhaps this may be occaſioned
by

374 The APPENDIX.

by feeing the *Plant* in two Stations, one when in flower, the other out.

6. Gramen pumilum loliaceo fimile *Pet. Conc. Gram.* N°. 27. *Raij Synop.* III. 395. *Fafc. Stirp.* II. Gramen exile duriufculum maritimum *Ejufd.* Ib. *Hift.* II. 1287. *Sch.Agroft.* 272. Gramen exile duriufculum maritimum foliolis circumvolutis veluti junceis brevibus *Pluk. Almag.* 173. *Phytog.* Tab. xxxii. **Dwarf=Darnel=Grafs.** On the fandy Shores. To this is referred by *Scheuchzer* the *Gramen minimum* J. B. III. 464. which *Magnol* makes to be the *Gramen exile durius Lob.* which he faith, grows about *Montpelier*; (and it is to this laft mentioned Grafs, that *Scheuchzer* refers the firft *Synonim* I here give from Mr. *Ray*; fo that from the Doctor's, expunge Mr. *Ray's* Name, and add that of *J. Bauhine* to *Lobel's*) Alfo by *Monti Prod.* 44. The gramen Phalaroides, alterum minimum *Park. Theat.* 1165. which neither in Figure nor Defcription agrees with it; and I conclude the like by another Reference of *Monti's*, viz. the *Gramen pufillum, unicaule panicula loliacea* Boc. Muf. di Piant. 69. Tab. lvii. whofe Figure fomething refembles that of *Parkinfon's*; but his Defcription is fo fhort as not to be conclufive; I fhould rather refer them to *Lobel's* Plant.

7. Gramen typhinum maritimum minus *Raij Hift.* II. 1267. *Synop.* III. 398. *Sch. Agroft.* 63. *Meth. Gram.* 14. *Pet. Conc. Gram.* 56. Gramen typhinum maritimum longius radicatum *Bar. Icon.* 717. *Obf.* 1183. Gramen fpicatum maritimum minimum, fpicâ cylindraceâ *Tourn. Inft.* 520. Gramen Phalaroides maritimum minimum *Mont. Prod.* 48. **Sea Cat's=tail=Grafs.** On the fandy Shores. Dr. *Scheuchzer* writes, that the *Gramen fpicatum, typhoides, glumis longioribus acuminatis & pilofis* Ponted. Comp. Bot. 48. differs from this only in largenefs and tallnefs.

8. Gramen paniculatum maritimum vulgatiffimum *Raij Synop.* III. 409. *Hift.* II. 1286. *Fafc. Stirp.* 11. *Hift. Oxon.* III. 202. Gramen loliaceum maritimum foliis junceis, paniculis minus fparfis *Mont. Prod.* 37. An Gramen maritimum alterum, five fecundum elatius *Lob. Illuft.* **Common panicled Sea=Grafs.** In the Salt Marfhes.

9. Gramen

9. Gramen caninum marinum paniculatum *Raij Hiſt*. II. 1286. *Faſc. Stirp.* 9. *Synop.* III. 410. *Tourn. Inſt.* 522. *Hiſt. Oxon.* III. 202. Gramen maritimum paniculis aſperis, criſtatis *Boc. Muſ. di Piant.* 135. Tab. xcv. Gramen loliacea panicula ramoſa maritimum *Mont. Prod.* 37. *C. B. Prod.* 19. *Pin.* 9. *Theat.* 130. 𝖕𝖆𝖓𝖎𝖈𝖑𝖊𝖉 𝕾𝖊𝖆= 𝕯𝖔𝖌'𝖘=𝕲𝖗𝖆𝖘𝖘. On the ſandy Shores.

II. *Cyperoides.*

GRamini cyperoidi ex monte Ballon ſimile humilius in mari- timis & arenoſis naſcens *Raij Hiſt.* II. 1297. *Faſc. Stirp.* 10. *Synop.* III. 423. *Pluk. Almag.* 178. *Phytog.* Tab. xxxiv. Gramen cy- peroides medium ſpicis turgidis brevioribus maritimum *Hiſt. Oxon.* III. 244. 𝕷𝖔𝖜 𝕾𝖊𝖆=𝕮𝖞𝖕𝖗𝖚𝖘=𝕲𝖗𝖆𝖘𝖘 𝖜𝖎𝖙𝖍 𝖆 𝖈𝖔𝖒𝖕𝖔𝖚𝖓𝖉 𝕾𝖕𝖎𝖐𝖊. On the ſandy Shores.

III. *Cyperus.*

CYperus vulgatior panicula ſparſa *Tourn. Inſt.* 527. Cyperus lon- gus inodorus latifolius ſpicis tumidioribus minus ſparſis *Hiſt. Oxon.* III. 238. Cyperus panicula ſparſa, ſpicis longioribus tenuiori- bus teretibus compoſita *Sch. Agroſt.* 398. Gramen cyperoides pa- luſtre panicula ſparſa *Park. Theat.* 1266. *Raij Hiſt.* II. 1296. *Sy- nop.* III. 425. Gramen cyperoides panicula ſparſa majus *C. B. Pin.* 6. *Theat.* 86. Gramen cyperoides vulgatius aquaticum *J. B.* II. 495. Gramen aquaticum cyperoides vulgatius *Ger. emac.* 22. 𝖂𝖆𝖙𝖊𝖗 or 𝕸𝖆𝖗𝖘𝖍=𝕮𝖞𝖕𝖗𝖚𝖘=𝕲𝖗𝖆𝖘𝖘 𝖜𝖎𝖙𝖍 𝖆 𝖘𝖕𝖆𝖗𝖘𝖊𝖉 𝖕𝖆𝖓𝖎𝖈𝖑𝖊. In the Marſh Ditches. Dr. *Plukenet* makes this the ſame with the *Cyperus ro- tundus littoreus inodorus* Lob. Icon. 77. but this being narrower leaved, a larger Plant, and the Spikes more divided ſhews the Dif- ference: Whether *Lobel's* Plant is to be found here, I am not cer- tain, but do ſuſpect it may, having found it in the like Places.

IV. *Juncoides.*

IV. *Juncoides.*

JUncoides parvum maritimum pericarpiis rotundis. Juncus parvus cum pericarpiis rotundis *J. B.* II. 522. quoad icon. *Vaill. Bot. Par.* 109. Gramen junceum maritimum vel paluſtre cum pericarpiis rotundis *Raij Synop.* II. 276. Gramen junceum vulgare *Park. Theat.* 1189. Gramen juncoides Junci ſparſa panicula *Ejuſd.* 1190. Gramen aquaticum vulgare *Ejuſd.* 1269. Gramen junceum aquaticum *Ger.* 11. *emac.* 12. Gramen junceum polyſtachion *C. B. Pin.* 5. *Theat.* 75. Gramen junceum junci ſparſa panicula *Hiſt. Oxon.* III. 227. ſruſh-ſraſs with round Seed-veſſels. In the Salt Marſhes. The Figure in *J. Bauhine* agrees with this Plant, but not the Deſcription nor the ſynonimous Names he quotes. I do not find that Mr. *Ray* hath this Plant in his Hiſtory, that which he deſcribes *Tom.* II. p. 1307. N. 6. with it Synonims belong to his *Juncus montanus paluſtris*, p. 1303. N. 6. aforegoing, and all the Figures belong to that. The Figure in *J. Bauhine* aforementioned, as likewiſe the two firſt quoted of *Parkinſon's* belong to this our Plant: And the third Figure of that laſt Author in *Vaillant's* Judgement belongs to this, but the Panicles of that are too large; and more reſembling thoſe of the great Bull-Ruſh.

V. *Juncago.*

JUncago maritima. Gramen marinum ſpicatum *Lob. Icon.* 16. *Park. Theat.* 1178. *Johnſ. Mer. Bot.* 40. *Phyt. Brit.* 53. *Mer. Pin.* 55. Gramen aquaticum ſpicatum *Ger.* 12. *emac.* 13. Gramen ſpicatum alterum *C. B. Pin.* 6. *Theat.* 82. Gramen ſpicatum cum pericarpiis parvis rotundis *Hiſt. Oxon.* III. 228. *J. B.* 508. Hyacinthi parvi facie Gramen triglochin *Ejuſd.* Ib. Gramen loliaceum ſpicatum ſive Hyacinthi parvi facie Gramen triglochin *Hiſt. Oxon.* III. 228. Sea-ſpiked-ſraſs. In Salt Marſhes plentifully. Mr. *Ray* feeing this Plant when old, blames *J. Bauhine* for calling it *cum pericarpiis parvis*, ſince thoſe he found when near ripe, were longiſh

and ftriate. Not only *J. Bauhine*, but Mr. *Ray* likewife, and Mr.
Bobart defcribe this Plant twice, being led thereto by the different State in which they found it ; the Figure given by moft Botanifts
is taken from the Plant while the Fruit is round: but when it is
ripe, it refembles the Seeds of *Caraway* in Colour, Shape and Bignefs. Dr. *Dillenius* faith, that the Fruit confifts of fix Seeds, firmly fticking together.

Arbor Nucifera.

CAftanea *J. B. I.* 121. *Chab.* 58. *Ger.* 1253. *emac.* 1442. *Mer.*
Pin. 23. *Raij Hift.* II. 1382. *Synop.* III. 440. Caftanea vulgaris *Park. Theat.* 1400. *Johnf. Mer. Bot.* 27. *Phyt. Brit.* 24. Caftanea fylveftris quæ peculiariter Caftanea *C. B. Pin.* The Chest=
nut=Tree. Whether any of thefe Trees grow in this Parifh I
know not, but I have feen divers of them in *Stour-Wood* in the
next Parifh ; and therefore it is not improbable, but that there may
be fome in this. The Fruit of this is binding, efpecially the inner fkin violently ftopping all manner of Fluxes. The Fruit boiled
and mixt with Honey, is good againft Coughs taken fafting,
They are eaten raw and roafted ; but either way they are not
good for thofe who are fubject to the Cholick.

FASCICULUS TESTACEORUM.

OUR Author here mentions *Shells* among the delightful things
that are to be found on the Sands of this Shore, but doth
not name any ; what follow are fuch as I have found when on
this Shore. The *Authors* who have written of this Subject are
divers ; yet there are but few of them, who have made any confiderable Progrefs therein, and fome of them have rather confounded than dilucidated the Subject. There are fome of late, who
have attempted to range *Shells* into a *Method*, among whom I think
Dr. *Lifter* deferves the firft Place: That *Gentleman* after the Publication of thofe which he found in the Northern Parts of *England*,

was

was at great Charge in publishing the Figures of all the Shells that he could meet with. This came forth first under the Title of *Historia Conchyliorum*, which he afterwards changed into that of *Historia five Methodus Conchyliorum*, it consists of the Figures of the *Shells* and their Names, but without Descriptions or References; for which Reason it should have only the Title of *Methodus*. Since him, *Langius*, a *Switzer* hath published a Book which he entitles *Methodus nova & facilis Testacea marina*, in which he hath quoted few Authors besides *Bonannus* and *Rumphius*, having not a dozen References from *Lister*; those few he hath are out of the *English Shells*, but none from the *Methodus*, tho' that Book was published thirty seven Years before his. What was done by *Bonannus*, seems only the Collection of some Cabinet in which are few but the very fine, and many of those polished from their outward and natural Coverings; they are divided into three Classes.

I. MONOVALVIA NON TURBINATA.

I. *Patella.*

PAtella ex livido cinerea, striata *List. Hist. Animal Angl.* 195. Patella maculosa, fere striata, modo levior *Ejusd. Meth. Conch.* Lib. IV. Sect. 1. Nᵒ. 14. Patella striata, vertice mucronato integro *Lang. Meth. Test.* 3. Patella *Bellon. Aquat.* 393. *Gesn. Aquat.* 626. Lepas five Patella Bellonii *Johnf. Exang.* Tab. XVII. Lepas *Rondel. Test.* 3. Lepas major Rondeletii *Aldrov. Test.* 546. Patella Nᵒ. 4. *Bonan.* quoad Fig. **The Flither, Limpet** or **Papshell**. This is sometimes, but rarely flung up on these Shores. I have seen these Fish sticking in great Plenty to the Chalk Cliffs at *Dover*. There is a good Figure of this in Dr. *Lister's Books*; from which the Figure in *Bonannus* seems to be copied, but he calls it *Patella Indica major*, &c. pag. 90. whereby it should be different.

II. TUR-

II. Turbinata seu Cochleata.

I. Cochlea.

1. Cochlea rufefcens fafciis maculatis maxime ad imos orbes diftinċta *Lift. Hift. Animal Angl.* p. 163. Tab. III. N°. 10. Cochlea fublivida ore fufco, ad bafin cujufque orbis, velut funiculus depingitur *Ejufd. Meth. Conchyl.* Lib. IV. Sect. 5. N°. 19. Cochlea umbilicata foramine fpirarum rotundo lævis *Lang. Meth. Teft.* 55. Cochlea umbilicata *Bonan.* 141. N. 225. An umbilicus *Rond. de Teft.* 104. Umbilicus Rondeletii *Androv. de Teft.* 398. *Gefn. de Aquat.* 741. **Sea-ſnail.** I have feen it brought up in the Fiſhermen's Nets. Dr. *Lifter*'s Figure in his *Methodus Conchyliorum* is much better than that in his *Hiftoria Animalium Angliæ.* If *Rondeletius* intended this our **Sea-ſnail** by his *Umbilicus* the Figure is not good.

2. Cochlea fubclava ima parte volutæ primæ leviter finuata, quem finum alba linea circumfcribit *Lift. Meth. Conchyl.* Lib. IV. Sect. 5. N°. 13.

3. Cochlea parva N°. 8. *Lift. Meth. Conchyl.* Lib. IV. Sect. 5. This I did fee dragged out of the Sea by the Fiſhermen among the Sea Weeds *Anno* 1699. At which time I found the foregoing alfo, on the coaft of *Harwich* among other things, *Philof. Tranf.* N°. 249. p. 50.

4. Cochlea nigricans denfe ac leviter ftriata *Lift. Meth. Coch.* Lib. IV. Sect. 5. N. 43. Cochlea fufca fafciis crebris anguftifque prædita *Ejufd. Hift. Animal. Angl.* 162. **Coubins, Perewinckles, Pinpatches.** They are eaten in moft Sea-Port Towns; at *Rochefter*, and other Places, I have feen them to be fold by the Fiſh Women.

II. *Nerita.*

II. *Nerita.*

NErita vel citrina vel coloris caſtanei *Liſt. Meth. Conch.* Lib. IV. Sect. 6. N. 39. Nerita ex fuſco virideſcens, aut ex toto flaveſcens, modò pallidè, modò intenſè ad colorem mali aurantii maturi *Ejuſd. Hiſt. Animal. Angl.* 364. Nerita parva flaveſcens *Aldrov. de Teſt.* 363. Nerita Æliani *Rond. de Teſt.* 94. *Geſn. Aquat.* 626. Nerita cochlea *Belon. de Aquat.* 417 Nerita lævis *Lang. Meth. Teſt.* 53. 𝕾mall 𝕾ea-ſnail. Theſe are to be found plentifully ſticking to the Stones when the Tide is out: There are divers Colours. The *Nerita cinerea & vulgaris* Bonan. 141. N. 219. I take to be our ſort. Dr. *Liſter*'s Figure is good, but that of the other Authors not ſo.

III. *Trochus.*

1. TRochus pyramidalis variegatus limbo anguſto in ſummo quoque orbe circumdatus *Liſt. Meth. Conchyl.* Lib. IV. Sect. 8. N. 1. Trochus albidus maculis rubentibus diſtinctus ſex minimùm ſpirarum *Ejuſd. Hiſt. Animal. Angl.* 166. Tab. III. N. 14. Trochus ore anguſto & horizontaliter compreſſo ſtriatus *Lang. Meth. Teſt.* 8. Strombus Margaritæ nitore condecoratus *Bon.* 124. N. 93. 𝕮he pyramidal 𝕾ea-ſnail. On theſe Shores, but rarely; I have ſeen them more plentifully at *Orford*, in *Suffolk*, on the Beach where the *Fiſum maritimum* grows; together with N. 3. following. This is well figured by *Liſter*, and likewiſe by *Bonannus*; but doth not agree with either N. 89. nor 97. of the laſt mentioned Author which *Langius Meth. Teſt.* p. 48. joins under the Title of *Trochus ore anguſto & horizontaliter compreſſo ſtriatus.* What the Figure is in *Rumphius*, Tab. XXI. N. 12. which *Langius* makes likewiſe ſynonimous, I do not know, not having that Author by me. I ſuſpect that *Langius* makes uſe of the *Italian* Edition of *Bonannus*, becauſe his Pages do not agree with thoſe of the *Latin* Edition; though the Numbers of the Figures on the Plates, I take to be the ſame in both.　　　　　　　　　　　2. Trochus

2. Trochus pyramidalis parvus ruberrimus fafciis crebris exaſperatus *Liſt. Meth. Conchyl.* Lib. IV. Sect. 8. N. 2. **The ſmaller Top-ſnail.** This is more rare than the former.

3. Trochus parvus ſtriatus undatim ex fuſco denſe radiatus *Liſt. Meth. Conchyl.* Lib. IV. Sect. 8. N. 21. Trochus crebris ſtriis fuſcis, & tranſverſè & undatim diſpoſitis donatus *Ejuſd. Hiſt. Animal. Angl.* 166. Tab. iii. Fig. 15. **The ſmaller umbilicated Top-ſnail.** This is commonly caſt up by the Sea on theſe Shores. *Langius* in his *Meth. Teſt.* p. 48. joins this of *Liſter* with the *Strombus admodum productus decorticatus colore margaritifero tranſverſis ſulcis corrugatus* Bon. N. 92. under the Title of *Trochus ore anguſto & horizontaliter compreſſo ſtriatus, rugoſus, papilloſus & tuberoſus*; neither of which agrees with my ſhell : Dr. *Liſter*'s Figure is good.

4. Trochus planior undatim ex rubro latè radiatus *Liſt. Meth. Conchyl.* Lib. IV. Sect. 8. N. 22. Cochlea-trochiformis ſtriata & umbilicata *Lang. Meth. Teſt.* 51. Cochlea umbilicata *Bon.* 133. N. 170. Umbilicus varius *Rond. de Teſt.* 104. *Geſn. de Aquat.* 241. *Aldrov. de Teſt.* 398. **The umbilicated Top-ſnail.** This I find among my Shells collected at *Harwich.*

IV. *Buccina.*

1. BUccinum album læve, maximum, ſeptem minimùm ſpirarum *Liſt. Hiſt. Animal. Angl.* 155. Tab. iii. N. 1. Buccinum roſtratum, majus, craſſum, orbibus paululum pulvinatis *Ejuſd. Meth. Conch.* Lib. IV. Sect. 14. N. 4. Buccinum majus canaliculatum roſtratum ore ſimplici ſtriatum *Lang. Meth. Teſt.* 36. item, Buccinum majus canaliculatum roſtratum ore labioſo læve *Ejuſd.* Ib. **The greater ſmooth Whelk.** This is fiſhed up in the Sea before this Place, and likewiſe the dead Shell found upon the Shore. Dr. *Liſter* hath given good Figures of this and the following.

2. Buccinum anguſtius tenuiter admodum ſtriatum, octo minimùm ſpirarum *Liſt. Hiſt. Animal. Angl.* 157. N. 4. Buccinum roſtratum gracilius *Ejuſd. Meth. Conchyl.* Lib. IV. Sect. 14. N. 5.

Buccinum

Buccinum majus canaliculatum roftratum ore fimplici læve *Lang.*
Meth. Teft. 36. Turbo feptem fpirarum anfraſtibus finitus ore valde
longo lævis ubique, *Bonan.* 119. N. 53. The leffer long and
fmooth Whelk. Dr. *Lifter* found this near *Scarborough* in *Yorkfhire*; I on the Shores near this Town.

3. Buccinum craffum rufefcens ftriatum & undatum *Lift. Hift.
Animal. Angl.* 156. Tab. 111. N. 2. Buccinum brevi-roftrum tenuiter ftriatum, pluribus undatis finubus diftinctum *Ejufd. Meth.
Conchyl.* Lib. IV. Sect. 15. N. 14. Buccinum majus canaliculatum,
fulcatum ftriatum & criftatum *Lang. Meth. Teft.* 37. Buccina intrinfecus livida, extrinfecus terrea *Bonan.* 136. N. 189. Rough-
Whelk. This is not fo common as the other. *Langius* refers this
to N. 191. of *Bonannus*, whereas it is N. 189. of that Author
as appears by comparing the Figures of both, which are to be feen
in them both, and are good. There is a Diffection of this Animal
publifhed by Dr. *Lifter* in his *Exercitatio Anatomica altera*, p. 68.

4. Buccinum brevi roftro magnum tenue leviter ftriatum *Lift.
Meth. Conchyl.* Lib. IV. Sect. 15. N. 15. Buccinum tenue, læve,
ftriatum & undatum *Ejufd. Hift. Animal. Angl.* p. 157. Tab. 111.
N. 3. Buccinum majus canaliculatum fulcatum & ftriatum *Lang.
Meth. Teft.* 37. Buccina fenis orbibus finita, minutiffimis filis tranf-
verfe ductis afpera *Bonan.* 137. N. 190. The moft common Whelk.
This is not only frequently caught here, but likewife to be found
on thefe Shores.

5. Buccinum minus albidum, afperum; intra quinas fpiras finitum *Lift. Hift. Animal. Angl.* 158. Tab. 111. Fig. 5. Buccinum
brevi roftro album denticulo unico ad imam columellam *Ejufd.
Meth. Conchyl.* Lib. IV. Sect. 15. N. 19. Buccinum parvum fulcatum & canaliculatum ftriatum & rugofum ore labiofo *Lang.
Meth. Teft.* 35. Turbo N. 52. *Bonan.* 119. Purpura Anglicana
major. The bigger English purple Fifh. On thefe Shores. This
is the Fifh which yields the *purple Colour*, mentioned in the *Philofophical Tranfactions*, N. 178. The Account whereof mentioned,
p. 86. aforegoing ought as belonging to this Place to be referred
hither. The Figure of this in Dr. *Lifter* is good. *Langius* confounds

founds this with the following making them but one. Dr. *Lifter* hath given a *Differtion* of this *Animal*, as likewife of the following in his *Exercitatio Anatomica altera*, p. 85.

6. Buccinum minus, ex albo fubviride ore dentato, eoque ex flavo leviter rufefcente *Lift. Hift. Animal. Angl.* 159. Tab. III. N. 6. Buccinum brevi roftro fupra modum craffum ventriofius, labro denticulato *Ejufd. Meth. Conchyl.* Lib. IV. Sect. 15. N. 18. 𝔠𝔥𝔢 𝔩𝔢𝔰𝔰𝔢𝔯 𝔈𝔫𝔤𝔩𝔦𝔰𝔥 𝔭𝔲𝔯𝔭𝔩𝔢 𝔣𝔦𝔰𝔥. This is likewife to be found with the foregoing. The Figure given by Dr. *Lifter* is good.

7. Buccinum brevi-roftrum cancellatum, denfe finuofum labro dentato *Lift. Meth. Conchyl.* Lib. IV. Sect. 15. N. 21. 𝔖𝔪𝔞𝔩𝔩 𝔠𝔥𝔢𝔮𝔲𝔢𝔯𝔢𝔡 𝔚𝔥𝔢𝔩𝔨. On the the Sea Shores.

III. Bivalvia.

I. *Pecten.*

PEcten fubruffus, ftriis viginti quatuor ad minimum donatus *Lift. Meth. Conchyl.* Lib. III. Sect. 1. Pecten ftriis valde minutis fignatus *Bonan.* Claff. 11. N. 5. Pectunculus vulgaris *Lang. Meth. Teft.* 62. Pectunculus *Rond. Teft.* 18. Pectunculus Rondeletii *Gefn. Aquat.* 691. 𝔖𝔪𝔞𝔩𝔩 𝔖𝔠𝔞𝔩𝔩𝔬𝔭. This is flung up by the Tide on this Shore, but more plentifully on the other Side on the Beach by *Landguard-Fort.*

II. *Oftrea.*

OStrea major fulcata inequaliter, utrinque ad cardinem denticulata *Lift. Meth. Conchyl.* Lib. III. Sect. 2. N. 30. Oftreum vulgare maximum, intus argenteo quodam fplendore albefcens *Ejufd. Hift. Animal. Angl.* 176. Tab. IV. N. 26. Oftrea pelagica *Rond.* 37. *Aldrov. de Teft.* 481. *Gefn. de Aquat.* 645. An oftreum roftratum fine ftriis five læve *Lang. Meth. Teft.* 81? 𝔠𝔥𝔢 𝔒𝔭𝔰𝔱𝔢𝔯. They are caught in the Sea before this Haven, but in no plenty. The Figure given by *Rondeletius* is copied by *Aldrovand* and *Gefner*, but

is not good ; thefe two laft Authors have added a better Figure,
but the beft is given by Dr. *Lifter* in his two aforementioned
Books.   The faid Doctor hath likewife given the *Anatomy* of this
Shell-fifh Hift. Animal. Angl. p. 176. as he hath taken it from
Willis de Anima Brutorum, p. 14. Edit. 1676. the fame he inferted into his *Exercitatio Anatomica tertia*, p. 62. and added Obfervations of his own, p. 68. he hath likewife publifhed in his laft
cited Book, and in his *Meth. Conchyl.* two Plates of the Diffection
of an **Opfter** both taken from the aforecited Book of Dr. *Willis.*
Concerning the Generation of **Opfters**, &c. Dr. *Lifter* hath publifhed fomething in *Latin* for the ufe of the learned in his aforecited *Hift. Animal. Angl.* p. 179.   But for the Benefit of the *Englifh* Reader, I fhall here tranfcribe it from the *Hiftory of the Royal
Society*, p. 307.

   In May *the* Oyfters *caft their* Spawn *(which the* Dredgers *call
their* Spat*) it is like to a Drop of a Candle, and about the Bignefs
of an half penny* [i. e. Silver not Copper] *The* Spat *cleaves to Stones,
old* Oyfter-Shells, *Pieces of Wood, and fuch like things at the Bottom
of the Sea, which they call* Clutch. *'Tis probably conjectured, that
the* Spat *in twenty four Hours begins to have a* Shell.   *In the Month
of* May *the* Dredgers *(by the Law of the* Admiralty Court*) have
liberty to catch all manner of* Oyfters, *of what fize foever.   When
they have taken them with a knife, they gently raife the fmall Brood
from the* Clutch, *and then they throw the* Clutch, *in again, to preferve the Ground for the Future, unlefs they be fo newly* Spat, *that
they cannot be fafely fevered from the* Clutch ; *in that Cafe they are
permitted to take the Stone or Shell,* &c. *that the* Spat *is upon, one
Shell having many times twenty* Spats.   *After the Month of* May
'tis Felony to carry away the Clutch, *and punifhable to take any other*
Oyfters, *unlefs it be thofe of fize,* i. e. *about the Bignefs of a half
Crown Piece, or when the two* Shells *being fhut, a fair Shilling will
rattle between them.   The Places where thefe* Oyfters *are chiefly
caught, are called the* Pont Burham, Malden, *and* Coln Waters
[In Effex.] *This Brood and other* Oyfters *they carry to* Creeks *of
the Sea at* Brickelfea, Merfey, Langno Fringrego, Wivenho, Tolefbury

lefbury and Salt-coafe [all in *Effex*] *and there throw them into the*
Channel, *which they call their* Beds *or* Layers, *where they grow
and faften, and in two or three Years the fmalleft Brood will be* Oyfters *of the fize aforefaid.* The Oyfters *when the Tide comes in lie
with their hollow Shell downwards, and when it goes out, they turn
on the other Side; they remove not from their Place unlefs in cold
weather, to cover themfelves in the* Cliffs. The Oyfters *are fick after they
have* Spat; *but in* June *and* July *they begin to mend, and in* Auguft
they are perfectly well: The Male-Oyfter *is* 𝕭lack-fick, *having a
black Subftance in the Fin*; *the* Female 𝕮hite-fick *(as they term it)
having a milky Subftance in the Fin.* This Obfervation of the Fifhermen, Dr. *Lifter* rejects, the white Sicknefs, being by him accounted the *milky Sperm* of the Male, and the other the *Ova* of the
Female newly effufed in the *Branchiæ.* The Doctor further obferves, that the Eggs of *Oyfters* upon their Ejection, are perfect
and foon form themfelves into *Congeries* fomething like *Hony-combs.*
This he hath figured *Tab.* vii. *Fig.* 6. and he likewife thinks it
plain both from the time which they carry thefe eggs within them,
and alfo from the fmallnefs of each Congeries, that tho' the Oyfters may perhaps emit many Eggs together, yet it may be at feveral times. After which each fingle *Ovum* or *Spat,* grows to the
Bignefs of a *Lentil* before they difunite. What the Doctor hath
here written, I am fomething in doubt of, becaufe thofe *Balls* or
Hony-combs are to be found with Animals in them at all Seafons
of the Year, and of the fame Bignefs and Subftance as to their outward Covering, &c. And even this feventeenth of *February* 1729.
I found them thus among *Oyfters:* Whereas, had they been the
Ova or *Spat* of *Oyfters,* they muft have been much more altered
from the precedent *May*; in which it is generally believed, that
Oyfters breed. *J. Bauhine* takes notice of thefe, and names them
Veficariæ marinæ, Tom. III. p. 818. *There are great Penalties by
the* Admiralty-Court, *laid upon thofe that Fifh out of thofe Grounds,
which the* Court *appoints, or that deftroy the* Clutch, *or that take* Oyfters *that are not of fize, or that do not tread under their Feet, or
throw upon the Shore, a Fifh which they call a* Five-finger, *refembling*

a Spur-rowel; *becaufe that* Fifh *gets into the* Oyfters *when they gape, and fucks them out.* The Reafon why fuch a Penalty is fet upon any that fhall deftroy the Clutch, is becaufe they find, that if that be taken away the Oufe will increafe, and then Mufcles and Cockles will breed there, and deftroy the Oyfters; they having not whereon to ftick their *Spat.*

Thofe Oyfters *which they would have green, they put into* Pits *about three Foot deep in the Salt* Marfhes, *which are overflowed only at Spring Tides, to which they have Sluices, and let out the Salt Water untill it is about a Foot and half deep.* Thefe Pits *from fome Quality in the Soil co-operating with the Heat of the* Sun, *will become green, and communicate their Colour to the* Oyfters *that are put into them in four or five Days, though they commonly let them continue there fix Weeks or two Months; in which time they will be of a dark Green.* To prove *that the* Sun *operates in the greening,* Tolefbury Pits *will green only in Summer, but that the Earth hath greater Power,* Brickel-fea Pits *green both Winter and Summer: And for a further Proof, a Pit within a Foot of a greening Pit* will *not green; and thofe that did green very well, will in time loofe their Quality.* Oyfters *are Salt in the* Pits, *falter in the* Layers, *but falteft at* Sea.

Feverfham in *Kent* is a Town of great Trade for *Oyfters,* which they fetch out of the Weft-country, and fatten them on their Layers, many of which are on the *fartheft* Shore of *Shippey* Ifland: Thefe the *Dutch* come every Year to buy, whofe buying them up is given as a Reafon of their Scarcity, and confequently of the dearnefs of them.

III. *Pectunculus fafciatus.*

PECtunculus fubfufcus tenuiter admodum fafciatus *Lift. Meth. Conchyl.* Lib. III. Part. II. 129. **The Clam.** This is to be found on this Shore. Dr. *Lifter* hath given the Diffection of a Sort of *Tellina* by the Name of *Tellina fafciata, compactile radiata, intùs ex parte fubaurea, interdum fubpurpurea, Hiftoriæ five Synopfeos noftræ Methodicæ Conchyliorum* Exer. Anat. tert. p. 25. Tab. III. Fig. 4. This, he faith, he found among *Cockles* brought out of *Effex,* but whether the fame with mine or not, I cannot be pofitive.

IV. *Tellina.*

IV. *Tellina.*

1. COncha parva fubrotunda ex parte interna rubens *Lift. Hift. Animal. Angl.* 175. N. 25. Tellina rofeo colore zona candida divifo *Bon. Claff.* II. 44. Tellina lævis intùs & extrà rubra ad latus finuofa *Lift. Meth. Conchyl.* Lib. III. Part. II. N. 251.
2. Tellina intùs ex viola purpurafcens in ambitu ferrata *Lift. Hift. Animal. Angl.* p. 190. Tab. v. N. 35. Tellina ex rufo maculata fafciis exafperata *Ejufd. Meth. Conchyl.* Lib. III. Part. II. N. 241. Both thefe are to be found on this Shore.

V. *Chama.*

CHama fufca ftriis tenuiffimis donata *Lift. Meth. Conchyl.* Lib. III. Part. II. N. 271. *Chama* 𝖕𝖚𝖗𝖗𝖘 *Anglicè* dicta *Ejufd. Exerc. Anat.* 3. p. 27. Concha quafi rhomboides, in medio cardine utrinque circiter tribus exiguis denticulis donata *Ejufd. Hift. Animal. Angl.* p. 171. Tab. iv. N. 20. 𝖕𝖚𝖗𝖗𝖘. Thefe are caught by the Fifhermen before the Mouth of the Haven, and found caft on thefe Shores. Dr. *Lifter* hath given a Diffection of thefe in his *Exercitatio Anatomica tertia* p. 27. Tab. iii. in which Fig. 5. is the live Animal; Fig. 6. the infide of the Shell; and Fig. 7. the feveral Parts of the Animal delineated; Fig. 8. the Heart.

VI. *Pectunculi Striati.*

1. PEctunculus vulgaris, albidus, rotundus, circiter viginti fex ftriis majufculis, at planioribus donatus *Lift. Hift. Animal. Angl.* p. 189. Tab. iv. N. 34. Pectunculus capite minore, rotundiore & magis equali margine *Ejufd. Meth. Conchyl.* Lib. III. Part. II. N. 171. Pectunculus ftriatus vulgaris, 𝕮𝖔𝖈𝖐𝖑𝖊𝖘 *Anglicè* dictus *Ejufd. Exer. Anat. tert.* p. 20. Tab. iii. Fig. 1. Pectunculus *Belon. Aquat.* 410. Concha ftriata prima *Rond. Teft.* p. 21. Concha ftriata prior Rondeletii *Aldrov. Teft.* 448. 𝕮𝖍𝖊 𝕮𝖔𝖈𝖐𝖑𝖊. This
is

is an Inhabitant of thefe Seas, and the dead Shell often found upon the Shore. Thefe are plentifully fold at *London*, being brought chiefly from *Suffex*, perhaps the beft come from *Selfea*, from whence they are frequently called **Selfea-Cockles**. Dr. *Lifter* hath given the anatomical Diffection of this Animal in his *Exercit. Anat. tert.* p. 20. Tab. III. where Fig 1. is the Animal in its *Shell* with its two *Tracheæ*; Fig. 2. the fame taken out of the *Shell*, that the feveral Parts may appear; Fig. 3. a chryftalline ftyle.

2. Pectunculus exiguus fubfufcus *Lift. Meth. Conchyl.* Lib. III. Part. II. N. 154. An concha ftriata umbone roftrata vinofo colore terreis maculis diftincto *Bon.* III. N. 94. This is much larger than any I have feen here, and is much fpotted which mine is not. **The fmaller triangular Cockle.** I have feen fome few of thefe on this Shore.

VII. *Mufculus.*

MUfculus ex cœruleo niger *Lift. Hift. Animal. Angl.* p. 182. Tab. IV. N. 28. Mufculus fubcœruleus fere virgatus *Ejufd. Meth. Conchyl.* Lib. III. Part. II. N. 200. Mufculus vulgaris marinus fubcœruleus ferè virgatus aut nigricans *Ejufd. Exer. Anat. tert.* 30. Mufculus *Bon.* p. 102. Mytulus *Rond. de Teft.* 48. *Belon. de Aquat.* 397. Mytulus Rondeletii *Aldrov. de Teft.* 512. **The Mufcle** or **Sea Mufcle.** It is to be found in this Haven. The Shells are found on the Shore. It is a common Fifh, and much eaten among the common People, but is thought not to be very wholfome, being fufpected of caufing Sicknefs and Inflammations; fome attributing this Quality to the *Seta* or *Hairs*, others to a fmall poifonous *Infect* found in them. Dr. *de Heide* hath publifhed a Tract *Anno* 1634. about the Anatomy of this Shell-fifh under the Title of *Anatome Mytuli.* Dr. *Lifter* hath likewife diffected it in his *Exerc. Anat. tert.* p. 30. in which he complains that he cannot well underftand the former's Figures, and hath Tab. IV. given divers Figures thereof with their Explanations.

IV. MUL-

IV. MULTIVALVIA.

I. Pholas.

PHolas ftriatus finuatus ex alterâ parte *Lift. Meth. Conchyl.* Lib. III. Part. II. N. 276. Pholas altè ftriata ex altera parte finuata, eademque mucronata *Ejufd. Exerc. Anat. tert.* p. 88. Tab. VII. Fig. 1. 2. Concha altera longa *Rond. de Teft.* p. 23. *Gefn. de Aquat.* 265. Concha longa fecunda Rondeletii *Aldrov. de Teft.* 453. Donax five Dactylus mas *Bellon. de Aquat.* 414. 𝕻𝖎𝖉𝖉𝖔𝖈𝖐𝖘. It is fometimes to be found on this Shore. Dr. *Lifter* hath in the Book laft cited given a Diffection of this Shell-fifh, in which he takes Notice of the Error of Writers, about the Number of *Shells* to this Fifh: Moft affirming that they have but two, as *Aldrovandus*; others three, of which Opinion was the Doctor himfelf; but they are really five, *viz.* two large ones on the Sides, two fmaller ones on the Back, and a fifth that is long and narrow, which is extended beyond the Cardo or Hinge. Thefe live in Chalk and foft Stones, where they burrow themfelves holes to live in, and therefore are more frequently to be met with on fuch Shores where fuch Stones abound. The manner of thefe Animals lying or burrowing in thefe Stones, are expreft by *Rondeletius*, p. 49. *Gefner* 713. *Aldrovandus* 526. and *Lifter*.

II. Concha Anatifera.

COncha anatifera margine lævi *Lift. Meth. Conchyl.* Lib. III. Part. II. N. 285. Concha anatifera dicta *Ejufd. Exerc. Anat. tert.* p. 94. Tab. VII. Concha anatifera *Aldrov. de Teft.* 543. Britannica Concha anatifera *Ger.* 1391. *emac.* 1587. *Park. Theat.* 1306. 𝕭𝖆𝖗𝖓𝖆𝖈𝖑𝖊𝖘. I gathered fome of thefe from the Side of a Ship which came from *Virginia*, and lay in this Harbour. *Gerard* in the Place above cited tells two ftrange Stories, the firft concerning thefe 𝕭𝖆𝖗𝖓𝖆𝖈𝖑𝖊𝖘; of which he relates, That in the North Parts

I

Parts of *Scotland*, and the Iſlands called *Orchades*, are certain Trees which bear *Shell-fiſh*, wherein are contained little living Creatures, which upon opening of the *Shells*, do fall into the Water and become Fowls, called *Barnacles*, *Brent-Geeſe*, or *Tree-Geeſe*. This *Gerard* confirms by his own Eye-witneſs; but the Abſurdity of this *fabulous Story*, is contradicted and refuted by *Johnſon* and *Parkinſon*, as utterly erroneous. The *Barnacle* or *Brent-Gooſe*, having been found to breed and hatch from Eggs as other Fowls, by ſome *Dutchmen* in a Voyage to the Northward *Anno* 1536. This is likewiſe confirmed by others to be done at this Day on the *Baſs Iſland* in *Scotland*. The other Story which *Gerard* brings to confirm his firſt, was concerning what he found upon the Trunk of an old rotten Tree, on the Shore between *Dover* and *Rumney* in *Kent*, viz. many long crimſon Bladders, in ſhape like Puddings newly filled, at the nether End whereof did grow a *Shell-fiſh* like a *Limpit*; bringing ſome of theſe home, he fancied that they contained *Birds*, &c. what his Puddings were, I ſuſpect ſome Sort of *Zoophytæ*, and his Shell-fiſh to be no other than *Limpits*; Multitudes of which, I obſerved ſticking to the Chalk Stones which tumble down from the Cliff on which ſtands *Dover Caſtle*.

III. *Balanus.*

BAlanus parvus ſtriatus *Liſt. Meth. Conchyl.* Lib. III. N. 287. Balanus cinereus, velut a ſenis laminis ſtriatis compoſitus, ipſo vertice alterâ teſtâ bifidâ, rhomboide occluſo *Ejuſd. Hiſt. Animal. Angl.* 196. Balanus primus ſeu Glandium *Rondel. Teſt.* 28. Balanus minor Rondeletii *Aldrov. de Teſt.* 522. *Geſn. Aquat.* 121. Balanus vulgaris *Liſt. Exerc. Anatom. tert.* p. 96. Balanus marina *Johnſ. Exang.* Tab. xv. p. 49. Balanus *Bellon. Aquat.* 395. Balanus ſeu calix *Bonan.* p. 98. N. 14. Balanus tintinnabuliformis *Lang. Meth. Teſt.* 4. **The Acorn-fiſh.** Theſe ſtick plentifully to Stones, and on the Shells of Oyſters and other Shell-fiſh. The Figure which is given by Dr. *Liſter* is good; who hath likewiſe given a *Diſſection* of this Fiſh in his Book above cited; and the Figure thereof magnified from *Leuwenhooke*, Tab. VIII. II. *Tubuli*

II. *Tubuli Vermiculares.*

1. **T**Ubulus vermicularis minor Oſtreorum aliiſque teſtis adnaſcens. **Small Worm-ſhells**. Theſe are ſometimes found ſticking to Stones, the Shells of Oyſters, &c.

2. Vermiculus exiguus albus nautiloides Algæ fere adnaſcens *Liſt. Meth. Conchyl.* Lib. IV. Sect. I. N. 5. **Very ſmall Worm-Shells**. Theſe are abundantly to be found ſticking to the Sea-Wracks, &c.

What our Author means by his many other ſtrange things, whether *Sanguineous* or *Exanguious* I am at a loſs to know; becauſe, beſides *Shells* he doth not name any other; however, we may therefore ſuppoſe, that the Tribes of *Zoophytæ* and *Moles* may here come in, as may likewiſe *Sea Inſects*; and I ſhall in the firſt Place begin with the *Zoophytæ*, or *Plant Animals* as ſome term them.

IV. ZOOPHYTÆ.

1. **U**Rtica marina major. **The greater Sea-blubber or Gelly**. Theſe are ſeen frequently ſwimming in the Salt Water when the Tides come in, and are often left upon the Shore, where they rot and conſume, when many purple Veins may be obſerved in them. They have on their upper Side five oval Marks, which the Fiſhermen call Eyes; when they ſwim it is in an oblique Poſture, they contracting and expanding their Verge or Brim; the Form reſembles that of a Diſh being round, thick in the middle, and thinner as they approach their Edge: What their under Part is I have not obſerved. Perhaps the *Urtica contracta*, and *Urtica explicata* of *Bellon. de Aquat.* 342. may be the ſame with this of ours; and the *Urtica rubra* Rond. de Piſc. p. 530. *Urtica rubra Rondeletii* Aldrov. de Zoop. p. 568. Jonſt. de Exang. Aquat. Tab. XVIII. *Urtica* III. *rubra, vel purpurea Rondeletii* Geſn. de Aquat. 1039. may be this Species in the State of Diſſolution aforementioned.

The

The *Seamen* are of Opinion, that they will make the Hands of those that touch them to itch, as tho' they were nettled, whence the *Latin* Name.

2. Urtica marina minor. 𝕿𝖍𝖊 𝖑𝖊𝖋𝖋𝖊𝖗 𝕾𝖊𝖆=𝖌𝖊𝖑𝖑𝖞. This is like the foregoing, only fmaller in all its Parts, and hath the fame manner of fwimming. The five Eyes in this are very confpicuous, and are well expreft by *Rondeletius* in his Figure, p. 533.

3. Mentula marina *Rond. de Zoop.* p. 128. Mentula marina *Rondeletii Aldrov. Zoop.* p. 589. *Jonft. Exang. Aquat.* Tab. xx. Pudendum marinum five mentula marina Rondeletii *Gefn. Aquat.* 758. 𝕿𝖍𝖊 𝕻𝖎𝖋𝖋𝖊𝖗. Thefe when they are taken up out of the Sea, refemble a Gut full of Water, which in a little time it will pifs out.

4. Pudendum muliebre marinum. 𝕿𝖍𝖊 𝕻𝖊𝖆𝖗𝖑 as the *Dredgers* call it. This is in the hollow *Shell* of an *Oyfter*, being fometimes brought up in their *Dredges*.

II. Molles.

1. S Epia *Bellon. Aquat.* 336. *Rond. de Pifc.* 498. *Salv.* 164. *Schon. Icthy.* 68. *Jonft. Exang. Aquat.* 7. Sepia Salviani *Aldrov. de Mollib.* 50. Sepia Rondeletii *Gefn. de Aquat.* 852. 𝕿𝖍𝖊 𝕮𝖚𝖙𝖙𝖑𝖊 or 𝕴𝖓𝖐𝖊=𝖋𝖎𝖋𝖍. This is to be met with in thefe Seas. The *Bone* is often caft upon the Shore. It is ufed in Medicine to dry up Humours, cleanfe the Teeth, and ftop *Gonorrhea's*; Farriers ufe it to cleanfe the Eyes of Horfes.

2. Loligo, *Bellon. Aquat.* 339. Loligo *Salv.* 196. *Schon. Icthy.* 68. Loligo major *Rond. de Pifc.* 506. *Aldrov. de Mollib.* 69. Loligo magna *Gefn. de Aquat.* 491. *Jonft. Exang. Aquat.* 8. 𝕾𝖍𝖊 𝕾𝖑𝖊𝖊𝖛𝖊. This is fometimes found in thefe Seas. Dr. *Lifter* hath given a Diffection of this in his *Auctarium* to the *Exercit. Anat. tert.* p. 19. and two Tab.

III. Insecta

The APPENDIX.

III. Insecta Marina.

I. *Apoda.*

1. **L**Umbricus marinus *Schon. Icth.* 76. **The Sea-worm.** It is about eight Inches long, the fore Part is red and fleshy, about the Thickness of a Finger; the hinder Part is pale and full of sandy Excrements. They use these in fishing for *Cod-fish* and *Whitings.* *Rondeletius* mentions two or three Sorts of *Sea-Worms,* but none of them seem the *Worm* here given from *Schoneveldius.*

2. Hirudo marina *Rond. de Insect.* III. *Jonst. de Insect.* 143. *Gesn. de Aquat.* 433. Hirudo marina altera *Aldrov. de Insect.* 733. An Insectum marinum Hirudini affine Cornubiense *Raij Hist. Insect.* p. 4. **The Sea-Leech.** This is found on the Stones when the Tide is out, and also brought up in fishing among the Recrements of the Sea. *Moufet* gives the Figure of this in *Rondeletius,* together with that of the *common Leech,* and of the two *Sea-worms* of that last mentioned Author, without any other Description than of the common Leech, so that thereby he takes them for one.

II. *Pedata.*

1. **P**Ediculus major *Schon. Icthy.* 55. Pediculus marinus *Rond. de Pisc.* 576. *Raij Hist. Insect.* 44. *Aldrov. de Insect.* 711. Pediculus marinus Rondeletii *Gesn. Aquat.* 694. **The Sea-Louse.** This is often found sticking to Fishes.

2. Pulex marinus *Rond. de Pisc.* 575. *Aldrov. de Insect.* 711. *Mouf. de Insect.* 322. *Raij. Hist. Insect.* 43. Pulex marinus Rondeletii *Gesn. de Aquat.* 759. **The Sea-flea.** This Insect is found skipping on the sandy Shores abundantly.

3. Scolopendra marina *Rond. de Insect.* 108. *Raij Hist. Insect.* 44. *Aldrov. de Insect.* 714. *Moufet de Insect.* 322. *Gesn. de Aquat.* 839. **The many Feet.** This I have seen among the Recrements of the Sea.

4. Eruca

4. Eruca marina fcolopendra marina nondum defcripta *Philof.* *Tranf.* N. 225. p. 405. Scolopendræ marinæ fpecies e mare Hyber-nico *Ib. Tab.* Vermis Aureus *Barth. Act. Med.* Vol. III. p. 88. *Obf.* 55. An fcolopendra marina lato corpore fubcaftaneo velut pe-dibus innumeris longiufculis aurei coloris *Aldrov. de Infect.* p. 636. **The Sea-Moufe.** Some of thefe Animals I did fee taken by the Fifhermen *Anno* 1699. being brought up among the *Recrementa marina.* D. *Molyneux* found two of them in the Stomach of a *Cod-fifh,* fold in the Market at *Dublin,* which he there defcribes as follows. It was bigger at the one End, and went taper or gradu-ally leffening towards the other. The length above four Inches, and where largeft an Inch and half broad. It's covering mem-branous. The upper Side or Back was roundifh, and covered with a thick fine foft Hair of a delicate Colour, among this foft Hair was thickly interfperfed, very many black fharp hard prickles. The Tail or fmalleft End was terminated on the Back by two *triangular* pellucid foft Scales, that covered the Orifice of the *Anus.* The other End, tho' it had nothing to diftinguifh it for a *Head,* be-fides a very large *Mouth,* which was not at the very End, but fomething underneath, and could not be feen when it lay on its belly; which was flat and covered with a fmooth naked *Skin,* of a lighter Colour than the Back, irregularly fpotted with darker brown Spots: On each Side of the Belly, from the Mouth to the Tail was a Row of *Feet,* the largeft were towards the Mouth, being there about a Quarter of an Inch long, and in number thirty fix; each Foot having five or fix ftiff Hairs paffing through them, and ftanding out like fo many *Claws* or *Toes.* Joining to the Feet, towards the *Back* was a range of fmall thin foft flat *Fins,* each Foot having a Fin. As to the inward Parts of it: The *Vif-cera* were but few, the *Gullet* about an Inch long, thin and mem-branous; the *Stomach* tough and thick, confifting of an outward and inward Membrane, refembling in Make, tho' not in Figure, the *Gizard* of fome Fowl; the *Inteftine* was of a different Colour, Cavity and Subftance from the Stomach with little *Circumvolution,* being almoft direct. Thus far D. *Molyneux* whofe Account I have
contracted,

contracted, but omitted little of the Subftance thereof. When I firft faw this *Animal*, I examined fevcral Authors of *natural Hiftory*, that I might find whether it was taken notice of by any of them; That which feemed to me to come neareft, was the *Phyfalus* of *Rondeletius*, p. 428. *Lib. de Pifc.* where he tells you, that *Ælianus* mentioned and defcribed the *Phyfalus* from *Leonides Byfantinus* in thefe Words. *In Mari rubro*, &c. by which it appears, that *Rondeletius* did not defcribe it from his own View of the *Animal*, but from the Publication of another, and he from a fecond. I was not infenfible that the Figure of the *Animal* in that Author was not good, yet the manner of the ftanding of the Feet induced me to fufpect that it was our 𝕾𝔢𝔞=𝔐𝔬𝔲𝔰𝔢 that was there intended *(N. B.* It is figured lying on the Back, and thofe Tufts of Hair are its Feet) and its being flender at both Ends doth anfwer to this Animal, which agrees with the Defcription afore given by Dr. *Molyneux*; except in the *Mouth*, which might be large in the Doctor's fubject, as it was dead; a like Inftance we have in another *Water Infect*, viz. *The Leach*, whofe Mouth while living is but fmall, but when dead very large. Nor doth *Rondeletius* mention any *Warts* or *Bumps*, upon the Back of the *Phyfalus*; but of the *Phyfa* of *Leonides*, which he defcribes towards the clofe of the Chapter, of which he faith *Cum Phyfalo eundem planè effe eum quem hic exprcffimus, non affrmamus*, p. 429. and perhaps thofe *Warts* were no other than the Feet, the *Belly* being miftaken for the *Back*. As to the Figures, thofe given by *Rondeletius* as I faid before are not good, and confequently thofe taken from him by *Gefn. de Aquat.* 722. *Moufet* in the firft Table at the End of his *Theat. Infect*, and *Jonfton Hift. Infect.* Tab. xxvi. give the fame Figures, but with this Difference; in the laft of them one of the *Animals* is figured on its Belly. I take *Bartholine's* Figure to beft reprefent our Animal as alive. The Figure of the *Scolopendra marina* of *Aldrovandus* is bad, no way agreeing to the 𝕾𝔢𝔞=𝔐𝔬𝔲𝔰𝔢; tho' by his Name it feems to be the fame.

Page 113. *Paragraph* the fecond, our *Author* mentions only fuch *Birds* or *Fowls* as are for *Kitchen* ufe, to which I fhall add fuch others as are frequently to be found or feen here. Fasci-

Fasciculus Avium.

HERE I will not give the Names of all the *Birds* that may be here found, but only fuch as are either mentioned by our *Author*; or fuch as are more rare, among which I account all fuch as frequent the *Sea*.

I. *Aves Rapaces*.

HAliætus feu aquila marina *Willoughb*. *Ornit*. 29. *Raij Ornith*. 59. *Gefn*. *de Avib*. 177. Haliætus feu Offifraga *Raij Synop*. A. 7. Haliætus *Bellon*. *de Orn*. 96. *Aldrov*. *Ornith*. 190. *Jonft*. *de Avib*. 3. **The Sea-Eagle** or **Ofprey**. Whether this Bird is at any time to be feen here I know not; but this being a Bird that frequents the Sea Coaft, and having feen the Cafes of two of them which have been fhot in this County, the firft at *Maldon* in the Houfe of one Mr. *Robjent*, killed near that Place; and the other at the Horn in *Braintree*; but kill'd at St. *Ofith* in *Tendring Hundred*; I do not doubt but fometimes they frequent this Place. This is a very large Bird, much larger than the *Bald-Buzzard*. There are two fabulous Stories relating to this *Bird*, the firft, that it hath one Foot webbed like a Goofe, and the other not, but neither of thofe two Cafes which I faw, had any webbed Foot. The other of the Oil or Fat about the Rump, which dropping into the Water, makes the Fifh fo aftonifhed or ftupified as that they may be eafily taken. Doubtlefs the *Oil* of *Ofprey*, which is fold at fome Shops to catch Fifh with, is nothing but an Impofition upon the too credulous. There is a good Figure of this Bird in Mr. *Ray*'s *Ornithology* or *Hiftory of Birds*, Tab. 1.

2. Otus five noctua aurita *Raij Synop*. A. 25. *Will*. *Ornith*. 64. Otus five Afio *Raij Ornith*. 100. Afio five Otus *Aldrov*. *Ornith*. I. 519. *Jonft*. *de Avib*. 30. Tab. xviii. Otus *Bellon des Oyf*. 138. *Gefn*. *de Avib*. 573. **The Horn-Owl**. I have feen of thefe caught in this County toward the Sea, fome of which may not unlikely be

be here: Thefe are that fort of Owl, which *Childrey* in his *Britannia Baconica*, p. 100. mentions: The Story is this. In the Year 1580. at *Allholland-tide*, an Army of *Mice* fo over-run the Marfhes of *Denge-Hundred*, near *South-Minfter*, that they eat up the Grafs to the very Roots, and fo poifoned it with their Teeth, that a great Murrain fell upon the Cattle that grazed there. But at length a great Number of *ftrange painted Owls* came and devoured all the *Mice*. The like happened again in *Effex* Anno 1648. The Figure in Mr. *Ray's Ornithology*, Tab. XII. is good.

II. *Gallinaceum genus fylveftre.*

1. PHafianus *Raij Ornith.* 163. *Ejufd. Synop.* A. 56. *Aldrov Ornith.* II. 45. *Bellon des Oyf.* 254. *Gefn. de Avib.* 618. *Jonft. de Avib.* 40. Phafianus a Phafide Colchidis fluvio dictus *Will. Ornith.* 117. **The Pheafant.** Thefe are Inhabitants of the Wood ; and are mentioned by Mr. *Tayler.* This is celebrated for the Goodnefs of it, flefh by all Authors both ancient and modern. Many have written and moft thinks faith Mr. *Ray*, that Pheafants and Partridges are far more favoury when taken by a *Hawke*, than in a Net or Snare.

2. Perdix cinerea *Raij Ornith.* 166. *Jonft. de Avib.* 46. Perdix *Gefn. de Avib.* 606. Perdix cinerea Aldrovandi *Raii Synop.* A. 57. *Will. Ornith.* 118. Perdix minor five cinerea *Aldrov.* II. 140. Perdix minor fulva *Bellon des Oyf.* 258. **The common Partridge.** This is likewife mentioned by Mr. *Tayler* among his *Kitchen Provifions.*

III. *Columbinum genus.*

1. COlumba domeftica feu vulgaris *Raii Synop.* A. 57. *Will. Ornith.* 130. Columba vulgaris *Raij Ornith.* 180. Columba domeftica *Bellon des Oyf.* 314. *Aldrov. Ornith.* II. 463. **The common or Dove-houfe Pigeon.** Thofe may be reckoned among the &c. of Mr. *Tayler's* Kitchen Provifion being frequently brought to Market for that Ufe. I 2. Palumbus

2. Palumbus torquatus *Raij Synop.* A. 62. *Ejufd. Ornith.* 185. *Aldrov. Ornith.* II. 487. Palumbus *Bellon des Oyf.* 308. *Jonst. de Avib.* 63. *Gef. de Avib.* 272. Palumbus torquatus *Aldrovandi Will. Ornith.* 135. 𝕮𝖍𝖊 𝕽𝖎𝖓𝖌-𝖉𝖔𝖛𝖊 or 𝕼𝖚𝖊𝖊𝖘𝖙. In the Woods.

3. Oenas five vinago *Raij Ornith.* 185. *Ejufd. Synop.* A. 62. *Will. Ornith.* 136. *Jonst. de Avib.* 64. *Aldrov. Ornith.* II. 497. 𝕮𝖍𝖊 𝕾𝖙𝖔𝖈𝖐-𝖉𝖔𝖛𝖊 or 𝖂𝖔𝖔𝖉-𝖕𝖎𝖌𝖊𝖔𝖓. Whether it is this or the foregoing, that Mr. *Tayler* intended by the Name of *Wood-pigeon* I cannot tell, but rather fufpect the *Ring-dove* to be it.

IV. *Aves minores roftris tenuioribus.*

1. A Lauda vulgaris *Raij Synop.* A. 69. *Ejufd. Ornith.* 203. *Will. Ornith.* 149. Alauda non criftata *Aldrov. Ornith.* II. 845. *Bellon des Oyf.* 269. *Jonst. de Avib.* 70. Alauda fine crifta *Gefn. de Avib.* 67. 𝕮𝖍𝖊 𝕾𝖐𝖞-𝕷𝖆𝖗𝖐 or 𝖈𝖔𝖒𝖒𝖔𝖓 𝕱𝖎𝖊𝖑𝖉-𝕷𝖆𝖗𝖐. It is a Bird well known, being as well kept in Cages for the Excellency of its finging, as brought to the Table for the Delicacy of its Flefh; which is very light and eafy of Digeftion.

2. Oenanthe five vitiflora *Raij Synop.* A. 75. *Ej fd. Ornith.* 233. *Aldrov. Ornith.* II. 762. Oenanthe five vitiflora *Aldrovandi Will. Ornith.* 168. Oenanthe *Bellon des Oyf.* 352. *Gefn. de Avib.* 567. *Jonst. de Avib.* 88. 𝕮𝖍𝖊 𝖂𝖍𝖊𝖆𝖙-𝕰𝖆𝖗. In *Suffex.* 𝕮𝖍𝖊 𝕱𝖆𝖑𝖑𝖔𝖜-𝕾𝖒𝖎𝖈𝖍; in other Places 𝖂𝖍𝖎𝖙𝖊-𝖙𝖆𝖎𝖑. This is alfo one of Mr. *Tayler*'s Kitchen Provifions.

II. A V E S A Q U A T I C Æ.

O F thefe our Author hath mentioned only fuch as are of *Kitchen* Ufe, which he calls The *Venifon of Fowls*, but there being many others that are not frequently or not at all to be fo accounted; I fhall therefore prefent my Reader likewife with fuch as do frequent the Sea Coaft almoft every where, to which may be added fome that frequent Rivers and other watery Places, and are of Kitchen Ufe likewife.

I. *Aves*

I. *Aves fiſſipedes.*

1. NUmenius five arquata *Raij Ornith.* 294. Numenius five arcuata major *Ejuſd. Synop.* A. 103. Numenius Aldrovandi five arquata *Will. Ornith.* 216. Arquata *Jonſt. de Avib.* 108. Arquata five numenius *Aldrov. Ornith.* III. 424. *Geſn. de Avib.* 196. Elorius *Bellon des Oyſ.* 104. **The Curlew.** For the Goodneſs and delicate Taſte of the Fleſh of this *Bird*, it may challenge the principal Place among *Water Fowl.* Mr. *Ray* mentions this Proverb among the Fowlers of *Suffolk.*

A Curlew, be ſhe white, be ſhe black,
She carries twelve pence on her Back.

2. Scolopax *Aldrov. Ornith.* III. 472. *Raij Ornith.* 289. *Will. Ornith.* 213. Scolopax, Gallinago maxima *Raij Synop.* A. 104. Scolopax & Aſcolopax, Gallinago *Bellon des Oyſ.* 273. Ruſticula vel Perdix ruſtica major *Geſn. de Avib.* 432. Scolopax ſeu Perdix *Jonſt. de Avib.* 110. **The Woodcock.** If this is not to be found here, yet doubtleſs it is one of the *Veniſon* of *Fowl*, that belongs to their Kitchen Proviſion. It is a Bird of Paſſage, coming into *England* in *Autumn*, and departing again in the *Spring.* The Fleſh is of high Eſteem, but eſpecially the Leg, in reſpect whereof it is preferred before the *Partridge*; according to the *Engliſh Rhythm :*

If the Partridge had the Woodcock's Thigh,
'Twould be the beſt Bird that ever did fly.

The Bird's Simplicity makes the Name *proverbial*, for a ſimple or fooliſh Perſon.

3. Gallinago minor *Raii Ornith.* 290. *Ejuſd. Synop.* A. 105. *Bellon des Oyſ.* 215. Gallinago minor Aldrovandi *Will. Ornith.* 214. Scolopax five Gallinago minor *Aldrov. Ornith.* III. 476. *Jonſt. de Avib.*

Avib. 110. Gallinago five Rufticula minor *Gefn. de Avib.* 448. 𝕮𝕳𝖊 𝕾𝖓𝖎𝖕𝖊 or 𝕾𝖓𝖎𝖙𝖍. This is found about Rivulets and running Springs, and without doubt is fometime Kitchen Provifion here. This is a Bird of Paffage being here in Winter only.

4. Barge feu Ægocephalus Bellonii *Will. Ornith.* 215. *Raij Ornith.* 292. *Ejufd. Synop.* A. 105. Barge feu Ægocephalus & Capricepa *Bellon des Oyf.* 206. Limofa Venetorum & Barge Gallorum *Aldrov. Ornith.* III. 434. 𝕮𝖍𝖊 𝕻𝖆𝖗𝖜𝖍𝖊𝖑𝖕 or 𝕻𝖆𝖗𝖙𝖜𝖎𝖕. This lives and feeks its Food on the fandy Sea Shores.

5. Totanus *Aldrov. Ornith.* III. 430. *Raij Ornith.* 293. Fodea fecunda *Will. Ornith.* 216. Fodea noftra fecunda five Totanus Aldrovandi *Raij Synop.* A. 105. Gallinula quam Angli 𝕲𝖔𝖉𝖜𝖎𝖙𝖙𝖆𝖒 vel Fodeam appellant *Gefn. de Avib.* 463. 𝕮𝖍𝖊 𝕲𝖔𝖉𝖜𝖎𝖙 or 𝕾𝖙𝖔𝖓𝖊=𝕻𝖑𝖔𝖛𝖊𝖗. This alfo feeds on the fandy Sea Shores, and in Salt Marfhes. *Bellonius* obferves, that moft of the Marfh-Birds feed in the Night. Mr. *Ray* formerly thought that the *Gotwit* or *Stone-Plover,* and *Yarwhelp* or *Yarwip* were the fame Bird, but he afterwards faw Caufe to divide them.

6. Hæmantopus *Bellon des Oyf.* 203. Hæmantopus Bellonii *Will. Ornith.* 220. *Raij. Synop.* A. 105. *Ejufd. Ornith.* 297. *Aldrov. Ornith.* III. 447. *Jonft. de Avib.* 106. 𝕮𝖍𝖊 𝕾𝖊𝖆=𝕻𝖎𝖊. This I have feen in *Malden* Channel, and no doubt but the fame is alfo here to be met with; it being a Bird that frequents the Sea Shore.

7. Gallinula Erythropus major Gefneri *Raij Ornith.* 299. *Will. Ornith.* 221. Erythropus major *Gefn. de Avib.* 449. Erythropus Ornitholog. major *Aldrov. Ornith.* III. 453. Erythropus major *Jonft. de Avib.* 110. Totanus Gefneri *Raij Synop.* A. 107. 𝕮𝖍𝖊 𝕽𝖊𝖉=𝕾𝖍𝖆𝖓𝖐 or 𝕻𝖔𝖔𝖑=𝕾𝖓𝖎𝖕𝖊. This is likewife a Frequenter of the fandy Sea Shores every where.

8. Tringa minor *Will. Ornith.* 223. *Raij Ornith.* 301. *Ejufd. Synop.* A. 108. Gallinula hypoleucos *Gefn. de Avib.* 454. *Aldrov. Ornith.* III. 469. Ancinclus fecundus five minor *Aldrov. Ornith.* III. 492. 𝕮𝖍𝖊 𝕾𝖆𝖓𝖉=𝖕𝖎𝖕𝖊𝖗. This likewife is to be found on the fandy Shores.

9. Arenaria

9. Arenaria *Will. Ornith.* 225. Arenaria noſtra *Raij Synop.* A.
109. The Sanderling or Curwillet. This is a Bird which much frequents the ſandy Coaſt, flying in Flocks.

10. Cinclus prior Aldrovandi *Will. Ornith.* 226. *Raij Synop.* A.
110. Schœniclos ſeu Junco Bellonii *Ejuſd. Ornith.* 305. Schœniclos *Bellon des Oyſ.* 217. Junco *Jonſt. de Avib.* 112. Junco Avis *Aldrov. Ornith.* III. 488. Cinclus ſive Moticilla marina *Geſn. de Avib.* 554. The Stint. Theſe Birds live upon the Sea Shores, and fly in Flocks.

11. Capella ſive Vannellus *Will. Ornith.* 228. *Raij Synop.* A. 110. *Ejuſd. Ornith.* 307. *Aldrov. Ornith.* III. 526. Capella & Parcus *Bellon des Oyſ.* 210. Vannellus *Geſn. de Avib.* 692. *Jonſt. de Avib.* 113. The Lapwing or Baſtard Plover, by ſome Tewit. In marſhy Places.

12. Pluvialis viridis *Will. Ornith.* 229. *Raij Synop.* A. III. *Ejuſd. Ornith.* 308. *Sloan. Hiſt. Jamaic.* Tom. II. p. 318. Tab. CCLXIX. Fig. 1. Pluvialis *Aldrov. Ornith.* III. 529. *Jonſt. de Avib.* 113. The green Plover. This is one of Mr. *Tayler's Kitchen Proviſions.* Its Fleſh is accounted a choice Diſh, being ſweet and tender.

13. Charadrius ſive Hiaticula *Will. Ornith. Sloan. Hiſt. Jam.* II. 319. Tab. CCLXIX. *f.* 2. *Raij Ornith.* 310. *Ejuſd. Synop.* A. 112. *Aldrov. Ornith.* III. 536. *Jonſt. de Avib.* 113. *Geſn. de Avib.* 224. *Bellon des Oyſ.* 183. Matuitui Braſilienſibus *Marcg.* 199. 217. Matuitui *Piſ.* 95. The Sea-Lark. This is commonly on the Shore. *Marcgravius* hath figured and deſcribed two Birds by this Name, the firſt of which hath a ſhorter Bill than the other, and is about the Bigneſs of a Lark; the other larger, and the Bill longer.

14. Fulica *Aldrov. Ornith.* III. 95. *Will. Ornith.* 239. *Raij Ornith.* 319. *Ejuſd. Synop.* A. 116. *Jonſt. de Avib.* 98. Fulica recentiorum *Geſn. de Avib.* 344. The Coot.

II. AVES AQUATICÆ PALMIPEDES.

I. *Roſtro anguſto.*

1. REcurviroſtra *Raij Ornith.* 321. *Ejuſd. Synop.* A. 117. *Will. Ornith.* 240. Avoſetta Italorum *Aldrov. Ornith.* III. 288. *Jonſt. de Avib.* 90. Avoſetta, Recurvi roſtro *Geſn. de Avib.* 205. 𝕮𝖍𝖊 𝕮𝖗𝖔𝖔𝖐𝖊𝖉=𝕭𝖎𝖑𝖑. In theſe Eaſtern Parts frequently. The firſt time I did ſee it was on an Iſland below *Maldon* called *Northey* Anno 1700. In the Summer-time.

2. Columbus five Podicipes minor *Will. Ornith* 258. *Raij Ornith.* 340. *Ejuſd. Synop.* 125. 190. *Sloan. Hiſt. Jam.* II. 322. Columbus minor *Aldrov. Ornith.* III. 259. 𝕮𝖍𝖊 𝕯𝖔𝖇=𝕮𝖍𝖎𝖈𝖐 or 𝕯𝖎=𝖉𝖆𝖕𝖕𝖊𝖗.

3. Larus cinereus maximus *Will. Ornith.* 262. *Raij Synop.* A. 127. *Ejuſd. Ornith.* 345. *Sloan. Hiſt. Jam.* II. 322. Guacaguacu *Braſilienſibus Marcg.* 205. 𝕮𝖍𝖊 𝕳𝖊𝖗𝖗𝖎𝖓𝖌=𝕲𝖚𝖑𝖑. This is very frequent here, Mr. *Ray* thinks it not deſcribed by Authors.

4. Larus cinereus minor *Raij Synop.* A. 127. *Ejuſd. Ornith.* 345. *Will. Ornith.* 262. 𝕮𝖍𝖊 𝖈𝖔𝖒𝖒𝖔𝖓 𝕾𝖊𝖆 𝕸𝖆𝖑𝖑 or 𝕸𝖊𝖜. This is a common Bird.

5. Larus cinereus *Geſn. de Avib.* 526. *Aldrov. Ornith.* III. 73. *Will. Ornith.* 274. Larus cinereus Ornitholog. *Raij Synop.* A. 128. *Ejuſd. Ornith.* 347. Larus cinereus tertius *Aldrov.* Ib. Larius cinereus primus & tertius *Jonſt. de Avib.* 83. Ceppus *Geſn. de Avib.* 221. *Tourneri.* 𝕮𝖍𝖊 𝕻𝖊𝖜𝖎𝖙 or 𝕭𝖑𝖆𝖈𝖐𝖈𝖆𝖕. While young they are eſteemed proper for the Table.

6. Larus fuſcus five hybernus *Will. Ornith.* 266. *Raij Ornith.* 350. *Ejuſd. Synop.* 130. 𝕮𝖍𝖊 𝕮𝖔𝖉𝖉𝖞 𝕸𝖔𝖉𝖉𝖞. It is a very common Bird.

7. Hirundo marina *Raij Synop.* A. 131. *Ejuſd. Ornith.* 352. *Aldrov. Ornith.* III. 80. *Will. Ornith.* 268. Sterna Turneri *Aldrov. Ornith.* III. 78. Speurer Argentoratenſis *Baltner.* 𝕮𝖍𝖊 𝕾𝖊𝖆=𝕾𝖜𝖆𝖑𝖑𝖔𝖜. It is a common Bird.

8. Mer-

8. Merganſer *Aldrov. Ornith.* III. 285. *Will. Ornith.* 253. *Raij Synop.* A. 134. *Ejuſd. Ornith.* 335. *Jonſt. de Avib.* 89. *Geſn. de Avib.* 119. Harle *Bellon des Oyſ.* 164. 𝕮𝖍𝖊 𝕲𝖔𝖔𝖋𝖆𝖓𝖉𝖊𝖗 or 𝕭𝖊𝖗𝖌𝖆𝖓𝖉𝖊𝖗. This is frequently to be met with here.

II. *Aves latiroſtræ.*

1. CYgnus ferus *Will. Ornith.* 272. *Raij Ornith.* 356. *Ejuſd. Synop.* A. 136. 𝕮𝖍𝖊 𝖜𝖎𝖑𝖉 𝕾𝖜𝖆𝖓, 𝕰𝖑𝖐 or 𝕳𝖔𝖔𝖕𝖊𝖗. This in Winter time is often ſhot upon this Coaſt. It is a large Fowl and different from the tame. Mr. *Willoughby* thought this Bird was not deſcribed before.

2. Anſer domeſticus *Raij Synop.* 136. *Ejuſd. Ornith.* 358. *Will. Ornith.* 273. *Geſn. de Avib.* 125. *Aldrov. Ornith.* III. 102. *Jonſt. de Avib.* 92. Anſer *Bellon des Oyſ.* 157. 𝕮𝖍𝖊 𝖙𝖆𝖒𝖊 𝕲𝖔𝖔𝖋𝖊. This is brought to Market for the Uſe of the Kitchen.

3. Anſer ferus *Raij Ornith.* 358. *Ejuſd. Synop.* A. 136. *Will. Ornith.* 274. *Geſn. de Avib.* 140. *Bellon des Oyſ.* 158. *Jonſt. de Avib.* 93. Anſer ferus Ornitholog. *Aldrov. Ornith.* III. 150. 𝕮𝖍𝖊 𝖜𝖎𝖑𝖉 𝕲𝖔𝖔𝖋𝖊. This is caught in Winter when it frequents this Coaſt.

4. Bernicla ſeu Bernacla *Will. Ornith.* 274. *Raij Synop.* A. 137. *Ejuſd. Ornith.* 159. Branta ſeu Bernicla *Aldrov. Ornith.* III. 165. Branta ſive Bernicla & Bernichia *Jonſt. de Avib.* 94. 𝕮𝖍𝖊 𝕭𝖊𝖗𝖓𝖎𝖈𝖑𝖊 or 𝕮𝖑𝖆𝖐𝖎𝖘. It breeds in the North of *England*, and no doubt but in Winter-Seaſon viſits theſe Parts. There are four Figures of this Bird in *Aldrovandus*, the firſt two of the *Bernacle*, and the other of the *Clakis*. The Production of this Bird hath been controverted by the learned, what its original is, I have already ſhewn among the *Shell-fiſh*, of which ſome will have it come.

5. Brenta *Raij Synop.* A. 137. *Ejuſd. Ornith.* 360. *Will. Ornith.* 275. Anas cingulum candidum in collo habens *Bellon des Oyſ.* 167. Anas torquata Bellonii *Aldrov. Ornith.* III. 214. 𝕭𝖆𝖚𝖒𝖌𝖆𝖓𝖋𝖌, i. e. Tree-Gooſe *Baliner.* 𝕮𝖍𝖊 𝕭𝖗𝖊𝖓𝖙-𝕲𝖔𝖔𝖋𝖊. Theſe no doubt are in Winter to be found here, having divers times ſeen them in

Braintree Market, being caught on the *Effex* Coaft. Mr. *Jonfton* thinks this to be only the Female of the foregoing, becaufe of their flying together in Company.

6. Brenthus *Raij Synop*. A. 137. Brenthus fortaffe *Ejufd. Ornith.* 361. *Will. Ornith.* 276. Brenta five Bernicla minor *Ejufd.* Tab. LXXVI. & *Raij.* **The fiat** or **Road-Goofe.** This I have fome Winters feen in *Braintree* Market.

7. Anas domeftica vulgaris *Will. Ornith.* 293. *Raij Ornith.* 380. *Synop.* A. 150. Anas domeftica *Aldrov. Ornith.* III. 188. *Jonft. de Avib.* 95. **The common tame Duck.** This no doubt in its Seafon the Town is fupplied with.

8. Bofcas major *Raij Ornith.* 371. *Will. Ornith.* 284. Anas torquata minor Aldrovandi *Raij Synop.* A. 145. Bofcas major feu Anas torquata minor *Aldrov. Ornith.* III. 212. Anas fera marina *Gefn. de Avib.* 105. Bofcas major *Jonft. de Avib.* 97. **The wild Duck and Mallad.** Thefe are in Winter time abundantly caught in *Decoy Ponds,* from whence they are carried to fupply Markets.

9. Penelope *Aldrov. Ornith.* III. 217. *Will. Ornith.* 288. *Raij Ornith.* 375. *Ejufd. Synop.* A. 146. **The common Wigeon** or **Weabre.** Thefe in Winter time are brought to Market from the *Decoys.*

10. Querquedula fecunda *Aldrov. Ornith.* III. 209. *Will. Ornith.* 290. *Raij Synop.* A. 147. *Ejufd. Ornith.* 377. **The Teal.** This is likewife with the foregoing: It is one of the fmalleft Sorts of *Ducks,* but for its pleafant Tafte, and wholefome Nourifhment is generally preferred before the reft.

11. Anas caudacuta *Aldrov. Ornith.* III. 234. *Gefn. de Avib.* 106. *Raij Synop.* A. 147. *Ejufd. Ornith.* 376. *Jonft. de Avib.* 98. *Will. Ornith.* 289. **The Sea-Pheafant** or **Cracker.** Mr. *Ray* faw this about *Orford* and *Aldborough* in *Suffolk,* and no doubt but the fame is to be met with here, by reafon of the Vicinity of thofe Places.

There are two other Sorts of *Englifh Ducks* that are fometimes taken at *Decoys,* and they are **The Gadwall** or **Grey** : And **The Summer Teal,** but whether they are at any time brought hither, I am not informed. The

The following are what are called 𝕾𝖊𝖆=𝕯𝖚𝖈𝖐𝖘, that is fuch as keep moftly at *Sea*, of thefe Mr. *Ray* hath mentioned about twelve forts that have been obferved either by Mr. *Willoughby* or himfelf; thofe which I have feen myfelf, or were fhot in the Neighbourhood, or that are common to thefe Seas, are as follow:

1. Tadorna *Bellon des Oyf.* 172. *Will. Ornith.* 270. *Raij Ornith.* 363. *Jonft. de Avib.* 98. Tadorna Bellonii *Raij Synop.* A. 140. Tadorna Gallorum *Aldrov. Ornith.* III. 237. 𝕮𝖍𝖊 𝕾𝖍𝖊𝖑𝖉𝖗𝖆𝖐𝖊 or 𝕭𝖚𝖗𝖗𝖔𝖚𝖌𝖍 𝕯𝖚𝖈𝖐. This I have feen at *Braintree*, brought from thefe Parts; it being very frequent on the Eaft-fide of *England*. To this ought to be referred the Vulpanfer *Aldrov. Ornith.* III. 159. *Bellon des Oyf.* 159. as being the fame Bird. The Figure of this Bird is twice in *Willoughby*, viz. Tab. LXX. and LXXI. the firft of which is taken from *Aldrovandus*.

2. Anas niger Aldrovandi *Will. Ornith.* 278. *Raij Ornith.* 363. *Ejufd. Synop.* A. 141. Anas niger, roftro nigro, rubro & luteo *Aldrov. Ornith.* III. 235. 𝕮𝖍𝖊 𝕭𝖑𝖆𝖈𝖐=𝕯𝖚𝖈𝖐. It was fent to *Braintree* fome Years paft from *Tendring Hundred*. The Figure of this in *Willoughby*, Tab. LXX. is taken from *Aldrovandus*; this Mr. *Ray* finds Fault with, and not without Reafon, the white that is on the Wings being made *Scallop* Fafhion.

3. Anas niger minor *Raij Ornith.* 366. Anas niger Eboracenfibus 𝕾𝖈𝖔𝖙𝖊𝖗 *Will. Ornith.* 288. Anas niger minor Eboracenfibus 𝕾𝖈𝖔𝖙𝖊𝖗 *Raij Synop.* A. 141. 𝕮𝖍𝖊 𝕾𝖈𝖔𝖙𝖊𝖗 or 𝕸𝖆𝖈𝖗𝖚𝖋𝖊. It hath been found in *Norfolk*, and on the Coaft of *Normandy*; and no doubt but here likewife. *Monfieur Cattier* in his *Traitè de la Macreufe* doth affirm, that the *Macreufe* is the *Fulica major* of *Bellon*, and the *French* calling it likewife *Macroul* or *Diable de Mer*, would induce one fo to think; but that *Bellon* p. 183. defcribes his Bird with a white Spot on the Head, and with Toes like the other *Coot* proves the contrary. Some alfo take it for the *Puffin*. This as well as the *Bernacle* hath been affirmed by fome to be generated, either of rotted Wood floating on the Sea, or out of certain Fruits falling into the Water, or from a kind of Sea Shells; but as to that of the *Bernacle*, I have already fhewn that it is produced

duced from an Egg, by Sir *Robert Sibbald*, *Prod. Hift. Nat. Scotiæ*, p. 21. Part II. the like is done againft the *æquivocal* Generation of the *Macreufe*, by *Monfieur Graindorge* in the *Hiftoire des Macreufes*. By Sir *Robert Sibbald* and the faid *Monfieur Graindorge*, the *Bernacle* and *Macreufe* are both made the fame Bird, as they are likewife taken to be by the *Anonymous* Author of the *Curiofities of Nature and Art*, who p. 316. writes, That the *Englifh* call thefe Fowls *Bernacles*, the *Scots* in their Language *Clakis*, and the *French Marguerolles*, and *Macreufes*; and in *Lent* they are eaten as Fifh; being brought out of *Normandy* to *Paris*, and there fold for Fifh. *Senguerdius* in his Anatomy of thefe Birds *(Macreufes)* hath found Numbers of Eggs in the *Ovarium* of the Females, and in the Male two Tefticles and a Penis; whereas the *Bernacle* is of the *Goofe*, and the *Macreufe* of the Duck-kind.

Dr. *Tancred Robinfon* in the *Philofophical Tranfactions*, N. 172. p. 1036. takes Notice of the Eating the *Macreufe* in *France* on Fifh-days, and all *Lent* thinking it a Sort of Fifh. *Wormius* likewife writes, *Muf.* 257. That in fome Places they are eaten as Fifh, as not having Flefh nor produced by Flefh. And he was informed by a *Frenchman* of Credit, That the Divines of the *Sorbonne* had publickly declared their Opinion, that the *Macreufe* was of the Genus of Fifh, and not of that of *Birds*.

The aforecited *anonymous* Author, p. 310. chargeth *Childray* of being wide of his Mark, in afferting that *Bernacles* are hatched from Eggs as other Birds, and terms it a mere Vifion; that he did not reflect that Animals whofe Blood is cold, as is the Blood of Fifh and (as he faith) of *Bernacles*, never Brood upon their Eggs, becaufe they themfelves are as cold as *Marble*, and therefore cannot be fuppofed to produce Heat; and thinks him under a Miftake in taking *Ducks* for *Bernacles*, confounding them together. Our Author boldly afferts, that *Bernacles* lay their Eggs as Fifh do theirs (they being nothing but *Fifh* under the Figure of *Birds)* and leave them to the Mercy of the Water to take their Fortune, and that the Sun hatches them; That thefe Eggs have no Shells (but only a Skin like the Eggs of Fifh) but are of a flimy Subftance like
thofe

thofe of *Frogs*, and as they float in the Water, they ftick to what they meet with, as *rotten Wood*, *Sea Weeds*, and other *Sea Plants*; all which are covered with a *glutinous* Subftance, or *vifcous* Matter. The Figures of the *Concha Anatifera* given by *Wormius Muf.* p. 256. and *Chioccous Muf. Calceol.* p. 28. are taken either from a Bunch of *Bernacle Shells,* as they ftuck to fome Ship (of which I have already taken notice) or as they clave to Sticks: And *Lobel* firft in his *Obfervationes Stirp.* p. 655. gives a Figure of thefe *Shell-fifh*, calling them *Britannicæ Conchæ Anatiferæ*, Gallis *Macreufes*, which is likewife in his *Icons*, Tom. II. p. 259. by the Name *Britannicæ Conchæ Anatiferæ*, to which from his *Dutch Herbal*, he added a Figure as they grow to Wood, and as they grow upon a Branch with a *Macreufe* by them: They are all figured and intended for the *Shell-fifh* called a *Concha Bernacle* or *Anatifera*, and not for a *Balanus* which our Author Figures, p. 311. for his *Anatiferous-Tree*, calling it a *Sea-nofe-gay*, fancying it not unlike one of our *Tulips*, affirming it of maritime Vegetation, and deferved no lefs to be placed among Plants, than the *Coralloides*, when it is really a *Shell-fifh* of the *teftaceous Kind*, and is fpecifically different from that Sort of *Shell-fifh* which hath been fabuloufly thought to be the Producer of the *Bernacle-Goofe*; the Difference between them may be feen among the Shells aforegoing, page 389.

This Author is at a Lofs after all, to know how this his fuppofed *Sea Plant*, and thofe little Inhabitants that are lodged in the Apartments thereof are formed; yet afterwards recollecting himfelf, he writes p. 315 That of the Egg aforementioned, which contains the firft Rudiments of the *Bird*, are formed the Shell and the little Fifh, to which Nature will in time give Feathers and Wings; and to ftrengthen this his Conjecture, he cites what *Du Turtree* faith about the Formation of *Oyfters*, (that is the *Tree-Oyfters* in *America)* no doubt, faith *Du Turtree*, the Seed of the *Oyfters* is fhed into the Sea when they fpawn and ftick to thofe Branches (or Roots of Trees) fo that the *Oyfters* form themfelves there, and grow bigger in Succeffion of time; and adds, That the Formation of *Bernacles* is exactly the fame; not confidering the *Seed*, *Spawn*

or

I

or *Spat* of *Oyfters* breed only *Oyfters*. And as himfelf in another Place rightly obferves, That the Shells of *teftaceous* Fifh, whether *Oyfters*, *Cockles*, &c. are known to grow proportionally, as the Fifh that are in them. And it is the fame with the *Snail* and its *Shell*; the Houfe grows according to the Bulk of its Inhabitants, p. 313. But it is now time to conclude this long Story, which the Author hath extended to about fifteen Pages; and, as he faith about the *Barametz* or *Agnus Scythicus*, p. 308 That this pretended *Prodigy* of Nature is at this Day allowed to be a Fable, fo it may as truly be faid of the *Bernacle* or *Macreufe* (as he makes them but one, though in reality diftinct Birds); for if we confider, *Firft*, that the Eggs of *Oviparous* Animals bear a proportional Bignefs to that of the Parents by which they are produced, but the Eggs of neither the *Concha Anatifera* or *Balanus*, whofe Eggs, tho' magnified with a *Microfcope* by the late Mr. *Leuwenhooke*, do not exceed the Bignefs of a *Millet Seed*, as may be feen in Dr. *Lifter*'s *Exercitatio Anatomica tertia*, Tab. VIII. Fig. 2. and are but of fmall Proportion to the *Balanus* itfelf; how then can they bear any comparative Proportion to that of either *Bernacle* or *Macreufe*, the firft of which is a Sort of *Goofe*, and the other of a *Duck* as already mentioned? To which laft the very *Balanus* itfelf (if it is allowed to be Eggs) can bear but a very fmall and inconfiderable Proportion to the Animal; no more can the *Concha Anatifera*, which is but very little larger than the *Balanus*, as may be feen in Dr. *Lifter*'s cited Book, Tab. VII. Fig. 4, 5. 8, and 9. *Secondly*, The *Macreufe* hath been obferved to be both Male and Female, *Philofophical Tranfactions*, N. 172. p. 1041. and as fuch hath all the Parts of either Sex as in other Birds, which are much different from thofe of *Oviparous Fifh*: And likewife, that they breathe thro' *Lungs*, which no Fifh befides thofe of the *Whale kind* do. *Thirdly*, That in the Egg of a Fowl on which the Hen hath fat but half the time, may be feen the Wings and all other Parts of a *Bird* tho' in *parvo*, when no Parts of a *Bird* can be clearly made out by the Figures of either the *Concha Anatifera* or the *Balanus*, in the *Tables* or *Diffections* of Dr. *Lifter*, Lib. cit.

2   P. 94.

p. 94. &c. *Fourthly*, The Eggs of no Fiſh whatſoever are covered or incloſed in any Shell of the ſame Subſtance with the *Teſta* of Fiſh; and our Author believes that thoſe of his *Bernacle* have no Shell, but a Skin as aforementioned; how then comes his *anatiferous Plant* to have Shells, and each compoſed of ſo many Parts; ſuppoſing it to be an Egg, tho' it is contrary to what is natural in all Eggs, the Shells of which are whole and generally of a longiſh round Form?

4. Anas fera fuſca vel media *Geſn. de Avib.* 101. *Aldrov. Ornith.* III. 221. Anas fera capite ſubruffo major *Will. Ornith.* 282. Anas fera fuſca *Raij Ornith.* 367. *Ejuſd. Synop.* A. 143. Anas fera 8. ſeu Erythrocephalus 1. *Schwenckf. Theriotroph.* 201. Penelope *Geſn. de Avib.* 94. *Aldrov. Ornith.* III. 217. *Jonſt. de Avib.* 98. Cane a la teſte rouffe *Bellon des Oyſ.* 173. 𝕮𝕳𝖊 𝕻𝖔𝖗𝖈𝖍𝖆𝖗𝖉 or 𝖌𝖗𝖊𝖆𝖙 𝖗𝖊𝖆𝖉-𝖍𝖊𝖆𝖉𝖊𝖉 𝖂𝖎𝖌𝖊𝖔𝖓. This is frequent in the Sea and Places adjoining.

5. Anas fera fuſca minor *Raij Ornith.* 367. *Ejuſd. Synop.* A. 143. Anas fera capite ſubruffo minor *Will. Ornith.* 282. Anas fuligula altera *Aldrov. Ornith.* III. 227. Glaucium *Bellon des Oyſ.* 166. Glaucius *Jonſt. de Avib.* 97. 𝕮𝕳𝖊 𝖑𝖊𝖘𝖘𝖊𝖗 𝖗𝖊𝖉-𝖍𝖊𝖆𝖉𝖊𝖉 𝕯𝖚𝖈𝖐. This probably is not uncommon here.

Page 113. Paragraph the third, our Author Mr. *Tayler* hath given a *Catalogue* or *Farrago* of Fiſh, of which they have good ſtore, and ſeveral Sorts according to their Seaſons; of theſe and ſuch others as I have here ſeen I ſhall give the following *Synopſis*, and divide them into

I. Such as breathe by Lungs, or the Whale Kind.

I. *Balæna*.

1. BAlæna vulgaris edentula, dorſo non pinnato *Raij Synop. Piſc.* 6. Balæna major laminas in ſuperiore maxilla habens, bipennis fiſtula carens *Sib. Phal.* 27. Balæna *Recch. Hiſt. Mex.* 568. Balæna vulgaris *Aldrov. de Piſc.* 688. *Jonſt. de Piſc.* 152. Balæna vulgo dicta ſive Muſculus *Rond. de Piſc.* I. 475. Balæna vulgo dicta

five

five Mysticetus Aristotelis, Musculus Plinii *Gesn. Aquat.* 114. Balæna Rondeletii, Gesneri & aliorum *Will. Icth.* 37. 𝕮𝕳𝕖 𝖂𝖍𝖆𝖑𝖊. This I take to be that Whale which hath the Whale-bone falsly so call'd in the Mouth. There is no good Figure of this *Fish* in any Author I have met with. That figured in *Martin's Spitzbergen*, Tab. II. Fig. 8. may be like this, but having a Spout cannot be the same, unless we suppose the *Male* to have a Spout, but the *Female* none.

2. Balæna edentula corpore strictiore dorso pinnato *Raij Synop. Pisc.* 9. Balæna *Schouf.* 24. Balæna vera *Rond. de Pisc.* I. 442. Balæna vera Rondeletii *Aldrov. de Pisc.* 677. *Gesn. de Aquat.* 115. 𝕮𝕳𝕖 𝕱𝖎𝖓𝖋𝖎𝖘𝖍. This seems to be that Sort of *Whale* which some Years ago was cast upon this Shore, according to the Account I received of it, which is as follows. *It had Fins in the Mouth, was blackish on the Back with whitish Scallops, one Fin on its Back, and that nearer its Tail than Head.* It seems to me to be the *Balæna prior* of *Aldrovand*, whose Figure may represent this, only it being made by Relation and not by Sight, it hath the horney Fins on each side hanging down without the Mouth like Barbles. Mr. *Ray* suspects that this is the *Physeter Veterum*; what the *Physeter* of the Ancients was I know not, but that which is so called by *Aldrovand*, and others cannot be our *Fin-fish*; that being described and figured with *Teeth* in both *Mandibles*, this hath none in either. The Figure in *Martin's Spitzbergen*, Tab. Q. lett. c. represents this Fish.

3. Balæna tripinnis nares habens cum rostro acuto & plicis in ventre *Sib. Obs. de Balænis* 29. *Raij. Synop. Pisc.* 16. 𝕮𝕳𝕖 𝖕𝖞𝖐𝖊ℎ𝖊𝖆𝖉𝖊𝖉 𝖂𝖍𝖆𝖑𝖊. Anno 1688. I saw this Fish in *Maldon* Channel; we could see it a Mile before we came at it, by its making the Sea froth and fly about, when the Head first emerged out of the Water to breathe or blow as the Seamen called it. All that we could for some time see of it was, first the Head by the blowing of the Water, (which was the Notice we had of sailing towards it) then the Back of a blackish Colour, like a great Boat or Lighter turned upside down; after that the back Fin, and last the Tail upon its immerging again into the Water; in this manner we

we faw it divers times, till being fhot at with a Sea-Mufket, it did not fhew its back Fin and Tail as before, but immediately finking, it foon rofe up with its Head out of Water about twelve or thirteen Yards from us; whereby we could difcover the Shape of the Head to be like that of a *Pike-fifh*, and the *Belly* to be white; and thus we faw it do at leaft thirty times, raifing itfelf fo high as to be near twenty Foot above the Water making towards the Sea, fo that it being then high Tide, 'tis thought it fwam over the Bar and went away. There is a Figure of this in *Sib. Phalais,* Tab. 1. D.

4. Balæna tripinnis edentula minor roftro parvo *Butskopf Mart. Spitzb.* p. 124. *Englifh* Edit. 𝕮𝖍𝖊 𝕭𝖔𝖙𝖙𝖑𝖊-𝕳𝖊𝖆𝖉 or 𝕱𝖑𝖔𝖚𝖓𝖉𝖊𝖗'𝖘-𝕳𝖊𝖆𝖉. This Fifh was caught at *Maldon September* 23. 1717. whither it came up with the Tide above the Bridge, but on the Return of the fame was there left. It was from the End of the Bill or Mouth to the End of the Tail fourteen Foot, and in the Girt or Circumference where biggeft feven Foot and a half. The Head was like that of the Dolphin, only the Bill or Snout was not half fo long, and in the Mouth no Teeth; from the End of the Bill to the Eye was twenty two Inches, the Eye was large but the Eye-lids fmall for the Bignefs of the Creature; and placed a little above the Line of the Mouth. The Spout-hole was of the Fafhion of a half Circle with the Points Tailwards placed on the Top of the Head, two Foot from the End of the Bill. The fore Fins were feventeen Inches long, and from the End of the faid Bill to the Fins three Foot, and from thence to the *Pudenda* or *Cloaca,* or common Vent three Foot nine Inches. The back Fin was a Foot long, but did not ftand in the Middle between Head and Tail, but neareft to the latter, being from the Extreme of the Tail but five Foot and four Inches. The Tail ftood *Horizontal* as in the Whale Kind, being three Foot and two Inches from one Extreme to another. The Colour of the Skin was brown on the Back, but on the Belly whitifh.

This Subject was a Female, and the Slit of the *Pudendum* was fourteen Inches long. It breathed by Lungs as all the Whale Kind do,

the

the *Larynx* like that in Dr. *Tyſon's Phocæna*, with which it likewiſe agreed in its Heart, Liver and other *Viſcera.* The Faſhion of the *Ventricle*, which in this Subject was ſingle and almoſt ſquare, was about a Span long; at the two upper Extremes were the *Pilorus* and *Oeſophagus*; the Kidneys did not join as in Dr. *Tyſon's* Subject, but lay far aſunder. Under the Stomach was a Bag in Shape like a Kidney, about ſix Inches long and four broad; it was ſoft and ſpongy, and in the Cavity a blackiſh Liquor, which taſted pungent but not bitter. My Neighbour Mr. *Allen* was at the opening it, to whom I am beholden for the *anatomick* Account. Another of this kind, but larger perhaps, the Male being twenty one Foot long, was caught about the ſame time at *Bradwell juxta mare*, near the Mouth of this Channel, from whence I believe they muſt have been before this Harbour. A Perſon who had been at *Greenland* call'd it 𝕮𝖍𝖊 𝕭𝖔𝖙𝖙𝖑𝖊=𝖍𝖊𝖆𝖉𝖊𝖉 𝕻𝖔𝖗𝖕𝖚𝖘.

The Figure of the Balæna *Bellon de Aquat*. p. 6. differs from this in having the Snout longer for the Proportion of the Body with Teeth in both Jaws, the Body deeper and ſhorter, and the back Fin nearer the Head.

The Figure of the 𝕭𝖔𝖙𝖙𝖑𝖊=𝖍𝖊𝖆𝖉 as taken from the Fiſh itſelf is repreſented, Tab. xiv. hereto annext.

5. Orca *Rond. de Piſc.* I. 483. *Aldrov. de Cetis* 657. *Will. Hiſt. Piſc.* 40. *Bellon de Piſc.* 18. *Raij Synop. Piſc.* 10. *Geſn. de Aquat.* 635. *Jonſt. de Piſ.* 153. *Schonf. Icth.* 53. Balæna minor utraque maxilla dentata, Orca dicta *Sib. Phal.* 6. *Raij Synop. Piſc.* 15. Cetacei generis piſcis quem noſtrates Grampus vocant *Mer. Pin.* 191. 𝕮𝖍𝖊 𝕲𝖗𝖆𝖒𝖕𝖚𝖘 or 𝕹𝖔𝖗𝖙𝖍=𝖈𝖆𝖕𝖊𝖗. This I take to be the Fiſh which about three Years ago was taken here; the beſt Account which I could get of it was from a Waterman, who told me that they call'd it a 𝕭𝖔𝖙𝖙𝖑𝖊=𝖓𝖔𝖘𝖊, that it was about twenty five Foot long, had Teeth in both Jaws, a Spout in the Head and Fin on the Back; that it was a Female, and had a young one in it which was about three Foot long. There is no good Figure of this Fiſh; thoſe in *Rondeletius, Aldrovandus* and *Geſner* better anſwer to their Deſcriptions, than doth that of *Bellonius*, which

is

Tab. XIV. P. 472.

Balæna tripinnis edentula. Minor vestro parve. The Bottle-Head or Flounders-Head Whale.
A. The Spout-hole. B. The Cloaca or Pudenda.

is figured to be a longer and flenderer Fiſh. This Fiſh is not the *Spermaceti Whale.* It is called by the *New England* Whalemen a **Killer.**

6. Balæna *Mer. Pin.* 190. Balæna macrocephala, quæ binas tantum Pinnas laterales habet *Sib. Phal.* 12. Balæna major, inferiore tantum maxilla dentata macrocephala, bipennis *Raij Synop. Piſc.* 15. Balænarum tertium genus *Purchaſ.* Balæna *Will. Icthy.* Tab. A. 1. Fig. 1. *Jonſt. de Piſc.* Tab. xli. xlii. Cetus Officinarum *Pharmacol. Noſtr.* 575. Cete *Will. Icthy.* 41. Cete admirabile aliud *Cluſ. Exot.* p. 131. Trompo *Park. Theat.* 1607. **The Parmacitty-Whale** or **Por-Wall-fiſh.** I do not hear that this Fiſh has been caught on this Coaſt, yet becauſe *Ambergreeſe* hath been ſaid by Mr. *Tayler* to be taken up here, I have therefore inſerted it. There are two noble Productions from this Sort of *Whale*, the firſt of which is the *Spermaceti* commonly call'd **Parmacitty.** What this is was formerly unknown, even *Caſper Hofman* in his *Paraleipomena Officinalia,* p. 678. ſaith, that what it was he did not know. Mr. *Dudley's* Spermacitty Whale differs from this in that he ſaith, there are fine Ivory Teeth in both Jaws, and a Bunch on its Back, which ours hath not; if it was not for the Teeth in both Jaws, it ſhould be the Balæna macrocephala tripennis, &c. *Sib. Phal.* 18. which hath them only in one Jaw. *Schroder* alſo in his *Pharmacopæia,* p. 440. put it among ſulphureous Bodies, ſaying, *Eſt & aliud genus Bituminis quod* Sperma Ceti Officinæ *vocant;* and afterwards in his *Chapter* lxxvii. p. 725. he writes *ex hoc animali ſunt qui* Sperma Ceti Officinarum *deſumi volunt ſed malè.* Some will have it to be what the Name makes it, *viz.* the *Seed* or *Spawn* of a *Whale,* [This Mr. *Martin* found after divers Eſſays not to be ſo, *Voyage to Spitzbergen,* p. 137, 138.] but their Notion thereof being wrong, it is univerſally rejected, it being known to be an Oil that comes from the Head of this and two other *Whales;* one of which was near thirty Years ago taken in the *Thames* and brought aſhore at *Blackwall,* which *Quiney* ſaith was accidentally diſcovered to be one of this Sort, by means of a Perſon buying ſome Quantity of the Oil which a poor Body ſcummed off the

Water,

Water, as it melted from it for a small Value, who set it out of the way, until some use it might be thought fit for should happen; but after a long time looking upon it, the Owner found it hardned into a Cake or solid Consistence, which a Person skilled in the Manufacture hearing of, bought it, and procured from it as good a *Parmacitty* as any yet met with in *London*. This as it comes from the Head of the Fish, is a brown and rank Oil, but by a peculiar Management or Preparation of some few *Druggists*, who carefully keep it as a Mystery, it is freed from that rancid Oil, and made white as sold in the *Shops*. The peculiar Property of this *Adeps Ceti* (which is its most proper Appellation or Name) is to shoot into Flakes, after it has stood a due time in a convenient Vessel; the best being that which is whitest and freest from Rancidity. It is good in many Cases, as in Bruises, inward Hurts, and after Delivery. It is an excellent *Balsamick* in many Distempers of the *Breast*, being good in *Coughs* from sharp *Rheums*, *Pleurisies* and inward *Impostumations*, *Erosions* and *Ulcerations*; and where the *Bowels* have been abraded by Acrimony and Choler, in *Diarrhœa's* and *Dysenteries*, Ulcerations of the *Kidneys* and *bloody Urine*. Outwardly applied it is emollient and healing, softning the Skin and filling up the Scars after the *Small Pox*. It hath been published as the Opinion of the late Mr. *James Petiver*, That it is only the *Male Whale* that doth produce the *Adeps* falsly call'd *Sperma Ceti*; how far this Observation of that diligent Searcher into natural Curiosities will be found right time must discover; but thus far it seems probable to be true, because of the three Sorts of *Whales* yielding that *Adeps*, described by Sir *Robert Sibbald*, two of them were Males, as to the third no notice is taken of its Sex. That *Cetus* of *Clusius* was also a Male.

I now come to the other noble Production from this *Whale*, and that is *Ambergreese*, what the Original thereof is hath been a Matter of much Controversy; it being by some referred to all the three Kingdoms, viz. *Mineral*, *Vegetable* and *Animal*.

1. That its Production is Mineral, a Species of *Bitumen* issuing from Fountains at the Bottom of the Sea was the Opinion of

Avicenna

Avicenna the *Arabian*, and *Plempius* in his *Scholia* as cited by Sir *Robert Sibbald's Phalainologia nova*, p. 42. who himſelf was of the ſame Opinion, as was likewiſe *Simeon Sethi* and *Ætius* among the *Greeks*, and *Garcias ab Horto*, and *Nicholas Monardus* among the more Modern; ſee *Cluſ. Exot.* 147. 300. *Helbigius Ephem. Germ. Dec.* 1. *Anno* 9. & 10. *Obſ.* 194. which laſt Account is tranſcribed into the weekly Memorials N. 49. p. 350. *Wormius* thinks that tho' it is found in the Sea, yet that its Original is from *Bituminous Fountains* as *Amber*, and condenſed by the Air *Muſ.* p. 33. and of the ſame Opinion is *Parkinſon Theat.* 1566. And in this Claſs is it ranged in my *Pharmacologia*, p. 57. The ſecond Opinion is that it is of *Vegetable* Extract. Dr. *Trapham* in his *Jamaica*, p. 147. believes it to be a *marine Plant* growing on Rocks or Shoals, not unlike the Species of *Caraganta* or *Manguel* or *Metle*, a large ſtrong thick leaved *ſucculent Plant*, whoſe Leaves if broke afford a thick roapy Juice, not unlike in Appearance to the white or black *Amber*, both which he ſuppoſeth from the ſame *Vegetable* : But that the black is the more recent dropped Juice, and therefore moſt heavy; the grey ſuch as by duration lying on the Sand near the Roots of its *Original* e're it be moved thence, becomes more light, as waſhed by the cleanſing Pickle of the Salt Waters from its more crude Parts: Thus far Dr. *Trapham*. The following Extract out of a *Dutch* Journal, belonging to the *Dutch Eaſt India* Company upon the ſame Subject, was communicated by the Honourable *Robert Boyle*, Eſq; " *Ambergreeſe* iſſues out of the Root
" of a Tree, which Tree how far ſoever it ſtands on the Land,
" always ſhoots forth its Roots towards the Sea, ſeeking the
" Warmth of it, thereby to deliver the fatteſt *Gum* that comes out
" of it; which Tree otherwiſe by its copious Fatneſs might be
" burnt and deſtroyed. Wherever that fat *Gum* is ſhot into the
" Sea, it is ſo tough, that it is not eaſily broken from the Root,
" unleſs its own Weight, and the working of the warm Sea doth it,
" and ſo it floats on the Sea. If you plant the Trees where the Stream
" ſets to the Shore, then the Stream will caſt it up to great Advantage, *Philoſophical Tranſactions*, N. 97. p. 6115. *Bartholine
" Acta*
2

" *Acta Med. Haffn.* Vol. II. p. 311. believes it to have the fame
" Original: Dr. *Hook* doth judge it the fame, *Philof. Exper.* p. 336.
" But as no Perſon has yet been ſo happy as to diſcover the Tree
" that produced it, there ſeems little probability of the Truth of
" it. *Garcias ab Horto* writes, that *Avicenna* Lib. II. cap. lxvii. &
" *Serapio* Lib. *ſimp.* cap. cxcvi. make this Drug to be a *Fungus* which
" grows on the *Sea-rocks,* and from thence tumbling down is by
" *Tempeſt* caſt upon the Shore, *Cluf. Exot.* 147." I now come
to the third Account about this precious *Drug, viz.* That it is of
animal Production, about which the Opinions are various. *Firſt,*
That it is the Work of an *Inſect,* This we have in an Account
ſent from *Jamaica* by Mr. *Robert Tredwey,* to Dr. *Leonard Plukenet,* the Account of which is in *Philof Tranſ.* N. 232. p. 711. as
follows. I ſhall only at preſent let you know the Account I received from *Ambergreeſe Ben;* for ſo the Man is called from the
vaſt Quantity of that valuable Commodity he found two Years
ago, *viz.* one Hundred and fifty Pound weight, *&c.* The way how
it is produced is from a *Creature,* as *Honey* or *Silk:* For I ſaw in
ſundry Places of this Body the *Beaks, Wings,* and Part of the
Body of the *Creature,* for this ignorant Fellow has ſeen the *Creature* alive ; and he believes they ſwarm as *Bees* on the Sea Shores
or in the Sea. Thus far Mr. *Tredway*'s Letters. *Klobius* in his
Hiſtoria Ambræ thinks that it is the *Dung* of a *Bird* (called in
the *Madagaſcar* Language *Aſchibobuch)* about the Bigneſs of a
Gooſe, curiouſly feathered with a big Head well tufted. Theſe
are affirmed by Authors to flock together in great Numbers, as
Cranes, and frequent high *Cliffs* near the Sea-ſide ; and there
void their Excrement, which the Sea waſhes thence, if it fall
not of itſelf into it, *Philof. Tranſ.* N. 28. p. 538. That it is the
Dung of a *Bird* in *Maldiva* called *Anacangriſpaſque,* is related by
Cluſius Exot. p. 148. from *Ferdinandus Lopez de Caſtagneda,* whoſe
Account is much to the foregoing Purpoſe. Others that it is the
Dung of the *Sperma Ceti Whale,* of which a Relation is in *Purchas,*
which gives an Account of a certain *Gentleman* (who had a Commiſſion to factor into *Greenland* for killing Whales and Morſes)
who

who takes notice of a Sort of Whale call'd *Trompa*, having but
one Trunk on his Head; This *Trompa* contains in his Head the
Sperma Ceti, and in his Entrails the *Ambergreese*, being in Colour like *Cows-dung*, *Philofophical Tranfaĉtions*, N. 28. p. 538.
That it is the *Dung* of a *Whale* there is an Account in *Cluf. Exot.*
p. 149. from one *Servatius Marel* a *Burgundian*; but he faith, that
it is from a *Whale* which hath no Teeth, but devoureth *Fifhes*
whole, fuch as the *Polypus*, *Sepia*, &c. whofe Bills or Beaks are
often found in it.   I have nothing more to add, but that the two
later Accounts which we have received about the Produĉtion of
this excellent *Drug*, affirm its being contained in a *Cyftis* or *Bag*,
and therefore not an Excrement proceeding from Food, or being
devoured by the Animal, but perhaps from a particular Secretion
fomething analogous to the *Scent-Bags* in fome *Quadrupedes*. The firft
of which Accounts given by Dr. *Boylfton Philof. Tranf.* N. 385. p.
193. is this.   Cutting up a Spermacitty Bull Whale, they accidentally found in him about twenty Pound weight of that Drug,
i. e. *Ambergreese*.   After which they and other fuch Fifhermen
became very curious in fearching all fuch *Whales* as they killed ; and
it hath fince been found in leffer Quantities, in feveral *Male Whales*
of that kind, and in no other.   They add further, that it is contained in a *Cyft* or *Bag* without any inlet or outlet to it, and that
they have fometimes found the *Bag* empty, but yet entire.   This
Bag is no where to be found, but near the *genital Parts* of the
Fifh.   The *Ambergreese* is, when firft taken out, moift, and of an
exceeding ftrong and offenfive Smell.   Thus far Dr. *Boylfton*'s Account.   The other Account fent by Efq; *Dudley Philof. Tranf.*
N. 387. p. 267. was taken from one Mr. *Atkins* as follows.   The
Ambergreese is found only in the *Spermacitty Whales*, and confifts
of *Balls* or *globular Bodies* of various fizes, &c. lying loofe in a
large oval *Bag* or *Bladder* of three or four Foot long, and two or
three Foot deep and wide, almoft in the Form of an *Ox's Bladder*,
only the Ends more acute or like a *Blackfmith's Bellows*, with a
Spout running tapering into and thro' the length of the *Penis*, and
a *Duĉt* or *Canal* opening into the other End of the *Bag*, and coming

H h h   from

from towards the *Kidneys*; this *Bag* lies juft over the *Teſticles*, which are above a Foot long, and is placed lengthways at the Root of the *Penis* about four or five Foot below the *Navel*; and three or four above the *Anus*. This *Bag* or *Bladder* is almoſt full of a deep orange coloured Liquor, not quite ſo thick as Oil, and ſmelling ſtrong or rather ſtronger of the ſame Scent with the Balls of *Ambergreeſe*, which float and ſwim looſe in it; the Inſide of the *Bag* is very deeply tinged with the ſame Colour as the Liquor, which may alſo be found in the *Canal* of the *Penis*; the Balls ſeem to be pretty hard while the *Whale* is alive, inſomuch that there are many times found upon opening the *Bag*, large concave *Shelves* of the ſame Subſtance and Confiſtence, that have ſcaled off from them, and the Balls themſelves ſeem to be compoſed of ſeveral diſtinct Coats incloſing one another, ſomething like the Coats of an *Onion*. He never found above four Balls in a *Bag*, and in the *Bag* where he found one that weighed twenty one Pounds, which was the largeſt he ever ſaw, there was no other in the Bag but that. That to one *Spermacitty Whale* that has any of theſe Balls, there are two that have nothing but the deep orange-coloured Liquor in their *Bags*. He never ſaw, nor certainly heard of a Female *Spermacitty Whale* taken in his Life; the *Cows* of that *Species* being much more timorous than the *Bulls*, and almoſt impoſſible to be come at, unleſs when happily found aſleep on the Water, or detained by their *Calves*. Thus far Mr. *Atkins*; to which Mr. *Dudley* adds from other *Whalemen*, That *Ambergreeſe* was only found in ſuch *Spermacitty Whales* as are old and well grown. And that the *Ambergreeſe* is only by the *Male* or *Bull Whale:* That the Boats can never come near the *Females* or *Cows* when they are awake; they are ſo very ſhy and fearful. The Reverend Mr. *Prince* of *Boſton* apprehends the *Bag* aforeſaid to be the *urinary Bladder*, and the *Ambergreeſe* Ball to be a *Concretion* formed out of the greaſy odoriferous Subſtance of the aforeſaid Liquor. Thus far the Account, concerning which I muſt add, that to me *Ambergreeſe* ſeems to be generated in the *urinary Bladder*, and is a Diſeaſe of the Animal, after the Manner as the

2   *Stone*

Stone in *human Bodies.* That the Whalemen who are ignorant in *Anatomy*, finding the *Ambergreefe* in the lower *Ventricle* or *Belly* of the *Whale*, did not diftinguifh the Place it was found in, but taking it for the Guts call'd it *Dung*, fuppofing it to be devoured by the Fifh. That the Reafon of its being found caft upon Shore by the Sea, muft proceed from the Death of the *Animal* containing it, which being of a light and oily Subftance floats on the Water until it is by the Waves left on the Shore.

II. *Delphinus.*

DElphinus *Bellon. de Aquat.* 9. *Rond. de Pifc.* I. 459. *Gefn. de Aquat.* 321. *Aldrov. de Cet.* 701. *Jonft. de Pifc.* 154. *Will. Hift. Pifc.* 58. Delphinus Antiquorum *Raij Synop. Pifc.* 12. **The Dolphin.** *Martin. Spitzbergen.* 123. This as it is to be feen on all Coafts, fo no doubt here. There is a good Figure of it in *Willoughby* Tab. A. 1. Fig. 1.

III. *Phocæna.*

PHocæna *Rond. de Pifc.* I. 473. *Mer. Pin.* 191. *Will. Hift. Pifc.* 31. *Jonft. de Pifc.* 155. *Raij Synop. Pifc.* 13. Phocæna five Turfio *Aldrov. de Cet.* 719. Turfio *Bellon. de Aquat.* 13. Turfio five Phocæna *Schon. Icth.* 77. Porcus marinus quem nautæ Harangivorum nuncuparunt *Mer. Pin.* 191. Phocæna vel Delphinus feptentrionalium *Ephem. Germ.* Anno 3. p. 25. Phocæna D. *Tyfon.* Turfio *T. Barthol.* **The Porpus.** This is every where about *England* and in all Havens. The Anatomy of this Fifh hath been done by feveral Perfons, *Firft*, By *Tho. Bartholinus Hift. Anatom. Cent.* II. *Hift.* 25. *Secondly*, By Mr. *Ray* Anno 1669. This you have in Mr. *Willoughby's* Hift. Pifc. *p.* 32. *Thirdly*, *John Daniel Major* in the *German. Ephem.* Anno 3. Obf. 20. And *Fourthly*, More copioufly by Dr. *Edward Tyfon* in his *Phocæna* or *Anatomy of a Porpus*, *Lond.* 1680. There is a good Figure in *Willoughby's Hift. Pifc.* Tab. A. Fig. 2.

II. Such

II. Such Fish as breathe by Gills.

I. Cartilagineous Fishes.

I. The Dog-kind, or such are as long.

1. **G**Aleus glaucus *Rond. de Pifc.* I. 378. *Will. Hift. Pifc.* 49. *Raij Synop. Pifc.* Galeus glaucusRondeletii *Gefn.de Aquat.* 609. *Aldrov.de Pifc.* 394. Glaucus*Charlt.Exerc.Pifc.* 8. Glaucus Æliani *Jonft. de Pifc.* 15. **The blue Sharke.** This being to be met with on the Coaft of *England*, is likely to be fometimes caught here. There is a good Figure of this in *Willoughby* Tab. B. viii. And here I cannot omit taking Notice, tho' I do not hear of its being caught or feen near this Place; That the Figure of the *Canis Carcharias* in *Willoughby* Tab. B. vii. is not good, being copied from *Gefn. de Aquat.* 175. who thus writes of it, *Hanc picturam Carchariæ Canis ad Sceleton olim fieri curavi.* And the manner of its Fins, Tail, &c. looking *fabulous.* There is a better Figure in *Bellonius de Aquat.* p. 60. which fhews the *Fifh* as alive. The Manner of the *Rictus* of the *Mouth* and ftanding of the *Teeth* are to be feen in many Places, being brought home by Seamen as Curiofities.

2. Canis galeus *Rond. de Pifc.* I. 377. *Will. Hift. Pifc.* 51. *Raij Synop. Pifc.* 20. *Aldrov. de Pifc.* 388. *Salv.* 130. Galeus Canis vel Caniculus *Gefn.de Aquat.* 167. Muftelus lævis fecundus, feu Canefa *Salv.* 132. **The Sweet-William.** This is often found in the *Britifh Ocean.* The Figure of it in *Willoughby* Tab. B. vi. N. 1. which is copied from *Salvianus*, is good. There is a Diffection of this Fifh in Dr. *Charlton's Mantiffa Anatomica*, p. 82.

3. Galeus acanthias five Spinax *Aldrov. de Pifc.* 399. *Will. Hift. Pifc.* 56. *Raij Synop. Pifc.* 21. Galeus acanthias *Gefn. de Aquat.* 607. *Rond. de Pifc.* I. 373. *Charlt. Exer.* 8. Galeus acanthias Gaze *Jonft.de Pifc.* 16. Muftelus Spinax *Bellon. de Aquat.* 69. *Salv.* 136. Canis acanthias *Schonf.* 29. **The Picked-Dog** or **Hound-Fifh, the Purfe.** This is caught fometimes on this Coaft. The Figure of it

in

in *Willoughby*, B. v. Fig. 1. taken from *Salvianus*, is good. The dried Skin of this is used by *Joyners, Turners*, &c. to smooth their Work with.

II. The Skate-kind, or such as are flat and broad.

I. *Paſtinaca.*

PAſtinaca *Rond. de Piſc.* I. 331. *Salv.* 144. *Schonf. Ieth.* 58. Paſtinaca marina lævis *Bellon. de Aquat.* 94. *Raij Synop. Piſc.* 24. Paſtinaca marina *Jonſt. de Piſc.* 19. *Geſn. de Aquat.* 679. *Charlt. Exer. Piſc.* 11. Paſtinaca marina noſtras *Aldrov. de Piſc.* 426. Paſtinaca marina prima Rondeletii *Will. Hiſt. Piſc.* 67. Aquila Piſcis ſeu Paſtinaca marina *Mer. Pin.* 185. 𝕿𝕳𝕖 𝕱𝕚𝕣𝕖-𝕱𝕝𝕒𝕣𝕖. I have ſeen this caught on this Shore, when to prevent Mischief the Fiſhermen inſtantly cut off the Tail. It is ſometimes brought to *Braintree* Market. *Salvianus* and *Willoughby* have each a good Figure of this Fiſh, Tab. C. III.

II. *Raia.*

1. RAIA lævis undulata ſeu cinerea Rondeletii *Raij Synop. Piſc.* 25. *Will. Hiſt. Piſc.* 69. Raia undulata *Charlt. Exer. Piſc.* 11. *Jonſt. de Piſc.* 21. Raia lævis *Mer. Pin.* 185. Raia undulata ſeu cinerea *Rond. de Piſc.* I. 346. *Geſn. de Aquat.* 791. *Aldrov. de Piſc.* 452. 𝕿𝕳𝕖 𝕾𝕜𝕒𝕥𝕖 or 𝕱𝕝𝕒𝕚𝕣𝕖. This is a very common Fiſh. There is a good Figure of it in *Willoughby* Tab. C. v.

2. Raia oxyrhynchos altera *Rond. de Piſc.* I. 348. Raia oxyrhynchos minor *Raij Synop. Piſc.* 26. *Aldrov. de Piſc.* 455. *Geſn. de Aquat.* 792. Raia oxyrhynchos minor Rondeletii *Will. Hiſt. Piſc.* 72. Oxyrhyncos minor *Jonſt. de Piſc.* 21. 𝕿𝕳𝕖 𝕤𝕙𝕒𝕣𝕡𝕖-𝕟𝕠𝕤𝕖𝕕 𝕾𝕜𝕒𝕥𝕖. I have ſeen this brought to *Braintree* Market.

3. Raia *Salv.* 148. *Schonf. Ieth.* 58. *Bellon. de Aquat.* 80. Raia clavata *Rond. de Piſc.* I. 353. Raia clavata Rondeletii *Raij Synop. Piſc.*

Pifc. 26. *Will. Hift. Pifc.* 74. *Gefn. de Aquat.* 795. Raia clavata *Aldrov. de Pifc.* 450. *Mer. Pin.* 185. *Charlt. Exer. Pifc.* 11. Cṭe Ṭịȯṙṅḃạꝛḳ. This is a very common Fiſh. The young ones of theſe are call'd Ⱦẽạịṭṡ.

4. Raia aſpera noſtras *Raij Synop. Pifc.* 26. *Will. Hift. Pifc.* 78. An Raia Fullonica *Rond. de Pifc.* I. 356? *Gefn. de Aquat.* 797. *Aldrov. de Pifc.* 462. *Jonft. de Pifc.* 22. Cṭe ẇḣịṭẽ Ḣꝛꞅẽ.

III. *Squatina.*

Ꞩ Quatina *Raij Synop. Pifc.* 26. *Will. Hift. Pifc.* 79. *Salv. Hift. Aquat.* 151. *Bellon. de Aquat.* 79. *Rond. de Pifc.* I. 367. *Charlt. de Pifc.* 12. *Jonft. de Pifc.* 23. Squatina Rondeletii *Gefn. de Aquat.* 899. *Aldrov. de Pifc.* 472. Cṭe Ⱦꝺṅḳ or Ⱥṅġẽḷ=ḟịꞅḣ. This is caught by the Fiſhermen on all Coaſts, and is carried with the aforementioned *flat Fiſh* to ſupply the Markets; but this being frequently very large, is not ſold whole, but cut into Pieces. There is a good Figure of it in *Willoughby* Tab. D. III.

IV. *Rana Piſcatrix.*

Ꞧ A N A piſcatrix *Will. Hift. Pifc.* 85. *Raij Synop. Pifc.* 29. *Salv. Hift. Aquat.* 140. *Schonf. Icth.* 59. *Rond. de Pifc.* I. 363. *Charlt. Pifc.* 11. Rana piſcatrix Rondeletii *Gefn. de Aquat.* 813. Rana marina *Bellon. de Aquat.* 85. *Jonft. de Pifc.* 22. Rana marina ſeu Piſcatrix *Aldrov. de Pifc.* 464. Cṭe Ḟꝛꝺġ or Cꝺạꝺ=ḟịꞅḣ, or Ꞩẽạ=ꝺẽṿịḷ. It is ſometimes caught by the Fiſhermen. The *Anatomy* of this Fiſh is among the *anatomical Prelections* of Sir *George Ent*, before the College of Phyſicians, *London*. It is pub-liſhed by Dr. *Charlton* in his *Mantiſſa Anatomica*, p. 73. and thence tranſcribed into Mr. *Willoughby's Hiſtory*, in which is a good Fi-gure, Tab. E. I.

II. SPINOSE OR OSSEOUS FISHES.

I. FLAT FISHES.

1. Rhombus maximus afper non fquamofus *Will. Hift. Pifc.* 94. *Raij Synop. Pifc.* 31. Rhombus *Mer. Pin.* 187. *Bellon. de de Aquat.* 140. *Charlt. Pifc.* 30. An Rhombus aculeatus *Rond. de Pifc.* I. 310? *Aldrov. de Pifc.* 248? *Jonft. de Pifc.* 66? *Schonf Icth.* 60? Rhombus aculeatus Rondeletii *Gefn. de Aquat.* 661? The Curbot or Brett. There is a good Figure of this in *Willoughby* Tab. F. 11.

2. Rhombus non aculeatus fquamofus *Will. Hift. Pifc.* 95. *Raij Synop. Pifc.* 31. Rhomboides *Mer. Pin.* 187. Rhombus fquamofus *Charlt. Pif.* 26. An Rhombus lævis *Rond. de Pifc.* I. 312. *Aldrov. de Pifc.* 249. *Jonft. de Pifc.* 66. *Schonf. Icth.* 60? Rhombus lævis Rondeletii *Gefn. de Aquat.* 663. Rhombus alter Gallicus *Bellon. de Aquat.* 141. The Pearl, Pril or Lug=a=leaf. The Figure of this is in *Willoughby* Tab. F. 1.

3. Paffer *Rond. de Pifc.* I. 316. *Schonf. Icth.* 61. Paffer vulgaris *Bellon. de Aquat.* 142. Quadratulus vulgò *Ejufd.* 143. Paffer lævis *Aldrov. de Pifc.* 243. *Jonft. de Pifc.* 66. *Charlt. Pifc.* 29. Paffer Aureus *Mer. Pin.* 187. Paffer Rondeletii *Gefn. de Aquat.* 664. Paffer Bellonii *Will. Hift. Pifc.* 96. *Raij. Synop. Pifc.* 31. The Plaife. It is a very common Fifh. This is figured in *Willoughby* Tab. F.

4. Paffer afper five fquamofus *Rond. de Pifc.* I. 319. Paffer afper five fquamofus Rondeletii *Will. Hift. Pifc.* 97. *Raij Synop. Pifc.* 32. *Gefn. de Aquat.* 665. *Aldrov. de Pifc.* 242. Rhombus afper *Schonf. Icth.* 61. Limanda *Bellon. de Aquat.* 145. Citharus *Mer. Pin.* 187. *Charlt. Pifc.* 26. The Dab or Sanderling. There is a good Figure of this in *Willoughby* Tab. F. IV.

5. Paffer fluviatilis vulgò Flefus *Bellon. de Aquat.* 144. Paffer fluviatilis vulgò Flefus Bellonii *Will. Hift. Pifc.* 98. *Raij Synop. Pifc.* 32. Paffer niger *Mer. Pin.* 187. *Charlt. Pifc.* 26. Pafferis tertia

tia fpecies *Rond. de Pifc.* I. 319. *Gefn. de Aquat.* 666. 𝕮𝖍𝖊 𝕱𝖑𝖔𝖚𝖓𝖉𝖊𝖗, 𝕱𝖑𝖚𝖎𝖙𝖊 or 𝕭𝖚𝖙. The Figure in *Aldrovand* 244. and *Gefner* 667. feems to be of this Fifh, tho' they call it *Solea.* There is a good Figure of it in *Willoughby* Tab. F. v.

6. Hippogloffus *Rond. de Pifc.* I. 325. *Raij Synop. Pifc.* 33. *Will. Hift. Pifc.* 99. Paffer Britannicus *Mer. Pin.* 187. *Charlt. Pifc.* 26. Pafferis major fpecies *Gefn. de Aquat.* 666. Paffer afper tertius Britannis 𝕳𝖊𝖑𝖇𝖚𝖙 dictus *Aldrov. de Pifc.* 243. Fletelatus *Bellon. de Aquat.* 144. 𝕮𝖍𝖊 𝕳𝖔𝖑𝖇𝖚𝖙 or 𝕮𝖚𝖗𝖇𝖚𝖙. Whether this is caught here, I am not certain, but it being frequently found in the *Britifh Ocean* there is no doubt but it is. There is a good Figure of this in *Willoughby* Tab. F. vi.

7. Solea *Mer. Pin.* 187. *Charlt. Pifc.* 26. *Bellon. de Aquat.* 145. *Jonft. de Pifc.* 57. Bugloffus vel Solea *Rond. de Pifc.* I. 320. *Will. Hift. Pifc.* 100. *Raij Synop. Pifc.* 33. Bugloffus vel Solea Rondeletii *Gefn. de Aquat.* 666. *Aldrov. de Pifc.* 235. 𝕮𝖍𝖊 𝕾𝖔𝖎𝖊. It is a common Fifh in thefe Seas. The Figure hereof in *Willoughby* Tab. F. vii. is good.

II. Fishes having only one pair of Fins.

I. *The Eel Kind.*

1. L Ampetra *Rond. de Pifc.* 398. *Will. Hift. Pifc.* 105. *Raij Synop.* 35. *Mer. Pin.* 188. *Charlt. Pifc.* 34. *Jonft. de Pifc.* 79. Lampetra major *Aldrov. de Pifc.* 539. *Salv. Hift. Aquat.* 63. *Schonf. Ictb.* 40. Muftela five Lampetra *Bellon. de Aquat.* 75. *Gefn. de Aquat.* 590. 𝕮𝖍𝖊 𝕷𝖆𝖒𝖕𝖗𝖊𝖞 or 𝕷𝖆𝖒𝖕𝖗𝖊𝖞 𝕰𝖊𝖑. There is a good Figure of this in *Willoughby* Tab. G. 11.

2. Anguilla *Bellon. de Aquat* 295. *Rond. de Pifc.* II. 198. *Gefn. de Aquat.* 40. *Aldrov. de Pifc.* 542. *Jonft. de Pifc.* 82. *Salv. Hift. Aquat.* 65. *Schonf. Ictb.* 14. *Mer. Pin.* 188. *Charlt. Pifc.* 34. Anguilla omnium Autorum *Will. Hift. Pifc.* 109. *Raij Synop. Pifc.* 37. 𝕮𝖍𝖊 𝕰𝖊𝖑. This is found in Salt as well as frefh Water Rivers and Ponds. Thofe which live in clear and running Waters, have

have the whiteſt ſhining Bellies, and are therefore call'd *Silver Eels.* Concerning the Generation of *Eels* the Learned are not agreed, for tho' *equivocal Generation* hath been juſtly exploded, yet whether they are *Hermaphrodites* or have diſtinct *Sexes*, hath not been yet fully determined; to me the latter ſeems moſt probable. Another Point controverted, is whether with the generality of *Fiſhes* they are *Oviparous* or with ſome few *Viviparous*; this latter hath been affirmed from the Obſervations of *Walter Chetwynd*, Eſq; in *Plot's Natural Hiſtory of* Staffordſhire, *p.* 242. *&c.* and Mr. *Benjamin Allen* in the *Philoſophical Tranſactions*, N. 231. p. 664. But this having been already handled, I will not here repeat it, but refer my Readers that deſire further Satisfaction therein to *ſome Conſiderations* thereon publiſhed in the *Philoſophical Tranſactions*, N. 238. p. 90. and all that I ſhall further add, is an *Obſervation* of *Signore Redi*, That all the *Eels* of the River *Arnus* in *Italy* do yearly in *Auguſt* go into the Sea, that there they may bring forth their young; which young ones do at certain times, between the Months of *February* and *April*, return into the River, and go up as high as *Piſa*. Mr. *Ray* remembred, that he had either read in ſome Book, or that it was told him by ſome Perſon whoſe Name he had forgot, that not only the *Eels* of the *Arnus*, but all in general did ſo, *Raij Synop. Piſc.* p. 37. To this I ſhall likewiſe ſubjoin another Account about the *Generation* of *Eels* from *Schwenckfeld*, to wit, that in *Sileſia* a Fiſh call'd *Alburnus*, or *Bleak*, doth not only breed its own *Species*, but alſo *Eels*; but the Part in which the *Eels* are ſaid to be bred, is ſo contrary to Nature, that it adds to the Incredibility of the Relation, tho' our Author ſaith it was confirmed to him by Eye-witneſſes ; and therefore I ſhall only refer the Reader who deſires a fuller Account thereof to the Relation itſelf *Theriotrophium Sileſiæ*, p. 414. There is a good Figure of an Eel in *Willoughby's* Tab.

3. Conger *Bellon. de Aquat.* 161. *Rond. de Piſc.* I. 394. *Salv. Hiſt. Aquat.* 67. *Geſn. de Aquat.* 250. *Aldrov. de Piſc.* 348. *Mer. Pin.* 188. *Charlt. Piſc.* 6. *Will. Hiſt. Piſc.* III. *Raij Synop. Piſc.* 37.

The

The Conger or **Conger-Eel.** The young ones are in some Places call'd **Elvers.** This is sometimes caught very large, some having weighed near thirty Pounds. The Figure of this in *Willoughby's* Tab. G. VI. is good.

4. Ammodytes *Gesn. Paralip.* 3. Ammodytes Gesneri *Will. Hist. Pisc.* 113. *Raij Synop. Pisc.* 38. Anguilla de Arena *Charlt. Pisc.* 27. Pisces *Sandilz* dictus *Salv. Hist. Aquat.* 70. *Sandilz* Anglorum *Aldrov. de Pisc.* 252. *Jonst. de Pisc.* 60. *Sandils* Anglorum *Mer. Pin.* 187. An Cicirellus Massanensis *P. Boccone.* **Sand-Eels** or **Launces.** They are rooted out of the Sand when the Tide is out. The Figure of this in *Willoughby's* Tab. G. doth not well answer, that being pictured with two *Fins* on its Back, when it hath but one; as likewise two Pair on the *Belly*, when it has only one Pair near the *Gills*, and none on the *Belly.*

5. Lupus marinus nostras *Schonf. Icth.* 45. Lupus marinus Schonfeldii *Jonst. de Pisc.* Tab. XLVII. Fig. 2. Lupus marinus *Charlt. Pisc.* 31. Lupus marinus nostras & Schonfeldii *Will. Hist. Pisc.* 130. *Raij Synop. Pisc.* 40. Anarrhichas *Gesn. Paralip.* 4. **The Wolf-Fish, Sea-Wolf** or **Woolf.** One of these Fishes some Years ago I saw in the Trunk of a Store-House next the Marsh on the West-side of the Town; it being caught in the neighbouring Sea. The *Dentes Molares* or *Grinders* are call'd **Toad-Stones,** and as Gems are set in Rings, as Dr. *Merret* well observed, *Pinax* 210. There is abundance of the Teeth of this Fish found Fossil, and are called *Bufonites*; see in Mr. *Lhwyd's* Lithóphyl. Britannic. p. 70, 71. &c.

6. Mustela *Lumpen* Antverpiæ dicta *Raij Synop. Pisc.* 40. Lumpen Antverpiæ dicta, Mustelæ species *Will. Hist. Pisc.* 120. **The Dutch Eel-pout.** This I have seen in *Braintree* Market, as well as caught in these Seas: In opening of which, I observed, that the *Liver* was pale and but of one Lobe, the Bottom of the *Ventricle* round the *Pylorus* had many *Cæca.*

II. *Globe-*

II. *Globe-Fiſh.*

1. **ACUS** Ariſtotelis *Aldrov. de Piſc.* 104. *Jonſt. de Piſc.* 36. Acus ſecunda ſpecies five Acus Ariſtotelis *Rond. de Piſc.*
I. 229. Acus ſecunda ſpecies five Acus Ariſtotelis Rondeletii *Geſn. de Aquat.* 9. *Will. Hiſt. Piſc.* 158. *Raij Synop. Piſc.* 46. Typhle marina *Bellon. de Aquat.* 446. **Che leſſer Cobacco=pipe Fiſh.** I have ſeen this not only brought up by the *Troylers* of *Harwich*, but likewiſe brought to *Braintree* Market among *Sprats*. The Figure in *Willoughby* Tab. I xxv. N. 6. doth repreſent this Fiſh.
2. Mola *Charlt. Piſc.* 9. Mola Salviani Orthragoricus Rondeletii *Will. Hiſt. Piſc.* 151. *Raij Synop. Piſc.* 51. *Aldrov. de Piſc.* 410. *Jonſt. de Piſc.* 17. Mola Rhinobatus five Quatraia *Salv. Hiſt. Aquat.* 153. Orthragoriſcus five Luna Piſcis *Rond. de Piſc.* I. 424. *Geſn. de Aquat.* 640. **Che Sun=Fiſh.** It is found in the *Britiſh* Sea. There is a ſhort *anatomical* Account of it both in *Willoughby* and *Ray*. It is figured in *Willoughby* Tab. I. 26.

III. FISHES WHICH HAVE THREE SOFT FINS ON THEIR BACKS.

I. *Aſellus.*

1. **A**Sellus major vulgaris *Raij Synop. Piſc.* 53. *Will. Hiſt. Piſc.* 165. Aſellus major *Schonf.* 18. *Charlt. Piſc.* 2. Aſellus Merlucius *Mer. Pin.* 184. Morhua vulgaris maxima Aſellorum ſpecies *Bellon. de Aquat.* 118. Molva *Rond. de Piſc.* I. 280. Molva vel Morhua altera ſpecies Rondeletii *Geſn. de Aquat.* 88. Morhua five Molva altera *Aldrov. de Piſc.* 289. *Jonſt. de Piſc.* 2. **Che Cod=Fiſh** or **Keeling.** It is to be caught in its Seaſon before this Harbour. Being ſalted it is call'd *Barrel Cod*, and *Salt-Fiſh*. The young ones are frequently ſold in Markets, and are call'd *Codlings*. The Bag by the Back is call'd the *Sound*. This is figured by *Willoughby* Tab. L. Mem. 1. N. 1. Fig. 4.

2. Afellus virefcens *Schonf.* 20. *Raij Synop. Pifc.* 53. Afellus Huitingo-Pollachius *Will. Hift. Pifc.* 167. **The Whiting Pol-lack.** This is fometimes brought to *Braintree* Market, it is like the Whiting, only larger, broader, but not fo thick, and greenifh on its Back.

3. Afellus mollis major feu Afellus albus *Raij Synop. Pifc.* 55. Afellus mollis major feu albus *Will. Hift. Pifc.* 170. Afellus candidus *Schonf. Icth.* 17. Afellus minor & mollis *Charlt. Pifc.* 3. Afellus mollis *Mer. Pin.* 184. Merlangus, altera Afellorum Species *Bellon. de Aquat.* 124. Secunda Afellorum fpecies Rondeletii *Gefn. de Aquat.* 58. **The Whiting.** This is here frequently, and is caught both by Nets and Hooks baited with Sea-worms, call'd in fome Places Spruling. It is a very tender Fifh and eafy of Digeftion. The young ones are call'd **Whiting Mops.** The Figure of this Fifh in *Willoughby* Tab. L. Mem. 1. N. 5. is good.

4. Afellus mollis latus *Raij Synop. Pifc.* 55. *Will. Hift. Pifc. App.* 22. Afellus fub mento barbatus *Mer. Pin.* 184. Afellus barbatus *Charlt. Pifc.* 3. **The Whiting-pout.** This is often brought to the Market at *Braintree* among *Whitings* and *Codlings.* There is a good Figure of it in *Willoughby* Tab. L. Mem. 1. N. 4.

5. Onos five Afinus *Turn. Epift.* ad *Gefnerum Will. Hift. Pifc. Raij Synop. Pifc.* 55. Onos five Afinus five Afellus *Aldrov. de Pifc.* 282. Onos nonnullis ὀνίσκ@ Afellus Plinio *Jonft. de Pifc.* 1. Afellus minor *Schonf. Icth.* 18. Tertia Afellorum Species *Rond. de Pifc.* I. 277. *Mer. Pin.* 184. Tertia Afellorum fpecies Eclefino Rondeletii *Gefn. de Aquat.* 86. Æglifinus tertia Afellorum fpecies *Bellon. de Aquat.* 126. **The Haddock.** This is a common Fifh in thefe Seas, but the Flefh is not fo good as the *Codfifh,* or *Whiting.* The Figure hereof in *Willoughby* is good. It is by fome call'd St. **Peter's Fifh.**

IV. FISHES

IV. FISHES THAT HAVE BUT TWO SOFT FINS ON THEIR BACKS.

MArlucius vulgaris *Bellon. de Aquat.* 124. Merlucius *Gefn. de Aquat.* 84. Afellus *Salv. Hift. Aquat.* 73. *Rond. de Pifc.* I. 272. Afellus major *Schonf. Icth.* 18. Afellus primus Rondeletii five Merlucius *Raij Synop. Pifc.* 56. *Will. Hift. Pifc.* 174. Afellus alter five Merlucius *Aldrov. de Pifc.* 286. Afellus fufcus *Mer. Pin.* 185. *Charlt. Pife.* 3. **The Hake.** This is fometimes caught here. When falted and dried, it is call'd **Poor Jack.** A good Figure thereof is in *Willoughby* Tab. L. Mem. 11. N. 1.

V. FISHES WHICH BESIDES THEIR TWO SOFT FINS HAVE DIVERS LITTLE ONES NEAR THE TAIL.

1. SComber *Bellon. de Aquat.* 100. *Rond. de Pifc.* I. 234. *Aldrov. de Pifc.* 269. *Gefn. de Aquat.* 841. *Schonf. Icth.* 66. *Will. Hift. Pifc.* 181. *Raij Synop. Pifc.* 58. *Mer. Pin.* 187. *Charlt. Pifc.* 27. Scombrus *Salv. Hift. Aquat.* 241. **The Mackrel.** Thefe in their Seafon are here to be caught. There is a very good Figure of this in *Willoughby* Tab. M. 111.

2. Eperlanus *Rond. de Pifc.* II. 196. *Charlt. Pifc.* 34. *Jonft. de Pifc.* 78. *Mer. Pin.* 188. *Raij Synop. Pifc.* 66. Eperlanus Rondeletii *Will. Hift. Pifc.* 202. *Gefn. de Aquat.* 362. *Aldrov. de Pifc.* 536. Eperlanus marinus *Bellon. de Aquat.* 290. Spirincus *Schonf. Icth.* 70. Viola & Perla *nonnullis.* **The Smelt.** This is both in Rivers and the Sea; tho' *Bellon* and *Gefner* make two different Sorts, and for the Second give a Figure no way anfwering. This is a very pleafant Fifh to eat. The Figure of this in *Willoughby* Tab. N. vi. N. 4. is good.

3. Gobius marinus niger *Bellon. de Aquat.* 233. *Raij Synop. Pifc.* 76. Gobius niger *Rond. de Pifc.* I. 200. *Jonft. de Pifc.* 35. *Will. Hift. Pifc.* 206. Gobius niger Rondeletii *Gefn. de Aquat.* 395. *Aldrov. de Pifc.* 97. Gobius, Gobio, & Gobio marinus *Charlt. Pifc.* 15. **The Sea-Gudgeon** or **Rock-Fifh.** This is a *Sea-fifh*, and

to

to be met with in many Places. The Figure of *Bellon's Sea-Gudgeon* hath but one Fin, and confequently not good, neither is there any fo in *Rondel*, *Gefner* or *Aldrovand*. There is a good Figure in *Willoughby* Tab. N. XII. N. 1. of which the Gobius albus of *Bellon*, p. 235. feems to be the fame, tho' not fo good.

4. Lumpus Anglorum *Gefn. Paralip*. 25. *Aldrov. de Pifc*. 479. *Jonft. de Pifc*. 24. *Mer. Pin*. 186. *Charlt. Pifc*. 12. *Will. Hift. Pifc*. 208. *Raij Synop. Pifc*. 77. Lepus marinus noftras Orbis fpecies *Schonf. Icth*. 41. 𝕿𝕳𝖊 𝕷𝖚𝖒𝖕-𝕱𝖎𝖘𝖍, 𝕾𝖊𝖆-𝕺𝖜𝖑 or 𝕮𝖔𝖈𝕶-𝖕𝖆𝖔-𝖉𝖑𝖊. This is often caught in fifhing, and is fold in the Market, but the Flefh not much efteemed. There is a good *Anatomy* of this Fifh from Dr. *Tyfon* in *Willoughby's Appendix*, p. 25. Alfo a good Figure of it Tab. N. 11.

5. Cataphractus *Schonf*. 30. Tab. 3. *Jonft. de Pif.* 77. Cataphractus Schonfeldii *Charlt. Pifc*. 35. *Will. Hift. Pifc*. 211. *Raij Synop. Pifc*. 77. 𝕿𝕳𝖊 𝕻𝖔𝖌𝖌𝖊, by the *Germans* 𝕲𝖆𝖑𝖇𝖊𝖗. I have feen this often brought upon this Coaft by the Fifhermen in their *Troyls*. In opening the Body of this I obferved, that the *Oefophagus* was large, as was likewife the *Ventricle* ending in a Point refembling a Pyramid or Cone: The *Pylorus* rifeth high; the Inteftines make two Circumvolutions before their *Exit*. The Liver was large, of a pale Colour and divided into two Lobes. This was firft publifhed by *Schonfeld*, and by him figured; afterwards *Jonfton* refigured them in his XLVI Table, N. 5, and 6. as he had done before in his Tab. XXIV. Fig. 2. but badly. There is likewife a good Figure in *Willoughby* Tab. N. VI. in which both the Back and Belly of the Fifh are well reprefented.

V. FISHES WHICH HAVE TWO FINS ON THEIR BACKS, OF WHICH THE FIRST IS THORNY THE OTHER SMOOTH.

1. MUgil *Aldrov. de Pifc*. 508. *Will. Hift. Pifc*. 274. *Raij Synop. Pifc*. 84. *Charlt. Pifc*. 32. Mugillis *Salv. Hift. Aquat*. 75. Cephalus *Jonft. de Pifc*. 72. *Rond. de Pifc*. I. 260. Cephalus feu Mugil *Bellon. de Aquat*. 210. Cephalus Rondeletii *Gefn. de Aquat*.

549. 𝕮𝖍𝖊 𝔐𝖚𝖑𝖑𝖊𝖙. Thefe are Inhabitants of the Sea, but the Delicacy of the Flefh, and the Difficulty of catching them enhance the Price; fo that they are not Food for every one's Table. Of the *Ova* or *Spawn* of the Females, falted and dried, is made *Botarg*, which quickens a depraved Appetite, excites Thirft, and a Guft to Wine. There is a good Figure of this Fifh in *Willoughby* Tab. R. 111.

2. Gornatus five Gurnardus grifeus *Will. Hift. Pifc.* 279. *Raij Synop. Pifc.* 88. Cuculus grifeus *Will.* Tab. S. 11. Fig. 1. Cuculus marinus *Charlt. Pifc.* 20. Cuculus *Mer. Pin.* 186. 𝕲𝖗𝖊𝖕 𝕲𝖚𝖗= 𝖓𝖆𝖗𝖉 or 𝕮𝖚𝖈𝖐𝖔𝖜=𝖋𝖎𝖘𝖍. This I have feen caught in the Sea before this Harbour. There is a good Figure of this in *Willoughby* Tab. S. 11. Fig. 1.

3. Lyra Harvicenfis pinna dorfali longiffima maculis cœrulefcentibus *Pet. Gaz.* Tab. xx11. N. 2. Cuculus lævis cœruleo flavefcens cui in fupremo capite bronchiorum opercula *Philofophical Tranfactions,* N. 293. p. 1749. 𝕮𝖍𝖊 𝖄𝖊𝖑𝖑𝖔𝖜=𝕲𝖚𝖗𝖓𝖆𝖗𝖉. This was caught near *Harwich.* It is figured both by Mr. *Petiver* and in the *Tranfactions.*

4. Lyra *Rond. de Pifc.* I. 298. *Mer. Pin.* 186. *Charlt. Pifc.* 21. Lyra prior *Raij Synop. Pifc.* 89. Lyra prior Rondeletii *Aldrov. de Pifc.* 146. *Will. Hift. Pifc.* 282. Lyra Rondeletii *Gefn. de Aquat.* 516. 𝕮𝖍𝖊 𝖕𝖎𝖕𝖊𝖗. It is figured in *Willoughby* Tab. S. 1. Fig. 4.

5. Trachurus *Aldrov. de Pifc.* 268. *Will. Hift. Pifc.* 290. *Raij Synop. Pifc.* 92. *Bellon. de Aquat.* 189. *Schonf. Icth.* 75. *Rond. de Pifc.* I. 233. *Jonft. de Pifc.* 63. *Charlt. Pifc.* 24. Saurus & Trahurus *Salv. Hift. Aquat.* 78. Lacertus Bellonii *Gefn. de Aquat.* 466. 𝕮𝖍𝖊 𝖍𝖔𝖗𝖘𝖊=𝔐𝖆𝖈𝖐𝖗𝖊𝖑 or 𝕾𝖈𝖆𝖉. This no doubt is here to be met with, being common in the *Britifh Seas.* There is a good Figure of it in *Willoughby* Tab. S. 12.

6. Perca *Rond. de Pifc.* II. 196. *Mer. Pin.* 190. Perca fluviatilis *Bellon. de Pifc.* 293. *Salv. Hift. Aquat.* 226. *Will. Hift. Pifc.* 291. *Raij Synop. Pifc.* 97. Perca fluviatilis Bellonii *Gefn. de Aquat.* 699. Perca major *Schonf. Icth.* 55. *Aldrov. de Pifc.* 622. *Jonft. de Pifc.* 107. *Charlt. Pifc.* 41. 𝕮𝖍𝖊 𝖕𝖊𝖆𝖗𝖈𝖍. This is plentiful in Rivers and

and Ponds, from whence it may be brought hither for the Use of the Kitchen, and may be therefore one of the *et cætera* of our Author Mr. *Tayler*. The Figure of this in *Willoughby* Tab. S. xiii. is good.

VI. FISHES THAT HAVE BUT ONE SOFT FIN ON THEIR BACKS.

1. **H**Arengus *Bellon. de Aquat.* 171. *Rond. de Pisc.* 222. *Mer. Pin.* 185. *Will. Hist. Pisc.* 219. *Raij Synop. Pisc.* 103. *Jonst. de Pisc.* 2. Harengus Rondeletii *Gesn. de Aquat.* 408. Harengus Flandricus *Aldrov. de Pisc.* 294. Harengus major *Schonf.* 36. Halec *Charlt. Pisc.* 4. **The Herring.** These are to be found in their Season; besides those that are eaten fresh, there are two Sorts, one salted call'd *white* or *pickled Herring*, being salted up in *Barrels*; and the other *Red-Herrings* from their being salted and dried in Smoke about *Yarmouth* in *Norfolk*. The manner of catching and curing of *Herrings*; See *Collings* of *Salt and Fishery*, p. 105. There is a good Figure of this Fish in *Willoughby* Tab. P. 1. The young ones are call'd **Sea Bleaks**; which Mr. *Tayler* rangeth among his Fishes. *Aldrovand* calls it *Harengus minor*. Mr. *Ray* thinks that Fish which the *Italians* at *Rome* call *Sardanus*, and *Bellon* a kind of *Chalcis* is only our *Herring*, they being larger in the *Ocean* than in the *Mediterranean*.

2. Harengus minor sive Pischardus *Will. Hist. Pisc.* 223. *Raij Synop. Pisc.* 104. Alosa minor *Mer. Pin.* 185. Harenga seu Alosa minor *Charlt. Pisc.* 4. Chalcis seu Sardina Gallis Celerinos dictus *Bellon. de Aquat.* 170. An Sardina *Rond. de Pisc.* I. 117. **The Pilchard.** These chiefly abound in the Western Parts of *England*, They have been sometimes but rarely brought among Herrings to *Braintree* Market. In *May* Anno 1714. I saw divers of them caught in their *Kettle-Nets* at *Dover* in *Kent*. Mr. *Ray* believes, that the *Sardina* of *Rondeletius*, *Gesner* and *Aldrovand*, call'd at *Venice Sardella*, and by *Bellon, Chalcis*, to be the same with our **Pilchard**. To this and not to the *Herring* is likewise to be referred the *Sardanus*

danus Italorum, of which Opinion was *Bellon*, p. 171. his Words are *Sardinam vel Sardallam maris Mediterranei eundem esse piscem quem celerrimum Oceani nemo dubitare potest, cujus natura ea est, ut paulo magis in Oceano, quam in Mediterraneo excrescat.* The Figure of this Fish in *Willoughby* Tab. P. 1. Fig. 1. is good.

3. Spratti & Sparlingi *Raij Synop. Pisc.* 105. Sarda *Mer. Pin.* 186. Sarda feu Sardella *Charlt. Pisc.* 24. Sarda feu Sardina *Aldrov. de Pisc.* 219. *Jonst. de Pisc.* 53. **The Sprat.** Thefe come upon this Shore in *January* and *February.* Mr. *Ray* thinks them to be only young **Herrings**, but the Fifhermen about *Harwich* are of another Opinion, affirming that they are a different Sort of Fifh from *Herrings*, tho' in Form they refemble one another; yet in this they differ, that in one the Belly is fmooth in the other rough. *Jonfton* will have them to be call'd *Sarda* and *Sardina* from being falted, and then the Name will ferve other falted Fifh befides.

4. Acus *Salv. Hift. Aquat.* 68. *Mer. Pin.* 186. Acus prima *Schonf. Icth.* 11. Acus major *Bellon. de Aquat.* 163. *Gefn. de Aquat.* 10. *Charlt. Pisc.* 16. Acus prima fpecies *Rond. de Pisc.* I. 227. Acus Oppiani *Jonst. de Pisc.* 37. Acus vulgaris feu Oppiani *Aldrov. de Pisc.* 107. *Will. Hift. Pisc.* 231. *Raij Synop. Pisc.* 109. **The Gar-fifh, Horn-fifh, Needle-fifh** or **Horn-beck.** This no doubt is to be found in thefe Seas. I have feen them at *Dover* taken in their *Kettle-Nets.* Mr. *Ray* writes, that the Fifhermen of *Cornwall* brought him two Sorts of this Fifh, one of which they called *Girrocks*, and the other *Skippers*; but doth not defcribe the Difference. There is a good Figure of this in *Willoughby* Tab. P. 2. Fig. 4.

5. Lucius *Bellon. de Aquat.* 196. *Rond. de Pisc.* II. 188. *Salv. Hift. Aquat.* 95. *Gefn. de Aquat.* 500. *Schonf. Icth.* 44. *Schw. Theriot. Silef.* 434. *Aldrov. de Pisc.* 630. *Jonst. de Pisc.* 109. *Mer. Pin.* 190. *Charlt. Pisc.* 42. *Will. Hift. Pisc.* 239. *Raij Synop. Pisc.* 112. **The Pike.** The younger **Pickrels.** This Mr. *Tayler* names as from the Flats in *Suffolk.* There is a good Figure in *Willoughby* Tab. P. v.

6. Sturio

6. Sturio *Bellon de Aquat*.98. *Aldrov.de Pifc*.517. *Jonft.de Pifc*.75. *Charlt.Pifc*.32. *Will. Hift. Pifc*.239. *Raij Synop.Pifc*.112. Sturio five filurus *Salv. Hift. Aquat*. 113. Acipenfer *Rond. de Pifc*. I.410. *Mer. Pin*. 188. Acipenfer Rondeletii *Gefn. de Aquat*. 2. Acipenfer five Sturio *Sconf. Icth*. 9. **The Sturgeon.** This fometimes coming up the great Rivers, as the *Thames* often, and not many Years ago *Maldon* Channel, I doubt not but it may be likewife found fometimes in this Haven. It is pickled, and then accounted as a Rarity at Gentlemens Tables. The Figure of this is in *Willoughby* Tab. P. vii.

VII. *Leather mouthed Fifhes.*

1. **C**Yprinus *Bellon. de Aquat*. 273. *Rond. de Pifc*. II. 150. *Salv. Hift. Aquat*. 92. *Schw. Ther. Silef*.427. *Aldrov. de Pifc*.635. *Mer. Pin*. 190. Ciprinus nobilis *Schonf. Icth*. 32. Cyprinus Rondeletii *Gefn. de Aquat*. 309. *Will. Hift. Pifc*. 245. *Raij Synop. Pifc*. 115. Cyprinus Oppiani *Jonft. de Pifc*. III. *Charlt. Pifc*. 43. **The Carp.** This is generally kept in Ponds, and perhaps makes one of thofe Fifhes which Mr. *Tayler* mentions as brought out of *Suffolk*, being much efteem'd at Gentlemens Tables. The Figure of this in *Willoughby* Tab. Q. I. Fig. 2. is excellent.

2. Tinca *Bellon. de Aquat*. 314. *Rond. de Pifc*. II. 157. *Salv. Hift. Aquat*. 89. *Schonf. Icth*. 76. *Schw. Ther. Silef*. 448. *Aldrov. de Pifc*. 646. *Jonft. de Pifc*. 115. *Mer. Pin*. 190. *Charlt. Pifc*. 43. Tinca Rondeletii *Gefn. de Aquat*. 984. Tinca omnium fere Autorum *Will. Hift. Pifc*. 251. *Raij Synop. Pife*. 117. **The Tench.** This I fuppofe is another of Mr *Tayler*'s intended Fifh, as being for Table ufe. In *Willoughby* there is a good Figure of this Fifh, Tab. Q. 2.

Scorpœna *Bellon. de Aquat*. 148. *Gefn. de Aquat*.848. Scorpœnæ Bellonii fimilis *Raij Synop. Pifc*. Scorpœnæ Bellonii p. 201. Edit. Gallicæ fimilis *Will. Hift. Pifc*. 138. **Father-lafher.** This was brought up in the Fifhermens *Troyls* or *Nets* Anno 1697. The *auricula Cordis* was very large, fo as to equalize the *Heart*; the *Liver* was of a deep Colour, confifting but of one Lobe; the Bottom

2   tom

tom of the *Stomach* was round; the *Pylorus* had divers *Cæca*; the Inteftines made two Turnings; the *Rectum* as large as the *Oefophagus*; the *Renes* long and flender; the *Spleen* large and red. In the Ventricle it had *Shrimps* and *Prawns*. Mr. *Willoughby* hath Tab. H. IV. Fig. 3. given *Bellon*'s Figure for this, nor is there fo far as I could obferve any great difference between this and that of *Bellon*, except that Mr. *Ray* faith, his hath no Scales; *Bellon*, that its Scales are fo fmall as fcarce to be obferved by the naked Eye.

Page 114. Paragraph 1. I come to Mr *Tayler*'s laft Part of his *Natural Hiftory*, viz. his *Shell-fifh*. Thefe as I in my Note on the Place obferved, were of two Sorts, *Cruftacea* and *Teftacea*, of this laft I have already taken Notice, p. 377. aforegoing; and fhall only here treat of fuch *cruftaceous Fifhes* as I have obferved at or near this Place.

1. Aftacus *Bellon. de Aquat.* 350. *Rond. de Pifc.* I. 538. *Aldrov. de Cruftac.* 108. Aftacus Rondeletii *Gefn. de Aquat.* 98. Aftacus marinus *Mer. Pin.* 191. *Charlt. Pifc.* 55. Aftacus marinus communis *Jonft. de Exang.* 23. **The Lobfter.** Thefe are caught in their *Troyls* in catching flat Fifh, but moft plentifully on what are call'd the *Weftern Rocks*, by Nets baited with Pieces of *flat Fifh*. When they firft come out of the Water, they are of a fine *mazarine* blew; but as they dry they turn black. They are looked upon as very reftorative. This is figured by moft Authors.

2. Squilla gibbea minor *Bellon. de Aquat.* 356. Squilla gibba prior feu parva *Schonf. Icth.* 72. Squilla gibba *Rond. de Pifc.* 549. *Aldrov. de Cruft.* 150. *Jonft. de Exang.* 17. *Charlt. Pifc.* 56. Squilla gibba Rondeletii *Gefn. de Aquat.* 507. **The Shrimp.** Thefe are taken with Nets on the fandy Shore.

3. Squilla altera *Schonf. Icth.* 72. Squilla parva *Rond. de Pifc.* I. 550. *Jonft. de Exang.* 18. *Charlt. de Pifc.* 56. Squilla parva Rondeletii *Gefn. de Aquat.* 908. *Aldrov. de Cruft.* 155. **The grey Shrimp.** This is very common on all fandy Shores. *Rondeletius* commends the *Shrimp* as a Reftorative in *Hecticks*.

4. Can-

4. Cancellus *Bellon. de Aquat.* 362. *Rond. de Pifc.* 553. *Aldrov. de Cruft.* 218. *Jonft. Exang.* 24. *Gefn. de Aquat* 161. *Charlt. Pifc.* 58. Cancer in teftis degens *Mer. Pin.* 192. **Ẅhe Wrong=Ḥeire or Ḅernarḍ the Ḥermit.** Thefe are found in all Sorts of turbinated Shells.

5. Pagurus *Aldrov. de Cruft.* 168. *Bellon. de Aquat.* 368. *Jonft. de Exang.* 21. *Charlt. Pifc.* 55. Pagurus decem libras pendens *Mer. Pin.* 192. Pagurus Bellonii *Gefn. de Aquat.* 155. **Ẅhe Ṗunger or Ḥammer=Crab.** This is found here of divers Magnitudes. The Claws of this are the *Chelæ Cancrorum* of the Shops; the black Tips of which are ufed. *Rondeletius* confounds this with the *Maia*, figuring one for the other.

6. Cancer marinus *Bellon. de Aquat.* 367. *Aldrov de Cruft.* 173. *Mer. Pin.* 192. *Charlt. Pifc.* 57. *Jonft. de Exang.* 20. Cancer anonymus *Rond. de Pifc.* I. 567. Cancer anonymus Rondeletii *Gefn. de Aquat.* 148. **Ẅhe Crab.** This is a very common Animal living not only in the Sea, but likewife in ftanding Salt Waters. The Figure of this in *Bellonius* is beft, it being by moft others confounded with the Figure of the River-Crab of the fame Author.

7. Cancer brachichelos Maiæ congener, licet minor multo *Aldrov. de Cruft.* 185. **Ẅhe long legged Crab.** This is frequently brought up in the *Troyl-Nets*.

8. Cancer Araneus. Araneus marinus *Mer. Pin.* 192. Aranea *Rond. de Pifc.* 575. Aranea marina Rondeletii *Aldrov. de Cruft.* 202. **Ẅhe Ṡea=Ṡpiḍer.** This is much fmaller than the laft, and the legs longer, fo that it feems different from it.

De Stellis.

1. Ṡ Tella lævis *Rond. de Zoophyt.* 120. Stella lævis Rondeletii *Jonft. de Infect.* 141. **Ẅhe fmall Ṡtar=Ḟifh.** The Figure in *Rondeletius* is good.

2. Stella quinque radiis latioribus. Stella marina Plinio *Schonf. Ictb.* 75. **Ẅhe Ḟive=Ḟinger.**

3. Stella

3. Stella duodecim radiorum Rofa marina dicta. **The Sea-ftofe.** Thefe are all brought up by the *Troylers*.

Echinus marinus *Mer. Pin.* 192. Echinus *Aldrov. de Teft.* 403. *Jonft. de Exang.* 39. Echinus Ovarius *Rond. de Pifc.* I. 578. **The Sea-Egg.** Thefe are abundantly to be found near *Walton-nefs*, being brought up in the Fifhermens *Troyls* and *Dreggs*.

Page 119. *Col.* 2. *Line ult.* add, I am informed that this *Ukwin* was Lord likewife of the Mancrs of *Caftle* and *Sible-Hedingham* in *Effex*.

Page 120. *c.* 2. *l.* 14. after the Word *Wife*, add, who is faid to be Daughter of *Harlowyn* Earl of ——— MS. penes *Edward* Earl of *Oxford* and *Mortimer*, fol. 53. and *dele* what follows from the faid Word *Wife* to the End of the *Paragraph*, which was inferted thro' Miftake: For I do not find that D. *Robert* the Father of D. *William*, call'd the *Conqueror*, had any other Child but him; tho' as fome Authors write, he was married afterwards to *Arlot* D. *William*'s Mother: And it is but reafonable to believe, that if the faid D. *Robert* had by any former Wife any Child living; he would not have recommended his Baftard to fucceed in his Dukedom before his legitimate Offspring: Nor do I find that he had any other Child by *Arlot* but this D. *William*; and therefore *Beatrix* aforementioned could be no Sifter to the *Conqueror*.

Page 121. *c.* 2. to the End of the Paragraph after 271. add, It is written of this Man, that he went into the *Holy-Land* with *Robert Curtois*, where he fought valiantly againft the *Saracens*, often overcoming them, and when by his Prowefs he had recovered St. *George's Banner* which the *Saracens* had gotten, all the Chriftian Princes gave their Confent that he fhould bear St. *George's Shield* in the firft Part of his Efcutcheon; or with his own Arms. And after, for his Valour, they gave him a *Star of Silver* to bear in the firft Quarter of his Shield, becaufe a certain Star did fhine fo clearly, that the Chriftian Army at dark Midnight did overcome the *Saracens*. MS. penes *Edw.* Earl of *Oxford* and *Mortimer*; which MS. calls the Wife of this *Aubrey* by the Name of *Alice* Daughter to *Geofrey Mandevyll*, Aunt unto *Geofrey Mandevyll* the firft

I

firſt Earl of *Eſſex*; but who his Wife was my following Note will ſhew. King *Stephen* in the firſt Year of his Reign ſeized upon this *Aubrey* with *Geofrey de Mandevyll* in his Court at St. *Albans*, and compelled them to ſurrender their Caſtles. At which time *Geofrey* ſurrendered the *Tower of London*, and the Caſtles of *Waleden* and *Pleiſſiz*: *Aubrey* only the Caſtle of *Caneveles*, reſerving to himſelf the Caſtles of *Hedingham* and *Caſtle-Camps* in *Eſſex* and *Cambridgeſhire*, Mills's *Cat. p.* 675.

Page 122. *c.* 2. *l.* 10. add, The following are the Charter of *Henry* I. and the Bull of *Pope Eugene* III.

Carta Henrici Regis de diverſis rebus quas Abbas Faricius adquiſivit.

Licèt omnia mundi regna ſint tranſitoria per ea tamen conquiruntur æterna ſi eorum divitiæ ritè traĉtentur & juſtè diſpenſentur. Fælix ſanè commercium ubi pro tranſitoriis ſemper manentia, pro terrenis cæleſtia commutantur. Unde ego Henricus *Dei gratia rex Anglorum* & dux Normanorum, *inter cætera quæ Deo auĉtore, pro ſalute animæ meæ & parentum meorum, uxoris meæ & filiorum in diverſis jam locis feci, concilio baronum meorum, hæc quæ infra leguntur Deo & ſanĉtæ genetrici ejus conceſſi in* Abbendonenſi *eccleſia perpetuo jure manentia, videlicet,* &c. *unam hidam in* Femcote (Fencote) *cum pratis & paſcuis & omnibus ſibi pertinentibus, ſicut* Adelina *de Suerio* (Iverio) *dedit eccleſiæ in elemoſina, &* Adeliza *filia conceſſit,* &c. *Et in villa de* Kinſuetona (Kinfington *call'd in ſome Deeds* Kinfintuna *and* Kinſentune) *eccleſiam & duas hidas, duodenis* xx. *acris & unam virgatam, quas* Albericus de Ver *& uxor ejus* Beatrix *& filii ejus dederunt eccleſiæ pro anima* Gaufridi (in the Donation Charter he is call'd *Godefridus,* but in that of King *Henry, Goisfredus) filii ſui* &c. *Signum Regis* Henrici. *Signum Reginæ* Matildis, *&c.* Dugd. Mon. Vol. I. p. 105.

The Charter of King *Henry* concerning divers Matters which were acquired by Abbot *Faricius*.

Though all the Kingdoms of this World are tranfitory, yet by them may we gain fuch as are eternal, if we rightly manage and juftly difpenfe their good things. Happy Commerce where things tranfitory are exchanged for fuch as are everlafting, and an earthly Inheritance for one in the Heavens; wherefore *I* Henry, *by the Grace of God King of* England *and Duke of* Normandy, *among other things which by God's Guidance I have done in diverfe Places for the Salvation of my Soul, and of my Parents, my Wife and Children, by the Advice of my Barons, I have granted what is hereafter fpecified to God and his holy Mother to remain for ever in the Church of* Abbendon, *viz.* one hide Femcote (Fencote) *with Meadows and Paftures and all Appurtenances, as they were given and granted by* Adelina *of* Ivery, *and* Adeliza *her Daughter,* &c. *And in the Villa of* Kinfington, *the Church and two Hides of twelve fcore Acres and one Yardland, which* Aubrey de Ver *with his Wife* Beatrix *and his Sons gave to the Church for the Soul of his Son* Geoffrey, &c. *The Seal of King* Henry. *The Seal of Queen* Matilda, &c.

Privilegium Eugenii Papæ tertii.

Eugenius *Epifcopus, fervus fervorum Dei, dilectis filiis* Ingulfo *Abbati Monafterii Sanctæ* Mariæ de Abbendona, *ejufque fratribus tam præfentibus quam futuris regularem vitam profeffis in perpetuum, falutem. Pia poftulatio voluntatis effectu debet fequente compleri, quatenus & devotionis finceritas laudabiliter enitefcat, & utilitas poftulata vires indubitanter affumat. Eapropter dilecti in Domino filii veftris juftis poftulationibus clementer aunuimus, & præfatam Sancti Dei Genetricis Ecclefiam in qua divino mancipati eftis obfequio fub Beati Petri & noftra protectione fufcipimus, & præfentis fcripti privilegio communimus, ftatuentes ut quafcunque poffeffiones quæcunque bona in præfentiarum jufte & canonice poffidetis, aut in futurum con-*

ceffione

ᶜeſſione pontificum, liberalitate regum, largitione principum, oblatione fidelium, ſeu aliis juſtis modis, præſtante Domino poteritis adipiſci, firma vobis veſtriſque ſucceſſoribus & illibata permaneant. In quibus *hæc propriis duximus exprimenda vocabulis: ipſum locum,* &c. *In* Fencota *unam hidam: In* &c. *Cunctis autem eidem loco ſua jura ſervantibus, ſit pax Domini noſtri Jeſu Chriſti, quatenus & hic fructum. bonæ actionis percipiant, & apud diſtrictum judicem præmia æternæ pacis inveniant,* Amen, Amen. ✝ *Ego* Eugenius *Catholicæ Eccleſiæ Epiſcopus ſubſcripſi* &c. *Datum Viterbi per manum Guidonis S.* Romanæ *Eccleſiæ diaconi cardinalis, & cancellarii, decimo Kalendas* Januarii, *indictione* IX. *Incarnationis Dominicæ Anno* MCXLVI. *pontificatus verò domini* Eugenii *Papæ anno ſecundo.* Dugd. Mon. Vol. I. p. 107.

Eugenius *Biſhop, and Servant to the Servants of God, to his beloved Sons* Ingulf *Abbot of the Monaſtery of the Holy* Mary *of Abbendon, and his Brethren as well preſent as future, profeſſing a regular Life, greeting. A pious Requeſt ought willingly to be complied with, ſo that both the Sincerity of Devotion may laudably ſhine forth, and that the Boon requeſted may be indubitably confirmed. Wherefore my beloved Sons in the Lord, we graciouſly conſent to your juſt Petition, and take the aforeſaid Church of the holy Mother of God, in which ye are bound to ſerve with an holy Obedience, into the Protection of St.* Peter, *and our own, and confirm it by this preſent Bull, ordaining, that whatever Poſſeſſions, or whatever Goods you juſtly and canonically poſſeſs at preſent, or whatever you may hereafter obtain by the Conceſſion of Popes, the Liberality of Kings, the Benevolence of Princes, and the Oblation of the Faithful, or any other lawful Means, may remain firm and entire to you and your Succeſſors. Which we have thought proper to ſpecify by their particular Names: The Place itſelf,* &c. *In* Fencote *one Hide: In* &c. *And may the Peace of our Lord* Jeſus Chriſt *be with all thoſe who maintain the Rights and Privileges of that Place, ſo that they may here receive the Fruits of Well-doing, and be hereafter rewarded with eternal Peace.* Amen, Amen. ✝ *I* Eugene *Biſhop of the Catholick Church have ſubſcribed,*

ed, &c. *Given at* Viterbo *by the Hands of* Guy *Cardinal-Dean,
and Chancellor of the holy* Roman *Church, the Tenth of the Ca-
lends of* January, *Indiction* IX. *In the Year of our Lord* MCXLVI.
and the second Year of the Pontificate of our Lord Eugene *the Pope.*

Page ead. *l.* 21. infert.

> *Terra uxoris* ROGERI DE IVERI
> In dimid. BESENTONE Hund,
> LETELAPE Iſſip.
> OTENDONE Oddington.

And blot them out in *Page* 123. as being there wrong placed.
Page 125. *c.* 1. *l.* 19. add,
And as a further Confirmation, I have tranfcribed the follow-
ing Charter.

Ego Robertus, filius Albrici Camerarii regis, terram de Twiwelle,
quamdiu vixero, de domino abbate Roberto *& monachis de* Thorneia
*per eandem conventiònem in feodi firmam teneo, per quam conventio-
nem pater meus ante me tenuit; & decimas de quinque carucis quas pater meus Deo & Sanctæ* Mariæ Thorneiæ *conceſſit, ſcilicet* Iſlep, *&*
Draitune, *&* Edinton, *Deo atque Sanctæ* Mariæ *atque Monachis*
Thorneienfibus *concedo. Hujus conventionis ſunt teſtes* Robertus de
Jakefley, *&c.* Dugd. Mon. Vol. I. p. 248.

I Robert *Son of* Aubrey, *Chamberlain to the King, grant to God
and the bleſſed* Mary, *and the Monks of* Thorney, *the Land in*
Twiwelle, *which I hold in Fee-farm during my Life of* Robert
Abbot and the Monks of Thorney, *by which Tenure my Father held
it before me; and the Tithes of five Ploughlands which my Father
granted to God and the Holy* Mary *of* Thorney, *namely* Iſlep, *and*
Draitune, *and* Edington. *Witneſs* Robert de Jakefley, *&c.*

Privilegium

Privilegium Domini Alexandri *Papæ tertii.*

Alexander *Epifcopus, fervus fervorum Dei, Dilectis filiis* Hereberto *Abbati ecclefiæ Sanctæ* Mariæ *& Sancti* Botulphi Thorney, *ejufque fratribus tàm præfentibus quàm futuris vitam religiofam profeffis in perpetuum. Juftis religioforum defideriis confentire & rationabilibus eorum petitionibus clementer annuere, apoftolicæ fedis, cui largiente Domino defervimus, auctoritas & fraternæ charitatis unitas nos hortatur. Quocirca, dilecti in Domino filii, veftris juftis poftulationibus clementer annuimus, & præfatam ecclefiam in qua divino mancipati eftis obfequio, fub beati* Petri *& noftra protectione fufcipimus, & præfentis fcripti privilegio communimus. Statuentes, ut quafcunque poffeffiones, quæcunque bona eadem ecclefia impræfentiarum juftè & canonicè poffidet, aut in futurum, conceffione pontificum, largitione regum, vel principum, oblatione fidelium, feu aliis juftis modis, Deo propitio, poterit adipifci, firma vobis veftrifque fuccefforibus & illibata permaneant. In quibus hæc propriis duximus exprimenda vocabulis. Infulam* &c. *in comitatu* Hampton, *&c. De dono* Alberici *de* Twywell, *duas garbas decimarum, fex carucarum trium villarum, fcilicet,* Iflep, Drayton, Adinton, *&c. Dat.* Turoni, *per manum* Hermanni *Sanctæ* Romanæ *ecclefiæ fubdiaconi & notarii* v. *Idus* Januarii. *Indictione* xi. *Incarnationis Dominicæ anno* MCLXII. *Pontificatus vero* Alexandri *Papæ tertii, anno quarto.* Dugd. Mon. I. 249.

Alexander *Bishop, Servant of the Servants of God, to his beloved Sons* Herbert, *Abbot of the Church of the blessed* Mary, *and St.* Botolph Thorney, *and to his Brethren,* &c. *The Authority of the Apoftolick See, and the Unity of brotherly Love exhort us to confent to the juft Defires of the Religious, and to grant their reafonable Requefts. Wherefore beloved Sons in the Lord, we gracioufly grant your reafonable Petitions, and receive the aforefaid Church to which you belong, into the Protection of the bleffed* Peter *and our own, and confirm it with this prefent Bull. We do therefore ordain, that whatever Poffeffions, and whatever Goods the fame Church at prefent lawfully and*

4   *canonically*

*canonically enjoys, or may acquire by the Bleſſing of God, the Conceſ-
ſion of Popes, the Munificence of Kings and Princes, the Oblation of
the Faithful, or any other lawful means, may remain firm and entire to you and your Succeſſors.* Among which we here thought proper
to particulariſe thoſe which follow. *The Iſle,* &c. In the County of
Hampton, *&c. of the Gift of* Aubrey, *of* Twywell, *two Sheaves
of the Tithes of ſix Ploughlands and three Villages,* viz. Iſlip, Drayton,
Adinton, *&c. Given at* Turone *by the Hands of* Herman *Sub-Dean
and Notary of the holy* Roman *Church,* &c.

Page 129. *l.* 10. after the Words *morte tua,* add,

Thetfordenſis *Prioratus in agro* Norfolcienſi *fundatus Anno* MCIII.
Annales NORWIC. *in Bibl. Cott.*

Carta Rogeri Bigot *Inter collectanea* Jac. Strangeman *in Bib.
Cotton. ſub. Effigie Vitellii F.* 4.

Ego Rogerus Bigot *concilio domini mei* Henrici *illuſtris regis, &
uxoris ejus* Matildis *reginæ, & domini* Hereberti *Epiſcopi, & uxoris
meæ* Adeliciæ, *& hominum meorum, pro communi ſalute, & remedio
animarum noſtrarum & pro anima domini* Willielmi *regis ſenioris, &
uxoris ſuæ* Matildis *reginæ, & filii eorum* Willielmi *regis, necnon,
pro ſalute aliorum liberorum ſuorum, dono Domino Deo, & beatæ* Mariæ *ſemper Virgini, beatis Apoſtolis* Petro *&* Paulo, *& Eccleſiæ Clu-
niacenſi, eccleſiam quam apud* Thetfordenſem *villam in honore ejuſdem beatiſſimæ ſemper virginis* Mariæ *conſtruere & edificare cœpi,
cum omnibus quæ ad eandem eccleſiam pertinent quæ* Oſbertus *eidem
contulit, & quæ tenuit tempore regis* Edwardi, *& cum omnibus quæ
ego & hæredes mei in præſentiarum donavimus, & quæ in poſterum do-
naturi ſunt hæredes & ſucceſſores noſtri.* Ego itaque Rogerus Bigot
dono imprimis, & reddo meipſum & uxorem meam Adeliciam *& omnes
liberos meos,* &c. *Deo & eccleſiæ beatæ* Mariæ *de* Thetford *ſicut fratres, & benefactores & advocatores ſepeliendos in fine. Quare confirmo
dictæ eccleſiæ totam terram quam* Alwi *tenet in* Thetford *ſicut eam*

à domino

à domino rege Willielmo *feniori habui.   His teſtibus Domino* Hereberto *epiſcopo, &* Gundulpho *epiſcopo, &* Roberto Bloet *epiſcopo, &* Aluredo *archidiacono, &* Gaufrido *archidiacono,* Rotoldo *comitis filio,* Ranulpho *cancellario, &* Eudone *dapifero,* Willielmo Malet, Euſtachio *de* Brettevill, *& aliis, dum rex moram fecit apud* Thetfordiam, *ubi & hoc* ✝ *Signum fanctæ crucis, & figillum fuum in teſtimonium appofuit.* Dugd. Mon. Vol. I. p. 664.

Thetford Priory in *Norfolk* founded A. MCIII. Annal. *Norwic.* in Bibl. Cotton.

The Charter of *Roger Bigot,* among the Collections of *James Strangeman* in the *Cotton* Library, under the Effigies of *Vitellius,* F. 4.

I Roger Bigot, *with the Confent of my fovereign Lord King* Henry, *and his Wife* Matilda, *and* Herbert *Lord Biſhop, and* Adelice *my Wife and my Tenants, for our common Salvation and the Health of our Souls, and for the Soul of our Lord King* William *the Elder, and his Queen Confort* Matilda, *and their Son* William *the King, alfo for the Salvation of their other Children,   I give to God and the bleſſed Virgin* Mary, *to the bleſſed Apoſtles* Peter *and* Paul, *and to the Church of* Cluniack, *the Church which I have begun to build at* Thetford *in honour of the bleſſed Virgin, with all Appurtenances given thereto by* Ofbert, *and which it held in the time of King* Edward, *together with every thing which I and my Heirs have at prefent given, and what our Heirs and Succeſſors ſhall hereafter give.*

Imprimis, I Roger Bigot *give myfelf and* Adelize *my Wife, and all my Children,* &c. *to God and the Church of the bleſſed* Mary *of* Thetford; *and to be there interred as Brothers and Benefactors and Patrons. Wherefore I confirm to the faid Church all the Land which* Alwi *holds in* Thetford, *as I had from King* William *the firſt.   Witneſs* Herbert *Biſhop,* &c. *and others while the King was at* Thetford, *who alfo bore Teſtimony by affixing his own Seal and the Sign of the Crofs.*

Carta

Carta Willielmi Bigot.

Sciant præfentes, & pofteri, Franci *&* Angli *& omnes fideles Chri-fiiani, quod ego* Willielmus Bigot *dapifer regis* Anglorum, *pro reme-dio animarum patris mei* Rogeri Bigoti, *& Matris meæ* Adelidis, *& pro falute mea, & Fratris mei* Hugonis, *& fororum mearum, & om-nium parentum meorum, vivorum & defunctorum; necnon pro falute* Domini *mei* Henrici *regis, & ftatu, & quiete regni fui, concedo & præfenti carta mea confirmo Deo & ecclefiæ beatæ* Mariæ Thedfor-denfis, *& monachis* Cluniacenfibus *in ea Deo fervientibus, in liberam & perpetuam elemofinam, quicquid pater meus* Rogerus Bigotus, *& homines fui, & mei, pro falute animarum fuarum eidem ecclefiæ do-naverunt; ecclefias videlicet, & decimas, & terras, & redditus, & alia beneficia, ficut carta ejufdem Patris mei* Rogeri Bigoti *eis tefta-tur. De dono itaque ipfius, ipfam ecclefiam beatæ* Mariæ, *in qua ipfi monachi primitus manferunt, cum omnibus quæ ad eam pertinent, quæ* Ofbertus *ibi dedit, & tenuit tempore regis* Edwardi; *& terram quam* Ailwi *tenuit in* Thetfordia, *cum molendinis, & pratis, & pafturis & omnibus rebus quæ pertinent ad eadem, ficut pater meus* Rogerus Bi-gotus, *a rege* Willielmo *feniore ipfam habuit; & manerium* Snare-fhelle, *cum advocationibus pertinentibus. Et fepulturam corporis mei, & hominum meorum in finem; ficut in carta patris mei continetur,* &c.

The Charter of *William Bigot.*

Know all Men both French *and* Englifh, *and all faithful Chri-fians, that I* William Bigot *Sewer to the King of* England, *for the Health of the Souls of* Roger Bigot *my Father and* Adeliza *my Mo-ther, and for the Salvation of myfelf, and my Brother* Hugh, *and my Sifters and all my Relations whether living or dead; alfo for the Sal-vation of my fovereign Lord King* Henry, *and for the Eftablifhment and Quiet of his Kingdom, I grant, and by this my prefent Charter confirm to God and the Church of the bleffed* Mary *of* Thetford, *and to the Monks of* Cluniack *ferving God therein, as a free and perpetual*

2   *Donation,*

Donation, whatever Roger Bigot *my Father, and his and my Tenants have given to the said Church for the Salvation of their Souls, viz. the Churches, Tithes, Lands and Revenues, and such other Benefactions, as are confirmed to them by the Charter of the said* Roger Bigot *my Father. His Grant therefore is the Church itself of the blessed* Mary, *in which the Monks first dwelt, with all its Appurtenances, which* Osbert *gave thereto, and which it held in the time of King* Edward, *and the Land which* Alwi *held in* Thetford, *together with the Mills, Meadows and Pastures, and all things else appertaining thereto, as my Father* Roger Bigot *had it of King* William *the first, and the Manor of* Snareshelle, *with the Advowsons appertaining. And the Burial of my Body and my Tenants, as is contained in my Fathers Charter.*

Carta regis Henrici *primi.*

H. *Dei gratia rex* Angliæ, *omnibus baronibus, & fidelibus suis,* Francis & Anglis *totius* Angliæ *salutem. Sciatis omnes, me concessisse* Deo, & sancto Petro de Cluniaco, & Sanctæ Mariæ de Thedford, *quicquid* Rogerus Bigotus *ei dedit, & quicquid in posterum ipsi ecclesiæ de* Tedford *meo consilio daturus est; scilicet in terris & decimis, & consuetudinibus & omnibus aliis rebus. Et volo, & præcipio ut ita bene, & quietè, & honorificè, ipsa ecclesia de* Tedfort *&* monachi *ibi* Deo *servientes omnia sua teneant sicut melius & quietius, & honorabilius ulla ecclesia & monachi de* Cluniaco *sua tenent alicubi in meo regno. Testibus* Roberto Bloiet *episcopo* Lincolniæ, & Rogero *episcopo* Salisburiensi, & Waltero *cancellario, &* Hammone *dapifero, &* Roberto Mallet *camerario,* Ursone de Abetot, & Willielmo de Torneio, & Willielmo Reinis, & Willielmo de Magnavilla *apud* Ramesei, *in Transitu regis, in proxima die ante festum Sancti* Valentini *martyris.*

The

The Charter of King *Henry* the Firſt.

Henry by the Grace of God King of England, *to all his Barons and faithful Subjects,* French *and* Engliſh, *greeting.* Know ye, that I have granted to God and Saint Peter of Cluniack, and the bleſſed Mary of Thetford, whatever has been given thereto by Roger Bigot, and whatever he ſhall hereafter give to the ſaid Church with my Conſent; namely, in Lands, Tithes, and all other things. And I will and ordain, that the Church of Thetford and the Monks therein ſerving God, enjoy their own as well, quietly, and honourably as any Church and the Monks of Clune enjoy their own any where in my Kingdom. Witneſs Robert Bloet Biſhop of Lincoln, &c.

Carta regis Henrici ſecundi donatorum conceſſiones recitans & confirmans.

Henricus *Rex* Angliæ & *dux* Normaniæ, & Aquitaniæ, & *Comes* Andegaviæ, *Archiepiſcopis,* &c. ſalutem. *Sciatis me* conceſſiſſe & confirmaſſe Deo & Sanctæ Mariæ & Monachis de Theodforda omnes antiquas tenuras ſuas ficut *Rex* Henricus avus meus illas eis conceſſit & per cartam ſuam confirmavit, & quicquid eis rationabiliter datum eſt vel donabitur in regno meo; videlicet Eccleſias & terras & decimas & homines & piſcarias & nemora & prata & molendina & omnia alia beneficia; & nominatim totam terram quæ fuit Alwi quam Rogerus Bigod tenuit, in qua ſitum eſt monaſterium Sanctæ Mariæ novum, & totam terram quam comprehenderunt, ad hortum ſuum & virgultum. Et de tota terra ſua extra burgum de Theoforda de qua non ſcottaverunt tempore Rogeri Bigod & Radulphi de Belfago, quæ fuit Alwi, & quæ eſt in Fagertoneſfelda : vel de aliqua terra quæ eſt circa Theodfordam, prohibeo ne ſcottent, &c. Teſte Nigello Helicuſe epiſcopo & R. Exonienſe, & Hillario Ciceſtrenſe epiſcopis, Thomæ cancellario, H. Comite Norfolciæ, Ricardo de Humez conſtabulario, Manaſſero Biſet dapifero, &c. Dugd. Mon. Vol. I. p. 666.

The

The Charter of King *Henry* the Second reciting and confirming the Grants of the Donations.

Henry *King of* England, *and Duke of* Normandy *and* Aquitain, *to the Archbiſhops,* &c. *greeting. Know that I have granted and confirmed to God and the bleſſed* Mary, *and to the Monks of* Thetford, *all their ancient Tenures as my Grandfather King* Henry *granted and confirmed to them by Charter, and whatever has been reaſonably granted, or ſhall be given in my Kingdom,* viz. *the Churches, Lands, Tithes, Vaſſals, Fiſh-ponds, Woods, Meadows, Mills and all other Benefactions: and particularly all the Land which was* Alwi's, *and which was held by* Roger Bigot, *on which is ſituated the new Monaſtery of the holy* Mary, *and all the Land which they have taken in as far as their Garden and Oſier-ground. And all their Land without the Town of* Thetford, *which was not taxed in the time of* Roger Bigod *and* Ralph *de* Belfage, *which belonged to* Alwi, *and which is in* Fagertone's *Field or any other Land about* Thetford, *I forbid being taxed,* &c. *Witneſs* Nigellus Helienſis *Biſhop,* &c.

Page 142. *Column* 1. *Line* 25. inſtead of *Alice* r. *Allſy, p.* 161. *c.* 1. *l.* 6. *r.* the Duke of *Hereford* ſaid, that not, *l.* 23. *r.* That in the *p.* 172. *c.* 2. *l.* dele *of, p.* 186. *c.* 2. *l.* 13. for *Survey* r. *Surrey,* the like *r. p.* 191. *c.* 2. *r. Aubrey's Surrey,* as alſo *p.* 192. *l.* ult. *p.* 198. *c.* 1. *l.* 14. for *long* r. *large, p.* 203. *c.* 2. after *Canterbury* make a Period.

Page 206. *c.* 1. *l.* ult. add, The *Infcriptions* mentioned above are as followeth:

On the Wall on the Weſt-ſide of *Bridewell* Hofpital.

> Mᴿ· WILLIAM WHITMORE
> LATE CITIZEN & HABBER˘.
> OF LONDON GAUE TOWARDS
> SETTING POORE PEOPLE TO
> WORRE IN THIS HOSPITALI.
> 200ᴸ·
> Mᴿˢ· ANN WHITMORE WID꞊
> DOW OF Yᵗ SAID Mᴿ· WHITMORE
> GAUE TO THE SAME USE 150ᴸ·

On a Table of the *Benefaɛtors* in the *Court Room*
1600 Mr. *William Whitmore*, 200 l.
1615 Mrs. *Ann Whitmore*, 150 l.

Page Ib. c. 2. *l.* 11. fill up the Blank with *Penelope*.

Page. 207. The *Paragraph* between the two *Epitaphs*, and alfo the *Epitaph* under it ought to have been fet after the following *Paragraph* of the *Efcutcheon*, which Error was occafioned by not receiving that laſt *Epitaph* until that Part of the Copy was out of the Publifher's Hands.

Col. 2. the latter Part of the *Paragraph* beginning with *William* his only Son, *&c.* which relates to the Burial of the faid *William*, unfortunately killed, I received from the late Reverend Mr. *Robert Rich*, Vicar of *Ramfey*, who informed me that he buried him under his own Pew in the Chancel clofe to his Father; and that there was a black Marble Stone laid-over him with an Infcription; but it is doubtful to me whether or no by reafon of his great Age, his Memory might fail him therein, for upon

fearching

fearching the *Regifter* of *Ramfey*, I could find there no Regiftry of his Burial; nor upon taking up the boarded Floor of the faid Pew, could I find there any more than one Stone, on which was the laft mentioned *Epitaph* and no other.

Page 208. *c.* 1. *l.* 2. and 3. *dele* (the Truftees who fold were) and *add* of, *l.* 6. read three of the Truftees aforementioned, *c.* 2. *l.* 28. and 29. *dele* (with the Addition of two Pendants.)

Page 225. and 26. After the Lift of the *Parliament Men*, who ferved for this *Borough* was printed, I received a more correct one from *Brown Willis*, Efq; which I will here prefent my Readers with, in the fame Manner as I received it, *viz.* digefted into the Years of each King's Reign; and the Place where held.

Anno Regni	EDWARD III.
17	At *Weftminfter*, *John But.* *Thomas de Eaton.*

JACOBI I.

| 21 | *Weftm. Nathaniel Rich*, Kt.   *Chriftopher Harris*, Efq; |

CAROLI I.

1	*Weftm. Edmund Sawyer*, Kt. *Chriftopher Harris*, Efq;
1	*Weftm. Nath. Rich*, Kt. *Chriftopher Harris*, Efq;
3	*Weftm. Nath. Rich*, Kt. *Chriftopher Harris*, Efq;
15	*Weftm. Tho. Cheeke*, Kt. *John Jacobs*, Kt.
16	*Weftm. Harbottle Grimftone*, Kt. and Bart. *Thomas Cheeke*, Kt. *Capell Luckyn*, Efq;

CAROLI II.

12	*Weftm. Capell Luckyn*, Efq; *Henry Wright*, Efq;
13	*Weftm. Henry Wright*, Kt. and Bart. *Tho. King*, Efq;
30	*Weftm. Anthony Deane*, Kt. *Samuel Pepys*, Efq;
31	*Weftm. Thomas Middleton*, Kt. *Philip Parker*, Kt.
32	*Oxford Philip Parker*, Bart. *Thomas Middleton*, Kt.

2

J A C O B I II.

1   *Weft. Anthony Deane*, Kt.   *Samuel Pepys*, Efq;

G U L I E L. E T M A R I Æ.

1   *Weftm. Thomas Middleton*, Kt.   *John Eldred*, Efq;
2   *Weftm.* Honourable *Charles Cheyne*, Vifcount *Newhaven.*
          Thomas Middleton, Kt.

G U L I E L M. III.

7   *Weftm. Thomas Daval*, Kt.   *Thomas Middleton*, Kt.
10   *Weftm. Thomas Daval*, Kt.   *Samuel Atkinfon*, Efq;
          in his Place expell'd the Houfe, *Thomas*
          Middleton, Kt.
12   *Weftm. Thomas Daval*, Kt.   *Dennis Lyddel*, Efq;
13   *Weftm. Thomas Daval*, Kt.   *Dennis Lyddel*, Efq;

A N N Æ.

1   *Weftm. Thomas Daval*, Kt.   *John Ellis*, Efq;
4   *Weftm. Thomas Daval*, Kt.   *John Ellis*, Efq;
7   *Weftm. John Leake*, Kt.   *Thomas Frankland*, Efq; In
          Sir *John Leake's* Place chofe for *Rochefter*,
          Thomas Daval, Kt.
9   *Weftm. Kendrick Edisberry*, Efq;   *Tho. Frankland*,Efq;
12   *Weftm. Thomas Daval*, Kt.   *Carew Harvey*, alias
          Mildmay, Efq; In Sir *Thomas Daval's*
          Place unduly elected *Kend. Edisberry*,Efq;

G E O R G I I I.

1   *Weftm. Benedict Leonard Calvert*, Efq;   *Thomas Heath*,
          Efq; In *Calvert's* Place, Sir *Philip Parker*,
          Bart.
8.   *Weftm. Philip Parker*, Bart.   *Humphrey Parfons*, Efq;

G E O R G I I II.

1   *Weftm. Philip Parker*, Bart.   *John* Vifcount *Percival.*
                    M m m 2   The

The Account fent by Mr. *Willis* ends with the Reign of Queen *Anne*, what remained I have fupplied in the fame Method.

Note, The Pages of Sheet G g are wrong numbered, for that which fhould be 225, is made but 217, fo that the Reader is defired to correct them for eight Pages, when they will be right again.

Page 228. *Line* 19. *dele* (yet) *p.* 238. *l.* 20. *r.* to the King here, *p.* 251. *l.* 2. after *Landguard-Fort* add; the prefent Governor thereof is *Bacon Morris*, Efq; Lieutenant Governor Captain *Hays*, Commandant Captain *James Bex*; and in it are thirty *Invalids* in Garrifon. *Col.* 2. *l.* 3. for in *r.* on.

Page 255. after the laft Paragraph add,

The *Sea* fo encroaching upon this Town, that it was feared it would be entirely loft and overflown, a Complaint thereof was made to the *Government*, and a *Commiffion* was *Anno* 1729. iffued thereupon to divers Gentlemen to make Inquiry; but what was done in it, I have yet had no certain Account.

Page 238. *l.* 17. The laft Part of the Paragraph beginning at the Word *fince*, is by miftake mifplaced, it not belonging to the original Text, but to the Annotations: And likewife after the Word *Kings*, add, *viz.* Mr. *Brown*, Mr. *James Ferne*, Captain *Thomas Allen*, Mr. *Daniel Wifeman*, Mr. *Thomas Allen*, Mr. *James Banks*, and Mr. *Thomas Coleby*; but whether they fucceeded in the Order they are fet in I know not.

Page 255. *c.* 2. *l.* ult. add,

Among the *Marian* Martyrs, I find one *George Eagles* commonly *Trudge-over*, who being apprehended for holding unlawful Affemblies, and praying *That God would either convert the Queen, or take her away*; and being found guilty of High-Treafon was thereupon executed, and one of his Quarters fent to be fet up in this Town, *Mag. Brit.* Vol. I. p. 734.

A SUP-

A

SUPPLEMENT

To the foregoing

APPENDIX.

PAGE 17. *Column* 2. *Line* ult. *add*, The prefent Officers are Bacon *Morris*, Efq; Governor, Captain *Hayes* Lieutenant Governor, Captain *James Bex* Commandant, under whom are thirty *Invalids* to do duty.

Page 259. *l.* 10. inftead of *Well*, infert a large Pit made in form of an *Amphitheater*.

Page 174. *l.* 19. before the Word *Ludus* at the Beginning of the *Paragraph* add, 5. and alter the feveral Figures before the fucceeding *Paragraphs*, by making the 5. *p.* 275. a 6. and fo on, *p.* 288. *l.* 23. read Lib. IV.

Page 289. *l.* 10. after Fig. 14. add, Turben albus oblongus ftriatus ex montibus erutus *Aldrov. de Teft.* 355. This is without doubt our *Foffil*, agreeing with it in the Shape, Colour, Number of Turns, with the Striae within, together with its being dug up in fome Mountain; but where, he is filent, tho' he likewife mentions it in another Place, *viz.* p. 353. cap. xx.

Page 296. *l.* 19. *r.* Cetaceous Kind, p. 301. after Line 14. add, *Cambden* was likewife of Opinion, that thefe are *Lapides fui generis*, as appears by his Words following. *Here are found certain* Stones, *refembling the Wreaths and Folds of a* Serpent, *the ftrange Frolicks of Nature, which as one faith fhe forms for Diverfion,*

2.   after

after a toilfome Application to ferious Bufinefs. For one would believe them to have been Serpents, *crufted over with a* Bark *of* Stone. *Fame afcribes them to the Power of* Hilda's *Prayers, as if fhe had transformed them,* Brit. 751. *Mr.* Nicholfon *affirms, the* Serpent Stones, *as they are call'd at* Whitby *in* Yorkfhire, *to be the fame with thofe the modern* Naturalifts *call* Cornua Ammonis. *Whether they be original Productions of Nature or* petrified Shell-Fifhes *of the* Nautilus *kind has been much controverted by feveral learned Men on both Sides. But he is of Opinion, that they are rather* Spiral Petrifications, *produced in the* Earth *by a Sort of Fermentation peculiar to* Allum-Mines. *Hence* (continues he) *they are plentifully found in the* Allum-Pits *at* Rome, Rochel *and* Lunenburgh, *Ib.* 765. *As to the Stones like* Cockles (continueth the faid *Mr.* Nicholfon) *he could never hear of any that were met with lying fingle and difperfed, but that plenty of them, as well here as in any other Places of the North, are found in firm Rocks and Beds of* Lime-Stone; *fometimes at fix or eight Fathom within Ground. Whence the* Miners *call them* Run-Lime-Stone; *they fuppofing thefe Figures to be produced by a more than ordinary Heat, and quicker Fermentation than they allow to the Production of the other Parts of the* Quarry. *And this perhaps is as rational an Account of thefe* Sports *of* Nature, *as any that our* Modern Virtuofi *have hitherto pitched upon,* Ib. 767.

Page 324. after *Line* 9. add the following Paragraph.

On the Tops of thefe Mountains, faith Cambden *(viz.* Richmond-fhire) *as likewife in other Places, there have fometimes been found, Stones refembling* Sea-Cockles *and other Water-Animals, which if they are not the* Miracles *of* Nature, *I cannot but think with* Orofius, *a* Christian *Hiftorian, that they are certain Signs of an* univerfal Deluge *im the times of* Noah. The Sea *(as the faid* Orofius *faith)* being in *Noah's* time fpread over all the Earth, and a Deluge poured forth upon it, fo that this whole World was overfloated, and the Sea furrounded the Earth; all Mankind was deftroyed, but only thofe few faved in the *Ark,* &c. That this was fo, they have alfo been Witneffes, who knowing neither times paft, nor the Author of them, yet from the Signs and Import of thofe *Stones* (which we foregoing APPENDIX. 455

we often find on Mountains diſtant from the Sea, but over-ſpread
with *Cockles* and *Oyſters*, yea oftentimes hollowed by the Water)
have learned it by Conjecture and Inference, *Ib.* 758, 759.
Page 326. *Line.* 13. *r. p.* 21. *l.* 25. *dele* which, *l.* 29. *r.* of fifty
Shillings per annum, *p.* 327. *l.* ult. dele *its native*, *p.* 328. *l.* 23.
r. violent Death.
Page 332. *l.* 31. after the Word *Sea* add, and not from
Rain and *Vapours*, among many other ſtrong Reaſons he concludes
from the *Perennity* of divers *Springs*, which always afford the ſame
Quantity of Water: Of this he gave an Inſtance of a *Spring* in
Upminſter; that in the greateſt Drought is little, if at all diminiſhed,
and in wet Seaſons no Increment of its Stream, except only after
violent *Rains* for a Day, and ſometimes but of a few Hours Continuance, and then the Water is diſcoloured with running into it
from the higher Lands.
Dr. *Sympſon* in his Appendix to *Hydrologia Chymica* concerning
the *Original* of *Springs* admits that *Rain* and *Snow-waters* are indeed the *proximate* Cauſe of *Land-ſprings*, and *ſudden Floods*, but
that the *Fontes perennes* or *Living-Springs* are from the ſame Cauſe he
abſolutely denies. He advanceth this *Hypotheſis*; That there is a Cir-
culation of Water in the *Terraqueous Globe*, whereby thro' *Sub-
terraneous Channels* it runs from the *Sea* to the Heads of *Springs*,
and from thence into *Rivulets* and *Rivers* returns into the *Sea*
again. *Hydrologia Chymica*, &c. *London* 1668.
Page 333. *l.* 32. *r. Years*, *p.* 339. *l.* 3. *r.* hath *no* Reſemblance.
Page 378. *l. ult.* add, in this Place they being wrongly inſerted,
p. 391. II. *Tubuli Vermiculares.*
1. Tubulus Vermicularis minor Oſtreorum aliiſque teſtis adnaſcens. 𝔖mall 𝔚orm-𝔰hell𝔰. Theſe are oftentimes found adhering to *Stones*, the Shells of *Oyſters*, &c.
2. Vermiculus exiguus albus nautiloides Algæ fere adnaſcens,
Liſt. Meth. Conchyl. Lib. IV. Sect. I. N. 5. 𝔙ery ſmall 𝔚orm-
𝔰hell𝔰. Theſe are abundantly to be found ſticking to the Sea-
wrecks, &c.

Page

456 A SUPPLEMENT, &c.

Page 379. *l.* 13. *r.* this for our, *p.* 382. *l. penult,* *r. p.* 286. *p.* 384. *l. ult. r. Langenhœ, Fingringhœ,* as being their true Names, and *p.* 385. *l.* 1. *r. Salcott, p.* 391. *dele* the firſt eight Lines, they belonging to *p.* 378. as aforementioned. *Ib. l.* 16. *dele* IV. and inſert I. *p.* 408. *l.* 22. *r.* to be only an Egg. *l.* 33. after *parvo* add, *And Dr.* Woodward *obſerves, that in the Formation of a* Chicken *in the* Egg; *That the firſt which appears are the Eyes and Brain, next is the ſpinal Marrow and* Carina *of the* Body, *then the* Wings *and* Legs *begin to bud forth before the* Lungs, Liver, Stomach *and* Guts, *or the* Muſcles *and* Integuments, *ſhew themſelves,* &c. *Holloway's Introduction* p. 19. For when *r.* But.

Page 409. add, *Another Argument to prove that neither the* Bernacle *nor* Macreuſe *can be* Fiſhes *is, becauſe they have two* Ventricles *in their* Hearts *with two* Auricles Appendant, *which no* Fiſh *have but thoſe of the* Whale-kind, *of which neither of theſe are pretended to be.*

Page 413. *l.* 2. after *Whale* add, *to which a late* Author *hath imprudently joined it, they being two different Animals.*

INDEX.

INDEX.

A.

	Page
A Bsinthium	359
Acus Aristotelis	427
Salviani	433
Adeps Ceti	413
Alauda	398
Alexanders	361
Alms-Houses	29. 56
Amber	275
Ambergreese	414
Ammodytes	426
Anas	404. 409
Andrasta	4
Anguilla	424
Anser	403
Apium palustre	362
Arenaria	401
Asellus marinus	427
Astacus	435
Aster	359
Atriplex	351
Avium Fasciculus	396

	Page
Bamford William	53
Barge	400
Barnacles	389
Beets-Sea	358
Bernicle	403
Bezoar Mineral	278
Bigod Hugh	125. 130. 132
——Roger	130. 133. 137
Bleaks Sea	432
Blite-Sea	354
Blubber-Sea	391
Bolingbrook Lord Visc.	223
Boscas	404
Bottle-Head	411
Bowper's Mustard	366
Brenta	403
Brenthus	404
Brotherton Thomas	144
——————Margaret	148
Buccinum	381
Bufonites	416
Burr Daniel, Esq;	210
The But	424

B.

	Page
Balanus	390
Balæna	409, 410, 411. 413

C.

	Page
Cakile	367
Campion Sea	371
Camulodunum	

Page

Camulodunum 3. 257
Cancellus 436
Cancer ibid.
Canis galeus 420
Capella 401
Carp 434
Carr Andrew 41
Caſtanea Arbor 377
Cataphractus 430
Cephalus ibid.
Cetus 413
Chama 387
Charadrius 401
Charles II. King 251
Chenopodium 354
Cheſſnut-tree 377
Cinclus 401
Clams 386
Clare Caſtle 11
Clark Sir William 39
Cochlea marina 379, 380
Cochlearia 365
Cockle 387
Cod-fiſh 427
Coddy-moddy 400
Coke Sir Edward 221
Coleman Roger 36
Colewort-Sea 367
Colts-foot 358
Columba 397
Columbus 402
Concha Anatifera 389
Conger 425
Coot 401

Page

Copperas-ſtones 111
Coralline 338
The Crab 436
Crambe 367
Creſſes Baſtard 366
Cuculus 431
Cunobeline King 2
Curlew 399
Cygnus 403
Cyperoides 375
Cyperus ibid.
Cyprinus 434

D.

The Dab 423
Danes 9
Daval Sir Thomas 207, 208, 209
Deane Sir Anthony 221. 239
Delphinus 419
Didapper 402
Dittander 366
Dobchick 402
Dog-fiſh 420
Dolphin 419
Dove 397
Dovercourt Church 73
————Pariſh 62
————Rood 81
Ducks 404, 405

Echinus

E.

	Page
Echinus marinus	437
Edward III. King	247
———Prince	245
The Eel	424
Eel-pout	426
Sand-Eels	ibid.
Sea-Egg	437
Elizabeth Queen 198. 200.	249
Elvers	426
Eperlanus	429
Eruca marina Herba	367
——— Insecta	394
Eryngium maritimum	363
Eryngo	ibid.
Exchange	58

F.

	Page
Fennel	363
Fin-fish	410
Finckle	363
The Flair	421
Flounder	424
Fœniculum	363
Fossil Bodies	297
——— Shells	284, 285, &c.
Frederick Prince	251
Fucoides	340
Fucus	341
Fulica	401

G.

	Page
Galeus	420
Gallinago	399
Gallinula	400
Gar-fish	433
Sea-gelly	391
Gild of St. George	82
Glass-wort	350
———Prickly	356
Glaucium	368
Glaux maritima	363
Goosander	403
The Goose	ibid.
———Road or Rat	404
Gornatus	431
Gramen	372
Grampus	412
Grass Rush	376
Grasses Sea	372, 373
Grimstone Sir Harbottle	223
Sea-Gudgeon	429
The Gull	402
Gurnardus	431
Gurnard	ibid.

H.

	Page
Haddock	428
Hæmantopus	400
Haliætus	396
Halimus	353
The Hake	429
Harengus	432
Harwich	

	Page
Harwich Cliff	18. 99
———— Church	30
———— Market Place	61
Henry VIII. King	249
𝕳𝖊𝖗𝖗𝖎𝖓𝖌	432
Hippoglossus	424
Hirudo marina	393
Hirundo marina	402
𝕾𝖊𝖆 𝕳𝖔𝖑𝖑𝖞	363
𝕿𝖍𝖊 𝕳𝖔𝖑𝖞𝖇𝖚𝖙	424
𝕿𝖍𝖊 𝕳𝖔𝖗𝖓-𝖋𝖎𝖘𝖍	433
Howard John Duke of *Norfolk*	179
———— *Thomas*	193, 194
———— *Henry*	193

I.

James I. King.	203
𝕴𝖓𝖐𝖊 𝕱𝖎𝖘𝖍	392
Isabel Queen	243
Juncago	376
Juncoides	ibid.

K.

Kali	356
𝕶𝖊𝖑𝖕	336
𝕿𝖍𝖊 𝕶𝖊𝖊𝖑𝖎𝖓𝖌	427
King's Yard for Building Ships	236

L.

Lactuca	358
Lampetra	424

	Page
𝕿𝖍𝖊 𝕷𝖆𝖒𝖕𝖗𝖊𝖞	424
Landguard-Fort	16
Langley Thomas	38
𝕿𝖍𝖊 𝕷𝖆𝖗𝖐	398
———— 𝕾𝖊𝖆	401
Larus	402
𝕾𝖊𝖆 𝕷𝖆𝖛𝖊𝖓𝖉𝖊𝖗	360
𝕾𝖊𝖆 𝕷𝖊𝖊𝖈𝖍	393
Lepidium	366
Limonium	360
𝕿𝖍𝖊 𝕷𝖔𝖇𝖘𝖙𝖊𝖗	435
Loligo	392
𝕾𝖊𝖆=𝕷𝖔𝖚𝖘𝖊	393
Lucius	433
Ludus Helmontii	274
Lumpen	426
Lumpus Anglorum	430
Lupus marinus	427
Lychnis maritima	371
Lyra	431

M.

𝕸𝖆𝖈𝖐𝖗𝖊𝖑	429
𝕳𝖔𝖗𝖘𝖊=𝕸𝖆𝖈𝖐𝖗𝖊𝖑	431
𝕿𝖍𝖊 𝕸𝖆𝖈𝖗𝖊𝖚𝖘𝖊	405
Market Place	61
Marlucius	429
Marquess of *Harwich*	252
Mayors	215
Medica	370
Merganser	403
𝕸𝖎𝖑𝖐𝖜𝖔𝖗𝖙	363
𝕸𝖔𝖈𝖐=𝕮𝖗𝖞𝖘𝖙𝖆𝖑	275
	Mola

4

	Page
Mola	427
Sea-Mouse	394
Mowbray Anne	175
———— John	149.151.167.172. 174
———— Thomas	151. 166
Mugil	430
The Mullet	431
Musculus	388
The Muscle	ibid.
Mustela	426

N.

Napus Sylvestris	364
Nasturtium	366
Wild Navew	364
The Needle-fish	433
Nerita	380
Nettle Roman	351
St. Nicholas's Chapel	30
Numenius	399

O.

Oenanthe	398
Onos	428
Orach-Sea	351
Orford Edward Earl of ——	224
Orwell Haven	13. 245
Osprey	396
Osteocolla Anglicana	19. 273
Ostrea	383
Otus	396
The Horn-Owl	ibid.

	Page
The Oyster	383
Oyster-green	350

P.

Pacquet Boats	241
Palumbus	398
Pap-shell	378
Parliament-Men	217. 279
Parmacitty	413
Partridge	397
Passer piscis	423
Pastinaca	421
Patella	378
The Perch	431
Pecten	383
Pectunculus	386, 387
Pediculus Marinus	393
Pellitory	356.
Penelope	404
Pepper-wort	366
Percival John Viscount	225
Perdix	397
Perewincles	379
Petrifications	107
Petrified Wood	109. 279
The Pewit	402
Phasianus	397
The Pheasant	ibid.
The Sea Pheasant	404
Philip King	249
Phocæna	419
Pholas	389
The Pick	433
Pickrel	

Page

Pickrel 433
Piddocks 389
The Sea-Pie 400
Pigeon 397, 398
Pinpatches 379
The Piper 431
The Pilchard 432
Plantegenet Richard Duke of
York 175
Sea Plantain 369
Buckhorn Plantain ibid.
Plantarum Fasciculus——— 336
The Plover 401
Pluvialis ibid.
The Pochard 409
The Pogge 430
Sea Poppy 368
The Pril 423
Pudenda marina 392
Pulex marinus 393
Purrs 389
Sea-purslain 353

Q.

Querquedula 404

R.

Raia 421
Rana Piscatrix 422
Reay Roger 41
Recurvirostra 402
Rhombus 423

Page

Sea Rocket 367
Rood at Dovercourt 81

S.

Saltwort 363
Sand-Eels 426
The Sanderling 401
The Sand-piper 400
Scallops 381
School-House 56
Scolopax 399
Scolopendra marina 393
Scomber 429
Scorpæna 434
Sea Scurvey-grass 365
Selenites 275
Segrave Elizabeth 149
——— John Lord de 148
Sepia 392
The Sharke 420
The Sheldrake 405
Shells a Fasciculus of — 377
Ships built 238
The Shrimp 435
The Skate 421
The Sleeve-fish 392
Smallage 363
The Smelt 429
Smith Henry, Esq; 89
Smyrnium 361
Sea-snail 379
The Snipe 400
The Sole 424
Solea

	Page
Solea	424
Spergula	371
𝔖𝔭𝔬𝔫𝔤𝔢	337
Spongia	ibid.
——*Lapis*	283
𝔖𝔭𝔯𝔞𝔱𝔰	433
Spratti	ibid.
𝔗𝔥𝔢 𝔖𝔢𝔞-𝔰𝔭𝔦𝔡𝔢𝔯	436
Springs their Original	332
𝔖𝔢𝔞-𝔰𝔭𝔲𝔯𝔤𝔢	368
𝔖𝔢𝔞-𝔰𝔭𝔲𝔯𝔯𝔶	371
Squatina	422
Squilla	435
𝔗𝔥𝔢 𝔖𝔢𝔞-𝔰𝔱𝔞𝔯	436
𝔖𝔢𝔞 𝔖𝔱𝔞𝔯-𝔴𝔬𝔯𝔱	359
Statice	361
Stella marina	436
𝔗𝔥𝔢 𝔖𝔱𝔦𝔫𝔱	401
𝔖𝔥𝔯𝔲𝔟-𝔰𝔱𝔬𝔫𝔢-𝔠𝔯𝔬𝔭	354
Stoure River	11
𝔗𝔥𝔢 𝔖𝔱𝔲𝔯𝔤𝔢𝔬𝔫	434
Sturio	ibid.
Succinum	275
𝔗𝔥𝔢 𝔖𝔲𝔫-𝔣𝔦𝔰𝔥	427
𝔗𝔥𝔢 𝔖𝔴𝔞𝔫	403

T.

𝔗𝔥𝔢 𝔗𝔢𝔞𝔩	404
𝔗𝔢𝔫𝔠𝔥	434
𝔗𝔥𝔢 𝔗𝔥𝔬𝔯𝔫𝔟𝔞𝔠𝔨	422
𝔗𝔥𝔯𝔦𝔣𝔱	361
Tinca	434
Tithymalus.	368

	Page
𝔗𝔬𝔞𝔡-𝔰𝔱𝔬𝔫𝔢𝔰	427
𝔗𝔥𝔢 𝔗𝔬𝔟𝔞𝔠𝔠𝔬-𝔭𝔦𝔭𝔢 𝔉𝔦𝔰𝔥	ibid.
Tadorna	405
Totanus	400
Town-Hall	221
𝔗𝔯𝔢𝔣𝔬𝔦𝔩	369
Trenchard George, Captain	37
Trifolium	369
Trochus	380
Tubuli vermiculares	283
𝔗𝔥𝔢 𝔗𝔲𝔯𝔟𝔬𝔱	423
Tuſſilago	358

V.

Ver, Vere, Veer	62. 64. 115. 120, 121
Vermiculi Foſſiles	283
Vicars of *Dovercourt*	73
Urtica marina	391
—— *Romana*	351

W.

𝔖𝔢𝔞 𝔚𝔢𝔢𝔡	349
𝔗𝔥𝔢 𝔚𝔥𝔞𝔩𝔢	410. 413
𝔗𝔥𝔢 𝔚𝔥𝔢𝔩𝔨	381
𝔗𝔥𝔢 𝔚𝔥𝔦𝔱𝔦𝔫𝔤	428
—————— 𝔐𝔬𝔭𝔭𝔰	ibid.
—————— 𝔓𝔬𝔩𝔩𝔞𝔠𝔨	ibid.
—————— 𝔓𝔬𝔲𝔱	ibid.
Whitmore George, Knight	203
——*William*	205,206,207
𝔗𝔥𝔢 𝔚𝔦𝔤𝔢𝔬𝔫	404. 409
William	

I N D E X.

	Page		Page
William III. King	251	Sea-Wreck	342
The Wolf-fish	417	Grafs-Wreck	348
Wood petrified	109. 279	The Wrong-heir	436
The Woodcock	399		
Sea-Worms	393	Y.	
Worm-shells	391		
—— Foffil	283	The Yarwhelpe	400
Sea Wormwood	359		

F I N I S.

Printed in Great Britain
by Amazon